ORACLE
Express OLAP

Sergei Arkhipenkov
Dmitri Golubev

A-LIST, LLC
295 East Swedesford Rd.
PMB #285
Wayne, PA 19087
mail@alistpublishing.com

This book is printed on acid-free paper.

Oracle Express OLAP
By S. Arkhipenkov, D. Golubev

ISBN: 1-58450-084-0

Printed in the United States of America
01 02 7 6 5 4 3 2 1

A-LIST, LLC titles are distributed by Charles River Media and are available for site
license or bulk purchase by institutions, user groups, corporations, etc. For additional
information, please contact the Special Sales Department at 781-740-0400.

CHARLES RIVER MEDIA, INC.
20 Downer Avenue, Unit 3
Hingham, MA 02043
781-740-0400
781-740-8816 (FAX)
info@charlesriver.com
http://www.charlesriver.com

Book Editor: Jessica Mroz

CONTENTS

Preface

What this Book is About

Data Warehouse and On-Line Analytical Processing (OLAP) are new information technologies, which provide business analysts, managers, and leaders of management groups with the ability to study huge volumes of interconnected data using fast, interactive viewing of information at different levels of detail and from various points of view according to the user's ideas on the area of business activity. Several years ago, only a few people had heard about these technologies. Today, however, data warehouses and OLAP have become an integral part of modern corporate support systems. It is one of the most rapidly developing areas in the software industry. Most of the leading software manufacturers—including Arbor Soft-ware, Cognos, IBM, Informix, Microsoft, Oracle, SAS Institute, and Sybase—compete in this market area. However, none of the OLAP software manufacturers provide a complete solution for the corporate analytical system, and their products are only a set of tools that form the basis for designing support systems.

The first edition of this book created intense interest among information technology professionals. As with any book describing particular software versions, this edition later required some revision and amendment. Initially, it was planned that this book would simply be a second edition. However, we were dissatisfied with the fact that the content of the book covered only "the tip of the iceberg", namely expert support systems, and the content did not show its "underwater part", which contains 90% of the work and problems.

Within the last five years, the media has intensively discussed this subject in various periodicals, and it was covered as well in a number of books, thanks largely to the fundamental work of R.Kimball [2]. IBM, Microsoft, Oracle, PricewaterhouseCoopers, and the SAS Institute have, in their methodologies, summarized particular project implementation experiences related to data warehouse development. Unlike the aforementioned edition, we tried to limit as much as possible the general ideas, and chose to discuss only one of the many possible approaches, and only one particular platform. We hope that this will allow our work to be as useful as possible to professionals and managers from information technology departments who are concerned with the practical problems of corporate information system development.

This edition is devoted to the theoretical, methodical, and practical construction aspects of analytical systems based on Oracle software. Our goal in this edition is not to comprehensively answer all or even most of the questions that will arise during the development of a corporate information analysis system, but only to address those questions that have most often come up in our experience, and that we believe deserve public attention.

We also aim to give the reader unfamiliar with these technologies a general idea about data warehouses and OLAP, about the theoretical and methodical aspects of their use during support system development, and about the content and features of the Oracle Express software family.

Who is this Book for?

Primarily, *this edition* is intended for IT department specialists and managers who are interested in various aspects and real-world practice of using data warehouse technologies and OLAP for corporate information systems. The first step begins a journey of thousand miles, and we hope this book will help you to make that first step towards the development of a corporate information analysis system.

What is Inside?

Regarding organization, this edition consists of ten chapters.

The *first chapter* is devoted to a brief view of data warehouses and OLAP, discussing the importance and place of these technologies in modern corporate information systems. It considers the conceptual problems of designing information analysis systems based on these technologies. The implementation strategy of such projects is also given.

In the *second chapter* of this edition, one possible approach to developing a corporate information analysis system is described. All stages of design, from making suggestions through to the introduction of a ready-to-use system, are discussed step by step.

The *third chapter* is devoted to the Oracle Warehouse Builder development package for developing multidimensional data warehouses based on an Oracle 8 relational database.

Chapter 4 discusses a number of questions related to the design and administration of data warehouses and data windows based on the specialized multidimensional database Oracle Express Server, which provides maximum performance while working with ad hoc queries.

Chapter 5 gives a detailed description of ways of working with the development tools for corporate record-making systems that Oracle Discoverer provides, and of how to create analytical applications using MS Excel spreadsheet from Express Spreadsheet Add-in.

Chapter 6 is dedicated to questions dealing with the creation of "easy" client applications—in particular, presenting data with the tools provided by Express Analyzer, as well as expanding them to the intranet/Internet with the help of Express Web Publisher.

The possibilities that are opened up to analytical system creators by the instrumental object-oriented environment Express Objects for developing "thick" clients are discussed in *Chapter 7.*

Chapter 8 describes how to build "thin" clients in the intranet/Internet networks. We look at the particular features of using Java technology in Oracle Express.

Chapter 9 gives an analysis of one attempt at developing a relatively complex application, as well as some research that was done, all with Oracle Express.

And, finally, *Chapter 10* turns your attention to a description of practical methods of building a corporate financial information analysis system based on the Oracle Financial Analyzer software.

Acknowledgements

Special thanks to Oksana Maksimenko, the author of *Chapter 10*. She is a consultant for the IDS company, and for the last five years has been actively working on planning and developing corporate information analysis systems based on Oracle software products.

The authors express their gratitude to the Oracle representatives for their help in preparing the manuscript and providing the necessary materials, in particular Roman Samokhvalov, business development manager, without whom this edition of the book would not be possible. The authors would also like to thank the Director of IBS's corporate information analysis system department, Aleksandr Saksin, for his help and cooperation with our work. Special thanks go to the readers, for their interest in this edition.

Introduction

A Picture Paints a Thousand Words...

Let's imagine that we are sales managers who handle the sales of audio-visual systems produced by Saturn Electronics. Our duty is to deal with sales of more than 30 items at once. Our customers are located in 60 cities in different countries, on all the inhabited continents. Our task is to evaluate business, to analyze positive and negative trends, and to determine future prospects for our business. To solve these problems, we shall use an Oracle Express multidimensional database which stores trade reports on each customer for the last year and a half.

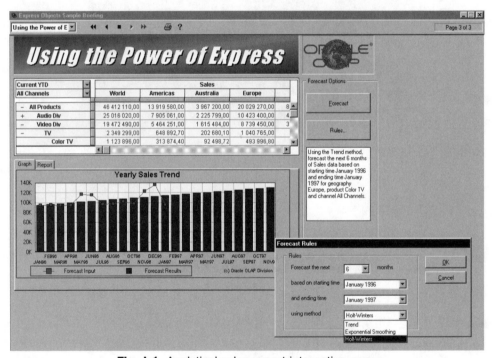

Fig. I.1. Analytical sales report interactive page

To get a general idea, we'll look at the view page, which includes total sales data grouped by continent for a five month period in the current year (Fig. I.1). Using Drill Down (clicking on the "+" symbol), we can easily receive more detailed information, for example, figure out the amount of sales with respect to a particular type of video system, or elaborate on information concerning sales in a particular country or city.

In the following diagram, we see not only a retrospective view of the indicated aspect for the last year and a half, but also a prognosis for changes that may occur before the end of the current year. In view of the considerable discrepancies between the predicted values and previous period data, we may not be satisfied with the accuracy of the sales prognosis, which was derived in accordance with the linear trend model.

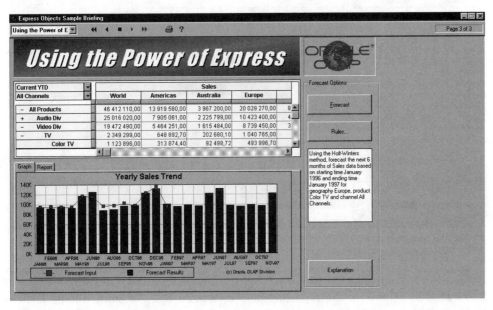

Fig. I.2. Updating the sales amount forecast according to the seasonal change variation method

To change the prediction model, you need only select the required item from the list, which appears after pressing the **Rules** button. A more accurate forecast for our time series is thus achieved, which takes into account seasonal changes (Fig. I.2).

However, discovering adverse tendencies is only half of our problem. It's more important to understand the reasons for them. Let's then proceed to another page of our analytical system, which allows us to carry out the analysis using the "What if..." pattern (Fig. I.3). Looking through the data, we can see that our biggest difficulty lies in Europe. By further specifying the query, we see that the most unfavorable decline in sales, as compared with the previous year, took place in Paris.

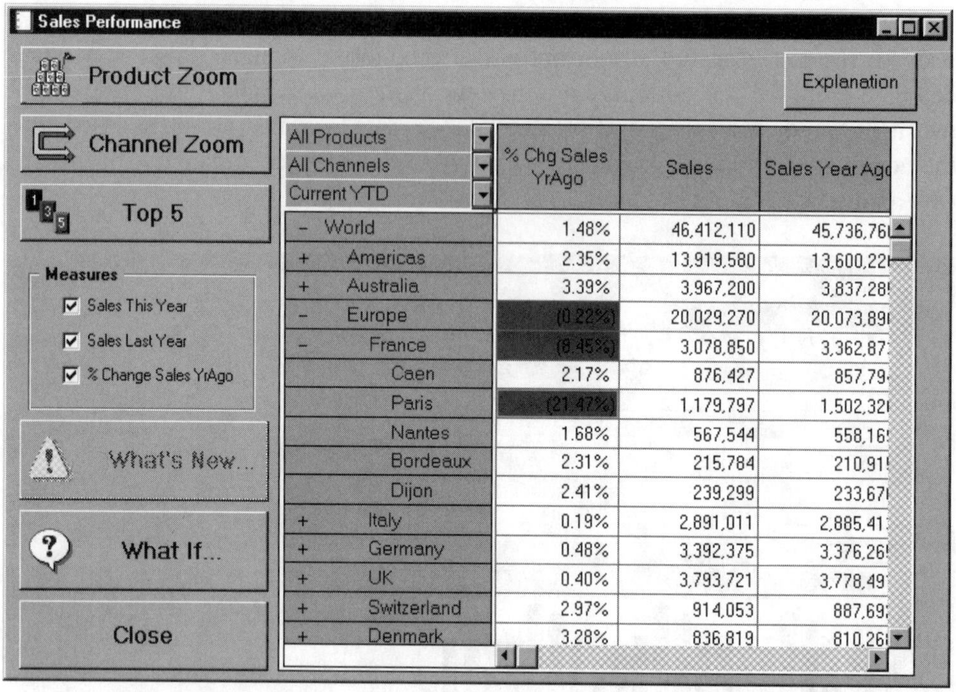

Fig. I.3. Page of the analytical report for carrying out the analysis under the pattern "What if..."

Let's click the **Top 5** button to understand the situation in the areas where we saw a rise in sales volume in the reporting period. We see that the sales volume leader is the Dallas, Texas department. Getting more information by pressing the **What's New** button, we find out that such a high level of activity has been achieved due to the introduction of the Oracle program that handles customer support using Internet technologies.

By clicking the **What If...** button, we can evaluate what would have happened if we had introduced such a program in Paris (Fig. I.4). It should be noted that, despite the considerable volume of data, the given analytical results can be obtained in less time than was required to familiarize oneself with the description of this process.

In spite of the fact that various queries were not regulated during the application's development, they are done with the click of a mouse, and require practically no time at all. All we need to carry out business activity analyses are retrospective data related to trade operations, and **OLAP** tools to handle the information effectively. It should also be noted that the above example demonstrates only a fraction of the opportunities that are provided by this software product family.

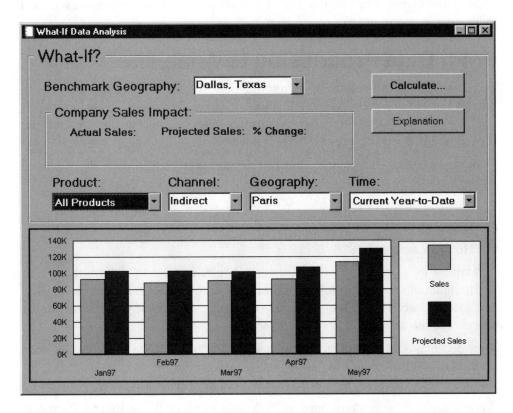

Fig. I.4. Results of the analysis according to the "What if..." pattern. Sales volume growth is connected with the introduction of a new client support service

It is clear that Oracle Express OLAP's possibilities are not limited to applications dealing with sales analysis, finances, or other types of business activity. Multidimensional Oracle Express databases can be used everywhere consolidation of disembodied sources and analysis of significant volumes of empirical data (from a few megabytes up to tens of terabytes) defined in a space with a large number of dimensions is required. Furthermore, the 4GL Server Programming Language (SPL)—which provides efficient multidimensional data handling—and the advanced Express Objects toolkit, allow us not only to analyze data but also to create powerful simulation models that take into consideration the large variety of determining factors and their complicated interactions, and to experiment with these models and analyze the results effectively. That is why applications of the aforementioned software can work in physics and chemistry, biology and medicine, ecology and complex technical areas, or any other area of research activity related to large-scale system analysis.

From Data Processing to Analysis

To remain competitive, those in business should be able to consider decisions in full, and determine the optimum financial strategy. Today, efficiently managing a middle- or large-sized business without using advanced information technologies (i.e., Decision Support System (DSS)) is not possible.

Generally speaking, the management process can simplified to the following three problems:

❏ Where are we?

❏ Where do we want to go?

❏ How can we get there?

It is typical for complicated systems that, as a rule, we have to manage them even under conditions such as a lack of information, ignorance of functional principles, and external factors that are constantly changing. That is why the management process is done iteratively.

After deciding on a controlled plan of action, it is necessary to again estimate the position of our system and to decide whether we are on the right track. If the deviations do not satisfy us, we should redefine the management process.

While searching for answers, modern technologies allow the analyst to formulate and solve tasks of the following classes.

Analytic tasks imply the calculation of the given parameters and statistical characteristics of business activity on the basis of retrospective information from the database.

A *Data view* is any graphic or tabular view of the available information.

Data mining is the definition of interrelations and business process interdependencies on the basis of existing information. It includes tasks such as statistical hypotheses checking, clusterization, and finding associations and temporary patterns. For example, by analyzing the economic and financial parameters of companies that have gone bankrupt, a bank can determine certain stereotypes, which can then be taken into account to evaluate risk when considering a loan lease.

Simulation tasks are implementations of experiments with mathematical models on a computer that describe the behavior of complicated systems during a given or formed interval of time. Tasks of this type are used to analyze the possible consequences of different administrative decisions ("What if..." analysis).

Synthesis of control is used to determine the permitted control actions, which ensure the achievement of a given goal. Tasks of this type are used to estimate the attainability of planned goals and to determine the set of possible control actions that will result in the stated goal.

Optimization tasks are based on the integration of simulated, controlled, optimized, and statistical methods of modeling and forecasting. Tasks of this class allow you to choose from a set of possible control actions those that prove to be the most efficient (taking a certain criterion into account).

It is unlikely that DSS complex software will ever implement all, or even a large part of the algorithms used to solve the classes of tasks listed above. Also, one should not think that we will see on the market in the coming years universal simulation model software for commercial enterprises that could be adapted and used in the DSS of a company. However, it is quite possible that to obtain the advantage in a competitive activity, a number of companies will pay more attention to their own simulation model development. Based on our own experience in the field of complicated system model development, we can prove that even with the presence of a qualified team of business analysts, mathematicians, and programmers, the execution time of a project will be no less than one-and-a-half to two years. From our point of view, until that moment, it is premature to discuss the real application of information technologies for solving tasks of the fifth and sixth types, since the algorithms in these areas require the presence of an adequately managed system model.

Models allow us to represent phenomena and objects in the real world by a set of abstract symbols and concepts, and to show object relationships as relationships between the appropriate abstractions (Fig. I.5). For example, the model allows us to forget about the actual diameter, length, and material of the conductor, and to describe it using some abstraction (i.e., R [resistance]). Then, after we measure the resistance value (after we receive the data), we will be able to take advantage of the model known as Ohm's Law, and predict that if we apply a voltage of U to the conductor's ends, the electric current in the conductor will be $I = \dfrac{U}{R}$.

Business represents a complex object, which is created from various subsystems with different properties, and between these subsystems exist a large number of heterogeneous links. Business activity consists of many business processes, which all essentially depend on a set of external factors (legislative, economic, social, political, etc.). In cybernetics, such objects are called *complex systems*, and they are studied using *systems analysis*. Though this science has been developing since the beginning of the 1940s—from the time when the armies of the USA and Great Britain began to recruit scientists to develop guidelines for WWII military operations, the essential practical results were only obtained from researching those operations, i.e., using quantitative mathematical methods to base the solutions on. But a mathematician can only start to work once the research worker has a model of the system ready. As a rule, mathematicians are rarely concerned with the origins of a formal model. They rightly assume that a model's build is connected to the competence of the experts in the specific application area.

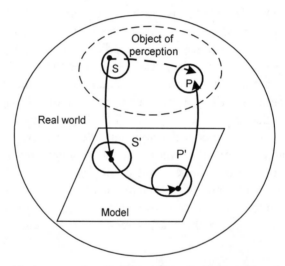

Fig. I.5. Relationship between the studied entity and its model. S is the set of source phenomena, P is the set of target phenomena

What is the origin of models and why are they practically non-existent for business management systems?

Taking epistemology into consideration, a common triad looks like this: *Hypothesis—Model—Solution*. A hypothesis about the correlation of certain phenomena and real world objects precedes any model. The hypothesis is a discovery. It's fundamentally new knowledge. The discovery cannot be calculated or obtained by logical deduction from already existing knowledge, since it would then be only tautology, a repeat of something that has been already done. From the point of view of modern psychology, a discovery is made through *intuition*, which originates in the area of the human subconscious, and is based largely on personal experience. Before Georg Ohm pioneered his law, he carried out experiments with conductors of different diameters, different lengths, and different metals, and analyzed and stored empirical data for many years. As a rule, not one, but a set of hypotheses precede the discovery. The model, which is a formal mathematical description, is defined in accordance with each hypothesis, and, as a result, a solution is discovered. Then, during experimentation, the obtained solution is checked and rejected if it is not confirmed. This process happens until the researcher is not able to falsify the hypothesis during an experiment (Fig. I.6). As a result, we obtain knowledge that we may use in our practical activities.

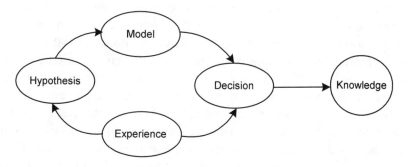

Fig. I.6. Cognition activity process

In business, adequate model definition is complicated by two problems.

First, the dynamism of economic circumstances takes some importance away from the businessperson's experience accumulated during his or her daily activity. There is simply no time to develop the intuition necessary to set up a business hypothesis.

The second problem is that in business activity, and moreover under free market conditions, there is no possibility of performing purposeful experiments, which necessarily precede the discovery of a hypothesis and allow it to be checked in practice.

Therefore, in reference to business activity, the knowledge process shown in Fig. I.6 has at least two major flaws: at the stage of hypothesis suggestion and at the stage of experimenting with and verifying the model.

In the actuality of business today one can only depend on complex software that realizes the first, second, and partially the third type of algorithms mentioned above. Nowadays, we can observe immediate progress in the development of the software commonly named OLAP (On-Line Analytical Processing). The main function of the new data warehouse technologies and OLAP is to objectively eliminate existing defects in cognitive activity. More than 100 of the largest software manufacturers compete in the given market sector.

Artificial Intelligence on the Manager's Desktop

One of the main ideas in the field of data warehouse technology is to compile all the information necessary for the manager to make a decision into one place (at least from the user's point of view)—into one large database, or superdatabase. Data sources for a warehouse are, first and foremost, data from uncoordinated transaction information systems based on various relational DBMSs that support everyday business activity. It is necessary to emphasize that a data warehouse is not intended to replace existing systems. It is more like a structure on a different, higher level. A data warehouse can include data concerning clients, staff, competitors, the demographic situation, economic indicators, etc. Newspapers, radio, television, Internet, and others might be the sources of the necessary information. Thus, it is supposed that the data should conform to a uniform standard beforehand; their contradictions should be resolved, and they should be structured and summarized, observing the required level of detail. The size of a data warehouse is estimated at roughly ten terabytes (1 terabyte $\approx 10^{12}$ bytes). To make this more clear, imagine a pile of encyclopedia-size books one kilometer high. This is the equivalent amount of information.

The idea of a data warehouse itself is not new. The distinctive feature of such storage areas is simply the predictable size of the stored information, which allows us, hopefully, to see a new, high-quality database property (i.e., to eliminate the defects in an analyst's cognitive activity mentioned in the previous section—lack of personal experience and the impossibility of carrying out purposeful experiments). It is not without basis in fact to say that when an analyst analyzes your commercial activity and a competitor's activity, taking into account internal and external factors, the analyst will obtain the intuition necessary to form a hypotheses. He or she will then be able to check the validity of the hypothesis, not by conducting a purposeful experiment, but by using stored information on experiments conducted by life itself.

OLAP development software is an on-line data analysis tool for data contained in a warehouse. From our point of view, the key feature is that these resources are intended for use not only by IT specialists or statistical experts, but by professionals in the area dealt with by the application (e.g., a credit department manager, budget department manager, a chief administrator, etc.). They are intended for connecting an analyst with a problem, not with a computer.

Having flexible mechanisms of data manipulation and visual mapping, the researcher generally first considers from different sides the data that may or may not be connected with the problem to solve. At this point, the researcher has no particular ideas, and is simply trying to notice any striking features. He compares various business figures trying to find hidden correlations. If an item attracts his interest, he can consider the data more carefully and elaborate upon it. He can sort the data by time, area, client, or, on the contrary, remove distracting details and summarize information. For example, he can form the hypothesis that the difference in asset growth among various branches of the bank depends on the ratio of employees with a technical education to those with a humanities background. The researcher can then request data from storage (not from the information department!) and map these ratios on one graph for all the branches that, in the current quarter, have either experienced a drop of more than 10%, or who have experienced a growth of more than 25% in comparison to the previous year. For this purpose, a research worker doesn't need to use a sophisticated SQL query, just make a simple choice from a menu. If the obtained results clearly break up into two distinct groups, this should become a stimulus for further checking the hypothesis put forward. And, perhaps in his subconscious, there will arise some new associations, and after receiving these results the search will start moving in another direction.

These days, it seems to me that we are witnessing a very unusual phenomenon—the wide application of artificial intelligence in practical activity, which is especially interesting for such a closed sphere as business. OLAP technology, however, does not try to simulate natural intelligence, but only strengthen its possibilities using the power of modern computing servers and data warehouses.

The universal applicability of the laws of psychology, on which the OLAP technology is partially based, allows the application developer to not worry about the nature of possible queries given by an end user. The laws of human thinking are poorly investigated. At the same time, hardly anyone doubts that common laws of thinking exist and operate. We can criticize the 12 OLAP system indicators stated by Codd [3] as much as we want, but they were in large part influenced by laws of human reasoning that have not yet been fully investigated or understood. We believe that the

OLAP indicators, which are based on the laws of psychology, should include the following:

❒ Division of data into measures and dimensions, defining the state and expanse of the business accordingly.

❒ Logical presentation of measure values as multi-dimensional cubes ordered by equivalent dimensions.

❒ Unlimited number of hierarchical link levels between dimension values.

❒ Flexible data manipulation. Possibility of constructing a subset of measure values using any discriminating rule defined by a value set of its dimensions. Possibility of constructing a subset of dimension values using any discriminating rule defined by a value set of any of the measures connected with it. Execution of logical operations with the resulting sets.

❒ Unlimited possibilities of aggregating the given subset of metric values. And thus the possibility of calculating not only the sum of values, but also any other functional defined by the user (minimum, maximum, average, median, etc.).

❒ Possibility of processing queries in real time (i.e., at the rate of the user's analytical comprehension of data).

❒ Developed resources of tabular and, more importantly, graphical data display for the end user.

I would like to emphasize the importance of graphical output. Such eminent scientists as Jacques Hadamard and Henri Poincaré, who tried using self-analysis to study the creative process of mathematical discovery, agreed that when they were solving a complex problem, they thought not in words or mathematical signs, but in geometrical images. Once a solution is found with these images, all that remains is to formalize it in writing or symbols so that it can be described to others. Also, modern psychology states that creative thinking is figurative. It is termed right-brain thinking. Without going too deeply into the psychological aspects of the problem, we shall state the widely-known fact that the human brain is capable of interpreting and analyzing much more information when it is represented as geometrical images than when it is in alpha-numeric form.

It is possible to give many examples confirming this fact. Imagine that it is necessary for you to analyze a chess position written in standard chess notation. If the number of figures is more than ten and you are not an experienced professional, you will spend significantly more time than if you were to analyze this on an actual chessboard. Even if the position is relatively simple.

Let's discuss another example. Suppose you need to find a picture of a person you know from a pile of a hundred different photos. You would probably not need more than a minute. Now imagine, however, that instead of photos, you are given one hundred written descriptions of the same people. It is doubtful that you will manage to solve the task at all.

Visual geometric images connected to a solvable problem enormously stimulate creative thinking and lead to discoveries in even such a formal area as number theory [4]. One of the leading experts in the field of an artificial intelligence, Professor D. Pospelov, has called systems like OLAP the "new window into the world of knowledge". Other experts [5,6] have also emphasized the importance of developing a graphic representation of information, and its influence on the intuition of the researcher.

OLAP technology is intended to increase efficiency in the informational, analytical, and administrative activity of management staff. Using these resources, it is possible to make quick and well-grounded operational and strategic decisions. The laws discovered with OLAP are then realized in economic models that allow us to glance into the future, which, in the words of Neil Raden, the president of Archer Decision Sciences Inc., "belongs to the one who can predict it and approach it first".[1]

According to the research done by the Meta Group Corporation, about 90% of the companies listed in the Fortune 1000 try to create data warehouses of various forms. For many companies, the main reason to create such a warehouse is the possibility of receiving information about the firm as a single unit. Warehouses help to perform operations on information much more reasonably. Besides, all the information related to the firm is actively included in the analysis, since the data used are stored in standard form, and their logical organization corresponds to business rules. Thus it is guaranteed that the various functions that support all aspects of the company's activity (product circulation, income, geographical allocation of production, etc.) form a complete, non-contradictory picture.

After three years of studying 62 organizations, an analysis carried out by International Data Corporation (IDC), has shown that these organizations have spent on average 2.2 million dollars on data warehouses—and received a 400 percent return on investment.

---

[1] *S.Arkhipenkov:* I believe it is necessary here to tell a story based on my own experience, a kind of a joke. Once I was making a presentation on the OLAP technology to the top managers of one of commercial banks. I had completed the report with this impressive, or so I thought, Neil Raden citation, and then there was an unexpected pause. After some time (30-45 seconds, which seemed to me like an eternity), the head bank representative said to me, "In my opinion, you are mistaken. The future belongs to whoever makes it." After that I realized that if these gentlemen really did have the keys to control the future, I should apologize that I had taken away their time, since they obviously do not require a tool for building models and predicting the future.

Chapter 1

Introduction
to Data Warehouses

1.1. Evolution of Corporate Information Systems

It just so happens that the introduction of information technology to the great majority of companies is carried out without a strategic development plan. It was initiated by separate entities, isolated from one another. This is due to the fact that the development of a company's information infrastructure was effected from the bottom upwards, as it came to light that this or that industrial or administrative area needed to be automated, and as the following objective conditions corresponding to the task arose:

❏   Information technologies

❏   Hardware-software support

❏   Human resources

❏   Financial resources

This led to the fact that today the majority of companies use a considerable number of diverse and poorly integrated information systems that function on various hardware platforms under different operating systems and use various DBMSs. First of all, these systems support the current daily activity of separate company divisions: warehouse, accounting department, staff, and others. In the documentation, such information systems are called transaction systems, or OLTP (On-Line Transactions Processing).

At the same time, the existing condition of corporate information systems is characterized by a considerably increased volume of data, obtained during the last five to ten years of active introduction of information technologies to industrial and administrative processes. This existing data allows you to formulate and solve problems connected not only with the daily activity of separate divisions, but also with tactical and strategic planning and management problems of not only separate divisions, but of the company as a whole as well.

In connection with this, the number of applied tasks intended for extracting, collecting, and presenting information necessary to the end user—be it a business analyst or a manager—for analyzing the current condition of business and predicting future development has significantly increased. Information systems oriented towards the settlement of just such a class of problems have been termed decision support systems. Historically, the first systems of this type became the so-called Executive Information Systems, or EISs. As a matter of fact, application packages that generated information in predetermined forms based on data received from transaction systems were somewhat similar to these. Each time you wanted to create a new report, the corporate divisions responsible for information support had to provide shared access to data in the transaction systems for both existing and new applications. This problem was usually solved using network equipment and operating system tools. While the number of corporate transaction systems, the volume of data circulating in them, and the number of reporting tasks were increasing, the connection topology associating isolated sources of data became more and more complicated and akin to "a plate of spaghetti" (Fig. 1.1 A). Further integration of corporate information resources in this manner has revealed a number of formidable problems with this approach:

❏ The constant increase in time and financial expenditures necessary to provide each new report form

❏ The necessity of continuously eliminating inconsistencies between semantically homogeneous data presented in different formats in various information sources

❏ The significant increase of the workload of the DBMS transaction system, which is connected with the parallel fulfillment of tasks related to report generation

❏ The absence in transaction systems of historical data (for a period of some years) necessary to effect strategic analysis and planning

In these days of dynamically changing market conditions and aggressive competition, it has become impossible to provide support for effecient corporate tactical and strategic management without first solving these problems.

Today, many people admit that in order to solve management tasks effectively, it is necessary to provide users with a unified view of corporate information, regardless of the place where it is physically stored. According to the strategic analysis performed by the Gartner Group [4], in large corporations today, information is integrated using a technique which allows you to retrieve, convert, and present information as a resource of the appropriate business processes (Fig. 1.1 B). This fact stimulated the appearance of data warehouses. The main purpose of such warehouses is to form a unified logical view of data located in different databases, or, in other words, to form a unified corporate data model.

A) Decentralized integration of sources   B) Centralized integration of sources

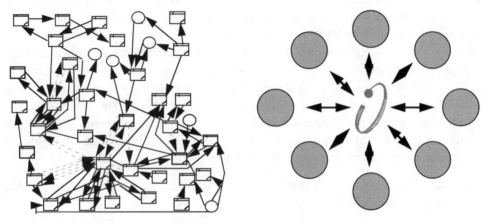

Fig. 1.1. Two approaches to corporate information integration

The information warehouse concept (originally named just that, Information Warehouse) arose in the 1980s in IBM. Nevertheless, it was William Inmon [1], the technical director of the Prism company, who is generally recognized as the "Father" of this technology. He published a number of articles that became an impetus for further research in this area. At that time, he gave the following definition of data warehouses:

> *"A data warehouse is a subject-oriented, integrated, time-variant, non-volatile collection of data in support of management's decision making process."*

In recent literature, however, the term "data warehouse" has been used in two senses [2,5].

First, the narrow sense, which differs little from Inmon's definition.

Second, the broad sense, when a data warehouse is regarded as a computer-based system oriented towards supporting administrative solutions that consist of an organizational structure, hardware, a database or collection of databases (a warehouse in the more narrow sense), and software, which generally executes the following functions:

❑ Retrieving data from separate sources, transforming them, and loading them into the warehouse

❏ Administering data and warehouse

❏ Retrieving data from the warehouse, analytically processing it, and presenting it to end users

As a rule, IBM, Oracle, PriceWaterhouseCoopers, and the book by R. Kimball [2] describe data warehouses in this broader sense. In our account, we used the terms decision support system (DSS) or OLAP system to denote this broader meaning, which, from our point of view, more accurately describes the subject discussed in the present edition.

We would like once more to stress that an OLAP system has different functional purposes than OLTP systems, and does not replace them, but is rather built on their basis, and uses transaction systems as data sources.

Generally, in a control circuit of a complex system, we can distinguish five interdependent functions (Fig. 1.2).

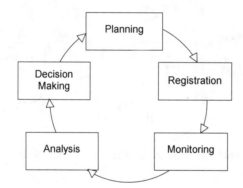

Fig. 1.2. Control circuit of a complex system

During the execution of these functions, it is required that the processes of data acquisition, data processing, and data viewing be implemented for the end user. While planning and registration functions are characteristic for transaction systems, management (monitoring), analysis, and decision-making support functions are characterized by:

❏ The collection, storage, and preparation of data formed at the planning and registration stages

❏ Support of administrative inventory taking and internal and external organization reporting

❏ The implementation of multi-criteria analysis of business

❏ A search for and simulation of a solution in different situations

Thus, there are two distinct classes of control circuits:

❏ On-line transaction processing systems (OLTP)

❏ Decision support systems (DSS)

The distribution of functions between analytical and transactional information systems is shown in Fig. 1.3.

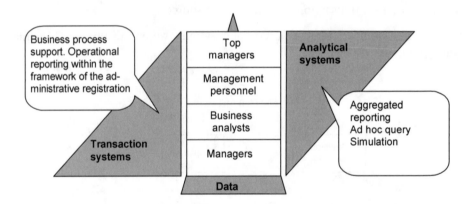

Fig. 1.3. The allocation of a functional between analytical and transactional information systems

This new stage of data warehouse development became possible due to the overall perfection of information technologies, in particular:

❏ The arrival of software intended for on-line data analysis and for users' ad hoc queries (OLAP)

❏ The appearance of new types of databases based on multidimensional models and parallel query processing, which, in turn, come from achievements in the field of parallel computers

❏ The appearance of middleware, which provides a connection between databases of different types

❏ The sharp fall in the cost of information storage

1.2. OLAP Technology

To this day, a canonical definition of OLAP does not exist. We shall not reiterate here the twelve OLAP tags formulated by Codd in 1993 [3] nor the six additions to them that were added later. The reader who is interested in this will find them easily in practically any article on the subject. We define OLAP as a "Fast Analysis of Shared Multidimensional Information". *We believe that this definition,* formulated in 1995, remains the most accurate, and concisely expresses the features of the given technology. As was emphasized in the introduction, when referring to the OLAP technology, the word *fast* is the most important thing. It means that the system should provide most answers to the users within approximately five seconds. Thus, the simplest queries are handled within one second, with very few exceeding 20 seconds. Recent research in the Netherlands has shown that end users believe the process to be unsuccessful if the results have not been obtained within 30 seconds. They might press <Alt>+<Ctrl>+<Del> if the system does not advise them that the data processing requires more time. Even if the system notifies the user that the process may last much longer, users can be distracted and lose their train of thought. Thus, the quality of the analysis will be worse.

The definition of the information as *shared* stresses the fact that OLAP applications are built above a common base—the data warehouse—which is the only "source of truth" when making administrative decisions.

The main feature of an OLAP system is that it is created based on a multidimensional data model, as opposed to OLTP systems, which are based on a relational model. Data stored in databases with a relational model have the appearance of tables consisting of rows and columns. Such data structures are the best way to provide efficient processing of constantly incoming information, but to a lesser extent are convenient for creating decision support systems based on them. OLTP systems are oriented towards applications that execute, in a relatively short period of time, a large number of transactions having to do with adding and updating small volumes of information dispersed among various interdependent tables (Fig. 1.4). For example, in a typical situation, you must refresh all data related to the given customer. Each relevant table contains the identification number of the customer, which is used to establish a relationship between different tables. When adding or changing data, such a simple relationship between records only allows for the updating of a small number of records during one transaction.

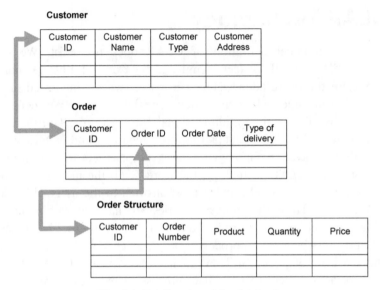

Fig. 1.4. Relational models of data view

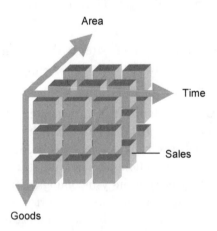

Fig. 1.5. Multidimensional model of data view

In a multidimensional model, data are represented as a multidimensional cube, where dimensions correspond to the axes of a cube, and variables correspond to the individual cells of a cube. For example, if we want to analyze the sales volume of a specific product, depending on area and time, we come to a multidimensional database model having three dimensions (the product, the region, and the month) and one variable, which is sales volume (Fig. 1.5).

The multidimensional model allows us to make plane sections of a data cube, and to turn it on whatever edge is convenient for us. Besides which, using the built-in queries construction tool, the researcher can put together a fairly refined selection of data. Using a multidimensional model, an analyst can easily see the kind of data display she or he needs to best accomplish the task (Fig. 1.3).

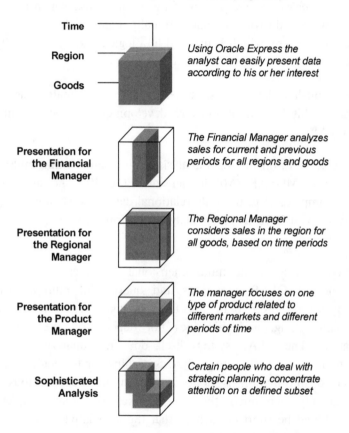

Fig. 1.6. Sections and rotations of a data cube in a multidimensional model

In the example above, multidimensional data can be also represented in a relational model under the "star" schema. At the center of "star" there is a main table containing facts; this table will contain rows for all existing combinations of "product", "area", and "month" values. Another column of this table will define the value of the sales volume. All data can be stored in one table, including columns with values for each of the three measurements; however, they are usually replaced by short numerical keys, which are used instead of indexes in smaller reference tables that form the points of the "star". As the numerical keys are usually shorter than the actual values of the measurements, you save space in the database.

Just as relational models consist of rows and columns, multidimensional models of cubes are simply *logical representations* of the information, which are used to understand what we can do with the data. Actually, data on the disk are stored in a kind of ordered structure, which is mapped in a logical model only while executing user queries.

This is why an on-line data analysis system can also be created based on a relational database. This branch of software development has been named **ROLAP** (Relational OLAP).

In contrast to **ROLAP**, on-line data analysis implemented with a multidimensional database is called **MOLAP** (Multidimensional OLAP). The question naturally arises: why is it impossible to use only relational databases when creating analytical systems; why do you have to store analyzed information in special multidimensional databases?

The basic argument for using multidimensional databases is their productivity. Execution time for OLAP operations and queries in multidimensional bases can be many times faster than the time it takes for a relational database to do the same thing, and this does not depend on the volume of data in the database. The OLAP system itself does not analyze the information. It is only a tool controlled by the analyst. Searching for the logic and correlation in the collected information is done in the human subconscious. Therefore, as we have already mentioned, the time it takes to execute a query is vitally important. It should be short enough so that the associative links in the analyst's brain that generated the given query are not forgotten. Otherwise, when a researcher obtains the result, he or she might not remember what was the aim of the research.

While constructing a DSS, a compromise solution is also possible, in which the aggregated data are stored in a multidimensional database, and detailed data, which are called rather rarely, are stored in the "star" schema-type relational tables. Such an approach has been named **HOLAP** (Hybrid OLAP) in certain literature.

1.3. Data Warehouses

1.3.1. General Properties

A data warehouse is created for the following purposes:

☐ To integrate data within a single location; coordination and possibly aggregation of previously disjointed detailed data:

    ☐ Historical archives

    ☐ Data from on-line systems

    ☐ Data from external sources

☐ Disjoining data sets used for on-line processing and data sets used for solving decision support tasks

☐ Providing overall information support to the maximum number of users

First and foremost, a data warehouse plays the role of an integrator and accumulator of historical data. The structure of the warehouse's organization is oriented towards data domains. A subject-oriented storage area contains data that come in from different on-line databases and external sources. The storage area is a set of data possessing the following characteristics:

☐ Based on a data domain or a number of data domains

☐ Integrated

☐ Time variable (chronology support)

☐ Non-volatile

Based on a Data Domain

The first feature of a data warehouse is the fact of its being grouped by subject. The subject orientation contrasts with the classic trend of applied applications to lean towards functionality and processes.

Applications always operate using functions, such as drawing up a contract, providing loans, issuing invoices, transferring to accounts, etc. A data warehouse is organized around facts and subjects, such as a business deal, credit amount, buyer, supplier, product, etc.

Integration

The most important aspect of a data warehouse is that the data contained in the warehouse is integrated. Integration comes through in many aspects:

❏   In coordination of names

❏   In coordination of units of measurement for variables

❏   In coordination of data structures

❏   In coordination of physical data attributes

The contrast between data integration in a data warehouse and in an application environment can be illustrated in the following manner.

The first reason for a possible application mismatch is a large number of development tools. Each development tool establishes definite rules to work with, and some of these are specific to each tool. It's no secret that each developer prefers one set of development tools to another. If two developers use different sets of development tools, then they, as a rule, use each set's individual properties, so there is the chance of non-conformity between the systems that they develop.

The second reason that applications may not properly match is that there are many ways for an application to be constructed. The way in which a certain application is constructed depends on the developer's style, when the application was developed, and also on a number of factors that characterize the actual conditions under which the application was developed. All this is reflected in the methods used in defining the key structure, ways of coding, data denotation, the physical characteristics of data, etc. Thus, if two developers create different applications using different sets of development tools, as well as different ways of constructing their applications, there is a high probability that complete coordination between these systems will not exist.

Data integration with respect to attributes' units of measurement can be explained thus. Application developers can approach the problem of defining production size in several ways. Sizes can be set in centimeters, inches, yards, and so on. Whatever the data source was, if the information goes into storage, it should be transformed into the units considered standard in the storage area.

Time-Variable

At any given moment, all data in storage are chronologically consistent. For on-line systems, this fundamental data characteristic corresponds to the compatibility of data at the moment of access.

When data are accessed in an on-line environment, it is expected that the data have common values only at the moment of access.

A data warehouse's dependence on time is shown in the following. The data in a warehouse covers a period of time anywhere from one to ten years. In an on-line environment, data are presented for an interval from the current time to several dozen days. For effective transaction processing, highly efficient applications should use only the minimum amount of data. Therefore, on-line applications are oriented towards using a short interval of time.

Another example of the data warehouse's dependence on time is found in its structure. Each warehouse structure includes—either obviously or implicitly— a time element.

The third way a data warehouse depends on time is in the necessity of strictly observing the rule that data, once they are correctly introduced to the warehouse, cannot be updated. Looking at it from a practical point of view, a data warehouse is a large series of snapshots. Naturally, if the data snapshot has been done incorrectly, it can be modified. But if the correct snapshot was received, then, once it has been obtained, it cannot be changed later. On-line data that is correct at the moment of access can be updated as required.

Non-Volatility

The fourth defining characteristic of a data warehouse is non-volatility. In an on-line environment, updating, adding, deleting, and modifying affect records regularly. Basic manipulation of data in warehouses is limited to the initial loading of data and accessing it later. In a data warehouse, data are not updated. Initial (historical) data, after these have been harmonized, verified, and brought into a data warehouse, remain constant, and are marked as read-only.

The difference between data processing in an on-line environment and data processing in a data warehouse leads to an important difference in outcome. As updates are not performed in data warehouses, there is no need to support mechanisms for the updating process at the design level of a data warehouse. This means that when solving problems of normalization and physical de-normalization at the physical level of design, access to data can be optimized without any limitations.

Another consequence of the simplicity of operations with data from a warehouse concerns data operation technology. Data operation technology in an on-line environment is noted for its great difficulty. It supports on-line backup and restoring functions, provides data integrity, and includes conflict- and deadlock-resolving mechanisms. These functions are not so very critical for information processing in a data warehouse.

Such data warehouse characteristics as being oriented on data domain during design, integration of data, dependence on time, and simplicity of working with data, determine the environment that differs significantly from the classical transaction environment.

On-line environments are the source of almost all warehouse environment data. You might get the feeling that there is a huge redundancy of data in both environments. However, in practice, the redundancy of data in the environments is minimal, since:

❏ When data are transferred from an on-line environment to a data warehouse, the data are filtered. A lot of data is never unloaded from the on-line environment. A data warehouse receives only information used for processing in a decision support system.

❏ The range of time in the environments differs considerably. Data in an on-line environment are always current. The data in a warehouse have a chronology. Taking into consideration this time range, the intersection between an on-line environment and a data warehouse environment is minimal.

❏ A data warehouse contains aggregated (final) data that will never be included in an on-line environment.

❏ There are fundamental conversions made when data are transferred from an on-line environment to a data warehouse. Upon arrival in the warehouse, most of the parts of the data have been somehow changed.

1.3.2. Warehouse Data

Generally, a modern DSS data model is created on the basis of five data classes:

❏ Data sources

❏ A data warehouse (in the narrow sense)

❐ On-line data store

❐ Data marts

❐ Metadata

Data Sources

On-line transaction systems, which support the everyday record-making activity of a company, are warehouse data sources. The necessity of including this or that transaction system as a source is defined by the business requirements put on DSS. Proceeding from these requirements, external systems, including the Internet, can be considered as data sources. Detailed data from sources can either be directly introduced into a warehouse or be drilled up to the required level of generalization.

Data Warehouse (in the Narrow Sense)

A data warehouse (in the narrow sense) is a subject-oriented database or collection of databases extracted from sources organized into segments that reflect the concrete data area of business: manufacturing, output, customers, suppliers, invoices, etc. As a rule, a data warehouse contains data that are rather weakly aggregated.

Operational Data Store

There are different definitions given for this class of data. In saying operational data store (ODS), we will take it to mean a technological element used to store data in DSS, which is an intermediate buffer between transaction data sources and the warehouse. As has already been mentioned, before data can be introduced to the warehouse, they need to be transformed to a uniform format, cleaned up, unified, and synchronized. For example, the data necessary for supporting decision-making can exist in a transaction system for a shorter time (hours or days) than the period of adding data to warehouse (days or weeks). Or, semantically homogeneous data are extracted from transaction systems at different times. In such a case, an ODS acts as an accumulator of data introduced from sources before their loading to warehouse. As opposed to a data warehouse, the information in an ODS can change over time, in accordance with changes that take place in the data sources.

ODS is created as an intermediate buffer between on-line systems and a data warehouse. This is a construction similar to that of a data warehouse. The similarity of an ODS and a data warehouse lies in their being subject-oriented, and in the fact that they store detailed data. An ODS is different from a data warehouse in that an ODS:

❏ has changeable contents

❏ contains only detailed data

❏ contains only current data values

Detailed data are data from on-line and external systems that has not been affected by generalization and addition operations (i.e., data that have not changed their semantics). Data from on-line systems and external sources are received by an ODS after going through transformation processes.

The data in an ODS are regularly updated. Each time the data are changed in on-line systems and in external sources, the corresponding data from the ODS should also be modified. The frequency of ODS updates depends both on the frequency of the source updates and on the regulations relating to loading data into the store.

Data Marts

Functionally-oriented data marts are data structures that provide a solution for analytical tasks in a specific functional area or in a particular company department, for example, profitability management, market analysis, resource analysis, and others. Data marts can be looked at as small warehouses created for information support of specific company administrative departments' analytical tasks.

The data source for data marts is data from the warehouse, which, as a rule, are aggregated and consolidated on various levels of a hierarchy. Detailed data can also be introduced into the data mart, or just be present in it as a link to warehouse data.

Different data marts contain different combinations and samplings of the same detailed warehouse data. It is important that the data in the marts is introduced from the central warehouse, which is the only "source of truth".

Metadata

Metadata are any data about data. Metadata play an important role in DSS creation. At the same time, it is one of most complex and least studied problems. Generally, it is possible to select at least three aspects of metadata that must be present in the system.

- ❏ From the users' point of view:
    - ❏ Metadata for business analysts
    - ❏ Metadata for administrators
    - ❏ Metadata for developers
- ❏ From the point of view of data domains:
    - ❏ Warehouse data structures
    - ❏ Business process models
    - ❏ User descriptions
    - ❏ Technological items
    - ❏ Other
- ❏ From the point of view of system functionality:
    - ❏ Metadata on transformation processes
    - ❏ Metadata on system administration
    - ❏ Metadata on applications
    - ❏ Metadata on data display for users

The presence of the three metadata aspects mentioned above suggests that, for example, applied users and system developers will have different visions of the technological aspects of source data transformation. For end users it will be semantics, structure, and periodicity of adding data from sources to the warehouse; for developers, it will be Entity-Relationship (ER) diagrams, rules of transformation, and the interface for access to a source's data.

Currently there is no uniform industrial technology for creation or support of metadata. Therefore, problems connected with metadata management are considered separately for each specific project of constructing a DSS.

1.3.3. Warehouse Components

Generally, at the top level, a warehouse consists of three subsystems:

- ❏ Data loading subsystem
- ❏ Query processing and data visualization subsystem
- ❏ Warehouse administration subsystem

Data Loading Subsystem

The given subsystem represents modular software, which, in accordance with the defined regulations, extracts data from sources and organizes them in the unified format defined for the given warehouse. The subsystem is responsible for the formalized logical coordination, quality, and integration of data loaded from sources into an ODS. Each data source requires the cultivation of its own load module. Each module should solve tasks of two classes:

❏ Initial loading of retrospective data

❏ Regulated addition of source data to the warehouse

Under the regulations, the subsystem also extracts detailed data from ODS, aggregates, consolidates, and transforms them, and moves data to the warehouse and data marts. It is in this subsystem that all business models of data consolidation by hierarchical measurements and of calculation of dependent business variables with independent input data should be defined.

Query Processing and Data Visualization Subsystem

ODS, data warehouses, and data marts are the infrastructure that provides for the storage and administration of data. To extract, analytically process, and present to end users the data, special software is provided. We can generally define three types of software for this:

❏ Software for regulated reporting, which is characterized by predetermined data queries and their presentation to business users. It is not necessary that this software have a fast response time. Taking into consideration cost efficiency, it is best to implement this with ROLAP technology.

❏ Ad hoc query user software. This software is the main means of dialogue between business analysts and the warehouse, where each subsequent query to data and type of representation is defined, as a rule, by the results of the previous query. Applications of the given type should perform query processing with a high rate of efficiency (within seconds). This software is realized using the MOLAP technology and special tools for complex ad hoc query construction, where such tools have a graphic interface that is intuitively clear to business analysts.

❏ Data mining software, which implements complex statistical algorithms and artificial intelligence algorithms intended to search logic hidden in data, to present this logic as a model, and according to it give various predictions of possible developments in the situation using the "What if...? " pattern.

Certainly, such a division is as a rule rather conventional, and the differences between appropriate applications can be slight.

Warehouse Administration Subsystem

This subsystem is responsible for all tasks connected with system support and providing its reliable operation and extension. It is possible to select at least four classes of tasks, the solutions of which should be provided by the subsystem:

❏ Data administration, which includes regular addition of data from sources and, if necessary, manual input, verification, and data correction in an ODS. Ordinarily, data administration is carried out by business users, and responsibility is allocated among the subject-oriented segments.

❏ Warehouse administration. The task of warehouse administration includes all problems connected with maintenance of the warehouse architecture, support of its effective and uninterrupted operation, and data protection and recovery after failures.

❏ Data access administration provides support for user profiles, discretionary control over access to confidential data, and protection of the information against unauthorized access.

❏ Administration of system metadata.

1.4. Oracle Software Review

The Oracle Corporation has defined data warehouses as one of the most important areas of their activity, and offers customers a complete and integrated tool and business application set to implement these technologies. Software intended for design, creation, and support of DSS include:

❏ Relational and multidimensional database servers

❏ Tools for developing transformational layer software, warehouse administration, ODS, and data marts

❏ An application server

❏ Software development tools

❏ Ready-to-use special applications

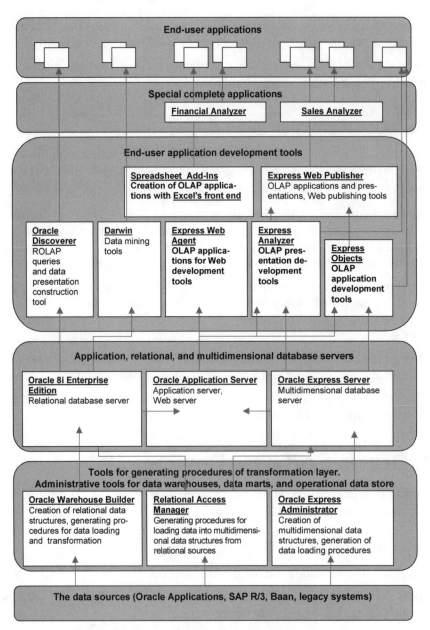

Fig. 1.7. Oracle general software and dataflow components

Let's discuss in brief the characteristics of the software components considered in this book.

1.4.1. Data and Application Servers

Oracle 8i Enterprise Edition

This is a reliable, scalable, high-performance corporate server for object-oriented and relational databases with built-in mechanisms for administration, automatic replication, and post-failure data recovery. It has tools to support these functions and structures, which are characteristic to the warehouse.

Query processing techniques other than OLTP applications are required for warehouse data structures, since they usually process complex ad hoc queries executed with large data volumes. To comply with these special requirements, Oracle has systematically developed their own DBMS over several years, which now has the ability to solve specific tasks of decision support system applications. Such leading technologies as concurrent execution of queries, effective bit indexing, and specialized query execution algorithms like hash connections, are included in Oracle 8i. It is also necessary to mention the inclusion of data sectioning and query optimization mechanisms, which provide effective, scalable, and concurrent execution of queries. To create and support repositories, some features have been specially added to the aforementioned DBMS version.

Also included is the direct capability of determining multidimensional data dimensions (the `CREATE DIMENSION` operator) and the set of dimension attribute hierarchies. Metadata established by this process (the data structure that describes the dimensions and is stored in the DBMS directory) are used during data manipulation.

Materialized Views: As opposed to regular views, which do not contain real data but only specify the operation for selecting and unifying data from other tables, materialized views really do contain data. Usually, materialized views are used to create and support tables of aggregates in their actual state. The data definition language allows you to set the update order for materialized views (after changes in the initial tables) and to allow their involvement in the mechanism for dynamic overwriting of queries.

The mechanism of query overwriting is the analysis of the initial data selection query for the possibility of using data stored in materialized views and overwriting the initial query, if that is an option. If for example the initial query contains data aggregating functions, and there are materialized views that already contain the indicated aggregates, the initial query will be overwritten, so that instead of processing a large number of records to determine these aggregates, the necessary aggregates will simply be selected from the materialized views. This mechanism significantly increases the system's data-handling capacity and is invisible to applications.

A set of specialized utilities that permit a user to control the frequency of data queries, and in particular, the frequency of calculating aggregates, is also included. This information is intended to assist in making a decision as to the necessity of creating or deleting materialized views.

Certain special extensions of the SQL query language were also implemented. In particular, the analytical functions of ranking, statistical analysis, aggregating, and lag/lead functions were added, and reporting tools were extended. The "Rollup" and "Cube" extensions allow you to set calculation of intermediate totals in conformity with dimension hierarchy levels.

Oracle8i Enterprise Edition includes Oracle Enterprise Manager, which is a tool specially designed to efficiently control the Oracle server. There are diverse tools for developing stored procedures and server applications in the Java and PL/SQL programming languages.

Express Server

Express Server is multidimensional database server. Thanks to its capability of modeling correlations between stored data, it allows us to broadly describe the business activity of any company.

It has advanced tools for analysis and time series prediction, which can be used for a wide range of OLAP applications. It includes the powerful programming language SPL 4GL, which is oriented towards multidimensional data processing that provides for the modification of large arrays using just several strings of program code. It provides business activity simulation tools, which allow for analyzing data in accordance with the "What if...? " pattern. Finally, it allows for submission of data as reports and diagrams defined by the user.

Oracle Application Server

This is a platform for developing multi-user network applications whose clients can be both standard browsers and Java applets and applications. To provide transport functions, popular Web servers from Netscape, Microsoft, or Apache optimized for effective network data transmission can be used together with Oracle Application Server. The main features of the Oracle Application Server are:

❑ *Close integration with Oracle and Oracle Express DBMS.* Oracle Application Server is a tool for publishing information stored in relational and multidimensional Oracle databases on the Web. Although writing programs and batch tasks in C and Perl is still possible, it defers to application development with PL/SQL or Java, which are more closely integrated with DBMS and are more effective in development, debugging, and support.

❑ *Scalability.* Oracle Application Server is accessible on many platforms, including basic versions of Unix, Linux, and Microsoft Windows NT. Since the product was created based on CORBA specifications, Oracle Application Server can arrange the user load, working on several computers at the same time within the framework of one logical node. This property is absolutely necessary for constructing scalable, fault-tolerant solutions, especially in cluster architectures. The built-in monitor manages component efficacy and will automatically restore in case of a failure.

❑ *Manageability.* The Administrator can control all Oracle Application Server functions using one console implemented as a Web application.

Oracle Application Server enables you to introduce "thin" clients—browsers and Java servers—into organizations of various sizes, and to move basic business applications to the network platform.

1.4.2. Administration Tools

Oracle Warehouse Builder

This is a special tool used to create data warehouses based on Oracle RDBMS, which provides a solution for the following tasks:

❑ Defining and initializing the warehouse schema, data sources, and operations that extract data from sources, converting them, and loading them into the warehouse or to an ODS

❑ Configuring and generating program code for warehouse creation: table and extraction operations, transformation, and data loading

❑ Creating a warehouse and transmitting control of regulated data loading to Enterprise Manager

Express Administrator

Oracle Express Administrator simplifies construction and support of Express databases, making the implementation of OLAP applications easier and faster. It provides some easy-to-use graphic tools for administration, which enable you to define and in the future work with database objects such as dimensions, variables, formula, ratio, programs, models, and dimension value sets. The interface, based on intuitive dialogs, simplifies the process of data loading and data drilling up to different dimension hierarchy levels. A graphic hierarchy editor, an SPL 4GL program editor, a multi-line command window, and tools for planning and monitoring tasks are also included with Express Administrator.

Express Administrator supports the import of data files in ASCII format, Express Interchange Format (EIF), and Discoverer format, as well as the import of relational database tables accessible through ODBC (obviously, when executing a loading program from Oracle DBMS, you can use the SQL*Net "native" interface).

Relational Access Manager

Relational Access Manager is an additional specialized tool that allows Express to access relational data sources. Using this tool, Express applications and tools can present relational database data in table and graphic form, and manipulate them in a multidimensional model context, providing simple data selection and analysis. Relational data can be visualized using descriptors, which help to hide the true complexity of internal relational structures. Thus the end users do not need to be familiar with the real structure of the relational schema.

The Relational Access Manager user interface is Relational Access Administrator (RAA), which includes tools that give the database manager the ability to build data models based on the analytical business requirements of end users. Using the RAA, managers can easily translate these requirements to the language of multidimensional modeling, which extracts data from accessible relational sources. Among the tools that are useful to the database administrator, we should note the following:

❒   The schema generator, which permits you to automatically set prototypes for a database with a "star" schema that supports the Express data model.

❒ The loading tool, which permits the administrator to define and save procedures for a database update, which can be done immediately or in accordance with a schedule (once or periodically).

❒ The query statistics module, which collects key statistics describing system performance. With it, the manager can find out whether there are any sore spots affecting the performance of the system, define which hierarchy level combinations should be aggregated in a relational database, figure out which combinations need to be stored in the Express database, decide which system resources should be reserved, and make corrections.

The following relational databases are supported:

❒ Oracle 7

❒ Oracle 8

❒ Oracle RDB versions 6.1 and 7.*x*

❒ Sybase System 11

❒ IBM DB2 versions 2.*x*

❒ Microsoft SQL Server 6.5 (or earlier versions)

❒ Teradata 2.*x*

❒ Red Brick 5.*x*

1.4.3. Application Development Tools

Discoverer

This is an end user business analyst tool, which is used:

❒ To build ad hoc queries to data

❒ To build regulated report forms

❒ To analyze multidimensional data

❒ To publish the results of analyses to the Web

Data for Discoverer are stored in a relational repository or in a data mart in tables organized according to a "star" or "snowflake" schema (ROLAP). Thus, the following standard OLAP mechanisms are accessible to the user: drilling up/down, slicing and rotating data cubes, and tabular and chart data presentation.

Express Analyzer

This is a tool environment for viewing and analyzing multidimensional data, and for creating briefings/OLAP applications in MS Windows. It also acts as an environment for running ready applications designed in Express Objects and Express Analyzer. Analyzer has access to any data that is stored in a multidimensional Express database.

Compared to Express Objects, Express Analyzer is an "easy" tool environment for an end user, in which OLAP application development for MS Windows is possible even for a layman, as it does not require you to use programming or know DBMS basics. Applications are developed by visually constructing them from predefined components and then setting their properties.

Oracle Express Analyzer enables you:

❐ To analyze data and create tables and graphics using data from a database, and to manipulate their presentation to study data from different perspectives

❐ To create and to edit presentations that can contain a few interrelated pages with tables and diagrams representing the information stored in a database with various dimensions

❐ To view applications prepared in Express Analyzer and Express Objects by other users

Express Objects

This is a professional tool environment for visual object-oriented development of OLAP applications in MS Windows. Using Express Objects, it is possible to create and to debug client-server applications, which allow an end user to effectively apply all the power of Express products.

Express Objects is a completely object-oriented development environment, which supports such necessary object mechanisms as encapsulation, inheritance, and polymorphism. In addition to this, Express Objects includes the standard containership mechanism, which is extremely useful for creating complex applications. During development, you can use the pre-prepared standard components set, and, according to your own needs, modify and customize their properties (object data), methods (object functions), and events (functions to handle messages from a user, hardware, the operating system, or other objects). Also, there is the possibility of developing new components, using the ready-made components as a base and adding new properties, methods, and event handlers to them. New components can be added to an existing set and be used in later developments as standard components.

The standard components provide the developer with the capability of using all the MS Windows interface components, buttons, main and pop-up menus, edit windows, toolbars, lists, images, standard dialogues, and other such things as needed. Also, certain powerful on-line components for managing and displaying multidimensional data such as tables and diagrams are included in the set. They not only display information stored in a multidimensional base in a convenient way for the end user, but also allow him or her to effectively gain flexible control, both of the data view on the screen and of the content of the displayed information, which is a necessary condition for on-line analysis.

Express Basic is a language for application development; it has a core similar to that of Visual Basic, as well as having similar functions and expressions. Dynamic data exchange (DDE), OLE embedding, and Visual Basic object embedding are also supported.

A set of special tools such as Object Browser, Database Browser, and Object Inspector provides efficient visual application development.

Spreadsheet Add-Ins

The given tool provides close integration of Express software with Microsoft Excel applications, and allows you to use them as an environment for developing on-line client applications with read/write access to multidimensional databases.

Express Web Publisher

Oracle Express Web Publisher is a Rapid Application Development (RAD) tool for developing OLAP briefings for the Web, as well as for publishing WWW briefings developed using Express Analyzer and Express Objects.

Web technologies provide a simple solution for the problem of integrating different platforms in information systems. Now, Web browsers for practically all platforms can be downloaded as shareware.

Express Web Agent

Oracle Express Web Agent is a library of standard objects, which allows you to create Express OLAP applications executed in the Internet/intranet with the help of any Web browser. The procedures that generate dynamic HTML pages are stored in the Express Database as objects. An HTML page can include interactive Java applets—tables, diagrams, and any other Java applets; JavaScript programs; and VRML scripts, which receive data from a multidimensional database as parameters. These functional capabilities allow you to develop interactive applications for a "thin" client of practically unlimited complexity.

Darwin

The tools included in the Darwin software are used for extracting knowledge from enormous databases. This package is an integrated product that includes various algorithms for computer generation of classification and prognostic models for the investigated problem. It is intended for analyzing practical problems in the field of on-line and strategic administrative business solutions based on the constantly growing volume of corporate information systems data. The package has an open architecture and provides parallel processing on different hardware platforms.

The given software is intended for solving tasks of the following two classes:

❐ Construction of complex models with considerable computing performance based on large industrial databases

❐ Construction of classification models and templates for a wide range of separate data classes

In the first case, generalized models for different practical situations are created, having information consolidated into one database. In the second case, computing models for each area or product type, etc., are created.

1.4.4. Ready-to-Use Special Applications

Oracle Financial Analyzer

Oracle Financial Analyzer is a distributed computing OLAP application system, which provides consolidation, management, planning, and generation of reports related to the company's financial activity. It is intended for a PC local area network and has access to any data that is stored in a multidimensional Express database.

Financial Analyzer allows one to solve the following tasks:

❑ Summarizing and analyzing corporate financial data and forming a budget

❑ Performing financial simulations

❑ Configuring a financial system, taking into consideration the concrete requirements of entrepreneurial activity

❑ Forming a hierarchical system of collection, analysis, support, and distribution of financial data on a corporation scale

Oracle Sales Analyzer

Oracle Sales Analyzer is an OLAP tool used to analyze corporate data for sales and marketing departments. It has access to any data that is stored in a multidimensional Express database.

It allows the user to evaluate development tendencies in different fields of entrepreneurial activity on the basis of corporate data, and provides:

❑ Detailed and competent data analysis

❑ Control over the speed of introduction and promotion of a new product

❑ The ability to compare price, distribution, and promotion of products in different areas

Using Sales Analyzer, it is possible to:

❑ Create a new document and edit a previously created one

❑ Assign a subset of dimension values to multidimensional data, on the basis of which a report or diagram will be generated

❑ Calculate new data according to information from a multidimensional database

❑ Edit the format of a document in an appropriate manner

❑ Print out, save, and/or send the contents of a document to another application

Chapter 2

Methodology

2.1. The Strategy of System Construction and Rational Unified Process

We will take the phrase "strategy of information analysis system construction" to mean a general plan that is necessary to implement in order to achieve the desired final result.

There are different approaches to the strategy of corporate data warehouse construction: top-down construction, bottom-up construction, dynamic data integration, *etc*. The subject of their advantages and drawbacks lies beyond the scope of this book. Based on experience from specific, successful projects, we consider the most efficient approach to be one where during the process of warehouse development and introduction, the database is built up, step by step, based on a uniform classifier system and a common environment for data transmission and storage. With each deployment step, one or two data marts are implemented in accordance with the following development stages:

❏ Inception

❏ Elaboration

❏ Construction

❏ Transition

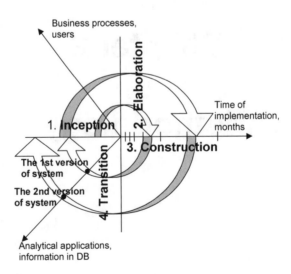

Fig. 2.1. DSS Building Strategy

The step-by-step building strategy allows us, upon completion of each cycle, to put the completed system with the defined limits of functionality into commercial operation with in the shortest period of time. The small size of each design cycle essentially minimizes losses in case of a project error, as opposed to what would happen if an error occurred while designing and creating the whole system all at once. Besids, since each cycle uses the same methodical and technological approaches and the same development tools are applied, the time it takes to implement each new piece of data is reduced. This is because the experience of the group of developers gradually increases, and the mechanism of interaction between the customers and system developers improves with time.

It is necessary to emphasize that this approach to creating DSS formed from our experience is close to the Rational Unified Process (RUP) [9], which uses an iterative approach while creating complex systems. This approach assumes gradual improvement and the construction of more and more capacious solutions after several cycles. According to RUP, each cycle consists of four phases similar to the stages of system development mentioned above:

❐ Inception: problem statement, define the purpose of the business system

❐ Elaboration: design, develop a system schedule and a system architecture

❐ Construction: system implementation

❐ Transition: delivery of the system to the end users

At the end of each phase, there is a strictly defined basic point where one evaluates to what degree the stated purposes were achieved, and whether it is necessary to make changes to the process before the next step.

At the *inception* stage, the system purpose and project framework is defined. The analysis of the purpose includes the definition of the criteria for project success and risk appraisal.

The *elaboration* stage includes analysis of the data domain and development of a basic architectural solution. As a rule, in large projects, a system prototype is developed, intended to confirm the viability of the selected architectural solutions. The prototype usually implements only one or a few of the most important scripts for system performance. At the end of the elaboration stage, methods to manage the most significant risks of the project are developed.

At the *construction* stage, a product ready for implementation is developed, and development and testing of the program complex is completed.

Transition includes the delivery of the system to the end users: business analysts, managers, and the support and maintenance groups.

These four main project stages form the development cycle. Each cycle is completed by the generation of a new version of the system.

The structure and content of each stage are considered more closely in the following chapters.

2.2. Project Start

This stage is not a part of the design cycle; however, as our experience shows, it has fundamental value for successfully executing operations in all subsequent stages of the project. The main purpose of this stage is to minimize the risks related to incorrect and/or inadequate estimation of results, sizes, periods, and cost of design operations by the customer and by the developer. At this stage we need to solve all required tasks before starting the actual work. First, we have to clearly define and stipulate the project framework in the contract documents. As a rule, this stage precedes the preliminary inspection, which should answer questions as to what are the business problems of the customer and what must be done to solve them. Within the framework of such a preliminary inspection, it is necessary to estimate the driving forces of the given project on the part of the customer, and his or her readiness to participate in the project. A clear understanding of all these factors can fundamentally affect the structure and the estimation of the complexity (and sometimes the expediency) of working under the contract. At this stage, along with the coordination of the contract documentation, a project management plan and an organizational structure (design group and executives) are formed. Coordination and confirmation of the working plan of the project, and the actual start of operation under the contract, are the last steps of the given stage.

2.2.1. Defining the Project Framework

Successful execution of the project is possible only if there is a clear understanding of the customer's needs, and if the project purposes are formulated clearly. We believe that it is necessary to define two aspects of the given problem.

The Driving Forces of the Project

The first aspect relates to the detection and clear understanding of the objective and subjective reasons that the customer wishes to construct the warehouse.

In practice, different situations are possible, and not only the complexity of work under the contract, but also the possibility of success as a whole can depend on them. Let's discuss some of them.

Objective reasons:

☐ Attempt to gain an advantage over competitors thanks to increased operational ability and increased validity of administrative solutions

☐ Attempt to increase business profit

☐ Attempt to reduce overheads

☐ Implementation of new information technologies within the framework of business reorganization

It is possible to refer to the subjective "driving-forces" in the following ways:

☐ The realization by a specific person from upper management (generally, the head of a department) that the company needs to obtain better access to information in order to make better decisions. This can be considered the best situation for control over the project, since on the one hand, the manager, etc. clearly sets the functional framework of the project, and on the other hand, he or she provides for close interaction between the implementers and the necessary experts from the customer's company. The project usually leads to the creation of one or more functionally-oriented data marts, and to a number of analytical applications above them.

☐ The real customers of the system are specific departments, and company management makes a decision to develop a unique integrated analytical system. As a rule, the given project takes the form of creating a large-scale corporate DSS. This situation is more complex than the previous one for a number of reasons. First off, the actual customers are mid-level managers who cannot assist the developers in overcoming the clash of interests between the owners and the information consumers. Secondly, the large-scale nature of the project requires a more careful study of general design solutions and a specification of priorities and the phases of implementation. Thirdly, as a rule, there are difficulties in organizing interaction between the implementers and the necessary customer company experts, since, due to certain objective reasons, it is difficult to draw the attention of upper management to the project in order to manage it.

☐ The system's customer is a person or department responsible for company information technologies that tries to follow modern trends. This situation comes up frequently enough, and occasionally leads to insurmountable problems. The most typical development of such a scenario is a situation in which the implementer doesn't consult the potential users of the system on matters of setting the tasks, but rather goes to the business analysts. These settings are then implemented in the system, and then the person whose idea it was attempts to prove to conservative-minded potential users (usually unsuccessfully), that "this system is just the thing they need". In such a situation, Kimball [2] does not recommend even starting the project, and advises you to look for real functional customers among the company management, and transform this situation into one of first two cases.

While drawing up the contract, a clear understanding of these driving forces allows you to more accurately define the purposes and tasks of the project, to figure out and to take into account possible risks, and to work out an adequate situation plan for managing the project.

Amount of Work

The second aspect relates to the correct estimation of the amount of work that will be necessary and its level of complexity.

Usually, one of the main purposes of a DSS is to satisfy customer's needs for regulated and unregulated corporate data analytical reporting. Therefore, a clear understanding of the amount and complexity of the report forms to be realized by the system is the first condition for defining the project framework. (There are cases when besides the tasks of analytical report construction, a data warehouse needs to solve tasks of on-line reporting of records.)

The second factor is knowledge of the number of sources, their condition, and the volume of data that needs to be loaded to the system.

The third factor defining a project's framework is the estimation of the complexity of converting source data that need to be transformed before they can be presented in report forms. For example, the task of bringing in various manuals on fixed capital stocks from independent accounting and technological registration systems might not be able to be expressed in an algorithm, and can require a significant amount of manual work. Or, the rules of financial report consolidation could be defined by hundreds, and occasionally thousands of formulas, each of which needs to be programmed and debugged.

Therefore, if it is possible, we recommend stipulating in the contract a concrete list of report forms to be developed, business models, and data sources used. At the "project start" stage, if everything is not clear in this matter, one possible solution is to move defining the project framework and cost of the work to the "problem statement" stage. You can elaborate on the framework in the system requirements section developed on the basis of a detailed system analytical inspection, and the project cost can be stipulated in an additional agreement in the contract.

To conclude this section, we shall give approximate estimations of project costs. According to the experts, the development of a warehouse for a small department can cost anywhere from $400,000 to $600,000; the automation of a large department in a large firm can run from $800,000 to $1.5 million; and a large corporation will likely have to spend about $15 million. Development periods can also vary, from six months to two years when a large data warehouse for a large firm is created.

One more guideline from the experts, which is desirable, but not always possible to follow in real life: "Each subsequent stage of work is to be financed only after the previous stage has been completed and accepted".

Working Plan

Generally, there are as many working plans as there are projects. Each real project has its own specifics and features. Therefore, drawing up an adequate detailed working plan is one of the stages that ensures the success of the project. To develop one, it is necessary to involve as many design team members and independent experts who have the necessary experience in implementing similar projects and can reasonably estimate possible design risks. As a guideline, we can give a crude working plan, which includes the most typical items in various projects.

Table 2.1. Approximate Working Plan for Creating a Corporate Information Analysis System

Stage	Work	Period	Results
Inception	System-analytical investigation Information analysis Definition of system requirements Definition of the general architecture Reason for general software choice	From 1 to 3 months	Report on system-analytical investigation System's design concept Demo prototype System requirements Plan for creating the first level of the system

continues

Table 2.1 Continued

Stage	Work	Period	Results
	Reason for system's technical infrastructure choice		
	Definition of structure and contents of system documentation		
	Definition of evolution strategy, creation, and system implementation stages.		
	Elaboration on the general system development plan, including functionality extension, database extension, and user number growth		
	Creation of a system demonstration model		
	Confirmation of the decisions made and the characteristics of the designed system during tests of the demonstration model		
	Planning of work for creating the first system project (elaboration on structure and time-consumption of work; allocation of work, and definition of co-implementers' cooperation; definition of priority and the time it will take for hardware delivery and adjustment; definition of priorities and of length of time of delivery of purchased mathematical software)		
Elaboration	Detailed system architecture design: logical view process view implementation view deployment view	From 1 to 3 months	System Project

continues

Table 2.1 Continued

Stage	Work	Period	Results
	Special software algorithm design: Data extraction, cleaning, coordination, and transformation subsystem Query processing and data view subsystem Warehouse administration subsystem		
Construction	On-line data warehouse creation Relational warehouse creation Creation of data marts Development of debugging and testing for special software Software complex debugging and testing Loading the data to the ODS and data marts Development of documentation on the subsystem (user guides, user manuals, troubleshooting, and modification instructions) Planning of stages of system implementation and acceptance tests	From 1 to 4 months	Data warehouse Transformation level software, data mart software, system administration software Project and user documentation on the subsystem Plan for implementing the system
Transition	Training of the company staff Installation, adjustment, and testing of system infrastructure (hardware, operational system, and communication software, data base management system software) Installation, adjustment, and testing of special system software	From 1 to 2 months	A trained team of employees Infrastructure of and software for the system Documentation on system usage Plans for system development Plans for moving to the second level of the system.

continues

Table 2.1 Continued

Stage	Work	Period	Results
	Documentation of software setup modifications and settings		
	Creation and documentation of system users' profiles		
	Documentation confirming the operability system		
	Beta test of the system		
	The analysis of the development experience; implementation and beta testing of the first system		
	Elaboration of proposals for further developing the system		
	Planning to proceed to the second system		
	Acceptance and tests		

The experience of such project implementation has shown that the minimum and maximum acceptable deadlines are estimated as three months to one year. There are a number of reasons that, if an information analysis system project is large enough, we strongly recommend that you divide it into steps, so that the time spent on each step does not exceed one year.

2.2.2. Project Organization Structure

For working on the project, a design group that includes experts from the implementer and the customer is organized. A working group is directly managed by managers from both the implementer and the customer.

A project management committee is organized to solve organization and technical problems, manage the work on the project as a whole, make decisions related to the structure and amount of work at each stage of the project, estimate the quality of the obtained results, and confirm reporting materials.

Design Group

Experience tells us that work on the project can be done most efficiently by an integrated design group, which, besides the experts from the company executing the project, also includes project implementers from the customer's company.

The group should include both business experts and information technology experts. The roles of members in charge should be clearly defined. Rights, duties, and qualification requirements are defined depending on the position. Obviously, the scale and conditions of the specific project define the make-up of the team. Therefore, we can only give general recommendations in this area.

Table 2.2. Design Group

Role in design group	Duties	Responsibilities	Rights
Representatives of the customer			
Head of the group	Project management Organize the design group's interaction with the necessary customer's departments Quality and deadline control	Organize and set deadlines for interviews in the customer's departments Present fully all the necessary input information to the members of design group	Assign work to members of the customer's design group Call design group meetings Raise questions before the managing committee of the project
Business expert	Define the functional requirements of the system	Assure quality and completeness of the functional requirements of the system	Raise questions before the managing committee of the project.
IT expert	Solve problems related to the operating system and network administration of the project's technical infrastructure Support of physical access to the data sources of the system	Access to the system's technical means for design group members Access to data sources	Raise questions before the managing committee of the project

continues

Table 2.2 Continued

Role in design group	Duties	Responsibilities	Rights
	Eliminate incorrect and failed data in sources Load the data to warehouse Warehouse administration Install system client software on workstations	Integrity of data in sources User profiles Access of design group members to workstations of system users Support of client software on users' workstations	
Representatives of the implementer			
Head of the group	Project management Work plan Support the design materials database Implement project work standards Quality and deadline control	Keep stage deadlines Quality of results	Assign work to members of the implementer's design group Call design group meetings Raise questions before the managing committee of the project
Systems analyst	Define the functional requirements of the system Develop requirements for system dataware Data source analysis Logical design of warehouse data structures	The functional requirements of the system Quality and completeness of data source description Content and logical data structure of warehouse	Propose an interview schedule for customer departments to the managing committee Raise questions before the managing committee of the project
Consultant/ developer	Develop program requirements to the system's technical tools	Quality of basic design solutions	Raise questions before the managing committee of the project

continues

Table 2.2 Continued

Role in design group	Duties	Responsibilities	Rights
	Develop specifications of the base system software Warehouse physical data structure design Custom software design Customer staff training	Quality of basic software specifications Quality of design solution implementation Quality of system user training	Define training plan and content Inspect design solutions implemented by developers
Database expert	Install the general system software Create warehouse's physical data structures Create transformation layer software Load data to the warehouse Develop manuals	Compliance of data structures and transformation layer software with the system reqirements Completeness and quality of operation instructions and warehouse support guides	Raise questions before the managing committee of the project
Application software development expert	Special system software and system user interface development Write user manuals	Compliance of special software with the system requirements Completeness and quality of user documentation for the system	Raise questions before the managing committee of the project

Only an approximate structure for the design group is mentioned here. Depending on the scale and specific conditions of the project, some roles can be executed by one expert, or, on the contrary, be shared by different experts.

The Managing Committee

The managing committee is formed from the representatives of the customer's top managers, representatives of the customer's functional sub-departments, representatives of the customer responsible for IT policy, and design group managers.

Table 2.3. The Managing Committee

Role in managing committee	Duties	Responsibility	Rights
The Head	Call committee meetings State the agenda for committee	Compliance of quality and volume of design work with the requirements of the contract	Approve work plans according to the project stages Issue instructions to the company about the organization of work on the projects on behalf of the General Director Approve project records
Committee members (representatives of the administrations of the departments who will be the functional customers of the system)	Manage the correspondence of the system functionality with end user requirements	Compliance of the system functionality with end user requirements	Coordinate project records related to functional and information system requirements
Committee members (representatives of the administrations of the departments responsible for company policy in the field of informatization)	Manage the quality of the project's main technical solutions Ensure the usage documentation's completeness and quality	Compliance of the system with hardware and software requirements	Coordinate project records with the hardware and software requirements
Committee members (design group leaders)	Provide information on the current state of the project	Present qualitative records in due time	Present project records and participate in discussions concerning them

It is advisable to determine who will make up the managing committee and design group, as well as their rules and plans, with appropriate documents from both the customer company and the implementation company.

2.2.3. Project Management

Project management consists of defining the following procedures:

❏ Risk and threat management

❏ Management of problems (disadvantages/errors)

❏ Modification management

❏ Monitoring and reporting on the state of the project

Risk and Threat Management

The process of risk and threat management will help to successfully complete a project; a "Journal of risks and threats" and a "Risk (threat) report" are used to aid this process, which consists of the following steps:

❏ *Detection of a risk or threat.* The risk or threat can be determined by a design group expert or by the customer. The registration information related to risk or threat are to be written into the "Journal of risks and threats" (Table 2.4), and detailed data are to be written in the "Risk (threat) report (Table 2.5)".

❏ *The risk or threat is analyzed.* Possible measures to decrease or eliminate risks or threats are developed, the influence of these measures on the plan and their cost is evaluated, and a project resolution is prepared. The information is written in the "Risk (threat) report".

❏ *The customer confirms the resolution.* Together with the customer, the resolution project is discussed, and its final variant is confirmed. The information is written to the "Risk (threat) report". If the resolution influences the project framework, working plan, or cost, the "Modification management" procedure begins.

❏ *Periodic risk examination.* The periodic analysis of all risks to guarantee appropriate measures of managing them.

During this procedure, strict registration of risk and threat status is carried out (open, sent out for analysis, analyzed, resolution recommended, resolution authorized, resolution postponed, no action to be taken).

Table 2.4. Journal of Risks and Threats

Section name	Contents
Project	Project Name
	Date
	Start date
	Customer
	Head of the project
	Project stage
Risk/Threat Description	Code
	Type of risk/threat
	Description
	Person who will carry out the analysis
	Priority
	Expected date of resolution
	Influence on other risks/threats
	Current status
	Resolution

Table 2.5. Risk (Threat) Report

Code		
Type (select)	Risk/Threat	
Priority (select)	Critical/High/ Medium/Low	
Detection	Implementer/Customer:	Date:
Analysis	Implementer:	Start date:
Status (select)	Open/ Sent out for analysis/Analyzed/ Resolution recommended/Resolution authorized/ Resolution postponed/No action to be taken	
Description		

continues

Table 2.5 Continued

Proposed actions that can be taken to decrease risks or to eliminate threats and the influence of these actions on the working plan, resources, and cost	Actions:	Influence:
	Actions:	Influence:
	Actions:	Influence:
Resolution		
Authorization of the resolution	Implementer: Date:	Customer: Date:
The code of the initiated project modification		

While far from a complete list of risks, the most common problems which we are frequently faced are mentioned below.

Table 2.6. Typical Project Risks

Risk	Possible solution
At the stage of elaborating the system dataware requirements, design group members cannot get a meeting with the persons responsible for the administration of specific data sources	Company management organizes the necessary meetings Company management includes in the design group the administrators responsible for data, and defines their rights, duties, and responsibilities The given source is moved beyond the framework of the project
The implementers can not get access to descriptions, structures, or electronic versions of sources	The management of the company issues an order to present the necessary data and makes sure that it is fulfilled

continues

Table 2.6 Continued

Risk	Possible solution
	Company management issues an order to export data from the sources to transit text files whose structure is in conformity with design group requirements, and makes sure that the order is fulfilled The given source is moved beyond the framework of the project
Incompleteness or inaccuracy of the system's input data (data loaded to the system)	Company management includes the employees responsible for data in the design group, and defines their rights, duties and responsibilities The source is moved beyond the framework of the project
The requirements to the functional software and/or dataware of the system cannot be realized by the deadline and/or does not fit into the project's budget	Company employees trained during project execution modify the corresponding system requirements and subsequently extend the system The budget, planned amounts of work, and deadline are revised
Change in the task defined by the customer during the development process (after completion or during designing a database, model input, etc.)	An accurate procedure to implement the changes is performed, and costs, the budget, the amount of work, and the deadline are revised The system is worked on after it is delivered to company employees trained during the project

Problem Management

The process of problem (disadvantage/error) management consists of the following steps:

☐ *Problem detection.* The problem can be detected by an expert of the design group or by the customer. The registration information related to the problem is to be written in the "Problem Journal" (Table 2.7), and detailed information is written in the "Problem Report" (Table 2.8).

☐ *Case study.* Possible measures to solve the problem are developed, the influence of these actions on the working plan and the cost are evaluated, and a resolution is prepared. If the resolution influences the framework, schedule, or cost of the project, the "Modification management" procedure is begun and the case is closed. The information is written in the "Problem Report".

☐ *Solution of the problem.* The actions planned to solve the problem are executed.

☐ *Testing the solution.* The expert who detected the problem checks if the solution is appropriate.

☐ *Periodic reviewing of unsolved problems.* Periodic analysis of all unsolved problems in order to determine how to solve them.

During execution of the procedure, a strict register of problem status is kept (open, sent out for analysis, analyzed, solved, closed, no action is to be taken).

Table 2.7. Problem Journal

Section name	Contents
Project	Project Name
	Code
	Start date
	Customer
	Head of the project
	Project stage
Problem Description	Code
	Area (detected location)
	Description
	Detected by:
	Date of appearance
	Priority
	Current status
	Closing date

Table 2.8. Problem Report

Code		
Priority (select)	Urgent/ Important/Insignificant	
Origin	Implementer/Customer:	Date:
Analysis	Implementer:	Start date:
Status (select)	Open/ Sent out for analysis/ Analyzed/ Solved/ Closed/ No action is to be taken	
Area (detected location)		
Description (including actions to be repeated)		
Results of the analysis		
Actions to take to solve the problem and the influence of these actions on the work plan, resources, and cost	Actions:	Influence:
Solution	Implementer:	Date:
Closing	Implementer: Date:	Customer: Date:
The code of the initiated project modification		

Project Modification Management

The procedure of project modification management uses a "Project Modification Journal" (Table 2.9) and a "Project Modification Report" (Table 2.10), and consists of the following steps:

❏ Declaration of a project modification that needs to be made. The need to change the project can be detected by an expert of the design group or by the customer, and can also be initialized by the "Risk and threat management" and "Problem management" procedures. The registration information on the required project modification is to be written in the "Project Modification Journal", and is to be detailed in the "Project Modification Report".

❐ Analysis of the necessary project modification. Definition of the necessary actions to be taken to execute the change, as well as an estimation of the influence of these actions on the plan and cost. The information is to be written to the "Project Modification Report".

❐ Approval of the modification by the customer. The modification is discussed with the customer and its final variant is confirmed. The information is to be written in the "Project Modification Report".

❐ Adjustment of the work plan while taking into consideration the confirmed changes to the project.

❐ Periodic review of the existing project modification requests. Periodic analysis of all open project modification requests with the purpose of managing their revision.

During execution of the procedure, a strict register of the status of the project modification is kept (open, sent out for analysis, analyzed, resolution recommended, resolution authorized, resolution postponed, no action will be taken).

Table 2.9. Project Modification Journal

Section name	Contents
Project	Project Name
	Code
	Start date
	Customer
	Head of the project
	Project stage
Necessary modification	Code
	Description
	Reason of appearance
	Date of appearance
	Priority
	Current status
	Date of confirmation

Table 2.10. Project Modification Report

Code		
Priority (select)	Critical/ High/Medium/Low	
	Requested by (indicate first and last name)/ Problem/ Risk/Threat	Date:
Analysis	Implementer:	Start date:
Status (select)	Open/Sent out for analysis/Analyzed/Resolution recommended/Resolution authorized/Resolution postponed/ No action will be taken (refusal)	
Description		
Results of the analysis	Necessary measures:	Influence on: Work plan Complexity Cost
The authorized modifications to the project	Authorized actions:	Adjustment to: Working plan Complexity Cost
Approval	Implementer: Date:	Customer: Date:
Interrelation (code)	Risk/ Threat:	Problem:

Project Status Monitoring and Reporting

DSS creation requires coordination of the work of different experts, who simulta-neously solve interdependent design tasks, and should achieve certain results on time. The procedure of managing the execution of work on the project should pro-vide a solution to the given task. We recommend that you manage project work through weekly, one-hour managing committee meetings, in which a "Project Status Report " (Table 2.11) is discussed and confirmed, and the results of the dis-cussion are laid out in the "Meeting Protocol".

Table 2.11. Project Status Report

Section name	Contents
Project	Project Name Code Start date Customer Head of the project Project stage
General project status	During the past accounting period, the project was fulfilled according to the operating plan. The following basic results were obtained: ... ...
Results and control states	The results planned in the contract, the project's control states (complete list), and any additional results or control states obtained from authorized changes in the project, are to be described in the following items: The contract/Necessary project modification Result code/control state Result/control state Scheduled deadline Predicted (actual) deadline Authorized by the customer? (Yes/No)
Problems, risks, and threats	Information on problems, risks, and threats that were discussed, detected, and/or solved in the past accounting period are to be described in the following items: Brought over from last period Appeared this period Solved this period Unsolved this period The following problems, risks, and threats from the past accounting period remain unsolved: Code

continues

Table 2.11 Continued

Section name	Contents
	Type (Problem/Risk/Threat)
	Description
	Current status[1]
	Note
Project modifications	Information on the project modifications for the past accounting period, which were considered, detected/initiated and/or authorized are to be described in the following items:
	Brought over from last period
	Appeared this period
	Authorized this period
	Not authorized this period
	The following project modifications changes for this past accounting period remain unauthorized:
	Code of the project modification
	Project modification
	Reason of appearance (Detected/Problem/Risk/Threat)
	Current status[2]
	Note
	The following project modifications for this past accounting period were authorized:
	Code of the project modification
	Project modification
	Reason of appearance (Detected/Problem/Risk/Threat)
	Authorization date
	Adjustment of the working plan

continues

---

[1] The risk and threat status can be one of the following: is open, sent out for analysis, analyzed, resolution recommended, resolution authorized, resolution postponed, no action to be taken. The status of a problem can have the following values: open, sent out for analysis, analyzed, solved, closed, no action will be taken.

[2] The status of a project modification can be the following: open, sent out for analysis, analyzed, resolution recommended, resolution is authorized, resolution postponed, no action to be taken.

Table 2.11 Continued

Section name	Contents
Work for the next quarter, month, etc.	Work code Work Work results Scheduled time of completion
Meteing for the next month, quarter, etc.	Date, time, and duration of meeting Purpose of meeting Meeting participants

2.3. Problem Statement

2.3.1. System-Analytical Inspection

This stage of inspection begins with the customer coordinating and giving approval to the inspection plan and program.

The inspection plan defines:

❑ Interviewees

❑ Correspondents

❑ Interview date, place, and time

The inspection program includes:

❑ Definition of main concepts

❑ Purposes and tasks of the project

❑ Technique of system-analytical inspection within the framework of the DSS project

❑ Project participant roles

❑ List of main questions to be answered during inspection

▼

During the inspection:

☐ The main project participants from the customer company and persons responsible for administrative decision making are interviewed

☐ The organizational structure is specified, and the organizational and functional frameworks of the project are determined

☐ The features and disadvantages of current information solutions are determined and documented

☐ The company business schema is formalized, taking into account the functional frameworks

☐ The existing account materials and other official documents directly related to implementation of the project are collected

In accordance with the results of the inspection, the strategic and operational tasks of company management to be solved by the DSS are specified, and the purposes and tasks of system creation are formalized.

While analyzing the information, interview materials are processed, the collected documents are analyzed, and detailed requirements for the developing system are defined. The purpose of the analysis stage is to obtain data models and a description of administrative decision procedures.

The stage is complete after drawing up a report on the system-analytical inspection. The report contains information shown in Table 2.12.

Table 2.12. Report on the System-Analytical Inspection

Section name	Contents
Business process analysis	Analysis of current and prospective company infrastructure in which the DSS will function: ☐ Organizational infrastructure and its components' dependencies ☐ Information infrastructure ☐ Business processes ☐ Purposes and functions

continues

Table 2.12 Continued

Section name	Contents
Data mart description	Description of a multidimensional logical data mart model: ☐ Determining prototypes based on an analysis of the business processes, purposes, and functions of the company ☐ Formalizing questions for which the system should provide answers ☐ Determining base and computed business indexes, as well as sections illustrating the answers to questions ☐ Determining business space measurement composition based on a list of sections ☐ Mutual coordination of measures and dimensions
Data warehouse description	Determining data that should be located in the warehouse and the data conversion processes: ☐ Description a high level logical data model ☐ Determining sources from which data will be imported to the warehouse ☐ Describing data conversion processes (extracting, cleaning, coordinating, aggregating, and synchronizing)
Data source description	Automated Information Management System (AIMS) designation AIMS description (its functionality and tasks solved by it) AIMS developer (department(s)/organization(s) responsible for AIMS development, support, and cultivation) Department responsible for AIMS exploitation (data actualization, data access, and application administration) Department responsible for AIMS administration (data structure generation, backup copying, DBMS management) AIMS future development (problems, proposals for additional work or replacements) Description of hardware and software tools (hardware platform, operating system, DBMS, development tools) Description of AIMS dataware (structure, content, and data formats)

continues

Table 2.12 Continued

Section name	Contents
Analysis of sources related to the external conditions of customer company activity	Classification of the external environment, analysis of data sources
Definition of data views	Classification of system users (by function, access to aggregated data) Description of data view types (table, graphics, etc.) Description of user interfaces Description of procedures for analytical data processing

2.3.2. Concept

At this stage alternate variants of basic approaches to DSS creation for meeting user requirements are developed, as well as implementation plans, an estimation of resources necessary for their implementation and support, and an estimation of the advantages and drawbacks of each variant.

Table 2.13. System Concept

Section name	Contents
General provisions	Basis for development Prerequisites for creation The purposes and tasks of system creation Role and place of the system Main methodical and technological principles of creation
Description of automation objects	Automated processes Decomposition of automated processes to functions and tasks Information flows that provide basic management processes Required qualitative system implementation characteristics

continues

Table 2.13 Continued

Section name	Contents
System architecture	Logical view
	Process view
	Implementation view
	Deployment view
Types of support	Dataware
	Software
	Hardware
	Organizational support
Construction plan	Creation strategy
	Creation and implantation prioritization
	Working stages and phases
Basis of software and hardware supplier choice	Definition of hardware and software requirements
	Definition of the criteria for choosing the software and hardware
	Analysis of the market and choices of hardware and software suppliers
Estimation of project cost	Special software development
	General software purchases
	Hardware purchases
	Expenditures on maintenance and support
Estimation of income due to system creation	*Expected profit*

2.3.3. System Requirements

System Requirements (SR) is one of the key project documents, which defines the requirements and the order of DSS creation. Our experience shows that if the time of system development exceeds twelve months, it makes sense to introduce prioritization into the system and begin with developing system requirements based on what is expected in the first phase of the system, which can be implemented within 3-9 months. Otherwise, dynamically varying business conditions, which are constantly improving information technology, will result in the fact that when the system is finally implemented, it will already be obsolete. If the project is of large enough scale, then besides the main SR for the whole system, individual technical requirements for its separate components can also be developed.

In the given section, we will only give some general comments related to certain areas of SR.

In the "Scheduled beginning and end times for system development" section, we recommend defining the following three stages: Technical project, Working documentation, and Commissioning.

Exact deadlines should be stipulated for each stage.

In the "Technical Project" stage, you should: develop design solutions for the whole system and its parts, including informational and functional models of automated processes; create documentation on the whole system and its parts; develop and prepare the documentation on technical software delivery for completing the system.

In the "Working Documentation" stage: develop working documentation on the whole system and its parts; develop and adapt programs, including developing database and user interfaces for workstations.

In the "Commissioning" stage: prepare the automation object, put the system into operation, train the staff, complete the system with delivered articles (including software and hardware), make sure the system starts up correctly, and run preliminary tests, beta tests, and acceptance tests.

After completing the "Commissioning" stage, the support stage should begin. Its requirements and conditions should be stipulated in a separate contract.

In the "System Designation" section, management processes subject to automation within the framework of the given system—including technological administration and system management processes—should be clearly defined. All functions related to the above-defined business processes and automated by the given system should be specified.

In the "System Design Goals" section, you can indicate that the main purpose of creation is to raise the efficiency of informational-analytical and administrative activity of company management and experts, which is achieved by the following:

❐ Structuring and unifying (standardizing) stored data and the processes of accessing them

❐ Increase of on-line availability of data and extension of the users' number

❐ Rise in quality and accuracy of data

❐ Highly developed tools of table and chart representation of data to users to support operational, tactical, and strategic decision making

❐ Integration of operational systems and distributed databases

❐ Rise in the amount of information used to solve administrative tasks

❐ Rise in reliability of data storage

❐ Protection against unauthorized data access

Some criteria that will indicate that you have reached this goal could be:

❐ Rise in motivation to make administrative decisions

❐ Reduction of the time it takes company managers and experts to access data

❐ Extension of the data content used to make administrative decisions

❐ Rise in data quality (reliability, instituting uniform standards)

❐ Reduction of expense and time required to prepare informational and analytical reports

Requirements for the subsystem and database content (data warehouse, data marts, and ODS) should be defined in the "Requirements for the Structure and Functioning of the System" section.

2.4. Design

Based on the analysis of the requirement for the system formulated in the System requirements, the main architectural solutions are developed at this stage of design. According to the RUP approach, the architecture of the informational system is considered in four aspects:

❐ *Logical view.* This presents the architecture of the system from the point of view of basic class packages and their interconnections. With reference to our practice of DSS design we, as a rule, carried out functional, and not object, decomposition of the system. Taking into consideration the goals of the system, we defined the processes and functions necessary to automate in order to fulfill these goals, which then were divided into separate tasks to be implemented in the development stage.

❑ *Process view.* As applied to DSS, this view determines the dataware of the system (i.e., the make-up and contents of the data transfer and conversion processes).

❑ *Implementation view.* Represents the architecture of system software, and its decomposition into subsystems and components.

❑ *Deployment view.* Describes the physical nodes of the system and the links between them.

In addition to these four aspects of the system architecture, in our practice we often studied one more aspect of the system architecture: organizational support. This looks at the aggregate of the customer's organizational structures involved in system maintenance, their composition, the roles of the staff, and the connections among them all.

2.4.1. Automated Processes and Functions

With respect to the form of automated activity, DSS is a data processing and transmitting system. Objects of automation are technological processes connected with the dataware for the administrative and analytical activity of managing staff, department specialists, and upper management of the company. The main tasks of the system are:

❑ Integration of detailed data that was previously disjoined:

    ❑ Historical archives

    ❑ Data from on-line systems

    ❑ Data from external sources

❑ Disjunction of data sets used for on-line processing and data sets used to solve decision-making problems

❑ Comprehensive information support for the maximum number of users

To realize the given tasks within the framework of the system, the following processes are subject to automation:

❑ *Data acquisition.* Data necessary for analyzing the state of business and for allowing upper management and departments of the company to make tactical and strategic administrative decisions are collected. The data sources are reports from the subordinate organizational structures and on-line transaction systems that allow for everyday activity.

❐ *Data transformation:*

    ❐ *Data cleaning.* Incorrect and contradictory data are made more accurate and harmonized. Examples of incorrect information are records with a company code that doesn't exist, a negative number of permanent staff members, or a non-zero sum of actual payments for the next year. Data should not be contradictory. For example, contradictory information can be the fact that the sum calculated using the entries does not correspond to the residual on the account.

    ❐ *Data coordination.* Data obtained from various sources, for example, companies, banks, regions and so on, can be indexed using the same measurements. However, there can be different directories, different coding, etc. in these sources. The task of data coordination is to organize all conformal measurements from different sources into a uniform pattern.

    ❐ *Unification of data.* All data are coordinated in accordance with a uniform system of classifiers, codes, structures, and directories. The unification is effected at the corporate standard level, the international standard level, and so on. Besides which, data are converted to uniformly accepted units.

    ❐ *Data aggregating.* For meeting the needs of most persons responsible for analysis and decision-making, completely detailed information is not necessary. Therefore, the aggregated variables that you can use are calculated in advance.

❐ *Data storage:*

    ❐ *Intermediate data storage.* As a rule, data don't come from low level operating systems simultaneously and require mutual checking and coordination. With this purpose in mind, intermediate, short-lived data storage is organized before their coordination and aggregation.

    ❐ *Accumulation of historical data* necessary for effecting retrospective analysis, and for making predictions and detecting various tendencies.

❐ *Presentation of data to customers.* Data and the method of their visualization are chosen to meet the requirements of analysts and persons responsible for making administrative decisions.

❐ *Metadata support.*

Table 2.14 describes the main processes and functions automated within the framework of DSS.

Table 2.14. DSS Processes and Functions

Processes	Functions
Data collection	Import of data from sources
	Definition of and modifications to the schedule for adding data to the warehouse
	Starting the procedure of importing data from the sources according to schedule
	Providing the necessary interface for manual data entry if the data do not exist in electronic form
	Logging data input to the warehouse
Data conversion	Checking of data from sources and automatic notification of the absence of imported data or a mismatch
	Data check results log
	Coordination of data imported from sources
	Synchronization of the imported data
	Aggregation and consolidation of imported data
	Loading of data to the warehouse
	Conversion and data loading log
	Data correction log
	Writing of appropriate metadata to the repository
Data storage	Data structure creation and support
	Data backup
	Data modification
	Data modification log
	Archiving seldom used information
	Data recovery after failures
	Writing the existing metadata to the repository
Delivery and presentation of data to end users	Interpretation of users' queries; search and retrieve necessary information
	Providing a unified strategy for differentiating access to confidential information for analytical application users

continues

Table 2.14 Continued

Processes	Functions
	Preventing access to confidential information by unauthorized persons
	Differentiation of legal warehouse and analytical applications users' access to information, software, and hardware resources
	Log of user access to the information and analytical applications
	Presentation of data as regulated report forms
	Interactive tabular and graphic data presentation
Logical definition of data and processes (metadata support)	Storage and allocation of of CASE resource Metamodels for simulation and design
	Storage and allocation of information related to warehouse data structure
	Storage and allocation of information related to on-line repositories data structure
	Storage and allocation of information related to multidimensional data structure
	Storage and allocation of information related to data sources
	Storage and allocation of information related to conversions of imported data
	Storage and allocation of information related to data corrections
	Storage and allocation of the DSS administration metadata
	Storage and allocation of information about DSS users

2.4.2. Dataware

In general, dataware includes data of five classes:

❑ Data sources   ❑ Data marts

❑ ODS   ❑ Metadata repositories

❑ Data warehouse

System dataware design is carried out from top to bottom. Data views for system application end users (made up of indices and their slices) are defined based on an analysis of system prototypes revealed in the system analytical inspection stage. The segmentation of data views is carried out in accordance with their problem orientation. Data marts are designed based on the presentation groups that support them. When designing data marts you need to define the following:

❏ Dimensions, their hierarchies, and their drilling level. For example, for the time dimension, a minimum time interval (day, week, or month) by which the variables in a mart will be indexed should be defined.

❏ Base variables, their indexing dimensions, and the rules of aggregation of each variable by hierarchy. The rules of aggregation by the hierarchy dimension depend on the variable. For example, if you want to determine income from sales, aggregation by time can be done with simple addition. To research product price, aggregation by time can be done by finding an average, maximum, or minimum value for the aggregation period.

❏ Variable derivatives and formulas for their calculation, based on basic variables.

Generally, the choice of a definitive way of representing ROLAP, MOLAP, or HOLAP data marts is fulfilled in the system implementation stage.

The detected dimensions and variables serve as source data for warehouse design.

First, all detected slices and their hierarchies are generalized. Based on these, warehouse business space is designed. Dimensions are usually tightly connected with the structured normative and directory information of the company. For example, warehouse dimensions normally act as an organizational structure of the company, an administrative and territorial directory, a plan of financial articles of the company, and more.

In the space given by business dimensions, base and derivative variables to be contained in the warehouse are designed. For large systems, it makes sense to carry out warehouse segmentation according to data domains.

In the next stage, the results of data source inspection are analyzed. When choosing the appropriate source, you need to take the following problems into consideration:

❏ If there is more than one source, it is necessary to figure out which is best.

❏ Which conversions are necessary to prepare a source for loading to the warehouse?

❑ Do the structure of the source and the structure of the warehouse match?

❑ To what extent do data from source and normative and directory information match?

❑ What happens if the source has several locations?

❑ To what extent are data from the given source accurate?

❑ How is the source updated?

❑ What is the age and availability of a source?

❑ To what extent are the data complete?

❑ What is required to integrate data from the source into the loading stream?

❑ What technology of data storage is used in a source?

❑ How effectively can access to source be realized?

Based on this analysis, the following architectural solutions can be found:

❑ The structure, content, and sources of the dataflows that will be introduced to the warehouse from the sources should be determined.

❑ Transformation of data (which should be done while the data are loading), as well as the periodicity of their loading to the warehouse should be determined.

❑ If it is necessary, the structure of the operating data warehouse and of transit files are designed.

❑ Data that are absent from information warehouse sources are determined. As a rule, procedures and rules are designed for manual input of such data to the warehouse.

The general structure of a warehouse is a kind of description of the main purpose of its construction, which is done to satisfy user requirements for this or that information as completely and as quickly as possible. Depending on users' information requirements, you can allocate the following basic types:

❑ Personal information is information exploited by the users with strictly defined duties and information requirements. Usually it requires a lot of preprocessing, or, in other words, has a high level of aggregation. It is most often stored in multidimensional databases.

❑ The information on business themes (i.e., information concerning specific subjects, like the financial activity of the organization). For organizations having close functional and organizational structures, it can be defined as the information for a department (for example, for the financial service). It has a wider spectrum, both in data domains and in time, but at the same time is directly used less often than information related to a specific person. They are usually stored in mixed structures: multidimensional databases and relational tables.

❐ Current detailed data are the most detailed information accessible in a data warehouse. Ordinary users access it rather rarely, only if it is necessary to clarify certain information in detail. Generally it is used in an analysts' field of activity for data mining (or searching for hidden dependencies in large volumes of information). As a rule, it is stored in relational structures.

Old detailed data has the same low level of aggregation as current detailed data, but it is allocated a special type for the following reason. On the one hand, detailed data frequently requires large storage resources, and on the other hand, detailed data that are a few years old are seldom used. The solution, then, in this case, is to use cheaper and more capacious methods of storage, for example, tape or library.

The most typical dataware architecture is shown in Fig. 2.2.

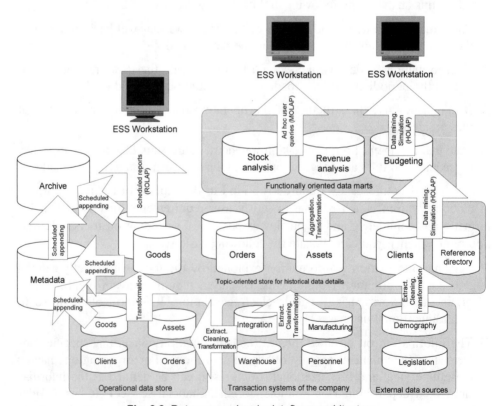

Fig. 2.2. Dataware and main dataflows architecture

2.4.3. Subsystem/Component Specification

As a rule, a system at the top level consists of software of two types: general-purpose software and special software.

Tools developed by Oracle that are classified as common software:

❏ *Middleware*, which provides network access to applications and databases—network and communication protocols, drivers, messaging system, and so on.

❏ *Loading and data preprocessing software*. This level includes a set of tools for loading data from OLTP systems and external sources. It is usually designed while doing additional processing: checking data integrity, consolidation, formatting, filtering, etc.

❏ *Server software*. Represents the kernel of the entire system. It includes:

   ❏ Relational database servers

   ❏ Multidimensional database servers

   ❏ Application (retrieval, analytical processing, data mining, etc.) servers

A number of programs developed during DSS creation make up what is known as special software. They are grouped into the following subsystems:

❏ The subsystem for extraction, conversion, transformation, and integration of data from sources

❏ Query processing and data view subsystem

❏ Repository administration subsystem

In this part the modules forming the subsystem and the algorithms of some procedures included in them should be designed.

Data Loading Subsystem

The goal of the design stage of this subsystem is to translate the requirements for the subsystem defined at the inception stage into concrete design solutions (i.e., into software packages specifications, modules, and algorithms). Ordinarily, the data loading subsystem consists of the following packages:

❏ *Extracting data*. This package is a set of program modules that connect to data sources, perform data retrieval from the required tables or files, and put into standard format data certain interface transit structures. These transit structures can be either simple text files or temporary tables in an on-line data warehouse.

The development of such interface structures isolates a specific character of the data source from the system we developed and simplifies its future support and modification. Even if an operating system acting as a source is replaced by a new one, we will only have to replace one unit from the given package, depending on the source. When creating an extracting module, most problems arise when accessing inherited systems no longer supported by developers. In this case, you need to consult with the customer's specialists that are responsible for support of the given systems, and together with them develop modules in the source language to unload the necessary data to transit files. You can find below descriptions of problems that arise in such a case as this in the "Management Support" section. Most modern databases provide standard means of accessing their sets, for example ODBC or JDBC drivers, which encapsulate the source's specific character and further simplify the creation of data extracting modules all the way up to automatic code generation using special tools.

❑ *Data conversion*. This package includes software that should fulfill the following functions:

    ❑ *Data cleaning*. There should be specified program modules and algorithms to determine incorrect and contradictory data, and that will automatically correct them if the appropriate business rules are defined. Mismatches detected during cleaning and the corrections made should be defined in the loading protocol.

    ❑ *Data matching and data unification*. You should specify the program modules and algorithms that determine conformal dimensions in different sources and coordinate them into a unified pattern on the basis of corporate and external (state and international) standards. The given software should coordinate all the data introduced to the warehouse into accepted uniform units of measurement.

    ❑ *Data aggregating*. Algorithms for aggregating input data by hierarchical dimensions should be specified for the given software. Aggregation can be either simple adding—for example, for the cumulative income of child companies, or other functional calculation—for example, the average, maximum, or minimum values for product prices by region.

While designing a data loading subsystem, you will usually have to develop specifications for software of two types: software for initial data loading to the warehouse, and software for regulated repository addition of data from sources.

Query Processing and Data Visualization Subsystem

This subsystem is DSS's "face", which applied users of an analytical system will see. Certainly, in many respects the appearance of this "face" depends on the "health" of all of the "organs" of our system. However, from our point of view, the success of the entire DSS project is about 90% determined by the demand for the DSS client applications. If the end users of the system are interested in the offered analytical applications, they will render a great amount of support to the project within the customer company, which can allow us to overcome all those organizational difficulties about which we have already spoken earlier and which we will come to again later.

The most typical tasks that can be solved by the presentation system are:

❏ Delivery of regulated reports

❏ New report generation

❏ Navigating metadata and execution of ad hoc queries

❏ Execution of an analysis according to the "What if ?" pattern

❏ Data mining

❏ Simulation

The main task when designing the system presentation is transformation into the presentation software specification of applied users' functional requirements, which were determined in the problem formulation stage, to the system. The approach to designing this part of the DSS differs little from the generally accepted approach to custom software design, about which there is plenty of literature. Here we shall discuss only features specific to DSS projects.

As a rule, three layers are singled out while constructing the presentation system. They are:

❏ *Data extraction layer.* This layer's software is responsible for access to warehouse data necessary for developing analytical applications. While designing the given software, you must determine the data volumes required by the analytical application, the degree of aggregation/detail, their presentation format, and the sources of extraction.

❏ *Data analysis layer.* While specifying the procedures of the given layer, it is required that you define the analytical conversions to be fulfilled above the data extracted from the warehouse before they are presented to the end user.

❏ *Data view layer.* While designing this layer, the view (tables, graphics, and so on) that will present the results of an analysis to the end user should be specified.

Warehouse Administration Subsystem

The majority of standard tasks related to warehouse administration is normally solved using the tools (Warehouse Builder, Express Administrator) supplied by Oracle. They allow you to:

❏ Define warehouse objects, their attributes, and their interdependencies

❏ Determine external source access

❏ Describe procedures of loading to the warehouse

❏ Set a physical warehouse model

❏ Execute loading procedures

❏ Regulate execution of loading procedures

❏ Generate metadata automatically

❏ Present warehouse structure in convenient graphic form

At the same time, data access administration, user profile support, differentiation of access to confidential data, and protection of the information against unauthorized access are usually performed by tasks of a particular character, and should be designed according to the specific requirements of the customer. While specifying the given special software, the algorithms of discretionary access control for different categories of users should be defined:

❏ For analytical applications.

❏ For the range of variables accessible for analysis. For example, the employees cannot have access to industrial stores data.

❏ For data defined by drilling level and completeness of presentation. For example, an employee in a regional branch cannot have access to the aggregated variables on the company as a whole, or to similar data from another regional branch.

2.4.4. Deployment View

The server software works under the control of application servers and database servers on UNIX or Windows NT platforms or on mainframes. The client software is installed on end users' PCs. In the past few years, the steady use of "thin" client technology has come about, where the PC user has only a Web browser, and all the functionality of the client software boots from an application server like JavaScript programs or applets. In many respects, the deployment view depends on the scale of the system and its productivity and reliability requirements. Depending on these, the system's server components can be either on only one computer or on several computers. Warehouse and data mart segments in large systems can be located on several computers. The approximate deployment view of the system and the set-up of software components are presented in Fig. 2.3.

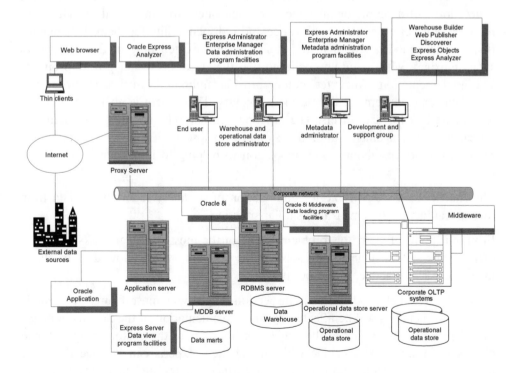

Fig. 2.3. Approximate deployment view

2.4.5. Organizational Support

Practice shows that the design of system organizational support is one of the most important and one of the most difficult aspects of design work. The complexity of the given problem lies in a social and not in a technical area. The solution of these problems is rather a task for psychologists and psychoanalysts.

We shall make only a few comments on this problem.

It can be psychologically explained that most people are inwardly conservative-minded concerning any changes in their daily activity. Therefore, the implementation of new technologies such as repositories and OLAP often meets with reluctance on the part of the customer's staff.

The most difficult problems to solve, in most cases, are those of interaction with the customer's specialists responsible for the access to data sources. They are normally IT experts who have worked for ten or more years with legacy systems. It is these people to whom top managers went when it was necessary to prepare a new form of a report or an unconventional query to available data. This promoted a sense of a personal significance and indispensability for them. It happened that the data models stored in the legacy system existed only in the notepad of such an expert, who "naturally" believed that they were his or her private property. The implementation of new technology provides unlimited direct access to corporate data for management and business analysts. Thus, there is no longer that intermediate link for data savers. These people are naturally afraid to lose their significance to management, and, occasionally, to lose their job. This is often the reason for cases of sabotage and opposition to helping to implement a new technology.

The staff that was responsible for compilation of summary reports with data from several transaction systems is in a similar situation.

From our point of view, this problem is one of the most significant risks of implementing the system. One way of solving this problem, which allowed us to eliminate this risk in practice, is laid out here.

First off, even before the design inspection stage, you must figure out exactly which staff members will be affected by the implementation of the new technology. Together with the sponsor of the project on the part of the customer, you should discuss the problem and decide who among these experts can be placed on the integrated design team, who can act as a business analyst and task producer, and who can work as an implementer. Systems analysts, whenever possible, should already during inspection be on good footing with these people. This can be achieved, first of all, by explaining what benefits system implementation will bring to the worker. There is a large number of options possible here: from getting a promotion and improving skills to lowering the burden on the eyes with an improved graphic interface. During the interview, these experts should not play the role of persons giving their knowledge, but the role of new system customers.

Secondly, it is in system organizational support that these people should be able to see a reputable position for themselves under the new conditions.

Often, therefore, system management support has to be designed not according to the best technical and financial solution, but by "following the path of least resistance"— appeasing the customer's staff as much as possible. For example, technically unreasonable warehouse segmentation may have to be introduced, and additional ODSs might need to be created to find a place for the experts, the former owners of data, in the new system.

It is therefore difficult to give general recommendations on planning organizational support. We will just mention that, in our opinion, organizational support should consist of the following sections:

❏ Changes in the structure of an organization

  ❏ Organizational structure changes and their justification

  ❏ Changes in interactions between departments

❏ Organization of new departments

  ❏ Organizational structure and departmental functions established with the purpose of supporting system performance

  ❏ Work regulations

  ❏ The list of employee categories and the number of staff

❏ Reorganization of existing departments

  ❏ Changes in organization structure

  ❏ Changes in department functions

  ❏ Changes in the rules of operation

  ❏ Changes in structure of staff

❏ User training

  ❏ Definition of the nomenclature and structure of training groups

❑   Definition of training programs and techniques

❑   Preparation of educational materials and manuals

❑   Preparation of the training plan

2.5. Construction

This stage of the project is directly connected with developing and testing information components and special system software with the architecture developed at the design stage.

The main results of this stage's work are:

❑ The system itself as common and special software, and as databases.

❑ The plan of system implementation, which should define all work related to system implementation for the customer, including packing the system, delivery to the customer, installing the system on the customer's facilities, testing, and adding final touches (see *Section 2.3.1*).

❑ Set of tests to be executed after installation and implementation on the customer's premises.

❑ User documentation and educational materials for the system users.

❑ In this chapter, the methodology of information analysis system development is not discussed in detail since the remaining parts of the book are generally devoted to this problem.

2.6. Transition

This phase includes fulfilling the plan for implementation developed in the previous phase.

At the system set up stage, mounting and installing the system and its separate components is carried out on the customer's premises. The initial loading of the warehouse is done with the necessary data, and the system is beta tested. Besides which, at the set up stage, users and technical support service employees are trained. The given stage ends when commercial warehouse operation starts.

Chapter 3

Creating a Data Warehouse Based on a Relational DBMS (Oracle Warehouse Builder)

I n the previous chapters, we looked at the methodical problems of corporate data warehouse construction. In this chapter, we shall discuss the technology of creating a data warehouse based on a relational DBMS supported by the Oracle Warehouse Builder software.

Oracle Warehouse Builder (OWB) is an integrated solution intended for designing and creating data warehouses and data marts. OWB is basically a tool for designing data warehouses, but at the same time it extracts, transforms end-to-enterprise planning, and loads data, which allows us to solve the following tasks:

❒ Defining the logical and physical data warehouse or data mart models

❒ Extracting, converting, and transforming data from relational databases, flat files, and various End-to-end Enterprise Planning (ERP) systems to the data warehouse database schema

❒ Automatically designing and installing data creation and loading scenarios and scripts in the data warehouse

❒ Administering, managing, and monitoring data warehouse status transition processes

Generally in OWB, this task can be solved by performing the following steps (Fig. 3.1):

Fig. 3.1. The standard diagram of the data warehouse creation process

❐ **Step 1. Define the Source**

In this step, we define and describe the main data sources using OWB. We can use different databases, ERP systems, and flat files as data sources.

❐ **Step 2. Designing the Target Warehouse**

In this step, we design the database data warehouse schema to which data will be loaded using OWB.

❐ **Step 3. Map Sources to Targets**

The third step connects the data sources defined earlier with the target database.

❐ **Step 4. Generate Code**

Here, we create scripts and scenarios based on definitions, in order to generate the database schema and data loading procedures.

❐ **Step 5. Instantiate Warehouse**

In this step, immediately before loading the data, we create a database schema and define its main objects.

❐ **Step 6. Extract Data**

In the last step, we load the data into the data warehouse.

Actually, the process of creating a data warehouse is much more complicated than the steps mentioned above. It also includes a rather significant number of tasks and subtasks that need to be solved during data warehouse creation. A detailed description of this process is provided by the Oracle Data Warehouse creation Methodology (DWM).

According to the given methodology, OWB is used at the defining, creating, and initializing stages of the data warehouse creation project. As a rule, these stages are always found in the project, regardless of its scale. Therefore, before we start to describe data warehouse creation, we shall consider these stages of data warehouse creation one by one, taking into consideration the tasks to solve, and then we will discuss in detail the process of creating a data warehouse from the technological aspect.

Note. OWB is intended for those experts who create data warehouses with Oracle software, and thus we assume that end users (designers) have the necessary knowledge of Oracle 8i Enterprise Edition and Oracle PL/SQL.

3.1. OWM Design Methodology

As with any other project, developing a data warehouse project starts with determining what end users require to be contained in the data warehouse. After these requirements have been defined and analyzed at the appropriate stage of the project, they can be described by the OWB tools. In accordance with DWM, reducing end user requirements to OWB terms is done at the definition stage.

3.1.1. Definition

The main goal of the given stage is to define the main data warehouse components and their interrelationships (Fig. 3.2). For this purpose, we should define the following, based on the end users' functional requirements:

☐ The type of main (or target) database schema, which will be based on a data warehouse, and also on various intermediate and on-line data warehouse schemas.

☐ We are to clearly define the quantitative content of data sources and their location, and we should form a general idea on the kind of information they contain.

☐ The quantitative composition and the contents of the procedures of data extraction, cleaning, and transformation from the data source.

Fig. 3.2. Dataflow diagram

3.1.2. Data Model Design

The role of OWB in this process consists of changing the conceptual model with formal definitions into a repository structure called a "data storage module". Then, using Warehouse Module Editor, we can define the main objects and their interrelationships to present the schema in a graphic view. As soon as the schema is complete, we can present it as DDL (Data Definition Language) scripts for direct loading into the data warehouse.

OWB allows us to design a data warehouse using business terms, while creating simple sets of logical concept definitions. Having then joined all of these representations into one metamodel, we can create different subject slices of these integrated representations in order to get data marts oriented towards concrete services or ones solving specific tasks.

When designing a data model, we recommend that you keep in mind the following rules.

General Approaches to Designing Data Models for Data Warehouses and Data Marts

Despite the fact that it is supposed that a data warehouse is implemented on a relational database, the basis of the data model for repositories and data marts is not the usual third normal form (3NF), but rather the "star" schema. This data model assumes that you will create, usually, just one table of facts, and several tables of dimensions linked to that table of facts by relations.

The basics of the design process, which can be called "multidimensional design", were described by Ralph Kimball in his book. This approach assumes the sequential execution of four main steps common for projects of any scale:

❏ Identify a business process and the operating system that supports it

❏ Formally state the fact table's grain

❏ Describe the fact table's dimensions

❏ Describe the fact table record

Identify a Business Process and the Operating System That Supports It

At this step, we must define and classify a set of objects and business processes that happen externally (from the warehousing online systems' data point of view). To simplify object and business process acquisition and classification, we recommend that you draw up and fill in an Objects And Business Processes Card, which will be the final document for the given step. Data acquired in this manner help us considerably in designing a data warehouse model.

For example, for an operating system that controls daily shipments of goods from a warehouse to the buyers, the Objects and Business Processes Card might look something like Table 3.1.

Table 3.1. Processes and Objects Card Example

On-line system	Business process	Dimension	Measures
On-line registration system for goods in a warehouse	Input of an order	Days Buyer Goods	Number of units sold Price Total goods sold
On-line registration system for goods in a warehouse	Income order input	Month Goods Supplier	Amount of goods acquired Price Delivery volume
Delivery planning system	Definition of monthly schedule for goods purchase	Month Group of goods	Delivery volume

Formally State the Fact Table's Grain

For this second step, we must describe in detail the main measures that will be used in the fact table, as well as state the grain of the information saved in the repository.

Choosing the grain level is one of the most important tasks in database and data warehouse design, since it influences the amount of the stored information, the productivity of the data warehouse, and the character of tasks to be solved with the data warehouse.

When specifying the grain for information stored in the data warehouse, it is necessary that you pay attention to the following circumstances:

❑ If we select a coarse grain, i.e., only load the information derived from detailed data to the data warehouse, we should realize that we won't be able to find these data when we need them. When indicating the level of detail required, we should not be guided by the number of current tasks. For example, in time, let's say that we plan to solve a number of analytical tasks belonging to the Data Mining class, which, as a rule, require detailed data. In such a case, we have to reconstruct the data warehouse in such a way to load detailed data too, but this is an undesirable process, since it is connected with many difficulties and necessitates that we design the data warehouse anew.

☐ If we select a high degree of specification (a fine grain), i.e., we load to the data warehouse all the information accessible to us, we must keep in mind that this can significantly increase the size of the stored data, as well as the time it takes to analytically process them. However, we will be able to find the necessary detailed data in our data warehouse at any moment.

To sum up, when choosing a grain, we recommend that you remember the following rule: "Load detailed data whenever you can and whenever there's no reason not to".[1]

Describe the Fact Table's Dimensions

At this third step, we have to define the following properties:

☐ Dimension attributes

☐ Hierarchies

☐ Primary keys

Dimension attributes are simply the properties of a dimension. For example, such properties as age, sex, and educational level can be used as attributes for the BUYERS dimension, and the quarter or month to which a day belongs can be used as attributes for the DAYS dimension.

Usually, a dimension contains one or more attributes that uniquely identify each object described by the dimension. Such attributes are known as "natural keys", since they are normally used for object identification.

When defining data attributes, we should always define the natural keys of a dimension, even if they are absent in the definition. It will help us to avoid inaccuracies when designing the data transformation procedures.

---

[1] Let me give an example from our personal experience. We were once discussing the question of level of detail with an upper-level manager. We suggested to him that he have only aggregated data in his personal mart since he, being a high level manager, would only require aggregated data to give him the big picture and thus the ability to make strategic decisions. But the manager stood his ground; he wanted data of even the tiniest detail, reasoning like this: "Of course I'm not going to analyze all that detailed data, but the fact that I can access it at any moment will keep the mid-level managers in line."

After describing the dimension attributes, we should define them in OWB and use them to construct a sketch of the data model diagram. This will allow us to determine whether the set of attributes we've defined is complete or not.

Hierarchies are "one-to-many" relations defined above dimensions, and are created, as a rule, for data aggregation.

From the physical aspect, Oracle 8i hierarchies are not separately stored objects, and are used by an internal server mechanism, Query Rewrite, to improve the processing capacity of aggregation requests.

For example, if a request aggregates daily variables to monthly variables, Oracle8i—using the Query Rewrite mechanism and the hierarchies we defined—can rewrite the request so that it will use the data already aggregated in another object (a table or material representation), instead of using detailed data to evaluate them each time.

When defining a hierarchy, we should:

❏   name the hierarchy

❏   define the hierarchy levels and name each of them

❏   define the relation between hierarchy levels

Primary keys are numerical columns that normally contain unique numerical values created by a special object of a database server—a sequence.

Generally, we can use a dimension's natural keys as primary keys. If more than one level of a hierarchy is defined above a dimension, we need to select the natural key of one hierarchy level and use it as the primary key of the dimension.

Describe the Fact Table Record

At this last step, we must define the structure of recording (the set of columns of) the fact table, which usually includes two sorts of columns:

❏   Columns that contain secondary keys that refer to dimension tables

❏   Columns that contain measures

When designing measures, it is necessary to distinguish the following types of measures:

❏   *Additive measures*—measures that can be totaled (and that make sense to total) by any dimension of the facts table.

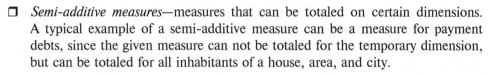

❏ *Semi-additive measures*—measures that can be totaled on certain dimensions. A typical example of a semi-additive measure can be a measure for payment debts, since the given measure can not be totaled for the temporary dimension, but can be totaled for all inhabitants of a house, area, and city.

❏ *Non-additive measures*—measures that cannot be totaled for any dimension.

When designing the fact table, don't forget about semi-additive and non-additive measures.

3.1.3. Data Sources

Creating a data warehouse is impossible without defining and analyzing the data sources used, and without mapping this information to the data warehouse project.

In this process, OWB's role consists of moving metadata from different sources to a repository structure called the "Source Module", and presenting this information in the form of the usual graphic and table representations for further processing.

Situations when metadata can not be imported from the data source because of its absence or inaccessibility arise rather frequently. This is typical for file-server applications and for data stored in flat files. In these cases, we can use the Flat File Importing Wizard to define and import the main attributes and the data contained in these sources.

3.1.4. On-Line Data Warehouse

Ordinarily, extracted data will contain, besides the necessary information, various "bad data" and/or unstructured data. Therefore, before loading data to the main schema of the data warehouse, they should be cleaned, edited, and put into common format.

To perform these operations, it is necessary to define with OWB a special container (module), to which data will load from the sources. The main purpose of this module is to prepare data for loading to the data warehouse and to solve the following tasks:

❏ Generating primary keys for data warehouse tables

❏ Cleaning and matching data obtained from different data sources

❏ Converting data to the data warehouse model

❏ Subsequent analytical data processing

In some cases, an on-line repository can be absent, and the data can be loaded directly to the data warehouse. This is possible if you don't need to solve any of the aforementioned tasks. In any other case, it makes sense to include an on-line repository into the architecture of the data warehouse in order to solve these tasks.

3.1.5. Data Conversion

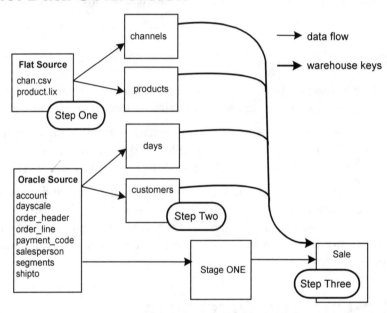

Fig. 3.3. Data conversion schema

After the main objects of the database target schema and the data source have been defined, we can start to describe how raw data is to be extracted, transformed, and saved in the target schema of the data warehouse.

If a data warehouse does not use an on-line repository, extracting and loading can be done in two steps. On-line repository use, as a rule, implies that you must create a set of intermediate tables. This somewhat complicates the conversion procedure, which can consequently be fulfilled in steps (Fig. 3.3):

❐ **Step 1. Extracting and loading data from sources**

At this step, for each object of the on-line repository, we describe, create, and execute procedures for extracting, cleaning, and transforming data from data sources, as well as procedures for creating primary keys for on-line repository tables.

❏ **Step 2. Loading dimension tables**

At this step, for each dimension of the data warehouse target schema, we describe, create, and execute procedures for extracting and transforming data from an on-line repository.

❏ **Step 3. Loading fact tables**

At this last step, for each fact table of the data warehouse target schema, we describe, create, and execute procedures for extracting data from the on-line repository and for matching data with dimension tables. This would also be a good time to execute procedures for aggregating fact tables in the target database schema.

Before beginning the process of describing transformation procedures, it is expedient to define their character and number. As a rule, there are tens or even hundreds of transformation procedures, even for a medium-sized data warehouse or data mart. To clear up this complicated combination of objects (Table 3.2) it is necessary to classify all procedures in such a manner:

Table 3.2. An Example of Data Transformation Procedure Classification

Name	Direction of data flow	Execution step	Type of execution
Accounts_to_stage_map	From an Oracle Application table to an on-line repository	Extraction and loading of data from sources	PL/SQL Package
Accounts_flat_to_stage	From flat files to an on-line repository	Extraction and loading of data from sources	SQL Loader
Accounts_to_customers	From an on-line repository to the Customers dimension	Loading of dimension tables	PL/SQL Package
Accounts_to_days	From an on-line repository to the Time dimension	Loading of dimension tables	PL/SQL Package
Accounts_to_Sums	From an on-line repository to the fact table	Loading of fact tables	PL/SQL Package

3.1.6. Generating a Project

After we have described the target schema of the database, all data sources, the on-line repository, and the data conversion schema, we can begin the following stage of data warehouse creation—generation.

Using OWB in this stage, we can:

- Create DDL scripts to generate:
  - References (Database Links)
  - On-line repository tables
  - Dimensions, fact tables, and materialized views of the database target schema
- Create PL/SQL procedures and SQL Loader scripts for extracting and loading data to the tables of the database target schema
- Create TCL scripts for Oracle Enterprise Manager

The process of project generation can be done in the following steps.

- For our first step, before launching the data warehouse object generating scripts, we should define the physical parameters of storage and maintenance for each of them. So, for example, we should create repetitive indexing for dimension tables, so as to reduce the time it will take later to search the data according to their index. Or we can partition fact tables by a certain key, and arrange the partitions in different table spaces.
- For the second step, after we have configured the database objects and environments, we should determine a creation order for scripts for generating data warehouse objects, and create them using the OWB script generation wizard.
- At the last step, we must establish a creation scenario for data warehouse objects and actually develop the system.

3.1.7. Loading, Testing, and Administrating

After we have completed the main work in the process of data warehouse creation and development in Oracle Enterprise Manager, we should set up the data update procedures that we created, and create procedures for and make an attempt at data loading.

3.2. Software Description

3.2.1. Product Architecture

OWB contains four tools: OWB Client, Repository Assistant, Runtime Assistant, and Runtime Audit Viewer (Fig. 3.4).

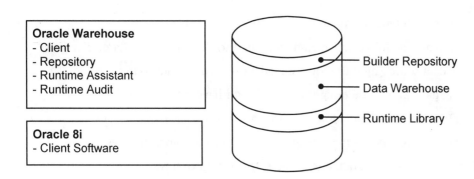

Fig. 3.4. Product architecture

❐   OWB Client is a Microsoft Windows application intended for defining, editing, and saving the main components and data warehouse objects in the OWB repository

❐   Oracle Warehouse Repository Assistant is a utility intended for manipulating (creating and deleting) OWB repositories

❐   Both Runtime Assistant and Runtime Audit Viewer are utilities intended for monitoring and collecting statistics on the processes that take place in the data warehouse

3.2.2. OWB Repository Structure

The OWB repository is a schema of the Oracle 8i database that contains a description of the main objects. The repository is divided into projects, and therefore, each time you connect to the OWB repository you must indicate the name of the project you are going to edit.

A *project* is a repository structure established by end users, which is intended to systematize the information on the data warehouse project. A project can contain information—about the module database target schema, data sources, schemas and methods of data transformation, and the scenario of loading to data warehouse—integrated into modules.

A *module* is a repository structure established by end users that is intended for defining dimensions, fact tables, materialized views, and other components of a data warehouse, such as data sources, on-line repositories, and the target schema of the data warehouse.

There are two types of modules in OWB:

❑   A target module stores metadata related to the target schema of database

❑   A data source module stores metadata related to data sources

During data warehouse design, a module can have one of three states:

❑   *Development*—the module is in the design stage

❑   *Quality Assurance*—the module is in the stage of alpha trial tests

❑   *Production*—the module is in the stage of beta trial tests

An *integrator* is an OWB component intended for supporting the integration of data from various sources. OWB now includes three integrators for importing data from flat files, Oracle applications, and SAP R/3 systems.

OWB Repository Installation

Before installing the OWB repository on a database server, you need to do the following:

❑   Make sure that the Oracle Database Server Enterprise Edition version installed on the server is 8.1.6. or higher

❑   Make sure that the user on behalf of whom we are going to install the repository has administrator's rights

❑   Define the main parameters of the database server: host name, SID, and listener port number

To install the OWB repository on a database server, you must follow these steps:

❑   Run the OWB Repository Assistant from the **Start —> Oracle** menu.

❑   At the first stage of the OWB Repository Installation Wizard (**Choose Operation**), select **Install a new Warehouse Builder Repository** from the "**Which operation would you like perform?**" field. The remaining values in the given field: **Upgrade Warehouse Builder Repository objects**—reinstallation or upgrade; **Drop Warehouse Builder Repository objects**—the repository will be deleted.

❑   In the second step (**Server Information** page, Fig. 3.5), fill in the necessary fields and click **Next**.

❑   In the third step (**New or Existing Schema** page), in the **Select one of the following choices** field, indicate the user's schema to which the new repository will be installed (either a new one (**Create and install into new user schema**) or an existing one (**Install into existing user schema**)), and then click **Next**.

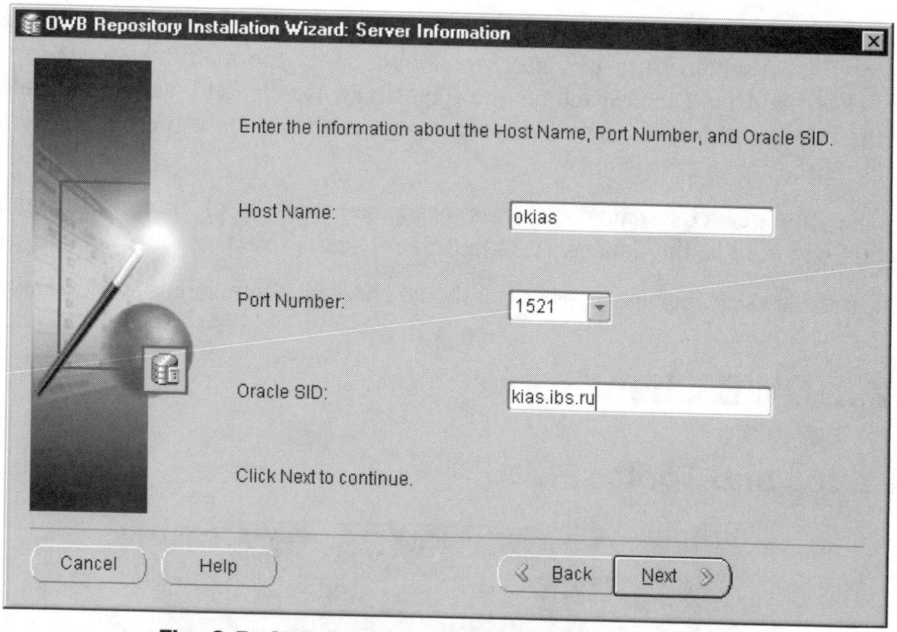

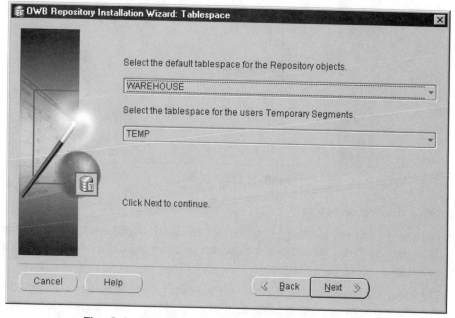

Fig. 3.5. OWB Repository Installation Wizard. Step 2

Fig. 3.6. OWB Repository Installation Wizard. Step 4

❑ For the fourth step (**Tablespace** page, Fig. 3.6), if we are installing the repository into a schema of a new user, we should select the main tablespace in the
Select the default tablespace for the Repository objects field, and in the **Select
the tablespace for the users Temporary objects** field choose the temporary table space. Then click **Next**.

❑ The fifth step (**Username and Password** page) consists of entering the name
and password of the database user and then clicking **Next**.

❑ For the last step (**Summary** page), you should check all information and click **Finish**.

3.2.3. OWB Client

Desktop and Tools

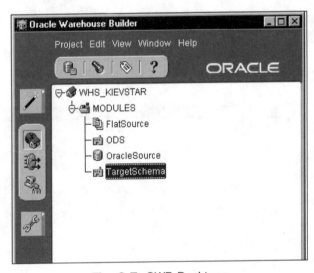

Fig. 3.7. OWB Desktops

The OWB desktop, shown in Fig. 3.7, has five main components:

❑ The main window, located in the center of the desktop, contains the navigation panel as a tree, which provides access to the main components of the data
warehouse

❑ The main menu, located at the top of the desktop, provides access to functions
that allow you to manipulate the main objects of the data warehouse, as well as
the desktop settings

❏   The main toolbox, located under the main menu, provides general functions for manipulating objects

❏   The Operation Switchboard, located in the left part of the desktop

❏   Separate buttons for calling wizards and OWB utilities, located above and below the toolbar

OWB Client Operation Modes

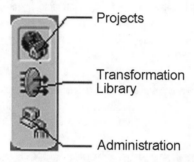

— Projects

— Transformation Library

— Administration

Fig. 3.8. Operation Switchboard

There are three modes for an OWB Client, each of which can be run from the switchboard, Fig. 3.8.

Project mode is the main operation mode. Working in project mode, we can:

❏   define data sources, the database target schema, and the main objects of the on-line repository

❏   transform data

❏   create and execute data loading scripts

To manipulate projects and integrators defined in OWB, we are provided with the administrative mode of operation. It can be run by clicking the appropriate icon on the operation switchboard.

The Transformation Library mode is intended for editing data conversion procedures and functions that are used, for example, during the migration of data from sources to the target schema of the database.

Configuring the Desktop

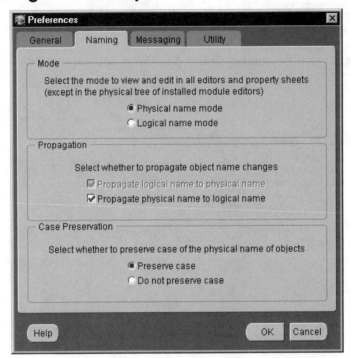

Fig. 3.9. Preferences window for OWB Client desktop

In OWB Client, we can customize the client desktop in different ways. For example, we can add different utilities to the client desktop, or install different modes for naming objects. We can call the window for editing the Oracle settings (**Preferences**) from the main menu **Projects** using the appropriate **Preferences** command. The given window contains the following tabs:

1. The **General** tab fixes the settings of the **Color Scheme** interface and of the **Wizard Welcome page on all windows** welcome window, which allows you to set a color scheme and the OWB Client welcome window display mode, respectively.

2. The **Naming** tab (Fig. 3.9) contains object naming controls and the following fields:

   ❐ **Mode**, which allows you to set the object naming mode

   The logical mode for object naming means that all object editors and wizards will display the logical names of objects.

The physical mode for object naming means that all object editors and wizards will display the physical names of objects.

❑ **Propagation** allows you to specify how the physical and logical names of objects will be propagated

❑ **Case Preservation** allows you to specify whether or not to save physical names of objects

3. The **Messaging** tab contains features to configure user activity logs. We can define the following:

❑ **Full Path**—protocol file name

❑ **Max Size**—maximum size of a protocol file

❑ **Log the follow messages**—the option of saving message types in the protocol file

4. The **Utility** tab contains a set of utilities that can be called from the toolbox using the **Utility** button. Using the given tab, we can configure already existing utilities or add our own.

To define utilities, do the following:

1. On the **Utility** tab of the **Preferences** dialog box in the field

❑ **Name**: specify an application

❑ **Full path Command**: state the utility's command line

❑ **Icon File**: select an icon for the utility

❑ **Description**: give a description of the launched utility

2. Use the **Add** button to add a new description of the launched utility to the list.

Object Creation Wizard

In an OWB Client, each object creation process has its own creation wizard. The wizard is a series of dialog boxes in which we define the attributes and properties of a specified object. Each object creation wizard contains a set of standard buttons:

❑ **Cancel**—cancels the wizard's action

❑ **Help**—calls context-oriented help for the given wizard's window

❑ **Back**—moves to the previous wizard window

❒ **Next**—moves to the next wizard window

❒ **Finish**—completes the wizard's activity, assuming its successful execution

> **NOTE**
>
> Each object creation wizard's window starts from a welcoming dialog box. A description of this dialog box is unnecessary. When describing dialog boxes related to object creation and editing wizards, we assume that you realize that you must click the **Next** button to get to the next step's dialog box.

3.3. Construction of a Data Warehouse— Step by Step

3.3.1. Step 1—Project Development

Configuring the Connection with the Server

Fig. 3.10. Configuring the connection with the database server

OWB Client is launched from the Oracle home product directory program group. After the application starts, the dialog box for configuring the connection with the repository (Fig. 3.10) appears on the screen. In it, you must enter the connection parameters in the appropriate fields and click **Logon**. Unlike other products,

OWB Client defines the connection string with the database as a set of the following five parameters:

- **User name**—name of database user
- **Password**—password of the given user
- **Host Name**—name of the computer on which the database server is installed
- **Port Number**—listening port number
- **Oracle SID**—name of the database where the OWB repository is installed

After connection with the OWB repository, the dialog box for project selection appears on the screen. It is necessary to select the name of the project which we are going to use from the **Project Name** list. By default, OWB contains the **My Project** project. To create a new project follow these steps:

1. Select the administrative mode by clicking the appropriate icon in the mode switchboard.

2. Move the cursor over the **Projects** item in the administrative object tree.

3. Run the **Create Project** command, which will start the Project Creation Wizard from the main or an auxiliary administrative menu.

4. At the first step of the Project Creation Wizard (**Name** page), specify the name and give a brief description of the new project.

5. At the next step (**Finish** page), check all the entered information and click **Finish.**

6. After we have created the new project, we can start to create and describe its main modules.

3.3.2. Step 2—Designing Data Models

Creating Modules

Before we design the data model, we have to create a module in which OWB will store all schema object definitions.

To create the module for the schema of the data warehouse database, do the following:

1. Select **Project mode** from the main panel.

2. Select the project that will contain the given module, having beforehand saved all changes, and position the cursor over the **Modules** element in the selected project.

3. Run the **Create Module** command from the main or an auxiliary administrative menu.

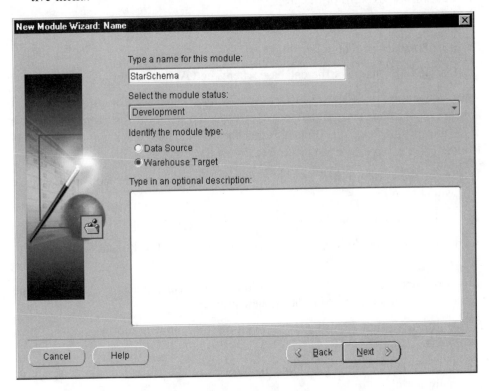

Fig. 3.11. New Module Wizard. Step 1

4. The New Module Wizard will execute the given command, and at the first step (**Name** page, Fig. 3.11) you should fill in the following fields:

   ❑ **Type a name for this module**—contains the module name that will be displayed on the main panel.

   ❑ **Select the module status**—contains information on the module's status.

   ❑ **Identify the module type**—contains information on the project type. Here you should select **Warehouse Target** since the given module should contain the data warehouse schema.

   ❑ **Type in an optional description**—contains help information on the given module.

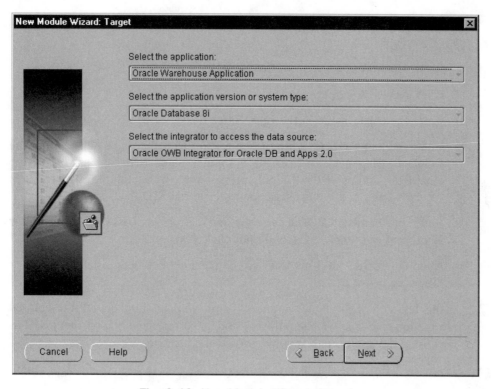

Fig. 3.12. New Module Wizard. Step 2

5. For the second step of the New Module Wizard (**Target** page), fill in the following fields:

   ❏ **Select the application**—contains a list of accessible system types

   ❏ **Select the application version or system type**—contains a list of accessible databases

   ❏ **Select the integrator to access the data source**—contains a list of integrators for connection with different data sources

   When creating the target database schema module, all of the items listed above can only accept default values.

6. In the following step of the New Module Wizard (**Connection Information** page), we should either select a connection with the database or create a new one. Making a new connection encompasses creating a database object—

`DbLink`—which establishes connections between different databases, including heterogeneous ones.

To create a new connection with the database:

1) Click **New** in the given window.

2) Enter the object name in the **Link Name** field.

3) Enter the name of the string of connection with the database server to the **Connect string** field, or give the computer name (database server) in the **Host** field, and enter the listening process port (by default, 1521 or 1527) in the **Port** field, and the database identifier in the **SID** field.

4) Enter the name of a database user and his or her password in the **User Name** and **Password** fields, and then click **Test**.

5) After the server confirms that the connection has been established, click **OK.**

7. At this last step of the New Module Wizard, you should check all the entered information and click **Finish**. If you find an error, go back to the previous steps using the appropriate key and correct the inaccuracy.

After we have defined the database schema module, we can begin defining its main objects.

Defining Module Content

Warehouse Module Editor

To define module contents, OWB includes the Warehouse Module Editor, which we can use to create, edit, and delete module contents. To call the Warehouse Module Editor, double click on the project module icon, or select **Edit Object** from the main or an auxiliary menu.

The Warehouse Module Editor window (Fig. 3.13) contains:

❑   A navigation toolbar located at the center of the dialog box, which provides access to the main objects grouped by type

❑   The main menu located at the top of the dialog box, which provides access to functions for manipulating the basic module objects

❑ The main toolbar located under the main menu, which contains the basic functions for manipulating objects

❑ Three main tabs intended for showing an object's various functional slices:

   ❑ The **Logical Tree** tab shows objects in end user terms

   ❑ The **Physical Tree** tab shows objects in database terms

   ❑ The **Business Tree** tab defines business areas

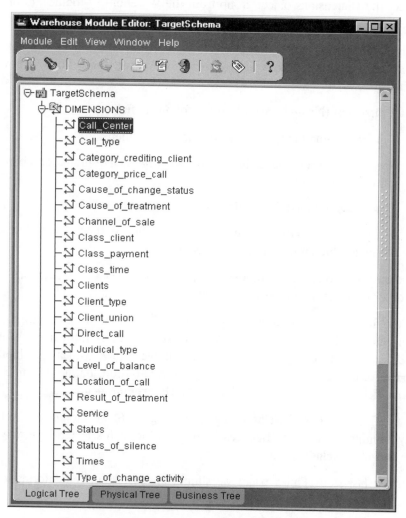

Fig. 3.13. The **Warehouse Module Editor** window

Dimension Creation and Editing

There are two types of dimensions in OWB—*time* and *simple*. The main difference between the two is that the `time` type is intended to describe the time dimension—days, weeks, months, or years—and the `simple` one is used to describe all other types of dimensions.

To create the time dimension:

1. Select the **Dimensions** object group from the Warehouse Module Editor object tree.

2. Using the right mouse button, select the **Create Time Dimension** command from the auxiliary menu, which will call the Wizard for defining a new time dimension, where:

3. In the first step (**Name** page), fill in the following fields:

   ❐ **Type in a name for the dimension**—name of dimension

   ❐ **Specify the prefix used in key names (optional)**—prefix or abbreviated name of dimension

   ❐ **Type in an optional description**—description of dimension

4. At the second step (**Levels** page), select from the list those levels that will be used to create hierarchies in the dimension.

5. At the third step (**Level Attributes** page, Fig. 3.14) check each level one by one in order to select additional level attributes from the list.

6. At the fourth step (**Hierarchies** page, Fig. 3.15), define the correlation between hierarchy levels by selecting the most suitable hierarchy from the existing list. If the given list does not suit us, we can supplement it with a new hierarchy. To do so, create a new hierarchy using the **Add** button, define its name in the **Name** field, and give its description in the **Description** field.

7. At the fifth step (**Level Relationships** page, Fig. 3.16) we should set the hierarchy defining levels in the **Selected levels** field for each selected hierarchy using the **Include/Exclude** buttons.

8. For the last step (**Finish** page) we should check all entered information and click **Finish**.

   After that, OWB will create and display the dimension in the object tree.

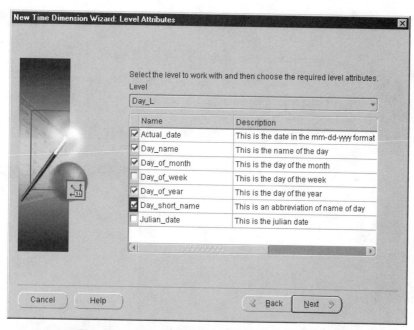

Fig. 3.14. New Time Dimension Wizard. Step 3

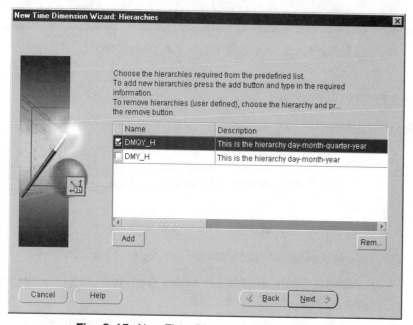

Fig. 3.15. New Time Dimension Wizard. Step 4

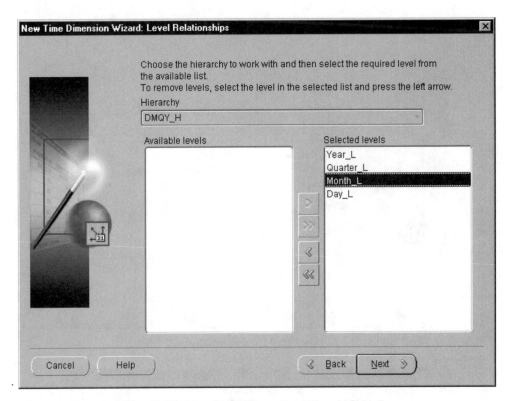

Fig. 3.16. New Time Dimension Wizard. Step 5

To create a simple dimension:

❏ Select the **Dimension** object group from the Warehouse Module Editor object tree

❏ Using the right mouse button, select the **Create Dimension** command from the auxiliary menu, which will launch the New Dimension Wizard, in which:

    1. For the first step (**Name** page), you should indicate in these fields:

        ❏ **Type in a name for the dimension**—name of the dimension

        ❏ **Specify the prefix used in key names (optional)**—prefix or abbreviated name of the dimension

        ❏ **Type in an optional description**—description of the dimension

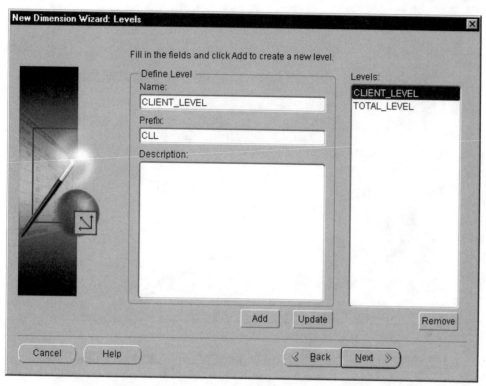

Fig. 3.17. New Dimension Wizard. Step 2

2. At the second step (**Levels** page, Fig. 3.17) you can define the hierarchy levels that will be used in the dimension. To create a hierarchy level, indicate its name in the **Name** field, its abbreviated name in the **Prefix** field, a description of the new level in the **Description** field, and click **Add** to add it to the list of levels.

3. At the third step (**Level Attributes** page, Fig. 3.18), create additional level attributes for each existing hierarchy level. To construct a hierarchy level attribute, indicate its name in the **Name** field, the type and length of the attribute for storage in the database in the **Data type, Length, Precision,** and **Scale** fields, and provide a description of the new level in the **Description** field. To add it to the level list click **Add**.

4. At the fourth step (**Hierarchies** page, Fig. 3.19), you can create a new hierarchy to define the interconnection between hierarchy levels. Specify the name in the **Name** field, an abbreviated name in the **Prefix** field, and a description in the **Description** field. Then click **Add** to add it to the list of hierarchies.

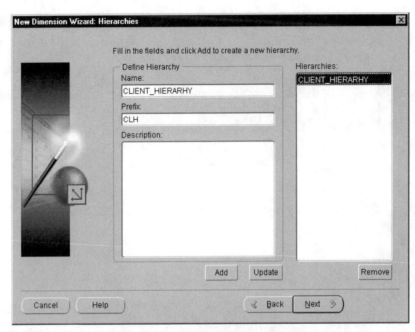

Fig. 3.18. New Dimension Wizard. Step 3

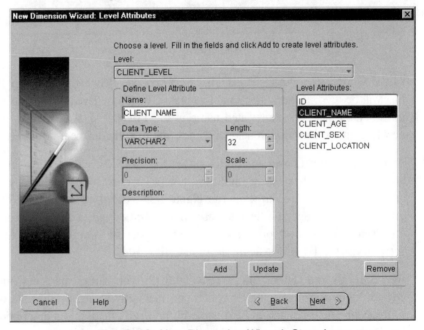

Fig. 3.19. New Dimension Wizard. Step 4

5. In the fifth step (**Level Relationships** page), define the dimension levels included in the hierarchy for each selected hierarchy in the **Selected levels** field using the **Include/Exclude** buttons. At the same time, you should pay attention to the order of the levels in the **Selected levels** field; a "parent—child" relation is defined between neighboring levels in the hierarchy.

6. In the last step (**Finish** page), check all the entered information and click **Finish**.

    After that, OWB will create and display the created dimension in the tree of objects.

After we have defined the dimension, we must set the properties of the table over which the dimension will be defined.

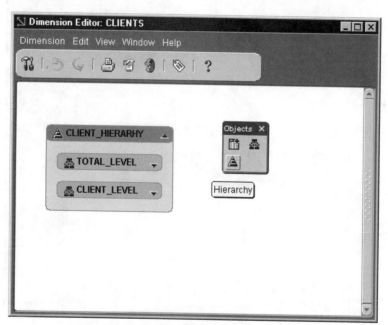

Fig. 3.20. The **Dimension Editor** window

To do so:

1. Select the required dimension in the Warehouse Module Editor navigation panel.

2. Using the **Edit Objects** command from the Warehouse Module Editor main menu, or the **Edit** command from the object edit menu, display the **Dimension**

Editor window, which shows hierarchies, levels, and dimension attributes in graphic form (Fig. 3.20).

3. In the **Dimension Editor** window, display the dialog box for editing table dimension properties using the **Edit** command from the main menu.

4. In the **Table Properties** window, **Columns** tab, you should check all previously entered information and, if necessary, indicate the order of columns in the dimension table in the **Position** field, which in many respects can influence the productivity of queries to the given table.

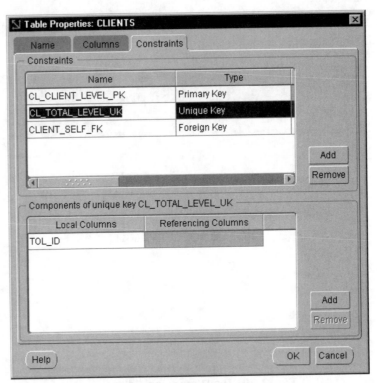

Fig. 3.21. The **Table Properties** dialog box for editing dimension properties

5. In the **Table Properties** window, **Constraints** tab, first define the primary key of the given table, and then the alternative primary keys (Unique keys), the secondary (Foreign) keys, and also the mandatory rules of integrity constraint for the given table. To do so, use the **Add** button in the **Constraints** field to create an empty row, where we should give the name of the integrity constraint

in the **Name** field, and its type in the **Type** field, which can accept the following values:

☐ **Check Constraint**—this integrity constraint is a test condition contained in the **Check Condition** field

☐ **Primary key**—this integrity constraint is a primary key

☐ **Foreign key**—this integrity constraint is secondary key, which references an object set in the **Referenced Application, Referenced Table,** and **Referenced Key** fields

☐ **Unique key**—this integrity constraint is a unique, or alternate primary, key

☐ In the **Components of... using** field, create an empty row using the **Add** button, in which you should select the column (attribute) of representation in the **Local Columns** field, and then select a column from another table in the **Referencing Columns** field, depending on the integrity constraint type

6. Finally, click **OK.**

Creating and Editing Fact Tables

After we have created all the dimensions, we can start to create fact tables. Take notice that fact tables in OWB Client are based on their hierarchy level rather than on dimensions.

To create a fact table:

1. Select the **Fact** object group from the Warehouse Module Editor object tree.

2. Using the right mouse button, select the **Create Facts** command, which will call the New Fact Wizard.

3. At the first step (**Name** page) of the New Fact Wizard, we should fill in these fields:

    ☐ **Type in a name for the fact table**—name of fact table

    ☐ **Type in an optional description**—description of fact table

4. At the second step (**Define Foreign Keys** page, Fig. 3.22), define what dimension levels will define the fact table. For this purpose, we should select the dimension, the dimension's hierarchy level, and a unique key for each foreign key in the **Dimension, Level,** and **Unique key** fields. Then, using the **Add** button, we should add the selected combination as a foreign key of the fact table.

5. At the third step (**Define Measures** page), define the measures that are to be contained in the fact table. To do this, create an empty row using the **Add** button, indicate the name of the measure in the **Name** field, and define its type and size in the **Data type, Length, Precision,** and **Scale** fields.

6. In the last step (**Finish** page), check all entered information and click **Finish**.

    OWB will then create and display the fact table in the object tree.

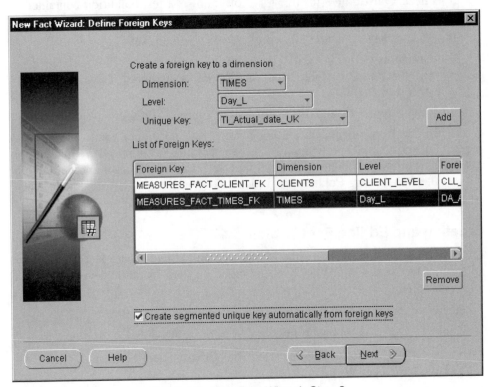

Fig. 3.22. New Fact Wizard. Step 2

To edit the fact table's contents, you can use:

☐ The **Edit** command from the object editing menu, which calls the fact table editing window in which the table itself and its interconnection with dimensions are presented in a graphic form

☐ The **Properties** command from the object editing menu, which calls the object edit window in which the steps of the New Fact Wizard described earlier are presented in the form of tabs

Creating Materialized Views

Materialized views are database objects intended for processing fact tables and saving the results of this processing. Like views, materialized views are defined by a query to the database, but in contrast to them, they store in their structure the results of a query's execution, instead of a reference to data.

To create a materialized view:

1. Select the **Materialized Views** object group from the Warehouse Module Editor object tree.

2. Using the right mouse button, select the **Create Materialized View** command, which will call the New Materialized View Wizard:

   1) At the first step (**Name** page), fill in the following fields:

   ❏ **Type in a name for the materialized view**—name of the materialized view

   ❏ **Type in an optional description**—description of the materialized view

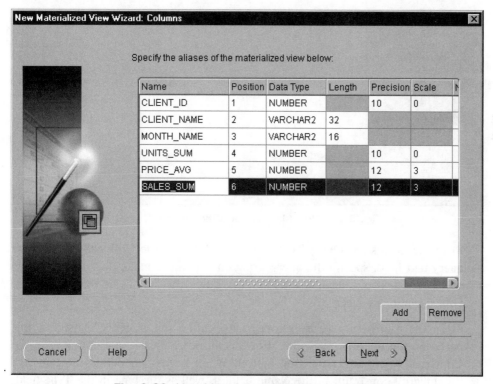

Fig. 3.23. New Materialized View Wizard. Step 2

2) At the second step (**Columns** page, Fig. 3.23), determine the set of columns that will define the materialized view. For this purpose, click the **Add** button to

create an empty description row, and give the column name in the **Name** field. Then define its type and size in the **Data type, Length, Precision,** and **Scale** fields, and its serial number in the **Position** field.

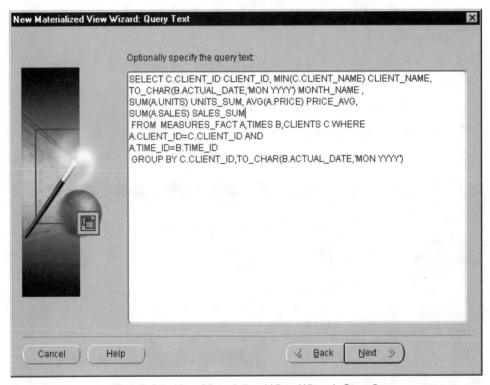

Fig. 3.24. New Materialized View Wizard. Step 3

3) In the third step (**Query Text** page, Fig. 3.24), in the **Optionally specify the query text** field, specify the query string on which the materialized view will be based. The text of query must be an SQL query that abides by the rules of the Oracle syntax analyzer.

4) In the fourth step (**Constraints** page), define the integrity constraint imposed on the materialized views. For this purpose, create an empty line in the **Constraints** field using the **Add** button. When necessary, define the name of the integrity constraint in the **Name** field, as well as the type in the **Type** field, which can accept the following values:

❏ **Check Constraint**—this integrity constraint is a test condition contained in the **Check Condition** field

❏   **Primary key**—this integrity constraint is a primary key

❏   **Foreign key**—this integrity constraint is a foreign key, which references an object defined in the **Referenced Application, Referenced Table,** and **Referenced Key** fields

❏   **Unique key**—this integrity constraint is a unique, or alternate primary, key

You should create an empty line in the **Components of**... field using the **Add** button, where you should then select a column (attribute) of the materialized view in the **Local Columns** field, and select a column from another table in the **Referencing Columns** field, depending on the integrity constraint type.

5) In the last step (**Finish** page), we should check all the entered information and then click **Finish**.

After that, OWB will create and display the materialized view in the object tree.

Creating Views

Views are objects of a database usually intended to hide from end users the complex structure of objects and present these objects in terms more familiar to end users.

To create a view:

1.   Select the **Views** object group from the Warehouse Module Editor object tree.

2.   Using the right mouse button, call the **Create View** command, which will call the View Creation Wizard:

3.   At the first step (**Name** page), indicate in these fields

❏   **Type in a name for the view**—name of the view

❏   **Type in an optional description**—description of the view

4.   At the second step (**Columns** page), set the columns that will define the view. Use the **Add** button to create an empty description line, and in the **Name** field, give the name of the column. In the **Data type, Length, Precision,** and **Scale** fields, define their type and size, and in the **Position** field, give the serial number.

5.   At the third step (**Query Text** page), we should specify the text of query on which the view will be based in the **Optionally specify the query text** field, and hit **Next**. The text of the query should be a proper SQL query according to the rules set by the Oracle parser.

6. At the fourth step (**Constraints** page), define the constraints imposed on the integrity representation. In the **Constraints** field, using the **Add** button, create an empty line in which you must indicate the name of the integrity constraint in the **Name** field, and the type in the **Type** field, which can accept the following values:

  ❑ **Check Constraint**—this integrity constraint is a test condition contained in the **Check Condition** field

  ❑ **Primary key**—this integrity constraint is a primary key

  ❑ **Foreign key**—this integrity constraint is a foreign key that references an object defined by the fields **Referenced Application, Referenced Table**, and **Referenced Key**

  ❑ **Unique key**—this integrity constraint is a unique, or alternate primary, key

  At the **Components of...** field, create an empty line with the **Add** button; select a column (attribute) of the view in the **Local Columns** field, and, depending on the type of integrity constraint, select a column from another table in the **Referencing Columns** field.

7. At the last step (**Finish** page), check the correctness of all of the entered information and click **Finish**.

OWB will then create and map the view in the object tree.

Creating Sequences

A sequence generates ordinal integer values and is usually used to create primary keys for a table.

Depending on how we load data, we either have the ability to create a sequence or not. If an object loads using SQL*LOADER, the control file of the given product itself defines the sequence. If a table loads with the PL/SQL package, we have to define a sequence for the loaded object.

To create a sequence:

1. Select the **Sequences** object group from the Warehouse Module Editor object tree.

2. Using the right mouse button, call the **Create Sequence** command, which will call the sequence creation wizard.

3. At the first step of the sequence creation wizard (**Name** page), define the following fields:

   ❐ **Type in a name for the sequence**—name of the sequence

   ❐ **Type in an optional description**—description of the sequence

4. At the last step (**Summary** page), check all entered information and then click **Finish**.

3.3.3. Step 3—Defining Data Sources

To define a data source, just as when defining the target schema of the database, we need to create a module.

Creating a Module for Data Sources

To create a module for the data warehouse database schema:

1. Select **Project mode** from the main panel.

2. To select the project that will contain the given module, having saved all changes beforehand, move the cursor to a position over the **Modules** element inside the selected project.

3. From the main menu or a supplementary menu of the manager, execute the **Create Module** command. This command will call the New Module Creation Wizard.

4. In the New Module Creation Wizard, fill in the following fields for the first step:

   ❐ **Name of the module**—contains the name of the module, which will be displayed on the main panel.

   ❐ **Status of the module**—contains information on the status of the module.

   ❐ **Type of the module**—contains the information on the type of the project. Here you should select **Data Source**, since the given module should contain a description of the data source

   ❐ **Description of the module**—contains help information on the given module.

5. At the second step (**Data Source Information** page), fill in the fields:

   ❐ **Select the application**—to select the type of data source

❑ **Select the application version or system type**—indicate the system version, depending on the selected type of data source

❑ **Select the integrator to access the data source**—indicate the integrator to be used

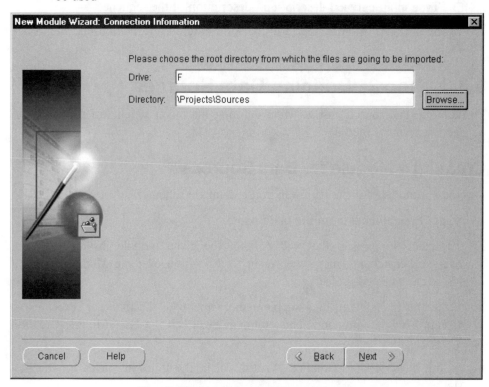

Fig. 3.25. New Module Wizard. Step 3

6. At the following step of the New Module Creation Wizard (**Connection Information** page), depending on the type of data source selected, you should:

❑ If the data source is a **Generic File Based Application**, indicate the complete paths to files in the **Drive** and **Directory** fields (Fig. 3.25)

❑ If the data source is a **Generic Oracle Database Application**, indicate the type of metadata dictionary and the database link in the **Source for Metadata Import** and **Database Link** fields

7. At the last step of the New Module Creation Wizard, check all of the entered information and click **Finish**. If you detect an error, return to the previous steps and correct the inaccuracy using the **Back** button. After we have finished

creating our new module, we can start the Metadata Import Wizard. To do this, you'll have to set the **Proceed to the Import Metadata Wizard after creating this module** option.

Importing Metadata from Oracle Databases

To define the main objects of the data source module:

1. Select a data source module from the OWB object tree.

2. Call the **Import Metadata** command using the right mouse button. This command will call the Import Metadata Wizard.

3. For the first step (**Filter Information** page), we can set various options and conditions for viewing data source objects.

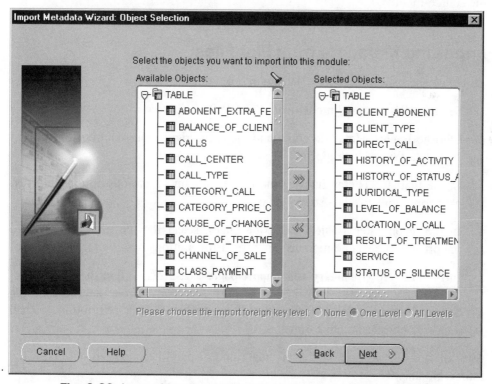

Fig. 3.26. Import Metadata Wizard (from Oracle databases). Step 2

4. At the second step (**Object Selection** page, Fig. 3.26), using the arrow buttons, select the objects that you want to import to the source module. With the

Please choose the import foreign key level option, we can set a nesting level for the imported objects:

☐ **None** means that only the object itself will be selected

☐ **One Level** means that the object and objects connected with it will be selected

☐ **All Levels** means that the object and all objects connected with it will be selected

5. In the last step (**Summary and Import** page), give a description to each imported object, and click **Finish**.

After that, OWB will import the metadata and will display the imported objects in the source module.

Importing Metadata from Flat Files

To define the main objects of a data source module:

1. Select the data source model from the OWB object tree.

2. Call the **Import Metadata** command using the right mouse button; the Import Metadata Wizard will appear.

3. In the first step (**Filter Information** page), we can set various options and display conditions for data source objects.

4. In the second step (**Object Selection** page), select the files that you want to import into the source module using the arrow buttons.

5. In the last step (**Summary and Import** page, Fig. 3.27), define the structure of the flat file (we will look at the *Import Flat File Wizard* later) using the **Sample** button, or select it from the **Same as** list. Give a description to each imported object and click **Finish**.

After that, OWB will import the metadata and display the imported objects in the source module.

OWB provides various methods for creating a file structure with specific (**Delimited**) separators between data attributes and files with fixed line length (**Fixedlength**).

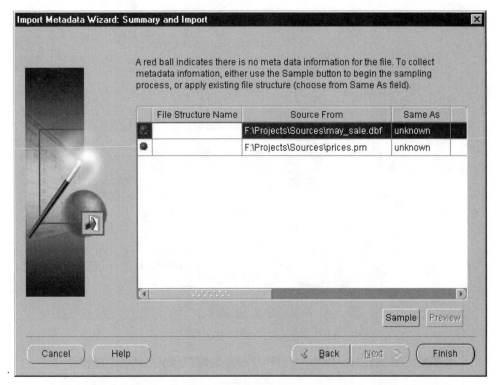

Fig. 3.27. Import Metadata Wizard (from flat files). Step 3

Creating a Description of a File Structure with Specific Separators

The given type of file structure is used when strings are divided by an operating system separator and data attributes are divided by a specific symbol.

To describe the structure:

1. In the Import Metadata Wizard, call the Flat File Sample Wizard on the **Summary and Import** page using the **Sample** button.

2. For the first step (**File Format** page), fill in the following fields as indicated:

   ☐ **Select File Format**—select the type of the imported file—**Delimited**

   ☐ **Character set**—select the type of data coding

3. At the second step (**Field Breaking** page, Fig. 3.28), in the **Field Delimiter** field, select or indicate a separator symbol for the attributes of the imported file.

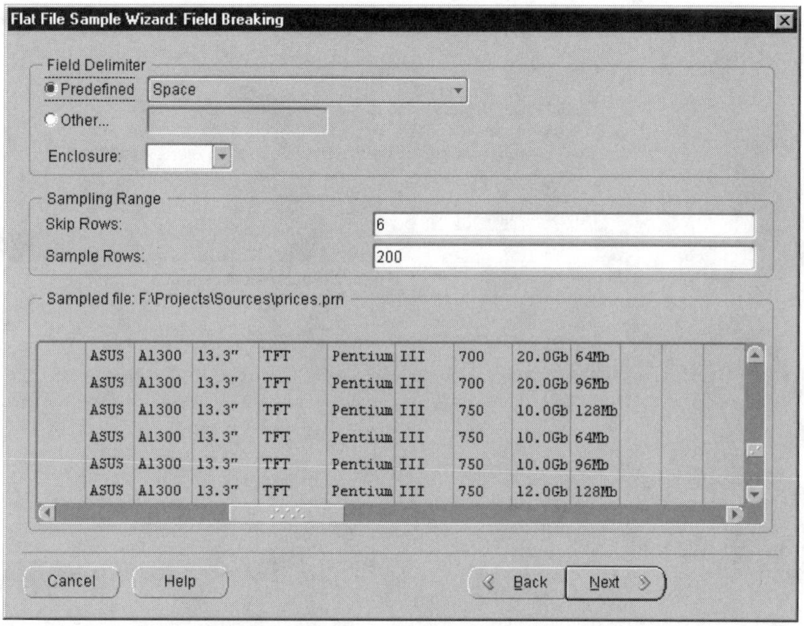

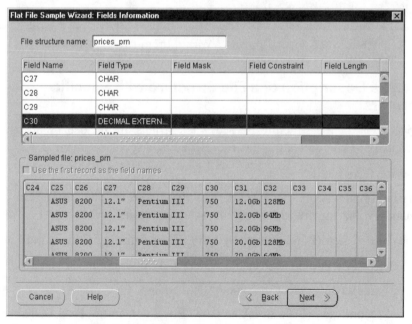

Fig. 3.28. Flat File Sample Wizard. Step 2

Fig. 3.29. Flat File Sample Wizard. Step 3

4. For the third step (**Fields Information** page, Fig. 3.29) we should indicate the following information for each attribute:

    ❏ **Field Name**—its name

    ❏ **Field Type**—data attribute type

    ❏ **Field Mask**—mask for the data attribute format (for example, 'YYYY-MM-DD')

    ❏ **Field Constraint**—determines how uncertain values will be interpreted

    ❏ **Field Length**—record attribute length

5. At the last step of the wizard, check the entered information and click **Finish**.

NOTE

The type of imported data coding should coincide or be compatible with the database coding. By default, OWB uses database coding.

Creating a File Structure Description with Fixed Line Length

This type of file structure is usable when strings are divided by an operating system separator, or when they have a fixed length. The most common type of this kind of structure is DBF, and using DBF files as an example, we will look at describing a structure with a fixed line length.

To describe a file structure with a fixed line length:

1. In the Metadata Import Wizard, on the **Summary and Import** page, call the Flat File Sample Wizard using the **Sample** button.

2. For the first step (**File Format** page, Fig. 3.30):

    ❏ Select the type of imported file—**Fixed Length**—In the **Select File Format** field.

    ❏ Select the type of data coding in the **Character set** field.

    ❏ In the **Physical Record Definition field**, either define the size of the **Physical Record Size** line, or indicate that the strings are separated from each other by the **Physical OS Record Terminator** operating system separator. If the source file is a file with a DBF structure, the **Physical Record Size** field should take a value equal to the sum of all the lengths of the DBF file columns plus one, and the **Support Logical Record** option should take the `Single` value (non-withdrawn value).

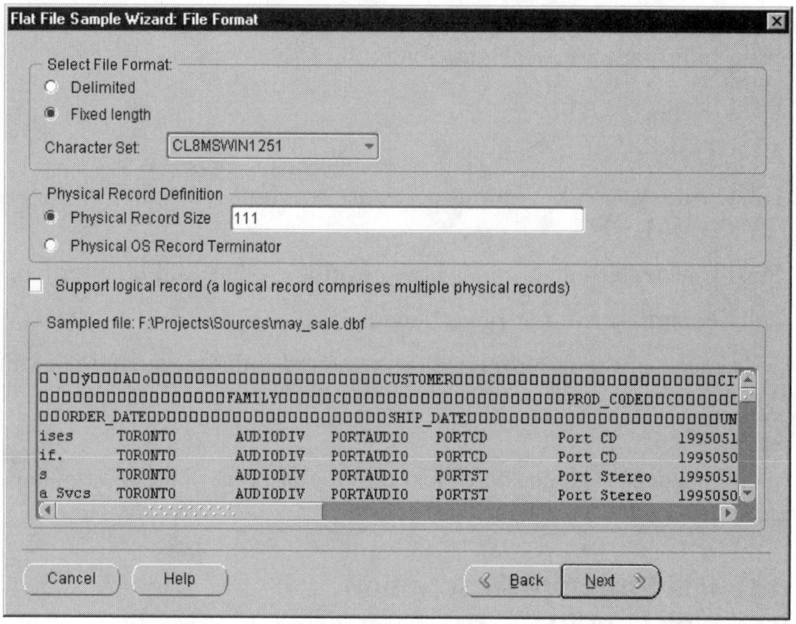

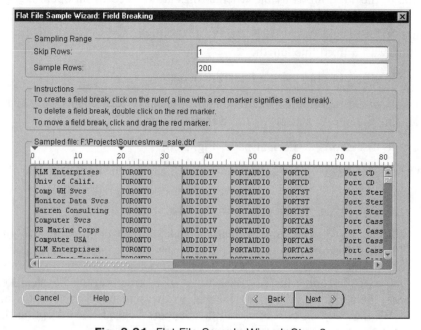

Fig. 3.30. Flat File Sample Wizard. Step 1

Fig. 3.31. Flat File Sample Wizard. Step 2

3. For the second step (**Filed Breaking** page), show the number of skipped (disregarded) strings in the **Sampling Range** field, and, according to the instructions, define the columns in our file. In our case, the **Skip Rows** field should take a value of 1, since the first string of the DBF file contains the data definitions.

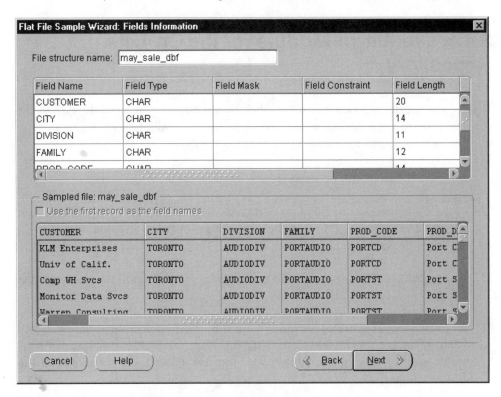

Fig. 3.32. Flat File Sample Wizard. Step 3

4. The third step (**Fields Information** page, Fig. 3.32), shows the following information for each column defined in the previous step:

    ❏ **Field Name**—its name

    ❏ **Field Type**—data attribute type

    ❏ **Field Mask**—mask of the data attribute format (for example, 'YYYY-MM-DD')

    ❏ **Field Constraint**—determines how uncertain values will be interpreted

    ❏ **Field Length**—records attribute length

5. In the last step of the wizard, check all the entered information and click **Finish**.

3.4. Creating an On-Line Repository and a Transformation Layer

3.4.1. Creating a Module for the On-Line Repository

Before you create a module for the on-line repository, you need to define the physical layout of the repository according to the data warehouse architecture we selected as it relates to the target schema of the database.

The on-line repository can be located:

❏ In the same database as the data warehouse target schema, but in another user schema. Here you should remember that we are creating an additional load on the target database.

❏ In another database, but on the same server as the data warehouse target schema.

❏ In a database of another server. This is the most preferable situation, since when we locate the on-line repository on other server, we isolate tasks connected with loading and cleaning data from the other tasks performed in the data warehouse.

❏ In the same server database as the data source. This architectural option is preferable only if there is only one data source, because if there is more than one data source in the architecture, each containing an on-line repository, you will have to integrate several data sources.

After setting the location of the on-line repository, regardless of the architecture, we must create a connection (a database link), and then create a module for it.

Creating a module for an on-line repository is identical to the process of creating a module for the data warehouse target schema (see "*Creating Modules*" in *Section 3.3.2*).

3.4.2. Creating a Transformational Data Loading Layer

A transformational data loading layer is a set of packages, procedures, and functions intended for extracting, transforming, and loading data from sources to the target base.

Generally, creating a data transformation procedure includes four main steps:

☐ Step 1. Creating a procedure description

☐ Step 2. Defining a set of transformation functions that will be used in the procedure

☐ Step 3. Creating a high-level description of the procedure

☐ Step 4. Creating a detailed description of the procedure

Creating a Description for Data Mapping

To define the main objects of the data source module:

1. Open the on-line repository module in the OWB object tree.

2. Place the mouse cursor over the **Mappings** module in the **Warehouse Module Editor** window.

3. Using the right mouse button, call the **Create Mappings** command, which will open the New Mapping Wizard, where:

4. For the first step (**Name** page), we should define mapping and indicate in the fields:

    ☐ **Enter a name for mapping**—the name for the mapping

    ☐ **Type in an optional description**—a description of the mapping

5. For the second step (**Source Modules** page, Fig. 3.33), select the modules that will be used in mapping using the arrow keys.

6. For the last step (**Summary** page), check all the entered information and click **Finish**.

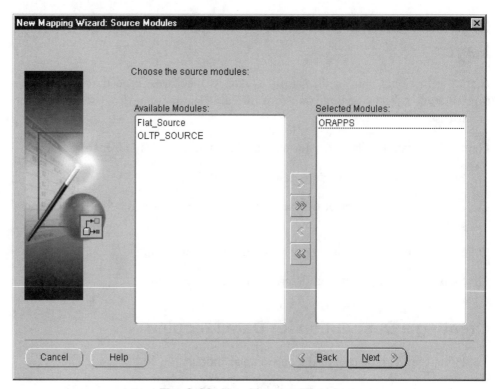

Fig. 3.33. New Mapping Wizard

Defining a Transformation Function Set

As a rule, functions for operation with character and numerical fields and data type fields, as well as functions for converting one data type to another, are classified as transformation functions, for example, TO_DATE, TO_CHAR, or DECODE.

By default, OWB contains a library that gives a set of standard data transformation functions separated into certain categories.

Besides using standard functions in the transformation procedure, we can use functions that should be either created beforehand or registered in the OWB repository. Before writing our transformation function, we should create a function library if one does not yet exist.

To create a custom function library:

1. Select the **Transformation Library** mode from the main client panel.

2. Select the module that will contain the given function library, and move the cursor to the **Transformation Category** item inside the selected module.

3. Execute the **Create Transformation Category** command from the main or supplementary menu.

4. This command will open the Create a Transformation Category Wizard, in which you should give a name for and a description of the category.

5. In the second step, check all the entered information and click **Finish**.

To create an appropriate function:

1. Select the **Transformation Library mode** in the main client panel.

2. Select the module that will contain the given transformation function, and place the cursor on the **Transformation** item inside the function library of the selected module.

3. From the main or supplementary menu, execute the **Create Transformation** command.

4. This command will open the Create Transform Wizard, where in the first step you need to define for the fields:

    ❏ **Type in a name for the transformation**—the name of the procedure or function

    ❏ **Check if this is a procedure**—checks whether the given transformation function is a procedure

    ❏ **Specify the return type of the transformation**—resets the data type

    ❏ **Type in an optional description**—gives a brief description of the given transformation function

5. In the second step (**Parameters** page, Fig. 3.34), define the input parameters for the given transformation function. For this purpose, add an empty line using the **Add** button, and in the fields:

    ❏ **I/O**—set the parameter type

    ❏ **Position**—define the position of the parameter in the header of a function or procedure

    ❏ **Name**—give a name to the parameter

    ❏ **Type**—define its data type

    ❏ **Required**—define whether or not it is mandatory

    ❏ **Default Value**—define the default value for the given parameter

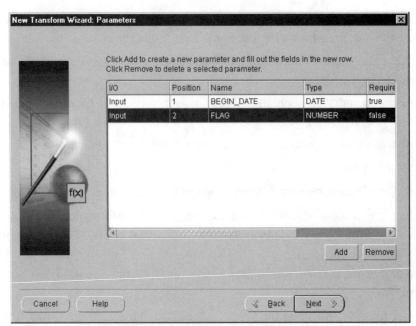

Fig. 3.34. New Transform Wizard. Step 2

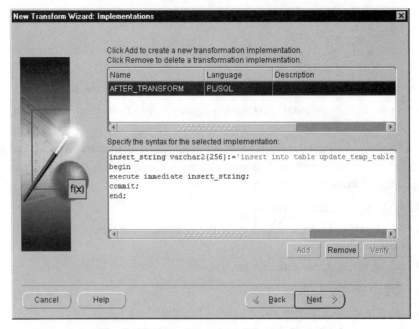

Fig. 3.35. New Transform Wizard. Step 3

5. For the third step (**Implementations** page, Fig. 3.35) in the fields:

    ❑   **Name**—indicate the transformation function's name

    ❑   **Specify the syntax for the selected implementation**—specify a procedure block in PL/SQL that is correct according to the rules of Oracle's parser

6. For the last step, check all the entered information and click **Finish**.

OWB will then create the transformation function and display it on the object tree.

Tools for Describing Data Extraction from Data Sources

To create a high-level description for the data extraction procedure:

1. Select the required mapping procedure in Warehouse Module Editor.

2. Call the **Mapping Editor** property editing window using the **Edit** command from the main or supplementary menu (Fig. 3.36).

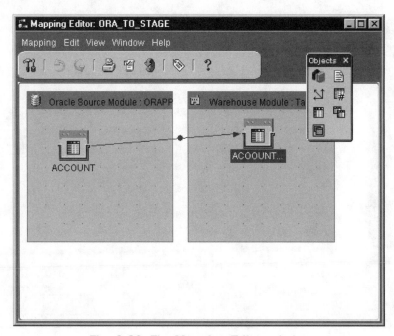

Fig. 3.36. The **Mapping Editor** window

3. Drag the data source object from the object panel to the data source area. If the data source is a flat file, the source object can be a file object. If the data source is a database application, the source object can be a table object.

4. Select one of the following options from the **Add Table** list which will appear:

   ☐ **Import Table**—you have to start the object import wizard (Importing Metadata from Oracle Databases) to define the source object

   ☐ **Select from existing table**—you should select the source object from the existing object list and then click **OK**

After defining the source object, you must define the target loading object. The target object can be defined in four ways:

☐ *Method 1. Cloning (copying) of source object.* To define the target object, do the following:

   ☐ While holding down the <Shift> key, drag the source object to the target region of the mapping properties editing window.

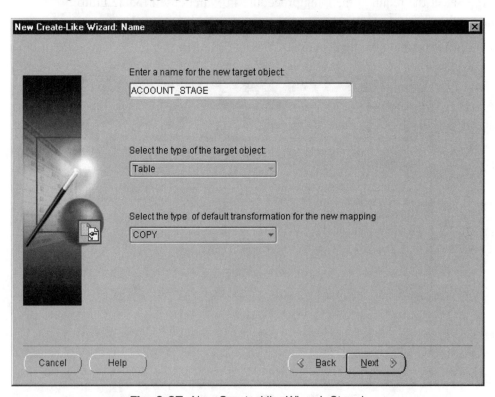

Fig. 3.37. New Create-Like Wizard. Step 1

❏ In the window of the Create-Like Wizard that appears, for the first step (**Name** page, Fig. 3.37), indicate the name in the **Enter a name for the new target object** field, the type in the **Select the type of the target object** field, and the type of target table transformation in the **Select the type of default transformation for the new mapping** field.

❏ For the second step (**Summary** page), check all the entered information, and after clicking the **Finish** button, the OWB Client will create an exact copy of the source object as a target table, and will define the relation between these two objects as an arrow.

❏ *Method 2. Creating a target object.* To define the target object, proceed in this manner:

  ❏ Drag the data source object to the data target area from the object panel.

  ❏ Select the **Create Table** option from the **Add Table** list that will appear.

  ❏ For the first step of the New Table Wizard (**Name** page), give the name of the target table.

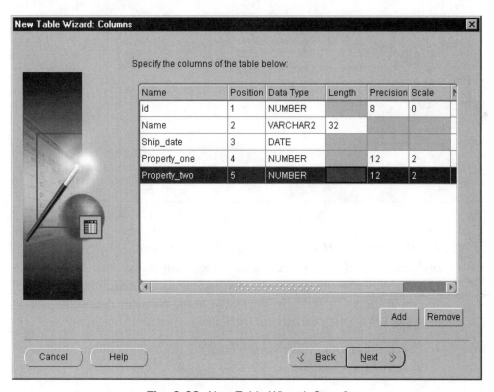

Fig. 3.38. New Table Wizard. Step 2

☐ For the second step of the New Table Wizard (**Columns** page, Fig. 3.38), define the table columns and click **Next**. To create a table attribute, use the **Add** button to create an empty line in which you should specify the name of the column in the **Name** field, define its type and size in the **Data type**, **Length**, **Precision**, and **Scale** fields, and the serial number in the **Position** field.

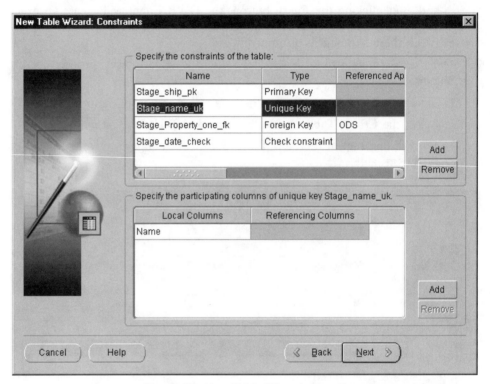

Fig. 3.39. New Table Wizard. Step 3

☐ For the third step (**Constraints** page, Fig. 3.39), define the rules of integrity constraint to be imposed on the table columns. For this purpose, create an empty line in the **Constraints** field using the **Add** button, in which you should name the integrity constraint in the **Name** field, and the type in the **Type** field, which can accept the following values:

- **Check Constraint**—this integrity constraint is a test condition contained in the **Check Condition** field

- **Primary key**—this integrity constraint is a primary key

- **Foreign key**—this integrity constraint is a foreign key, which references an object defined by the **Referenced Application**, **Referenced Table,** and **Referenced Key** fields

  - **Unique key**—this integrity constraint is a unique, or alternate primary, key

❐ For the last step, we should check all the entered information and click **Finish**.

❐ *Method 3. Select from an existing table.* To define the target object in this way:

❐ Drag the data source object to the data target area from the object panel using the mouse.

❐ Choose the **Select from existing table option** in the **Add Table** window that will appear, and click **OK**.

❐ Select the target table from the **Add Table** list that will appear and click **OK**.

❐ *Method 4. Importing the table.* In this case:

❐ Drag the table object to the data target area from the object panel with the mouse.

❐ Select the **Import table** option from the **Add Table** list that appears and click **OK**.

❐ In the **Database Link Information** window that will appear, select an object for linking with the database from list in the **Database Link** field, or create it with the **New DB Link** button.

❐ Select a target table from the list in the **Object Selection** window, and click **OK**.

When all objects have been defined, link the source object to the target object using the mouse, if such a link was not already defined when establishing the target object.

When concluding the procedure of determining a high-level definition for the transformation, check for the presence of the following target table attributes and create them if they are not there:

❐ A column to contain the primary key of the table

❐ A unique key for the column that will contain the primary key of the data source table

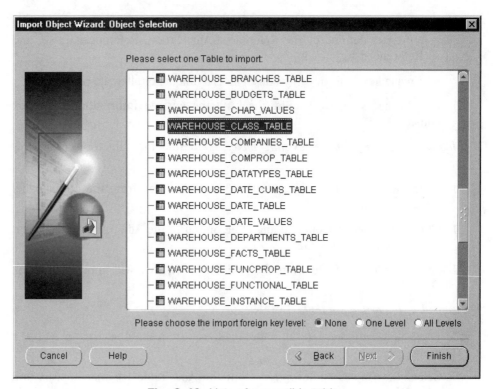

Fig. 3.40. Lists of accessible tables

To create or to delete a data column or the integrity constraint rules of the table, we can use the standard table property editing dialog described in *"Dimension Creation and Editing"* in *Section 3.3.2.*

After we have created a high-level description of the data transformation procedure, we can begin a detailed description of the data loading process.[1]

The detailed description (the **Detail Mapping Editor** window) determines the order and the terms of the projection of data source table columns onto intermediate table columns of the on-line repository.

---

[1] Objects created in the process of describing the transformation procedure in detail are an interpretation of the SQL and PL/SQL syntax constructions to which they will be converted at the script generation stage. For example, the **Filter** object will eventually be converted into the WHERE phrase, and the sorting condition will be converted into the phrase ORDER BY.

To call the detail window from the high-level description window, double-click on the arrow that defines the relation between the source object (table or flat file) and the target object. As a result of this, the **Detail Mapping Editor** window (Fig. 3.41) that contains transformation objects (the source and target objects), as well as the toolbar, will appear on the screen.

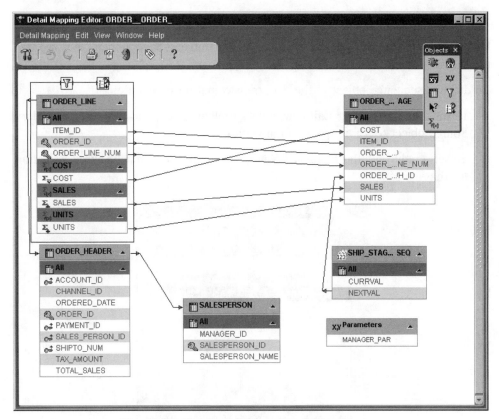

Fig. 3.41. The **Detail Mapping Editor** window

To complete the data definition process, we should:

❏ First, define or reassign all the existing data display operations (displayed by arrows in the **Detail Mapping Editor** window)

❏ Secondly, if necessary, define additional transformation objects for the data import procedure

Using the detail window tools, we need to describe the following objects:

❏ Sequences and foreign keys

❏   Transformation functions

❏   Local and global variables

❏   Filters and sorting conditions

❏   Parameters and descriptors

Very often during the data transformation procedure, you have to move data located in several different sources to the target table. To implement this, we can use the Secondary Source tool.

To define a sequence object in the data transformation procedure:

1.   In the **Detail Mapping Editor** window's toolbar, select and drag the Secondary Source object to a free space in the window.

2.   Select a value for the **Sequence Source** from the **Secondary Source Selection** list that appears.

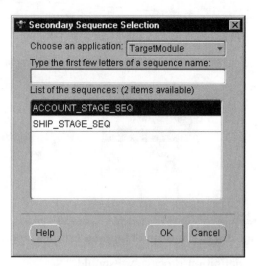

Fig. 3.42. The list of accessible sequences

3.   Select a sequence that will create unique values for the column from the **List of the Sequences** in the **Secondary Sequence Selection** window (Fig. 3.42).

4.   Using the mouse, link one of the Sequence object's values (NEXTVAL or CURRVAL) to a primary key of the target table in the **Detail Mapping Editor** window.

With the Secondary Source object, you can supplement the transformation procedure schema with a second object—a table. To do this:

1. In the toolbar of the **Detail Mapping Editor** window, select and drag the Secondary Source object to a free space in the window.

2. Select **Foreign key related Source** from the **Secondary Source Selection** list that appears and click **OK**.

3. Select a source object from the **Choose a source with foreign key** list in the **Secondary Source Selection** window, and from the list that appears, select a foreign key and click **OK**.

4. Link one or more secondary object columns to the target object columns in the **Detail Mapping Editor** window using the mouse.

The Transformation tool is intended for describing transformation for the data source columns. It can also be used for performing preparatory operations over the data.

For example, it can be used if in the transformation data task you have to link (concatenate) values of two columns of a source table in one column of the target table.

To solve the given task:

1. Select the Transformation object from the toolbar of the **Detail Mapping Editor** window and drag it to a free space in the window.

2. In the first step of the New Transform Usage Wizard (**Transformation Selection** page, Fig. 3.43), select the transformation function (in our case, CONCAT).

3. In the second step (**Select Parameter** page, Fig. 3.44), we should define the value of the transformation function's first parameter (in our case, AC_NAME).

4. For the third step (**Select Parameter** page, Fig. 3.45), give a value for the second parameter of the transformation function (in our case, AC_POST_CODE).

5. In the fourth step (**Select Return Value (CONCAT)** page, Fig. 3.46), indicate the reset transformation function value (in our case, AC_FULL_NAME of the Stage_table table).

6. In the last step (**Finish** page), check all entered information and click **Finish**.

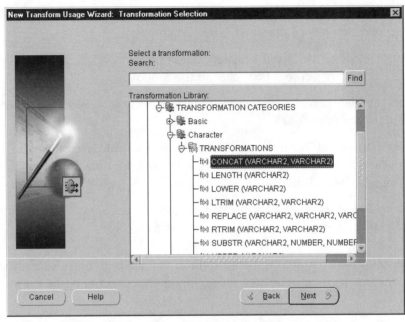

Fig. 3.43. New Transform Usage Wizard. Step 1

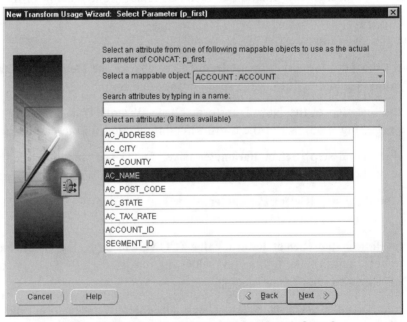

Fig. 3.44. New Transform Usage Wizard. Step 2

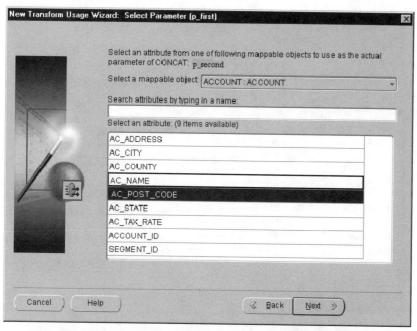

Fig. 3.45. New Transformation Usage Wizard. Step 3

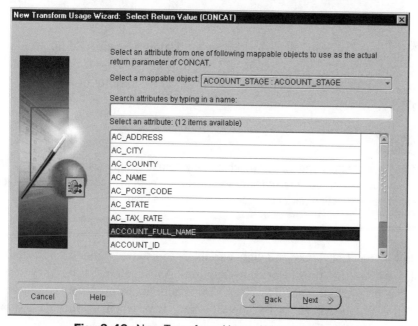

Fig. 3.46. New Transform Usage Wizard. Step 4

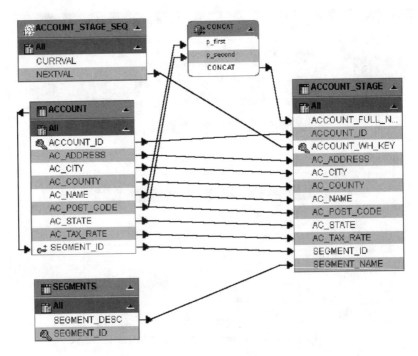

Fig. 3.47. An example of transformation function display

As a result of the operations performed in the **Detail Mapping Editor** window, the AC_NAME and AC_POST_CODE columns will be connected by the transformation function, and will be connected to the AC_FULL_NAME column of the Stage_table (Fig. 3.47).

NOTE

The number of steps and their content in many respects depends on the transformation function you select, but the order of their execution—which consists of defining each transformation function parameter for all functions—is identical.

The **Local** and **Global Variables** tools are intended for describing variables within the transformation function. As a general rule, they are used for storing or tracking specific values. For example, local variables can be used for defining unique values of the table primary keys when loading data from flat files.

To add a second object to the schema transformation procedure:

1. Select the **Local Variable** object from the toolbar of the **Detail Mapping Editor** window and drag it to a free space in the window using the mouse.

2. In the **New Local Variable Wizard** window that appears, indicate a name for and the description of the given local variable in the first step. Otherwise, OWB won't create the correct control file for the SQL Loader package.

3. For the second step, select the type of the local variable from the list (in our case, Number).

4. For the third step, set an expression for the given variable (in our case, SEQUENCE (MAX, 1)).

5. In the last step (**Finish** page), check all the entered information and click **Finish**.

6. After the local variable has been displayed on the monitor, connect it to the primary key of the target table.

The Filter tool is intended for limiting the data set to be loaded. For example, we can load only data that fall within the specified range of values.

To solve this task:

❑ First, set two parameters to describe the value range

❑ Second, create sampling conditions for the source object that will contain these two parameters

To create a parameter:

1. In the toolbar of the **Detail Mapping Editor** window, select and drag the **Parameter** object to a free space in the window.

2. In the first step of the New Parameter Wizard (**Name** page), give a name for and a description of the parameter.

3. For the second step (**Data Type** page), indicate the parameter's data type.

4. In the third step (**Attribute** page), fill in these fields:

   ❑ **I/O type**—indicate the parameter type

   ❑ **Type in the position**—define a tracing order for the given parameter in the transformation procedure header

- ❐   **Type in the default value**—define a default value for the given parameter

- ❐   **Required parameter**—state whether or not the given parameter is mandatory

6.   In the last step (**Finish** page), check all entered information and click **Finish**.

To create the filter:

1.   In the toolbar of the **Detail Mapping Editor** window, select the **Filter** object and drag it to the data source using the mouse.

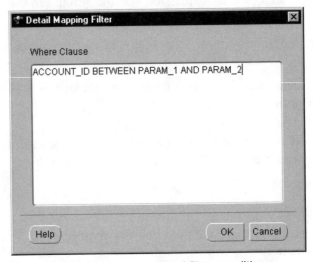

Fig. 3.48. An example of filter conditions

2.   In the **Detail Mapping Filter** window that appears (Fig. 3.47), set the filter conditions and click **OK**.

The **Aggregation** tool is used for defining in a query aggregation functions residing within the transformation procedure body.

To create a grouping (or aggregating) query:

1.   Select the Aggregation object from the toolbar of the **Detail Mapping Editor** window and drag it to a data source column.

2.   In the **Aggregation Selection** window that appears (Fig. 3.49), define the function and click **OK**.

Fig. 3.49. Choosing the bunching function

3.4.3. Creating a Description of the Dimension Loading Procedure

When creating a high-level description for the procedure of loading data to a dimension:

1. Select the required procedure in the Warehouse Module Editor.

2. Call the **Mapping Editor** window using the **Edit** command from the main or supplementary menu.

3. Drag the table object from the toolbar to the data source area.

4. Select one of the following options from the **Add Table** list that appears:

    ❑ **Import Table**—launch the Object Import Wizard to define the source object (see "*Importing Metadata from Oracle Application*" in *Section 3.3.3*)

    ❑ **Select from existing table**—select the source object from the list of existing objects, then click **OK**

5. After defining the data source table, you need to determine the dimension to which the data will load. For this purpose, drag the object dimension from the toolbar to the data target area using the mouse.

6. Select one of the following options from the **Add Dimension** list that will appear:

    ❑ **Create dimension**—start the New Dimension Wizard for the target object definition (see *"Dimension Creation and Editing"* in *Section 3.3.2*)

❑ **Create time dimension**—define the target object by launching the New Time Dimension Wizard (see *"Dimension Creation and Editing"* in *Section 3.3.2*)

❑ **Import dimension**—launch the Import Dimension Wizard for defining the target object

❑ **Select from existing dimension**—select the source object from the list of existing objects, and then click **OK**

Just as with the data extraction procedure, when creating transformation functions for loading data to a dimension, we should define:

❑ Which data are to be loaded to the dimension from the intermediate area tables, and in what manner

❑ How the primary key of the dimension table will be defined

To solve these tasks, we can also use the **Detail Mapping Editor** window's tools described in *"Tools for Describing Data Extraction from Data Sources"*, *Section 3.4.2*, and present the description in graphic form (Fig. 3.50).

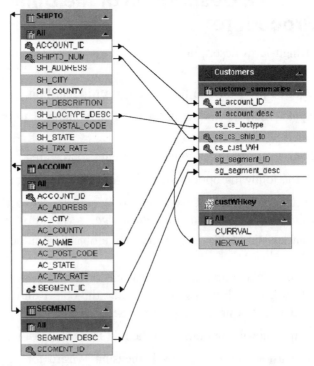

Fig. 3.50. An example of a graphic representation of the transformation of data to dimensions

3.4.4. Describing the Fact Table Loading Procedure

Creating a High-Level Description

To create a high-level description of loading data to dimensions:

1. Select the required procedure from the Warehouse Module Editor.

2. Call the **Mapping Editor** window using the **Edit** command from the main or supplementary menu.

3. Drag the table object from the toolbar to the data sources area.

4. Select one of the following options from the **Add Table** list that appears:

    ❏ **Import Table**—launch the Import Object Wizard to define the source object (see Importing Metadata from Oracle Databases)

    ❏ **Select from existing table**—select the source object from the list of existing objects and click **OK**

5. After defining the data source, you need to define the fact table to which the data are to be loaded. To do this, drag the fact table object to the data target area from the toolbar using the mouse.

6. Select one of the following options from the **Add Fact** list that appears:

    ❏ **Create fact**—launch the New Fact Wizard to define the target object (see Creating and Editing Fact Tables)

    ❏ **Import fact**—launch the Import Fact Wizard to import the fact table

    ❏ **Select from existing facts**—select the source object from the given list of objects, then click **OK**

Creating a Detailed Description

When creating a transformation function for loading data to the fact table, as well as when extracting data, we should define which data are to be loaded from the intermediate area tables to the fact table, and in what manner.

❏ How the primary key of the dimension table will be defined

❏ How the foreign keys of the fact tables will be loaded

To solve these tasks, we can use the tools from the **Detail Mapping Editor** window described in *"Tools for Describing Data Extraction from Data Sources"*, *Section 3.4.2*, and present the description in graphic form (Fig. 3.51).

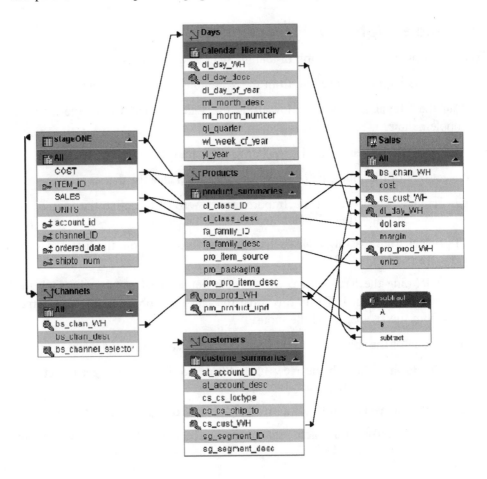

Fig. 3.51. Example of a graphic representation of data transformation to the fact table

3.5. Generating a Data Warehouse

After we have finished describing the main objects of the data warehouse and its processes, we can start generating scripts for creating the data warehouse database schema and for data loading.

However, before we start generating these scripts, you need to:

❒ Thoroughly configure the main objects of the data warehouse target schema

❒ Once more check the data sources, the target database, the transformation procedures, and the cleaning and data loading definitions

Only after these steps can we generate scripts, and then start data warehouse loading and administration.

3.5.1. Configuring Data Warehouse Objects

The descriptions of the data warehouse's main objects in the data warehouse target module define the logical data model which can be physically realized in several ways.

Physically implementing a logical data model is a procedure that sets the parameters and properties for each data model object and the module itself, and also creates the necessary scripts according to these descriptions.

Configuring Data Warehouse Object Properties

To set the data warehouse object's properties, call the property setting window and do the following:

1. Select **Project mode** from the main panel.

2. Select the project module that contains the object to be configured, and call the Warehouse Module Editor for it using the **Edit Objects** command.

3. Select the **Physical Tree** tab of the Warehouse Module Editor.

4. Select the required object from the object tree and call the **Configure** command using the right mouse button, which will open the property editing window for the given object (Fig. 3.52).

This window is divided into two columns that contain the titles and values of object properties.

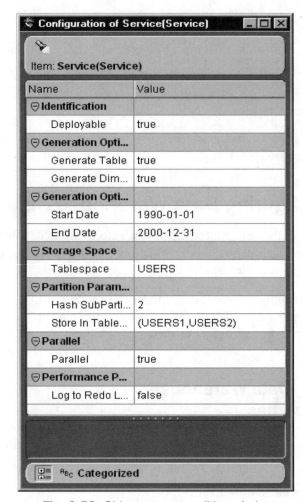

Fig. 3.52. Object property editing window

NOTE

If we change an object's properties after generating and executing the scripts defining it in the data warehouse schema, we will have to re-create and execute these scripts anew in order to have these changes be reflected in the data warehouse schema. When doing this, we advise you to be especially cautious, since re-creating an object can change the data in the object.

Configuring the Data Warehouse Module

Configuring the data warehouse module consists of defining the directory that will contain scripts created by OWB Client, as well as these scripts' starting and registration parameters in Oracle Enterprise Manager. To configure the data warehouse module, simply define the nine main properties (Table 3.3).

Table 3.3. Properties of the Data Warehouse Module

Property	Property description
Top Directory	Defines the file system directory where OWB containing the object definition scripts will be located
OEM Directory	Defines the file system directory in which Oracle Enterprise Manager is located
OEM User	Defines the Oracle Enterprise Manager user name
OEM Password	Defines the password for an Oracle Enterprise Manager user
OEM Domain	Defines the name of the server on which Oracle Enterprise Manager is installed
OEM Target Name	Defines the name of a database for the data warehouse registered in Oracle Enterprise Manager
OEM Target Job User	Defines a name for the data warehouse database owner (user)
OEM Target Job Password	Defines a password for the data warehouse database owner (user)
OEM Target Job Connect String	Defines the data warehouse database connection string

Configuring the Database Link Object

Before developing a physical copy of the data warehouse database schema, we should check the definition and test all remote database links. The Database Link object is defined by the following set of properties:

Table 3.4. Database Link Object Properties

Property	Property description
Deployable	Defines whether the given object will be initialized in the data warehouse or not
Schema owner	Contains information on the name of the remote database schema owner

continues

Table 3.4 Continued

Property	Property description
Schema password	Contains information on the password of the database schema owner
Connect string	Contains the string for connection with the remote database
Machine	Contains the name of the computer (server) on which the database is installed
Port	Contains the database's listening port process to which connection is realized
SID	Identifies the name of the database to which connection is realized

NOTE

When defining the connection with a remote database object, you simply need to define either the **Connect string** property or the **Machine**, **Port**, and **SID** properties.

Configuring Object Dimensions

From the point of view of Oracle 8i, the OWB dimension object is basically just two Oracle 8i server objects: Dimension and Table, which contain definitions for attributes, hierarchies, and data. Therefore, when creating scripts, the OWB Client generates two scripts for a simple dimension: one to create the Dimension database object, and the other to create the Table database object.

For a time dimension, OWB can create a third script that puts values into the dimension table according to the defined parameters. The dimension configuration parameters determine how the scripts defining the dimension object will be created and developed in the database.

To configure this object, you must define these properties:

Table 3.5. Dimension Object Properties

Property	Property description
Deployable	Defines whether or not the given object will be initialized to the data warehouse

continues

Table 3.5 Continued

Property	Property description
Generate Table	Defines whether the table for the given dimension will be created or not
Generate Dimension	Defines whether the dimension object will be created or not
Start Date	Defines the start date for the time dimension
End Date	Defines the end date for the time dimension
Tablespace	Defines the main tablespace for the dimension table
Hash Subpartition number	Defines the number of hash partitions in the dimension table
Store in Tablespaces	Defines the tablespaces in which the hash partitions of the dimension table will be located
Parallel	Defines whether or not the Parallelism mechanism will be applied to the given object
Log to redo log file	Defines whether or not the Redo mechanism will be used with the given object
Analyze table: Estimate Percent	Defines the percentage of strings for which statistics for the given object will be created

Configuring the Loader Mapping Object

The Loader Mapping object represents a mapping procedure intended for importing data from flat files with SQL Loader. When generating scripts, OWB creates two types of scripts: the control file script of the SQL Loader package, and the registration script in Oracle Enterprise Manager.

We can define the contents of these scripts using OWB. To do this, we must set the following properties:

Table 3.6. Loader Mapping Object Properties

Property	Property description
Identification	—
Deployable	Defines whether or not the given object will be initialized in the repository
Loader Parameters	—

continues

Table 3.5 Continued

Property	Property description
Data File name	Contains the data loading file name
Direct Mode	Defines whether or not the direct mode will be used for data loading
Errors Allowed	Defines the number of errors allowed in the strings when loading to the database
Bind Size	Defines the size of the data reference array
Rows to Commit	Defines the number of read-out and saved strings per one data loading operation
Records to Skip	Defines the number of beginning strings to skip
Records to Load	Defines the generally acceptable number of loaded strings
Parameters for Direct Path Load	—
Read Buffers	Defines the number of read buffers for the direct data loading mechanism
Operation Recoverable	Defines whether or not the recovery mechanism will be used after a direct data loading failure
Re-enable Constraints	Defines whether the rules of integrity constraint will be activated
Exception Table	Defines the name of the table to which rejected strings will be loaded
Presorted Data	Defines the Index name of the table, which will be used by the Pre-Sorted mechanism when loading data
Parameters for Control File	—
Method of Loading Table	Defines the method of loading data to the table. This property can accept the following values, which define the data loading method: INSERT—adds new strings to the table. It is used to load data to an empty table APPEND—appends new strings to the table without changing the existing strings REPLACE—adds new strings to the table, deleting all existing strings

continues

Table 3.5 Continued

Property	Property description
	TRUNCATE—adds new strings to the table, deleting the existing strings. As opposed to the REPLACE method, TRUNCATE executes the TRUNCATE TABLE command before loading data, which can increase data loading productivity but requires that the owner schema have the DELETE ANY TABLE privilege
Preserve Blanks	Defines whether empty characters in columns will be truncated
Nls Character set	Defines data coding
Record Terminator	Defines the separator symbol for data file strings
Field Terminator	Defines separator symbol for data file columns

NOTE

SQL Loader does not allow you to update data while loading. To update data, you will have to create an intermediate table into which you should load data, and then, using the SQL UPDATE command, refresh the target table.

Configuring the Table Object

Configuring the Table object consists of setting properties related to the object and creating and configuring table partitions and indexes. Creating and effectively managing these objects in many respects determines the productivity of queries to the table.

To configure the Table object, define these properties:

Table 3.7. Properties of the Table Object

Property	Property description
Identification	—
Deployable	Defines whether the given object will be initialized in the repository
Storage space	—
Tablespace	Defines the main tablespace of the table

continues

Table 3.5 Continued

Property	Property description
Partition Parameters	—
Hash Subpartition number	Defines the number of hash partitions in the table
Store in Tablespaces	Defines the tablespaces where the hash partitions of the dimension table will be located
Parallel	Defines whether the Parallelism mechanism will be applied to the given object
Log to redo log file	Defines whether the Redo mechanism will be applied to the given object

Partitions are Oracle 8i database objects used for dividing large database objects (tables, materialized views, and indexes) in order to increase query productivity and improve control over these objects.

When dividing a table or a materialized view, you can use one of three methods of object partitioning:

❏ Range partitioning—defines table partitions based on a range of values

❏ Hash partitioning—defines table partitions based on hash function values

❏ Composite partitioning—a combination of the first two methods

Before dividing the table into partitions, you need to define a partition key. The *partition key* is a column or set of columns, each value (or combination of values) of which will form one partition of the table or materialized view.

To create the partition key:

1. Select the **Physical Tree** tab in Warehouse Module Editor.

2. Move the cursor over the **Partitions Keys** item inside the table in the object tree.

3. Execute the **Create Partition Key** command from the main or supplementary menu, which will call up the window for defining the partition key.

4. Define a table column to be the partition key in the **Create Partition Key** window, and click **OK.**

5. After OWB creates the partition key, you must define the partition method—**Hash** or **Range**—in the properties window (the **Type** property).

Having created the partition key, you can determine the table partitions. To do this:

1. Select the **Physical Tree** tab in Warehouse Module Editor.

2. In the object tree, place the cursor over the **Partitions** item inside the table.

3. From the main or supplementary menu, execute the **Create Partition** command, which will call the window for defining the partition name.

4. Define the name of the partition in the **Create Partition** window and click **OK.**

5. After OWB creates a partition, for partitions defined using the `Range` method, we should define the appropriate limit value in the property window (the `Value Less Than` property).

As opposed to OLTP systems, creating indexes plays a primary role in analytical systems, and determines a query's efficiency in many respects. Therefore, creating indexes has a generally redundant character in decision support systems.

However, when indexing tables, one should not create indexes for each column of each table. Indexes can occupy a large amount of memory and decelerate data addition and update operations in the table. Usually, a set of indexes is defined basing on the prospective user's queries to the data warehouse, but can later be corrected basing on an analysis of query statistics and the data character in the base's tables.

To create an index:

1. Select the **Physical Tree** tab in Warehouse Module Editor.

2. Move the cursor over the **Indexes** module inside the table in the object tree.

3. Execute the **Create Index** command from the main or supplementary menu.

4. Define the name of the index in the **Create Index** window and click **OK**.

5. After OWB has created the index, we should define its type—**Unique** or **Bitmap**—in the property window (the `Index Type` property).

6. After defining the index itself, define the set of columns on the basis of which it will be created. For this purpose, execute the **Create Index Column** command using the right mouse button.

7. Define the table column in the **Create Index Column** dialog window and click **OK**.

Configuring the Materialized View Object

Configuring a `Materialized View` object, just as with configuring a `Table` object, consists of setting of the properties related to the object, as well as creating and configuring the table partitions and indexes. Therefore, everything related to `Table` object configuration can be used for the `Materialized View` object.

To configure the `Materialized View` object, you must define these properties:

Table 3.8. Properties of the Materialized View Object

Property	Property description
`Identification`	—
`Deployable`	Defines whether the given object will be initialized in data warehouse
`Storage space`	—
`Tablespace`	Defines the main tablespace of the table
`Materialized View Parameters`	—
`Build`	Defines how data will be loaded to the given materialized view
`Refresh`	Defines the update method for the materialized view
`Query Rewrite`	Defines whether or not to use the Query Rewrite mechanism
`Partition Parameters`	—
`Hash Subpartition number`	Defines the number of hash partitions in the table
`Store in Tablespaces`	Defines the tablespaces to which the hash partitions of the table dimension are to be located
`Parallel`	—
`Parallel`	Defines whether or not the Parallelism mechanism will be applied to the given object
`Performance Parameters`	—
`Log to redo log file`	Defines whether or not the Redo mechanism will be applied to the given object

3.5.2. Validation

After we have defined each object's parameters, we should check our object definitions. OWB checks object definitions based on their internal consistency and data type correspondence, and shows the results of the check in a separate window (Fig. 3.53).

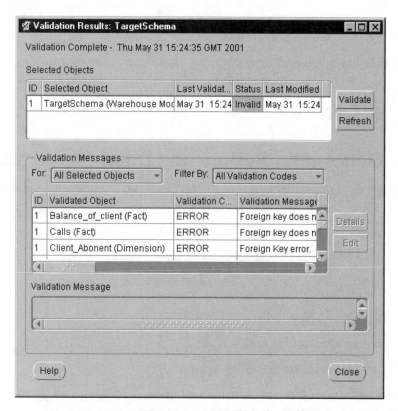

Fig. 3.53. The window containing the results of the check

To execute the definition validation procedure:

1. Select **Project mode** from the main panel.

2. Select the module that contains definition procedures, and call the Warehouse Module Editor for it using the **Edit Objects** command.

3. Select the **Physical Tree** tab in Warehouse Module Editor.

4. Select a module or concrete object from the object tree, and execute the **Validate** command from the main menu, which performs the check and displays its results in a special window (Fig. 3.53).

The check result window contains these fields:

❏ **Selected Objects**—the name of the selected object, its status, and the last check date

❏ **Validation Messages**—object name, validation project status (**Error** and **Warning**), and the ways of correcting an error

If the **Validation Messages** field does not contain any errors (warnings are allowed), you can consider the given object to be valid. Otherwise, you must correct all errors and remove all warnings. After all object definitions have an acceptable status we can start generating scripts.

3.5.3. Generating Scripts and Database Schemas

The process of script generation can theoretically be divided into the following stages:

❏ Creating scripts that use object descriptors

❏ Putting scripts in the file system or database

❏ Recording scripts in Oracle Enterprise Manager

Creating Scripts

To start the procedure for creating scripts:

1. Select **Project mode** from the main panel.

2. Select the module that contains the definition procedures and call the Warehouse Module Editor for it, using the **Edit Objects** command.

3. Select the **Physical Tree** tab in Warehouse Module Editor.

4. Select the module or specific object from the object tree, and from the main menu, execute the **Generate** command.

As a result of the generation procedure, a list of OWB scripts will appear in the results window (Fig. 3.54):

❏ DLL database object creation scripts

❐ PL/SQL extracting, mapping, and data loading package creating scripts

❐ Control files of SQL Loader procedures

❐ TCL Oracle Enterprise Manager job registration scripts

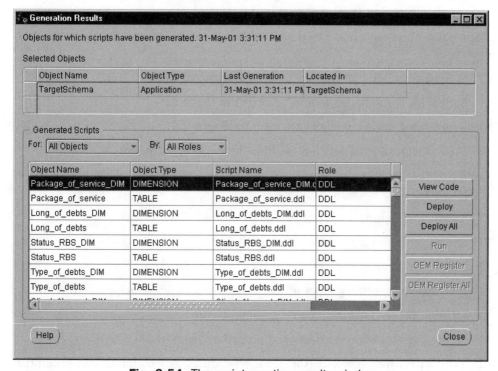

Fig. 3.54. The script creation results window

NOTE

According to the product's ideology, OWB itself controls all object definitions, and thus you can only view the script code using the **View Code** button. To change the text object definition, we should find the required object in the main object tree and change its properties or definitions using the utilities built into OWB.

OWB creates various script sets, depending on the object type.

The Database Links object is used in extraction and data loading procedures. The data transfer mechanism looks like this:

❐ OWB creates scripts for the database links and puts them in the target database

❑ For each data source table, a synonymous object is created in the data target schema that contains a reference to the connection with the database other than the name of the data source object

❑ Extraction and the data loading scripts (PL/SQL scripts) refer not to the source object, but to its synonym in the target database

Depending on its settings, OWB creates the following scripts for the dimension object:

❑ Scripts for creating dimension tables and their partitions

❑ Scripts for defining the dimension object in the table

❑ Scripts for creating indexes and index partitions

❑ Additional scripts for loading the time dimension type values

OWB creates the following scripts for the `Table` and `Materialized View` objects, depending on their settings:

❑ Scripts for creating an object and its partitions

❑ Scripts for defining the object's integrity constraint

❑ Scripts for creating indexes and index partitions for the object

OWB creates the following types of scripts for extraction and mapping procedures:

❑ DLL scripts for creating data source object synonyms

❑ Scripts for creating procedures and procedure libraries

❑ TCL scripts for registering the given procedures as jobs for Oracle Enterprise Manager and Oracle Workflow

Deploying Scripts to a File System or a Database

To deploy scripts to a file system or on a database server:

1. Click the **Deploy** button in the **Generation Results** window to move the selected scripts, or **Deploy All** to deploy all scripts of the given module.

2. Select the final script location in the **Deployment Types** window (Fig. 3.54) using the **Where do you want to deploy the selected scripts?** option, and click **OK**. The values are:

   ❑ **In Database**—the scripts are to be executed on the database server

   ❑ **In File System**—the scripts will be deployed to a particular directory

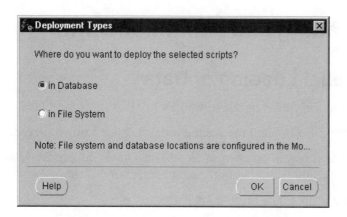

Fig. 3.55. Types of data script deployment

3. The action you will take in the next step depends on the value selected in the previous step:

☐ For the **In Database** value—define the principal parameters of connection with the database server on the **Connection** tab of the **Database Deployment** window, as well as the name and password of the schema owner, and click **Create** on the **General** tab

☐ For the **In File System** value—click **Save** in the **File System Deployment** window

After we deploy the scripts to the file system or database server, dialog windows will display the results of the operation.

Script Registration in Oracle Enterprise Manager

Finally, we can register data definition procedures as jobs to be fulfilled in Oracle Enterprise Manager.

To register jobs in Oracle Enterprise Manager, click the **OEM Register** button in the **Generation Results** window to register the selected script, or click the **OEM Register All** button to register all scripts of the given module.

3.6. Loading and Administrating

3.6.1. Initial Loading of Data

To load data to the data warehouse, we should:

❑ First, define a set of and the tracing order for data loading procedures

❑ Second, register the procedures as jobs in Oracle Enterprise Manager if they were not already registered in the script generation stage

❑ Third, make up a data loading schedule

❑ Fourth, fulfil all jobs one by one using OWB resources or independently

Defining the Structure of the Procedures

Generally, when defining a set of procedures that we want to use for loading data to the data warehouse, we should classify all procedures by the sort of the changes they will bring to the data warehouse. We should also define the procedure order in the general schema of data loading based on their interrelations, as shown in Table 3.9.

Table 3.9. An Example of a General Schema of the Data Loading Process

Procedure name	Change object	Step of execution	Dependencies
Accounts_to_stage_map	Account_stage	Extracting and loading data from sources	Does not depend on the execution of any procedure
Accounts_flat_to_stage	Account_stage	Extracting and loading data from sources	Does not depend on the execution of any procedure
Accounts_to_customers	Customers	Loading the dimension tables	Depends on loading to the intermediate table
Accounts_to_days	Days	Loading the dimension tables	Depends on loading to the intermediate table
Accounts_to_Sums	Fact_sums	Loading the fact tables	Depends on loading to the intermediate table
Sums_to_MV	Sums_materialized_view	Loading the fact tables	Depends on loading to the fact table

After we have defined a set of and an order for the procedures in the data loading general schema, we can start to make a schedule of these procedures.

Developing a Data Loading Schedule for the Data Warehouse

To make up a schedule for a data loading procedure registered as a job:

1. Run the Console utility from **Start —> Programs —> Oracle —> Oracle Enterprise Manager**.

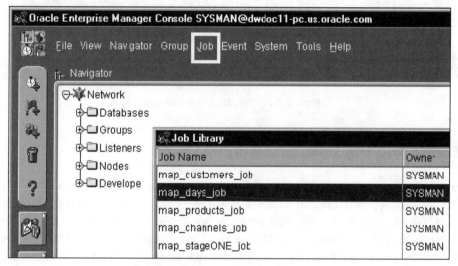

Fig. 3.56. The **Job Library** window

2. Run the **Job** command from the main menu, which will return a list of registered jobs in the **Job Library** window (Fig. 3.56).

3. Select the required job from the **Job Library** list and click **Edit.**

4. Select the **Schedule** tab from the **Edit Job** dialog box (Fig. 3.57), and in the fields:

    ☐ **Run Job**—define how frequently the given procedure will be fulfilled

    ☐ **Start Execution** and **End Execution**—define the date and time of the start and end of the data loading procedure

5. Using the **Submit** button, place the given job in the job queue.

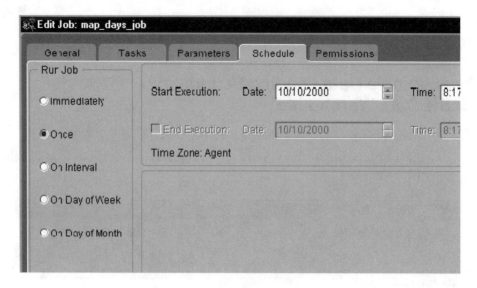

Fig. 3.57. The **Edit Job** window

Monitoring the Data Loading Process

To control the progress of jobs related to the process of loading data to the data warehouse, and also to analyze possible errors and the reasons for their origin, we can use the Oracle Builder Audit Viewer utility. This utility is launched from the program group of the Oracle products home directory. After starting, you will see the window for configuring the connection with the repository (Fig. 3.58), in which it is necessary to indicate the connection parameters and click **Logon**.

After successfully connecting with the OWB repository, **Run Time Audit's** main window appears on the monitor (Fig. 3.59). The window contains two panels. The left panel displays jobs, loading procedures, and data mapping procedures as the lower layer of the object tree. The right panel, depending on the type of object selected, displays job execution statistics or a list of errors that have arisen during execution.

To see statistics and error messages for a specific job, select its name from the left panel of the **Run Time Audit** window using the mouse. Oracle Builder Audit Viewer will return statistics on the given job in the right panel. The example in Fig. 3.59 shows that as a result of executing the MAP_CUSTOMER procedure,

61 strings have been selected, and none of them have been loaded to data warehouse, owing to certain errors that have arisen.

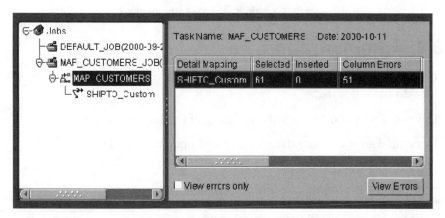

Fig. 3.58. The window for configuring the connection with the repository

Fig. 3.59. The main window of the Oracle Builder Run Time Viewer utility

To analyze the errors that have appeared during this job, point the cursor to the data mapping procedure in the object tree on the left panel, which is located on the lowermost level. Oracle Builder Audit Viewer will return the error list in the right panel, from which we can call a window containing a detailed description of a specific error (Fig. 3.60) using the **View Errors** button.

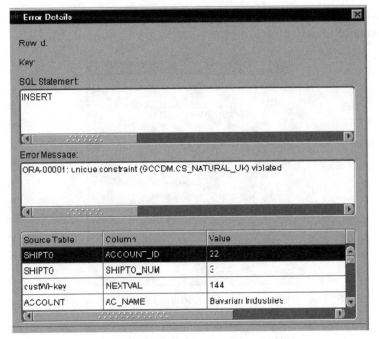

Fig. 3.60. The **Error Details** window

3.6.2. Administration

After we have initialized the data warehouse and have loaded the initial data to it, we must do the following:

☐ Develop a scenario for periodic updating of the data warehouse

☐ Draw up data warehouse data loading and update schedules

☐ Make a data storage system

☐ Develop measures to increase the data warehouse's productivity

Periodic Updates

As a rule, the data warehouse and data marts are periodically updated every day, week, or month. The process of renewing data in a data warehouse is divided into two components:

☐ Updating dimension tables

☐ Updating fact tables (usually, adding data)

We should stress that updating dimension tables should be done before updating fact tables, since updating the dimensions generates new values for the foreign keys of the fact table. For example, a certain company has taken to producing a new product, the activity of which is to be shown in the fact table or in the dimension table. To indicate data on this new product in the data warehouse, we should first load its description to the dimension table, and only after that add the results of operations with the given product into the fact table. Otherwise, the adding of new strings will be rejected during data loading, since the foreign keys will not be defined for them.

When developing dimension table update procedures, a situation often arises where the description of one of the essential attributes in the data source system has changed. The reason for this can be either a user error, or a completely conscious decision. Regardless of the reason, there is now a problem for the designers of data warehouse: how to reflect such changes.

Ralph Kimball described a similar problem in his book [2], and gave us three methods of updating dimension tables that would solve the problem.

❑ Replace the existing attribute description with a new one. When updating a dimension table by this method, remember that we are not simply replacing an old description of the object with a new one. A retrospective analysis will later show that all the previous facts will have already been indexed by the new value of the dimension, and the history of the old value will cease to exist.

❑ Add a new string that contains a modified description of the essential attributes. This method implies that the new description of the essential attribute will be brought to the dimension table as a new string. Thus, the old description remains unchanged.

❑ Add a new column to the dimension table. This method implies that the modified attribute description will be put into a new column of the same string. The value of the old attribute remains unchanged.

When designing update procedures for fact tables, a situation can also arise in which data already defined in the data warehouse are changed in the data source. In this case, we have a similar problem: how to reflect such changes in the data warehouse.

To solve this task we should define whether or not to save old data, and on the basis of this decision we should design our procedures for loading data to the data warehouse.

Data Loading and Data Update Schedule

After we have defined the character of data change in the data warehouse, and according to it developed the necessary set of procedures for data warehouse update, we should register them in Oracle Enterprise Manager and make up the loading schedule just like we did when loading the initial data. When developing the data update schedule in the data warehouse, we can use the approach described in Developing a Data Loading Schedule for the Data Warehouse, or use the tool for developing the data loading and update schedule—Oracle Workflow.

Organization of Data Storage System

As a rule, data are not deleted from the data warehouse and data marts, and thus in the course of time their volume can considerably increase. To control the growth of data:

❏ Estimate the increase in data volume beforehand for a specific period of time

❏ According to this estimation, define the size of tablespaces in the Oracle 8i server so as not to allow a situation where they are completely filled or one where there is an unjustified excess of free space

When creating tablespace for data storage systems, we recommend that you follow these rules:

❏ Divide tables and indexes into different tablespaces

❏ Divide dimension tables and fact tables into different tablespaces, since these types of objects have a tendency to grow differently

❏ Plan how you are going to partition the fact tables and other large objects beforehand. For example, it makes sense to partition the fact table according to a temporary key (year), having arranged the partitions in different tablespaces. If we do so, we needn't delete historical data from the system, but just store them elsewhere, leaving them in the system

Productivity of a Data Warehouse

The main factors that affect the productivity of a data warehouse and data marts are:

❏ The correspondence of the data warehouse data model to the "star" or "snowflake" schema

❑   The organization of object indexing

❑   The use of materialized views

❑   The organization of the data storage system and the use of the concurrent query execution mechanism

❑   The configuration of the Oracle8i server database

The process of indexing objects entails the creation of two classes of indexes: one for dimension tables and one for fact tables.

To index the dimension table correctly:

1.   Define a set of table columns that will be most often used for searching.

2.   From this set of columns, select the columns with a rather small number (< 100) of unequal values, and create bitmap indexes for them.

3.   For the remaining dimension table columns, create the typical B-Tree indexes.

Afterwards, based on an analysis of user queries, we can still repeatedly change the set of table indexes. Defining the optimal set of indexes is an iterative process, both for fact tables and for dimension tables.

After defining the dimension values that will satisfy user demand, the Oracle 8i database server starts to retrieve the appropriate values in the fact table. To perform this process most productively, it is good to use the "star-shaped query conversion" mechanism, which assumes the use of an appropriate operator (hint) in the body of a query, as well as the execution of the following preparatory operations:

❑   Creation of a bitmap index for each foreign key of the fact table

❑   Setting a True value for the STAR_TRANSFORMATION_ENABLED parameter in the init.ora settings file of the database server

❑   Using a cost-based query optimizer

❑   Analysis of the fact table and all dimension tables

Configuring Oracle 8i's Parameters

Finally, we present the parameter list of the database's init.ora initialization file (Table 3.10), which can significantly affect the productivity of a data warehouse realized on the basis of Oracle 8i DBMS.

Table 3.10. Parameters of the Oracle 8i Server

Parameters	Parameter description	Recommended value
`DB_BLOCK_SIZE`	Defines the size of the data package with the smallest data storage structure. The parameter can be defined only during the stage of creating the database	8 or 16 KB
`DB_FILE_MULTIBLOCK_READ_COUNT`	Defines the number of data packages read out by an operation system in one call to the database	Is defined on the basis of the formula `DB_FILE_MULTIBLOCK_READ_COUNT = 64 / DB_BLOCK_SIZE`
`HASH_MULTIBLOCK_IO_COUNT`	Defines the number of data packages used when reading /writing hashed connections in one call to database	4 or 8
`DB_BLOCK_BUFFERS`	Defines the number of data packages that form Oracle database's hashing area	Is defined on the basis of the formula: `DB_BLOCK_BUFFERS =` `MAX` (Size of transaction) / `DB_BLOCK_SIZE`
`SORT_AREA_SIZE`	Defines the size in bytes of the storage area intended for sorting. It is a dynamic parameter, and depends on system resources and the query being executed	~ 2 MB and more
`HASH_AREA_SIZE`	Defines the size in bytes of the storage area intended for executing hash connections. It is a dynamic parameter, and depends on system resources and the query being executed	Defined by default on the basis of the formula: `HASH_AREA_SIZE= SORT_AREA_SIZE*2`
`PARALLEL_MAX_SERVERS`	Defines the maximum number of query servers in the system	8 (depends on system resources)
`PARALLEL_MIN_SERVERS`	Defines the minimum number of query servers in the system	2
`SHARED_POOL_SIZE`	Defines the size in bytes of the storage area used for queries	~ 50 MB and more
`STAR_TRANSFORMATION_ENABLED`	Defines the usage of the Star Transformation mechanism, used for demand processing in the star schema	`True`

continues

Table 3.10 Continued

Parameters	Parameter description	Recommended value
QUERY_REWRITE_ENABLED	Defines the usage of the Query Re-write mechanism	True
OPTIMIZER_MODE	Defines the mode of the query optimizer	ALL_ROWS or FIRST_ROWS
COMPATIBLE		8.1.0 and higher
ALWAYS_ANTI_JOIN	Defines how to analyze the NOT IN operator	HASH
HASH_JOIN_ENABLED	Defines the use of the hash connection mechanism (HASH JOIN)	True

Chapter 4

Oracle Express
Multidimensional
Database Server

4.1. Multidimensional Database Design Concept

In this chapter, we will look at the main approaches to multidimensional database design. The material is presented in comparison to relational database design methodology, and therefore we assume that the reader is familiar with the given methodology.

4.1.1. Database Express Typical Structure

Express database is a unified file containing objects that allow you to organize, save, and manipulate data for an analytical system.

The Express Server multidimensional database stores objects such as:

Table 4.1. Express Server Multidimensional Database Objects

Dimensions	The range of values by which data is indexed in a multidimensional database (MDB); for example, time, company departments, sales regions, types of products, etc.
Variables	Arrays of business data indexed by dimensions
Relations	Relations link values of one dimension with values of another. Relations allow the database administrator to create hierarchical dimensions on which subsequent data analysis, aggregation, or data view drilling will be carried out. Time is a typical example of a hierarchical dimension; it can be aggregated and drilled by day, month, quarter, and year
Formulae	Formulae define expressions in the Express SPL language whose values are calculated "on the fly" and can be used like stored data, or variables. In this book, the term "variable" is used for a group title of variables and formulae
Programs	Programs provide storage for series of Express SPL commands
Models	Systems of interdependent equations whose solution is found using iteration methods. For example, using profit and expenditure values, the model first calculates income, and then sales
Subsets	Subsets contain a sample of values related to one of the dimensions
Working tables	Interface objects supporting text import/export of data

4.1.2. Measures

The *measure* is the main Oracle Express Server object, intended for storing business data. At the logical level, the measure is a multidimensional cube. The dimensions by which the given measure is defined represent the edges of the cube. We shall discuss dimensions later. Usually, quantitative measures of analyzed information—such as, for example: Sales, Profit, Price, and Budget—are created as measures. Measures are used to store data of different types, such as logical, integer, long, string, date, and identifier. Although as a rule measures make up the main part of a database, this object is the most simple to understand and does not require additional description.

From the physical point of view, a measure represents a set of memory pages. As opposed to relational databases in which tables are also divided into pages, one page of memory in Oracle Express can contain data related to only one measure. This kind of memory organization is what causes the increased speed of multidimensional databases, since while executing queries Oracle Express works with data related to a defined address within the memory instead of searching through all of the available space.

Generally, the size of the measures determines the size of the database. If we can evaluate the size of each measure correctly, we shall be very close to the correct estimation of the size of the entire database, since dimensions and other objects don't take up much space at all when compared to measures.

4.1.3. Dimensions

The set of dimensions defines the *space* in which our business activity is carried out. The correct choice of the structure, type, and values of dimensions is extremely important, as they index all the variables stored in the database. Data is selected and analyzed in accordance with dimension values. In an example illustrated by Figs 1.4 and 1.5, a three-dimensional business space is shown. In this case, the specific dimension values may be represented by:

Table 4.2. Example of the Three-Dimensional Business Space

Product	Region	Time (Hierarchical dimension)		
Cadillac	Texas	January		
Ford	Maine	February	1st quarter	1999
Dodge	Pennsylvania	March		

continues

Table 4.2 Continued

Product	Region	Time (Hierarchical dimension)		
		April	2nd quarter	
		May		
		June		
		July	3rd quarter	
		August		
		September		
		October	4th quarter	
		November		
		December		

When doing an analysis, managers can have the following statistics on sales volume:

Table 4.3

Financial manager

  Sales volume

March 1999

	Texas	Maine	Pennsylvania
Cadillac	---	---	---
Ford	---	---	---
Dodge	---	---	---

Regional Manager

Sales volume

Pennsylvania

	January 1999	February 1999	March 1999
Cadillac	---	---	---
Ford	---	---	---
Dodge	---	---	---

continues

Table 4.3. Continued

Sales Manager			
Sales volume			
Ford			
	January 1999	February 1999	March 1999
Texas	---	---	---
Maine	---	---	---
Pennsylvania	---	---	---
Financial manager			
Sales volume			
March 1999			
	Texas	Maine	Pennsylvania
Cadillac	---	---	---
Ford	---	---	---
Dodge	---	---	---
Regional Manager			
Sales volume			
Pennsylvania			
	January 1999	February 1999	March 1999
Cadillac	---	---	---
Ford	---	---	---
Dodge	---	---	---
Sales Manager			
Sales volume			
Ford			
	January 1999	February 1999	March 1999
Texas	---	---	---
Maine	---	---	---
Pennsylvania	---	---	---

Different variables can be indexed by identical dimensions, different dimensions, and/or separated dimensions (Fig. 4.1).

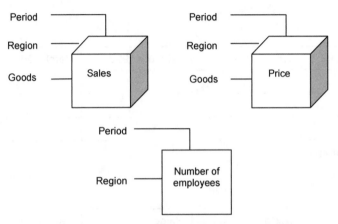

Fig. 4.1. Sharing dimensions between variables

Dimensions can have any type of value; for example, text, identifier (a short text value of fixed length), integer, or date.

A text or identifier dimension value is used when it is required that data have a descriptive (readable) label when viewing the data in the application. A dimension value related to time can be of the following types: day, week, month, quarter, or year. Integer dimension values are used when the interpreted label for data cannot be found, for example, when indexing the sequence of data coming into the system without binding to a definite time. Integer dimension values always start with "1" and are positive integers "1, 2, 3, ..., N".

From the physical point of view, a dimension is a set of measure indexes by which a certain subset is selected with the LIMIT command (the LIMIT command will be discussed in detail later). While creating measures, Oracle Express Server creates an index table containing all possible combinations of dimension values by which the measure is defined. The address of one of the memory pages into which the measure is divided is added for each combination.

If we want to reduce the size of the index table, and consequently the search time and the physical number of memory pages, it makes sense to use whenever possible the minimum quantity of dimensions to define the measure. This is usually done by integrating dimension values into hierarchy levels, by creating additional hierarchies, or by using attributes, which will be considered in the following sections.

It is also necessary to stress that the order of the dimensions following a measure is not important, since it defines the physical model of measure construction, and therefore defines the size and processing time of the given measure.

Specialized types of dimensions, such as the time dimension and conjoint dimensions, are of particular interest to us.

☐ Time Dimension

To create dimensions that contain information related to time, Oracle Express Server has defined special data types that correspond to a certain type of time data: day, week, month, quarter, or year. Using these types, we can easily manipulate time data, since dimensions defined in such a manner have a number of useful properties:

☐ First of all, all time dimensions have internal connections, which help in data retrieval. For example, the following series of commands:

```
LIMIT year to 'YR99'
LIMIT month to 'YEAR'
```

will give us the 12 months of the year 1999.

☐ Secondly, the standard arithmetic operations of addition and subtraction can be used with time dimensions. So, the following commands

```
LIMIT month to 'DEC99'
LIMIT month to month-12
```

will give us the value of December, 1998.

☐ Thirdly, only time dimensions can be used as arguments of specialized time series processing functions, such, for example as LAG, CUMSUM, etc.

☐ Conjoint Dimensions

Conjoint dimensions are associations of two or more simple (base) dimensions, whose values are combinations of base dimension values. Conjoint dimensions can be used to create hierarchies, to define many-to-many relations between dimensions, and also to solve problems concerning data discharge, since they can contain only the required combinations of values.

4.1.4. Relations

Relations define a "one-to-many" relationship between values of one or two dimensions, and can be applied to construct dimension hierarchies and attributes.

4.1.5. Hierarchies

The concept of a hierarchy is a foundational one for the concept of multidimensional database construction. Therefore, we shall consider its different aspects in detail. A hierarchy represents a database object—a tree of dimension values—and is mainly intended for two things: obtaining detailed data and summarizing. A hierarchy can only be organized for one dimension, but several hierarchies can be defined for each dimension.

First, we shall consider a simple case where only one hierarchy for the given dimension is defined, and then we shall discuss more complex schemas which include multiple hierarchies.

4.1.5.1. Simple Hierarchies

Before creating a hierarchy, we must define groups of dimension values, which will be at different levels of the hierarchy. For example, while creating a time hierarchy, months will be on one level and days will be on another, since day data will drill month data.

After we have defined the groups of values that form the hierarchy levels, we should define links between levels as "parent—child" type relations.

As an example of hierarchy definition, we will show an example of creating a simple hierarchy from a relational table.

Table 4.4. Example 1

Model_id	Model_make	Model_mark	Model_name
7	Foreign	Audi	A6
8	Foreign	Audi	A8
16	Foreign	BMW	316
40	Foreign	BMW	530i
150	Foreign	Mercedes	600E
151	Foreign	Mercedes	600SEL
287	Domestic	Cadillac	3110
328	Domestic	Ford	21065
345	Domestic	Ford	21099i
346	Domestic	Ford	Escort

In the given example, the table containing car model descriptions is considered. Besides model name, the table contains attributes related to the manufacturer and to the type of manufacturer.

Before creating a hierarchy, it is necessary to:

❏ Define data sets and the order in which they will be used to create the hierarchy. In this case, you'd be wise to use columns of the given table as hierarehy levels. Use the `Model_id` column as the Car model level, the `Model_make` column as the Place of production level, and the `Model_mark` column as the Car brand level. The `Model_name` column, as well as the `Model_id` column, are used to identify the automobile model, and thus can be used as a dimension attribute, which will be discussed a little bit later.

❏ Make sure that the data sets we have selected are complete and adequately describe the data domain.

❏ Make sure that the values of the selected sets can be uniquely defined as values related to only one hierarchy level.

After all necessary conditions are fulfilled, we can structure the hierarchy as follows:

❏ All cars

❏ Country of origin

❏ Brand of car

❏ Model of car

To establish the given structure, we must make sure that each value of the Car model field has only one value of the Car brand field, which in turn should have only one value for the Country of origin field. After this condition is confirmed, we can start creating and loading the hierarchy by data.

Multiple Hierarchies

Suppose that the `Model_color` column is added to the simple hierarchies table of automobile models from example 1, and the structure and the values of other columns have not been changed. Let's say we want to include it in the existing hierarchy of car models.

Table 4.5

Model_id	Model_make	Model_mark	Model_name	Model_color
7	Foreign	Audi	A6	Metallic
8	Foreign	Audi	A8	Black
16	Foreign	BMW	316	Blue
40	Foreign	BMW	530i	Blue
150	Foreign	Mercedes	600E	Metallic
151	Foreign	Mercedes	600SEL	Metallic

Before including a new column to the hierarchy, it is necessary to examine the relations between the Car brand color level we are including into the hierarchy, and the Country of origin, Brand of car, and Car model levels that already exist. Our reasoning could look something like this:

We could put the Car color level between the Brand level and the Model level. But then rule 2 would be violated, since the relation between the Car color and Car model levels are many-to-many, and thus not allowed when creating hierarchies. Sequentially having sorted out the remaining combinations of relations between hierarchy levels, we come to precisely the same result, which means that it is impossible to add the new Car color hierarchy level to the already existing hierarchy without destroying it.

This problem is frequently encountered when constructing hierarchies, and there are 4 ways to solve it:

❑ *Method 1.* Creating a new dimension

We could create a new dimension connected with a measure. However, we must keep in mind that creating new dimensions inevitably results in increasing the size of the database and thus lengthening the query processing time. In our case, for example, we have a Sales measure containing 200 MB. If we add a new dimension with a value of 4, the size of the Sales measure will now be 4 times what it was, 800 MB, which is an unacceptable value from a productivity point of view. In this case, therefore, the approach of adding a new hierarchy will certainly solve the hierarchy problem, but it is not the optimal one.

❒ *Method 2.* Creating a new hierarchy

We could create a new hierarchy above the existing one with the same dimension. The new hierarchy would look like this:

❒ All cars

❒ Color of car brand

❒ Car model

The given approach is the most simple and most optimal solution to our problem. However, when you create multiple hierarchies, you need to keep in mind that the data aggregating process depends on their number, so the more hierarchies you have, the more time will be required for data aggregation.

❒ *Method 3.* Creating a new hierarchy level

As we mentioned previously, we can not include the new hierarchy level Car brand color without destroying the entire hierarchy, since between the values of the new hierarchy level and the old values there are inadmissible, many-to-many relations. However, we can solve the problem artificially if we create a hierarchy level that is a unique combination of new and old hierarchy levels, for example a combination of the Car brand and Car brand color levels.

Thus, the hierarchy will look like this:

❒ All cars

❒ Country of origin

❒ Car brand + Car brand color

❒ Car model

This method causes the distortion of the data domain and we can not, for example, determine any summarized information using car brand or car brand color separately.

❒ *Method 4.* Creating dimension attributes

We could create a new dimension, not connected to the Car brand color measure, and connect it using a dimension attributes relation, which will be discussed in the following section. However, here you should remember that

▼

attributes are used mainly to select data, and it will thus be impossible to construct a total value using them.

4.1.6. Dimension Attributes

Attributes represent database objects connected with dimensions, whose primary goal is to drill data down to a certain dimension. From the physical point of view, attributes represent additional dimension indexes and, as a matter of fact, are another way of indexing variables without increasing the number of dimensions. Drawing a parallel with relational databases, attributes are identical to a specified table connected with the main one by a basic relation.

Using attributes can considerably increase the efficiency of query execution, because attributes do not immediately index data, and thus do not increase the size of the index table.

Going back to example 1, let's assume that we only need to receive the car model name for a particular car brand color, and we needn't aggregate data according to car brand color. In this case we could simply not include the Car brand color level in the existing hierarchy, nor create a new hierarchy, but simply do the following:

- ❏ Create a new `Car brand color` dimension and load data into it
- ❏ Create a relation between the `Car model` dimension and the `Car brand color` dimension
- ❏ For this relation, each value of the `Car model` dimension takes on the value of the Car brand color dimension

Thus, users can now select all values of the `Car model` dimension that correspond to a definite value of the `Car brand color` dimension.

4.1.7. Programs

These types of objects allow for storing in the database a sequence of Express commands that manipulate data stored in the database. The formulae can define only relatively simple data conversions. As opposed to these though, programs in Express can define data conversion algorithms of practically unlimited complexity. Besides, the RETURN directive, which returns converted or calculated data (including multidimensional), can be used in the program. Such programs define functions. If you are defining a function, the program call can be used in any Express expression, including the expression defining formula.

4.1.8. Analytical Abilities of Oracle Express Server

As opposed to some other multidimensional databases, Oracle Express Server is not only a database, but a calculation tool as well. A relatively wide range of calculation functions—from statistical and financial analysis to prediction—are realized in Oracle Express Server. Therefore we shall first consider the more simple and more frequently used calculation methods, and then discuss the more complex ones.

Simple Formulae

A formula is an object set by an Express expression that defines a certain set of data. From the application client's point of view, the Formula object does not differ at all from the Measure object, and can be used anywhere where operations with measures are valid. However, unlike measures, the data assigned by the formula are not stored in the database, but are calculated "on the fly" when the first call of the application client to this formula is made, and are then put in the operating cache. For example, a database can contain data on the amount of units sold, and the price of the goods. Then, the obtained sales income can be expressed by the formula: INCOME = AMOUNT x PRICE. In this case, if the Price measure is indexed by the Time dimension and the Amount measure using both the Time and Region dimensions, the data defined by the Income formula will also be indexed using both the Time and Region dimensions.

From the physical point of view, a formula represents an Oracle Express Server stored procedure, which is indexed just like a measure. Thus, when we call the given formula from Oracle Express Administrator or from the client application, the given stored procedure will be automatically executed for the required combinations of dimension values. For example, if we limit each Time and Region dimension to 10 values, Oracle Express Server will execute the stored procedure 100 times in order to calculate the Income formula. Rules for multidimensional operations in the Express language are considered in more detail in *Chapter 6.*

Measure or Formula?

Very often when constructing a database, designers have to solve the dilemma of whether to save computed data in a measure, or calculate them each time "on the fly" using the formula. On the one hand, saving data requires some time to calculate and save the results, but the server is not heavily loaded. On the other hand, using formulae sometimes requires a significant amount of time to calculate, which can seriously affect server performance.

The difference in speed between formulae and measures is directly connected with the complexity of the procedure function called inside the formula. This complexity is determined in many respects by the number of data pages that the internal procedure of the formula must access: the less data pages, the faster the formula is evaluated.

To therefore solve the given dilemma, we recommend using the following rule: "If using the formula significantly reduces server performance, you should use a stored measure".

Complex Formulae

In Oracle Express, complex formulae are classified as the following:

- Formulae using built-in Oracle Express 4GL functions
- Formulae using logical operators
- Formulae using Oracle Express 4GL programs

Formulae Using Built-in Oracle Express 4GL Functions

The majority of the formulae that use built-in Oracle Express 4GL functions deal with series processing, those such as LAG, LAGIF, LEAD, etc. When using these formulae, pay attention to:

- The amount of defined formula arguments. It should be equal to the amount of arguments for the called function.
- The logical order of values in the dimensions used in the formulae. For example, we define the LAG function (Sales, 12, Time) as the formula to calculate the sales volume one year ago. Here, Sales is a variable containing the sales volume values, and Time is a text dimension containing temporary values. In this case, Oracle Express Server will return values of the Sales variable for a period of time equal to the current period minus 12. Obviously, the variable will not always correspond to exactly a year ago.

NOTE

To change the order of the dimension values, use the MAINTAIN MOVE command. Keep in mind that some Oracle Express Server functions depend on the order.

Formulae Using Logical Operators

Oracle Express formulae can use logical operators and provide data output based on conditional transitions. For example, using logical operators, we can change the formula from the previous example so that it determines the current level of a temporary dimension and, depending on its current status, uses a certain function to calculate the Sales variable.

The formula will look like this:

```
If Time.leveldim eq "Year"
Then Lag(Sales, 1, Time)
Else if Time.leveldim eq "Quarter"
Then Lag(Sales, 4, Time)
Else Lag(Sales, 12, Time)
```

In addition, we should stress that the above example can be used for constructing partitioned variables as well, which will be discussed in detail later.

Formulae Using Oracle Express 4GL Programs

When defining formulae in Oracle Express, we can use our own functions alongside the predetermined ones. They will be programs written in Oracle Express 4GL.

For example:

```
Define F.SALES formula decimal <PROD GEOG TIME> Eq f.sales.prg
Dfn F.SALES.PRG
Prg
Vrb result dec
limit D_PROD to PROD_DATA
limit D_GEOG to GEOG_DATA
limit D_TIME to TIME_DATA
result = total(DATA_SALES, -
DATA_PROD PROD DATA_GEOG GEOG DATA_TIME TIME)
return result
end
```

This significantly increases the user's capabilities and provides truly unlimited abilities for analytical data processing.

Models

A model represents a set of interdependent equations (equalities) based on values of the given dimension. Models are used in those cases when it is impossible to calculate values by aggregating functions, or when computed values cannot be presented as new dimension values.

4.2. Creating Databases and Stored Objects

4.2.1. Customizing the Connection with the Server

After the software is installed in our local network, it is necessary to customize the connection between client and server. This is done using the special Connection Editor utility, which is installed from the distribution kit. A reference for the utility is placed into the program group for Express client applications. The application's main window, which is displayed after the utility starts, is shown in Fig. 4.2. The utility sets the parameters of connection with Personal Express and remote Express server. If Personal Express is installed on the same PC as the client applications, the connection to it will be set automatically.

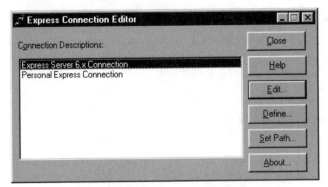

Fig. 4.2. Connection Editor

The first thing you need to do when customizing the connection with Express server is to define which directories will contain the files with the connection setting parameters (XCL extension), and which directories will be searched later on when making the connection with Express. This is done with the dialog box called by the **Set Path** button. The defined paths to the directories will be saved in the xconnect.ini file. The connection is customized in the dialog called by clicking the **Define** button (Fig. 4.3).

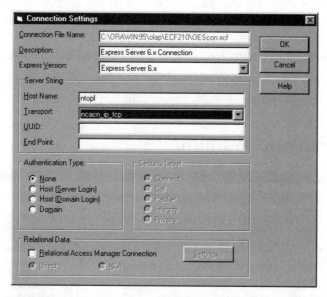

Fig. 4.3. Dialog for setting parameters of the connection with the server

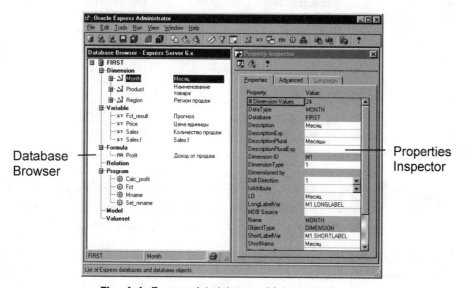

Fig. 4.4. Express Administrator Main window

In the simplest case (without setting discretionary access control) you need to set a filename in the **Connection File Name** parameter. Select the **Express Server** item from the **Express Version** drop-down list, and then in the **Host Name** parameter, set the name of the computer network on which the Express server software is installed. Then select the Transport protocol to call from the list the remote procedures needed for the configuration of your network. To check the correctness of the connection setup parameters, simply start Express Administrator.

To install a more complicated connection, you can find the necessary information in the accompanying Help system, or from the Express Administrator manual.

4.2.2. Express Administrator

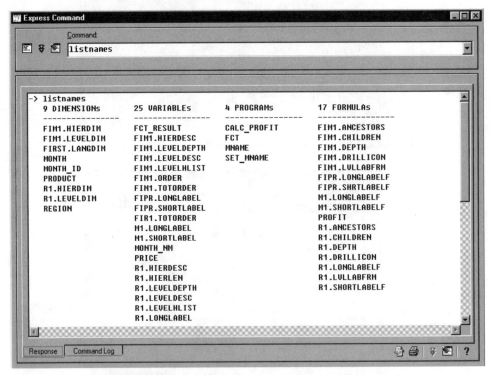

Fig. 4.5. Executing commands with Express Command

Express Administrator Windows application is an Express Server client that provides a convenient interface for creating, configuring, and supporting multidimensional databases. The given application is installed from the distribution kit, and its reference is is placed into the program group of Express client applications. The product contains a Help system, which provides a detailed description of rules and methods for working with this application. After starting the program, a dialog box for selecting the type of connection with Express appears automatically. If the connection is established successfully, the application's main window, shown in Fig. 4.4, will appear.

In this application, multidimensional databases are created and edited after starting the tools found in the main menu that convert user actions into a sequence of commands appropriate for the server. For example, attaching the existing demo.db database can be done using the **File/Open** menu command. The DATABASE ATTACH demo.db command will then be generated and executed on the server. A number of databases can be open simultaneously, but only one of them can be current.

A database browser window, in which objects in the form of a hierarchical list stored in the open database are displayed, is located in the Administrator's main window.

It is hardly possible to predict all that will be required of the user concerning data manipulation on the server. That's why, in order to provide fully functioning access to the service offered by Express, Administrator includes a built-in mechanism for inputting and executing commands on the server. Starting the given subroutine is done using the **Run/Express Command** menu item. This dialog is shown in Fig. 4.5.

The dialog box is divided into two parts. In the top part of the window you will find the Express command input window, and in the lower part you'll see the results of command execution after you click the **Run** button. This tool is extremely useful for debugging programs and learning commands in the Express language. Most often, information commands must be executed using Express Command. For example, Fig. 4.5 shows the results of the LISTNAMES command that provides information related to all objects defined in the current database. To get the result calculated by the Express Command function, you need just use the REPORT or SHOW command on its result. For example, after the command

```
REPORT EXISTS ('MONTH')
```
is executed, we receive the following result:
```
EXISTS (
'MONTH')
YES
```

These are the most frequently used information commands and functions:

Table 4.6. The Most Frequently Used Commands and Functions

Name	Type	Description
DESCRIBE [name list]	command	Displays information related to descriptions of one or more objects defined in the database
EXISTS ('name')	function	Allows you to find out whether the given object is defined in the current database or not
LISTBY list of changes	command	Displays information related to current database objects indexed by data dimension
LISTNAMES [DATABASE name / *] [type list/ ALL]	command	Displays the names of all objects from the indicated database, provided that these objects are of types defined in the list
OBJLIST ['DB name']	function	Allows you to get a list of objects defined in all attached databases or in the given database
REPORT expression	command	Displays in standard tabular representation all values of a multidimensional expression. The command has a flexible mechanism for setting the data view (see the User's Manual)
SHOW expression	command	Displays a single expression value or message, for example, SHOW 'This is a message'
STATUS name1 [, name2, ...]	command	Outputs all values of the dimensions that index the given objects and belong to the current status

The **Express Command** dialog can be effectively used to define the values of a measure. For example, to change all values of the SALES measure to zero, just execute the command SALES = 0. Executing the SALES = 1000*RANDOM command allows you to fill in the SALES measure with random values taken from the interval (0,1000). Thus, if the SALES measure is indexed by one or more dimensions, a random number will be generated for each combination of indexes (see rules of multidimensional operations in *Chapter 5*).

Working with Express Administrator is discussed in more detail the remaining sections of this chapter.

4.2.3. Creation of Objects

Dimensions

The dialog box for determining dimensions (Fig. 4.6) is displayed using the **Edit —> Define —> Dimension** menu item.

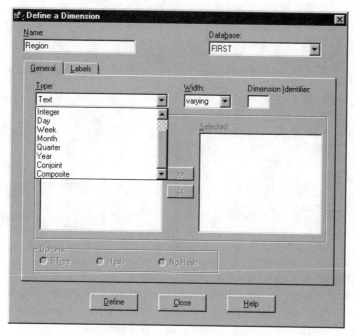

Fig. 4.6. The **Define a Dimension** dialog box (main)

The name, which is saved in the database dictionary and is for reference to the given dimension in commands and programs, is set in the **Name** input box. The Express language is not case-sensitive, and therefore names identical in all ways but case will act in the same manner. The name of a database object can not contain foreign alphabet characters. However, this limitation is not relevant to client applications, since their reference to a dimension is made using long or short labels set in the second part of the given dialog box (Fig. 4.7). The **Type** list is used to select values for the defined dimension.

Fig. 4.7 shows the second part of the **Define a Dimension** dialog box.

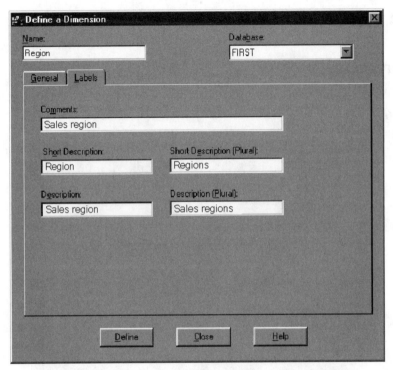

Fig. 4.7. Dialog box for determining dimensions (labels)

Here, the **Description** field gives the description of the given object, which can be detailed. It is displayed in the client application Object Inspector. By default, short and long labels are generated automatically, according to dimension name. However, they can be modified in the given dialog if necessary.

To save the dimension in the database, click the **Define** button. Pay attention to the fact that it will not be saved directly to a disk file. To save changes, you need to select **File —> Save**.

In addition, the following objects, whose names start with the x*n* prefix (where x is the first character of dimension name and n is a unique number for the given character), will be created in the database: measures, formulae, and subsets.

Measures

x*n*.LONGLABEL contains the full descriptive variable name in the language that will be used in client applications when referencing the given dimension in tables, dimension lists, and in the **Selector** tool.

X*n*.SHORTLABEL contains a short descriptive variable name in the language that will be used in client applications when referencing the given dimension in tables and graphs.

Formulae

X*n*.LONGLABELF defines a long label for dimension values according to their short label when a long label is not set.

X*n*.SHORTLABELF determines a short label for dimension values according to the value itself when a short label is not preset.[1]

Subsets

X*n*.VALUESET*n* provides support for saving values related to the given dimension subset.

You can see these objects if the **Show options designed as not user visible** and **Show all metadata** options are set in the **Administrator options setting** dialog box, which is on the **DB Browser** page. It should be stressed that you should not change names or delete data objects from the database manually. However, when redefining formulae for long and short labels, it is possible to customize the way the value is presented in table and graph views in client applications.

As a rule, in real analytical systems, specific data values are introduced to the multidimensional database by importing the information from already existing relational databases (see *Chapter 6*). However, it is possible to set or change specific dimension values interactively. For this purpose, you will need to select from the database browser the list of objects for the dimension you are interested in and select the **Edit/Values** item, which will call the dialog window in which you can set definite values for the dimension (Fig. 4.8).

Dimension values of the text type are set arbitrarily and can contain any characters, including spaces and foreign language characters. It is necessary to remember, however, that there can not be two identical dimension values.

For a time dimension (DAY, WEEK, MONTH, QUARTER, YEAR) its values represent a continuous part of a time series constantly moving in time, and they are set by an initial dimension value, for example, 01.01.99 (type DAY), and by a number of

---

[1] The automatically generated text, which defines the algorithm for determining the label dimension value, can be modified according to your preferences.

sequential values after or before this value, for example, 364. Thus, in this case, we will have a continuous segment of a time series having 365 values from 01.01.1999 to 12.31.1999.

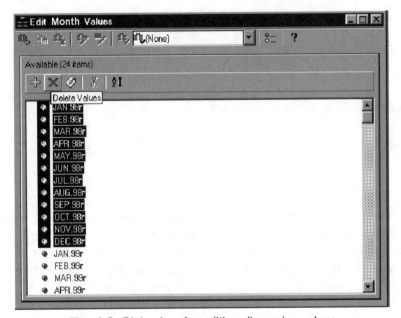

Fig. 4.8. Dialog box for editing dimension values

If the dimension has the integer type, its values are set by a unique integer, which represents the number of values for the given dimension.

Adding dimension values is done in a similar manner.

To delete values for the previous year from the TIME dimension, such as DAY, for example, check these days in the list of values and click the **Delete values** button in the edit dialog box. You could use the MAINTAIN command for this as well, which is executed using the Express Command tool. The command: MAINTAIN TIME DELETE FIRST 365 will delete the first 365 values from our TIME dimension.

The syntax of the given command looks like this:

```
MAINTAIN dimension name    ADD         [arguments]
                           DELETE
                           RENAME
                           MOVE
                           MERGE
```

The arguments of the MAINTAIN command depend on the types of dimension and operation, and are described in detail in the *Express Language Reference guide.*

Relations

Relations set a "one-to-many" relationship between values of two dimensions or values of the same dimension. In the first case, for example, two dimensions— PRODUCT, with the values "APPLE, ORANGE, BANANA, POTATO, CARROT", and CATEGORY, with the values "FRUIT, VEGETABLE"—can be created.

Then, using the **Edit/Define/Relation** menu item, we can define the PROD.CAT (product category) relation with the following values:

```
PRODUCT                 PROD.CAT
--------------          ----------
APPLE                   FRUIT
ORANGE                  FRUIT
BANANA                  FRUIT
POTATO                  VEGETABLE
CARROT                  VEGETABLE
```

The **Type** field sets the parent dimension in the given relation, and the **Selected** list sets the dimension containing child values.

Now we can use the constructed relation to select the sales values related to the VEGETABLE category using the SALES measure, which is indexed by the PRODUCT dimension. With this purpose in mind, we can execute the following Express Command sequence of commands:

```
LIMIT CATEGORY TO VEGETABLE
LIMIT PRODUCT TO PROD.CAT
REPORT SALES
```

As a result, we shall see the following in the Express Command output window:

```
PRODUCT           SALES
--------------   ----------
POTATO            100.00
CARROT            55.00
```

Using the LIMIT command is considered in more detail in the following chapter.

To set the dimension hierarchy, click the **Add Hierarchy** button in the dialog box that allows for editing its values (Fig. 4.9). Let's define, for example, the hierarchical dimension REGION. In this case, the dialog box to edit dimension values will look as it does in Fig. 4.9. Here in the REGION list, dimension values for all hierarchy levels are set. It is possible to set and change links between hierarchical relations by using the simple drag and drop method.

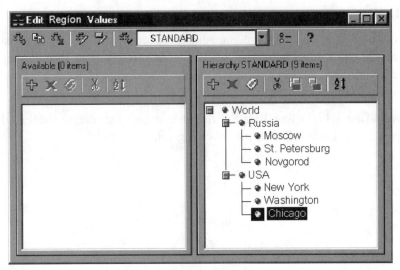

Fig. 4.9. The dialog box used to set values for a hierarchical dimension

The relation we've set has to do with the hierarchy diagram with the standard name of STANDARD, which is defined in the hierarchy list. Using the **Rename Hierarchy Levels** button, we can set descriptive names for three hierarchy levels of the given schema we've created, which will make our client applications clearer. Besides, using the **Add Hierarchy** button located in the same dialog box, we can similarly define more schemas for hierarchical relations between the values of this dimension. Supplementary object relations that describe the defined hierarchy diagrams will be formed in the database according to our definition.

After we define a hierarchy dimension diagram, we shall be able to use the ROLLUP Express command to calculate aggregated data at all higher levels (see *The User's Guide*) when we set the values of a certain measure related to the lowermost hierarchy level.

Measures

The dialog box that allows us to define a measure is called using the **Dictionary/ Define/Variable** menu item. Fig. 4.10 shows the main part of this dialog box. The **Name** field defines a measure's name. The item selected from the **Database** list defines the attached database in which the given measure will be created. The **Type** list defines the type of a measure, which can be:

```
INTEGER (4 bytes) / SHORTINTEGER (2 bytes)
DECIMAL (8 bytes) / SHORTDECIMAL (4 bytes)
ID (8 bytes)
BOOLEAN (accepts values YES/NO) (2 bytes)
DATE (4 bytes) from 01.01.1000 to 31.12.9999
TEXT (up to 256 bytes)
```

The **Width** field allows us to reduce the amount of disk space needed to store data for such measures as TEXT.

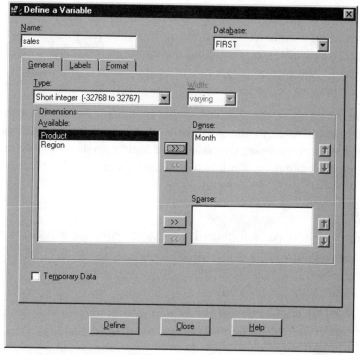

Fig. 4.10. Dialog box for defining variables (main part)

The **General** section of the dialog box sets the dimensions by which the defined measure will be indexed. In the list on the left, the dimensions that are defined in the database are listed, and the right section contains those selected dimensions by which the defined variable will be indexed. The order in which the indexing dimensions are set influences the sequence in which the measure values are laid out in the memory, as well as the results of certain commands' execution (like FETCH or REPORT). Thus, the dimension that changes the fastest is the first one in the list, and the slowest dimension would be the last. Let's take a look at an example. If the SALES measure is indexed first by the MONTH dimension, and then by the PRODUCT dimension, after executing the REPORT command the prices for all months for the first product will be outputted first, then those for the second one, and so on. If the SALES measure is indexed first by the PRODUCT dimension, and then by the MONTH dimension, then executing the REPORT command will produce first the prices on all goods for the first month, then for second month, and so on.

The second section of the measure definition dialog box—**Labels**—is similar to that which was described above in the dimension definition dialog box.

The third section of the dialog box sets the parameters of the text presentation to which the values of a numerical measure will be converted when being output (the SHOW, REPORT commands, etc.). Defining the appropriate settings in the given dialog allows you to control the data view for tables and graphs effectively. More detailed information can be found in the Administrator help.

For measures of all types, the special NA value is defined, which is interpreted as an absent or uncertain value in the given cells of a multidimensional cube. For the given value, special rules for mathematical and logic operations are defined, which, in many respects, facilitate multidimensional data processing.

Formulae

As was already mentioned, a formula is an object set by an expression in the Express language which defines a certain set of data. The formula definition dialog box in many respects is similar to the measure definition dialog box (Fig. 4.11). Here we describe only a few features.

The type of formula values should be defined in accordance with the type of the measures involved in its definition.

In the **Equation** field, the Express language expression that defines the calculated formula values is set. For example, in the case shown in the figure, the PROFIT formula is determined by the expression NAFILL (PRICE*SALES CALC_PROFIT (REGION)), where the PRICE measure sets the price for an item, and the SALES measure sets the amount of units sold. If the list of dimensions by which the given formula is indexed remains empty, it is defined according to the rules for multidimensional operations (see *Chapter 5*). For example, if the SALES measure is indexed by the MONTH, PRODUCT, and REGION dimensions, and the PRICE measure is indexed by the MONTH and PRODUCT dimensions, the resulting PROFIT formula will be indexed by the MONTH, PRODUCT, and REGION dimensions.

In a more complicated case, the list of indexing dimensions can be defined as a subset of the list that would index the formula by default. For example, our PROFIT formula can be indexed by the PRODUCT and REGION dimensions. In this case, the formula will represent the appropriate slice of the initial time expression: a range of income values laid out by area and goods for a specified month (the first one from the current MONTH dimension status; see the description of the LIMIT command). Therefore, the values defined by such a formula will depend on the current MONTH dimension status.

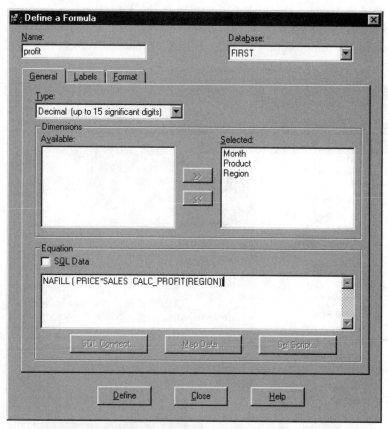

Fig. 4.11. The **Define a Formula** dialog box (main part)

Setting the **SQL Data** option allows you to create formulae that import their values from relational data sources.

4.2.4. Copying, Renaming, and Deleting Objects

The information on objects created in a database is stored in a data dictionary. The dictionary is dynamic, and therefore information on database objects can be modified easily at any moment. Using a data dictionary, we can copy, rename, and delete objects.

To copy the object, select it from database browser, select the **Edit/Copy** menu item, and set a name for the new object. Remember that only the descriptive information contained in a data dictionary will be copied to the new object, and not the object's content.

It is possible to rename the object by selecting the **Edit/Rename** menu item. Deleting objects is done using the **Edit/Delete** menu item. Here, keep in mind that before deleting a dimension, you must delete all database objects indexed by this dimension.

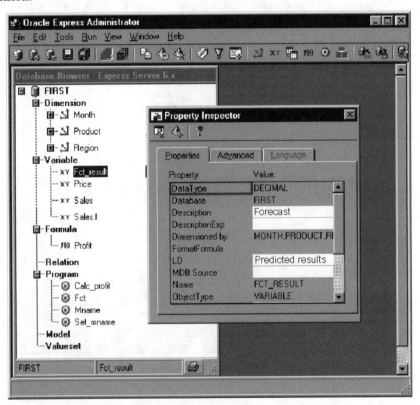

Fig. 4.12. Express Administrator Property Inspector

Property Inspector is an additional Express Administrator service resource (Fig. 4.12), which can be selected from the **Tools —> Property Inspector** menu item. Using this tool, we can see information on objects stored in the database and edit some of their properties.

The second page of the properties inspector (**Advanced**) contains additional help information related to the allocation of the disk memory assigned to the object.

4.2.5. Setting Database Properties

Setting database properties allows you to define additional features related to the interaction between server and client applications. The dialog box for setting properties can be called using the **Properties** button from the **Database Setup** dialog box, which in turn is called from the **File/Setup** menu item. Among other properties, the following important ones can be defined for the database:

Table 4.7. Important Database Properfies

Attach Order	While establishing the connection on the part of the client, it defines the position of the given database in the list of automatically connected databases (in this case AutoAttach property is to be set to YES)
AutoAttach	If for the given property the value YES is set, the given database will join automatically each time the client application starts. For example, the automatically connected database can contain information and data that we want to make accessible to all users of our analytical system
Pre-Attach Program	This variable can contain the name of an Express program to be executed before database attachment (in this case the program itself should be contained in another database, which remains attached)
Pre-Detach Program	This variable can contain the name of an Express program that will be executed before the database is detached (the program itself can be contained in this database or in another attached database)
Post-Attach Program	This variable can contain a name of an Express program that will be executed immediately after database attachment (the program can be contained in this database or in another attached database)
Post-Detach Program	This variable can contain name of the Express program, which will be executed immediately after database detaching (the program should be contained in other database, which remains attached)
ReadOnly	With the help of this property, we can deny client applications writing access to the database
User Data	By default, this property is YES. However, if we set it to NO, we can make even those objects for which the "Visible" option is set invisible to client application database browsers

For example, using these settings, we can customize the import from a relational database so that new information is periodically added to the multidimensional cube. For this purpose:

☐ Let's create a simple variable in our database, in which the date of the last data update will be saved automatically

☐ At the beginning of its execution, the data import program will compare the date of the last data update and the current date according to the necessary criterion (see the TODAY and TOD Express Language functions), and, if necessary, it will load new data and correct the date of their last update

☐ Let's use Post-Attach Program as the name of our import program

4.3. Data Selection and Creation of Subsets

4.3.1. The *LIMIT* Command

The main feature of a multidimensional analysis is the ability of flexibly manipulating large data volumes. The LIMIT command is probably the command used for this purpose most frequently. This command is used both in Express Administrator and in programs. The multiple ways of applying this command allows you to retrieve data from a multidimensional cube of practically any level of complexity. The LIMIT command controls the dimension status or defines the values that a database subset object will contain. The current dimension status defines the values that are currently "in operation". From a practical point of view, it is possible to imagine that all database variables are at that moment indexed not by a complete set of values defined for a dimension, but only by those values that belong to the current dimension state.

The syntax of the command looks like this:

LIMIT	*Dimension name*	*TO*	*[argument]*	*[IFNONE label]*
	Subset name	*ADD*		
		INSERT		
		KEEP		
		REMOVE		
		COMPLEMENT		
		SORT		

The LIMIT command operates with two dimension sets or a subset (database object). The first set, designated as **C** (C for Current), consists of dimension values defined by its current status. The second set, designated as **A** (A for Argument), is defined by an argument of the command. Let's designate as **M** the set of all values preset for the given dimension. The new status of the dimension is defined by the third set, **R** (for Result), which is the result of the set-theoretic operation over the **C, A,** and **M** sets assigned by one of keywords: TO, ADD, INSERT, *etc.*, of the LIMIT command. The table below explains the actions of the main command operations.

Table 4.8. Main Operations of the LIMIT Command

Operation	Formula	Result
TO	$R = A$	
ADD	$R = A \cup C$	
KEEP	$R = A \cap C$	

continues

Table 4.8 Continued

Operation	Formula	Result
REMOVE	R = not A ∩ C	
COMPLEMENT	R = not A	

The INSERT and SORT keywords allow you to control the order of the values belonging to the current status. The value order definition selected in the status defines the sequence in which these values will be shown to the client application.

The keywords

INSERT FIRST—inserts into the beginning of the list

LAST—inserts into the end of the list

BEFORE *position*—inserts before the given list position

AFTER *position*—inserts after given list position

allow us to expand the status, by inserting new values in the defined position of the list of values already selected in the status. The value FIRST can be omitted. The argument of the LIMIT command can define both new dimension value and values already present in the status. In the latter case they will simply be transferred to the indicated place.

The argument of the LIMIT command for the SORT keyword defines the order in which dimension values will make the current status. For example, if, for the

REGION dimension, the values "EAST, CENTRAL, WEST" are preset, then the execution of these commands:

```
LIMIT REGION SORT 3,2,1
REPORT REGION
```

will result in:

```
REGION
WEST
CENTRAL
EAST
```

As has already been stressed, an argument of a command defines a range of dimensions. A large number of ways of defining this set are provided for. Let's consider the most important of them in detail.

Value List

The set of dimensions defined by an argument can be set in one of 16 ways:

Integer1, *Integer2*—a list of integer variables, which sets dimension values according to their positions in the whole list of its values.

Text expression—the Express language expression that defines a set of strings, provided that each of these strings sets a value of the given dimension.

Value1 TO *Value2*—defines a continuous subset of the given dimension values.

Value, *Value*—set of values defined by direct enumeration.

Subset name—a set of values selected in the database object subset (see next section).

ALL—defines set dimensions by default.

Logical condition—defines a logical condition that should be indexed by a dimension whose status is defined by the LIMIT command. Only those conditions defined by an argument whose expression value is TRUE will be reflected in the value set. For example, LIMIT REGION TO SALES GT 1000.

BOTTOM *n* BASEDON *expression*—defines a set consisting of exactly n values of the given dimension, for which the size defined by the expression indexed by the given dimension has the lowest numeric value.

TOP *n* BASEDON *expression*—similar to the previous case, but for n of the greatest values.

BOTTOM *n-percent* PERCENTOF *expression*—is similar to the previous case; however, it defines a given percent of the dimension values defined by an argument instead of a given number.

TOP *n-percent* PERCENTOF *expression*—is similar to the previous case; however, it defines a given percent of dimension values defined by an argument instead of a given number.

FIRST *n*—defines a set from the first *n* dimension values of the entire list (TO, ADD, COMPLEMENT, and INSERT) or in the current status (KEEP and REMOVE).

LAST *n*—defines a set from the last *n* dimension values of the entire list (TO, ADD, COMPLEMENT, and INSERT) or in the current status (KEEP and REMOVE).

LONGLIST—allows you to define a list of more than 300 arguments; the list can contain up to 2000 arguments.

NTH *n*—indicates the value numbered n in the whole list of values (TO, ADD, COMPLEMENT, and INSERT) or in the current status (KEEP and REMOVE).

NULL—sets an empty set of values (can not be used together with the keyword IFNONE; see later).

Relation or Dimension

Here, the argument of the LIMIT command is set by the name of a relation or dimension connected by a relation with the dimension defined in the LIMIT command. Let's look at an example of how to define an argument. Suppose we have three dimensions—MONTH, QUARTER, and YEAR—which are connected by a hierarchical relation. The following sequence of commands:

```
LIMIT YEAR TO 1, 7
LIMIT MONTH TO QUARTER YEAR
```

will first select in the current status of the YEAR dimension the first and seventh values from the list, then set the status of the QUARTER dimension according to the status of YEAR dimension. It will then select the values appropriate to the QUARTER dimension status in the current status of the MONTH dimension, and upon completion of this operation, it will restore the former status of the QUARTER dimension.

Family

Here, the argument looks as follows:

```
PARENTS                    DESCENDANTS

CHILDREN                   USING relation [value list]

ANCESTORS
```

PARENTS (by default)—allows you to select those dimension values which are parents to the defined list of values in the relation whose name is defined by the USING keyword. If a list of values is not set, the selection is defined in accordance with the current status of the child dimension.

CHILDREN—allows you to select those dimension values derived from a preset list of values in the relation whose name is defined by the USING keyword. If a list of values is not set, the selection is defined in accordance with the current status of the parent dimension.

ANCESTORS—allows you to select all "ancestors" for the values set in the list.

DESCENDANTS—allows you to select all "descendants" for the values set in the list.

There are a number of possibilities for defining ways of setting arguments for the LIMIT command. They are considered in detail in the description of the given command in the user reference guide.

The last, optional, IFNONE keyword defines the program's label in the Express language to which handling will be transferred after applying the LIMIT command in the program if the current dimension status is empty. If a transition to a label is not provided for, setting an empty status will cause the program to abort.

We should mention another useful command—ALLSTAT—which allows us to include all values in the current status of all dimensions.

4.3.2. Creation of Valuesets When Retrieving Data

Valuesets allow us to define a set of values for the preset dimension and then to use it in the LIMIT command for faster data selection. Similar to other variables (measures, formulae, relations), subsets can be (or not be) indexed by one or several dimensions. For example, let's say the following values are preset for the PRODUCT dimension: APPLE, ORANGE, BANANA, POTATO, CARROT. Then, if we define the SWEET valueset for the PRODUCT dimension, we can place all products that contain more than a certain level of sugar into this valueset using the LIMIT command:

```
LIMIT SWEET TO 1,2,3,5
```

and use this valueset every time it is necessary to select sampling data related to sweet products. To accomplish this, we need just execute the following command:

```
LIMIT PRODUCT TO SWEET
```

This is only a simple example of valueset usage. In practice, valuesets are created as a result of relatively long chains of the LIMIT command, and represent a complex multidimensional object that contains a neutral sampling of the dimension values for which the given valueset was defined.

4.3.3. Assigning the Data of One Object to Another

Assigning values to an object is done using the SET command or its equivalent, the "=" command. The syntax of the commands looks like this:

```
SET name expression
name = expression
```

You should keep in mind the features of multidimensional operations, namely for those cases when there is a database object indexed by a number of dimensions in the left part of the assignment, because the assignment will be executed for all combinations of indexing dimension values selected in the current status. Similarly, the values of the expression from the right part of the assignment will also be evaluated for all combinations of dimension values that index the left part, even if it is not indexed by these dimensions.

For example, executing the following commands:

```
LIMIT MONTH TO FIRST 12
SALES = 0
```

will cause all SALES measure values of the first 12 months to take on a value of zero (for all regions and all goods related to the current status of these dimensions). Executing the following commands:

```
LIMIT MONTH TO LAST 12
SALES = INTPART(RANDOM(100))
```

sets the values of the SALES measure that concern the last 12 months. An individual value of the whole part of a random variable evenly distributed among an interval of (0, 100) will be brought into each cell of our multidimensional cube, since, as we said earlier, the right part will be calculated for each combination of dimension values selected in the current status.

4.4. Programming in the Express Database

4.4.1. Creating, Compiling, and Executing Programs

Programs are stored database objects. A program's behavior is similar to the behavior of the Express command, which means that it can be called from another program. If a program contains the RETURN command and return data, it can be used as a function everywhere the Express language syntax permits using functions.

A program can be defined with the help of a dialog box called using the Express Administrator **Edit/Define/Program** menu item. The dialog box for editing a program is called with the **Edit/Modify** menu item. The program is a sequence of Express commands and does not require heading or ending lines (such as BEGIN, END).

The Express language is a powerful resource for creating OLAP applications, loading data from external files and relational databases, executing complex analytical calculations, and converting multidimensional data. *Command, expression,* and *option* are the basic concepts of the language.

Executing Command calls a predetermined sequence of operations on the part of the server. As practically any command can be used in the program (except commands that require console editing of data outside of Administrator), any database objects can be created, modified, and removed in the program. From a programmatic point of view, one attractive opportunity is that one program can create and execute another program, since this is done with a sequence of commands. An example of using this Express language feature is considered in the sections of *Chapter 5* that describe the xCommander applet, an analogue of the Express Command tool for Web applications.

The name of practically any Express command can be reduced to three characters according to these rules:

❑ Vowels, except for the first one, are discarded, beginning from the end

❑ Then, consonants are discarded, beginning from the end

❑ When you are left with three characters, you have finished

For example,

Command	Abbreviation
LIMIT	LMT
VARIABLE	VRB
DATABASE	DTB
MAINTAIN	MNT

Executing a *function,* just as with a command, calls a certain sequence of operations, but it also returns definite data.

Options are global variables whose values influence server operation in a definite way.

A comment in the program starts with the " character and continues until the end of the line:

```
"This is a comment
```

String values are enclosed in single quotes:

```
'This is a string value'
```

To prolong a program line, you need to put two characters, a space and a minus sign (-), at the end.

```
LIMIT REGION TO — "This is an example of string prolongation
'TEXAS' —
'MAINE' —
```

You can compile the program by selecting the **Tools/Compile** menu item, which becomes accessible when the edit window of the program is active. Another way of compiling is to execute the following command in Express Command:

```
COMPILE program name
```

If the compilation is successful, an additional object containing an executable program code will be created in the database. Otherwise, an error message will be generated.

To execute a program, execute the following command in Express Command:

```
CALL program name
```

or

```
program name
```

If the program has not been compiled, or its text has been modified after compilation, the program will be compiled on the Express server before program execution, and after this is has completed successfully, the program will be executed.

4.4.2. Expressions and Operators

An expression consists of constants, variables, data references, functions, and operators. Five categories of operators are permitted in expressions:

1. *Arithmetic operators* are used in numerical expressions that operate with numerical data or date-type data and return the appropriate numerical or date type result.

Operator	Use
+	Addition
-	Subtraction
*	Multiplying
/	Division
**	Exponentiation

It should be stressed that if one of the operands in an arithmetic expression has an uncertain value (NA), the result will be also be an uncertain value. For example, when executing in Express Command the command

```
SHOW NA - NA
```

in the output window we will receive:

```
NA
```

In the Express language, an uncertain value can even be divided by 0, in which case the result will be an uncertain value.

2. *Comparison operators* compare two values of two corresponding types and return a logical value.

Operator	Use
EQ	Equals
NE	Not equal

continues

Continued

Operator	Use
GT	Greater than
LT	Less than
GE	Greater than or equal to
LE	Less than or equal to
IN	Whether date belongs to the defined interval
LIKE	Whether text value satisfies the defined template

If one comparison operator operand has an uncertain value, the result will also be an uncertain value. For example, the expression NA GT 0 gives NA. However, if an uncertain value is compared with another uncertain value, the result of the expression is defined and accepts YES or NO values.

3. *Logical operators* are applied to convert logical values and also reset a logical result.

Operator	Use
AND	Logical And
NOT	Logical Not
OR	Logical Or

4. *If statements* evaluate and reset a certain value that belongs to of one of the fundamental types, depending on the value returned according to the logical condition.

Operator	Use
IF...THEN...ELSE	If the logical expression after IF is equal to TRUE, then the value of the expression defined by the THEN keyword is evaluated and returned; otherwise, ELSE is executed. If the value of the logical expression is not defined (NA), the returned value is also not defined

5. *The substitution operator* (&) is used to calculate the value of an expression and to substitute it.

The operators' priorities are the ones traditional for programming languages (see *The Reference Guide*).

The type of the expression is defined by a returned value. It in turn depends on the data types, operations, and functions making up the expression. To convert one data type to another, the CONVERT function is used.

An expression is indexed by combining the dimensions of all variables, functions, and data references included in it.

A variable (measure, formula) is indexed by the dimensions set when it was defined. The dimension by which a data reference is indexed is defined depending on how it was set (see the following section). The dimensions indexing the function are defined in accordance with the expression set in the RETURN command. The PARSE command allows us to receive information on dimensions that index expressions. For example, as a result of executing the following commands:

```
PARSE 'TOTAL (SALES REGION)'

SHOW INFO (PARSE DIMENSION)
```

we will receive the following result in the output window:

```
REGION
```

4.4.3. Data References

References to data represent a "slice" of a multidimensional data cube by one or more dimensions. For example, let's say the SALES measure is indexed by the MONTH, REGION, and PRODUCT dimensions (Fig. 4.13). The SALES (MONTH 03.99) reference will address a two-dimensional data array, SALES (MONTH 03.99, REGION 'TEXAS') a one-dimensional array and, lastly, SALES (MONTH 03.99, REGION 'TEXAS', PRODUCT 'FORD') a single cell of the initial cube. In the item containing dimension value, you can indicate an integer number of this value from the list of current status values, for example SALES (PRODUCT 3).

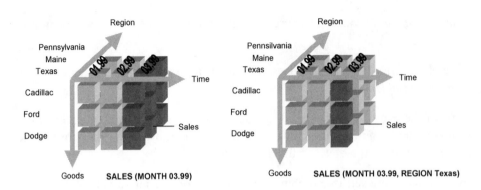

Fig. 4.13. Data references

4.4.4. Local Variables

The VARIABLE command declares variables that can be used inside a program. Declaration of local variables should precede all other commands of the program. Local variables can not be indexed by any dimensions, and they contain only one value. The syntax of the command looks like this:

```
VARIABLE name       data_type
dimension_name
VALUESET dimension_name
```

The name sets a local data name accessible only inside the given program. Data_type can accept any base value:

INTEGER	TEXT
SHORTINTEGER	ID
DECIMAL	BOOLEAN
SHORTDECIMAL	DATE

If *dimension_name* is set as a type, the variable can contain one of its values.

The *dimension_name* with the VALUESET keyword means that the local variable is the list of values for the defined dimension.

If the local variable is not assigned a value, it is equal to the NA empty value.

4.4.5. Program Arguments

The command

```
ARGUMENT    name    data_type
dimension_name
VALUESET dimension_name
```

declares an argument—a local variable whose value the given program expects. The syntax is exactly the same as when declaring local variables. Declaration of arguments precedes all other commands of the program. The order of argument declaration defines the order of their value transmission when the program is called. All program arguments are transferred by value.

Let's consider an example of a simple program with arguments. Let's create in our database a new PGM object, such as PROGRAM. Open the created object for editing and input the text:

```
ARG CAPTION TEXT
ARG X DECIMAL
SHOW CAPTION
SHOW IF (X GT 0) THEN X*X ELSE 0
```

Remember that ARG is the abbreviation of the ARGUMENT command name. While the edit window is open, let's call the **Express Command** dialog box using the **Tools/Execute** menu item. Then let's type the following command in the input window

```
CALL PGM('Square number =' 12)
```

and click the **Execute** button. In the output window we will see the following:

```
Square number =
144.00
```

Pay attention to the fact that when calling an argument, both a comma and a space can act as a separator, but only in those cases where it will not cause a misunderstanding. For example, an attempt to execute the command

```
CALL PGM('Square number =' -12)
```

will cause a message on an attempt to execute an invalid operation to appear, instead of the expected output of 0.00

```
ERROR: (MXOPERR) You are trying to perform an invalid operation. You
cannot subtract TEXT data in the expression that begins with Square
number =
```

since the text in parentheseses is perceived as an expression, and when calculating its value this error arises.

If we use a comma as an argument separator when using the

```
CALL PGM call ('a Square number = ', -12)
```

the expected result will be obtained:

```
Square number =
0.00
```

We should stress that if arguments are not set when the program is called, then the local variables corresponding to them will be equal to NA.

4.4.6. The Substitution Operator (&)

If the "&" character is contained in an Express command, Express will substitute the current value for the text expression before executing the command immediately following the ampersand. To understand the functioning of the substitution operator, let's create the simple program PGM1:

```
ARG VAL TEXT
REPORT VAL
```

and execute the following command in Express Command.

```
CALL PGM1('SALES')
```

As was expected, we receive the value of the internal variable VAL:

```
VAL
-------------------------------------------------------------------
SALES
```

Now we shall add the & character to the second line of our program before the variable name:

```
REPORT &VAL
```

and execute the command once again.

```
CALL PGM1('SALES')
```

The result will look like this:

```
REGION: TEXAS

------------------------------------------------------------------------
---------------------SALES----------------------------------------------
---------------------------MONTH----------------------------------------
PRODUCT    JAN99    FEB99    MAR99    APR99    MAY99    JUN99    JUL99

---------  ------   ------   ------   ------   ------   ------   ------

CADILLAC   77.00    24.00    32.00    49.00    13.00    36.00    16.00
FORD       49.00     7.00    38.00    58.00     6.00    72.00    53.00
DODGE      63.00    50.00    74.00    21.00    86.00    88.00    78.00
REGION: MAINE

------------------------------------------------------------------------
---------------------SALES----------------------------------------------
---------------------------MONTH----------------------------------------
PRODUCT    JAN99    FEB99    MAR99    APR99    MAY99    JUN99    JUL99

---------  ------   ------   ------   ------   ------   ------   ------
...
```

In other words, before executing the REPORT command, its text value was substituted for a variable, and as a result we receive a report on the SALES measure, which is one of our database objects.

This operator provides considerable opportunities for the programmer. For example, we may transfer a command or the name of another program to the program as an argument:

```
ARG PGM_NAME TEXT
CALL &PGM_NAME
```

4.4.7. Control Transfer Commands

The *IF* Command

As with other programming languages, the IF command allows you to execute one or more commands only if the logical expression is YES. An alternate command or group, which will be executed if the condition is NO, can also be set. The syntax of the command looks like this:

```
IF logical_expression
THEN command1
```

```
[ELSE command2]
The group in brackets can be set as a command:
DO
Command1
    ...
CommandN
DOEND
```

As opposed to the IF ... THEN ... ELSE (see above) conditional statement, which is written in one row, the command keywords THEN and ELSE in IF should start new lines, and the following command or DO bracket is to be placed on the same line.

We should mention one more feature of the IF command. If the logical condition is not defined, it will be interpreted as false. In other words, after execution of the following program:

```
IF NA
THEN SHOW 'TRUE'
ELSE SHOW 'FALSE'
```

in the output window we will receive

```
FALSE
```

The *FOR* Command

The FOR loop command has the following syntax:

```
FOR dimension_name1 [ dimension_name2]
    command
```

and defines one or more dimensions for which an exhaustive search of values will be carried out. For each combination of dimension values selected in the current status, a preset command or the DO ... DOEND group will be executed. Let's look at a simple example. Execute the program:

```
VRB M INTEGER
M=0
LIMIT MONTH TO FIRST 3
LIMIT PRODUCT TO FIRST 3
FOR MONTH PRODUCT
    DO
            M=M+1
            SHOW M
            SHOW MONTH
            SHOW PRODUCT
    DOEND
```

As a result, in the Express Command output window we shall see:

```
1
JAN99
CADILLAC
2
JAN99
FORD
3
JAN99
DODGE
4
FEB99
CADILLAC
5
FEB99
FORD
...
```

The *WHILE* Command

The syntax of the WHILE loop looks like this:

```
WHILE       logical_expression
                Command
```

A preset command or the DO ... DOEND group will be executed so long as the *logical_expression* is YES (true). Executing the given loop in the Express language has no features that can compare with other programming languages.

The *CONTINUE* and *BREAK* Commands

The CONTINUE command allows you to bypass executing commands located at the end of the DO ... DOEND group, and to begin a new iteration of FOR or WHILE loops. The application of the command is similar to other languages, for example, the following program

```
FOR MONTH
DO
IF TOTAL (SALES, MONTH) GE 1000
THEN CONTINUE
```

```
"report generating commands
              ...

DOEND
```

will produce a report only for those months for which the total amount of sales was less than 1000 units.

The BREAK command allows you to interrupt the execution of a DO ... DOEND group set in FOR or WHILE loops, or in a SWITCH switch (see the following section). Control will be transferred to the command immediately after the DOEND bracket.

The *SWITCH* Command

The SWITCH command has the following syntax:

```
SWITCH control_expression
DO
CASE expression1:
Command1.1
[Command1.2]
                    ....

[BREAK]
CASE expression 2:
Command2.1
[Command2.2]
                    ....

[BREAK]
                 ....

[DEFAULT:
CommandN.1
[CommandN.2]
                 ...

BREAK]
DOEND
```

Using the SWITCH command allows us to organize the branching of program execution in certain cases. In comparison with other programming languages, the SWITCH command in the Express language has a number of features. The first feature is that the controlling expression and the expressions after the CASE keyword can have not only integer values, but also other fundamental types of values (types of expressions should correspond to each other). The second feature can be found in the fact that calculating expressions and matching their values is effected during run time, and is carried out top-down until the first match; therefore, expressions after CASE can have basically identical values.

Let's consider these ideas in a program example:

```
ARG SW MONTH
ARG CS MONTH
VRB M TEXT
SWITCH SW
DO
CASE CS:
M = 'MARCH 1999'
BREAK
CASE 01.99:
M = 'JANUARY 1999'
BREAK
CASE 02.99:
CASE 03.99:
M = 'FEBRUARY 1999'
DEFAULT:
M=NA
BREAK
DOEND
SHOW M
```

The program results that concern various argument values are shown in the table:

Value of argument	Result
01.99	JANUARY 1999
02.99	FEBRUARY 1999
03.99	FEBRUARY 1999
04.99	NA
03.99,03.99	MARCH 1999

4.4.8. Other Commands and Functions

The power of modern high-level languages is seen in many respects by the ready-to-use program libraries accompanying them, which allow you to create complex applications by simply gathering available components from them. From this point of view, the

Express language is a kind of Eldorado with its huge gold deposits. The entire two volumes of the *Express Language Reference Guide*, which simply list descriptions of command and function syntax in alphabetical order for the current version of the language, has 1245 pages. Besides, there is on-line Help system whose volume is 1.5 MB. Even simply browsing the existing abilities will move us far beyond the scope of our book. Therefore, if we are going to use all the power of the language and not reinvent the wheel, we need to access these documents and search the available components, whether we want to or not, before we start developing real applications.

In this section, we don't plan on covering everything, just some of the most frequently used functions and commands from those a developer of real-world analytical systems will almost certainly need.

Database Operations

Many database operations can be done using Express Administrator commands. However, when relatively complex applications are created, program control over database association and update is generally required.

The DATABASE command allows us to create a new database, open an existing one, close an open one, and change the current multidimensional database to another.

The UPDATE command saves the disk changes effected in a database open for reading and writing. Before executing the UPDATE command, all implemented changes are stored in the temporary cache of the current session and can be undone by detaching the database without executing the UPDATE command.

Operations with the Database Dictionary

The commands for operation with the database dictionary allow the program to create and update all objects stored in it. The most frequently used commands for object manipulation are listed below.

Command	Usage
DEFINE	Defines a new database object
DELETE	Removes an object from the database
EQ	Allows you to set an expression that defines a formula object
EXISTS	Checks for object existence in all attached databases
RENAME	Changes object name

Multidimensional (Cell-by-Cell) Functions

Multidimensional cubes of numerical data are arguments of the functions related to the given group. A multidimensional function is sequentially applied to each cell of a cube, and the returned result is placed in an appropriate cell of a cube that is "similar" to the initial one.

Let's consider an example. The following command sequence is executed in Express Command:

```
LIMIT MONTH TO FIRST 3
LIMIT REGION TO FIRST 2
LIMIT PRODUCT TO FIRST 2
REPORT SALES
REPORT SQRT(SALES)
```

and as a result we will receive:

```
REGION: TEXAS
------------SALES--------------
------------MONTH--------------
PRODUCT     JAN99          FEB99          MAR99
--------    --------       --------       --------
CADILLAC    49.00          7.00           38.00
FORD        48.00          24.00          30.00


REGION: MAINE
------------SALES--------------
------------MONTH--------------
PRODUCT     JAN99          FEB99          MAR99
--------    --------       --------       --------
CADILLAC    33.00          74.00          4.00
FORD        79.00          3.00           26.00


REGION: TEXAS
----------SQRT(SALES)-----------
------------MONTH--------------
PRODUCT     JAN99          FEB99          MAR99
--------    --------       --------       --------
CADILLAC    7.00           2.65           6.16
FORD        6.93           4.90           5.48
```

```
REGION: MAINE
-----------SQRT(SALES)-----------
-------------MONTH--------------
PRODUCT       JAN99           FEB99           MAR99
--------     --------        --------        --------
VOLGA         5.74            8.60            2.00
ZHIGULI       8.89            1.73            5.10
```

A list of multidimensional functions is shown in the following table:

Function	Result
ABS	Absolute value
INTPART	The integer part
LOG	Napierian logarithm
LOG10	Brigg's logarithm
MAX	Maximum value of two numbers
MIN	Minimum value of two numbers
RANDOM	The pseudo-random uniformly distributed value
REM	Division remainder
SQRT	Square root

Pay attention to the fact that the MAX and MIN functions for the indexed values of arguments compare each cell of one cube with each cell of the other cube.

Data Aggregating

Aggregating functions calculate the value of a certain functional (average, maximum, minimum values, *etc.*) in the defined set of data.

Function	Result
AGGREGATE	According to aggregation card, aggregates data "on the fly
ANY	Returns YES, if even one of the values satisfies a defined condition; otherwise NO
AVERAGE	Evaluates the average value

continues

Continued

Function	Result
COUNT	Allows you to perform an exhaustive search of values that satisfy a defined condition
EVERY	Returns YES if all values satisfy a defined condition; otherwise NO
LARGEST	Evaluates the maximum value
NONE	Returns YES if any value does not satisfy a defined condition; otherwise NO
SMALLEST	Evaluates the smallest value
STDDEV	Evaluates the standard value of standard deviation using an unbiased estimator (N-1)
TALLY	Calculates the number of values for a defined dimension that are included in the current status or in the appropriate dimension connected with the initial relation
TCONVERT	Evaluates the values of one temporary dimension through another
TOTAL	Evaluates the sum of values

TCONVERT and AGGREGATE are functions of special interest, as they allow us to evaluate values "on the fly".

The *TCONVERT* Function

The TCONVERT function allows us to aggregate (calculate the summarized value of) variable values from one temporary dimension to another "on the fly". Using the given function, we can considerably reduce database size. For example, the Sales variable contains data by month for 2 years. To aggregate these data by quarters and years, we have to store 8 additional values of a temporary dimension. Using the TCONVERT function, we needn't store these values, since we can evaluate them "on the fly", thus saving in the database only 24 values of the temporary hierarchy instead of 34.

```
Define MONTH dimension month
Define QUARTER dimension quarter
Define YEAR dimension year
Define V.SALES variable decimal <PRODGEOG <PROD GEOG> MONTH>
Ld Where the data is stored
```

```
Define Q.SALES formula decimal <PRODGEOG <PROD GEOG> QUARTER> Eq
TCONVERT(V.SALES, QUARTER, SUM)
Define Y.SALES formula decimal <PRODGEOG <PROD GEOG> YEAR> Eq
TCONVERT(V.SALES, YEAR, SUM)
```

Using the TCONVERT function complicates the application, but this complexity can be hidden from users. For example:

```
Define F.SALES formula decimal <PROD GEOG TIME>
eq if isvalue(TIME YEAR) then Y.SALES(YEAR TIME ) else
If isvalue(TIME QUARTER) then Q.SALES(QUARTER TIME)
else if ISVALUE(TIME MONTH) then V.SALES(MONTH TIME) else NA
```

The AGGREGATE Function

The AGGREGATE function is another useful function (analogous to the Aggregate command). The AGGREGATE function allows you to aggregate the values of a measure for all levels of a hierarchical dimension "on the fly", using the "aggregation card". The "aggregation card" represents an internal database object that defines a data set which is to be aggregated. For example:

```
DEFINE sales.agg AGGMAP <time, product, geography>
AGGMAP
RELATION time.r PRECOMPUTE (time ne 'YEAR99')
RELATION product.r PRECOMPUTE (product ne 'ALL')
RELATION geography.r
CACHE STORE
END
REPORT AGGREGATE (actuals USING sales.agg)
```

Another useful command is the ROLLUP command, which allows us to aggregate measures for all levels of the hierarchical dimension by which it is indexed.

Analyzing Time Series

Functions of this category allow you to work with time series segments and to evaluate their most common characteristics.

Function	Result
CUMSUM	Evaluates the sum of time series
LAG	Returns the value of the time series segment for the previous period

continues

Continued

Function	Result
LAGABSPCT	Evaluates the difference in percentage between the values of the time series for the current period and the previous period, taking into account the sign of change
LAGDIF	Calculates the difference between the values of time series for the current period and the previous period
LAGPCT	Calculates the difference in percentage between the values of time series for the current period and the previous period
LEAD	Returns the value of a time series segment for the subsequent period
MOVINGAVERAGE	Moving average
MOVINGMAX	Moving maximum value
MOVINGMIN	Moving minimum value
MOVINGTOTAL	Moving total

The FORECAST and REGRESS commands also concern the analysis of time series. The FORECAST command allows you to estimate values for certain time series in accordance with one of the built-in statistical trend models—linear, exponential model, or model—that takes into account seasonal variations. The REGRESS command provides multidimensional linear regression analysis of two or more sample ranges. To estimate regression coefficients, standard deviations and confidence intervals are evaluated.

Functions for Date and Time Processing

Function	Result
BEGINDATE	Returns the first value of the time dimension (DAY, WEEK, MONTH, QUARTER, or YEAR) for which the expression has an uncertain value (NA)
DAYOF	Returns the number of the day of the week for the defined date
ENDDATE	Returns the last value of the time dimension (DAY, WEEK, MONTH, QUARTER, or YEAR) for which the expression has an uncertain value (NA)

continues

Continued

Function	Result
ISDATE	Allows you to define whether the text expression is allowed to be converted to the value of the given type
MAKEDATE	Converts three integer values (number, month, and year) to the value of the DATE type
TOD	Returns the current time for the current day
TODAY	Returns the current date
VNF	Allows you to change the text data view for data of DATE (DAY, WEEK, MONTH, QUARTER, YEAR) type
YYOF	Returns the year that corresponds to the defined date

Text Data Conversions

The Express language contains a large number of functions that allow for flexible text data manipulations. The functions used most frequently are shown below.

Function	Result
BLANKSTRIP	Deletes leading and ending blanks
CHANGECHARS	Replaces one sequence of characters with another one
FINDCHARS	Finds and returns the text position in which the defined character sequence is located
JOINCHARS	Connects two strings
LOWCASE	Converts all text characters to lower case letters
NUMCHARS	Returns the number of characters in a text expression
REMCHARS	Deletes from the text all appearances of the defined character sequence
UPCASE	Converts all text characters to capital letters

Data Type Conversion

The CONVERT function, which allows us to convert one data type to another, is used frequently. The syntax of the CONVERT function looks like this:

```
CONVERT(expression, type [arguments])
```

The expression defines an expression or variable whose type is to be transformed. The type to which the expression is converted can be one of the following:

TEXT BOOLEAN	DATE	BYTE	PACKED
ID	SHORTINTEGER	INFILE	BINARY
INTEGER	DECIMAL	SHORTDECIMAL	

The TEXT, ID, DATE, BOOLEAN, INTEGER, SHORTINTEGER, DECIMAL, and SHORTDECIMAL types set data conversion to fundamental Express data types. The BYTE, INFILE, PACKED, and BINARY types provide additional opportunities for data manipulation. If the TEXT, ID, or DATE types are set, you can specify conversion with the help of an argument.

The result of command execution depends on the initial expression type, on the type to which the expression is converted, and on the command arguments (see *The User's Reference Guide*). Most frequently, conversions are made from text type to another type, and vice versa. For example, after executing the following commands

```
SHOW CONVERT('1/3/98' DATE 'MDY')
SHOW CONVERT('1/3/98' DATE 'DMY')
```

we shall receive the following result:

```
03JAN98
01MAR98
```

Or, if the current date corresponds to December 26, 1999, then the command

```
SHOW CONVERT(TODAY TEXT '<DD>-<MM>-<YY>')
```

will give the following result:

```
26-12-99
```

4.4.9. Saving and Restoring Environment Parameters

A large number of environmental parameters—i.e., options—that allow us to flexibly customize and use the characteristics of the majority of Express commands and functions are defined in the Express language. As an example, let's consider how the DATEFORMAT option, which stores templates such as DATE defining data conversion to the text type, is used. The option is set by simply assigning some text constant to it, for example:

```
DATEFORMAT = '<DD><MTXT><YY>'
```

The given template is the default one. The template consists of four components, which define the type of text presentation for the day, month, year, and day of week, and also probably some additional characters. Possible template component formats are shown below:

Format	Description	March 1, 1999	November 12, 2051
Day			
<D>	One or two digits	1	12
<DD>	Two digits	01	12
<DS>	Two digits, or one digit with a space	1	12
<DT>	With upper case ending	1ST	12TH
<DTL>	With lowercase ending	1st	12th
Month			
<M>	One or two digits	3	11
<MM>	Two digits	03	11
<MS>	Two digits, or one digit with a space	3	11
<MT>	The first character in upper case	M	N
<MTXT>	The first three characters in upper case	MAR	NOV
<MTXTL>	The first three characters in lower-case	mar	nov
<MTEXT>	Full name in upper case	MARCH	NOVEMBER
<MTEXTL>	Full name in lowercase	march	november
Year			
<YY>	Two or four digits	99	2051
<YYYY>	Four digits	1999	2051
Day of the week			
<W>	Numerical	4	1
<WT>	First character in upper case	W	S

continues

Continued

Format	Description	March 1, 1999	November 12, 2051
`<WTXT>`	The first three characters in upper case	WED	SUN
`<WTXTL>`	The first three characters in lower-case	wed	sun
`<WTEXT>`	Full name in upper case	WEDNESDAY	SUNDAY
`<WTEXTL>`	Full name in lowercase	wednesday	sunday

As an example of another controlling option, we can look at the `DECIMAL` option, which sets the amount of digits after the decimal point for the text representation of a fractional number. For example, if we set `DECIMAL = 0`, we shall receive an integer text representation for all decimal data related to commands and programs connected with the appropriate conversion type.

Let's take a look at a list of some of the most frequently used options.

Option	Type	Description
Numerical		
`DECIMALOVERFLOW`	`BOOLEAN`	Permits arithmetic overflow. The `NA` value is the result of the overflow
`DIVIDEBYZERO`	`BOOLEAN`	Permits division by 0. The `NA` value is the result of dividing by 0
`NASKIP`	`BOOLEAN`	If the option value is `NO`, then the `NA` value is the result of `NA` aggregation. Otherwise, uncertain values will be ignored
`NASKIP2`	`BOOLEAN`	If the option value is `NO`, then the `NA` value will represent the result of "+" and "−" operations using `NA`. Otherwise uncertain values will be interpreted as 0
Date		
`DATEFORMAT`	`TEXT`	Defines the template for text data conversion such as `DATE`
`DAYNAMES`	`TEXT`	Contains a list of days of the week
`MONTHNAMES`	`TEXT`	Contains a list of months of the year
`SECONDS`	`INTEGER`	Counts seconds since January 1, 1970

continues

Continued

Option	Type	Description
Text		
_XLTCASE		Sets a pair of tables that define conversion from one register to another
COMMAS	BOOLEAN	Controls the presence of the comma that divides thousands and millions when outputting numerical data
DECIMALS	INTEGER	Controls the number of characters after the decimal point when numerical data are output
DECIMALCHAR	ID	Defines a separator between the whole and fractional part when numerical data are output
NASPELL	TEXT	Contains the text that will be output for data whose value is NA
NOSPELL	TEXT	Contains the text that will be output for the NO logical value
THOUSANDSCHAR	ID	Defines a separator between thousands when numerical data are output
YESSPELL	TEXT	Contains the text that will be output for the YES logical value

Some options connected with program debugging will be discussed in the following section. The complete list of options and a description of their formats is described in *The Reference Guide*.

Any program in the Express language can change an option. As options are "global" data, changing an option in one program will influence the operation of all other programs connected with this option. Sometimes, such an effect can be undesirable. The simplest mechanism that allows us to remove side effects when changing an option consists of saving the values of all options that are changed in the program in the beginning of program execution and restoring them before it completes. For example, a program that changes the DATEFORMAT and DECIMAL options can look like this:

```
PUSH DECIMAL DATEFORMAT "save values in stack
DECIMAL=...
DATEFORMAT=...

...

POP DECIMAL DATEFORMAT "retrieve values from stack
```

Similar problems arise when using the LIMIT command in programs, since changing any dimension's current status executed with its help will have global consequences. To save and restore a dimension's current status, the PUSH and POP commands can also be used:

```
PUSH PRODUCT REGION
LIMIT PRODUCT...
LIMIT REGION...
...
POP PRODUCT REGION
```

4.4.10. Program Debugging

Let's discuss the most simple ways of program debugging. Debugging programs in Express is done with certain special commands, functions, and options.

When a run-time error occurs, a standard message is displayed. We can supplement this output, adding to it information about the line in which this error has taken place. For this purpose, it is enough to assign a YES value to BADLINE option.

The BACK function returns a list of currently running programs and allows you to control the stack of calls. For example, if in one of our programs an error occurs and we want to find out from which program the given program was called when this error took place, we need only include the SHOW BACK command in the beginning of the program, and we will receive the list of nested calls.

Sometimes it is useful to trace program execution completely. To do this, use the PRGTRACE option, by setting the YES value for it. Every time it is executed Express will produce a string. For example, if the FOR loop is executed 3 times, the command contained in this loop will be displayed in the output window three times. It is necessary to stress that when working with Express Administrator, the value of the given option should be changed in the program, instead of in Express Command.

When tracing programs in Express Administrator, the text output is routed by default to the **Command Result** window of the Express Command tool. The text output can be readdressed to the file using this command:

```
DBGOUTFILE [APPEND] file_name [NOCACHE]
            [EOF]
```

Using the optional APPEND keyword in the command allows for adding new debug information to the end of the existing file. The NOCACHE keyword makes Express write to the file for each output. The DBGOUTFILE EOF command restores output by default.

More complex debugging methods can be realized using a command line (XCA connection) in Personal Express (see *The Reference Guide*).

4.4.11. Methods of Increasing Productivity

The Problem of Measure Dispersion

Those measures for which the majority of dimension value combinations have no data are referred to as disperse measures. For example, take the Sales measure, which has 100 Product dimension values, 12 Time dimension values, and 10 Geography dimension values. At the initial moment we can define data for only one of the 12 Time dimension values. Therefore, only 1,000 (100×1×10) of 12,000 (100×12×10) cells will be filled, and the remaining 11,000 (100×11×10) cells will be empty.

The problem of measure dispersion arises in view of the fact that multidimensional databases, as opposed to relational databases, back up physical memory measure space for each possible dimension combination, which thus increases the time it takes to fetch data, and reduces server productivity.

There are three approaches to solving this problem of data dispersion.

☐ *The first approach* is usable in those cases where we can predict with a high probability the character of measure data filling, and it is grounded on the fact that Oracle Express Server does not save measure memory pages that do not contain any data. Thus, to reduce the number of physical memory pages related to the given measure, we need to fill sequentially only those memory pages that contain data. This is achieved by changing the dimension order in the measure.

☐ *The second approach* can be applied in cases where we cannot define the character of a measure filled with data, or when the dispersion is random. In this case, to decrease the number of physical memory pages, we can use conjoint dimensions, which are basically a combination of several dimensions. Thus the effect of decreasing the number of memory pages is achieved by reducing the number of physically stored dimension values, since using joint dimensions assumes indexing a measure only by existing combinations of dimension values.

❏   *The third approach* assumes integration of Oracle Express Server with relational databases.

Sectioning in Oracle Express

One of the adopted technologies which allow us to raise database productivity is the technology of sectioning, or physically splitting data into sections (parts). This technology is based on the fact that, as a rule, the time necessary for computing these sections is much less than the time required to compute an entire data set, which thus provides for a rise in system productivity.

As opposed to other databases, the given possibility is not provided for in Oracle Express Server, but we ourselves can use the given technology. To construct sections in Oracle Express Server, we need to execute the following sequence of operations:

1. Define the dimensions that will be sectioned.

2. Define a set or a range of dimension values that will define each section, and define the total number of sections.

3. Create a measure for each section.

4. Design procedures for data update so that.

Integrating and presenting data from various measures as a single unit can be done with the following formula:

```
Define F.SALES FORMULA DECIMAL <PROD GEOG TIME>
Eq if isvalue(DB1_PROD PROD) and isvalue(DB1_GEOG GEOG and
isvalue(DB1_TIME TIME)
then DB1_SALES(DB1_PROD PROD DB1_GEOG GEOG DB1_TIME TIME)
else if isvalue(DB2_PROD PROD) and isvalue(DB2_GEOG GEOG) and
isvalue(DB2_TIME TIME)
then DB2_SALES(DB2_PROD PROD DB2_GEOG GEOG DB2_TIME TIME)
Else na
Define DB1_SALES VARIABLE DECIMAL <DB1_PROD DB1_GEOG DB1_TIME>
define DB2_SALES VARIABLE DECIMAL <DB2_PROD DB2_GEOG DB2_TIME>
```

4.5. Data Import and Export

Efficient usage of on-line analysis resources assumes the presence of significant information content in multidimensional databases. Therefore, one of the first tasks of Oracle Express software users is the task of filling the database. At the same time, apparently, we should not think that one product includes all the resources necessary for an end user to effect a manifold analysis of information and to satisfy all his or her specific requirements. Therefore, exporting data from a multidimensional database is also an important task. Let's consider in detail some possible practical solutions for problems related to importing information to a multidimensional Express database from text (TXT files), MS Excel spreadsheets (XLS files), and relational Oracle DB, and also exporting information to MS Excel from a DB Express.

4.5.1. Importing Data Using Administrator

Loading data to an Express multidimensional database can be done most simply using the Express Administrator application. A main menu item becomes active after a new database has been created. If we select the **File/Import** item, we will see that four kinds of import are provided:

Text—text files import

Relational—import using built-in SQL queries

EIF—import from Express databases

Discoverer—import of data from an Oracle Discoverer 3.1 application

Let's consider the first two.

Importing Data from Text Files

Suppose we need to import data from an ImpTxt.txt ASCII-file:

COMPANY	PRICE	TRADE_DAT
Alaska Corned Beef	1.13	01-SEP-94
Webbe Trucking	5.77	01-SEP-94
Dinosaur Toys	5.28	01-SEP-94
GUI Intl.	5.32	01-SEP-94
Ultimate Lighting	4.35	01-SEP-94
OJ Sporting Goods	1.42	01-SEP-94
Oracle Corp.	49	01-SEP-94
Victoria Apparel	35.77	01-SEP-94
Microsoft	7.02	01-SEP-94

```
Volvo                          28.55   01-SEP-94
Cisco Systems                  20.5    01-SEP-94
Alaska Corned Beef             18.25   31-AUG-94
Webbe Trucking                 22.5    31-AUG-94
Dinosaur Toys                  5.45    31-AUG-94
...
```

To import data from this file, it is necessary to go through the following steps:

☐ Limit the company title field and data field by double quotes, or any other unique characters, and save the edited file

☐ Call a dialog (Fig. 4.14) using the **File/Import/Text** item from the main menu and define the parameters for text import

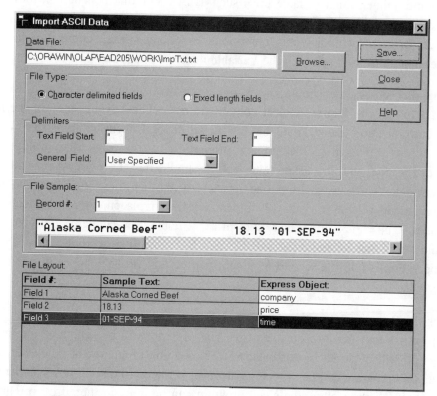

Fig. 4.14. Dialog box for customizing the import of a text file

☐ Select an alternative to character delimited fields in the **File Type** group (un-limited character fields)

❒ In the **Delimiters** group, set the initial (**Text Field Start**) and final (**Text Field End**) delimiters for text boxes (in our case they are quotation marks), select the **User Specified** alternative from the **General Field** list, and set a space character in the additional input box

❒ Set a name for the imported file in the **Data File** field, or select it from the dialog box opened with the **Browse** button

After that, a file line's content with a number indicated in the **Record#** field will appear in the **File Layout** window as an example.

While the customization dialog is open, select the **Dictionary/Define** item from the main menu and define a time dimension such as Day, a company such as Text, and a multidimensional variable price such as Decimal that depends on these dimensions. In the hierarchical list that displays the contents of our database in the **Object Browser** window, the appropriate subitems—time, company (in the **Dimension** item), and price (in the **Variable** item)—will appear.

Using the mouse, we should select the company subitem and drag it to the **Field 1** row of the **Express Object** column from the **File Layout** group of the import customization dialog. After that the modal dialog **Dimension properties (Text)** will appear for setting the import properties of the dimension values. In this dialog, the **Add dimension value** option should be set. If necessary, you can set character conversions from one register to another there, and you can also customize up to 100 variants of context-sensitive replacement of character sequences. The Time dimension and price variable are similarly dragged. We should stress that an imported variable can be transformed through an arithmetic operation, while the second argument can be any variable stored in our database.

Click the **Save** button and set in the dialog the name of the program that will load data from a text file into our database. The program will be generated automatically and will be saved in our database. The loading program can be executed at once. This program can be executed whenever we need to display possible changes in our ASCII file. Calling the given program can be done in the AUTOGO program. In this case, data will be updated every time we open our database. The loading protocol and messages concerning possible errors during data import will be written in the ImpTxt.log and ImpTxt.err files.

Importing Data from Relational Oracle Databases and MS Excel Spreadsheets

As was already mentioned, the built-in SQL-queries mechanism can be used to import data to the Express database. Before using the given mechanism, make sure that ODBC (Microsoft's Open Database Connectivity) support was set when the Express software was installed.

The SQL queries mechanism is a universal one, and provides access to any database for which appropriate 32-bit ODBC drivers are supported on your PC. Installing the ODBC driver for a remote relational Oracle database is done during installation of Oracle for Windows 95 products. A large number of ODBC drivers for popular databases can be installed when installing Microsoft Office software on your PC. It is necessary to state that these drivers, as a rule, are not included in the standard product configuration selected upon installation. You can install ODBC support by directly defining the appropriate item when installing the product with user settings.

Before using the help of Express DB administrator for data SQL Import, you must first define the ODBC data source:

❐ Start the ODBC Administrator application (the Odbcad32.exe file from the **Control Panel** program group).

❐ Click the **Add** button from the **Data Source** dialog box to start the dialog that allows you to select the ODBC data source to be added.

❐ Select Oracle73 (or another appropriate driver) from the **Installed ODBC Drivers** list.

❐ Display the dialog for setting the parameters appropriate to the selected driver; click the **OK** button. By clicking the **Help** button, you can get more information about features related to installing the selected driver.

❐ Save the definition of the data source and go back to the **Data Source** dialog box; set the necessary parameters and click the **OK** button. The source name and its description can be anything you like.

❐ Click the **Close** button.

As soon as the ODBC data source is defined, we can use the tools provided by the DB Express administrator. To import data from an ODBC source, we must first start Oracle Express Administrator, open (or create new) multidimensional databases, and do the following:

☐ Select the **Import SQL Data** dialog (Fig. 4.15) using the **File/Import/Relational** item from the main menu.

☐ Click the **SQL Connect** button and select the **SQL Connections** dialog box to install a connection with the SQL server.

☐ Click the **Connect** button to display the **Select Data Source** dialog box.

☐ Select from the **Select a Data Source** list an item with the required data source name (in our case, it is **Oracle7**) and click the **OK** button to start the program that will set the connection with the defined data source.

☐ In the standard dialog displayed, set the parameters of the **Scott/Tiger** connection with the demonstration database available in any installation of Oracle DB. Click **OK** and return to the **SQL Connections** dialog box. If the connection is successful, a row with **Oracle7** as the data source name will appear in the **Select Current Connection** list.

☐ To return to the **Import SQL Data** window, select **Oracle7** and click **OK**.

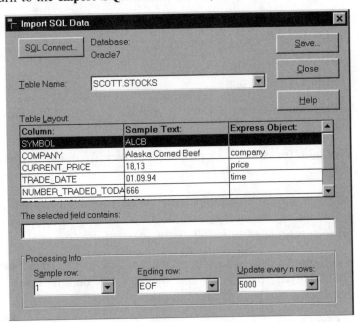

Fig. 4.15. Import SQL Data dialog box

In the list of tables (**Table Name:**) all tables for the logged on user will be displayed. Select the required table (SCOTT.STOCKS, for example). After that, you can see in the **Table Layout** group the contents of the STOCKS table record, whose number is indicated in the **Sample row** drop-down list.

Connection between table columns and objects (dimensions, variables) of a multidimensional database, as well as importing information, is carried out in a way similar to the one described in the section on importing data from text files.

Importing data from spreadsheets is also done in a similar manner, i.e., by setting an ODBC data source according to an Excel 7.0 file (*.xls). We only need to stress here one feature of the given procedure. Before saving the file in the MS Excel application, you have to assign unique names to all the tables from which data is to be imported. Otherwise, the list of tables will not be displayed in the **Import SQL data** dialog box. To assign a name to the table, highlight it, click the mouse button in the field where you usually find the address of the table's current cell, and give the required name. Column names are set in the first row of the table.

4.5.2. Programming Data Import

Adding New Data from an Excel Table

Using the Express DB administrator when importing data is not always possible or effective. It might be, for example, that fully loading a large data volume to a multidimensional database when actualization of the database state is required will lead to unacceptable time expenditures.

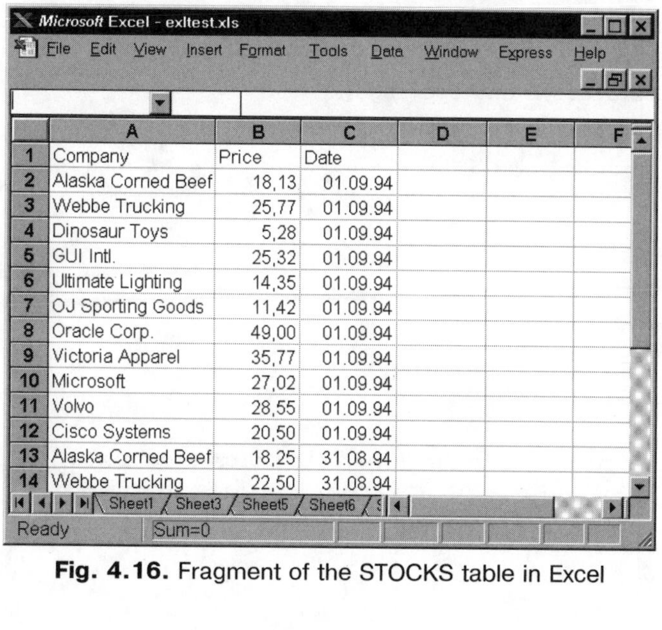

	A	B	C	D	E	F
1	Company	Price	Date			
2	Alaska Corned Beef	18,13	01.09.94			
3	Webbe Trucking	25,77	01.09.94			
4	Dinosaur Toys	5,28	01.09.94			
5	GUI Intl.	25,32	01.09.94			
6	Ultimate Lighting	14,35	01.09.94			
7	OJ Sporting Goods	11,42	01.09.94			
8	Oracle Corp.	49,00	01.09.94			
9	Victoria Apparel	35,77	01.09.94			
10	Microsoft	27,02	01.09.94			
11	Volvo	28,55	01.09.94			
12	Cisco Systems	20,50	01.09.94			
13	Alaska Corned Beef	18,25	31.08.94			
14	Webbe Trucking	22,50	31.08.94			

Fig. 4.16. Fragment of the STOCKS table in Excel

Obviously, when data is actualized, it would be desirable to simply add them instead of completely reloading them. The given task can be performed using the Express Language. As an example, let's create the EXLADD procedure for loading and adding new data to an Express DB from the STOCKS table, which was considered in the example we used when importing data from an ASCII file. However, the table will now be located in the Excel file (Fig. 4.16). We should remember that, as we said above, the given table should be named, and the XLS file in which it is located should be contained in the ODBC data sources list. The text of the EXLADD procedure is shown below. The procedure is quite efficient, and will add new data to the Express database from the STOCKS table of the file, which is indicated in the ODBC source under the name ExlTest:

```
"Working Variable declaration
VRB _DAY     DATE            "date
VRB _COMPANY      TEXT       "company name
VRB _PRICE          DECIMAL  "price value
PUSHLEVEL 'EXLADD'           "area name assignment in stack
PUSH SQLMESSAGES             "saving current value in stack
SQLMESSAGES = YES            "permission on SQL message output
_DAY = STATLAST(DAY)         "definition of the last date
"in the day dimension
IF _DAY EQ NA                "if there is no data
THEN _     DAY = 0           "then first load
ODBC.SOURCE = 'EXLTEST'      "ODBC-data source definition
SQL CONNECT                  " setting connection
"cursor declaration and opening
SQL DECLARE CSR1 CURSOR FOR -
SELECT -
COMPANY, -
PRICE, -
DATE -
FROM STOCKS -
WHERE DATE > :_DAY
SQL OPEN CSR1
WHILE SQLCODE EQ 0
DO
"exhaustive search of strings selected from a database
SQL FETCH CSR1 INTO -
:_COMPANY -
:_PRICE -
```

```
: _DAY
    IF      SQLCODE NE 0
    THEN    BREAK
"addition of new dimensions and variable values
MAINTAIN DAY    MERGE _DAY
MAINTAIN COMPANY MERGE _COMPANY
PRICE (COMPANY _COMPANY, DAY CONVERT(_DAY,DATE DAY)) = _PRICE
DOEND
SQL CLOSE CSR1            "close cursor
SQL DISCONNECT           "disconnect database
POPLEVEL 'EXLADD'        "return values from stack
RETURN
```

To understand how the given procedure works, you simply need to familiarize yourself with the comments. We must point out that new data will be added successfully even if records are not ordered by time in the STOCKS table.

It is supposed that adding information to the table is done simultaneously for all companies. Otherwise, to limit the amount of time, you should select not the last, but the minimum date for which there are empty cells related to the price variable in the database. To make the EXLADD procedure complete it should naturally be supplemented with code handling of possible errors, which are shown by the global SQLCODE variable.

"On the Fly" Data Import from a Relational DBMS

The presence of stored objects—*formulae*—in Express DB provides the user with an attractive possibility: not saving certain unfrequently used detailed data in a multi-dimensional database, but rather extracting them from accessible relational databases only if a detailed analysis is necessary. The formula for this is created using the administrator thusly:

1. Display the **Define a Formula** dialog box (Fig. 4.17) by selecting the **Edit —>** **Define a Formula** item from the main menu.

2. Set a name, the type of returned value, and the dimension by which the formula is defined. Set the **SQL Data** option in the **Equation** group. After that, three additional buttons will appear in the bottom of the dialog box.

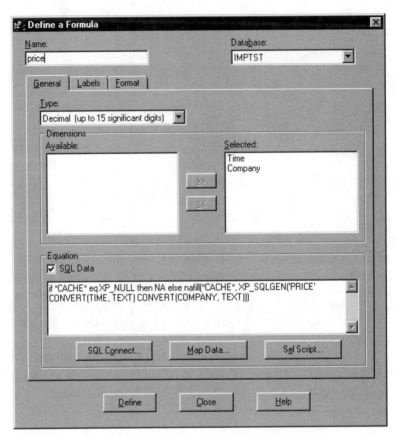

Fig. 4.17. The **Define a Formula** dialog box

3. Click the **SQL Connect** button and set the connection with the ODBC data source if it was not already set earlier. The connection procedure is exactly the same as the one discribed in the "*Data Import Using Administrator*" in *Section 4.5.1.*

4. Click the **Map Data** button to call the data mapping dialog (Fig. 4.18).

5. Select the table from which additional data will be loaded "on the spot" from the **Data Table** drop-down list. In our case it is, as before, the demonstration table STOCKS. After that, the structure of the table with the added **Express Object** column will appear in the **Database Map** window.

6. Using the drop-down lists located in each row of the **Express Object** column, set the required correspondence between DB Express objects and the columns of the STOCKS table. The data_variable item corresponds to a variable defined by the formula.

7. To display the dialog box (Fig. 4.17) again, click the **OK** button. In the **Equation** group of the given dialog, an automatically generated code of the formula will appear.

8. Click the **Define** button.

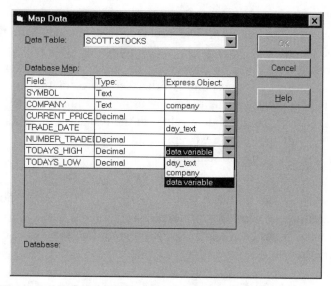

Fig. 4.18. The dialog box that allows you to define the connection between Express DB objects and a relational database

To provide for correct performance of the created formula of the client application, you must connect to the required relational data source before you use it. Programming here is a must. You have to create two procedures. The first one will provide connection with the ODBC data source. Its code in many respects is the same as the fragment described above. In our case, the difference is that when connecting to a relational Oracle DB, it is necessary to define the user login and password. The following code is an example of such a program:

```
PUSHLEVEL 'SETUP'              " saving the option
PUSH SQLMESSAGES               "in stack and set mode to
SQLMESSAGES = YES              "display SQL messages
ODBC.SOURCE = 'ORACLE7'        "name of ODBC data source
"connection with the server
SQL CONNECT 'SCOTT' IDENTIFIED BY 'TIGER'
"Definition of the format to convert date into text
DATEFORMAT='<DD>-<MTXT>-<YY>'
POPLEVEL 'SETUP'               "option restoring
RETURN
```

To correctly terminate the operation of the client application with a formula, you have to detach the source: SQL DISCONNECT. Also, you should keep in mind that all of the dimension values by which we define our formula are to be set before using it, for example, by importing values from a database.

It is necessary to mention a problem that the developer has to face when he or she uses this version of the software. The problem is connected with the incorrect functioning of the undocumented XP_SQLGEN function with such fields as DATE. Settling this problem is done by converting the date's text representation in the Express product so that it corresponds to the text representation for the date defined for the Oracle database client, and by using an additional DAY_TEXT dimension such as *text*, which contains date values in the text form by which the formula is defined. A view of the date's text representation in the Oracle 7 client can be gotten in SQL Plus by using the sentence:

```
SELECT TO_DATE ('31.01.97', 'DD-MM-YY') FROM DUAL
```

In our case it looks like this: 31-JAN-97. To correspond to it, a line of code, setting the necessary format of conversion (DATEFORMAT = ' < DD > - < MTXT > - < YY > ') has been added to the program that makes the connection to the Oracle database.

4.5.3. Exporting Data from Express to Excel

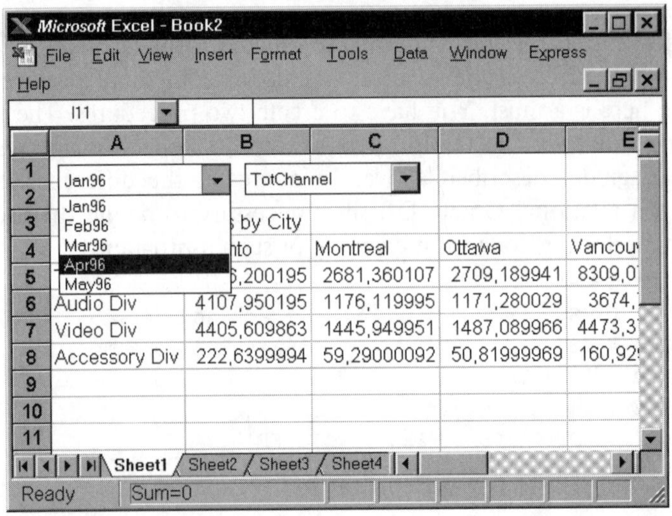

Fig. 4.19. Fragment of a multidimensional data view exported from the Express DB in Excel

If this component was installed when the Express product was installed, the folder X:/ORAWIN95/OLAP/XSA230 will contain a file for adding to Excel—Xpaddin.xll. To install the given addition, do the following:

❐ Open the Excel application.

❐ Open the Add-Ins dialog box by selecting the **Tools\Add-Ins** item from the main menu.

❐ Using the standard dialog box that will be opened after you click the **Browse** button, select the Xpaddin.xll file. After that, the Express Wizard item will be added to the list of accessible additions.

❐ Click the **OK** button. If Express SpreadSheet Add-In (32 bit) was successfully installed, the Express Wizard item will appear in the Excel main menu, and additional items for displaying help information on Express Wizard will appear in the Help menu.

❐ To open the dialog box that allows you to set the export of multidimensional data from Express DB, select the **Express\Run Express Wizard** menu item.

❐ Using the **Attach Database** button, attach the demo Express DB from the xademo.db file.

❐ Select the Sales by City measure from the **Choose Measures** list and add it to the right list by clicking the **Add > >** button.

❐ To open next dialog box, click the **Next >** button.

❐ Drag the dimensions of our variable, and using the data selector, set the multi-dimensional variable view in the Excel table.

❐ To open next dialog box click the **Next >** button.

❐ Define the Excel page cell in which the upper right corner of the multidimensional data view will be placed, and click the **Finish** button.

Fig. 4.19 shows a fragment of the Excel data view exported from Express DB. Look at the two drop-down lists located in the left corner of the page. Selection of the hypercube slice of interest to us—the one that contains sales data by city—is accessed using these lists. Thus, we have access to all information related to the multidimensional measure **Sales by City**, and not just to one slice, as we saw in the previous example.

Moreover, if we set Express Wizard options in the appropriate manner, we shall have access to Express DB not only for reading, but also for writing, and any data changes effected in Excel will be displayed adequately in the Express DB.

These examples of solving problems related to importing and exporting information in Oracle Express describe only the most common methods, and obviously do not cover all of the possibilities.

4.6. An Example of Simple Database Creation

In the first part of this book we looked at the problems of designing, creating, and modifying multidimensional databases that had to do with database administration functions. The majority of examples we used related to the simplest FIRST.DB database. Certainly, for all examples, the demonstration databases included in the standard package, for example DEMO.DB, could be used. Later, we will actively use the FIRST.DB database when discussing the creation of presentations with Express Analyzer and applications with Express Objects.

In this chapter, we consider step by step the process of creating a FIRST.DB database. First of all, this will help us to improve our multidimensional database administration skills, and second, it will allow the interested reader to repeat examples described in this and subsequent parts of the book.

4.6.1. Step 1—Creating a New Database

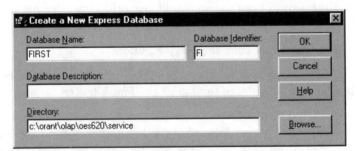

Fig. 4.20. The **Create a New Express Database** dialog box

To create new database, you have to run Express Administrator and connect Express server with the help of the standard dialog displayed either when the application starts or when we call it with the **File/Connect to Express** menu item. After the server connection is made, call the dialog box for creating a new database using the **File/New** menu item (Fig. 4.20). The FIRST database (the FIRST.DB file) will be created in the standard directory C:\orant\olap\oes620\service, which is located on the computer functioning as the OLAP server.

4.6.2. Step 2—Dimension Definition

All the examples discussed above were devoted to three-dimensional business spaces with the Time, Goods, and Locale dimensions.

Let's define the Goods text dimension. To do so, call the dialog box using the **Dictionary/Define/Dimension** menu item. Input product in the **Name** field as the dimension name, and select **Text** from the **Data Type** list as the type of our dimension values. Cancel the **Install** option in the **Options** section (an additional service provided for the given dimension). Let's now go to the second page of our **Labels** dialog (Fig. 4.21). Set the object description and long and short labels for naming the given dimension in client applications. Click the **Define** button.

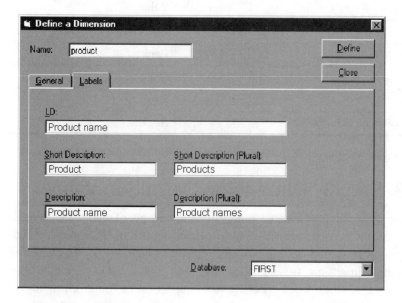

Fig. 4.21. Defining the description for the PRODUCT dimension

The second dimension we shall define is the dimension named MONTH, with the MONTH type defining the time coordinate for our business space. As opposed to the

PRODUCT dimension, let's leave the **Install** option selected. Now set the following descriptions for the MONTH dimension:

Field	Name
LD:	Sales period
Short Description:	Month
Short Description (Plural):	Months
Description:	Month
Description (Plural):	Months

Finally, let's define the last dimension, which we shall name REGION, and set the Text type for it. As our hypothetical business is carried out in different cities of two countries (Russia and the USA), let's include the **Hierarchical** option in the **Options** field, which will allow us to define hierarchy relations for the values of our dimension. Set the following descriptions for the REGION dimension:

Field	Value
LD:	Sales Region
Short Description:	Region
Short Description (Plural):	Regions
Description:	Region
Description (Plural):	Regions

To close the dimension definition dialog, click **Define**, and then the **Close** button.

4.6.3. Step 3—Dimension Definition Values

All value sets related to created dimensions are empty. To start defining the values related to the PRODUCT dimension, just select it from the database browser list and open the dialog for dimension editing (Fig. 4.22). To call the dialog for adding dimension values, click the **Add** button. Let's enter three values: Ford, Cadillac, and Dodge, clicking the **Add** button of the given dialog after each input.

Note that, in general, the Express language is not sensitive to the case in which data are set, and therefore when defining value dimensions both capital and lower case letters can be used.

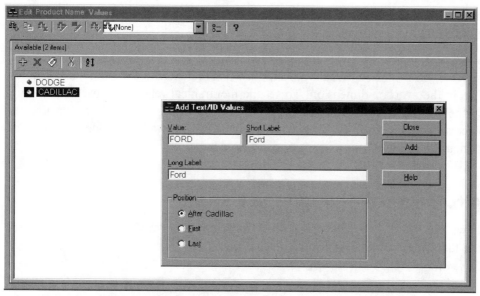

Fig. 4.22. Additing the PRODUCT dimension value

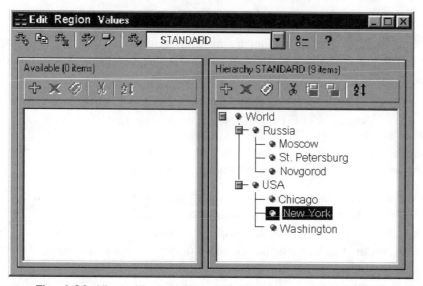

Fig. 4.23. Hierarchical relation setting for the REGION dimension

The dialog for setting the Month definition values looks somewhat different. You needn't introduce each month value, just set the first month, which in our case is 01.98, and the number of time periods to be added to the first value, in our case 23. Thus we shall define the Month dimension values for the time period from 01.98 to 12.99, inclusive.

Let's now define the text dimension values for REGION: World, Russia, USA, Moscow, St.Petersburg, Novgorod, New York, Washington, and Chicago, just like in the PRODUCT dimension. To set the hierarchical relations between the values of the given dimension, fill in the **Parent** column in the value editor, selecting the necessary values from the drop-down list that contains all the values of the given dimension (Fig. 4.23).

4.6.4. Step 4—Language Usage

If we execute the REPORT MONTH command from Express Command, we shall see the following list of values for the given dimension:

```
MONTH
----------------------------------------------------------------------------------
JAN98
FEB98
...
DEC99
```

To change a date view to another language, just redefine the MONTHNAMES option using the following command, replacing the English names of the month shown here with their equivalents in the chosen language

```
MONTHNAMES =
'January\February\March\April\May\June\July\August\September\October\
November\December
```

Remember that the command should be placed in one row. Now, when we repeat the REPORT MONTH command, we shall see the view in the new language.

However if we close and then open again Express Administrator, we shall see the previous English names of the months. This happens because of the fact that MONTHNAMES option is stored in the Express service database, and its changes are valid only within the limits of the current connection with the server. To receive the desired result of the month names in another language, we shall create a simple SET_MNAME program in our database, which will consist of one string specifying the new value for the MONTHNAMES option. Then, using **File/Setup** menu item, we should call the **Database Setup** dialog box and click the **Properties** button. Then set in the **Post-Attach Program** parameter the name of our program, i.e. SET_MNAME. Now each time the client application (Express Analyzer or Express

Objects) opens our FIRST.DB database, this program will be executed and we shall see the names of the months in a language other than English. Pay attention to the fact that this property of our database does not spread to the Express Administrator, and therefore if we wish to see the names of months in our second language when working with it, we should execute the SET_MNAME program using Express Command.

We may not to be satisfied with the text view of the date shown above. To change it, we can use the special command VNF:

```
CONSIDER MONTH
VNF <MTXT>.<YY>г
```

and receive a view closer to German grammar:

```
MONTH
------------------------------------------------------------------------------------
Jan.98

Feb.98

...

Dez.99
```

The VNF command defines the text view template for such values as DATE for a specified dimension, and can be fulfilled only once.

The short and long labels, which we see in the tables and graphs of client applications, correspond to each dimension value. In view of the fact that the **Install** option was set during definition, two additional formula objects—M1.LONGLABELF and M1.SHORTLABELF—as well as two additional measures indexed by the MONTH dimension—M1.LONGLABEL and M1.SORTLABEL—were automatically created for the MONTH dimension. Note that if we want these objects to be visible in the database browser list, it is necessary to call the **View/All Objects** menu item. The M1.SHORTLABELF formula is defined by the following automatically generated Express language expression:

```
NAFILL (M1.SHORTLABEL MONTH)
```

which means that if the M1.SHORTLABEL value is not defined, the value of the text representation for the appropriate month will be returned. For example, if we were to execute the REPORT M1.SHORTLABELF command, we would receive:

```
MONTH       M1.SHORTLABELF
-------     --------
Jan.98      Jan.98
Feb.98      Feb.98
...
Dez.99      Dez.99
```

In most cases, a similar short date view in client applications will satisfy us. The formula for the long label M1.LONGLABELF value is set in a like manner

    NAFILL (M1.LONGLABEL M1.SHORTLABELF)

which will provide the same result as the short label.

If you want to have something else as long label value, simply edit the formula. For example:

    NAFILL (M1.LONGLABEL CONVERT (MONTH TEXT '<MTEXT> <YYYY>'))

Now, if we use the commands:

    COLWIDTH=24

    REPORT M1.LONGLABELF

then the returned formula values will be the following:

```
MONTH        M1.LONGLABELF
--------     -------------
Jan.98       Januar 1998
Feb.98       Februar 1998
...
Dez.99       Dezember 1999
```

The appropriate values will be used in client application tables and graphs.

4.6.5. Step 5—Creating Measures

Let's define two main measures for our business: PRICE as DECIMAL and SALES as INTEGER. Let's assume that the given measures vary depending on good, time, and region. Therefore, when defining measures, we shall index them by the MONTH, PRODUCT, and REGION dimensions. Define the given measures by setting the following descriptions for PRICE:

Field	Value
LD:	Price for an item
Short Description:	Price
Description:	Unit price

For SALES:

Field	Value
LD:	Number of items sold
Short Description:	Sales
Description:	Number of Sales

The multidimensional cubes we created will have uncertain NA values in thir cells. To avoid manual input of measure values, we shall fill multidimensional cube cells using a command sequence that will be executed in Express Command:

```
LIMIT MONTH TO FIRST 18
LIMIT REGION       TO LAST 6
LIMIT PRODUCT TO ALL
PRICE (PRODUCT 1) = 4000.0*(1.0 - 0.05*CONVERT(MONTH DECIMAL) + -
0.25*RANDOM)
PRICE (PRODUCT 2) = 6000.0*(1.0 + 0.35*RANDOM)
PRICE (PRODUCT 3) = 5000.0*(1.0 + 0.05*CONVERT(MONTH DECIMAL) + -
0.25*RANDOM)
SALES (PRODUCT 1) = INTPART(40.0*(1.0 - 0.05*CONVERT(MONTH DECIMAL) + -
0.25*RANDOM + 0.01*CONVERT(REGION DECIMAL)))
SALES (PRODUCT 2) = INTPART(60.0*(1.0 + 0.25*RANDOM))
SALES (PRODUCT 3) = INTPART(80.0*(1.0 + 0.05*CONVERT(MONTH DECIMAL) + -
0.25*RANDOM - 0.05*CONVERT(REGION DECIMAL)))
LIMIT REGION TO ALL
ROLLUP SALES OVER REGION
```

Remember that the space and minus character combination at the end of a line indicates prolongation of the line. The given command sequence simulates (probably not very intelligently, but in a neutral enough way) the dynamics of our business for the first 1.5 years, depending on time and geography. Pay attention to the fact that the ROLLUP command is fulfilled only for the SALES measure, since adding the price of the goods (PRICE measure) by locale is not relevant.

4.6.6. Step 6—Creating Formulae

Suppose our hypothetical analysts are interested not only in price changes and the amount of sales, but also in sales income changes which depend on the first two measures. Let's create the formula PROFIT of the DECIMAL type, which will charac-terize sales income, depending on area, goods, and time. Set its descriptions as the following:

Field	Value
LD:	Sales income
Short Description:	Income
Description:	Sales income

At the lowermost level of the hierarchical dimension, REGION (the city level), sales income will be defined by the simple formula: PROFIT = SALES * PRICE. Remem-ber that for higher levels of goods, prices are not defined, and therefore the un-certain value NA is the result of the given formula at the whole world and country levels. To calculate income from sales on the country level, we should summarize the incomes of all cities of the country. Therefore, we define the PROFIT formula as follows:

```
NAFILL (PRICE*SALES CALC_PROFIT(REGION))
```

The standard NAFILL function returns the value of the first argument if it is de-fined; otherwise, it returns the value of second argument. In this case, the function call we are to create is set as the second argument. For the current region dimen-sion value the given function defines all its derived values and summarizes their incomes.

The LIMIT command can not be used in a program for formula calculation, since when performing iteration on the REGION dimension values its status cannot be changed. To solve this problem, we can use the TEMPSTAT command; however, it is a bit more difficult to demonstrate the peculiarities of the LIMIT function. The LIMIT function, as opposed to the command of the same name, does not change the dimension status, but returns an appropriate list of its values. Let's create the CALC_PROFIT program in the database, which will return the DECIMAL value. Type the following text of the program into the editor:

```
ARG REG          REGION
VRB SUM          DECIMAL
VRB CHILDRENS    TEXT
VRB I            INTEGER
VRB IMAX         INTEGER
PUSH RECURSIVE
"Allow recursive  RECURSIVE=YES
```

```
I=1
SUM = 0
"We obtain a list of all child values for REG for the REGION —
"dimension
CHILDREN = LIMIT(REGION TO CHILDREN USING R1.PARENT REG)
"Number of child values"
IMAX = NUMLINES(CHILDREN)
WHILE (I LE IMAX)
DO
SUM = SUM + PROFIT(REGION EXTLINES(CHILDREN I 1))
I = I+1
DOEND
POP RECURSIVE
RETURN SUM
```

The EXTLINES function used in the program allows us to extract one or more values from the list according to the defined I index.

You need to pay special attention to the recursive used. We can not simply multiply the appropriate values of the SALES and PRICE measures as in the formula itself, since when calculating worldwide incomes we have to use a SALES measure value for the country, which, as we have already stated, is not defined. The standard value of the RECURSIVE option is NO, and therefore before executing a recursive call of the PROFIT formula, we should permit it.

4.6.7. Step 7—Defining Prognostic Models

As was mentioned above, there are three types of standard models for time series forecast in the Express language: linear trend, exponential trend and forecast, which takes into account seasonal variations. Let's use a simple exponential trend model. For this purpose, we shall create a program to predict measure values for 6 months ahead using the 18 previous months. We shall give the measure name (SALES, PRICE, or PROFIT) to the program as a parameter. We'll now create the FCT_RESULT measure of a DECIMAL type, in which we shall save the results of the forecast. Then we index the given measure by the MONTH, PRODUCT, and REGION dimensions. Since we don't need to store the measure values in a file, select the **Temporary** option from the **Storage** section of the measure definition dialog. If we look at the **Advanced** page of the objects inspector (the **Window/Inspector** menu item), we see that the given object does not occupy any disk space. Thus our prediction program will look like this:

```
ARG VAR TEXT
PUSH MONTH PRODUCT REGION
LIMIT PRODUCT TO ALL
LIMIT REGION TO ALL
LIMIT MONTH TO ALL
FCT_RESULT = NA
LIMIT MONTH TO FIRST 18
LIMIT REGION TO &VAR NE NA IFNONE END
FOR REGION PRODUCT
FORECAST LENGTH 6 METHOD EXPONENTIAL -
TIME MONTH FCNAME FCT_RESULT &VAR
POP MONTH PRODUCT REGION
END:
RETURN
```

Since the FORECAST command only predicts a time series for the first values of the dimensions included to the status, a loop for all REGION and PRODUCT dimension values is used to make a forecast for all goods and locales in the program.

To see the results of the FCT program execution, call the following set of commands in Express Command:

```
CALL FCT('SALES')
LIMIT REGION TO 'USA'
LIMIT PRODUCT TO 'Dodge'
LIMIT MONTH TO LAST 12
REPORT FCT_RESULT
```

and we receive the forecast of a decrease in sales for Dodge cars in the USA by the end of the year:

```
REGION: USA
---------------------------FCT_RESULT----------------------------
----------------------------MONTH--------------------------------
PRODUCT      jul.99  aug.99  sep.99  oct.99  nov.99  dec.99
----------   ------  ------  ------  ------  ------  ------
Dodge         33.32   30.57   28.05   25.74   23.61   21.66
```

Chapter 5

Creating Summary Reports
(Oracle Discoverer)

5.1. Product Description

5.1.1. Primary Goals

Relational databases were designed in order to provide high efficiency transaction processing, which is more characteristic for data capturing tasks than for analytical ones. This does not mean, however, that relational databases were not used for solving analytical tasks such as estimating manufacturing costs or list prices, or selecting the most profitable vendor(s). As a matter of fact, relational databases can be used for solving analytical problems. However, when solving such tasks using relational databases, the user will face both procedural and technological problems, which can hardly be solved using standard reporting tools:

- First of all, relational database design is based on ER modeling (Entity/Relationship modeling). Generally, an ER model is a complex schema with a cryptic structure of tables and views. In fact, most times it is very complex and confusing for business analysts who need to examine the data as a limited set of values essential to their decision-making process.

- Secondly, the data used in analysis are generally distributed across different databases. In order to include the data in reports, it is necessary to group this data within a single integrated data source or, alternatively, use specialized tools for providing connectivity with different databases.

- Finally, the process of solving analytical tasks using standard reporting tools is extremely time-consuming. This is due to the fact that these tools are not oriented towards such tasks. This, of course, is not a satisfactory solution from the end user's point of view.

It is therefore advisable to solve such problems using a powerful and flexible specialized reporting tool such as Oracle Discoverer.

Oracle Discoverer is intended for creating analytical reports and summaries. It provides business analysts with a set of functional capabilities allowing them to easily find answers to various analytical requests.

5.1.2. Product Architecture

Oracle Discoverer comprises two main components (Fig. 5.1).

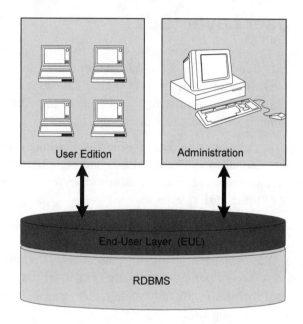

Fig. 5.1. Oracle Discoverer Architecture

Oracle Discoverer User Edition—a data access tool that allows analysts in various departments of the company to design reports and analyze relational data. Oracle Discoverer User Edition provides an easy-to-use wizard interface for creating and managing *ad hoc* queries and viewing the results of those queries. It provides data analysis capabilities, including full drill down, rotate, and slice. Oracle User Edition allows you to process reports in batch mode, present data in the form of graphs and diagrams, and much more.

This product is integrated with metadata (known as End-User Layer, EUL) intended for describing and preparing data for analysis. Thanks to the EUL, end users working with Oracle Discoverer User Edition view the data in the business terms of their respective fields of activities and therefore don't need to understand the actual design of the database.

Oracle Discoverer Administration Edition—this is a tool to create EUL metadata, which encapsulates the entire data architecture (no matter how complex it may be) and presents the data in the generally accepted terms of the appropriate field of activity.

5.1.3. End-User Layer (EUL)

End-User layer is a set of database objects, which, in turn, are user-created descriptions of the field of activity. The EUL insulates end users from the complexity of database object relationships that exist in actual databases used in analytical queries, and provides multidimensional representation of the data based on terms that end users are familiar with and easily understand.

When creating reports and analyzing data, business professionals formulate queries using these multidimensional model terms. EUL interprets user queries into SQL commands, which are then executed at the database server. A special application then gets the results of these SQL queries.

EUL is established for the database user, who in Oracle Discoverer terminology is known as the EUL owner. By default, only the EUL owner can access his or her metadata. However, the owner can grant other users access permissions to his or her EUL. You modify access permissions to the End-User Layer using the Administration Edition Privileges utility. Alternately, you can select the appropriate installation type when installing EUL.

> **NOTE**
>
> A database user can own only one End-User Layer. If you already have an EUL and attempt to create another one, Oracle Discoverer displays a message informing you that you need to delete an existing EUL. If you click **OK** in this message box, Oracle Discoverer deletes the existing EUL.

EUL Installation Types

Oracle Discoverer provides two options for EUL installation.

Public—if you create an EUL using this option, any database user will have permission to view and edit objects within the end-user repository without having access rights to that repository. This installation type is recommended for use at the first stages of designing the metadata layer.

Private—this installation type allows users to view and edit objects only after the repository administrator grants them the appropriate permissions.

The private installation type is appropriate for the following cases:

❐ When a newly created business area undergoes testing

❐ When a business area contains confidential data intended for a limited audience

❐ When the application under development is maintained and supported by the same department for which it was created

NOTE

Oracle Discoverer provides the capability of creating several repositories for a single database. In this case, access to each instance of a public repository is defined using the Administration Edition Privileges utility.

Creating the End-User Layer

Before you start creating the EUL for the database user, make sure that the user in whose schema you are going to create the EUL has the following database system privileges.

In the Oracle database:

❐ Create Session

❐ Create Table

❐ Create View

❐ Create Sequence

❐ Create Procedure

❐ Create User

❐ Grant Any Privilege

NOTE

To get the above listed privileges, contact the database administrator.

If the user already owns the schema in this database, you'll need to perform the following operations in order to create the End-User Layer:

1. Establish connection to the database server.

2. After establishing the database connection, select the EUL Manager command from the **Tools** menu.

3. Start the Create EUL Wizard (Fig. 5.3) by clicking the **Create an EUL** button in the **EUL Manager** window (Fig 5.2).

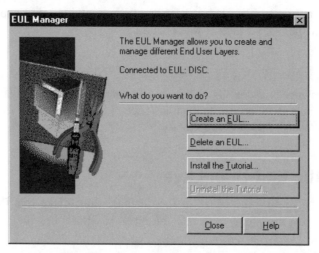

Fig. 5.2. The **EUL Manager** window

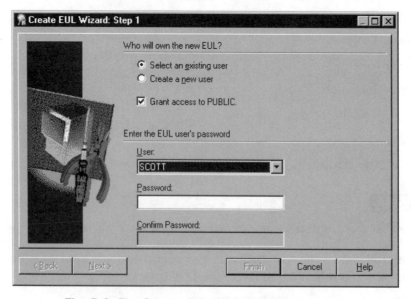

Fig. 5.3. The **Create EUL Wizard: Step 1** window

4. The next window of the Create EUL Wizard will appear. Set the **Select an existing user** radio button in the **Who will own the new EUL?** option group.

5. Depending on the selected installation type, set or clear the **Grant access to Public** checkbox.

6. In the **Enter the EUL user's password** option group, select the required username and specify the password.

7. Click **Finish** to continue.

When creating the metadata layer for the new user, you should do the following:

1. Connect to the database server.

2. After establishing the database connection, select the **EUL Manager** command from the **Tools** menu.

3. The EUL Manager window will appear (see Fig. 5.2). Click the **Create an EUL** button to start the Create EUL Wizard (see Fig. 5.3).

4. The **Create EUL Wizard Step 1** window will appear. Select the **Create new user** option in the **Who will own the new EUL?** option group.

5. Depending on the selected installation type, set or clear the **Grant access to Public** checkbox.

6. Go to the **Enter the EUL user's password** option group and specify the user name and password; then click Next.

7. The next window of the Create EUL wizard will appear (Fig. 5.4). In this window you'll need to define the names of the default and temporary tablespaces for the new user.

8. To continue, click **Finish**.

NOTE

This type of EUL installation is only applicable for Oracle databases, and can be created on behalf of a user having database administrator permissions. To create an EUL for other databases, you'll need to create database users before installing EUL into their schema.

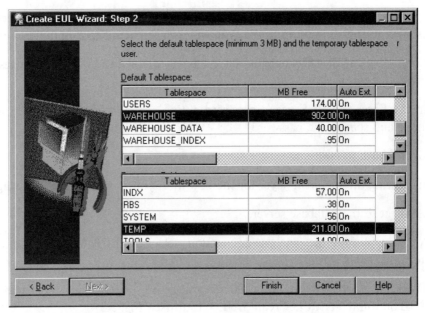

Fig. 5.4. The **Create EUL Wizard: Step 2** window

5.2. Creating the Metadata Layer (Oracle Discoverer Administrator Edition)

5.2.1. Setting up Connection to the Server

To start Oracle Discoverer Administration Edition, double-click the appropriate icon in the Oracle Discoverer 3.1 program group.

The application will then display a prompt, and you'll then need to click the **Start** button to continue. The dialog for setting up the connection to **Oracle Discoverer Administration Edition** (Fig. 5.5) will then appear. Here you'll need to enter the following information:

❑ **Username**—login name of the database user

❑ **Password**—password for that user

❑ **Connect**—in this field you'll need to specify the data source. If you are connecting to the Oracle database server, specify the SQL*Net connection string in this field; otherwise specify ODBC:<*data source name*>

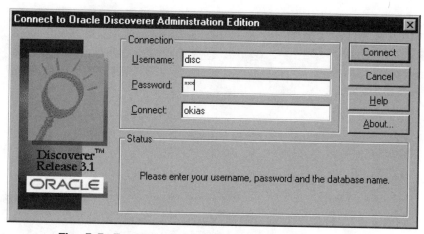

Fig. 5.5. Establishing connection to the database server

5.2.2. Work Area and Tools

Work Area

After establishing a connection to the server, the Oracle Discoverer Administration Edition main window, also known as the *work area,* will appear (Fig. 5.6). The work area is intended for viewing and editing main or auxiliary objects of the End-User Layer. It also contains a set of tools allowing you to manage these objects. Main objects of the work area are organized in the form of a hierarchical tree of *business areas* containing *folders.* Each folder, in turn, can contain various data description objects, such as data items, joins, and conditions. All objects within the work area are represented by icons.

The work area is divided into the following four pages:

❒ **Data**—this page is intended for editing basic End-User Layer objects and data items

❒ **Hierarchies**—this page is intended for editing hierarchies of EUL elements

❒ **Item Classes**—enables the user to edit data class elements of the EUL

❒ **Summaries**—this page allows the user to edit summary folders of the EUL

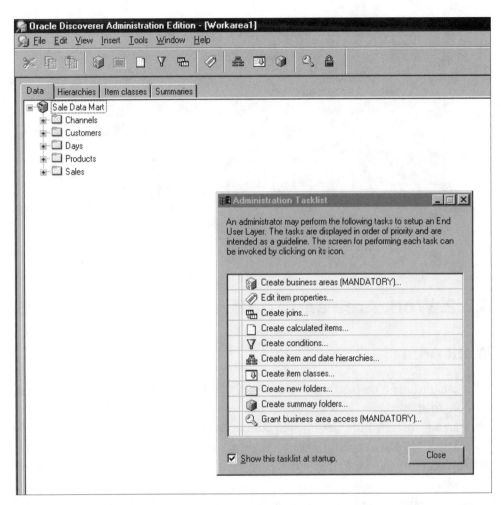

Fig. 5.6. Main window of the Oracle Discoverer Administration Edition

The Administration Tasklist

Oracle Discoverer provides special control intended to simplify the process of creating and editing basic objects—Administration Tasklist (Fig. 5.7). The **Administration Tasklist** window lists all basic procedures of creating and editing End-User Layer objects.

To start a wizard for creating or editing an object associated with the icon in the Administration Tasklist, simply double-click the appropriate icon in the list.

To open or close the **Administration Tasklist** window, select the **Tasklist** command from the **View** menu.

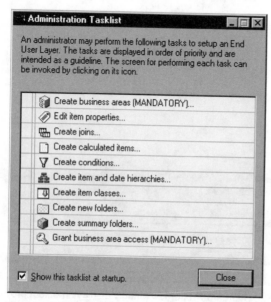

Fig. 5.7. The **Administration Tasklist** window

The Standard Properties Window

The **Properties** window, which provides custom setup capabilities for any object (Fig. 5.8), can be opened by selecting the **Properties** command from the right-click menu of the appropriate object. Or you could open this window by double clicking on the icon of the object to be edited.

This window has the following two tabs:

❏ **General**—this tab provides the list of object attributes

❏ **Dependents**—provides the list of objects that reference the selected object

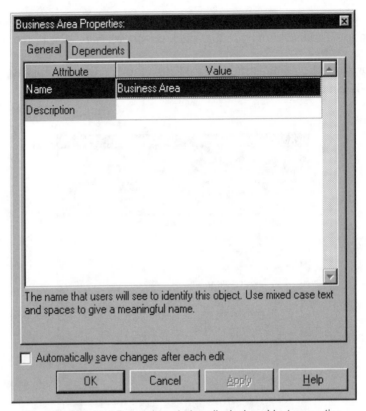

Fig. 5.8. Standard Properties window displaying object properties

5.2.3. Creating Objects

Business Area

Business area is the basic concept in Oracle Discoverer. Each business area is a group of Oracle Discoverer objects (folders, dimensions, hierarchies, variables, etc.) that apply to a specific type of task or problem to be solved by a specific group of users. From this point of view, the business area is very much like the concept of a *data mart* in data warehousing methodology. For example, when implementing the Decision Support System (DSS) of a large company, it is advisable to create several subject-oriented data marts in order to provide discretionary control over access permissions granted to different user groups.

The business area is aimed at solving the following tasks:

❏ Providing a systematic approach to user views

❏ Insulating analytical system end users from the complexities of database implementation

❏ Differentiating user access permissions to various forms of analytical information representation

When designing a business area, it is necessary to have a clear understanding of the fact that we are manipulating user views over the database objects rather than the database objects themselves. This provides us with a certain freedom of choice when designing a business area. It also allows us to satisfy various user requirements and make data representation more suitable for representing business processes. For example, instead of creating a complex set of object identifiers usual in database designing, we can identify business area objects by concepts easily understandable to the users. We also can create various joins and unions of data stored in different databases. The database tables will be displayed as folders in the business area. Notice that the business area can contain folders from a single as well as from several heterogeneous databases. Relationships between database tables will be displayed as special Oracle Discoverer objects, such as relationships, hierarchies, calculations, and conditions.

Before you start creating the business area, it is necessary to determine its basic properties as well as its goals. Thus, before you proceed any further, it is recommended that you do the following:

❏ Identify user requirements and the goals for the new business area.

❏ Identify the data sources that can be used for creating the business area.

❏ Identify database tables and views that will be used for creating the new business area.

❏ Identify the approximate number and contents of the required folders, as well as the necessary joins between these folders. For example, the Employees folder can be included into both the Sales business area and the Human Resources business area.

❏ Identify user rights and access privileges for the new business area.

❏ Identify ways of changing your business area in case you need to introduce modifications into the data area over which this business area is built.

To create a new business area, you can use the appropriate Wizard.

The business area creation wizard (Load wizard) solves the following tasks:

❏ Creates a name and description for the business area

❏ Loads metadata into the business area

❏ Automatically creates joins between business area folders, which are based on the existing joins between database tables

❏ Automatically creates lists of values for data items

The Load wizard starts every time you establish connection to the database server.

You can also start this wizard using the following methods:

❏ By selecting the appropriate menu item from the Administration tasklist

❏ By selecting the following menu commands **Insert** —> **Business Area** —> **From Database**

❏ By right-clicking the **Data** tab and selecting the appropriate item from the context menu

Step 1. Identifying the Data Source

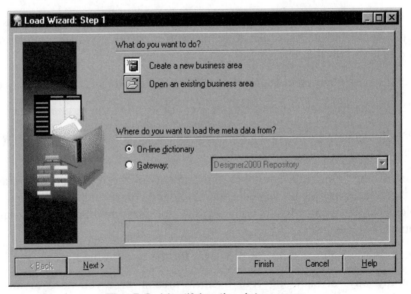

Fig. 5.9. Identifying the data source

At first the Load wizard prompts you to specify data sources from which to load metadata (Fig. 5.9). Besides this, we can not only create a new business area, but also open an existing one. To do so, select the **Open an existing business area** option in the **What do you want to do?** option group.

To create a new business area, proceed as follows:

☐ In the **What do you want to do?** option group, set the **Create a new business area** option.

☐ Next, go to the **Where do you want to load the meta data from?** option group and specify the data source type. This option group allows you to select one of the following options: **On-line dictionary** or **Gateway**. If you select the **On-line dictionary** option, the wizard will load metadata from the current database dictionary. If you set the **Gateway** option instead, the wizard will load metadata from the registered gateway. This option is only available when there is an Oracle Designer repository or registered gateway on the database server.

Depending on the option selected from this group, Oracle Discoverer implements different methods of creating new business areas.

Method 1. Creating a business area based on the on-line dictionary

When you choose to create a business area based on an on-line dictionary, the wizard will create it using schema objects of the current user and (optionally) schema objects belonging to other users. To implement this method you need to select the **Create a new business area** option and specify the **On-line dictionary** option as a source for data import.

Method 2. Creating a business area based on the EUL Gateway mechanism

When you choose this method, a business area is created based on metadata from other object systems. The EUL Gateway can also be used for accessing:

☐ Data warehouses

☐ Packages for retrieving, converting, and transferring data

☐ Systems for converting queries, such as Business Objects

The standard edition of Oracle Discoverer is supplied with the following gateways:

☐ Oracle Applications Data Warehouse Gateway

☐ Business Objects Universe Gateway

To implement this method, you need to set the **Create a new business area** option, specify the **Gateway** option as a source of data import, and then select the appropriate gateway from the drop-down list.

Method 3. Creating a new business area based on the Oracle Designer repository

The main advantage of using Oracle Designer metadata is the fact that the data is loaded from the business-modeling system. Therefore, you won't need to describe the existing objects.

To implement this method, you need to set the **Create a new business area** option, specify the **Gateway** option as a source of data import, and then select the Oracle Designer repository from the list of available gateways.

> **NOTE**
>
> If Oracle Designer is not installed on the database server, or if the schema owner is not registered as an Oracle Designer user, you won't be able to load metadata from Oracle designer. You can check this fact by calling the database information from the administrative menu. If the schema owner is not a registered Oracle Designer user, then Oracle Discoverer will issue the message: "Designer/2000 is unavailable". To get access to Oracle Designer, start the Oracle Designer Administration Utility and add the schema owner to the list of Oracle Designer users. Don't forget to grant that user write privilege.

Step 2. Selecting Schemas to Be Loaded

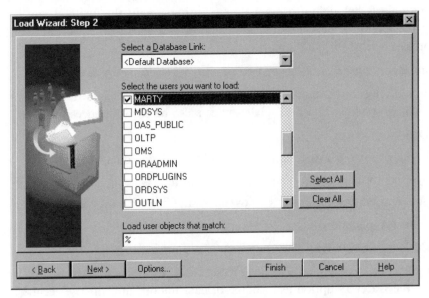

Fig. 5.10. Selecting the owners of the schemas to be loaded

For this step (Fig. 5.10) we need to specify the owners whose metadata will be loaded into the new business area. To perform this task, proceed as follows:

❏ Select the data source name from the **Select a Database Link** list

❏ Select one or more users from the **Select the users you want to load** list

The **Load user objects that match** field allows you to limit the list of displayed users. The default value (%) means that the **Select the users you want to load** list will display all users. To limit this list, you can use one of the following options briefly described below:

❏ *A%*—this limits the list of displayed users to user names starting with the letter A.

❏ *%ES*—this limits the list of displayed users to user names ending with the letter combination ES.

❏ Combination of _ _ _—this limits the list of displayed owners to users whose names have three arbitrary letters.

At this step we can also define the type (tables or views) of the objects that will be available for loading. To do so, click the **Options** button to open the **On-Line Dictionary Options** dialog (Fig. 5.11).

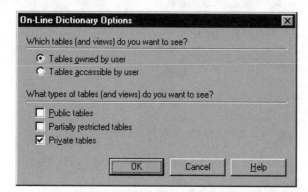

Fig. 5.11. The **On-Line Dictionary Options** dialog

Radio buttons in the **What tables (and views) do you want to see?** option group allow you to define which objects can be loaded into the business area.

The **Tables owned by user** radio button sets an option which allows you to load only the schema objects owned by the selected user.

If you set the **Tables accessible by user** radio button, you'll be able to load all schema objects available for the selected user, including objects from schemas owned by other users to which the current user has at least read access.

The checkboxes in the **What type tables (and views) do you want to see?** option group allow us to specify the type of the objects to be loaded into the business area.

❑ If you set the **Public tables** checkbox, the wizard will load schema objects from the schema owned by the current user, which are also available to the PUBLIC schema.

❑ If you set the **Partially restricted tables** option, the wizard will load schema objects from the schema owned by the current user, which are also available to a limited number of other users. This limited list of other users includes users who have been explicitly granted access to the objects owned by the current user.

❑ If you set the **Private tables** checkbox, the wizard will load the objects available to the current user only. This means that objects available to other users will not be loaded

Step 3. Selecting Schema Objects

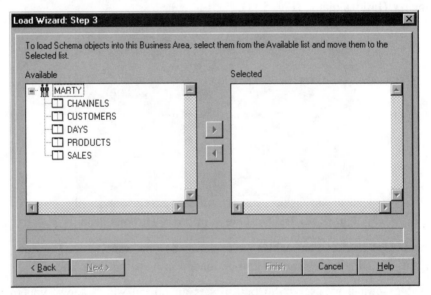

Fig. 5.12. Selecting schema objects

When performing the third step (Fig. 5.12), you need to browse the list of objects grouped by schema owners and select only the objects that need to be loaded into the business area.

The **Available** field contains a hierarchical list of schema objects available for loading into the business area. As you can see, the list is grouped by schema owner names.

The **Selected** field contains the list of objects selected for loading into the business area.

To move an object from the **Available** field to the list of selected objects in the **Selected** field, use the **Include/Exclude** buttons, or simply drag the selected object with the mouse.

Step 4. Specifying Options for Creating the Business Area

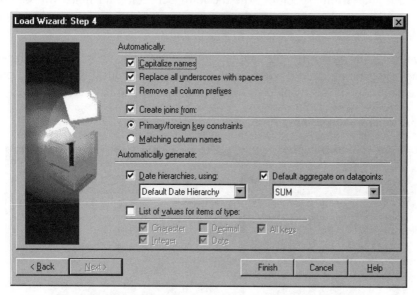

Fig. 5.13. Specifying the options for creating the business area

This step of the Load wizard (Fig. 5.13) allows you to define which data items are to be created automatically and which aren't (Fig. 5.13). At this step we are able to specify the following options:

❐ Which database columns are to be converted to data items

❐ How joins are created between data items

❐ How data item hierarchies are generated

❐ How data aggregation (drill-up) is performed

❑   Which data items must create value lists

The options available in this step are described below:

❑   **Capitalize names**—this option specifies the display format of the item labels (lower- or upper-case letters)

❑   **Replace all underscores with spaces**—specifies whether or not all underscore characters must be replaced by spaces

❑   **Remove all column prefixes**—specifies whether or not all column prefixes should be removed

❑   **Create joins from**—specifies how the joins between data items will be created (according to the primary or foreign key constraints, or by matching column names in the tables)

❑   **Automatically generate**—this option group allows you to specify the hierarchy and aggregate function used by default. The options from this group also provide the capability of specifying data item types that need to have lists of values

Step 5. Naming the Business Area

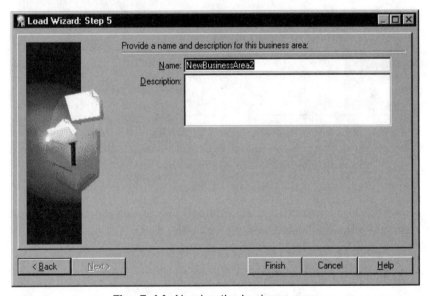

Fig. 5.14. Naming the business area

When performing this step, which is the last step of the Load Wizard (Fig. 5.14), we need to specify a name and description for the newly created business area.

Bear in mind that the name must be unique, otherwise Oracle Discoverer will display an error message and won't create the business area.

After creating the business area, you can activate the **Properties** window to edit the properties of this business area. To do so, double-click the icon of the appropriate business area. The **General** tab of the **Properties** window contains the following fields:

Table 5.1. Fields Available on the General Tab of the Properties Window

Name	Contains the unique identifier of the business area. The contents of this field are displayed in the **Oracle User Edition** dialog, allowing you to select business areas. The business area name must be unique within the End-User Layer
Description	Contains a description of the selected business area. The contents of this field are displayed on the description line of the User Edition's Query Wizard

Folders as Standard Units for Viewing User Data

Having created a new business area, you can proceed with creating main units for viewing user data, known as *folders*. Each folder is a set of data items containing information on a specific entity. From this point of view, the concept of folder is very similar to the concept of table or view in relational database theory. Actually, the folder represents the SQL query stored in the End-User Layer and executed any time the user opens that folder.

The folder represents a method of describing data. It can be related to one or more business areas. In Oracle Discoverer, there are four types of folders, which differ in their functions and aims:

Simple folders. Simple folders represent sets of attributes precisely matching a specified database table or view. Oracle Discoverer provides a special wizard for creating simple folders, which performs steps similar to steps 2 to 5 of the Load wizard used for creating a new business area. To start this wizard, select the **New Folder From Database** command from the business area right-click menu or, alternately, select the **Insert —> Folder —> From Database** commands from the Oracle Discoverer Administration Edition main menu.

Custom folders. Custom folders represent sets of SQL query attributes created by the business area developer. Notice that the set of attributes will precisely match the set of attributes in the SQL query.

Most times, you can manage custom folders the same way as you do simple folders, because their behavior is essentially the same. However, you need to bear in mind the following exceptions:

❐ Custom folders are refreshed when validating existing SQL queries, while simple folders are refreshed when validating the business area.

❐ Data items generated in the custom folder have no **Item Formula** property, which is for editing the item formula.

❐ Properties for custom folders don't include information on the database, schema owner, or table name. However, they do have a property containing the custom SQL statement.

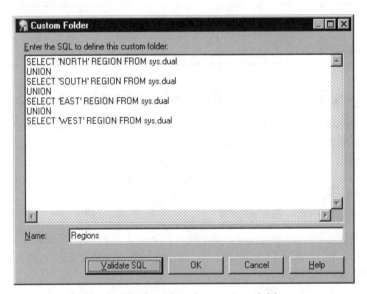

Fig. 5.15. Creating the custom folder

To create the custom folder, proceed as follows:

1. Select the **Custom** command from the **Insert —> Folder** menu.

2. The **Custom Folder** dialog will open (Fig. 5.15). Go to the **Enter the SQL to define this custom folder** field and enter a correct SQL query (see *Oracle SQL Reference Guide* for description of Oracle SQL syntax). The specified SQL query must contain the SELECT statement (i.e., it must be a query for reading data from the database). This query can contain any operators, qualifiers, and functions supported by Oracle server, as well as optimizer hints.

3.　Go to the **Name** field and specify a name for the new folder.

4.　Click the **Validate SQL** button to validate the syntax of the SQL query just entered.

5.　Click **OK** to save your changes.

Complex folders. Complex folders represent sets of data items from one or more folders. Complex folders provide a convenient way of simplifying the business logic of the application being developed. For example, to join two entities, such as **Departments** and **Employees,** we can create a complex folder named **Departments—Employees** containing data items from both folders. This will enable users to select data by department and employee from a single folder rather than from two separate folders.

Notice that data items contained in complex folders are inherited from other folders rather than copied from them. This means that the properties of complex folders change when modifications are introduced to the properties of the folders from which the complex folder inherits its properties.

To create a complex folder, it is sufficient to create a new empty folder, specify a unique name for that folder, and drag the data from another folder to it.

"Orphan" folders. "Orphan" folders are ones that exist in the EUL but are not used in the business area. Such folders are not available in Oracle Discoverer User Edition.

You can correct the folder properties any time after the folder has been created. To open a window allowing you to edit the folder's properties, double-click it with the mouse. The **General** tab of the **Properties** window contains the following fields:

Table 5.2. General Properties of Complex Folders

Name	Contains the unique identifier of the folder. The contents of this field are displayed in the folder selection dialog of the Oracle User Edition. The folder name must be unique within the End-User Layer. You can't have two folders with the same name, even if these folders belong to different business areas
Description	Contains the folder description. The contents of this field are displayed on the description line of the User Edition's Query Wizard
Visible to user	Specifies whether the content of this folder is visible to users. You can use this property to hide objects that must be kept from the end user but still need to be included into the business area because of joins or calculations. Folders invisible to the end-user are displayed in gray
Database	Specifies the name of the data source

continues

Table 5.2 Continued

Owner	Specifies the database object owner name
Object	Specifies the object name
Optimizer hints	Specifies the optimizer hint
Custom SQL	Contains the SQL query used to create the folder

Main Items of Data Description

In contrast to other OLAP products, Oracle Discoverer doesn't use the concepts of dimension and variable. More precisely, these concepts are joined by another, more general concept—the *data item*. From Oracle Discoverer's point of view, the same data item can be defined both by dimension and by variable. Certainly, this approach is different from the generally accepted one, but it also provides several advantages when managing data.

Physically, the data item is simply an attribute of the table, view, or database synonym.

Item Classes

For the sake of convenience, we can classify items. An item class represents a grouping of items of the same type. Item classes can be useful when you need items belonging to different folders to share the same attributes. For this purpose, we need to create the item class and specify the reference to this class in the Item Class property of the data items.

Oracle Discoverer has the following three item classes:

❏ *List of Values*—item class intended for selection of specified values from a list.

❏ *Alternative Sorts*—item class intended for sorting data items using the order specified by another data item. Alternative order enables users to sort item values practically in any order. For example, we can display the values for regions such as "South", "East", "West", and "North", or "East", "North", "South", and "West", or vice versa. Alternative sorts require no additional user input. Actually, the end user may even be unaware of the existence of alternative sorts.

❏ *Drill to Detail links*—item class that allows you to drill down or up for data items belonging to the current class.

Creating Item Classes

To create a new item class, do the following:

1. Go to the **Item Class** tab in the Oracle Discoverer Administration Edition work area.

2. Select the **Item Class** command from the **Insert** menu.

3. The **New Class Wizard. Step 1** window will appear (Fig. 5.16). Select the type for the class you are going to create and click **Next**.

4. At the second step of this wizard, depending on the selected type of item class, you need to select either a data item from which list of items will be created (**List of Values**, **Alternative Sort**), or data items that will use the current class (**Drill to Detail**), and then click **Next** to continue.

5. At the third step, depending on the selected item class, it is necessary to select either data items that will use this class (**List of Values**, **Alternative Sort**) and then click **Next**, or provide the name and description for the item class to be created (**Drill to Detail**) and click **Finish**.

6. The final step of the Item Class Wizard requires that you enter the name and description for the newly created item class and then click **Finish**.

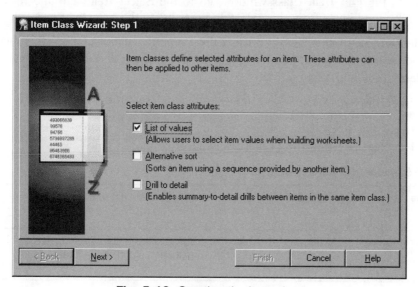

Fig. 5.16. Creating the item class

Adding Items to the Class

We can use one of the following methods for adding items to the class:

1. The first method is based on adding items to the class using the Drag and Drop method. To implement this method, do the following:

   1) Open a new work area window using the **New Window** command from the **Window** menu.

   2) In the new window, go to the **Item Classes** tab and select the class to which you are going to add new items.

   3) Return to the first window, go to the **Data** tab, and position the cursor over the item to be added. Select one or more items that you are going to add to the item class and drag them to the **Item Classes** tab of the second work area window.

2. The second method does this operation using the **Edit Item Class window**. To use this method, proceed as follows:

   1) Go to the **Item Classes** tab and select the required item class with the mouse.

   2) To open the **Edit Item Class** window, select the **Edit Item Class** command from the right-click menu or choose the Edit command from the Edit item in the main menu.

   3) In the **Edit Item Class** window, go to the **Select Items** tab and move the required items from the **Available items** list to the **Selected items** list.

3. The third method is based on using the **Properties** dialog. To use this method, open the Properties window of the item to be added and edit the value in the **Item Class** field as appropriate.

Item Properties

To activate the **Properties** window for an item, simply double-click that item's icon. The **General** tab of the **Properties** window contains the following fields:

Table 5.3. General Item Properfies

Name	Contains the unique identifier (Unique ID) of the item
Description	Contains the description string of the folder. The content of this field is displayed in the description string of the Create Query Wizard

continues

Table 5.3 Continued

Data type	Contains information on the data type. This property is not editable, since its value is inherited from the metadata dictionary of the database server
Formula	Contains a reference to the database column of an object or to the data item
Database column	Contains the names of the schema owner, table, and column. If this field is blank, it means the column was created from a formula. *Note*: this property is intended for tracking the status of the data source field. For example, if changes are introduced to the main database or data dictionary, this field will store information on the initial data source
Visible to user	This field can take one of two values: Yes or No. If this field is set to the Yes value, the current item will be available for use in queries. If the value in this field is No, the current item is hidden from end users. Normally, hidden items are used for internal calculations or in order to hide confidential information from end users
Item class	This property is active for items defined as a dimension and hidden for the items defined as a variable. The value of this property defines the class to which the current item belongs
Date Hierarchy	Contains the list of date hierarchies that can be added to the current item. This property becomes inactive if the item has a data type other than Date
Default position	Default location for displaying the item in reports
Default aggregate	Specifies the type of the function that will be used as the default aggregate function for items declared as variables
Sequence	Specifies the order in which the items will be displayed in the User Edition Query Wizard
Heading	Specifies the heading for the item when used in a summary
Format mask	Specifies the default data format. You can get more detailed information on data formats in the *SQL Language Reference* document
Alignment	Specifies the alignment type to be used in summaries
Word wrap	Specifies whether the word wrap feature will be used for the item
Case storage	Only used with text data types. Specifies the text display in summaries, independent of the method of storing that text
Display case	Specifies the case for the displayed text

continues

Table 5.3 Continued

Default width	Specifies the default width of the text field in summaries
Show NULL as	Specifies how to display NULL values
Content type	Specifies the drill-down type of the external application. The FILE value means that drill-down output will be redirected to the external file (Microsoft Excel file, for example). The Blob value means that the current item is a large binary object containing multimedia data (such as sound or video). The drill-down process in this case will display multimedia data within the summary body. If the value of this field is set to None, there will be no external drill-down for the current item
Max char fetched	Specifies the maximum number of characters for the current item that will be retrieved from the database

Additional Elements of Data Description

Joins

When analyzing data or generating a summary, it is often necessary to use data from different folders. To make this possible, you need to connect the folders with a join. A join represents an Oracle Discoverer object intended for defining relationships between data folders. The concept of a join is similar to the concept of a relationship in relational database theory, which relates database tables using common columns.

Like the concept in relational database theory, a join between folders means that the row from the *master* folder contains one or more rows from the *detail* folder. The join may have the "one-to-many" or "one-to-one" type. Oracle Discoverer does not support a "many-to-many" relationship, which, consequently, must be transformed to multiple "one-to-many" relationships.

When creating joins between folders, make sure that you have correctly defined the join. Notice that incorrectly defined joins may lead to incorrect query results or significant performance degradation.

To create a new join, proceed as follows:

1. From the **Insert** menu, select the **Join** command.

2. The **New Join** window will appear. Select the folder that will be the master folder of the newly created join, then click **OK**.

3. In the next window (Fig. 5.17), specify the data item of the master folder in the **Master Folder** field. Then go to the **Operator** field and specify the operator defining relationship between two folders. Next, go to the **Detail Folder** field and specify the name of the detail folder of the join. Enter the name of the relationship into the **Name** field, and a description of the relationship into the **Description** field.

4. Having finished with the operations described above, click **OK**.

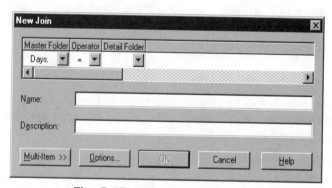

Fig. 5.17. The **New Join** window

To specify additional options for the join, click the **Options** button. The **Join Options** window will open (Fig. 5.18), allowing you to specify the join type and set the options for including NULL values for foreign keys.

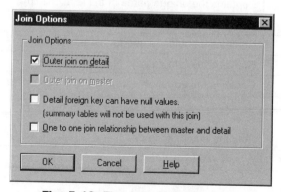

Fig. 5.18. The **Join Options** dialog

If you set the **Outer join on detail** option, the query will return all the records (rows) that satisfy the join condition and all the rows from the master folder.

If you set the **Outer join on master** option, the query will return all the rows satisfying the join condition and all the rows from the detail folder.

If you specify the **Detail foreign key can have null values** option, records from the detail folder may contain undefined (NULL) values. Note that a situation where foreign keys of the table contain NULL values is quite rare in relational databases. In most cases this means that the database contains incorrect data. Because of this, we recommend that you use this option with care.

If the **One to one join relationship between master and detail** option is set, then a "one-to-one" relationship between master and detail folders will be used instead of a "one-to-many" relationship.

> **NOTE**
>
> Joins between folders may be created automatically, based on relationships between respective database objects. The Load Wizard will do this if you specify the appropriate option when creating the folder.

To create joins with a multi-item key, click the **Multi-Item** button in the **New Join** window and define the join conditions. Remember that all items from the left part of the join condition must belong to the same folder. The same applies to items in the right part of the join condition.

A brief description of join properties is provided below.

Table 5.4. Join Properties

Name	Contains the unique name of the relationship
Description	Contains a text description of the relationship
Master	Contains the folder name for the master item
Detail	Contains the folder name of the detail item
Formula	Contains the equation specifying the relationship between the two folders
Join Relationship	Specifies the join type
Outer join on	Sets the outer join to on
Detail item values	Allows you to include NULL values

Hierarchies

Hierarchies are an integral part of practically any analysis. When performing analysis of financial information, you will often you need to get aggregate data for the current month, quarter, year, or for a certain group of customers or goods.

In Oracle Discoverer, a hierarchy of items represents a logical linking created for defining relationships between general and more detailed data, such as: "Year to Quarter", "Quarter to Month", or "Month to Day".

You can create hierarchies based on elements contained within the same folder, as well as on elements belonging to several folders. Note that to create a hierarchy based on items contained in different folders, you need to connect these folders with joins.

Oracle Discoverer provides the following two types of hierarchies: *item hierarchy* and *date hierarchy*.

An item hierarchy joins several items in a specific order, which allows you to drill down in different hierarchical levels when creating a summary. For example, we can join several items, such as country, region, and retail stores into a geographical hierarchy. In this model, each item at the higher level of the hierarchy is a superset of the items at a lower level. When generating a summary, we can easily move up or down these hierarchical levels.

The specific feature of the date hierarchy, which distinguishes it from the item hierarchy, is the fact that it can only be created for items of the date or time data type. It is intended to simplify the process of creating hierarchies over these data types (Fig. 5.19).

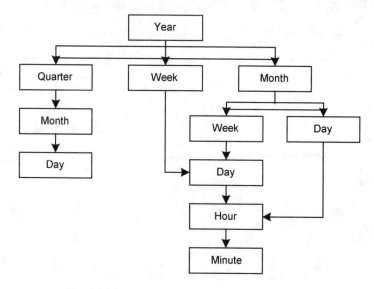

Fig. 5.19. An example of the Date hierarchy

The default template of the date hierarchy is applied to the database columns of the date or time data type whenever such an object is loaded to the End-User Layer, provided that you have set the appropriate option in Load Wizard. When we create a new date hierarchy, Discoverer automatically creates the corresponding template. A Load Wizard option allows us to select the default template or redefine an arbitrary date hierarchy.

To create an item hierarchy for items of any type, proceed as follows:

☐ From the **Insert** menu select the **Hierarchy** command.

☐ The **Hierarchy Wizard: Step 1** window will appear. Specify the type of hierarchy you are going to create and click **Next**.

☐ The **Hierarchy Wizard: Step 2** window will appear (Fig. 5.20). In this window you need to specify the positions of the entries within the hierarchy by adding items from the left pane of the window to the list in the right pane one by one. Having accomplished this task, click **Next**.

☐ In the **Hierarchy Wizard: Step 3** window you will be prompted to name the newly created hierarchy and provide it with a description. To complete the procedure, click **Finish**.

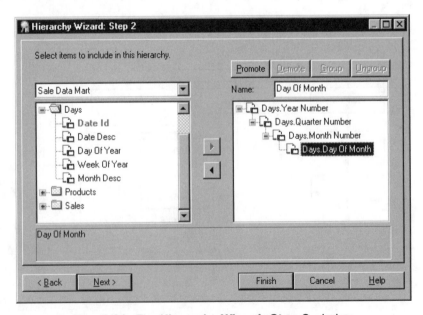

Fig. 5.20. The **Hierarchy Wizard: Step 2** window

Conditions

The aim of the *condition* object is to limit the set of records returned by the query. Conditions represent criteria stored in the database and used for selective filtering of data returned by the query. For example, if we need to display data related only to a single branch of the company within our summary, we'll need to create a condition containing an equation, and activate that condition when executing the query. Queries can be useful when it is necessary to restrict information provided to the end user or make the query faster. Oracle Discoverer allows you to create any number of conditions for one data item. However, you need to make sure that such conditions are consistent, because inconsistent conditions may lead to incorrect query results.

As queries are executed at the database server, conditions are represented by the WHERE clause in the SELECT statement. There may be static conditions containing a limited set of values, as well as subqueries containing an unlimited set of values. Conditions can also contain various comparison operators supported by the database server, such as <, >, IN, NOT IN, LIKE, BETWEEN, etc.

Oracle Discoverer supports two types of conditions:

☐ A *mandatory condition* is applied automatically any time the user selects a specific item from the folder. The system doesn't warn the user and doesn't display the mandatory conditions it applies, and therefore the user can't turn them off or otherwise interfere with such conditions. For example, you can associate mandatory conditions with company affiliations, thus providing them access to information within their area of competence.

☐ An *optional condition* is applied according to user requirements. Users of the Oracle Discoverer User Edition can see the condition formula, but can't edit it.

Comparison of these two types of conditions is provided in the table presented below.

Table 5.5. Comparison of Mandafory and Optional Conditions

Mandatory conditions	Optional conditions
Always influence the query results in a folder	Applied to the query results when selected
Are used as mandatory conditions when executing queries	Applied optionally
Are invisible in Oracle Discoverer User Edition	Visible (but not editable) in Oracle Discoverer User Edition

continues

Table 5.5 Continued

Mandatory conditions	Optional conditions
When created in complex folders, can relate only to items from source folders	When created in complex folders, can relate only to items from a complex folder
When added, changed, or deleted, influence the dependent objects	When added, changed, or deleted, don't influence the dependent objects

To create a new condition, proceed as follows:

1. Select the **Condition** command from the **Insert** menu.

2. The **New Condition** window will appear (Fig. 5.21). Select the folder or item to which this condition should be applied, and click **OK.**

3. The next dialog will appear, where you'll be prompted to specify the condition type in the **Type** field, the item to which the condition is applied in the **Item** field, the comparison operator in the **Condition** field, and data set values in the **Values** field. Next, you'll need to provide a name for the newly created condition in the **Name** field and a description string for the condition in the **Description** field.

4. Having defined all the fields, click **OK.**

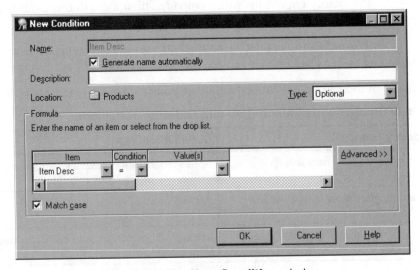

Fig. 5.21. The **New Condition** window

NOTE

To create complex conditions combining several simple ones, click the **Advanced** button in the **New Condition** window and sequentially define each condition.

The list of condition object properties is provided below.

Table 5.6. Condition Object Properties

Name	Contains the unique name of the condition
Description	Contains a text description for the condition
Type	Specifies the condition type which can take one of the following two values: `Mandatory` or `Optional`
Sequence	Specifies the order or the position in which this item appears when designing the query in Oracle Discoverer User Edition
Formula	Contains the formula that specifies the condition

Formulae

Oracle Discoverer provides a special object for defining formulae and other calculations. This special object is known as a *Calculated Item*. The calculated item represents that item for which the Formula property is a user-defined formula rather than a reference to a database column. The function can be one of the standard functions supported by the database server or any registered user function. Like any other item, calculated items can be used within conditions, joins, and other calculated data items.

Oracle Discoverer provides three types of formulae, which differ from one another by their purpose:

❐ Derived Items

❐ Aggregate Calculation

❐ Aggregate Derived Items

Derived Items

Derived items are expressions that contain no aggregate functions, for example: SALARY= CONSTANT PART + 0.1*COMPANY PROFIT. Derived items are static, which means that their values depend only on the values of the data items used in their definitions and don't depend on the conditions or result set (number of rows returned by the query).

Aggregate Calculation

Aggregate calculations represent a formula containing an aggregate function, for example: TAX=SUM(SALARY)*0.13. Aggregate calculations are dynamic, since their values depend not only on the values of the data items used, but also on the conditions and the result set. For example, in order to calculate the margin on all company divisions, it is necessary to use the SUM(Profit)/SUM(Sales) formula rather than the SUM(Profit/Sales) formula. Notice that if you use the latter formula, Oracle Discoverer will produce incorrect results, because it will first calculate the Profit/Sales value for each row satisfying the query, and only then will it produce an aggregate value (which will be incorrect).

Notice the following restrictions that you should observe when using aggregate calculations:

☐ They can be represented only as data points

☐ They cannot be used in joins

☐ They cannot be used in mandatory conditions

☐ They cannot be used in hierarchies

☐ They cannot belong to the item class

☐ They cannot be items of a complex folder

☐ They cannot be used in further aggregation functions.

Aggregate Derived Items

Aggregate derived items are calculations created in a complex folder that contains items from one or more folders. Aggregate derived calculations are similar to ordinary derived items with the exception that they can contain aggregate functions and influence the result set.

NOTE

Sometimes, using formulae can result in significant performance degradation of the application, since data processing is more time-consuming than data selection. Because of this, we recommend that you pay special attention to the process of creating formulae.

To create a new calculated item or formula, proceed as follows:

1. Select the **Item** command from the **Insert** menu.

2. The **New Item** window will appear (Fig. 5.22). Select the folder that will contain the new item and click **OK.**

3. The **Edit Calculation** window will appear. Enter the name for the new calculated item in the **Name** field, then go to the **Calculation** field and provide the function to perform the calculation using the operator buttons directly below this field. Click **OK.**

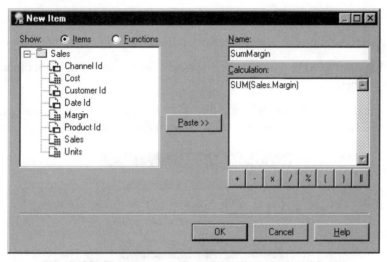

Fig. 5.22. The process of creating the calculated items

Using External Functions in Calculated Items

In the course of analytical data processing the situations often arise where the task of data processing can't be completed using only the built-in procedures and functions. Product flexibility is determined by the capability of using external libraries of procedures and functions for data processing.

Oracle Discoverer provides a mechanism for using external functions that allows us to use PL/SQL functions for solving tasks of different levels of complexity. To make an external function available in Oracle Discoverer, it is necessary to register this function in the End-User Layer. After the function has been registered, it appears in the *database functions list* in the **Edit Calculation** window (see "*Formulae*" in *Section 5.2.3*) and can be used when defining calculated items.

Oracle Discoverer supports two methods of registering external functions:

1. *Manual registration* assumes that all the actions necessary to register an external function will be performed by the application developer.

2. *Import* assumes that all the actions related to the process of external function registration will be performed by a special import procedure. This method

is preferable to manual registration, since the import procedure automatically registers all the required information, including all names, links to other databases, return data type, and list of function arguments. Import guarantees that this information will be loaded correctly.

To register external functions using the import procedure, do the following:

1. From the **Tools** menu, select the **Register PL/SQL Function** command.

2. The **Import PL/SQL Function** window will open. Go to the **Functions** tab and click **Import.**

3. The next window containing the list of PL/SQL functions will open (Fig. 5.23). Select the function to be imported and click **OK.**

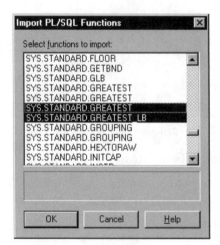

Fig. 5.23. The list of PL/SQL functions

To register an external function(s) manually, proceed as follows:

1. Select the **Register PL/SQL Function** command from the **Tools** menu.

2. The **PL/SQL Function** will open (Fig. 5.24). Go to the **Functions** tab, click the **New** button and define the required attributes of the external function manually.

3. If the external function takes arguments, then go to the **Arguments** tab and sequentially define all the required arguments.

4. Having accomplished all the required actions, go to the **Functions** tab and click **Validate**. If the system displays a message informing you that the opera-

tion was completed successfully, you can consider the registration process over; otherwise you'll need to locate and correct the error.

5.   Having completed the above-described procedure, click **OK.**

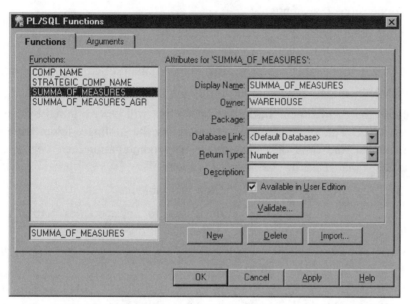

Fig. 5.24. The **Functions** tab of the **PL/SQL Functions** window

Summary Folders and Data Aggregation Procedures

Summary folders are database objects (tables and Materialized Views) of the End-User Layer that contain aggregate data along with the results of frequently executed queries normally requiring quite a long time for execution.

Once calculated, they subsequently allow for significant improvement of the Oracle Discovery analytical applications, since executing queries over the result set is significantly faster than executing the same query to the database itself.

In order to design an efficient summary folder, you'll need to do the following:

1.   Investigate user queries, group them by type (or by frequency of use), and identify for each query type a set of combinations within the summary folder.

While designing a summary folder, it is recommended that you observe the following rules:

- ❏ For the most frequently executed queries, it is advisable to create combinations containing a few (no more than three or four) items declared as dimensions (axis items)
- ❏ For other queries, it is recommended that you create combinations that contain no more than 5-7 dimensions
- ❏ For "unpredictable" queries, provide a combination containing all items
- ❏ Include all data points in all of the Summary Combinations

2. Identify the approximate amount of space that will be consumed by the Summary folder. The amount of space required by the summary folder depends on the number and time of the used summary combinations, as well as on the data items that make up that summary folder.

3. Define the refresh properties of the summary folders.

4. Make sure that summary redirection is used for most queries. Summary redirection is a process of automatic redirection of queries to summary folders instead of original detail data. Summary redirection is used only when the following requirements have been met:

- ❏ Data items and joins used in the query exist in the single summary combination or can be joined to a summary table using foreign keys existing in the summary combination
- ❏ The **Available for queries** property of the summary folder is set to **Yes**
- ❏ The time of the last refresh of the summary folder is less than the value specified in the *Query governor* options
- ❏ The user who runs the query has SELECT access to the summary table

5. Use an SQL Plus application to create procedures for collecting and analyzing statistics of the summary table.

Before creating a new summary folder, make sure that the following requirements have been met:

- ❏ The database where the End-User Layer is installed must support PL/SQL
- ❏ The DBMS_JOB package must be installed on the database server
- ❏ Database users must have the following privileges:
  - ❏ Create Table
  - ❏ Create View

❑ Create Procedure

❑ Create Materialized View (for Oracle 8.1.6 or later)

❑ Global Query Rewrite (for Oracle 8.1.6 or later)

To create a new summary folder, we can use the Summary Wizard. To start this wizard, select **Insert —> Summary** commands from the menu, or start it from the Administration tasklist.

Step 1. Selecting the Method of Creation

For the first step, the Summary Wizard prompts you to choose the method of creating the summary folder (Fig. 5.25). You'll need to select one of the following three options from the **How do you want to create this summary folder?** group:

❑ **From items in the End User Layer**—when this option is set, the summary folder will be created based on the items in the business area folders

❑ **Using query performance statistics**—if you set this option, the summary folder will be created based on query statistics

❑ **Registering an external summary table**—if you select this option, the summary folder will be created on the basis of an existing table

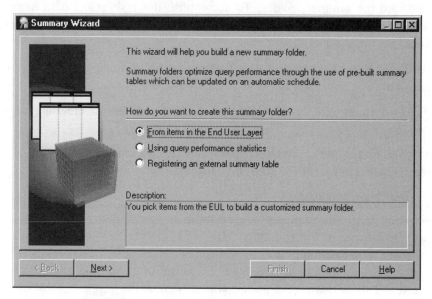

Fig. 5.25. The **Summary Wizard** window, Step 1

Step 2. Selecting Data Items

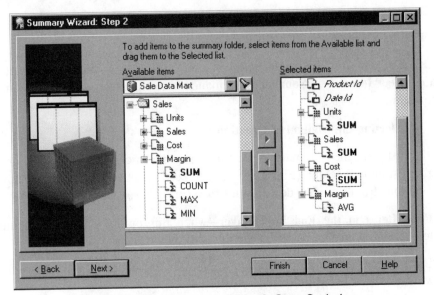

Fig. 5.26. The **Summary Wizard: Step 2** window

When performing step 2 (Fig. 5.26), you'll need to select data items that will be included into the summary folder. To accomplish this task, select data items that you need to process in the summary folder from the list of available items grouped by folders.

The **Available Items** field represents a hierarchical list of folders or items available for selection.

The **Selected Items** field contains the list of items selected for creating the summary folder.

To move an item from the **Available Items** field to the **Selected Items** field, use the **Include/Exclude** buttons or the standard Drag and Drop mechanism.

Step 3. Defining Combinations

For the third step, the Summary Wizard prompts you to define the combinations that will be present in the summary folder (Fig. 5.27). To accomplish this step, click the **Add Combination** button to add a new combination, then select the data items that will be present in the new combination by setting the appropriate checkboxes. This window also allows you to define the properties of summary tables. To calculate the space for the summary folder, click the **Estimate Space** button. By clicking **Storage Properties**, you can specify the parameters for the summary folder. Appropriate settings for these parameters can significantly improve application performance.

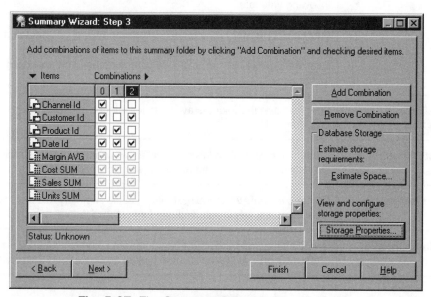

Fig. 5.27. The **Summary Wizard: Step 3** window

Step 4. Specifying the properties of the summary folder

In this step, the Summary Wizard allows you to define the refresh mechanism for the summary folder (Fig. 5.28) and provide a name for the new folder. Specify the creation date and time of creation of the summary folder in the fields of the **When do you want to build this summary folder?** group, then go to the **How often do you want to repeat this refresh?** group, and specify the time period after which the summary data will be refreshed. Having accomplished this, go to **Name** and enter the name for the new summary folder.

Summary folder properties are listed below.

Table 5.7. Summary Folder Properties

Name	Contains the unique identifier of the folder. The content of this field is displayed in the folder selection dialog of Oracle User Edition. The folder name must be unique within the End-User layer
Description	Contains the folder description

continues

Table 5.7 Continued

Type	Specifies the type of the summary folder. This attribute takes the following values: **Managed summary**—the folder was created based on data items **External summary**—the folder was created based on an external table
Available for Queries	Specifies that the folder is available for queries in Oracle Discoverer User Edition
Last Refresh	Contains the date when this summary folder was last refreshed. This property is only available for managed summary folders
Next Refresh	Contains the date when the next refresh of the summary folder will take place. This property is only available for managed summary folders
Refresh Interval	Specifies how often the summary folder must be refreshed. This property is only available for managed summary folders

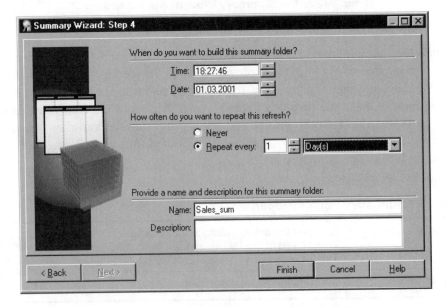

Fig. 5.28. The **Summary Wizard: Step 4** window

Additional Data Administration Utilities: Object Manager, Security Manager, Privilege Manager

Oracle Discoverer implements protection of objects from unauthorized access by granting users access privileges for performing actions over business area objects. Access rights and privileges define whether or not the information is available for user requests in Oracle Discoverer User Edition.

By default, the EUL schema owner is the system administrator who has all access rights to all objects. All the other users of the database server have no access rights to the objects. To grant other users access and privileges, Oracle Discoverer provides two utilities: Security Manager and Access privileges administrator

Security Manager

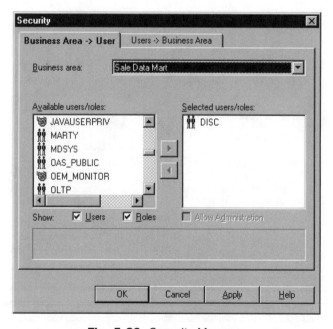

Fig. 5.29. Security Manager

This utility (Fig. 5.29) can be started by selecting **Tools —> Security** from the administrative menu. It allows the application administrator to grant users or roles access privileges for viewing and querying the business area in User Edition. Note the following rules:

☐ Only the business area owner can change or edit objects within that business area

☐ Oracle Discoverer doesn't allow granting access to a separate object within a business area

☐ Access rights in the database have priority over access rights in the End-User Layer

Access Control and Privileges

This utility (Fig. 5.30) can be started by selecting the **Tools —> Privileges** commands from the menu. This tool allows you to grant users privileges for performing specific operations and functions over the business area and its related objects. The first two tabs, **Privileges** and **User/Role**, allow us to manage user privileges in privileges or user slices, respectively. Depending on the selected tab, we add either privileges for users or a user to be granted a specific privilege.

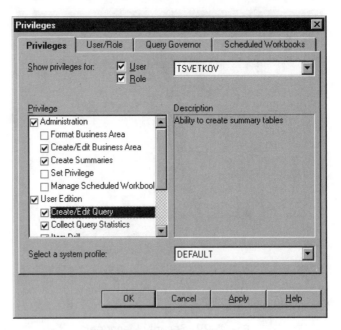

Fig. 5.30. Privileges Manager

The third tab of the **Privileges** window, **Query Governor**, allows you to set restrictions to queries executed by end users. Restrictions can be set both for users and roles.

To set a restriction, proceed as follows:

❏ Go to the **Show query limit for** option group and specify the user and/or role for whom the restriction will be set.

❏ In the **Query Governor** option group we can set the following restrictions:

   ❏ **Warn user if predicted time exceeds**: this option specifies the time limit for query retrieval. When this time limit has been exceeded, the system will warn end users.

   ❏ **Prevent queries from running longer than**: if the query runs longer than the time interval specified by this option, the system stops that query.

   ❏ **Limit retrieved data to**: specifies the maximum number of rows that can be returned by the query.

The privileges existing in Oracle Discoverer are listed below.

Table 5.8. Oracle Discoverer Privileges

Administration	This privilege allows the user to start Administration Edition. Administrative functions of the users depend on the privileges granted to users. If a user has no privileges at all, that user is able to perform only a limited set of functions, such as registration of PL/SQL functions
Format Business Area	This privilege allows the user to format the business area and the objects it contains
Create/Edit Business Area	This privilege allows the user to create and edit a new business area and any objects it may contain
Create Summaries	This privilege allows the user to start Summary Wizard. The user must also have the Resource privilege on the database server
Set Privilege	This privilege allows the user to manage privileges. By granting users this privilege, you provide them full access to Oracle Administration Edition. The user who has been granted this privilege can grant any privileges to other users. Although Oracle Discoverer allows you to grant administrative permissions to several users, it is strongly recommended that you have only one administrator for each business area
Manage Scheduled Workbooks	This privilege allows the user to start and manage scheduled workbooks
User Edition	This privilege allows the user to start User Edition and create reports
Create/Edit Query	This privilege allows the user to create and edit queries. Without this privilege users can only run pre-calculated summaries and can't create their own custom summaries

continues

Table 5.8 Continued

Collect Query Statistics	This privilege allows the user to collect query statistics by running Query Statistics
Item Drill	This is the privilege for using Drill up/Drill down operations
Drill Out	This privilege allows the user to start other applications from User Edition. By default, it is granted to all users
Grant Workbook	This privilege allows users to distribute stored workbooks
Schedule Workbooks	This privilege provides the capability of creating and editing the processing schedule for user workbooks
Save Workbooks to Database	This privilege allows for saving workbooks in the database

5.2.4. The EUL Gateway Mechanism

Aims of the EUL Gateway Mechanism

The issue of standardizing metadata is one of the most important problems in designing Decision Support Systems and Data Warehouses. Currently, each database vendor develops proprietary standards for metadata format. This, of course, results in problems when integrating different data sources within a single data warehouse.

EUL Gateway represents a mechanism intended for importing metadata from other data sources into Oracle Discoverer data repository. The availability of this mechanism simplifies the process of designing Decision Support Systems and reduces investment, since the EUL Gateway mechanism assumes that metadata from other data sources will be copied into the Oracle Discoverer repository. Therefore, we needn't worry about creating and loading this metadata.

EUL Gateway Architecture

Physically, EUL Gateway is a set of database tables and views that fulfil the role of a buffer between external metadata repositories and the Oracle Discoverer metadata repository. Oracle Discoverer uses this buffer for importing metadata from external systems into business area objects (Fig. 5.31).

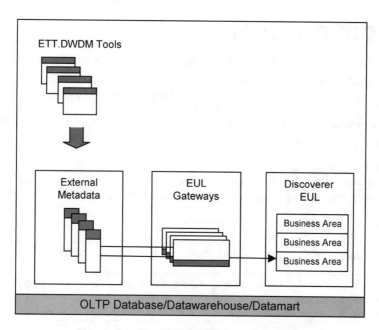

ETT.DWDM Tools

External Metadata

EUL Gateways

Discoverer EUL

Business Area

Business Area

Business Area

OLTP Database/Datawarehouse/Datamart

Fig. 5.31. The EUL Gateway architecture

Since the EUL Gateway is a set of tables, it requires a special procedure for refreshing these tables any time metadata from external systems change. When the EUL Gateway presents a set of views, such a procedure is not needed, because views automatically display metadata changes in external systems. Therefore, this type of EUL Gateway implementation is considered preferable.

Installing and Registering EUL Gateway

Usually, EUL Gateway is supplied along with other software products in the form of SQL scripts that run automatically during product installation. If it isn't, you can manually install EUL Gateway by running the appropriate SQL scripts. Before implementing this type of EUL Gateway installation, carefully read the installation manual supplied with the specific software product.

To make the EUL Gateway mechanism available for use, it is necessary to register it in the Oracle Discoverer End-User Layer. The registration procedure implies that you insert one row into a specific table of the Oracle Discoverer End-User Layer.

5.2.5. ODBC Support

Besides Oracle databases, Oracle Discoverer can be used with databases from other vendors via an ODBC mechanism. However, it should be noted that not all functions will be available to users when working with ODBC data sources.

The tables provided below summarize the functions that are only partially usable or totally unsupported when connecting to the database via ODBC mechanism.

Table 5.9. Unsupported Functions

Oracle Discoverer Functions	Features and limitations implied by ODBC data sources
Date hierarchies	N/A
Summary management	Summary folder management not supported
Automatic join creation using primary/foreign key constraints	Depends on the database support for specific constraints
Privileges and security	Roles not supported
Collect Query Statistics	N/A
Grant Workbooks	N/A
Query prediction	N/A
Query Governor—"warn if predicted time exceeds"	N/A
Oracle Designer	N/A
EUL facility for creating a new EUL database owner	N/A
List of database functions in calculation	Certain database functions are unavailable

Table 5.10. Functions that Have Support Limitations

Function	Support limitation
EUL Management	Users can create an EUL only for an existing database user
Count All Rows	For determining all the rows that satisfy the query condition, Oracle Discoverer uses proprietary internal mechanisms that are not supported by ODBC. For this reason, this function may sometimes produce incorrect results

continues

Table 5.10 Continued

Function	Support limitation
Available Functions	Users can create any formula, but the list of available functions when working with ODBC sources will be significantly reduced in comparison to the list available when working directly with Oracle databases

5.3. Creating Summaries (Oracle Discoverer User Edition)

5.3.1. Application Description

Oracle Discoverer User Edition Purposes

Oracle Discoverer User Edition is an instrument intended for viewing and analyzing data stored in relational databases.

Oracle Discoverer User Edition allows us to do the following:

- Find and analyze data stored in relational databases
- View data in any form
- Create standard reports
- Export data to other applications

Basic Concepts and Terms

A *business area* is a logical grouping of database tables or views that relate to the specific sphere of activity (*Chapter 3* covers the concept of business area in more detail).

A *workbook* is a report or a set of reports oriented towards solving a specific task.

A *query* is a set of database server commands intended for searching data in the database.

5.3.2. Work Area and Tools

Work Area

Work area is the main window of the Oracle Discoverer User Edition application (Fig. 5.32). It contains all data management tools and reports presented as worksheets in a workbook.

The **Main Menu** contains basic commands for managing data and user interfaces of the Oracle Discoverer User Edition application.

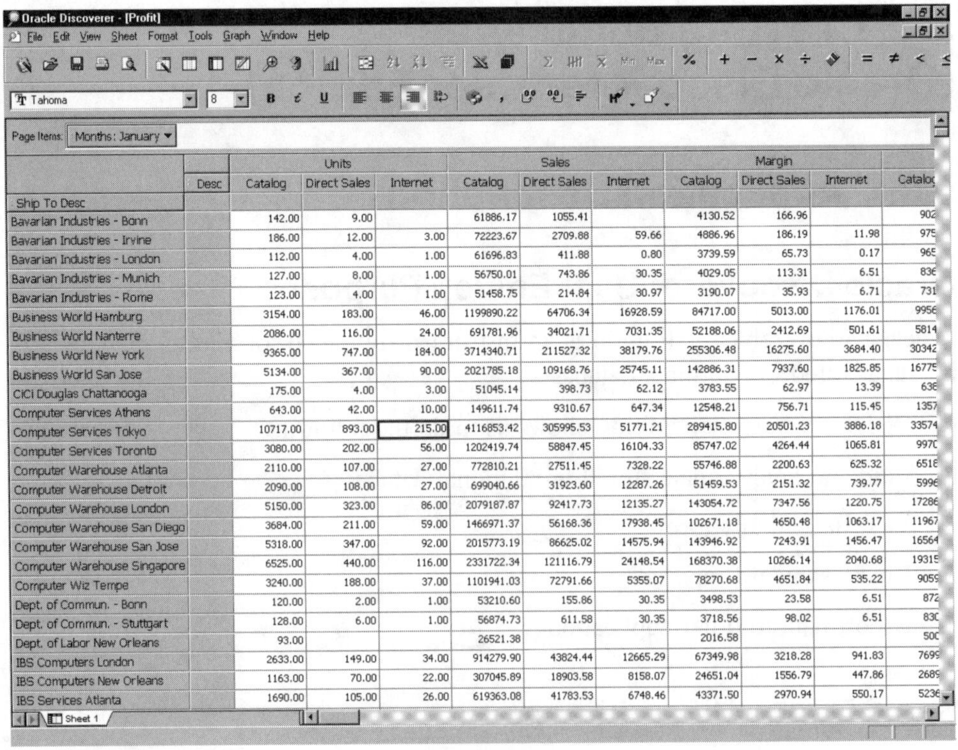

Fig. 5.32. The Work Area

The **Tool Bar** contains tools for creating and managing workbooks, such as Open or Sort tools.

The **Analysis Bar** contains tools for analyzing data contained in a workbook, such as finding minimum or maximum values within a column or finding the sum of the values of a specified column.

The **Formatting Bar** contains data formatting tools intended to format data within a report, such as an alignment tool or a font formatting tool.

The **Axis Item** displays data that can present dimensions.

Data Points represent actual data residing within a worksheet. Usually, data points are numeric values.

Worksheet Tabs represent bookmarks in the workbook. Each worksheet tab represents a page within a report.

Tab Scroll Buttons are visual controls intended for scrolling worksheets within a workbook.

Page Scroll Bars are visual controls intended for page scrolling in relation to the display.

Right-Click Menus

Besides the main menu, Oracle Discoverer provides a set of popup menus, which you normally access by right-clicking on specific objects. Generally, these menus contain data manipulation commands and commands for managing data display formats (Fig. 5.33).

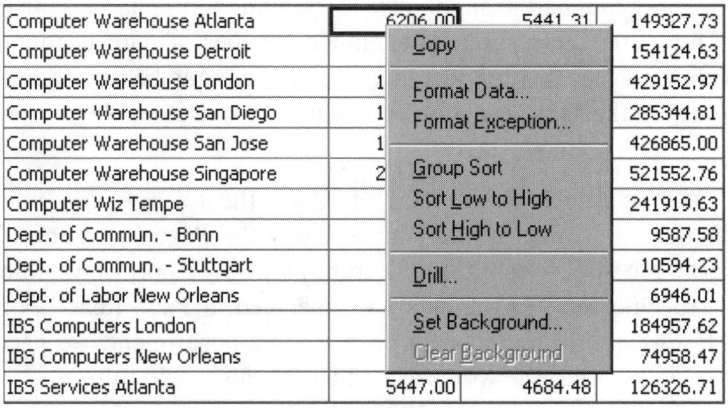

Computer Warehouse Atlanta	6206.00	5441.31	149327.73
Computer Warehouse Detroit	Copy		154124.63
Computer Warehouse London	1 Format Data...		429152.97
Computer Warehouse San Diego	1 Format Exception...		285344.81
Computer Warehouse San Jose	1		426865.00
Computer Warehouse Singapore	2 Group Sort		521552.76
Computer Wiz Tempe	Sort Low to High		241919.63
Dept. of Commun. - Bonn	Sort High to Low		9587.58
Dept. of Commun. - Stuttgart	Drill...		10594.23
Dept. of Labor New Orleans			6946.01
IBS Computers London	Set Background...		184957.62
IBS Computers New Orleans	Clear Background		74958.47
IBS Services Atlanta	5447.00	4684.48	126326.71

Fig. 5.33. The Right-click menu

Forms of Data Presentation

Oracle Discoverer supports two forms of data presentation for viewing and analyzing, namely, graphical and table.

Table layout is the most familiar two-dimensional representation of the multidimensional data of the analytical report. Based on an SQL query, it allows the user to select any order of data layout at the worksheet.

The table layout has the following structure:

❑ Axis—this is an edge of a virtual cube created at the stage of building a query on the basis of data items. Items that we select for our query are displayed on these axes. Oracle Discoverer uses the following three axes:

   ❑ **Top axis** is the axis of a sheet that runs horizontally, across the top of a sheet.

   ❑ **Side axis** runs vertically across the left side of a sheet (it is only used in crosstabs).

   ❑ **Page axis** is the axis that displays page items. It appears above the top axis.

❑ Axis items are data items that appear on one of the sheet axes.

❑ Data points—these are values of data items that appear in cells of a sheet within the report area.

Oracle Discoverer provides the following four types of presenting table layout.

Table

Table is the most familiar form of data presentation. Similar to other systems, an Oracle Discoverer table contains a limited number of named columns representing database object attributes and an unlimited number of numbered rows (Fig. 5.34). Thus, the table can display a database object (table or view) exactly as it is.

Page-detail table is a table (Fig. 5.35) in which the role of page items can be played by any column of an ordinary table. Using the **Page Items** control, we can set data display criteria in such a way as to display in a report only those data that relate to the specific value of the data item specified in **Page Items**. For example, it we need to display in a report data on a specific department, we need to place the Department item into the worksheet and select a specific value.

Crosstab is a table (Fig. 5.36) that can have an unlimited number of rows and columns. Crosstab rows and columns are data items that are dimensions of data, while the cells of this table represent relationships between these dimensions. In contrast to table layout, the crosstab layout allows us to display relationships between two or more dimensions by placing them on the row axis (side axis) or on the column axis.

	Department	▸ Region	▸ City	▸ Store Name	Sales SUM
▸ 1	Beverage	East	Atlanta	Store No. 3	449.03
▸ 2	Game Rental	East	Atlanta	Store No. 3	8756.08
▸ 3	Laser Disc Rent	East	Atlanta	Store No. 3	7731.61
▸ 4	Snacks	East	Atlanta	Store No. 3	206.93
▸ 5	Video Rental	East	Atlanta	Store No. 3	27229.69
▸ 6	Video Sale	East	Atlanta	Store No. 3	49103.38
▸ 7	Beverage	East	Boston	Store No. 19	359.34
▸ 8	Game Rental	East	Boston	Store No. 19	8697.9
▸ 9	Laser Disc Rent	East	Boston	Store No. 19	6439.94
▸ 10	Snacks	East	Boston	Store No. 19	220.69
▸ 11	Video Rental	East	Boston	Store No. 19	27705.45
▸ 12	Video Sale	East	Boston	Store No. 19	48609.47
▸ 13	Beverage	Central	Chicago	Store No. 2	63.43
▸ 14	Game Rental	Central	Chicago	Store No. 2	4533.58
▸ 15	Laser Disc Rent	Central	Chicago	Store No. 2	3616.87
▸ 16	Snacks	Central	Chicago	Store No. 2	99.74
▸ 17	Video Rental	Central	Chicago	Store No. 2	13177.65
▸ 18	Video Sale	Central	Chicago	Store No. 2	28856.23
▸ 19	Beverage	Central	Cincinnati	Store No. 11	810.05
▸ 20	Game Rental	Central	Cincinnati	Store No. 11	19355.59
▸ 21	Laser Disc Rent	Central	Cincinnati	Store No. 11	14272.32
▸ 22	Snacks	Central	Cincinnati	Store No. 11	567.66
▸ 23	Video Rental	Central	Cincinnati	Store No. 11	61710.98
▸ 24	Video Sale	Central	Cincinnati	Store No. 11	107448.35
▸ 25	Beverage	Central	Dallas	Store No. 10	167.76
▸ 26	Game Rental	Central	Dallas	Store No. 10	3550.98
▸ 27	Laser Disc Rent	Central	Dallas	Store No. 10	3034.54
▸ 28	Snacks	Central	Dallas	Store No. 10	138.99
▸ 29	Video Rental	Central	Dallas	Store No. 10	14480.42

Fig. 5.34. An example of an ordinary table

Page Items: Department: Beverage ▼

	▸ Region	▸ City	▸ Store Name	Sales SUM
▸ 1	East	Atlanta	Store No. 3	449.03
▸ 2	East	Boston	Store No. 19	359.34
▸ 3	Central	Chicago	Store No. 2	63.43
▸ 4	Central	Cincinnati	Store No. 11	810.05
▸ 5	Central	Dallas	Store No. 10	167.76
▸ 6	West	Denver	Store No. 15	296.65
▸ 7	West	Los Angeles	Store No. 4	189.82
▸ 8	Central	Louisville	Store No. 13	519.66
▸ 9	East	Miami	Store No. 18	210.69
▸ 10	Central	Minneapolis	Store No. 12	119.52
▸ 11	Central	Nashville	Store No. 20	32.71
▸ 12	East	New Orleans	Store No. 8	99.35
▸ 13	East	New York	Store No. 1	1402.14
▸ 14	East	Philadelphia	Store No. 6	552.48
▸ 15	West	Phoenix	Store No. 14	307.94
▸ 16	East	Pittsburgh	Store No. 7	318.56
▸ 17	West	San Francisco	Store No. 5	635.88
▸ 18	West	Seattle	Store No. 9	439.38
▸ 19	Central	St. Louis	Store No. 16	415.1
▸ 20	East	Washington	Store No. 17	730.32

Fig. 5.35. A page-detail table

		Sales SUM					
		Beverage	Game Rental	Laser Disc Re	Snacks	Video Rental	Video Sale
▶	Central	2128.23	58632.28	47751.07	1938.36	208072.52	342361.18
▶	Chicago	63.43	4533.58	3616.87	99.74	13177.65	28856.23
▶	Store No. 2	63.43	4533.58	3616.87	99.74	13177.65	28856.23
▶	Cincinnati	810.05	19355.59	14272.32	567.66	61710.98	107448.35
▶	Store No. 11	810.05	19355.59	14272.32	567.66	61710.98	107448.35
▶	Dallas	167.76	3550.98	3034.54	138.99	14480.42	18335.11
▶	Store No. 10	167.76	3550.98	3034.54	138.99	14480.42	18335.11
▶	Louisville	519.66	15309.48	12292.17	551.9	58639.66	86799.7
▶	Store No. 13	519.66	15309.48	12292.17	551.9	58639.66	86799.7
▶	Minneapolis	119.52	3160.63	3911.52	129.81	14177.66	25125.66
▶	Store No. 12	119.52	3160.63	3911.52	129.81	14177.66	25125.66
▶	Nashville	32.71	4081.77	3693.7	171.35	13874.53	18549.83
▶	Store No. 20	32.71	4081.77	3693.7	171.35	13874.53	18549.83
▶	St. Louis	415.1	8640.25	6929.95	278.91	32011.62	57246.3
▶	Store No. 16	415.1	8640.25	6929.95	278.91	32011.62	57246.3
▶	East	4121.91	96495.59	79236.24	3042.66	326317.25	534766.85
▶	Atlanta	449.03	8756.08	7731.61	206.93	27229.69	49103.38
▶	Store No. 3	449.03	8756.08	7731.61	206.93	27229.69	49103.38

Fig. 5.36. A crosstab example

Page Items: Region: Central ▼

		Sales SUM					
		Beverage	Game Rental	Laser Disc Re	Snacks	Video Rental	Video Sale
▶	Chicago	63.43	4533.58	3616.87	99.74	13177.65	28856.23
▶	Store No. 2	63.43	4533.58	3616.87	99.74	13177.65	28856.23
▶	Cincinnati	810.05	19355.59	14272.32	567.66	61710.98	107448.35
▶	Store No. 11	810.05	19355.59	14272.32	567.66	61710.98	107448.35
▶	Dallas	167.76	3550.98	3034.54	138.99	14480.42	18335.11
▶	Store No. 10	167.76	3550.98	3034.54	138.99	14480.42	18335.11
▶	Louisville	519.66	15309.48	12292.17	551.9	58639.66	86799.7
▶	Store No. 13	519.66	15309.48	12292.17	551.9	58639.66	86799.7
▶	Minneapolis	119.52	3160.63	3911.52	129.81	14177.66	25125.66
▶	Store No. 12	119.52	3160.63	3911.52	129.81	14177.66	25125.66
▶	Nashville	32.71	4081.77	3693.7	171.35	13874.53	18549.83
▶	Store No. 20	32.71	4081.77	3693.7	171.35	13874.53	18549.83
▶	St. Louis	415.1	8640.25	6929.95	278.91	32011.62	57246.3
▶	Store No. 16	415.1	8640.25	6929.95	278.91	32011.62	57246.3

Fig. 5.37. An example of the page detail crosstab layout

For example, Fig. 5.35 shows a crosstab that displays a relationship of five dimensions, three of which (Region, City, and Department) are placed on the column axis, while the values that form this relationship (Sales SUM) are stored in the table cells.

Like a page detail layout, the page detail crosstab (Fig. 5.37) enhances crosstab functionality by adding the ability to have multiple pages for representing data. The **Page Items** control, like rows or columns, can contain one or more dimensions. By placing dimensions on the page element, we group report data on separate pages according to the specified values of specific dimensions.

To conclude, let us note that the crosstab layout is intended for more detailed analyses and provides a wider range of data manipulation capabilities in comparison to the table layout.

Graphs

Graphs provide for graphical data representation, and are intended for displaying multidimensional report data. Like table data, data represented on graphs are not static. This data is refreshed any time you start the report. However, in contrast to tables, graphs don't support data management mechanisms such as pivoting, drilling, and sorting. Graphs can be created only on the basis of an existing table (a workbook sheet), and there can be only one instance of a graph. This means that you can create only one graph per worksheet. If you need to create another graph, you need to first create a new worksheet and define your new graph there.

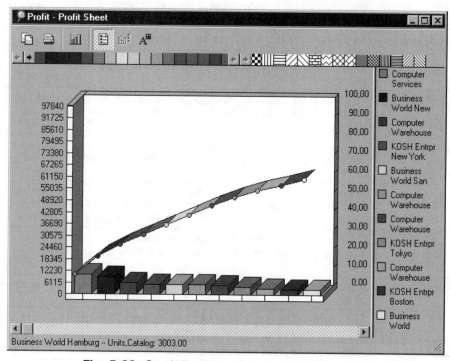

Fig. 5.38. Graph implemented in a separate window

A graph implemented in a separate window is shown in Fig. 5.38:

❑ **Tool Bar** contains buttons that allow you to perform various operations on the graph, such as printing or modifying it.

❏ **Y-Axis Scale** contains the scale of the dimension under analysis.

❏ **Titles** specifies the names of the dimensions under analysis.

❏ **Legend** specifies the graph legend, such as color and labels for the data.

❏ The **Data** field displays the dimensions under analysis, showing them as lines, curves, 3D bars, etc.

Oracle Discoverer provides the following types of graphs:

Table 5.11. Graph Types in Oracle Discoverer

Graph type	Description
Area	Shows deviations in data values among all categories
Bar	Shows data values in all categories and classifies data by categories
Cube	Shows deviations in data values among all categories, displays data classified by categories and values
Fit to Curve	Shows deviations in values among all categories. The points display specific data values, classified by value and category. To represent trends in your data, the points are connected with curves
Hi-Low Close	Displays the data in comparison to the initial and final values. This method of representation is especially convenient when working with financial data
Horizontal Bar	Shows deviations in data values among all categories, and classifies data by categories. Values are placed on the Y-axis, categories on the X-axis
Line	Shows deviations in data values for all categories. Points represent data separately by values and categories. However, to make the trends in data changes more evident, these points are connected by a line
Pareto	Shows values in all categories, classifies data by categories. To make the trends in categories more evident, there is a line for each value
Pie	Shows values in all categories. Each value is represented as a fraction of the total sum
Point	Specifies deviations in data among all categories. The points display data separately by value and category
Polar	Displays the angular extent of your data points
Scatter	Shows changes in data values as related to another value. The X- and Y-axes must correspond to numeric values
Doughnut	Displays deviations in values among all categories. Each value is represented as a fraction of the total sum
Surface	Shows deviations in values among all categories

More detailed information on the use of specific graph types is provided the part dedicated to Oracle Analyzer.

5.3.3. Creating a New Workbook

Oracle Discoverer simplifies the task of creating reports by providing the special Workbook wizard. To start this wizard, select the **New** command from the **File** menu or from the **Sheet** menu. The Workbook wizard provides a series of dialogs, where we can define the form of the new report, specify the query and conditions for this report, and, finally, execute it.

To create a new report using the Workbook wizard, follow the instructions provided below.

Step 1. Selecting the Report Type

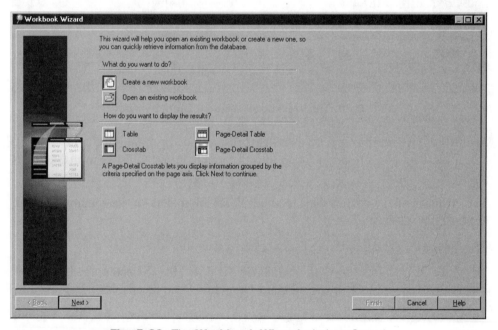

Fig. 5.39. The **Workbook Wizard** window, Step 1

The Workbook wizard first prompts you to specify the report type. To accomplish this step, go to the **How do you want to display the results?** option group and select the report type by clicking any of the available icons. To continue, click **Next**.

Step 2. Selecting Data Items

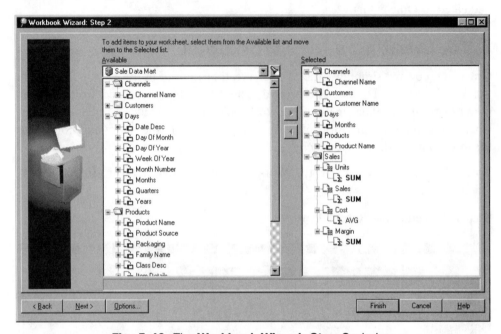

Fig. 5.40. The **Workbook Wizard: Step 2** window

At this step, we need to specify data items that will be displayed in the new report. Select the data items to be included into the report from the list of available items grouped by folders.

The **Available** field contains a hierarchical list of folders or data items that are available for selection.

The **Selected** field contains the list of selected data items.

To move data items from the **Available** field to the **Selected** field, use the **Include/Exclude** buttons or the standard Drag-and-Drop mechanism.

To specify more advanced settings of the report attributes, click the **Options** button.

Step 3. Arranging the Report Layout

In the third step, the Workbook Wizard allows us to arrange the report layout. To do this, use the standard Drag-and-Drop mechanism to place data items selected in the previous step to the proper rows, columns, or page axes. Notice that this layout is not necessarily always the same. Later, we can change it in the course of work by using the pivoting mechanism.

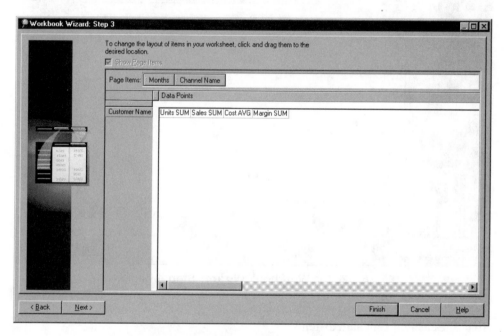

Fig. 5.41. The **Workbook Wizard: Step 3** window

Additional options of data display that we can specify in this step are listed below:

❏ **Show Page Item**—toggles the display of the page axis of the report

❏ **Hide Duplicate Rows**—toggles the display of the duplicate rows in the report

Step 4. Selecting Conditions

Here, we must select the conditions that we need to use in our report. To accomplish this, go to the **View Condition for** field and select the required data item or the **All Items** option. The list of available conditions will appear in the field below. Select the required conditions from this list and click **Next**.

You can also create new conditions or edit existing ones. To create a new condition, click the **New** button. To edit an existing condition, select it from the list and click **Edit**.

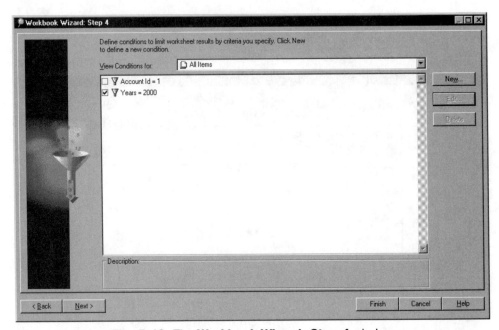

Fig. 5.42. The **Workbook Wizard: Step 4** window

Step 5. Selecting Calculated Items

To accomplish the final step of the Workbook Wizard, you need to select the calculated items or formulae that you need to use in the report. Select the required item (or set the abstract option labeled **All Items**) from the **View Calculation for** list, then select the required formula from the list of available calculations and click **Next**.

This window also allows you to create new formulae or edit existing ones. To create a new formula, click the **New** button. Instructions for creating new formulae are exactly the same as those that were described earlier in this chapter.

NOTE

When creating reports, you can use existing programs for defining analytical queries. To do this, select the **Import SQL** command from the **File** menu, then select the program that you need to import.

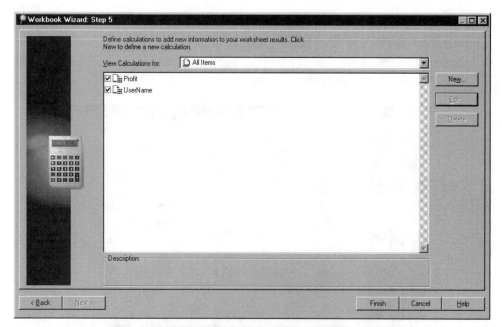

Fig. 5.43. The **Workbook Wizard: Step 5** window

5.3.4. Creating Graphs and Diagrams

To create graphs, start the New Graph wizard by selecting the **Graph —> New Graph** commands from the menu, then proceed as follows:

Step 1. Selecting the Graph Type

The New Graph wizard first prompts you to select the type of the graph to be created (Fig. 5.44). Select the appropriate graph type and click **Next**.

Step 2. Formatting the Graph

Next, the wizard prompts you to specify a format for the new graph (Fig. 5.45):

❐ **2D**—displays two-dimensional graph data

❐ **3D**—displays 3D graph data

❐ **2D Stacked**—displays 2D graphs, grouping series vertically

❐ **2D Stacked 100%**—displays 2D graphs, grouping series vertically and displaying values in percentages of the total sum

❐ **3D Stacked**—displays data in 3D format, grouping series vertically

❑ **3D Stacked 100%**—displays 3D graphs, grouping series vertically and displaying values in percentages of the total sum

❑ **Clustered**—displays data in 3D format, and groups series vertically, displaying the next series under the previous one

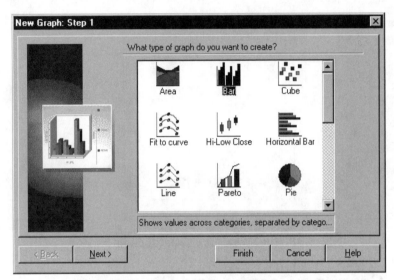

Fig. 5.44. The **New Graph: Step 1** window

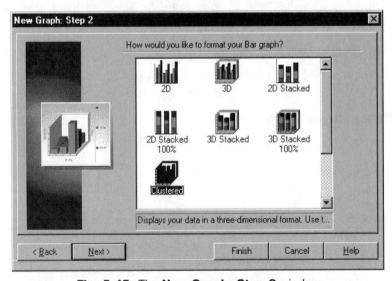

Fig. 5.45. The **New Graph: Step 2** window

Step 3. Defining the Graph Attributes

For this third step, the wizard prompts you to define the following Graph attributes (Fig. 5.46):

☐ The **Titles** group allows you to specify one or more titles for the graph. Enter the titles into appropriate text fields and format this text by clicking the buttons located to the right.

☐ The **Legend** options allow you to change the graph's legend display mode.

☐ The **Axis Label Fonts** group allows you to change the format of the axis labels.

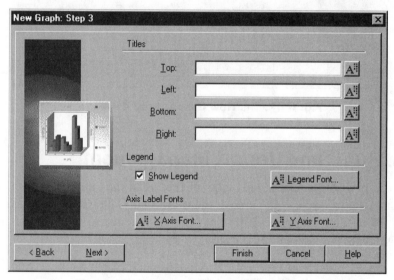

Fig. 5.46. The **New Graph: Step 3** window

Step 4. Specifying the Graph Settings

For the final step, the wizard prompts you to specify the following graph options (Fig. 5.47):

☐ The **Y Axis Scale** option group allows you to set minimum and maximum values on the vertical axis

☐ The **Show Gridlines** checkboxes allow you to toggle the grid lines display mode

☐ The **Graph Series By** radio buttons allow you to specify the data items that will be displayed on the horizontal axis

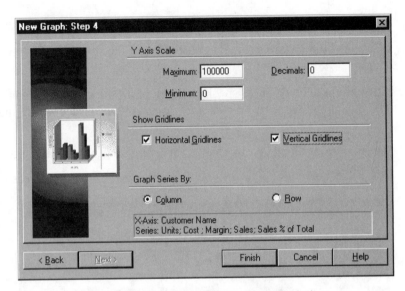

Fig. 5.47. The **New Graph: Step 4** window

5.3.5. Run-Time Report Management

One of the most important components of the visual data analysis process is data presentation upon display. Obviously, there are many alternatives of data layout, and not all of them can necessarily help the analyst in his investigations by correctly displaying the internal relationships of the data.

To simplify the process of creating the required data presentation, Oracle Discoverer implements the following data manipulation mechanisms:

❑   Pivoting data

❑   Drilling up/down operations

❑   Sort operation

Pivoting Operation

The pivoting mechanism rotates the multidimensional data presentation and displays another edge of the hypercube on the user screen. To pivot a data set in Oracle Discoverer, select the item from either the report body or heading and drag it to the desired position (Fig. 5.48, for example).

When performing this operation, you can move the data to any position and in any direction.

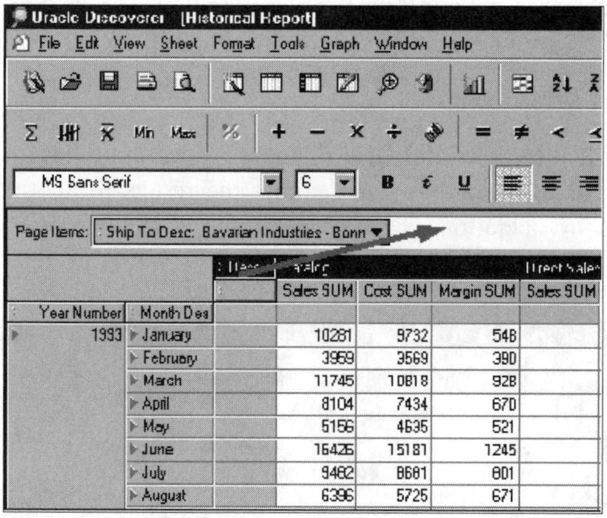

Fig. 5.48. Example of pivoting data in a table

Working with Hierarchies (Drill up/Drill down)

Changing the current hierarchical level provides the ability to get more detailed information on the object under investigation. It changes the data set by adding or removing displayed hierarchical levels. To be able to use this operation, you need to define at least one hierarchy in Oracle Administration Edition.

Oracle Discoverer implements two methods of retrieving more detailed data.

Drilling down Directly from the Report Body

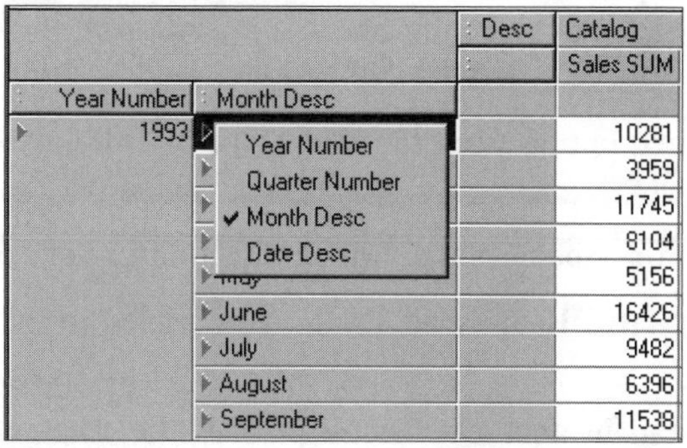

Fig. 5.49. Example of the drilling down operation

To implement the drilling down operation when working with a hierarchy, move the mouse cursor to the desired item. Then click the **Drill** icon to display a list of available hierarchical levels and select the required level from that list. When you have finished, the current hierarchical level will change.

Drilling from the Drill Dialog

Data drilling with the use of the **Drill** dialog provides more advanced drilling options. Using the **Drill** dialog, we can redirect the results to another worksheet or perform the drilling operation over any hierarchy rather than being limited to the current one.

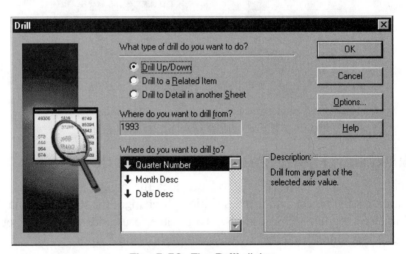

Fig. 5.50. The **Drill** dialog

To perform drilling with the use of the **Drill** dialog, proceed as follows:

1. Open the **Drill** dialog by selecting **Sheet —> Drill** from the User Edition main menu, or simply double-click the cell that you want to drill.

2. Select the required option from the **What type of drill do you want to do?** option group:

   ❏ **Drill Up/Down**—specifies the drilling direction (up or down)

   ❏ **Drill to a Related Item**—specifies an item related to the current one to be drilled

   ❏ **Drill to Detail in another Sheet**—specifies the sheet of the workbook to which the drilling results will be redirected

3. The **Where do you want to drill to?** field allows you to specify the level to which the data will be drilled. For example, if we are performing the drill operation for the year 1993, and select drilling by days, Oracle Discoverer will then display data values for all the days of year 1993.

Collapsing Data (Drilling up)

To collapse the drilled data, you can use one of the following two methods:

❏ First, you can use the **Drill** operation to change the current hierarchical level to a higher one

❏ Second, you can use the **Collapse** command from the **Sheet** menu after selecting the data item that you need to collapse

Sorting the Data

Data sorting in Oracle Discoverer is the process of rearranging data according to value. This operation depends on the data type: for example, character data can be sorted in ascending or descending alphabetical order, while numeric or time data can be sorted in ascending or descending order according to their value. Typical examples of using sort are creating a list of the best (or worst) customers according to a specific criterion, determining the most efficient salesman of your company, etc.

Oracle Discoverer provides several methods and types of sorting, all of which will be described below.

In the most general case, you can sort the data by clicking the **A_Z** toolbar button. To use this method, first select the data item that you want to sort by clicking it with the mouse, then select one of the two options (ascending or descending sort order) provided by this tool.

To use more advanced sort options, you can use special wizards that exist for each type of table.

To sort a report presented in table layout, proceed as follows:

1. Select the **Sort** command from the **Tools** menu.

2. The **Sort Table** window will appear (Fig. 5.51). Use the **Add** button to add sort criteria.

3. The **Direction** field defines the sort order for the table column. This field accepts two values used to identify the sort order: **Lo to Hi** specifies ascending sort order while **Hi to Lo** corresponds to descending sort order.

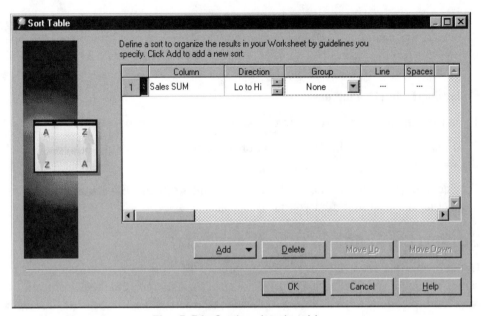

Fig. 5.51. Sorting data in tables

4. The **Group** field defines the grouping and display of the sorted data. This field can accept one of the following values:

    ❏ **Group Sort**—if you set this value, the data will be sorted within each group. The group name is specified once, at the heading of the ordered group of data

    ❏ **Page Break**—if this value is set, data of the same type will be grouped by pages, and a group name will appear at the top of the page

    ❏ **Hidden**—this value means that this column will not be displayed within the report.

    ❏ **None**—the current column will not be sorted

5. The **Line** field specifies the width of the grid lines separating data groups.

6. The **Spaces** field specifies the number of spaces between the groups.

7. If you need to sort only a single column, the sort operation can be considered complete, and you can click **OK**. If not, use the **Add** button to add another sort criteria, then repeat the above listed steps.

The difference between sort operations for crosstab data and for table data is that crosstab data can be sorted not only by column values, but also by values contained in the rows.

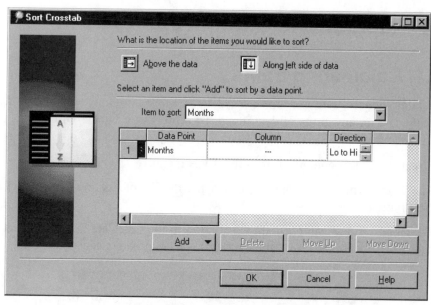

Fig. 5.52. Sorting crosstab data

To sort crosstab data, follow the instructions presented below:

1. Select the **Sort** command from the **Tools** menu.

2. The **Sort Crosstab** window will appear (Fig. 5.52). Specify the sort type by selecting the appropriate option in the **What is the location of the items you would like to sort?** option group:

   ❐ **Above the data**—sets sorting for the data contained in the crosstab rows

   ❐ **Along left side of data**—sets sorting for the data contained in the crosstab columns

3. Go to the **Item to sort** field and specify the item for which to create the sort condition.

4. Use the **Add** button to add sort criteria.

5. Go to the **Column/Row** field and select the data item according to which the data will be sorted.

6. Use the **Direction** field to specify the sort order.

7. If you need to sort only a single column, you can consider the sort operation complete and click **OK**, otherwise, use the **Add** button to add another sort criterion and repeat the above described procedures.

5.4. Calculations within Reports

5.4.1. Calculating Sums

Calculating the total sum is one of the typical tasks encountered when analyzing or reporting data on any group of data items. To do this with Oracle Discoverer, proceed as follows:

1. Select the **Totals** command from the **Tools** menu.

2. The **Totals** window will appear, displaying the list of existing sums. Click the **New** button.

3. The **Total** window will open (Fig. 5.53). Go to the **Calculate** field and select the aggregate function and the data items that will be used to calculate the total.

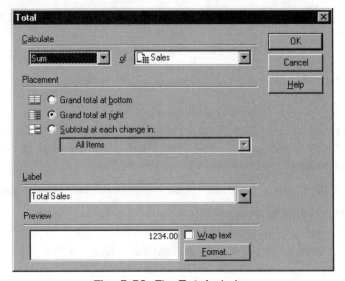

Fig. 5.53. The **Total** window

The following functions can be used for data aggregation:

- ❑   **Sum**—calculates the total sum of values

- ❑   **Average**—calculates an average value

- ❑   **Count**—calculates the number of values

- ❑   **Count Distinct**—calculates the number of distinct values

❏ **Minimum**—finds the minimum value

❏ **Maximum**—finds the maximum value

❏ **Standard Deviation**—calculates the standard deviation (the square root of the variance)

❏ **Variance**—calculates the variance

❏ **Percentage of Grand Total**—calculates the percentage of the grand total

4. Go to the **Placement** field and select one of the following values:

❏ **Grand total at bottom**—calculates the percentage as a ratio of the current value to the grand total (for the specified columns). This option is only applicable to the table data layout.

❏ **Grand total at right**—calculates the percentage as a ratio of the current value to the grand total for all columns.

❏ **Subtotal at each change in**—calculates the percentage as the ratio of the current value to the grand total for the specific data item, which you need to select from the list.

5. Go to the **Label** field and specify the label for the percentage measure and its visual attributes.

6. Having accomplished the process of defining the current percentage measure in the **Total** window, click **OK.**

7. Having accomplished the process of defining all percentage measures in the **Totals** window, click **OK.**

5.4.2. Calculating Percentages

Calculating percentages is another important task of data analysis within reports. There are two methods of performing this task:

❏ You may define the percentage as a calculated item when designing the business area in Oracle Discoverer Administration Edition or when creating a report using the Workbook Wizard.

❏ You may use the special tool provided by Oracle Discoverer User Edition for creating percentages. This section covers this tool in more detail.

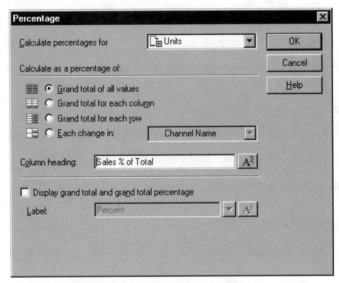

Fig. 5.54. Defining percentages

To define a percentage, proceed as follows:

1. Select the **Percentages** command from the **Tools** menu.

2. The **Percentages** window will appear, displaying the list of existing percentages. Click the **New** button.

3. The **Percentage** window will open. Go to the **Calculate percentages for** field and select the item that will be used when calculating the percentage.

4. Next, go to the **Calculate as a percentage of** field and select one of the following values:

   ☐ **Grand Total**—specifies the percentage as a ratio of the current value to the grand total of the specified column. This operation is only applicable to the table data layout.

   ☐ **Grand total of all values**—specifies the percentage as a ratio of the current value to the grand total for all columns.

   ☐ **Grand total for each column**—specifies the percentage as a ratio of the current value to the grand total of the current column.

   ☐ **Grand total for each row**—specifies the percentage as a ratio of the current value to the grand total of the current row.

   ☐ **Each change in**—specifies the percentage as a ratio of the current value to the grand total for a specified item, which you must select from a list.

5. Go to the **Column heading** field, specify the heading for the percentage, and specify its visual attributes.

6. If necessary, go to the **Display subtotal and subtotal percentage** and **Display subtotal's percentage of grand total** fields and provide separate names for these measures.

7. Having accomplished the process of defining the current percentage in the **Percentage** dialog, click **OK**.

8. Having accomplished the process of defining all percentages in the **Percentages** dialog, click **OK**.

5.4.3. Exceptions

One of the most important analytical tasks is the task of finding within a report a set of data that meets a specified requirement. For example, suppose that we need to find and highlight all the goods for which yearly profit has exceeded $1,000. The condition tool is not suited to solving this task, since this tool will simply exclude the values that don't meet this requirement and won't show them in the report. Therefore, Oracle Discoverer provides a special tool, known as *exception*, for performing this task.

Finding exceptions comprises the following two steps.

❏ Specifying the exception type, for example: "greater than 1,000" or "less than 1,000".

❏ Specifying the exception data format, which will be used for displaying the data that meets the exception condition.

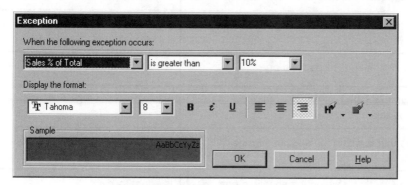

Fig. 5.55. Defining an exception

To define an exception, proceed as follows:

❐   Select the **Exceptions** command from the **Format** menu.

❐   The **Exceptions** window will appear, displaying the list of existing exceptions. To create a new exception, click **New**.

❐   The next dialog will appear, allowing you to specify the new exception parameters:

    ❐   **When the following exception occurs**—specify the exception condition, which consists of the data item to which the exception applies, a set comparison operator, and the set itself

    ❐   **Display the format**—specify the display format for the values that meet the exception requirements

❐   Having accomplished the operation of specifying exception attributes, click **OK**.

❐   Having accomplished the process of creating all exceptions in the **Exceptions** window, click **OK**.

The table below lists several examples of formulating the condition based on a user query.

Table 5.12. Examples of Formulating Exceptions

If you want to find	Use the following expression
A value greater than the specified one	Is greater than `<value>`
The text alphabetically following the specified text	Is greater than `<text>`
A value less than the specified one	Is less than `<value>`
The text that alphabetically precedes the specified text	Is less than `<text>`
A value that is within the specified range	Is between `<minimum value>` and `<maximum value>`
A value exactly matching the specified one	Is equal to `<value>`

5.4.4. Creating Reports with Parameters

Like conditions, parameters are intended for limiting the set of displayed records. However, in contrast to conditions, you need to specify parameters any time you run a report containing them.

Parameters can be used simultaneously by more than one user working with the same report of the same workbook. In this case, each user can specify his or her own values for report parameters, and these individual settings won't influence the results produced by other users working with the same report.

Oracle Discoverer provides the following two types of parameters:

❏   *Workbook parameters* are applicable to all reports of the workbook

❏   *Report parameters* are applicable only to the current report within a workbook

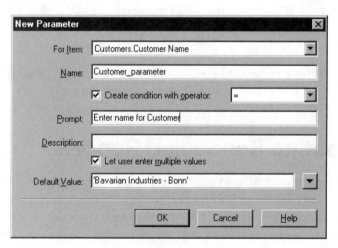

Fig. 5.56. Defining a new parameter

To create a new parameter, proceed as follows:

1.   Select the **Parameters** command from the **Tools** menu.

2.   The **Parameters** window will appear. Click the **New** button.

3.   The **New Parameter** window (Fig. 5.56) will appear. Here you need to specify the following options:

❏   **For Item**—selects the data item to which the new parameter will be applicable

- ❐ **Name**—specifies a name for the new parameter
- ❐ **Create condition with operator**—specifies the set comparison operator
- ❐ **Prompt**—enters the text that will be displayed any time Oracle Discoverer prompts you to specify the parameter value
- ❐ **Description**—specifies the parameter description
- ❐ **Default Value**—selects the default value for the new parameter
- ❐ **Let user enter multiple value**—specifies whether the user can use multiple values for the parameter, or if only a single value is allowed
- ❐ **What is the value of this parameter if it is used in more than one sheet?**—specifies the type of the new parameter

4. Having accomplished all the required operations, click **OK**.

5. Having created all parameters in the **Parameters** window, click **OK**.

NOTE

Any time you run a report with parameters, Oracle Discoverer will display a window prompting you to specify the values for the report parameters.

5.5. Creating Scheduled Reports

A report schedule is a set of workbook sheets or a set of workbooks that need to be processed at a specified time. It is convenient to schedule reports to run overnight, which would allow you to decrease the database server workload. Besides, end users won't need to wait until the reports are completed. Application administrators and end users must carefully plan the schedule for running reports in order to schedule only the most complex ones requiring the most significant processing operations. When determining the reports to be included into the schedule it is recommended that you observe the following rule:

If the report consumes a large amount of time for processing or must be run at regular intervals, such a report is a candidate for inclusion into a schedule.

For example, if you need to produce a monthly report containing various financial parameters of the business activity of your company for several thousands of analyzed items, it will obviously require a long time to run. Therefore, you must schedule such a report.

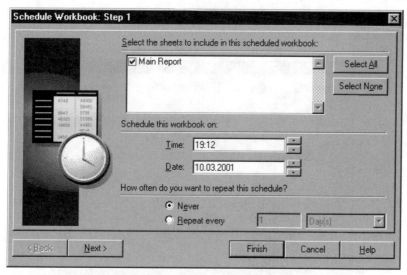

Fig. 5.57. The **Schedule Workbook: Step 1** window

In order to create a schedule for your reports, proceed as follows:

1. Select the **Schedule** command from the **File** menu.

2. The **Schedule Workbook: Step 1** window will appear (Fig. 5.57). Go to the **Select the sheets to include in this scheduled workbook** field and select the worksheets to be included into the schedule.

3. Next, go to the **Schedule this workbook on** field and specify the time which you would like to schedule the report to run.

4. The go to **How often do you want to repeat this schedule?** and set the refresh period for the report. Having accomplished this, click **Next**.

5. The **Schedule Workbook: Step 2** window will appear. Specify the name and description for the newly created schedule by filling in the **Name** and **Description** fields, respectively. Next, go to the **Scheduled workbooks save result each time they run**, specify the time period for which the results will be stored, and click **Finish**.

5.6. Customizing Oracle Discoverer User Edition

To customize the user interface and functionality of Oracle Discoverer User Edition, select the **Options** command from the **Tools** menu. The **Options** window will appear (Fig. 5.58). The options that you can specify in this window are grouped on the following tabs:

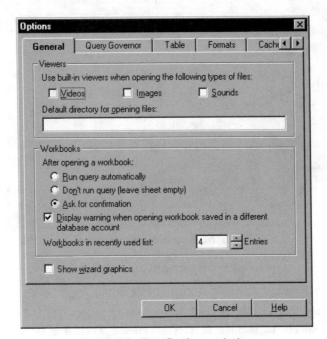

Fig. 5.58. The **Options** window

The **General** tab contains the following set of options intended for specifying general properties of the Oracle Discoverer user interface:

Table 5.13. General Properties of Oracle Discoverer User Interface

Option	Description
Viewers	Specifies file types and locations for files that can be opened for viewing by the built-in multimedia viewer
Workbooks	Specifies the mode of executing queries when opening a workbook (**Run query automatically**; **Don't run query**; **Ask for confirmation**). It also allows you to specify the number of the most recently used workbooks displayed in the **File** menu
Show wizard graphics	Allows you to disable graphics in the Workbook wizard

The **Query Governor** tab contains a set of options intended for query management.

Table 5.14. Query Governor Options

Option	Description
Summary Data	Specifies the mode of using summary folders (**Always, when Available; Only when summary data is not out of date; Never**)
Warn me if predicted query time exceeds	Specifies the time interval after which the system displays a warning if the query exceeds the specified limit
Prevent queries from running longer than	Cancels a query and prevents it from running if the query runs longer than the time limit specified by this option
Limit retrieved data to	Limits the amount of data retrieved by the query to the specified value
Retrieve data incrementally in groups of	Defines the number of rows displayed at once within a report. If this option is set correctly, you'll be able to save a significant amount of time, especially if the query retrieves a lot of rows
Cancel value retrieval after	Cancels data retrieval if the specified time limit has been exceeded

The **Crosstab** tab contains a set of options intended for managing data display when using the crosstab layout.

Table 5.15. Crosstab options

Option	Description
Show	Specifies the attributes to be shown in the crosstab
Style	Specifies the crosstab display style

The **Formats** tab contains a set of options intended for specifying data display formats.

Table 5.16. Oracle Discoverer Data Display Formats

Option	Description
Default Format	Specifies the default display format (font and background color) for the main elements of the table
Show NULL values as	Specifies the display format for NULL values

The **Cache** tab contains a set of options managing the data cache.

Table 5.17. Data Cache Option

Option	Description
Cache	Specifies the data cache size in RAM and on the local hard drive

continues

Table 5.17 Continued

Option	Description
Disk Cache Directory	Specifies the directory for storing the disk cache
Clear this amount from cache when full	Specifies the cache percentage that must be cleared when Oracle Discoverer clears the cache automatically
Cache Status	Displays information on the current cache status

The **Connection** tab contains a set of options intended to manage the connection between Oracle Discoverer User Edition and the EUL.

Table 5.18. Oracle Discoverer Connection Options

Option	Description
Connect to standard EULs	Specifies that the connection must be established directly to the Oracle Discoverer End-User Layer
Connect to applications EULs	Specifies that the connection be established to the Oracle Applications EUL
Connect to both standard and applications EULs	Specifies that the connection be established to both Oracle Applications and Oracle Discoverer EULs

The **Advanced** tab contains a list of options intended for managing the process of running queries.

Table 5.19. The Advanced Tab Options

Option	Description
Disable Automatic Querying	Set this option if you need to prevent Discoverer from repeatedly querying the database when editing the worksheet
Disable Fan-Trap Detection	If this option is disabled, Discoverer automatically detects and breaks fan-trap queries into several SQL statements. If you set this option (i.e., disable fan-trap detection), the results of your queries may contain Cartesian products or incorrect results
Multiple Join Path Detection	Disables a complex relationship between folders, which sometimes may produce incorrect results

The **EUL** tab contains the single option **Select the default EUL**, which defines the default schema of the End-User Layer.

5.7. Oracle Express Spreadsheet Add-In

5.7.1. Purpose of the Product

The Express Spreadsheet Add-in component (from now on, let's refer to it as simply Component) extends the functionality provided to spreadsheet users by including OLAP functionality. Using the Microsoft Excel add-in technology, Component includes itself as a menu item of the Excel spreadsheet and provides direct access to the data stored in Oracle Express Server databases or other databases accessible via Express Server.

When creating reports, you often need to modify the report form or content. The Component provides you with ease of data manipulation and presentation without having to write a program. For example, in order to change your point of view to multidimensional data (the slice according to which you analyze the information), it is sufficient to reverse the dimensions used within the table or place one or more dimensions into the columns and rows of the table. If the task operates with hierarchical dimensions, we can drill the data up or down by simply expanding or collapsing hierarchical items. To do so, simply double-click the value of interest, no matter where it is placed—in a row or in a column.

Most frequently, users like to view multidimensional data in the two-dimensional presentation to which they are the most accustomed, rather than in a classic multidimensional format. The Component provides us with the capability of building "asymmetric" data representation. Starting with multidimensional representation, we can easily build a simplified representation of our information with the use of commands such as **Delete Data Row** or **Delete Data Column**. At the same time, when working with such asymmetric report formats, we are still able to use all the advantages of manipulating multidimensional data (for example, change to new sets of values for dimensions, slicing, pivoting, drilling up/down operations).

For some types of financial applications, it is important to have the capability of saving the modified data into the multi-user database. The Component provides the user with the capability of querying the database for subsequent analysis, such as answering the "What if ?" question, both with and without saving the modifications in the database.

The Component has its specific Application Programming Interface (API), which can be used for developing more complicated applications based on standard spreadsheets. Using this interface, we can create macros for automation purposes.

5.7.2. Product Installation

Before you start installing Oracle Express Spreadsheet Add-in at the workstation, make sure that both the hardware and the software configuration of the workstation meet certain requirements.

Hardware Requirements

❏ IBM-compatible PC with an Intel 80486DX processor (or better)

❏ 16 MB RAM

❏ 8 MB of free disk space

Software Requirements

❏ Microsoft Windows 95, Windows 98, or Microsoft Windows NT 4.0

❏ Access to Personal Express or Express Server

❏ Microsoft Excel for Windows 95 version 7.0; Microsoft Excel 97 or Microsoft Excel 2000

To successfully accomplish Oracle Express Spreadsheet Add-in Setup at the client workstation, you'll need to do the following:

First of all, install the product itself and all the required libraries. To accomplish this step, follow the instructions listed below:

1. From the distribution CD (or from the directory containing the OLAP Express Client distribution), start the Setup.exe program. The **File Locations** window will open, where you need to go to the **Destination** field, select the Oracle home directory, specify its location within the file system, and then click **Next**.

2. The Available Products window will then open. Select the **Oracle Express OLAP Client Products and Utilities** option and click **Next**.

3. The **Installation Types** window (Fig. 5.59) will open. Here you'll need to select either the **End-user** or **Custom** installation type, then click **Next**. If you select **Custom** installation type, select the **Oracle Express Spreadsheet Add-In** item from the list of available products.

4. Answer the questions and select the options prompted by the installation wizard as you complete the installation steps. When you get to the final window, which summarizes the options selected by the user, click **Install**.

5. When the installation completes, click **Exit** to exit the installer.

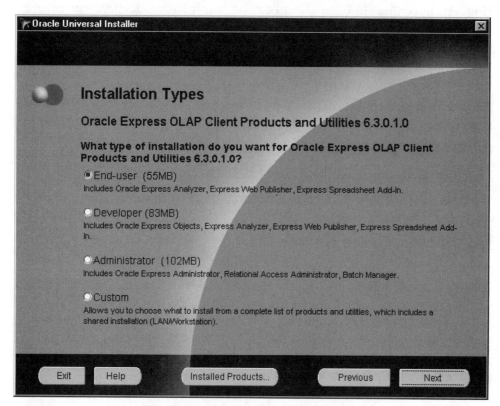

Fig. 5.59. Installing the client products

Second, you'll need to register the add-in with Microsoft Excel.

To do this, follow these steps:

1. In Excel, select the **Settings** command from the **Tools** menu.

2. The list of components will appear. Use the **Browse** button to select the xpad-din.xll file, which is located in the *oracle-home*\olap\xsa630 directory, then click **OK**.

5.7.3. Main Principles of Developing Reports

From a client—server architecture point of view, the Component is a client that provides connection to the server and data processing. As any other client component, this one uses the SNAPI mechanism for data exchange with the server. However, in contrast to other client components, it has no development environment and is simply a set of Microsoft Excel procedures and functions (henceforth called methods) that provide the capabilities of processing data from Oracle Express Server.

You can create a report both using the Workbook wizard and using API methods. Either way, the process of creating a report assumes that you perform the following steps:

❐ Establishing a connection to the database server

❐ Creating a query to retrieve data and its conditions

❐ Presenting and formatting the query results on the worksheet

Connecting to the Server

Before you can start processing data from the server or developing a report, we need to establish a connection to the database server. If you are creating a report using the Workbook wizard, the wizard will only request the server name, and then establish the connection automatically. If you use API calls of the Component, you need to call the `XPConnect(DisplayDialog)` method, where the `DisplayDialog` parameter (either `True` or `False`) specifies whether the Component needs to display the standard **Connect to the Database Server** window.

Creating the Query

After establishing the connection to the server we can start to create the report. The report is a Microsoft Excel workbook and can contain one or more queries. If you need to create several queries on the same worksheet, keep in mind that the results of the queries must not intersect, because such a situation can produce incorrect results.

Creating a query supposes that you select measures from the attached databases and their associated dimensions, create the conditions of this selection, and define their layout on the worksheet.

To create a new query and determine the conditions under which it will be executed, you'll need to perform the following steps:

❐ Start the `XPCreateQuery()` method to create the query identifier.

❑ Using the XPAttachDatabase() and XPDetachDatabase(), attach the required databases.

❑ Using the XPAddMeasure (QueryID, MeasureName, DBName) and XPRemoveMeasure (QueryID, MeasureName), retrieve the measures from the attached databases. Here QueryID is the query identifier, MeasureName specifies the name of the measure, and DBName is the name of the database.

❑ Using the XpCreateCube() and XPSetDimensionEdge (QueryID, DimName, Edge, Dim, Exchange) methods, create the DataCube object and determine the measure positions within that cube.

❑ Use the XPSetScript (QueryID, DimName, SelScript, SortScript) method to define the selection script—SelScript and sort script—SortScript, necessary for displaying the values of the DimName dimension.

❑ If necessary, use the XPSetOption (OptionName, OptionValue) method to determine the options required for execution of this query.

❑ Use the XPSetStartingCell (QueryID, Row, Col, Sheet) and XPRunQuery() method to determine the initial position of the query results in the Microsoft Excel worksheet, and execute the query.

Formatting the Query Results

When formatting the query results after retrieving the query data from the server, you can do the following:

❑ Apply various formatting styles to the data

❑ Create graphs based on the data

❑ Perform additional calculations

❑ Perform various manipulations over the data (for example, pivoting or drilling up or down)

5.7.4. Creating a Report Using the Worksheet Wizard

To simplify the process of creating reports, the Component provides a special wizard, which can be started by selecting the appropriate menu item in Express, or using the XPStartWizard method. The wizard displays a series of dialogs where you can create a connection to the Express server, visually determine data sources (databases) that will be used in a query, and specify the query and the conditions of its execution.

To create a report using the wizard, you need to perform the steps described below.

Step 1. Specifying the Server Connection

First of all, you need to establish the server connection. Select the required data source in the standard **Connect** window (Fig. 5.60). The required data source is the server containing the databases that you are going to use in report.

If for any reason you are unable to connect to the server, make sure that the connection settings are determined properly. To do this, use the Oracle Express Connection Edition utility.

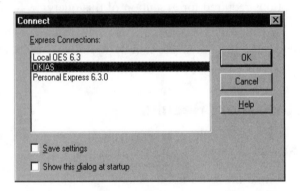

Fig. 5.60. Establishing connection to the server

Step 2. Selecting the Measures

After successfully connecting to the Oracle Express Server, you'll see the **Choose Measures** window, where you can do the following:

❏ Use the **Attach Database/Remove Database** buttons to attach or remove the database required to produce the report

❏ Use the **Add/Remove** buttons to determine the measures to retrieve from the selected databases

Finally, click the **Next** button to open the **Page Layout** window.

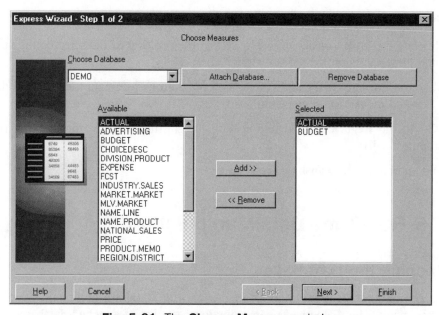

Fig. 5.61. The **Choose Measures** window

Step 3. Specifying the Page Layout for the Report

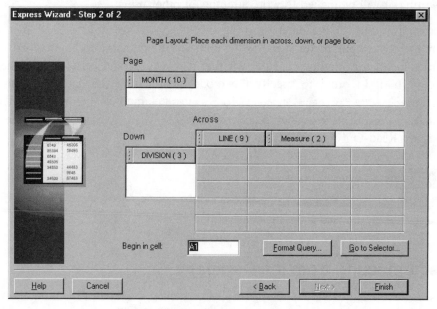

Fig. 5.62. The **Page Layout** window

At this final step of the wizard we can do the following:

1. Specify the layout of our report by setting the position of the selected measures and dimensions on the worksheet.

2. Use the **Format Query** and **Go to Selector** buttons to create the required data slice and format the dimension labels.

3. Go to the **Begin cell** field and specify the starting position for the data (left topmost cell).

4. When done, click **Finish**.

5.7.5. Run-Time Data Manipulation

Attaching the Database

To attach another database at run-time, select the **Database** command from the **Express** menu. The dialog will open, containing the list of attached databases. Use the **Attach Database** button to select the required database, then click **OK**. Pay special attention to the database connection mode. When you attach the database for writing, it will be locked to write attempts of other users.

We can also connect the database using the `XPDatabaseAttach(DBName)` method, where the `DBName` parameter specifies the name of the database to be attached. The return value of this method specifies whether it was successful (`True`) or whether it failed (`False`). In order to specify the mode of attaching the database, call the `XPSetOption ("DefaultAttachMode", OptionValue)` method before starting the `XPDatabaseAttach(DBName)` method. Here the `OptionValue` parameter can take the values `RO` (Read-Only) or `RW` (Read-Write).

> **NOTE**
>
> Don't attach several databases containing objects with the same name simultaneously, since this may produce undesirable results.

Disconnecting from the Database

Besides connecting to the database, the Component provides an operation allowing you to detach the database.

To detach the database, perform the following:

1. Select the **Database** command from the **Express** menu.

2. A dialog will appear containing the list of attached databases. Select the databases that you need to detach, and click the **Remove Database** button.

3. A message box will appear, prompting you to confirm database disconnection. Click **OK**.

4. To disconnect the database, you can also use the XPDatabaseDetach (DBName) method, where DBName specifies the name of the database to be detached. The return value of this method specifies whether the operation has been completed successfully (True) or has failed (False).

> **NOTE**
>
> Before you disconnect the database, make sure that you have deleted all queries that use that database, otherwise the Component won't allow you to detach the database.

Creating a Query

To create a new query that contains a data view different from the current one, you can use the above described Express Wizard or call the XPCreateQuery() method. This method returns the identifier of the newly created query, which can later be used when calling other query-processing methods. Notice that in contrast to the Express Wizard, the XPCreateQuery method only creates the query identifier. Thus, in order to determine all the parameters of the query, you must also use other methods.

Refreshing a Query

If you need to undo the changes that you have introduced when editing, you can use the **Refresh** command from the **Express** menu or call the XPRefresh (Row, Col, Sheet) method, where the Row, Col, and Sheet parameters correspond to the row, column, and Microsoft Excel worksheet name, respectively.

Deleting a Query

To delete the query from the current worksheet, proceed as follows:

1. Position the cursor to any cell containing data retrieved by the query.

2. Select the **Delete Query** command from the **Express** menu.

To perform the same command programmatically, use the XPDeleteQuery (Row, Col, Sheet) method, where the Row, Col, and Sheet parameters correspond to the row, column, and Microsoft Excel worksheet name, respectively.

Creating an Asymmetric Report

The Component allows you to delete rows or columns from the query results in order to create an asymmetric data view. This can be useful if you need to create a standard report form and fill it with data. For example, suppose that you need to create data on actual sales, expenses, and net profit for the first quarter, and provide capabilities for entering new data for the 2nd quarter.

To achieve this goal, you need to define a query that will select the data for the 1st and the 2nd quarters by retrieving the values for Results: Sales, Expenses, and Net profit for the measures Actual and Planned.

	1 Quarter		2 Quarter	
	Actual	Planned	Actual	Planned
Sales	7,000.00	6,000.00	NA	NA
Expenses	4,000.00	5,000.00	NA	NA
Net Profit	3,000.00	1,000.00	NA	NA

Next, use **the Delete Data Column** command to delete the Planned data for the first quarter and Actual for the 2nd Quarter. As a result, you'll get a report containing the values of two measures for two different dimensions.

	1 Quarter	2 Quarter
	Actual	Planned
Sales	7,000.00	8,000.00
Expenses	4,000.00	3,000.00
Net Profit	3,000.00	5,000.00

NOTE

Remember that the commands that delete rows or columns provided by the Component are different from the analogous commands provided by Microsoft Excel. The commands provided by the Component are intended for manipulating the query.

Drilling up and down

To drill the data down to the next hierarchical level or drill it up to the previous level, proceed as follows:

1. Select the cell containing the value of the hierarchical measure.

2. Double-click the selected cell or select the **Drill** command from the **Express** menu.

> **NOTE**
>
> If you are drilling at the lowest hierarchical level, the Component will prompt to you to further specify your actions by displaying the standard **List** dialog of the **Selector** tool. You'll be able to use that tool to select other values of the dimension at the same hierarchical level.

To perform data drilling programmatically, call the XPDrill (Row, Col, Sheet) method, where the Row, Col, and Sheet parameters designate the row, column and Microsoft Excel worksheet name, respectively. If the call completes successfully, the return value is True, otherwise the method returns False.

Using the Pivoting Mechanism to Change the Presentation of the Query Results

Pivoting is another important operation widely used in multidimensional analysis. The main idea of this operation is to manipulate query results after they have been displayed in your report.

To perform the pivoting operation interactively, proceed as follows:

1. Select a cell containing the query data.

2. Select the **Rotate** command from the **Express** or right-click menu.

3. A dialog will appear in which you can use the drag and drop method to define the required position of the dimensions within a report.

> **NOTE**
>
> The Component does not save the query formatting that you create when performing the pivot operation. Therefore, to avoid the necessity of formatting the query twice, format the results after you have changed the query results presentation.

Pagination of the Query by Workbook Sheets

Normally, queries created by users contain more than two dimensions. Therefore, there may be problems with printing reports creating such queries. To avoid such problems, you can use the query pagination function to present the pages on separate workbook sheets.

When performing query pagination, bear in mind the following features of this procedure:

❏ The Component will create a separate page for each combination of dimension values placed at the Page slice. Thus, the total number of pages will be equal to the product of dimension values on each page slice. For example, if your query has two dimensions containing 5 values per Page slice, you'll get 25 worksheets (5×5), and if you have one dimension containing 20 values, you'll get 20 worksheets.

❏ Any formatting applied to the query is inherited in all additional worksheets.

❏ If the worksheet contains two queries, the Component will only extend the query to which the extension is applied. The pages of the second query will not be extended.

❏ The extended worksheets are not so-called "dynamic" worksheets and can't be refreshed by data retrieved from the database.

❏ The process of extension may be time-consuming. To make this process faster, reduce the number of extendable pages by decreasing the number of values in each dimension within the Page slice of the data cube.

❏ The Component automatically numbers the pages in the course of the extension operation.

To subdivide the query by workbook sheets, proceed as follows:

1. Select the query that you want to expand.

2. From the **Express** menu, select the **Expand Pages to Workbook** command.

3. In the **Expand Pages to Workbook** dialog (Fig. 5.63), specify where to place the expanded pages: in the current workbook or in the workbook specified in the field below.

NOTE

Note the total number of pages that will be expanded. If this number is quite large, use the **Selector** tool to decrease it.

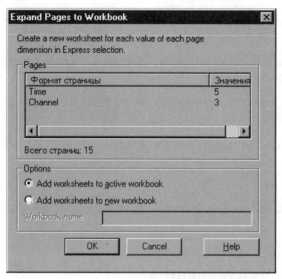

Fig. 5.63. The **Expand Pages to Workbook** dialog

Saving Changes in the Database

Besides read and data manipulation operations, the Component saves data in the database. When performing this operation, pay special attention to the following:

1. Check the file system access rights to the database. If you have no access rights, you won't be able to do this.

2. Look at the database connection mode, since the mechanism of this operation depends on the database connection mode.

To complete the write operation having connected to the database in **read-write mode,** you need to proceed as follows:

1. Within the report body, use the cursor to position the query that you are going to save.

2. Perform the **Write** command from the **Express** menu.

After this command completes successfully, the modified data will be saved in a special database cache, but won't be saved in the database. To save the data in the database, select the **Commit** command from the **Express** menu. You can also undo the data save operation by selecting the **Rollback** command from the **Express** menu.

To complete the save operation in **read-only mode** or in **shared read-only mode,** proceed as follows:

1. Make sure that **Permanently write changes to databases attached read only** is set in the **Options** dialog.

2. In the report body, use the cursor to position the query that you are going to save.

3. Select the **Write** command from the **Express** menu.

> **NOTE**
>
> In this mode, you can't use the **Rollback** command to undo the changes introduced into the database.

Creating Custom Measures

When executing queries, you can use predefined measures and create your own *custom measures*. To create a custom measure, proceed as follows:

1. Select **Custom Measures** from the **Express** menu.

2. A dialog will appear where you can select the database that you need to use.

3. Click the **New** button to open the dialog, which allows you to define custom measures. Start defining custom measures in this window.

To define a new custom measure, proceed as follows:

1. Specify the name for the new custom measure.

2. Next, specify the expression to be used to calculate the new custom measure. Selecting the objects, functions, and operators from the lists provided in this window is the easiest method of defining expressions.

> **NOTE**
>
> If you are creating a new custom measure in **read-write mode**, the new custom measure becomes available to all users. If you create the new custom measure in the **read-only mode**, the new custom measure will be available only to you.

Notice that you can't use any aggregation functions when creating custom measures.

5.7.6. Functions for Customizing Query Results

Redefining the Undefined Data

The database can store some undefined values. By default, the Component displays such values as NA. If you need to represent undefined values otherwise, you can specify an alternative designation or present them as a blank string.

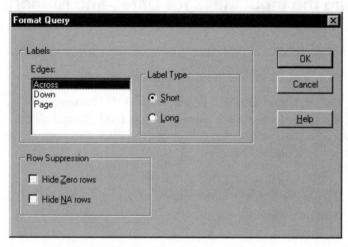

Fig. 5.64. The **Format Query** window

To specify the default value for all undefined values, select the **Options** command from the **Express** menu. The **Options** window will open. Go to the **Format** tab and specify an alternative value in the **Substitute for NA** field, then click **OK**. After accomplishing these operations, all undefined values of all types will be represented using the value specified here. The same operation can be performed programmatically by calling the XPSetOption("NASpell", "Value") method.

In addition to the above, notice that you can hide undefined values or values equal to zero. To specify this option, use the **Express** menu to open the **Format Query** window (Fig. 5.64). In this window, set the required option: **Hide NA rows** or **Hide Zero rows**. Notice that NA or zero rows suppressed by setting these options are hidden, but are not deleted. Formatting is not applicable to such rows.

To set the row suppression option programmatically, use the XPSetRowSuppression (QueryID, HideNARows, HideZeroRows) method, where QueryID is the query identifier, while the HideNARows and HideZeroRows parameters specify the suppression options and can take a value of `Yes` or `No` (default). If this method completes successfully, the return value is `True`, otherwise the return value is set to `False`.

NOTE

Suppressed rows can't be restored using Microsoft Excel tools.

Redefining the Input Mask for Dates and Numeric Values

To redefine the mask for entering dates and numeric values, proceed as follows:

1. Select the **Options** command from the **Express** menu.

2. A dialog with multiple tabs will appear. Go to the **Format** tab, and then enter the required mask to the **Date Format** or **Decimal Format** fields. To view the list of available date or decimal format masks, click the **Format** button next to the right of the required field.

To redefine the format mask programmatically, use the `XPSetOption` (`"DateFormat"`, `"mask"`) method for dates or `XPSetOption` (`"DecimalFormat"`, `"mask"`) for numeric values.

NOTE

You can set any date mask supported by Microsoft Excel.

Determining the Database Attachment Mode

Depending on the task you are solving, you can connect to the database using various modes. The selected connection mode will influence the features of the multi-user environment.

The **Read only** mode is used when you only need to view and analyze the data (the "what if" analysis). Using this mode, you can't introduce permanent changes into the database. If you connect to the database using this mode, other users will be able to change the data stored in the database. Note that you'll need to refresh the report to view these changes.

The **Public Read only** mode is used when you need to introduce minor changes into the database and retain shared write access for other users.

To view the changes introduced by other users, do one of the following operations:

❏ Select the **Refresh** command to refresh the data in your report

❏ Select the **Write** command to save the data in the database

❏ Manually disconnect from the database, then reconnect to the same database

The **Read write** mode is used when you need exclusive write access to the database. This mode is useful when you need to perform a massive loading of data into the database.

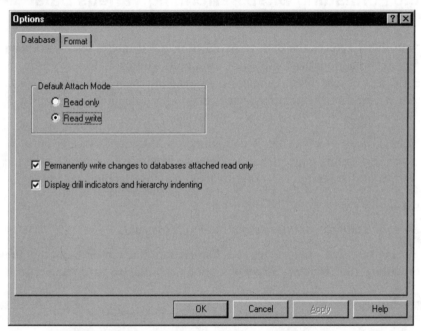

Fig. 5.65. The **Database** tab of the **Options** window

To define the default database access mode interactively, proceed as follows:

1. Select the **Options** command from the **Express** menu.

2. A dialog box will appear. Click the **Database** tab and select the required option from the **Default Attach Mode** option group. You can set one of the following options: **Read only** or **Read write**. If you need to set the **Public read only** mode, set the **Read only** default attach mode, and set the **Permanently write changes to databases attached read only** option.

To set the attach mode programmatically, use the following methods:

❏ XPSetOption("DefaultAttachMode","RW")—to set the read-write mode

❏ XPSetOption("DefaultAttachMode","RO")—to set the read-only mode

❏ XPSetOption("DefaultAttachMode","RO") and XPSetOption ("WritePermanent", "True")—to set the public read-only mode

> **NOTE**
>
> The selected attach mode does not influence access to the main database objects.

Saving Formatting when Performing Various Data Manipulations

After your query returns the data retrieved from the database server, you can perform any manipulations over this data using both Microsoft Excel commands and Oracle Express Spreadsheet commands. By default, the report formatting data is saved when performing operations such as drilling, selecting, or pivoting. Sometimes, however, we don't need to save the format.

For example, if we create a report containing several queries located next to each other when performing a pivoting operation, we would like to preserve the location of the results of these queries in order to avoid data overlapping.

To prevent data overlap, do the following:

1. Select the **Options** command from the **Express** menu.

2. A dialog box will open. Click the **Format** tab and set or clear the **Preserve Formatting after Drilling/Selection** option according to your requirements.

> **NOTE**
>
> Report formatting (font size and color) will not be preserved when manipulating data, no matter how the **Preserve Formatting after Drilling/Selection** option has been set.

Improving Performance

To increase the throughput and allow the Component to work with large amounts of data, change the automatic calculations to manual. To do this, select the **Options** command from the Microsoft Excel **Tools** menu, go to the **Calculation** tab, and set the **Manual** option.

To avoid errors when displaying more than 5,000 data rows or when running a query retrieving a large amount of data, use the xpaddin.ini file, where you can set the `RowFetchData` parameter, which specifies the maximum amount of rows that can be retrieved by the `Component`.

5.7.7. Oracle Express Spreadsheet Add-In API Reference

Table 5.20. Oracle Express Spreadsheet Add-In API Methods

Method	Description
Methods processing Express-calls	
XPSetCustomWriteCommand	Defines the procedure that will run when the user selects the **Write** command from the Express menu
XPSetPreCommitCommand	Defines the procedure that will be executed before saving data in the database
XPSetPrePageChangeCommand	Defines the procedure that will be executed before changing the query page
XPSetPreRefreshCommand	Defines the procedure that will be executed before refreshing the database query
XPSetPreUpdateCommand	Defines the procedure that will be executed before updating the data
XPSetPostAttachCommand	Defines the procedure that will be executed after attaching the database
XPSetPostUpdateCommand	Defines the procedure that will be executed after the command for updating data
Methods for processing database description	
XPAddMeasure	Adds an existing measure to the query
XPConnectHandle	Defines the existing SNAPI descriptor to be used for establishing connection to the Express Server
XPGetDatabase	Returns the name of or full path to the attached database
XPGetMeasure	Returns the measure name
XPGetMeasureDesc	Returns the measure description
XPGetMeasures	Returns the total number of measures available for selection in the attached database. You can use this method before calling the XPGETMEASURE or XPGETMEASUREDESC methods

continues

▼

Table 5.20 Continued

Method	Description
XPGetServerDesc	Returns a description of the current Express Server connection
XPGetServerHost	Returns the server name
Methods of query processing	
XPGetCellQDR	Returns the data definition script (QDR) for the current cell
XPGetChangeScript	Returns the data definition script for the current sheet
XPGetDimCount	Returns the number of dimensions associated with the value of a specific cell in the report
XPGetDimEdgeCount	Returns the number of dimensions associated with the cube edge for a specific report cell
XPGetDimensionDesc	Returns the description of the dimension for a specific edge associated with the report cell
XPGetDimensionName	Returns the name of the dimension for a specific edge associated with the report cell
XPGetDimStatus	Returns the number of dimension values associated with the cube edge value for a specific report cell
XPGetFirstDataCellColumn	Returns the column number of the starting (upper leftmost) cell of the specified query
XPGetFirstDataCellRow	Returns the row number of the starting (upper leftmost) cell for a specific query
XPGetFirstDataCellSheet	Returns the sheet number of the starting (upper leftmost) cell of a specific query
XPGetMeasureCount	Returns the number of measures for a specific report cell
XPGetMeasureDatabase	Returns the name of or complete path to the database for a specific measure
XPGetMeasureName	Returns the measure name for a specific cell
XPGetPage	Returns the position of the dimension in the list of dimensions for a specific cell

continues

Table 5.20 Continued

Method	Description
XPGetQueryID	Returns the internal query identifier for a specific report cell
XPGetQueryStartCell	Returns the starting cell of a specific query
XPGetSelectionScript	Returns the text of the data query script for a specific dimension
XPGetSelectionSortScript	Returns the text of the sort script for a specific dimension
XPIsMeasureDimension	Defines whether or not the specified dimension is a dimension of a measure of the selected cell
XPChangePage	Changes the position of the specified dimension in the dimension list for a specific cell
XPClose	Closes the session to the server
XPCreateCube	Creates a cube with dimensions for the specific query
XPCreateQuery	Creates the query identifier
XPDeleteQuery	Deletes the query
XPGetEdgeLabelType	Returns the type of the edge label
XPIsNASuppressed	Specifies whether blank row suppression is enabled
XPIsZeroSuppressed	Specifies whether zero row suppression is enabled
XPRemoveMeasure	Deletes the measure from the query
XPRunQuery	Runs the query
XPSetDimensionEdge	Moves the dimension from one edge to another
XPSetEdgeLabelType	Specifies the label type for the edge
XPSetRowSuppression	Sets the row suppression mode
XPSetScript	Sets the script text for the data query for a specific dimension
XPSetStartingCell	Sets the starting cell for the query
Methods duplicating the Express menu commands	
XPCommit	Commits database changes

continues

Table 5.20 Continued

Method	Description
XPConnect	Connects to the database server
XPDatabaseAttach	Attaches the database
XPDatabaseDetach	Detaches the database
XPDisconnect	Disconnects from the database server
XPDrill	Performs the data drilling operation
XPExecute	Executes an Oracle Express Server command
XPRefresh	Refreshes the data in the current sheet
XPRollback	Performs rollback
XPRotate	Performs data rotation
XPSelector	Starts the Selector tool
XPStartWizard	Starts the Query wizard
XPWrite	Writes data to the database
Methods for processing component parameters	
XPGetOption	Returns the value of the specified Oracle Express SpreadSheet Add-in option
XPSetOption	Sets the value of the specified Oracle Express SpreadSheet Add-in option

5.7.8. Example of Using API Calls in Microsoft Basic

```
' Declaring functions from the component library
Private Declare Function XPAddMeasure Lib "XPADDIN.XLL" (ByVal QueryID
As String, ByVal Meas As String, ByVal Database As String) As Boolean
Private Declare Function XPChangePage Lib "XPADDIN.XLL" (ByVal Row As
Integer, ByVal Col As Integer, ByVal Sheet As String, ByVal Dimension
As Integer, ByVal Offset As Long) As Boolean
Private Declare Function XPCommit Lib "XPADDIN.XLL" (ByVal Row As
Integer, ByVal Col As Integer, ByVal Sheet As String) As Boolean
Private Declare Function XPConnect Lib "XPADDIN.XLL" (ByVal Dialog As
Boolean) As Boolean
Private Declare Function XPCreateCube Lib "XPADDIN.XLL" (ByVal QueryID
As String) As Boolean
```

```
Private Declare Function XPCreateQuery Lib "XPADDIN.XLL" () As String

Private Declare Function XPDatabaseAttach Lib "XPADDIN.XLL" (ByVal
Database As String) As Boolean

Private Declare Function XPDatabaseDetach Lib "XPADDIN.XLL" (ByVal
Database As String) As Boolean

Private Declare Function XPDeleteQuery Lib "XPADDIN.XLL" (ByVal Row As
Integer, ByVal Col As Integer, ByVal Sheet As String) As Boolean

Private Declare Function XPDisconnect Lib "XPADDIN.XLL" () As Boolean

Private Declare Function XPDrill Lib "XPADDIN.XLL" (ByVal Row As
Integer, ByVal Col As Integer, ByVal Sheet As String) As Boolean

Private Declare Function XPExecute Lib "XPADDIN.XLL" (ByVal Script As
String) As String

Private Declare Function XPGetCellQDR Lib "XPADDIN.XLL" (ByVal Row As
Integer, ByVal Col As Integer, ByVal Sheet As String) As String

Private Declare Function XPGetChangeScript Lib "XPADDIN.XLL" (ByVal
Row As Integer, ByVal Col As Integer, ByVal Sheet As String, ByVal
Line As Integer) As String

Private Declare Function XPGetDatabase Lib "XPADDIN.XLL" (ByVal iDB As
Integer, ByVal bFullPath As Boolean) As String

Private Declare Function XPGetDimCount Lib "XPADDIN.XLL" (ByVal Row As
Integer, ByVal Col As Integer, ByVal Sheet As String) As Integer

Private Declare Function XPGetDimEdgeCount Lib "XPADDIN.XLL" (ByVal
Row As Integer, ByVal Col As Integer, ByVal Sheet As String, ByVal
Edge As Integer) As Integer

Private Declare Function XPGetDimensionDesc Lib "XPADDIN.XLL" (ByVal
Row As Integer, ByVal Col As Integer, ByVal Sheet As String, ByVal
Edge As Integer, ByVal Dimension As Integer) As String

Private Declare Function XPGetDimensionName Lib "XPADDIN.XLL" (ByVal
Row As Integer, ByVal Col As Integer, ByVal Sheet As String, ByVal
Edge As Integer, ByVal Dimension As Integer) As String

Private Declare Function XPGetDimStatus Lib "XPADDIN.XLL" (ByVal Row
As Integer, ByVal Col As Integer, ByVal Sheet As String, ByVal Edge As
Integer, ByVal Dimension As Integer) As Long

Private Declare Function XPGetFirstDataCellColumn Lib "XPADDIN.XLL"
(ByVal QueryID As String) As Integer

Private Declare Function XPGetFirstDataCellRow Lib "XPADDIN.XLL"
(ByVal QueryID As String) As Integer

Private Declare Function XPGetFirstDataCellSheet Lib "XPADDIN.XLL"
(ByVal QueryID As String) As String

Private Declare Function XPGetMeasure Lib "XPADDIN.XLL" (ByVal iMeas
As Integer) As String

Private Declare Function XPGetMeasureCount Lib "XPADDIN.XLL" (ByVal
Row As Integer, ByVal Col As Integer, ByVal Sheet As String) As Integer

Private Declare Function XPGetMeasureDatabase Lib "XPADDIN.XLL" (ByVal
Row As Integer, ByVal Col As Integer, ByVal Sheet As String, ByVal
Measure As Integer, ByVal FullPath As Boolean) As String
```

```
Private Declare Function XPGetMeasureDesc Lib "XPADDIN.XLL" (ByVal
iMeas As Integer) As String

Private Declare Function XPGetMeasureName Lib "XPADDIN.XLL" (ByVal Row
As Integer, ByVal Col As Integer, ByVal Sheet As String, ByVal Meas As
Integer) As String

Private Declare Function XPGetMeasures Lib "XPADDIN.XLL" (ByVal sDB As
String) As Integer

Private Declare Function XPGetOption Lib "XPADDIN.XLL" (ByVal
OptionName As String) As String

Private Declare Function XPGetPage Lib "XPADDIN.XLL" (ByVal Row As
Integer, ByVal Col As Integer, ByVal Sheet As String, ByVal Dimension
As Integer) As Long

Private Declare Function XPGetQueryID Lib "XPADDIN.XLL" (ByVal Row As
Integer, ByVal Col As Integer, ByVal Sheet As String) As String

Private Declare Function XPGetQueryStartCell Lib "XPADDIN.XLL" (ByVal
QueryID As String) As String

Private Declare Function XPGetSelectionScript Lib "XPADDIN.XLL" (ByVal
Row As Integer, ByVal Col As Integer, ByVal Sheet As String, ByVal
Edge As Integer, ByVal Dimension As Integer) As String

Private Declare Function XPGetSelectionSortScript Lib "XPADDIN.XLL"
(ByVal Row As Integer, ByVal Col As Integer, ByVal Sheet As String,
ByVal Edge As Integer, ByVal Dimension As Integer) As String

Private Declare Function XPGetServerDesc Lib "XPADDIN.XLL" () As
String

Private Declare Function XPGetServerHost Lib "XPADDIN.XLL" () As
String

Private Declare Function XPIsMeasureDimension Lib "XPADDIN.XLL" (ByVal
Row As Integer, ByVal Col As Integer, ByVal Sheet As String, ByVal
Edge As Integer, ByVal Dimension As Integer) As Boolean

Private Declare Function XPRefresh Lib "XPADDIN.XLL" (ByVal Row As
Integer, ByVal Col As Integer, ByVal Sheet As String) As Boolean

Private Declare Function XPRemoveMeasure Lib "XPADDIN.XLL" (ByVal
QueryID As String, ByVal Meas As String) As Boolean

Private Declare Function XPRollback Lib "XPADDIN.XLL" (ByVal Row As
Integer, ByVal Col As Integer, ByVal Sheet As String) As Boolean

Private Declare Function XPRotate Lib "XPADDIN.XLL" (ByVal Row As
Integer, ByVal Col As Integer, ByVal Sheet As String) As Boolean

Private Declare Function XPRunQuery Lib "XPADDIN.XLL" (ByVal QueryID
As String) As Boolean

Private Declare Function XPSelector Lib "XPADDIN.XLL" (ByVal Row As
Integer, ByVal Col As Integer, ByVal Sheet As String) As Boolean

Private Declare Function XPSetDimensionEdge Lib "XPADDIN.XLL" (ByVal
QueryID As String, ByVal DimName As String, ByVal Edge As Integer,
ByVal Dimension As Integer, ByVal Swap As Boolean) As Boolean

Private Declare Function XPSetOption Lib "XPADDIN.XLL" (ByVal
OptionName As String, ByVal OptionValue As String) As Boolean
```

```
Private Declare Function XPSetCustomWriteCommand Lib "XPADDIN.XLL"
(ByVal ExpressCommand As String) As Boolean
Private Declare Function XPSetPostAttachCommand Lib "XPADDIN.XLL"
(ByVal ExpressCommand As String) As Boolean
Private Declare Function XPSetPostUpdateCommand Lib "XPADDIN.XLL"
(ByVal ExpressCommand As String) As Boolean
Private Declare Function XPSetPreCommitCommand Lib "XPADDIN.XLL"
(ByVal ExpressCommand As String) As Boolean
Private Declare Function XPSetPreUpdateCommand Lib "XPADDIN.XLL"
(ByVal ExpressCommand As String) As Boolean
Private Declare Function XPSetScript Lib "XPADDIN.XLL" (ByVal QueryID
As String, ByVal DimName As String, ByVal SelectionScript As String,
ByVal SortScript As String) As Boolean
Private Declare Function XPSetStartingCell Lib "XPADDIN.XLL" (ByVal
QueryID As String, ByVal Row As Integer, ByVal Col As Integer, ByVal
SheetName As String) As Boolean
Private Declare Function XPStartWizard Lib "XPADDIN.XLL" (ByVal
QueryID As String, ByVal WizStep As Integer) As Boolean
Private Declare Function XPWrite Lib "XPADDIN.XLL" (ByVal Row As
Integer, ByVal Col As Integer, ByVal Sheet As String) As Boolean
Option Explicit
Sub test()
Dim b As Boolean
Dim Rw As Integer
Dim Cl As Integer
Dim SheetName As String
Application.ScreenUpdating = False
' Establishing connection to the server
If XPConnect(False) Then
  ' Set up Attach options
  Dim OptionVal As String
  OptionVal = XPGetOption("DefaultAttachMode")
  If OptionVal = "RO" Then
    Call XPSetOption("DefaultAttachMode", "RW")
  End If
  'Setting report parameters
  OptionVal = XPGetOption("DATEFORMAT")
  Call XPSetOption("DateFormat", OptionVal)
  OptionVal = XPGetOption("DECIMALFORMAT")
  Call XPSetOption("DecimalFormat", OptionVal)
  OptionVal = XPGetOption("FETCHSINGLEPAGE")
  Call XPSetOption("FetchSinglePage", OptionVal)
  OptionVal = XPGetOption("NASPELL")
```

```
Call XPSetOption("NASpell", OptionVal)
OptionVal = XPGetOption("RESIZECOLUMNS")
Call XPSetOption("ResizeColumns", OptionVal)
OptionVal = XPGetOption("SHOWDROPDOWN")
Call XPSetOption("ShowDropdown", OptionVal)
OptionVal = XPGetOption("PRESERVEFORMAT")
Call XPSetOption("PreserveFormat", OptionVal)
OptionVal = XPGetOption("WRITEPERMANENT")
Call XPSetOption("WritePermanent", OptionVal)
MsgBox XPGetServerDesc() + "      " + XPGetServerHost()
' Attaching the database
If XPDatabaseAttach("XADEMO") Then
  ' Activating the report sheet on which to place the query results
  Sheets("Sheet1").Activate
  ' Printing measures
  Dim iNumMeas As Integer
  iNumMeas = XPGetMeasures(XPGetDatabase(0, False))
  MsgBox str$(iNumMeas)
  Dim iMeas As Integer
  For iMeas = 0 To iNumMeas - 1
    Debug.Print XPGetMeasure(iMeas), "    ", XPGetMeasureDesc(iMeas)
  Next iMeas

  ' Creating a query
  Dim QueryID As String
  QueryID = XPCreateQuery()

  ' Adding measures
  If XPAddMeasure(QueryID, "F.UNITS", "XADEMO") Then
    XPAddMeasure QueryID, "F.SALES", "XADEMO"
    ' Deleting a measure
    XPRemoveMeasure QueryID, "F.UNITS"
    ' Creating a DataCube object
    If XPCreateCube(QueryID) Then
      ' Moving dimensions
      b = XPSetDimensionEdge(QueryID, "GEOGRAPHY", 1, 1, False)
      ' Setting the script for the GEOGRAPHY dimension
      b = XPSetScript(QueryID, "GEOGRAPHY", "LIMIT GEOGRAPHY TO -
FIRST 2", "SORT GEOGRAPHY A GEOGRAPHY")
      ' Setting the starting cell for the query
```

```
    b = XPSetStartingCell(QueryID, 5, 10, "Sheet1")
    ' Running the query
    b = XPRunQuery(QueryID)


    Application.ScreenUpdating = False


    Rw = XPGetFirstDataCellRow(QueryID)
    Cl = XPGetFirstDataCellColumn(QueryID)
    SheetName = XPGetFirstDataCellSheet(QueryID)
    ' Changing the report page
    Dim Count As Integer
    Count = XPGetDimEdgeCount(Rw, Cl, SheetName, 2)
    If Count > 0 Then
      Dim Status As Long
      Status = XPGetDimStatus(Rw, Cl, SheetName, 2, 1)
      If Status > 2 Then
        b = XPChangePage(Rw, Cl, SheetName, 1, 2)
  Application.ScreenUpdating = False
        Debug.Print "Page: " + Str$(XPGetPage(Rw, Cl, SheetName, 1))
      End If
    End If
    ' Changing the data cell
    Cells(Rw, Cl).Select
    ActiveCell.Value = 50
    ' Writing the changes to the database
    XPWrite Rw, Cl, SheetName
    Application.ScreenUpdating = False


    ' Rollback operation
    XPRollback Rw, Cl, SheetName
    Application.ScreenUpdating = False


    ' Repeated data modification
    Cells(Rw, Cl).Select
    ActiveCell.Value = 50

MsgBox XPGetChangeScript(Rw, Cl, SheetName, 0)
    ' Writing the changes to the database
    XPWrite Rw, Cl, SheetName
    Application.ScreenUpdating = False
```

```
' Committing the changes
XPCommit Rw, Cl, SheetName
Application.ScreenUpdating = False


' Displaying the query identifier
MsgBox XPGetQueryID(Rw, Cl, SheetName) + "     " + -
XPGetQueryStartCell(QueryID)
     ' Publishing data on the query
     Debug.Print "Dim Count: " + Str$(XPGetDimCount(Rw, Cl, -
SheetName))
        Debug.Print "Dimension Name: " + XPGetDimensionName(Rw, Cl, -
SheetName, 1, 1)
        Debug.Print "Dimension Description: " + XPGetDimensionDesc(Rw, -
Cl, SheetName, 1, 1)
        Debug.Print "Selection Script: " + XPGetSelectionScript(Rw, -
Cl, SheetName, 1, 1)
        Debug.Print "Sort Script: " + XPGetSelectionSortScript(Rw, Cl, -
SheetName, 1, 1)
        Debug.Print "Cell QDR: " + XPGetCellQDR(Rw, Cl, SheetName)
        Debug.Print "Is it the measure? " + -
Str$(XPIsMeasureDimension(Rw, Cl, SheetName, 0, 0))
    Debug.Print "Database: " + XPGetMeasureDatabase(Rw, Cl, SheetName, -
0, False)
    Debug.Print "Database: " + XPGetMeasureDatabase(Rw, Cl, SheetName, -
0, True)
        If XPGetMeasureCount(Rw, Cl, SheetName) > 0 Then
          Debug.Print "Measure Name: " + XPGetMeasureName(Rw, Cl, -
SheetName, 0)
        End If


' Refreshing the query
Call XPRefresh(Rw, Cl, SheetName)
Application.ScreenUpdating = False


' Drilling
Call XPDrill(Rw, Cl - 1, SheetName)
Application.ScreenUpdating = False


' Rotation
Sheets("Sheet1").Activate
Call XPRotate(Rw, Cl, SheetName)
Application.ScreenUpdating = False
```

```
        ' Calling the Selector tool
        Call XPSelector(Rw, Cl, SheetName)
        Application.ScreenUpdating = False

        ' Starting the Query wizard
        Call XPStartWizard(QueryID, 0)
      End If
    End If
  End If
End If
' Deleting the query
Application.ScreenUpdating = False
Call XPDeleteQuery(Rw, Cl, SheetName)
' Executing the database server command
MsgBox XPExecute("DTB LIST")
' Detaching the database
Application.ScreenUpdating = False
XPDatabaseDetach ("XADEMO")
' Disconnecting from the server
Call XPDisconnect
Application.ScreenUpdating = True
End Sub
```

Chapter 6

Creating Briefings
(Express Analyzer)

6.1. Product Description

6.1.1. Product Aims

Express Analyzer is the client application of the Express server. It is an instrumental environment intended for the following purposes:

❏ Viewing and analyzing multi-dimensional data

❏ Creating OLAP briefings

❏ Demonstrating ready-to-use end-user applications developed using Express Analyzer or Express Objects

In comparison to Express Objects, Express Analyzer is a "lightweight" end-user instrumental environment that enables non-programmers to develop OLAP applications for MS Windows, since it does not require programming. This application is installed from the distribution media, and the Setup program places its shortcut in the Express clients program group. The distribution package includes an on-line Help system providing a detailed description of the rules and principles of working with the application.

Development of the application (briefing) involves visual design based on pre-defined ready-to-used elements and subsequent tuning of their properties.

The briefing consists of a set of pages containing multidimensional data in table and graphical representation. An end user, such as a business analyst, can start the briefing and view it like a hard copy of a report. At the same time, he or she is able to manage both the presentation and the content of the data by drilling the information up or down. A typical view of the briefings is shown in Figs 1—4 (see the *Introduction*).

Briefings are composed of building blocks—components—which may include:

Component	Description
Pages	The page is the fundamental building block of the briefing. All other components are built into the pages
Tables	The components displaying the data in table view
Graphs	The components displaying the data in graphical view

continues

Continued

Component	Description
Express Output	Special objects enabling the user to run any command on the Express server and view the results of its execution
Embedded objects (OLE)	Display interactive information from other MS Windows applications, such as Excel, Word, etc.
Banners	Display text blocks
Buttons	Allow you to provide specific built-in commands

Objects are characterized by properties that specify their contents and view. The process of developing a briefing involves placing objects on the pages and tuning their properties. The briefing is saved in special file, which can at any time can be opened for viewing or editing.

6.1.2. Workspace and Tools

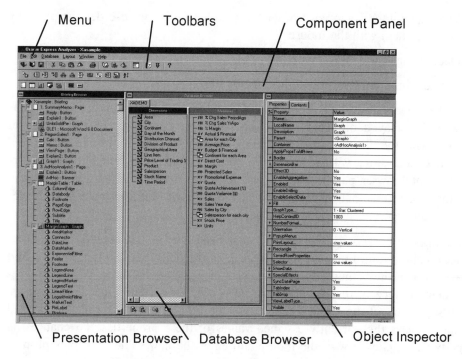

Fig. 6.1. Express analyzer workspace and tools

Fig. 6.1 shows the Express Analyzer interface. Express Analyzer workspace can include several child windows, the most important of which are shown in the illustration. The main window includes a menu, a toolbar, and the Component Panel. The application menu provides access to the main Analyzer functions, such as creating, editing, and executing briefings, establishing connection to the server, establishing the database connection, and many more.

The main window may contain the following three built-in toolbars:

❏ Buttons for quick access to the main menu

❏ Selector buttons

❏ Object layout buttons

You can specify the toolbars to be displayed in the main window by selecting the **Toolbars** command from the **Window** menu. The component panel contains buttons allowing you to create components and embed them into applications.

The presentation browser contains a hierarchical listing of all currently opened applications. Using this list, you can:

❏ View the contents and page order for each briefing, and re-order the pages by dragging them with the mouse

❏ Open a page for editing by double-clicking it with the mouse

❏ Create a link, copy, or move the page by dragging it from briefing to briefing

Using the database browser, you can select the required data from any opened database and display it on the briefing pages in table or graph view. The browser window shows the dimensions (left pane of the browser) that index variables stored in the database, along with relationships between dimensions, measures, and formulae (right browser pane). Having selected one or more dimensions, you can view the dimensions that index specific variables, since variables related to the selected dimensions are highlighted in blue.

Object inspector is comprised of two tabs: **Properties** and **Contents**. The object properties allow you to manage many aspects of the object's visual presentation and behavior when interacting with other objects or with the end user. When you create a new instance of the object, all its properties are assigned the default values. The first column of the **Property** table lists the property names, while the second column displays the currently assigned values of these properties. To change the property value, click it with the mouse and enter the new value. Complex properties can be edited in special dialogs. The complex properties that require special dialogs are designated with an ellipsis (...) following the property name. To open the dialog, simply double click the property name.

All objects have the following standard properties:

Property	Description
Name	The name of the object instance is used for referencing the current object from within another objects or from the Express Basic programs (which will be described in detail in *Chapter 7*). For example, the page name is displayed in the presentation browser. Only characters of the Latin alphabet are allowed in the names
LocalName	Local name is an additional name of the object instance, which can be specified in national languages
Description	Object description displayed by the presentation browser
Parent	Name of the parent object. The current object is a descendant of the parent object from the object-oriented point of view (see *Chapter 7* for more details)
Container	Name of the container object that contains the current object according to the nesting hierarchy. For example, the page containing a table or graph is a container for that table or graph. You can start editing the container object by double-clicking it with the mouse

Some properties can be combined within sets. For example, the Line property of the graph contains other properties, such as LineColor, LineStyle, LineTransparent, and LineWidth. Such properties are marked with a "+" or "-" icon to the left of its name.

The **Contents** tab contains the list of names of all object instances nested within the current object. For example, the **Contents** tab for the page will contain all the tables, graphs and buttons placed on this page. The **Contents** tab enables you to view the list of nested objects and edit their properties by simply double-clicking the required item in the list.

In the next sections of this chapter, we will look at how to use these tools to create data briefings in more detail.

6.2. Designing and Creating Briefings

6.2.1. Determining the Goals

As we mentioned before, briefings of multidimensional data are intended for applied specialists, such as sales managers, regional executives, financial analysts, and other persons responsible for making strategic decisions. Therefore, the most important task to be solved at the first stage of designing the briefing is to determine for whom it is intended. Express Analyzer provides you with the ability to flexibly tune applications according to specific end-user requirements. Based on these specific user requirements, we can determine the method of navigation within the briefing under development, data manipulation capabilities the user may require when performing on-line data analysis, and additional operations that the end user may perform when viewing the briefing.

In the second stage of development, which is as important as the first one, we need to determine the purposes of the briefing we are creating.

The briefing may have the form of a simple report representing in a specific format the current values of the most important business variables. This briefing form is aimed at enabling business analysts to monitor business processes. Such briefings are similar to navigation devices that allow you to constantly monitor the speed of movement in a specified direction, the available amount of fuel and other resources, the level of expenses, etc. The main goal of such briefings is to inform the person responsible for making decisions about unfavorable deviations of critically important business variables from the planned route, and provide them with the ability to timely correct them.

Another type of briefing is generally intended for searching possible business solutions, evaluating their efficiency, and selecting the optimum solution, rather than controlling the current processes. When solving this kind of task, the analyst usually requires the ability to send non-standard queries to the database and perform complex manipulations with the retrieved data, and also to represent this data in table or graphical views. In this situation, the user normally requires the capability of performing a "What if?" analysis based on business models stored in the database. For example, the user may wish to know how income would change if the sales amount increased by 50 % in the next quarter.

Having determined the intended audience and the aims of the briefing to be constructed, we will be able to make key decisions about the design of our briefing, such as:

❑ Determining the aggregation level and contents of the data presented in the pages of our briefing.

❑ Determining the format of data presentation, such as types of graphs and tables, their mutual interrelations, positioning of the dimensions, additional information, etc.

❏ Determining the required functionality of our briefing. For example, we need to determine the capabilities of manipulating data and their views, or other operations available when the user clicks specific buttons.

❏ Planning the briefing pages (page number, informational content, and placement of the add-on function buttons).

❏ Determining user navigation capabilities for viewing the briefing. For example, you can classify users by categories—those that require all of the information and the ones that require only the pages containing summary data.

Later in this chapter we will discuss how you can create briefings using Express Analyzer tools and achieve the specified goals while taking into account specific end-user requirements.

6.2.2. Creating Briefings

Starting Express Analyzer

Oracle Express
Analyzer   Express Analyzer is a client Express application designed for MS Windows. You can start it by double-clicking the appropriate icon in the **Express Clients** program group from the Windows main menu. After starting this application, a prompt will appear (Fig. 6.2). This dialog allows you to select one of the following Express Analyzer modes:

❏ **Run an Application or Briefing**—opens the standard **Open File** dialog and allows you to start the briefing file (XBR filename extension) or an application file (XPJ filename extension) created using Express Objects

❏ **Create a new Briefing**—opens a dialog allowing you to create a new briefing

❏ **Change an existing Briefing**—opens the standard **Open File** Windows dialog and allows you to select the briefing file and open it for editing

❏ **Analyze Express Data**—allows you to connect to the Express server and open one or more databases for analysis

❏ **Start where I left off last time**—Analyzer will open the briefing file with which you were working during the last session for editing

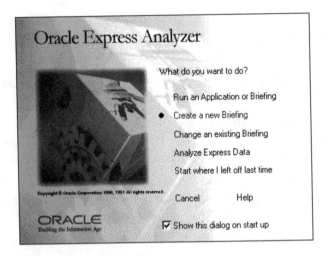

Fig. 6.2. The Oracle Express Analyzer welcome screen

To quit Express Analyzer, select the **Exit** command from the **File** menu.

Attaching Databases and Analyzing Data

To open the dialog allowing you to attach a database, select the **Analyze Express Data** mode in the starting Analyzer window, or select the **Database/Attach** commands from the main application menu and then open the required file (for example, FIRST.DB, as shown in Fig. 6.3).

Note that the database can be attached both in the read-only mode and in read-write mode. To specify the database attachment mode, select the appropriate option in the **Open File** dialog.

In the database browser window, you'll see the lists of dimensions and variables (measures and formulae) that you have created. Notice that both dimensions and measures are represented in the browser window by their long labels. Additional information on the selected database object (indexing measures, value type, descriptions, etc.) can be viewed in the **Object Inspector** window. Before you can view the variable values, it is necessary to create a new briefing (Fig. 6.4) (if you have not done this already) by selecting the **File/New Briefing** items from the menu. Then select the required database object (for example, the Sales income formula), right-click on that object, and select the desired format from the **Inspect/Table/Graph** menu (see Fig. 6.3) (for example, you may wish to select the table format).

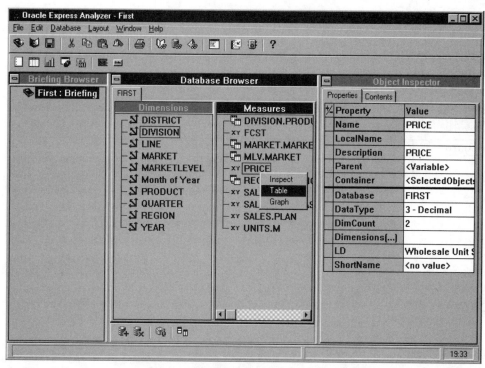

Fig. 6.3. Analyzing the data from the FIRST.DB database using Express Analyzer

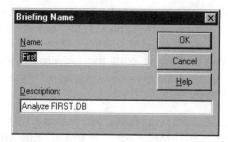

Fig. 6.4. The **Briefing Name** dialog allows you to create a new briefing

After performing this operation, a new page will be added to our briefing. This new page will contain a table view of the sales income (Fig. 6.5). Note that sometimes you may not be able to see national language characters in the table. To view such characters, you will need to perform two operations. First, you need to modify as necessary the font names (for example, change `Arial` to `Arial Cyr`) in the `[FONT]` section of the Xanalyze.ini file. This file contains the default settings of the Express Analyzer application and resides in the [*ORA_HOME*]/OLAP/OEA220 directory.

The new settings will come into force after restarting the application. Next, you'll need to set the Font property for all table objects containing national characters. Pay special attention to the fact that the information on the measure values is represented in the table as short and long labels.

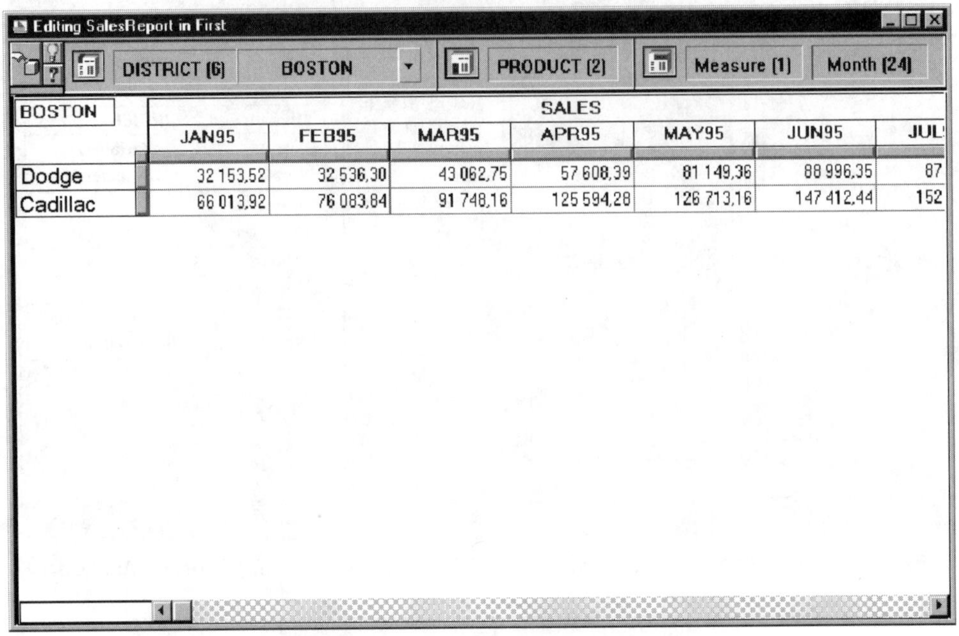

| Editing SalesReport in First | | | | | | | | _ | □ | X |

| DISTRICT [6] | BOSTON ▼ | | PRODUCT [2] | | Measure [1] | Month [24] |

BOSTON	SALES						
	JAN95	FEB95	MAR95	APR95	MAY95	JUN95	JUL
Dodge	32 153,52	32 536,30	43 062,75	57 608,39	81 149,36	88 996,35	87
Cadillac	66 013,92	76 083,84	91 748,16	125 594,28	126 713,16	147 412,44	152

Fig. 6.5. The briefing page containing the table view of the data

Setting table properties and working with the **Selector** object will be covered in following chapters. Graphical data representation can be viewed and analyzed in a way similar to that of the table view.

Saving the briefing implies that you write to the hard disk the components you have created along with their properties in a special file with the XBR filename extension. To perform this operation, select one of the following commands from the menu: **File/Save**, **Save As**, or **Save All**.

The *Briefing* Component

The Briefing component encapsulates the main properties of the briefing (Fig. 6.6). After the new briefing has been created (see the previous section), the presentation browser will display the root element of the hierarchical list:

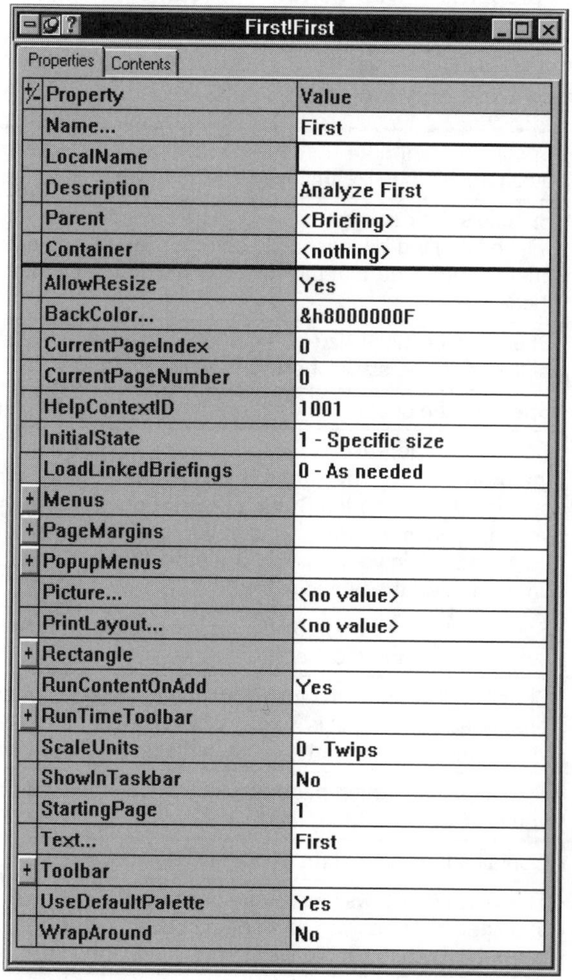

First!First	
Property	**Value**
Name...	First
LocalName	
Description	Analyze First
Parent	<Briefing>
Container	<nothing>
AllowResize	Yes
BackColor...	&h8000000F
CurrentPageIndex	0
CurrentPageNumber	0
HelpContextID	1001
InitialState	1 - Specific size
LoadLinkedBriefings	0 - As needed
+ Menus	
+ PageMargins	
+ PopupMenus	
Picture...	<no value>
PrintLayout...	<no value>
+ Rectangle	
RunContentOnAdd	Yes
+ RunTimeToolbar	
ScaleUnits	0 - Twips
ShowInTaskbar	No
StartingPage	1
Text...	First
+ Toolbar	
UseDefaultPalette	Yes
WrapAround	No

Fig. 6.6. The properties of the `Briefing` component

This root element will have the name (the **Name** property) and description (the **Description** property) specified when the component was created. The values of these and other properties of the components may be changed in the **Object Inspector** window shown in Fig. 6.5.

Specifying the Properties

Unfortunately, the limited volume of this book doesn't allow us to provide detailed descriptions for all properties of all objects and components. It should be noted, however, that the purpose of most properties are self-evident from their names. All these properties are described in detail in the reference manual supplied with the product. Therefore, we will only look at the most frequently used properties.

AllowResize	Specifies whether or not the end user can resize the briefing window by changing the size that was specified when it was first created
BackColor	Specifies the background color. The color specified by this property will be inherited by most child objects that will be nested within the briefing, provided that this property has not been explicitly changed for these objects
InitialState	Specifies the initial size of the briefing window (full-screen or a window of the specified size) when starting the briefing
PageMargins	Specifies the briefing fields (in inches) for the briefing page
Picture	Contains a reference to the Picture object (if specified) and defines the picture surrounding the briefing pages in the briefing window. Pay special attention to the **Saving in Briefing** option in the dialog allowing you to select the picture. This option specifies whether the picture will be stored within your briefing or opened from the specified file any time you start the briefing
Rectangle	Specifies the size and position of the briefing window. Normally, you set these with the mouse
ScaleUnits	Specifies the scale unit for coordinates and sizes of graphical objects. The default scale unit is Twips, which is equal to 1/1440 of an inch. If you change this property, all nested objects will inherit this change
StartingPage	Specifies the starting page at which the briefing will be opened when you start it
Text	Contains the title text for the briefing window
Toolbar	This property allows you to customize the toolbar within the briefing, and specify its position and some specific parameters (more detailed information on this topic will be provided later in this chapter)
WrapAround	This property specifies whether or not cyclic navigation will be used when using the navigation buttons on the toolbar

The Toolbar

The briefing toolbar (Fig. 6.7) is a standard object that can be built into the briefing for the end user's convenience (see the **Toolbar** property described in the previous section). The toolbar contains a drop-down list containing the names (the values of the **Text** property) of all pages contained in the briefing, buttons allowing you to perform navigation, **Print** and **Help** buttons. The rightmost position of the toolbar displays the current page indicator (unfortunately, this indicator can't be localized). The presence and initial position of the toolbar in the briefing window is defined by the complex **Toolbar** property. Using this property you can, for example, delete the current page indicator from the toolbar by specifying the value of 0 in the **TextPaneWidth** field. At run-time, the user can move the toolbar or open it in a floating window.

Fig. 6.7. The briefing toolbar

Briefing Editor

The briefing editor is another useful tool, complementing the presentation browser, database browser, and object inspector's functionality, and allowing you to significantly reduce the time required to design a client application. To open the editor, double-click the briefing name in the browser. The briefing browser displays the briefing window at design time in a way very similar to the look it will have at run-time.

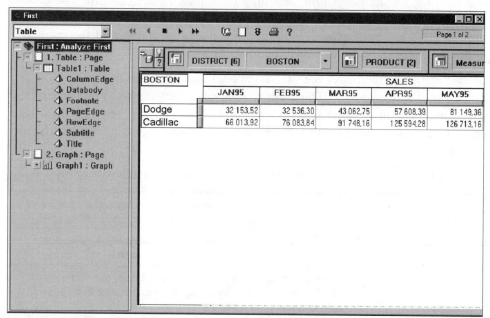

Fig. 6.8. The Briefing editor window

The editor can contain the built-in toolbar described in the previous section. However, in the editor window this toolbar contains three additional buttons, which allow you to start the briefing, create a new page, and open the presentation browser in the editor window (Fig. 6.8).

The editor allows you to significantly reduce the time required to navigate from window to window, switch from page to page, create new pages, and select objects for setting their properties both within pages and in the presentation browser window.

6.2.3. Creating and Editing Pages

The Page component is the basic building block for briefings. Like a book, any briefing usually contains one or more pages. All the other visual components, such as tables, graphs, text fragments, control buttons, etc., are placed within pages. A new page can be created by clicking the appropriate button in the briefing editor. As with any other component, a new page can be nested within an existing page. To do so, click the **Page** button on the component toolbar, and then position the mouse cursor at the point where the new window should be placed, click and hold the left mouse button, and drag the cursor to designate the rectangular area where the new page will be placed. After you release the left mouse button, the new page will be displayed within the designated rectangle, and the respective Briefing component will appear in the browser list.

Most common properties of the Page component are the same as for the Briefing properties described earlier. Once again, remember that the Text property of the page will appear in the drop-down list at the briefing toolbar. Therefore, make sure you take into account the end-user requirements when specifying a value for this property.

Listed below are some useful properties of the Page component:

AutoSize	If this property is set to YES, the page will be resized proportionally, which will result in automatic re-scaling of all tables and graphs placed at this page
Effect3D	Allows for managing the style of the page border
Enabled	If you set this property to NO, you can disable for the end-user all actions that were previously available when viewing this page, such as changing the type of graph, etc.

continues

Continued

`ExpressCommands`	Allows you to specify and execute on the server any command of the Express language (and, consequently, any stored program you have created) any time you initialize, display, or close this page. For example, the specified command may be responsible for data updating or for accumulating server statistics on the page's usage
`PageBorder`	Manages the presence and style of the page border. Also enables or disables user-specified resizing of the page at run-time
`Visible`	Allows you to make the page invisible to the end user at run time

Quite often you may need to change the order of pages within a briefing. You can do this in the presentation browser by dragging the pages with the mouse. Note that when using this method you need to position the cursor at an interval between the list items.

To delete the page from the briefing, select it in the browser list and press the <Delete> button on the keyboard.

6.2.4. Component Nesting

As we mentioned before, the briefing page can contain the following nested components: graphs, tables, Express Output (the results of executing Express commands on the server), OLE objects, text fragments, and buttons. To place the component on the page, click the appropriate button in the component bar (the mouse cursor will change), and then drag it with the mouse to the position on the page where you wish to place the upper left corner of the built-in component. Thus, you will create an object instance with the default size. You can drag with the mouse within a page to designate a rectangular area intended for the built-in component. Setting the components for visual representation of multidimensional data (graphs and tables) will be covered in another chapter. Now let's consider the remaining components.

Banners

Banner1 This component is intended for placing text banners and comments into a page.

The properties of this component provide for flexibly tuning its content and format. Besides the common properties listed above, such as `BackColor`, `Enabled`, `MouseIcon`, `MousePointer`, `Picture`, `Rectangle`, and `Visible`, you can set the following properties:

`FillColor`	Allows you to set the page border color
`Font`	Specifies the font style, size, and color
`Gutter`	Specifies the gutter width
`Style`	Manages the presence of the component border, its style, and shading
`WordWrap`	Enables or disables the word wrap feature

Fig. 6.9. shows an example of `Banner` component usage.

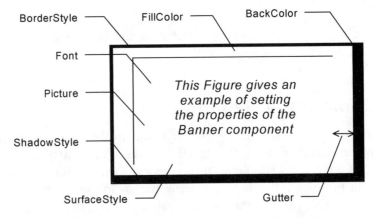

Fig. 6.9. Properties of the `Banner` component

Embedded OLE objects

The briefing page can contain a window served by another Windows application. This feature can be used only with applications supporting OLE (Object Linking and Embedding) technology. Express Analyzer allows us to embed OLE objects into its applications. However, Express Analyzer objects cannot be embedded into other applications. Most popular Windows applications, such as MS Word, MS Excel, MS Power Point, Adobe Acrobat, Adobe Photoshop, and other applications, support OLE. Objects created using any of these applications can be embedded into your briefing. An application window embedded into the page will look as if, for example, an MS Excel worksheet were part of our application (Fig. 6.10).

Using OLE objects, you can create quite complex Analyzer applications that can include additional capabilities as compared to those of Express, including graphical capabilities, editable text, multimedia, and many more.

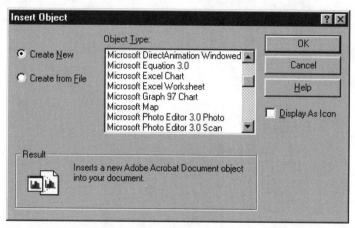

Fig. 6.10. The **Insert Object** dialog allows you to embed OLE objects into the briefing

After you insert an OLE object into the briefing, Express opens the **Insert Object** dialog (Fig. 6.10), which lists all OLE objects available at the local PC. You can select the type of the object to be inserted from the **Object Type** list, or simply open the file created using the required application (for example, an MS Word document, or an MS Excel workbook, or *.AVI animation). After this, the application will start in embedded mode. This application will take all responsibility for redrawing the embedded window and supporting the user interface when the embedded window gets the input focus.

We have flexible capabilities for customizing interaction between our application and an embedded object by changing the properties of OLE object in Object Inspector. Besides the standard properties common for most objects, OLE objects have the following important properties:

ActivateVerb	Defines the event (such as application start, window activation, double-clicking with the mouse within a window), which activates a specific action to be taken on the embedded object. This action is specified by the DefaultVerb property
DefaultVerb	Specifies the action that will be taken in the case of the event specified by the ActivateVerb property. The list of available actions depends on the specific application (for example, MS Excel provides **Edit** and **Open** capabilities)

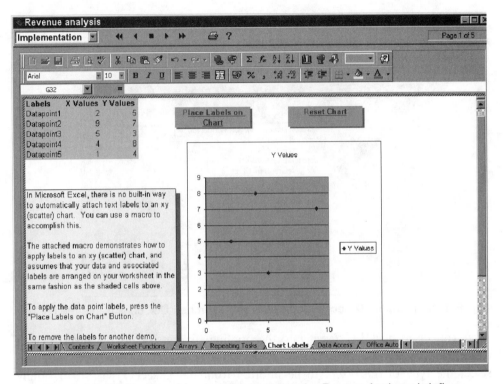

Fig. 6.11. MS Excel workbook embedded into the Express Analyzer briefing

This technology allows for complex tuning of the interaction between Express and other applications that you can develop using other programming languages and development environments such as Delphi, C++ Builder, etc. Independent software developers already supply OLE components for Express. For example, Open Map supplies an OLE component for Express that supports data display on geographical maps.

Buttons

Buttons represent one of the most common standard interface components in MS Windows. By default, the `Button` component looks as follows:

By changing the properties of this component, you can make this object look as you want it to. Besides the standard properties you can specify values for the following specific properties of this component:

`BevelWidth`	Sets the bevel width at the 3D button, thus imitating a 3D look
`BorderStyle`	Specifies if a border around the button is present
`Cancel`	Links the button to the <Esc> key and allows you to redefine the default action of the application when the user presses this key
`CornerStyle`	Allows you to select the button style (you can choose between MS Windows 3.11 style and Windows 95 style)
`Default`	Links the button to the <Enter> key and allows you to redefine the default action of the application when this key is pressed
`FitToPicture`	Allows you to adjust the button size automatically according to the size of the icon specified for this button

Fig. 6.12 shows one of the possible button styles which you may choose to specify in your briefing.

Fig. 6.12. Example of the button component

The `Button` component implements the `QuickAction` mechanism, which enables you to develop an advanced briefing functionality without having to do any programming. This mechanism allows you to select and customize parameters for more than 30 predefined actions. To open the dialog allowing you to define an action linked to the button, select the appropriate button at the briefing page or in the browser window, and then select the **Set QuickAction** command from the right-click menu. If you are interested in this topic, you can find a detailed description of all customizable actions in the *Reference Manual*. Here we will provide only a brief description of the most frequently used ones.

Action	Description
`Execute OLE Verb`	Allows you to assign specific actions in embedded OLE objects. For example, it is possible to customize the button in such a way as to play an inserted video clip when the user clicks that button
`Goto Page`	Allows you to perform quick navigation by going to the specified page of the briefing

continues

Continued

Action	Description
Launch Application	Starts an application
Show Custom	Opens the dialog for editing properties of the specified Express object (for example, the `Text` property of the `Banner` component)
Print	Allows you to specify the printer settings and print the contents of the briefing
Show Message	Displays the standard Windows message box with the specified message text
Create View	Creates a data view related to the existing data view. For example, you can insert a button displaying a table data view corresponding to the current graph on the current page
Execute Express Command	Runs one or more Express commands on the server. For example, you can use this action to run a program that calculates the predicted values of the specified business variable and displays the results as a graph on the briefing page
Export Table	Exports data from the table to the Excel file or to the text file
Format Measure	Opens the standard dialog allowing you to format the parameters of the text view
Show Drill Tool	Opens the standard dialog allowing the user to customize the required aggregation level of the data presented
Swap Dimensions	Swaps the specified dimensions
Execute Action List	Allows you to specify and execute several actions when the button is pressed

You set the customizable parameters for the action in action-specific dialogs.

Aligning Components

The buttons located at the Layout Toolbar provide for quick customization of the layout of the components on the briefing page. To display this toolbar in the main window, select the **Window/Toolbars** menu item and set the **Layout Toolbar** option in the dialog that will appear. The buttons of this toolbar become active if the current briefing page contains several components. Using these buttons, you can display the grid helping you to customize the component layout. All objects placed on the page can be snapped to this grid, which means that the objects will be moved within a page discretely, by increments equal to the grid unit. To set the scaling units for the grid and the value of the grid step, open the **Options** dialog by selecting the **Edit/Options** menu item.

Using the **Align** button, you can align object centers horizontally or vertically. This button also allows you to align objects near the left, right, top, or bottom window borders. To do so, first select the components to be aligned by clicking them with the mouse while pressing and holding the <Shift> key on the keyboard. After selecting the components, click the **Align** button and select the required option from the popup menu. Then position the mouse cursor over the object that will be used as an alignment prototype, and click it with the left mouse button.

The **Same Size** button allows you to align the sizes of several components by height, width, or by both of these dimensions. The alignment by size operation is similar to the above-described positioning procedure. First, select the group to be aligned, then set the alignment option, and the sample object according to which the new object sizes will be set.

The **Even Spacing** button is used for moving one object an equal distance from two other objects. To perform this operation, select the object to be aligned, select the alignment type by pressing the **Even Spacing** button, and then, one by one, click the first and the second objects in relation to which you need to perform the alignment operation.

The components within a briefing page can overlap each other. The redrawing order is defined by the order in which these objects were created. However, you can change this by clicking the **Z-Order** button and selecting the appropriate option from the menu. The selected object can be placed in front or behind all other objects or moved to the required position within the redrawing queue.

Having finalized the position and size of all components on the current page, you can lock them by clicking the **Lock Contents** button.

6.2.5. Print Settings

To print the briefing, click the **Print** button on the toolbar. The **Print** dialog will appear (Fig. 6.13), allowing you to customize the print settings. Using this dialog, you can print any graph or table located anywhere within your briefing (the **View** option), on the specified briefing page (the **Page** option). Using the **Briefing** option, you can print a specified range of pages or the whole briefing. Furthermore, you can specify the number of copies, set their order (the **Collate Copies** option), or scale the output according to the current paper size set for the selected printer.

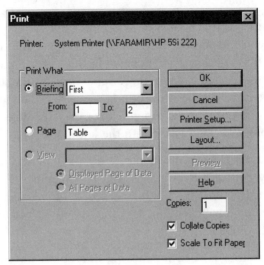

Fig. 6.13. The **Print** dialog allows you to customize printer settings for printing your briefing

The **Displayed Page of Data** and **All Pages of Data** radio buttons allow you to output the current page only or all data pages presented in the data cube (the data cube will be covered in the next chapter) corresponding to the graph or table on the briefing page.

To specify the page layout options, such as margins, titles, and other text labels, click the **Layout** button to open the **Layout** dialog that allows you to set these options.

If you don't want to make print settings available to the end user, you can specify preset values for all print options and assign them to a special button, which will be available for the end user for printing the required data. To do this, use the above-described **Print** action.

6.2.6. Publishing Briefings

List of Published Files

Once the briefing has been created, you need to make it available to the end users (business analysts). To make this possible, make sure that the Express Analyzer software is installed at the end-user workstation. This software is used as an environment for starting and executing briefings. Furthermore, since each briefing operates with data stored in the Express database, you need to provide access from the client workstation to the server (Express Server or Personal Express). To provide the required connectivity, set up the XCL file as appropriate.

The main file that must be available from the client computer is the briefing file with the XBR filename extension. Sometimes, however, publishing the briefing file alone is not sufficient. For example, if your briefing starts other briefings using the **Quick Action** operation, make sure that all required files are available to the end user.

Besides, if your briefing has pictures, such as button icons, background patterns, etc., and these pictures are not saved within the briefing file, you'll also need to publish all bitmaps (BMP files) with the briefing.

Also notice that all files inserted into the briefing using OLE components (for example, Excel workbooks or AVI files) must also be published along with the briefing.

If you assume that end users won't be saving the changes that they introduce into the briefing (for example, they may create new pages or change the current view), you can store the briefing in one of the shared network directories. If you want to provide end users with the capability of changing the briefing according to their preferences and saving these changes for future use, distribute the briefing files to the end-user workstations.

Viewing Briefings

To simplify the process of starting our briefing for end users, you may wish to create an icon or shortcut at the client computer. When specifying the shortcut properties, you need to create a command line starting Express Analyzer. For example, let us assume that your briefing is saved in a file named FIRST.XBR, located in the WORK directory. Then you can specify the following command line in the shortcut properties:

```
C:\ORAWIN95\OLAP\OEA220\XANALYZE.EXE /Q /Z FIRST.XBR
```

You'll also need to specify the working directory (for example, C:\ORAWIN95\OLAP\OEA220\WORK). The command line switches (/Q and /Z) manage the Express Analyzer start parameters (more detailed information on this topic can be found in the "*Using Run Switches*" topic of the on-line help system).

Publishing Databases in the WWW

Express software allows application developers to easily publish graphs and tables created using Express Analyzer on the Web. All aspects related to publishing the analytical systems in the intranet/Internet will be covered in detail in *Chapter 4* of this book. As for this section, let us consider the publishing functionality provided by Express Analyzer.

To enable the developers to publish data from multidimensional databases on the Web, you need to install Web support both on the server side (this includes Oracle software components such as Oracle Express Web Agent and Oracle Application Server), and on the client side (this includes the Oracle Express Web Publisher software component). Before publishing your data on the Web, you need to use the Express Web Publisher application to create a WWW site for publishing your data. Start Express Web Publisher and select the **File/New WebSite** menu item to create the Web site. To register the newly created site, select the **File/Publish All** menu item.

Having completed creation of the Web site, close Express Web Publisher and start Express Analyzer. Open any of the available briefings and select the object (graph, for example) that you intend to place on the WWW page. Right-click the graph and select the **ExportToWeb** command from the popup menu. Follow the instructions provided by Express Analyzer to create a WWW briefing containing the page with the Java graph presenting our multidimensional data. Do the same for publishing the table data view created using Express Analyzer.

6.3. Structured Multidimensional Data Queries

Currently, Express client applications provide two types of multidimensional data representation for the end users: tables (`Table` objects) and graphs (`Graph` objects). Both presentations are based on the `DataCube` object that encapsulates multidimensional structured queries to the Express database. By customizing the cube parameters, we can flexibly manage table and graph data views. The `DataCube` object, in turn, is related to the `Selection` objects, whose settings determine the informational content retrieved from the database. To efficiently use the Express family of products as a powerful OLAP tool, you need to have a clear understanding of the above mentioned objects and manage them skillfully.

6.3.1. Managing the Layout of the Displayed Data

Structure of the Data Cube Object

The `Data Cube` Express object used for logical representation of multidimensional data has exactly three dimensions (Fig. 6.14): COLUMNS, ROWS, and PAGES. For each dimension (with the possible exception of pages) there may be one or more related edge nodes—dimensions or variables defined in the database. Thus, each cube dimension is defined by a set of values representing the Cartesian product of the groups of values (dimension value set), related to that dimension of the cube.

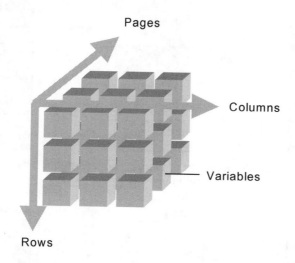

Fig. 6.14. Three dimensions of the data cube

Let us suppose that the PAGES dimension is related to the PRODUCT and MONTH dimensions. The PRODUCT dimension has three values: Dodge, Ford, and Cadillac. The MONTH dimension has five values: Jan98, Feb98, Mar98, Apr98, and May98. The PAGES dimension is then defined by the following fifteen values (Fig. 6.15).

If there are variables related to the data cube dimension, then there is exactly one value corresponding to each variable (Fig. 6.16).

There is no standalone data cube object in the set of standard Express components. However, the data cube is created for each table or graph included into the application. Customization of the data cube and, consequently, data view in a table or graph is done using the built-in dimension bars. Dimension bars represent three dimensions of the data cube and the database dimensions related to it. Fig. 6.17 shows the dimension bars of the table and graph. Each dimension bar comprises three parts reflecting the respective dimension of the data cube.

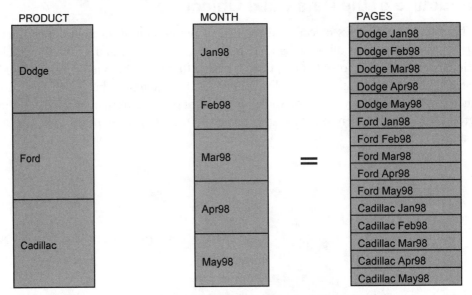

Fig. 6.15. The dimension value set of the data cube is defined by Cartesian product of related dimension value sets

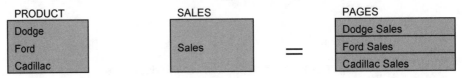

Fig. 6.16. Determining the dimension value set of the cube when one variable is related to the dimension

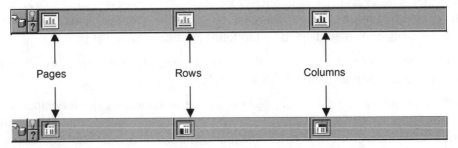

Fig. 6.17. Dimension bars of the table and graph reflecting the data cube dimensions

Let's illustrate this explanation with an example. Create a new project in Express Analyzer. Use the database browser to attach the xademo.db database. Drag the **Sales** variable from the browser to the main window of the newly created application, and then select the **Table** item from the list of available views. To make this example more general, drag one more variable—**Sales YrAgo**—into the newly created table. These variables are indexed by the following dimensions: **Geog.Area**, **Product**, **Channel,** and **Time**. The default view of the dimension bar for this table will look as shown in Fig. 6.18. Notice that the specified variables are joined within the **Measure** edge node.

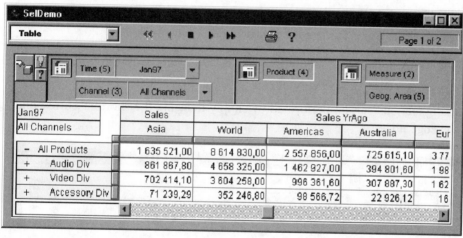

Fig. 6.18. The dimension bar for the table displaying the Sales and Sales YrAgo variables

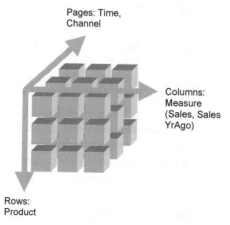

Fig. 6.19. Dimensions of the data cubes and their related edge nodes

The data cube will be automatically created for this table, and the appropriate dimensions and variables will be related to the dimensions of this cube (Fig. 6.19).

Managing the Data Cube

If you are not satisfied with the data view created by default, you can easily change it according to your personal preferences. Especially for this purpose, Express provides a visual mechanism for editing the correspondence between the data cube dimensions and their related edge nodes. Using this mechanism, you can do the following:

❏ Change the order of the edge nodes within a dimension

❏ Move the edge node from dimension to dimension

❏ Swap two edge nodes between two different dimensions

These operations can be performed by simply dragging the shortcut corresponding to the edge node.

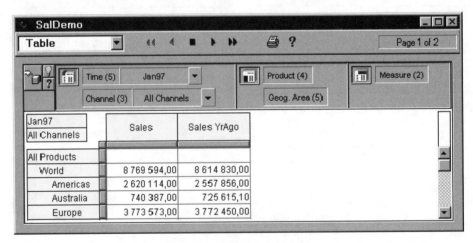

Fig. 6.20. Changing the data view by moving the `Geog.Area` from the `Columns` dimension to the `Rows` dimension (compare this view to the view shown in Fig. 6.18)

To move the edge node, first position the mouse cursor over the desired edge node in the dimension bar, click the left mouse button, and drag it with the mouse to the desired position. For example, if we move the **Geog.Area** dimension from the **Columns** dimension to the **Rows** dimension, the table shown in Fig. 6.18 will change to the one shown in Fig. 6.20.

To swap two edge nodes, the process is the same. For example, to swap the **Measure** and **Channel** edge nodes, click the **Measure** edge node and drag it to the **Channel** edge node. If you perform this operation with the table shown in Fig. 6.18, you will get the result shown in Fig. 6.21.

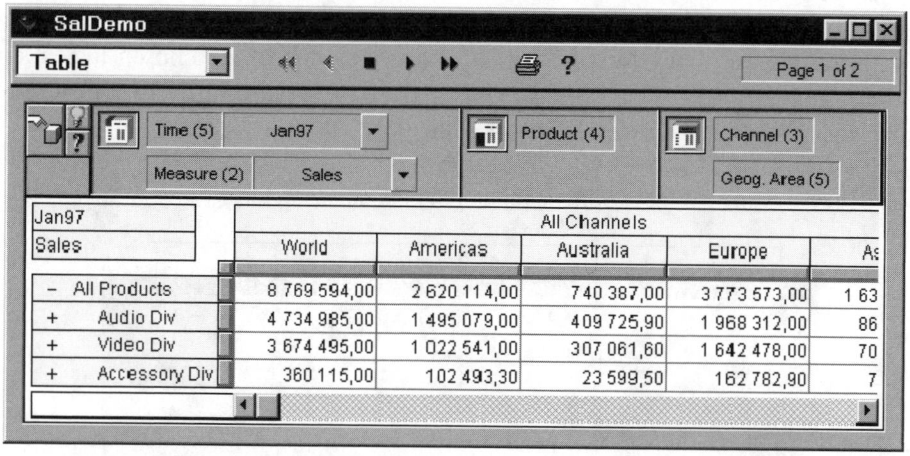

Fig. 6.21. The result of swapping the Channel and Measure edge nodes (compare this table to the one shown in Fig. 6.18)

6.3.2. Managing the Contents of the Displayed Data

Data Selection (Selector Object)

When creating the data view (table or graph) for each edge node related to the cube dimension, the system creates another object—the Selection Object. This object selects specific values of the dimension or variable from the set of available ones in the Express database to include them into the related edge node. For example, if the database contains data on product sales for several years, we can select and display only the data related to the last five months. Notice that the number of values or variables actually selected into the edge node is displayed in the dimension bar as a number in parentheses immediately following the name of the respective edge node. For managing the settings of the Selection objects, Express provides very powerful and flexible set of tools combined within the **Selector Object** dialog (Fig. 6.22). To open this dialog, click the  button in the dimension bar.

This interface object is intended for visual editing of the LIMIT statement (see *Chapter 4*) that will be executed on the server. All selection operations implement a similar schema. The operation is applicable to the selected edge node in the dimension list. For each operation, there is always a value set already present in the edge node being defined. The second set (let us designate it as **A**) is defined by applying the specified selection operation to the set of values defined in the database for respective dimension. The result of applying one of the chosen logical operations (Select[1], Add, Keep, and Remove) to these two sets will give us a new set of dimension values that will determine its state.

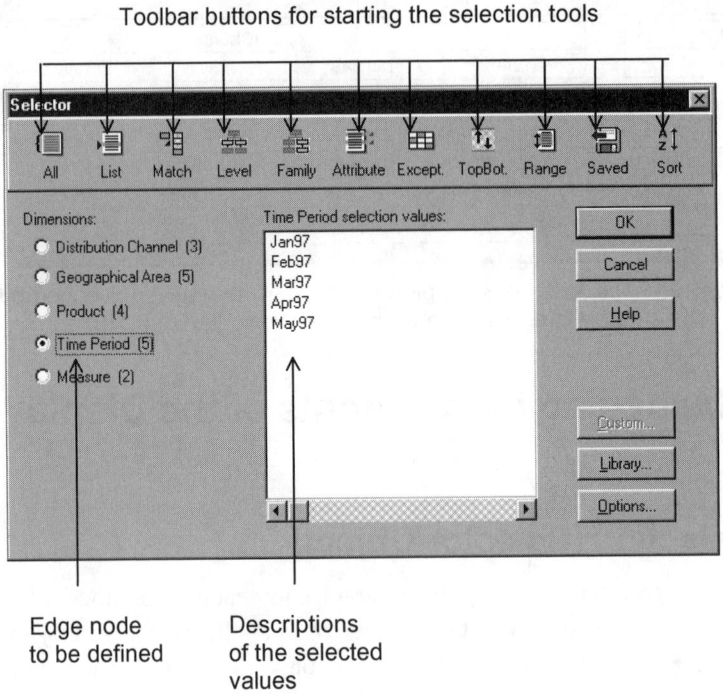

Fig. 6.22. The **Selector** dialog allows you to set the selection of data from the Express database

To understand the results of applying specific Selector tools, it is necessary to determine the value set it selects from the complete value set of the dimension being determined, and find the result of the selected logical operation over this set and

---

[1] In the LIMIT statement the SELECT operation corresponds to the TO keyword.

the set defining the current state. Note that for each dimension it is possible to define one or more types of hierarchies, each of which might contain a specific number of levels. A specific type of hierarchy can be defined only for a certain part of all possible dimension values. Therefore, the dimension values related to a specific hierarchy type or to one of its levels define the subset of all dimension values.

Because this mechanism takes the key position in on-line analysis with the use of Express products, let us consider brief descriptions of the services provided by each of the selector tools.

All—selects all dimension values for the current hierarchy type (Fig. 6.23).

All   In this case, the **A** set is the subset of dimension values related by the hierarchy type (if it is defined for the current dimension) selected from the **...in hierarchy** list.

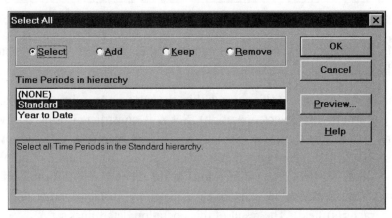

Fig. 6.23. The **Select All** dialog

List—selects the specified values from the list (Fig. 6.24).

List   The **Available**... list in the left part of this dialog displays the subset of values defined by the hierarchy type selected from the **Hierarchy** list. Set **A** is defined by selecting the required values from the **Available**... list. The **Select** and **Add** operations are applicable to both set **A** and the current value set (designated as **C**) displayed in **Selected**...

Set **A** can also be defined in the right list. You can keep only the selected values in the current list (by clicking the **Keep** button) or leave anything except for the selected ones (by clicking the **Remove** button).

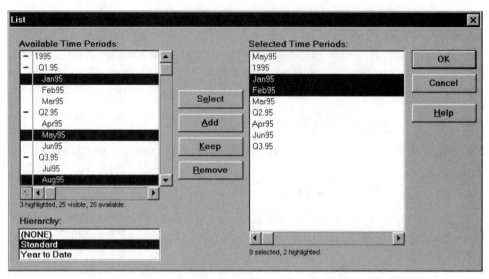

Fig. 6.24. The **List** dialog

🔲 **Match**—selects the values containing the specified set of characters
Match   (Fig. 6.25).

In this case, the current set of values within the edge node is ignored (practically, you are performing the Select operation). Set **A** is constructed using the two-step procedure. At the first step, the selected type (the **in hierarchy** list) and level (the **at level(s)** list) of the hierarchy select a specific subset from the set of all available dimension values for the current dimension. At the second step, this subset is further limited by selecting the values containing a matching character string (specified in the **the character(s)** field). The result of this operation determines set **A**.

The ...**that** group determines the method of checking for the matching string. The following options are available:

❑ **contain**—checks for any match

❑ **start with**—checks the starting characters

❑ **end with**—checks the ending characters

❑ **match exactly**—checks an the exact match

❑ **Ignore Capitalization**—specifies whether or not the comparison operation is case sensitive

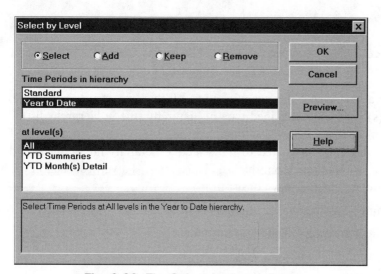

Fig. 6.25. The **Select by Matching Characters** dialog

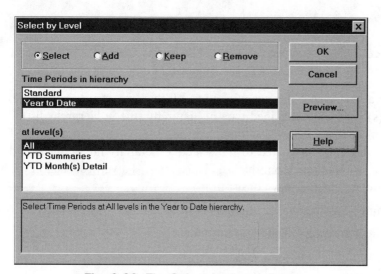 **Level**—selects all values for the specified hierarchy level (Fig. 6.26).

Level

Fig. 6.26. The **Select by Level** dialog

Select specific values from the **in hierarchy** and **at level(s)** lists to determine the subset of dimension values at the specified hierarchical level of a specific hierarchy. This subset makes up the **A** subset (the horizontal section of the given type of hierarchy).

Family—selects all the values of the specified hierarchy node (Fig. 6.27).

Family

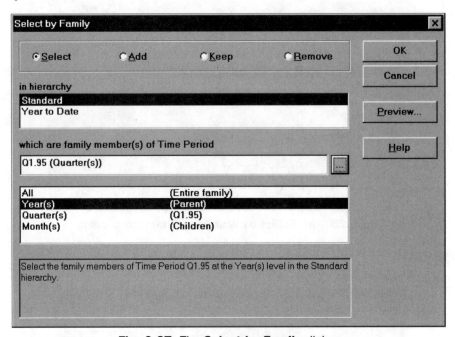

Fig. 6.27. The **Select by Family** dialog

This operation selects the specific node of the tree structure from the **Family Member(s)** list for the specified type of hierarchy (the **in hierarchy** list). The list at the bottom of this window lists the ancestors, the parent, the node itself, its children, and descendants related to the selected hierarchy node. Set **A** is defined by selecting a specific item from this list. Thus, set **A** is a vertical section of the specified hierarchy type and may consist from:

❑   All family members (from direct ancestors to direct descendants)

❑   All direct ancestors of the current node

❑   The parent of the current node

❑   The node itself

❏ All children of the current node

❏ All direct descendants of the current node (grandchildren, great grandchildren, etc.)

 ☰ **Attribute**—selects the values by specified attribute (Fig. 6.28).
Attribute

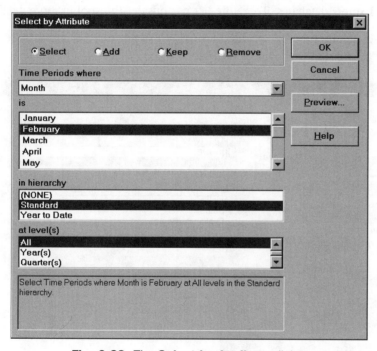

Fig. 6.28. The **Select by Attribute** dialog

Besides hierarchies, the values of the current dimension may be related by means of relations to the values of another dimension. For example, TIME dimension values such as Jan95, Jan96, and Jan97 can be related to the Jan value of the additional MONTH dimension. Various goods that make up the GOODS dimension may be joined by the RED attribute, which is the value of additional GOODS COLOR dimension. The **Attribute** tool allows you to define set **A** by selecting all values joined by a common attribute value at the specified hierarchy level. For example, you can select February for all years defined in the TIME dimension.

 ⊞ **Exception**—selects the dimension values based on comparison of the
Except. variable values.

Value selection for the dimension is performed by comparing the values of a specific variable indexed by the current dimension to the specified value or to another variable defined within the same dimension. The comparison operation checks all the values of the dimension being determined and selects the ones that satisfy the specified condition. The values of other dimensions that influence the variable(s) will be locked. The result is set **A**. This tool represents a powerful instrument for data selection from Express databases. Therefore, let us consider this tool in more detail.

The first selection type—by specified level (the **Numeric** radio button is selected)— is defined by the dialog shown in Fig. 6.29.

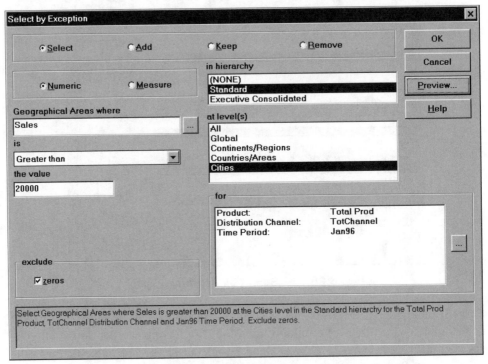

Fig. 6.29. The **Select by Exception** dialog (the Exception tool)

The **...where** list is used to specify the variable whose values will take part in the comparison operation (in our example, this is the `Sales` variable). The **is** drop-down list is used to select the comparison type and contains the following items:

`equal to`	$=$
`less than or equal to`	$\le$

greater than or equal to	$\geq$
not equal to	$\neq$
between	within a range
greater than	$>$
outside	outside the range
less than	$<$

The **the value** field determines the constant to which the variable values will be compared. The **for** window locks the values of other dimensions for which the variable is defined. You can exclude variables containing zero values by setting the **zeros** option. The **in hierarchy** and **at level(s)** lists allow you to specify the hierarchy type and the level at which the check will be performed. For example, using this dialog, we can select the *cities* where *total sales* have exceeded *$20,000* for *January 96.*

The second selection type (when the **Measure** radio button is selected) allows you to create an even more complicated query (Fig. 6.30). If the **Value** item is selected from the drop-down list and the specific constant value has been specified, this dialog will allow you to select dimensions for which:

❏ The first variable exceeds the second variable (**Above**) by a value greater than (**Greater than**) the specified one

❏ The first variable exceeds the second variable (**Above**) by a value less than (**Less than**) the specified one

❏ The first variable is below the second variable (**Below**) by a value greater than (**Greater than**) the specified one

❏ The first variable is below the second variable (**Below**) by a value less than (**Less than**) the specified one

❏ The first variable differs from the second variable (**Above or Below**) by a value greater than (**Greater than**) the specified one

❏ The first variable differs from the second one (**Above or Below**) by a value less than (**Less than**) the specified one

Thus, using this dialog, you can, for example, select the cities for which *total sales* for *January 96* have decreased by more than *$2,000*, as compared to the previous year.

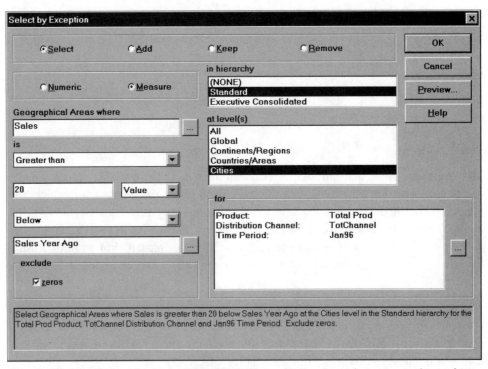

Fig. 6.30. The **Select by Exception** dialog for selection based on comparison of two variables (the Exception tool)

When you select the **Percent** item from the drop-down list, you'll get similar results. However, here, the difference will be evaluated as percentage in relation to the first variable.

Thus, using this dialog, we can select the cities, for which *total sales* for *January 96* have dropped by more than by *20 %*, as compared to the previous year.

Top/Bottom—selects the specified number (or specified percentage of the total amount) of dimension values for which a certain variable has maximum or minimum values.

TopBot.

For example, using this tool, we can select 10 cities where the total amount of sales was at maximum, and 5 cities for which this variable was at minimum.

Range—selects a contiguous range of values for the time dimension.

Range

Saved

Saved—allows for using the dimension value set that was previously saved in the special database selection library (the **Library...** button of the **Selector** dialog, see Fig. 6.22).

Sort—provides the sorting capability for the selected values of the dimension being defined.

You can choose one of the following sorting modes:

☐ **Alphabet**—sorts alphabetically (from A to Z or from Z to A)

☐ **Database**—sorts the values according to the order in which the dimension values are stored in the database

☐ **Data Value**—sorts in ascending or descending order by the value of the specified variable indexed by the current dimension

☐ **Dragdrop**—manual sorting of the value list

☐ **Hierarchy**—sorting according to the hierarchy

☐ **Level**—sorting by hierarchical levels

☐ **Time**—sorting the time dimension in ascending or descending order

The **Custom...** button in the Selector Object enables the user to create new calculated variables defined by a formula, and displays them in a table or graph.

The Selector Object set of tools is a very powerful and flexible instrument allowing you to build queries that will be used for selecting the required information from the Express multidimensional database. Combining these tools with logical operations enables you to answer the most complex questions that may arise when performing on-line data analysis.

Data Aggregation

Any data can be drilled up (aggregated) by one or more groups of selected dimension values defined in the data cube. The standard context menu that appears when you right-click the desired edge node in the dimension bar provides the following functionals for aggregating the selected data:

☐ Total—sum of values

☐ Average—average value

❏ Smallest—minimum value

❏ Largest—maximum value

❏ Median—the median

❏ Standard deviation—the standard deviation from the average value

The value selected from this list will be calculated for the dimension being defined by all current values selected into the group. This mechanism allows for drilling up the data under analysis and identifying the general trends. For example, aggregation helps us find an answer to questions such as "what are the minimum values of average monthly sales for the cities in each country?".

6.4. Table View

6.4.1. Tables

The table component is one of the two Express Analyzer objects intended for displaying multidimensional data in the briefing pages. It is very important to understand that the data presented in a table are interactive and display the database content that existed at the moment the briefing was created. As we already mentioned in the previous chapter, tables display the specified data cube. Using the tables, end users can do the following:

❏ View data in a flat table using the scroll bars

❏ Navigate from page to page in the data cube

❏ Rebuild the table layout by moving edge nodes between cube dimensions

❏ Use the Selector set of tools for changing the parameters defining the result set retrieved from the database, and view the new data

❏ Copy the data from the table to other Windows applications

❏ Perform a "What if?" analysis using business models

❏ Modify the table layout using the right-click menu

A typical table is shown in Fig. 6.31. This table displays the SALES and SALES YEAR AGO measures from the XADEMO database included with the standard product.

Fig. 6.31 also illustrates the correspondence between the data cube dimensions (rows, columns, pages) and their representation in a table.

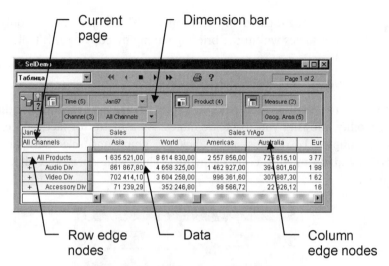

Fig. 6.31. Table view of the data

Navigation within a table is performed using the standard keyboard shortcuts common for most Windows applications. For example, to go to the last cell of the table and click <Ctrl>+<End>.

6.4.2. Creating Tables

We have already discussed one of the possible methods of creating a table representing the data from the database. Another convenient way assumes that you insert a blank table into the briefing page, in a way similar to the one used to insert other Express Analyzer components. Having inserted the blank table, you can then fill it with data retrieved form the database. To accomplish this operation, proceed as follows:

1. Click the **Table** toolbar icon

2. Within the briefing page, click and drag the cursor to designate the rectangular area intended for the table

3. Attach the database, if you have not done this already

4. In the database browser, select one or more variables (measures or formulae) and drag them to the table

You can also create a new table based on an existing one. This method may be useful if the values of the table properties are significantly different from the default ones. Having created and customized a "standard" table layout, you can create all the other tables within the briefing simply by copying this table.

To add one or more variables to the existing table, simply drag them with the mouse from the database browser into the table.

Besides the above-mentioned methods, Express Analyzer provides another interesting capability allowing you to create tables. As a matter of fact, you can create tables from graphs. To do this, right-click the graph and select the **Create New View** command from the context menu. This will open the dialog shown in Fig. 6.32.

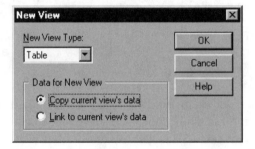

Fig. 6.32. The **New View** dialog allows for creating tables from graphs

When you create a table from a graph, you can choose one of the following two options: either copy the data from the graph or link the table data with the data presented on the graph. If you select the second alternative, you'll have two interrelated representations of multidimensional data within your briefing. Any time you change the contents of one of these views using the Selector tools, the related view will also change.

Notice that the table will be created on a new page that will be added to the briefing. Often, it may be useful to place the table view of the data on the same page as the related graph. To achieve this, go to the briefing browser and drag the newly created table from the new page to the page containing the source graph.

6.4.3. Customizing Table Properties

The `Table` object has more than 100 properties, all of which are described in detail in the *Reference Manual*. Here we will consider the most frequently used table-specific properties.

Border	The `Border` group property provides flexible customization capabilities for setting up the line color, type, and width of various borders surrounding table elements. A value of `"0-Not Used"` disables table borders
CellEditing	Enables the user to edit table cells and allows you to change cell formatting by specifying custom fonts and colors
CellSizing	Manages the sizing of table cells. The cell size can be fixed or automatically selected from a specified range determined by minimum and maximum values
DataSpell	Allows for specifying the text labels that will appear in table cells when displaying non-existent (`NA`) data, `NULL` values, or `YES`/`NO` logical data
DimensionBar	Using this property, you can hide the dimension bar from the end user or customize its layout
EnableAggregation	Manages the user's access to the data aggregation functions
EnableDrilling	Manages the drilling capabilities provided to end users when drilling hierarchical dimensions up or down
EnableSelectData	Manages user access to the Selector tool
Font	Specifies the default font for all titles within a table
Highlighter	Manages the availability and layout of the buttons intended for highlighting table rows and columns
HorzAlign	Sets the horizontal alignment of the table text elements
NumberFormat	This group of properties provides flexible capabilities for managing the text representation of numeric data
PrintLayout	Allows you to customize the print settings
Selector	By double-clicking this property in the object inspector, you can start editing the properties of the individual Selector object related to the current table. By setting the properties of this object, you can manage both the layout and content of the available tools (see the next section)
ShowHGrid	Toggles the display mode for the horizontal grid lines separating the table cells
ShowPages	Toggles the display mode for the drop-down list containing the values of the `PAGES` dimension of the data cube associated with the table
ShowVGrid	Toggles the display mode for the vertical grid lines separating the table cells

continues

Continued

`SuppressRows`	Allows you to suppress the display of blank table rows containing zero or `NULL` values
`ZoomFactor`	Provides the zooming capability for all table elements, including fonts, cells, buttons, etc

Fig 6.33 provides an example of the table view properties for the table shown in Fig. 6.31.

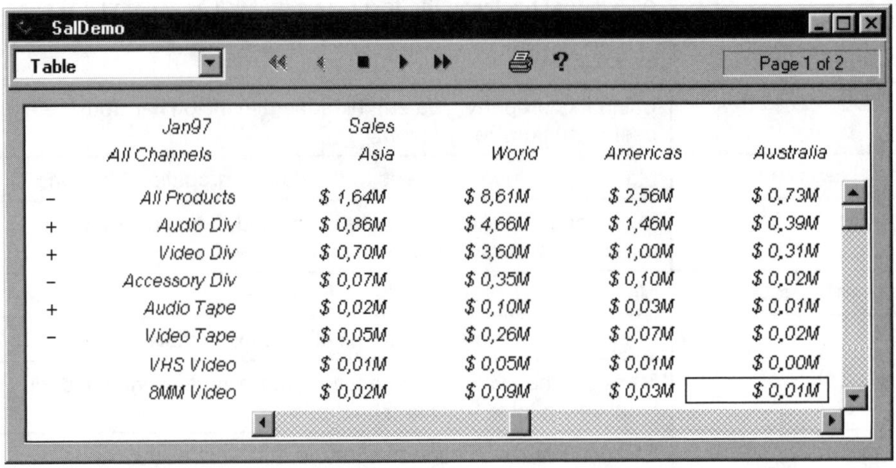

	Jan97	Sales			
	All Channels	Asia	World	Americas	Australia
–	All Products	$ 1,64M	$ 8,61M	$ 2,56M	$ 0,73M
+	Audio Div	$ 0,86M	$ 4,66M	$ 1,46M	$ 0,39M
+	Video Div	$ 0,70M	$ 3,60M	$ 1,00M	$ 0,31M
–	Accessory Div	$ 0,07M	$ 0,35M	$ 0,10M	$ 0,02M
+	Audio Tape	$ 0,02M	$ 0,10M	$ 0,03M	$ 0,01M
–	Video Tape	$ 0,05M	$ 0,26M	$ 0,07M	$ 0,02M
	VHS Video	$ 0,01M	$ 0,05M	$ 0,01M	$ 0,00M
	8MM Video	$ 0,02M	$ 0,09M	$ 0,03M	$ 0,01M

Fig. 6.33. The example illustrating the settings of the table properties

6.4.4. Customizing the Properties of the Table Elements

The `Table` component is a container object that contains other objects. You can access these objects from the object inspector. To achieve this, go to Object Inspector when editing the table properties and click the **Contents** tab (Fig. 6.34).

To start editing the properties of the objects listed on the **Contents** tab, double-click the object that you are going to edit. These objects manage the layout of the table elements. The correlation between table elements and these objects is illustrated in Fig. 6.35. The properties that determine the visual style of each of these objects are listed below.

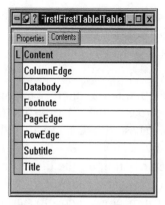

Fig. 6.34. Objects contained within the `Table` component

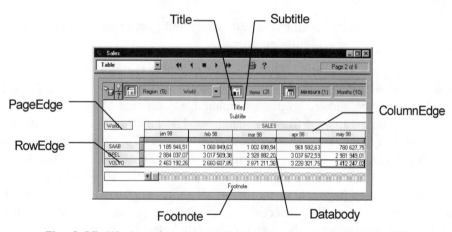

Fig. 6.35. Window elements related to the objects contained within the Table component

AutoViewLabelType	Defines the text that will appear when displaying dimension values. For example, you can specify the dimension name or its label (either long or short)
Border	Specifies the type of the border limiting the current object
FillColor	Specifies the fill color
Font	Specifies the font name, size, and color
HorzAlign	Sets the type of horizontal alignment
VertAlign	Sets the type of vertical alignment
Visible	Toggles the visibility mode for the object within a table
WordWrap	Enables the word wrap feature

When changing similar properties of the `Table` component, you set the same values for the components included within that table. By changing similar properties of the individual objects within a table, you can individually customize the display of each table element.

It is necessary to pay special attention to another important table component—the `Selector` object. It plays the role of the UI (user interface) when creating multi-dimensional queries to the database (see *Chapter 4*). When a new table is created, this field gets a blank value by default (`<no value>`). To create an individual Selector object, click the **Selector** button on the dimension bar. The `Selector` property of the `Table` object will then get a value of `SelectorN`. Double-click the `Selector` property in the object inspector window to start editing the `Selector` object properties.

The `DimLabels` property specifies the text (name and long or short labels) that will appear when displaying object descriptors.

The `SelectorType` property defines the type of dialog that will appear when the user clicks the **Selector** button on the dimension bar. If the type value is set to 2, the end user will be allowed to use a simplified selector that allows him or her to select one or more variables from the database. The functionality of this dialog is determined by the `SelectorMini` group of properties. The first property of this group specifies the text that will be displayed within the dialog, while the second property sets the list type. The list may contain either the name of the variable presented in a table (type 3), or the list of all variables available in the database (type 4). The list may allow selection of one item (types 0, 2) or several items (type 1). Fig. 6.36 shows the shorthand form of the selector with a list of type 1.

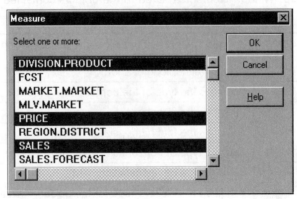

Fig. 6.36. The simplified form of the **Selector** dialog

If the type of `Selector` object is set to 1, the end user will see the common **Selector** dialog. The type and functionality of this dialog is defined by the `SelectorMain` property group. The properties included within this group are listed below.

`AvailableTools`	Manages the availability of individual selector buttons
`ShowCustomMeasure`	Determines if the button starting the dialog for editing formulae is available in the selector dialog
`ShowDimsListBox`	Specifies the type of description for the cube dimensions (list or radio buttons)
`ShowLibrary`	Toggles the availability of the **Library** button in the **Selector** dialog. The **Library** button is used for saving, restoring, and managing the preset selections
`ShowOptions`	Toggles the availability of the **Properties** button used for customizing selector properties. Presents a convenient alternative for customizing selector properties
`ShowSelectionValues`	Toggles the display mode for the list of selected values

Fig. 6.37 shows the result of customizing the `Selector` object properties. It is recommended that you compare this dialog to the standard **Selector** dialog shown in Fig. 6.22.

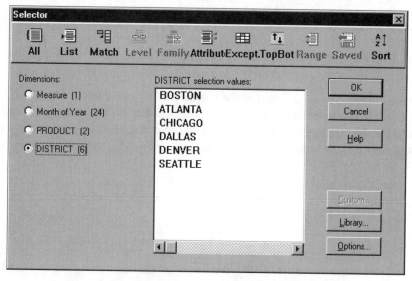

Fig. 6.37. Example of the custom **Selector** dialog

6.4.5. Copying Data to Other Applications

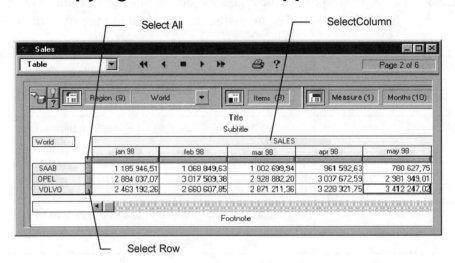

Fig. 6.38. Selecting the table data

Express Analyzer provides the end user with the ability to select the table data and copy it into another Windows application, such as MS Excel or Word. This can be done using various methods. First, you need to select the data that you are going to copy. To select all table cells, click the topmost left button within the data area (Fig. 6.38).

To select one or more rows (columns), click the appropriate leftmost or topmost buttons (Fig. 6.38) while pressing and holding the <Shift> key on the keyboard. To select a rectangular table fragment, click the left mouse button at one of its corners and drag the mouse to the opposite corner of the rectangular area you are going to select.

Having selected the required data, use the standard Clipboard **Copy** (<Ctrl>+<C>) and **Paste** (<Ctrl>+<V>) operation to copy the selected data to the Clipboard, and then paste it to another application. The listing below shows the result of pasting the selected data fragment from the table presented in Fig. 6.38 to the Microsoft Word application.

```
Boston
     Sales revenue
            Jan.98          Feb.98
Dodge       207008,044624  195185,914564
Cadillac    442580,907726  497550,900757
```

Notice that the appropriate dimension values (page, row, and column) are copied along with the data values, and the precision of the numeric data is exactly the same as in the database.

6.4.6. Using the "What If...?" Analysis

Tables can be used as an End-user interface to the business models enabling a "What if...?" analysis. The simplest schema of applying tables for such an analysis looks as follows.

First, we need to define a certain formula or model calculating the value of the dependent measure based on the values of several other independent measures. For example, in the FIRST database described earlier, we have the INCOME formula (the dependent variable) and the PRICE and SALES measures—independent variables that determine the INCOME.

Next, we need to create a table, where one row will be the dependent variable, while others will contain one or more independent variables. Now, using the CellEditing table property, provide the access for changing the row values representing independent variables. This will enable us to change the values of independent variables and view the changes in the dependent variable.

Let's continue with our example. Create a table where the first row is calculated using the INCOME formula, and the second row represents the PRICE measure (this is the retail price of an item). Now provide access for editing, and you'll be able to analyze *what happens* to the income *if* the retail price changes (Fig. 6.39).

SALES	JAN95	FEB95	MAR95	APR95	MAY95	JUN95	JUL95
FORD							
BOSTON	32 153,52	32 536,30	43 062,75	57 608,39	81 149,36	88 996,35	87 273,84
ATLANTA	40 674,20	44 236,55	51 227,06	78 469,37	93 633,88	110 765,24	123 304,32
CHICAGO	29 098,94	29 010,20	39 540,89	48 782,59	66 584,09	70 908,96	73 822,46
DALLAS	47 747,98	50 166,81	67 075,44	87 295,16	115 401,75	128 692,56	143 961,80
DENVER	36 494,25	33 658,24	45 303,93	57 447,92	79 548,78	91 717,46	102 806,98
SEATTLE	43 568,02	41 191,28	51547,230000	77 025,15	104 357,76	113 806,48	118 660,40
OPEL							
BOSTON	66 013,92	76 083,84	91 748,16	125 594,28	126 713,16	147 412,44	152 727,12
ATLANTA	49 462,88	54 209,74	67 764,20	96 333,28	92 656,62	106 327,17	110 503,68
CHICAGO	45 277,56	50 595,75	63 576,53	86 262,94	89 231,94	108 039,05	98 711,55
DALLAS	33 292,32	37 471,29	43 970,59	60 042,05	59 551,38	71 899,23	69 421,42
DENVER	45 467,80	51 737,01	58 437,11	79 612,71	80 860,50	99 099,20	95 858,62
SEATTLE	64 111,50	71 899,23	83 943,86	114 383,90	120 624,84	143 037,62	150 254,58

Fig. 6.39. Using the table for a "What if...?" analysis

Of course, this business model, where the income is proportional to the retail price, is very simple. Therefore, it can't be expected to produce a valuable result. However, it would become more practical if we could take into account the influence of the retail price on the sales amount and reflect this dependence in our formula (for example, it would be logical to expect a reduction in sales if we increase the price) and dependence of sales on the season and on the sales rate for the recent few months. In this case, the results of analysis based on a "What if...?" schema would not be so evident.

6.5. Graphs

6.5.1. Creating Graphs

The `Graph` visual component, like the `Table` component, is intended for displaying multidimensional data on briefing pages. The flexible capabilities of graph customization enable the user to visually display numeric data. Like table data, the data displayed in graphs are updated (read from the database) any time the user starts the briefing. A graph displays a certain data cube, where data are ordered by pages, rows, and columns. With graphs, end users can do the following:

❐ Change the type of graphical data presentation using the right-click menu

❐ Navigate between pages within the data cube

❐ Customize the graph view by moving edge nodes from dimension to dimension

❐ Use the Selector tools to modify parameters determining the data selection and view the new data

To create a new graph, go to the database browser, select one or more variables, and drag them to a blank briefing page. Next, select the **Graph** command from the popup menu.

Another convenient method assumes that you insert a blank graph into the briefing page, just the same as you insert other Express Analyzer objects, and then place there the required data from the database. To use this method proceed as follows:

❐ Click the graph icon in the toolbar

❐ In the briefing page, drag the cursor with the mouse to determine a rectangular area for the graph

◻ Attach the database, if you have not done this already

◻ Go to the database browser, select one or more variables (measures or formulae), and drag them with the mouse to the graph

You can also create a new graph based on a copy of an existing one. This method may be useful if the graph properties differ significantly from the default ones. If this is so, you can create a new graph, customize its "standard" view according to your requirements, and then create all the other graphs within a briefing based on this one.

To add one or more variables to the existing graph, drag them from the database browser to the graph area.

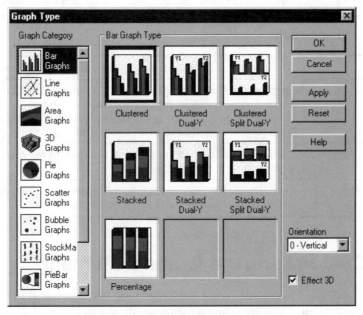

Fig. 6.40. Selecting the graph type

Express Analyzer provides another way to create graphs. Besides all the other methods, you can create a graph based on an existing table. To achieve this, right-click the table and select the **Create New View** command from the context menu. A dialog allowing you to create a graph will appear (Fig. 6.40). This dialog provides two options, the first of which copies the data from the table, while the second one relates the graph data with that represented in the table. If you select the second alternative, your briefing will contain two interrelated views representing the multidimensional data. Any time you change the content of one of these views using the Selector tool, the contents of the related view will change automatically.

Note that the new graph will be created on a new page, which will be added to the briefing. Quite often it may be useful to place the graph view on the same page as the related table. To do so, go to the briefing browser and drag the newly created graph from the new page to the page containing the source table.

6.5.2. Customizing Graph Properties

The total number of graph properties that can be customized by the developer according to his or her requirements is about 70. Most of these properties are analogous to the table properties described in the previous chapter. The graph-specific properties are listed below:

Effect3D	Specifies the availability of the 3D effect for the graph view
GraphType	Specifies the type of the graph view. This property can be customized using a special dialog (Fig. 6.40), which can be opened by double clicking this property in Object Inspector. Currently, Express Analyzer provides about 39 types of graphs
SpecialEffects	This property allows us to use bitmap images for filling graph elements
ViewLabelType	Defines the label type for the graph. The dimension may be represented by its value name or by its short or long label

6.5.3. Customizing the Graph's Elements

Besides the capabilities of customizing the graph, the developer is able to customize the properties of 26 individual elements of the graph (Fig. 6.41). Fig. 6.42 shows the correlation between the graph's properties and its display. By customizing an individual graph's properties, you can flexibly manage the graph display in order to make it more illustrative.

Customizable graph properties allow the developer to specify an individual font and color for the text labels within a graph (such as titles, names of the axes, etc.) and for properties of the grid displayed in the graph field, and to toggle the presence and specify the view of the text labels along the axes. Furthermore, for each point of our graph we can also display a corresponding numeric value.

Fig. 6.41. Properties of the graph components

Fig. 6.43 illustrates the results of individual customization of specific elements of the graph, which by default looks as shown in Fig. 6.42.

6.5.4. Using Various Graph Types

As was already mentioned, you can specify one of 39 available display types for the graph component. Using various graph types, you can present specific informational aspects more illustratively. For example, a graph in the form of broken lines are most suitable for analyzing trends, while pie charts are best for analyzing relations between percentages. All available graph types are grouped into the following two categories:

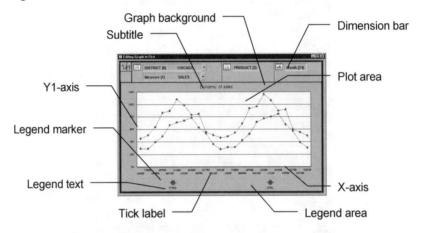

Fig. 6.42. Graph elements and their view in a graph

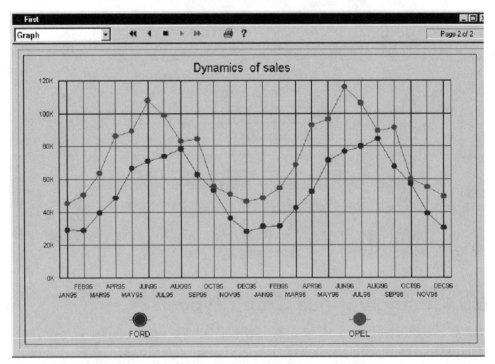

Fig. 6.43. Individually setting the graph elements

Standard types:

- ☐ Bar charts
- ☐ 3D Graphs

- ☐ Line graphs
- ☐ Pie charts

- ☐ Area graphs

Complex types:

- ☐ Scatter graphs
- ☐ Scatter graphs with value display
- ☐ Stock Market graphs

Bar Charts

Bar charts display data as a series of bars, the height of which corresponds to the values they represent. This type of graph can be used to represent the following data aspects:

Data aspect	Example
Trend over time	Sales for the last 12 months
Comparison of several values at the same time	Sales of different goods for different regions
Changes in percentage	Changes (in percentage) of incomes from the sales of different goods
Relationship between the part and the whole value	Identifying the goods that have the most significant influence on the general sales trend
Relationships between several parts of the whole	Changes in relationship between incomes for different divisions depending on time

To illustrate the usage of different types of bar charts, let us use the data from the FIRST database that we have used in other examples.

If you need to analyze the time trend for the income from different product types, we can use the **Clustered Bar Graph** type of the graph object (Fig. 6.44).

If you are interested in the relative value of monthly income from the sales of different lines of products, you can use a **Percentage Bar Graph**, shown in Fig. 6.45.

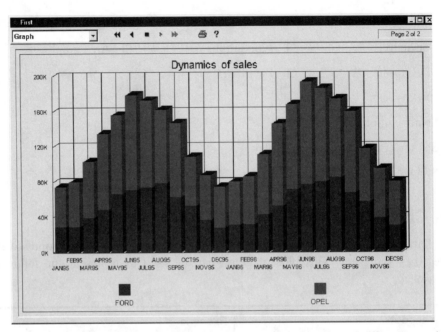

Fig. 6.44. Analysis of the time trend for the income from sales of different goods

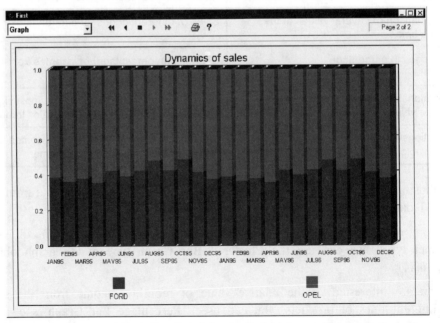

Fig. 6.45. The Percentage Bar Graph is convenient for analyzing relative values

For example, this graph shows that the relative part of monthly income from Ford sales grows with time, just as does the absolute value.

Line Graphs

Graphs of this type display data stored in the database as a series of data points connected with sections of a straight line. Using this type of graph, you can represent the following data aspects:

Displayed data aspect	Example
Trend over time	Sales for the last 12 months
Comparison of several values at the same time	Sales of various groups of products for different regions
Data change rate	Evaluation of the change rate of the market share
Changes in percentage	Changes in the income share that comes from different product groups
Relationship between the part and the whole value	Identifying the goods that have the most significant influence on the general sales trend
Relationships between several parts of the whole	Changes in the relationship between incomes for different divisions, depending on time

Fig. 6.43 presents an Absolute Line Graph. This graph displays the time trend of the revenue coming from the sale of different lines of products.

Area Graphs

This type of graph allows us to present data as filled-in area. Data aspects that can be analyzed using graphs of this type are exactly the same as for line graphs.

Fig. 6.46 shows the time dependence of the total sales revenue coming from different product groups. The width of the filled-in areas corresponds to the absolute sales revenue coming from different product groups.

3D Graphs

Graphs of this type represent data as a series of 3D bars. The current version of the software provides only one type of 3D graph. Though 3D graphs usually look attractive, this type of display is rarely used in real-world analytical tasks. However, they can be used efficiently if you need to make the representation of an identified trend more illustrative.

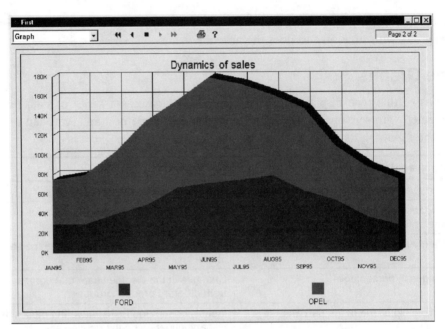

Fig. 6.46. Trend analysis for the total sales revenue

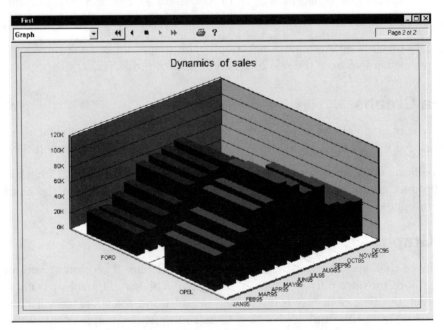

Fig. 6.47. Representation of revenue trends as 3D graphs

The example of a 3D graph shown in Fig. 6.47 represents the time dependence of the sales revenue for various types of products.

Pie Charts

Pie charts represent data as filled sectors of circles. The whole circle represents the whole, while the sectors represent shares of each part of the whole. Graphs of this type look like a sliced pie (hence its name). Traditionally, pie charts are used for displaying parts of the whole in percentages.

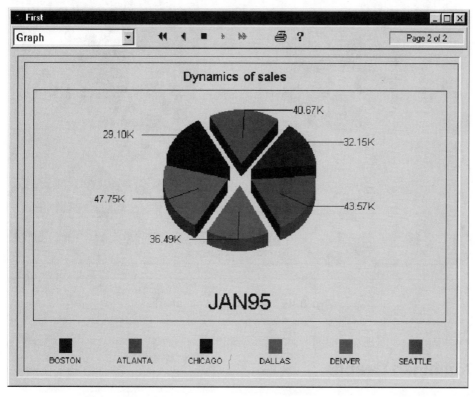

Fig. 6.48. Pie chart representing Ford sales revenue for different cities

Fig. 6.48 illustrates the relative percentages of the total revenue from the Ford monthly sales in different cities.

Proportional pie charts represent another type of pie chart. The graph shown in Fig. 6.49 provides you with the capability of comparing the values of the parts by cities and viewing the relationship of the cumulative revenue values for different types of products.

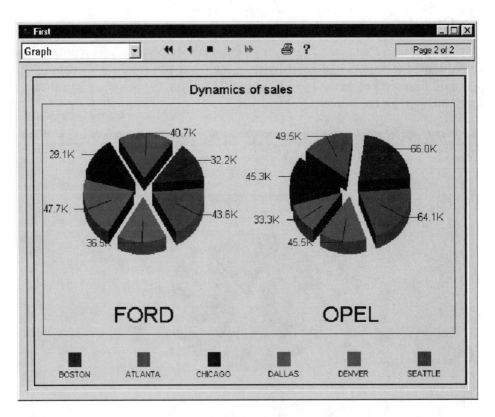

Fig. 6.49. Proportional pie charts

Combined Graphs

This type of graph represents data as a pie chart, next to which additional data for one of the pie sectors is presented. For example, the graph shown in Fig. 6.50 presents the relationship of the revenue coming from the sales of two types of goods for the specified month by all cities. Next to the pie chart is a bar chart displaying the relative revenue distribution by cities for the smallest "slice of the pie", which corresponds to the Opel revenue share.

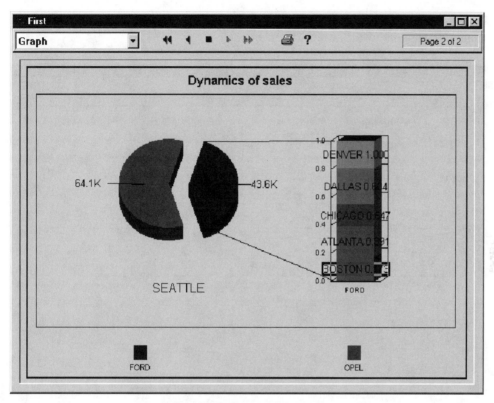

Fig. 6.50. Combined graph

Scatter Graphs

This type of graph is very convenient for analyzing the correlation between various measures. Let's explain the usage of these types of graphs in an illustrative example. The FIRST database contains data on the retail prices of the goods and revenues obtained from the sale of these goods. Fig. 6.51 represents the distribution of these measures for the first 10 months of the year 1998 for Boston.

By carefully analyzing these results, we can suggest that for the Dodge there is a strong correlation between the retail price and the resulting revenue. Similar correlations also exist both for Ford and Cadillac, but for Ford this correlation is not so strong, while for Cadillac it is practically non-existent.

Naturally, we could not consider all types of graphs. Furthermore, most types of graphs considered here have sets of subtypes, which were not considered either.

If you are interested in this topic, you can find detailed information in the documentation supplied with the software product.

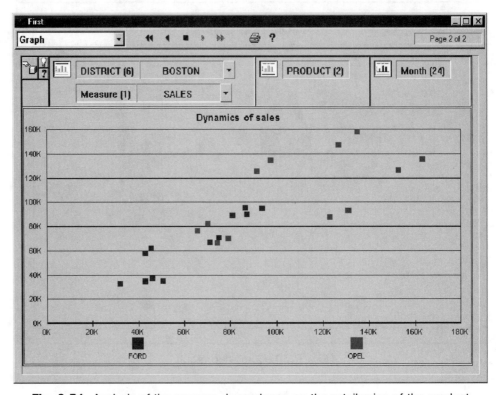

Fig. 6.51. Analysis of the revenue dependence on the retail price of the product

Chapter 7

Creating Analytical
Applications
(Express Objects)

7.1. Product Description

7.1.1. Product Aims

We have already considered the usage of the Express Analyzer application, which represents a "lightweight" end-user development environment in comparison to Express Objects. This development environment enables end users to develop OLAP applications for MS Windows, since it doesn't require programming experience. In contrast to Express Analyzer, Express Objects is a professional development environment for visual object oriented development of OLAP client/server applications for Microsoft Windows. Using Express Objects, you are able to create and debug applications enabling the end users to take full advantage of the Express OLAP software. Express Objects provides access to any objects stored in the multidimensional database managed by Personal Express or Express Server, and to relational databases available from those servers.

Express Objects is an object-oriented development environment fully supporting all required mechanisms, such as encapsulation, inheritance, and polymorphism. Additionally, Express Objects provides the standard containership mechanism useful for creating complex applications. In the course of development, we can use the ready-to-use set of standard objects, such as customizable visual components, methods (object functions), and events (message functions for processing messages from the user, hardware, operating system, or other objects). Furthermore, we can develop new objects on the basis of the existing ones, by adding new properties, methods, and event handlers. New objects can be included into the set and used in further development just the same way as the standard objects.

Standard objects provide the ability to use all the required Windows interface components, such as buttons, main menus, popup menus, editor window, toolbars, comboboxes, icons, standard dialogs, etc. The toolbox also includes powerful interactive data manipulation objects intended for working with multidimensional data: tables and graphs. Besides displaying the multidimensional database information in user-friendly and easily understandable format, these components provide flexible capabilities of efficient data management. End users can manipulate both the on-screen data view and informational content, which is the most important requirement for efficient on-line data analysis.

Express Objects uses Express Basic as its main programming language. Express Basic has much in common with Visual Basic, including the Basic core, functions, and expressions. Besides which, Express Basic supports Dynamic Data Exchange (DDE) along with embedding OLE and Visual Basic objects.

The efficiency of the visual development is provided by the following set of tools: Object Browser, Database Browser, and Object Inspector.

Using Express Objects, you can do the following:

❏   Create new projects or briefings

❏   Edit projects or briefings

❏   Execute projects or briefings

❏   Analyze multidimensional data using table or graph views

7.1.2. Creating Applications

Work Area and Tools

 To start Express Objects, double-click the appropriate icon in the Oracle OLAP Client 2.*x*. program group.

When the application starts, it displays a prompt similar to the prompt displayed by Express Analyzer, which was discussed and described in detail in *Chapter 6*. After selecting one of the alternatives available in this dialog, you'll get to the main application window. The Express Objects user interface is very similar to that of the Express Analyzer application. The main application window contains the main menu and toolbars (Fig. 7.1). The application main menu provides access to the basic Express Objects functions, such as creating, editing, and executing briefings and applications, connecting to the server, attaching databases, and many more.

The main application window may contain the following three toolbars:

❏   Menu access toolbar

❏   Selector buttons

❏   Object location buttons

The contents of the displayed toolbars is determined using the dialog opened by selecting the **Window/Toolbars** menu item. Besides menu and toolbars, the main application window provides the developer with the following tools: object browser, database browser, and object inspector. You can open or close these panes by clicking the appropriate toolbar buttons or by selecting the appropriate commands from the **Window** menu. The usage of these tools is very much like the usage of similar tools in Express Analyzer.

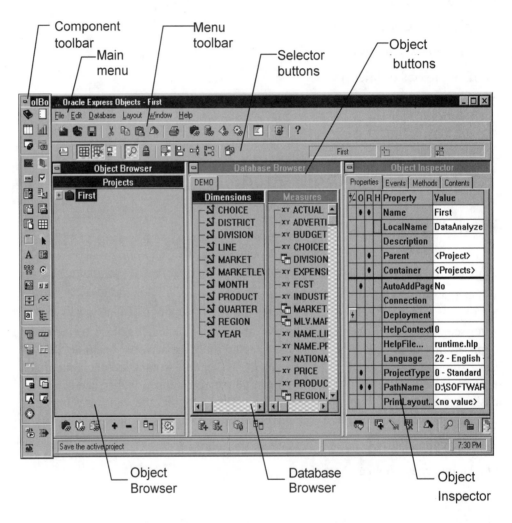

Fig. 7.1. Express Objects main window and its components

The component toolbar (Fig. 7.1) contains a set of ready-to-use standard visual objects that can be used when creating an application.

Creating and Editing Projects

The first step that you need to take when starting the development process is creating a new project. To create a new project, select the **File/New Project** command from the main menu. The **New Project** dialog will open (Fig. 7.2).

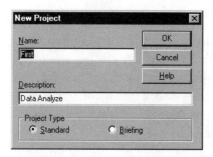

Fig. 7.2. The **New Project** dialog

The **Name** field of this dialog specifies the filename of the file storing the project data. The **Descriptions:** field allows you to specify the project description that will be displayed in the object browser. The **Project Type** group of radio buttons enables you to specify the type of the newly created project: an application (the **Standard** option) or briefing (the **Briefing** option). Notice that Express Analyzer is only able to edit projects of the **Briefing** type (XBR files). You can open the existing project for editing by selecting the **File/Open Project** item from the menu and specifying the path and filename of the file where you have saved the project.

The basic principles of application development are very similar to the principles described in *Chapter 3*. The project must contain one or more briefings, each of which may consist of one or more pages containing all the other application components. You can customize the data view and object behavior by changing object properties, methods, and event-handling procedures.

Inserting Components

The features and capabilities of the standard components that the developer can include into his or her applications will be covered in more detail later in this book. In this section we will consider common rules of usage and customization, applicable to all standard components. As was already mentioned, the first component that you'll find in any application is the Briefing component. To include the Briefing component into our application, double-click the **Briefing** icon in the component bar (notice that the cursor will change), then click the icon of our application in the object browser. The "+" icon will appear to the left of the application icon. If you click the "+" icon, a hierarchical list will open, and you'll notice that our application contains the Briefing object, which, in turn, contains the automatically inserted Page object.

If you double-click this page in object browser, the window will open, displaying the newly created briefing page. Click the **Button** icon in the component bar, then click somewhere within the newly created briefing page. The standard button with the default properties will be inserted into the page, as shown in Fig. 7.3. To customize the properties and behavior of the Button components, go to the object inspector. Some properties can be edited using the popup menu appearing when you right-click the button. For example, the **Button** properties listed below the popup menu separator (Fig. 7.3) can be edited without using the object inspector.

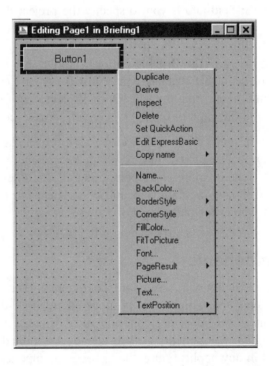

Fig. 7.3. The Button component and its related right-click menu

The **Set QuickAction** command from the right-click menu allows you to specify an action that will be performed in the case of a specific event (Fig. 7.4):

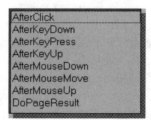

Fig. 7.4. The list of events displayed by the **Set QuickAction** command

For example, we can define the reaction to the AfterClick event as the display of the "Hello World!" message. To achieve this, double-click the **AfterClick** option in the displayed list and select the **Show Message** option from the list of available actions (Fig. 7.5). Go to the **Message** text field and specify the text of your custom message.

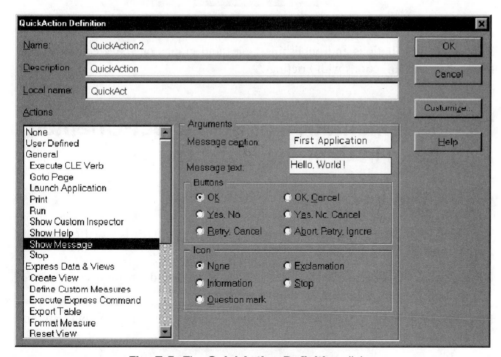

Fig. 7.5. The **QuickAction Definition** dialog

Click **OK** in the **QuickAction Definition** dialog. To save your project, select the **File/Save** item from the menu.

7.1.3. Starting the Application

The application can be started using Express Objects or Express Analyzer. To start an application, it is sufficient to select the appropriate option in the **Welcome** dialog displayed by both of these applications. If you need to run the project opened in Express Objects (for example, the one that we have created and saved in the previous section), select the **File/Run** item from the menu, or click the appropriate toolbar button. For example, if you start the First project and click the **Button1** button in the application window, you'll get the message shown in Fig. 7.6.

Fig. 7.6. The message displayed by the **First application**

Application distributions and publishing tables and graphs on the Web are no different than similar actions with briefings.

7.2. Implementation of the Object-Oriented Approach in Express Objects

7.2.1. OOP Paradigm

The classic approach to Object-Oriented Programming (OOP) is based on the following three concepts:

❑ *Encapsulation*—hiding the data (object properties) and program code (object methods) within a single programmable object.

❑ *Inheritance*—creating a new object on the basis of an existing one but with enhanced properties and methods.

❑ *Polymorphism*—modification of the behavior depending on the object type. For example, we can define the Figure object that will be responsible for representing itself on the screen (using the Draw method). Having done this, we can generate its child objects such as Rectangle and Circle. If we properly redefine the `Draw` method for the new objects, the program responsible for re-drawing the window will be able to call the `Draw` method for each of the built-in figures without needing to determine which figure it has to redraw. The `Rectangle` object will be displayed as rectangle, and the `Circle` object will be displayed as circle.

OOP is the natural enhancement of the procedural and structural programming paradigm. For the moment, OOP represents the most advanced technology allowing you to implement (design, develop, test, and support) complex software projects from tens to hundreds of thousands of lines of code written in a higher-level language.

Programmers acquainted with the object-oriented approach implemented in programming languages, such as C++, are used to the implementation of this approach on the basis of special language constructs—classes. In the Express Basic language, however, you'll never need to use this concept, since each object of this language can be considered a class. Each newly created object can be saved on the component toolbar, and you can generate child objects from any existing object.

Now let us consider the specific features of OOP implementation in Express Objects.

7.2.2. Objects and Their Components

As was already mentioned, objects represent a certain software abstraction that encapsulates both specific data (properties) and software code (methods) responsible for manipulating the object data. Programmer-defined objects implement the concept of modeling real-world objects, for example, such as pages, tables or graphics.

The OOP approach implemented in Express Objects is based on a concept that enhances the object concept and considers the object as a set of the following five interrelated components (Fig. 7.7):

❏ *Properties*—the data describing the object characteristics, such as button size and color.

❏ *Methods*— the program code that determines the actions performed by the object.

❏ *Events*— user actions such as clicking the mouse button, or the operating system actions, which the object recognizes and to which it reacts with the pre-defined action.

❏ *Implementation*—new and redefined methods and event handlers.

❏ *Content*—objects implemented outside the current object, to which the current object contains references. For example, the title contained within the graph object represents the `Title` object.

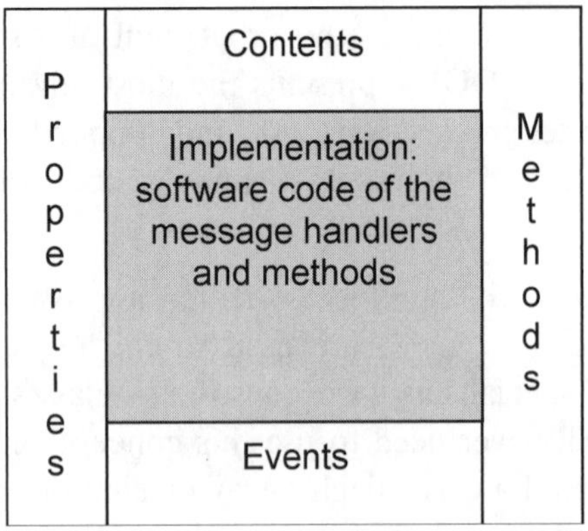

Fig. 7.7. Object structure in the Express Objects application

7.2.3. Properties

`Properties` represent a set of data contained within an object. In Express Objects, each object has the following five common properties:

Name	Unique name of the object used to reference that object from within other objects or from the program code of methods and event handlers
LocalName	Alternative name, which can represent a translation to the national language
Description	Description string (written in any language) displayed in the object inspector
Parent	Specifies the parent object from which the current object was generated
Container	Specifies the container object containing the current object

When managing objects, you are able to view and change their properties. Some properties can be joined into groups. For example, the `Rectangle` group property includes the coordinates of the upper left corner, width, and height. Object inspector marks such properties with the "+/-" button that enables the user to expand or collapse the list of properties that make up the current group. Group properties have no value, since the values are assigned only to the properties that make up that group.

Some properties in object inspector are displayed in angular brackets, for example, the `Font` property may be assigned the `<Font1>` value. This means that the current property is an object with the `Font1` name rather than a simple variable (integer or numeric value, string, etc.).

The so-called ambient properties are another important type of property. If you change such properties, the change will influence the values of the analogous property of all objects contained within the current object. For example, if you change the `BackColor` property for the page object, the change will propagate to the analogous properties of all labels, buttons, tables and graphs contained within that page, provided that you have not redefined the `BackColor` property for the nested objects. To determine if a specific property is ambient, search the detailed information on that property in the on-line Help system.

7.2.4. Duplicating and Deriving Objects

Express Objects provides two methods for creating new objects: duplicating and deriving. The differences between duplication of the existing object and deriving a new object from the existing object deserve careful consideration, since they might not necessarily be obvious for programmers without previous OOP experience. In Express Objects, when you select an object from the component toolbar and place it into the application, you are creating a new object by deriving it from the parent object. The derived object inherits all features of its parent object. An inheritance parent—child relationship exists between these objects, and, for example, if you change the fill color of the button in the parent object, this change will propagate to all child buttons, provided that you did not manually override these properties for the child buttons. The duplicate object also inherits the properties of the original object (prototype); however, after the duplicate object has been created, there is no relationship with the original object. Thus, when you change the properties of the original object, no changes will be applied to duplicate objects.

Duplication and derivation are powerful mechanisms allowing for significant improvement of the implementation efficiency for complex projects. For example, having created the Table object with the properties meeting specific requirements (for example, localized fonts for its components) and custom behavior, you can reuse this object in all your applications.

On the other hand, the derivation mechanism enables you to control the properties of all derived objects via the properties of the parent object, and customize the behavior of the derived objects as appropriate. For example, you can override methods and event handlers as needed (consider the example with the Figure object mentioned earlier).

Thus, these mechanisms enable you to reuse once created objects in all subsequent projects while providing flexible capabilities for customizing their behavior by enhancing their properties and methods.

Object browser is a convenient tool for controlling the inheritance hierarchy of the objects used in specific project. By clicking the **View Hierarchy** button at the browser toolbar, you can open the dialog displaying the hierarchical list of all Express Objects built-in objects, along with all user-defined objects and hierarchical inheritance relationships between them.

In Express Objects the following inheritance rules are in effect for objects:

☐ The parent object can have any number of child objects.

☐ Any objects, including child objects, can be used as parents.

☐ Child objects inherit *all* properties and methods of their parent objects. We can't exclude them from the derived objects.

☐ The parent object methods can be overridden in child objects. Overriding methods in child objects has no effect on the behavior of the parent object.

7.2.5. Object Nesting

The built-in containership mechanism is another important feature of the OOP implementation in Express Objects, distinguishing it from other object-oriented language implementations. This mechanism provides another scheme of hierarchical relationships between objects, and plays an important role when you need to implement complex applications. For example, the page represents a container that nests all the other built-in objects, such as tables, graphs, buttons, etc. This enables the user to manage the page and all its contents as a single object. For example, we can move, delete, duplicate, and derive new child objects from the page, and these child objects will inherit the contents of its parent. The objects included within a container can be added or deleted.

Notice that in Express Objects, containership and inheritance are mutually exclusive mechanisms of establishing hierarchical relationships. This means that the container object can't nest its parent or child objects within itself.

The **Projects** window in object browser displays hierarchical relationships between objects, in contrast to the inheritance hierarchy that can be viewed in the **Object Inheritance** window of the browser.

Each object that plays the role of container inherits the built-in methods of controlling its contents — the Add, AddLink, Remove, Count, Item, and Index functions. The containership mechanism also plays an important role in object identification in the Express Basic language, which will be covered in detail later.

7.2.6. Object Sharing via the Links Mechanism

The Links mechanism allows you to reuse the same object instead of duplication and derivation techniques. For example, if different briefings can contain the same pages, you don't need to create a copy of such pages for each of these briefings. It is sufficient to create a single page object within one of such briefings, and place the links to that page into all the other briefings that need to reference that page. To achieve this, go to the object browser, drag the page from one briefing to the other, and then select the **Link** command from the popup menu. This mechanism simplifies the development and support of applications having duplicated parts.

The Links mechanism is also very helpful for specifying the property of the object whose value itself represents an object. For example, if you place a table to the briefing page, the Font property for its components, such as page, row, and column names, will have its own value for each of them. We can replace the Font property values by linking to the object we have already customized according to our requirements. To do so, click the required Font object in the object browser and drag it with the mouse to the appropriate cell of the Font property in object inspector.

7.2.7. Event Handling and Methods

Each object may (but not necessarily does) contain the software code of some methods or event handlers. Event handlers are called any time this object gets the appropriate message from the operating system (for example, the mouse button was clicked) or from the Express Objects built-in objects (for example, the page is opened).

The handler name starts with a prefix determining when this handler gets control. Express Objects provides the following four types of prefixes:

Prefix	Handler gets control	Comment
Request	Before action	Allows the programmer to enable or disable this action
Do	Before action	Allows you to enable or disable the standard reaction to this event
Before	Before action	Only sends a warning message. The action can't be disabled
After	After action	Only sends a warning message. The action can't be disabled

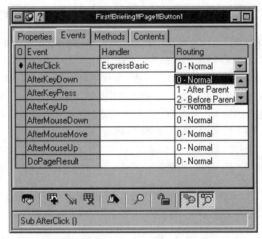

Fig. 7.8. Viewing and defining event handlers for the Button object

To view the predefined event handlers for a specific object, double-click that object in object inspector and go to the **Events** tab (Fig. 7.8). To define the software code for a specific event, double-click the required cell in the **Handler** column. The **Express Basic Editor** window will open, displaying the automatically generated starting and ending lines of code for the event handler (Fig. 7.9). Enter the required Basic operators in this window.

Pay special attention to the **Routing** column displayed at the **Events** tab in the object inspector (see Fig. 7.8). Using the drop-down list appearing in this column nest to the event handler that you are defining; you can specify the calling order for the event handlers specified for our object and its parent object (the **Before Parent** and **After Parent** options). To disable handling of this event by the parent object, select the

Normal option. If you want this event to be handled by the parent object, disable the custom event handler code by specifying the **None** option in the **Routing** column.

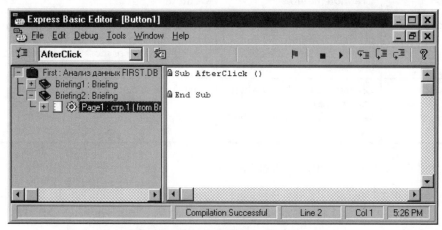

Fig. 7.9. The **Express Basic Editor** window

You can also make our object react to other events not included in the predefined event list. To achieve this, go to the **Events** tab, click the **Add Item** button, and add a new event to the list of events recognized by the object.

The **FireEvent** function allows you to dispatch the event to a specific object, and the **BroadcastEvent** function dispatches the event to all objects contained within the current object.

Object methods are Express Basic procedures that can be called from the event handlers or from other methods. All other aspects of working with methods are very similar to aspects of working with event handlers.

7.3. Express Basic: the Basic Concepts

7.3.1. Modular Structure

The module is the fundamental building block in the Express Basic language. Each module is compiled separately. The language supports the following three types of modules:

Type	Creation method	Contents
Code	Created automatically for each object	Contains the user-defined code for event handlers, methods, and local procedures related to the object

continues

Continued

Type	Creation method	Contents
Library	Created by dragging the **Module** icon from the component toolbar to the object browser	Contains the code that can be used anywhere within an application. The project can contain one or more library modules
Global	Created automatically when you first select the **Window/Global** item in the Express Basic editor	Contains a declaration of the global variables. The project can contain only one global module

All modules are saved in the project file.

The main program unit of the language is the procedure contained in the object code module or in the library module. You can create the following two types of procedures:

Type	Return value	Coding
Sub	None	Enclosed in procedural brackets: sub [...] end sub
Function	Yes	Enclosed in procedural brackets: function [...] end function

Express Objects automatically generates the program module for each object. The module is assigned a name corresponding to the object name. Object module contains the code for all procedures related to that object, including:

❐   Event handlers

❐   Object methods

❐   Local procedures that can be called only from within that module

Because procedure names of the event handlers and methods are registered within an object, their procedural brackets are protected from eventual deletion. To disable this protection, go to the **Express Basic Editor** window, position the cursor somewhere within the method or event handler code and click the **Detach Code** button. The current procedure will be unregistered within the object, thus enabling you to delete its code from the module.

Procedures contained within a library module can be called anywhere from within the project. To avoid name conflicts, library procedures must be called using the qualified names prefixed by the name of the library module. For example, to call the procedure named p1 from the Lib1 module use the following name: Lib1!p1. The exclamation mark here is used for separating the container name from the name of the nested object.

7.3.2. Naming Conventions

All objects or variables must be named according to the naming conventions standard for most programming languages:

❑ The first character of the name must be a letter

❑ Only letters, digits, and underscore characters are valid characters in a name

❑ The name length must not exceed 31 characters

Names of object methods or properties must be prefixed by the object name. For example, to reference the BackColor property of the Page1 object, specify the following name: Page1.BackColor. Here the period is used as a delimiter separating the object name from the member name. Some objects may be assigned another object as a property; for example, consider the Font property of the Page object. To reference the logical property named FontBold of the Font object, which, in turn, is the member of the Page object named Page1, use the following name format: Page1.Font.FontBold

The object name may be qualified. In this case it contains a sequence of container names nesting this object according to the nesting hierarchy. For example, the following reference:

```
pjSample!pgSample!btnSample.move
```

will refer to the move method of the btnSample button placed at the pgSample page of the pjSample project. This reference represents the fully qualified name. The exclamation mark in this case delimits the container names in accordance to the nesting hierarchy, while the period separates the method name from the object name.

Within a module, all the references to the properties and methods of the object to which the current module belongs can be used without the qualifying prefix. In principle, the name of any method or property of any object may be available within the whole application. However, to refer to the object member from within a module not belonging to it, it is necessary to consider the name visibility area.

This task can be solved by using fully qualified names, starting the name listing from the project name. However, this solution limits the capabilities of reusing the code. Let us consider this concept in an example.

Suppose that you have created a page named `Page1` and placed on this page the following objects: a title — `Banner1` and a button — `Button1`. Furthermore, you need the banner fill color to change to white when the button is clicked. To achieve this, the `AftrClick` event handler for the button must contain the following line:

```
Project1!Briefing1!Page1!Banner1.FillColor = white
```

where `Project1` is the name of our project and `Briefing1` is the name of the briefing that includes the page. Start the project to make sure that we have achieved our goal. Now suppose that we want all the pages of our briefings to have similar buttons changing the banner color. Certainly, it would be natural to use the once created object as a prototype for the newly created briefing pages.

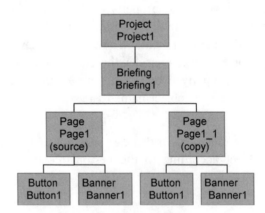

Fig. 7.10. The object nesting hierarchy

Create the new page by copying the `Page1` page. However, if you start the application and click the button in the second page of the briefing, this action will change the banner color at the first briefing page rather than at the second page, as you would expect. Correcting this "feature" is not a hard task. To do so, you need to edit the code relating to the button duplicate in the second page, and change the page name in the qualified reference to the `FillColor` property. However, this would be a tedious task if you needed to create several copies of the first page. To improve our project, observe the following name visibility rules:

❑ If the specified name can be found when searching the object nesting hierarchy in an upward direction starting from the object using the reference, then the reference doesn't require additional qualification.

❑ If the specified name can be found when searching the object nesting hierarchy in a downward direction starting from a specific point, then this reference requires additional qualification. You'll need to specify the containers downwards starting from the point where the search direction changes.

Like in any programming language, in Express Basic, object names must not coincide with the language keywords.

According to these rules, we can specify the reference in our event handler as follows:

```
Banner1.FillColor = white
```

This allows us to achieve the desired result, since the `Banner1` object is present in the first page as well as in each of its copies. Therefore, searching the object nesting hierarchy in an upward direction starting from the button object (no matter whether the button is located in the source page or at any of its copies) will give you this name at the next nesting level (Fig. 7.10).

7.3.3. Data

The Express Basic language supports the following basic data types:

Data type	Size (bytes)	Minimum value	Maximum value
integer	2	-32,768	32,767
long	4	-2,147,483,648	2,147,483,647
single	4	For negative values: -3.402823e+38 For positive values: 1.401298e-45	For negative values: -1.401298e-45 For positive values: 3.402823e+38
double	8	For negative values: -1.79769313486232d+308 For positive values: 4.94065645841247d-324	For negative values: -4.94065645841247d-324 For positive values: 1.79769313486232d+308

continues

Continued

Data type	Size (bytes)	Minimum value	Maximum value
string	From 0 to 32767	0 characters	32767 characters
object	Undefined	Undefined	Undefined
record	Undefined	Undefined	Undefined
variant	20	Depends on the stored value	Depends on the stored value

Some data types may require explanatory notes. The record data type is a data structure containing other data as its members. Before this structure can be used in variable declarations, it must be described using the type directive enabling the developer to define his or her own data types.

The variant data type defines the data of variable type. A variable of this type may contain data of any other type. The current data type of this variable is determined by the value it currently contains, and can be defined programmatically using the VarType function.

Express Basic has no built-in logical data type. Integers are used instead of the Boolean data. The value of 0 corresponds to a FALSE value, while any other value is interpreted as TRUE.

Express Basic supports dynamic data type conversion. However, if long integers are converted into short integers with the loss of significant digits, this causes an overflow interrupt. Loss in accuracy resulting from conversion of float data to an integer or of double to single does not cause an error condition.

You can also create data arrays consisting of data of the same type, for example, integer arrays or record arrays.

7.3.4. Expressions

Expressions are the fundamental building block of the language. Each expression consists of constants, variables, functions, and operators. The Express Basic compiler is case-insensitive. Therefore, you can type the names and keywords both in upper- and lowercase letters.

The sequence of operator execution is determined by the presence of parentheses or by the operator's priority. The first priority level is specified by the operator type: numeric, string, comparison, and logical (the types are listed according to their priority in descending order). The second level is determined directly within the same type by the operator itself.

For numeric operators, the priorities (in descending order) are as follows:

Operator	Description
^	Exponentiation
-, +	Unary minus and plus
*, /	Multiplication and division
\	Integer division. The operands must be of Integer or Long data types
Mod	The remainder from division (modulus). The operands must be Integer or Long
-, +	Addition and subtraction

String concatenation operators & and + are synonyms and have the same priority. Since the + operator is used also in numeric expressions, its usage when combining the operand types may lead to misinterpretation. Therefore, using the & operator in string expressions is safer.

Comparison operators in Express Basic are as follows:

Operator	Description
>	Greater than
<	Less than
=	Equal to
>=	Greater than or equal to
<=	Less than or equal to
<>	Not equal to

Express Basic supports logical operators that can be applied to Integer and Long types:

Operator	Description
Not	Negation
And	Logical AND

continues

Continued

Or	Logical OR
Xor	Exclusive OR (XOR)
Eqv	Equivalence: A Eqv B ≡ Not (A Xor B)
Imp	Implication: A Imp B ≡ (Not A) Or B

Logical operations are performed bitwise, therefore it is necessary to use them carefully. For example, if you expect that since any integer other than 0 is interpreted as TRUE, the Not 1 operator will produce 0 (logical FALSE), you'll have made an error. As a matter of fact, the result of this operation will be −2 (TRUE). This happens because the logical operation is performed bitwise:

```
1  ≡ 00000001b
Not 1 ≡ 11111110b ≡ -2
```

To avoid such mistakes, it is recommended that you use the predefined TRUE and FALSE (YES and NO) constants for assigning logical values.

7.3.5. Passing Parameters

All programming languages have two different techniques of passing parameters when calling procedures and functions: by value and by reference. When passing parameters by value, it is supposed that a new local variable of the same type as the argument will be created, and this variable will be assigned the argument value. All modification of that argument within the procedure body will be performed over the local variable and won't influence the value of the variable that was specified as an argument in the procedure call. In contrast, passing the argument by value enables you to change within the procedure the value of the variable passed as an argument from the calling procedure.

By default, in Express Basic it is supposed that the parameters are passed by reference. If you want to pass parameters by value, you need to specify this explicitly by enclosing the parameter in parentheses:

By reference	By value
call mysub (x,y)	call mysub ((x),(y))
mysub x,y	mysub (x),(y)
z = myfunction(x,y)	z = myfunction((x),(y))
Call myfunction(x,y)	call myfunction((x),(y))

For procedures belonging to an object, there are two limitations when passing parameters:

❑ The argument can't be an array

❑ The argument can't have the user-defined data type

This limitation doesn't concern the procedures whose code is defined in library modules.

The order in which arguments are listed in the procedure call is determined by the order of arguments in the procedure declaration. Notice that Express Basic provides another capability for passing parameters. The order of parameters may be arbitrary, if you explicitly specify the names of arguments passed to the procedure.

For example, if the procedure declaration is as follows:

```
sub mysub(aa, bb, optional cc, optional dd)
```

the following calls will be equal:

```
call mysub(1, 2, , 4)

mysub aa := 1, bb := 2, dd :=4

call mysub(aa := 1, dd:=4, bb := 2)

mysub 1, 2, dd:=4
```

From our point of view, this variety demonstrates the rich capabilities and power of the language. However, it certainly doesn't improve the code's readability. Therefore, we recommend that you observe the traditional syntax of calling procedures accepted in most programming languages.

Besides Express Basic procedures, we can call external procedures from MS Windows Dynamic Linked Libraries (DLL). These external procedures can be written using other programming languages, and may include the functions of the operating system itself. This feature provides practically unlimited capabilities for development of client applications, both in efficiency and functionality. Before calling procedures from external DLLs, you must declare them, and, furthermore, you should always pass the arguments by value.

7.4. Programming Express Basic

7.4.1. Creating, Compiling, and Executing Procedures

As was already mentioned before, Express Basic provides a special built-in multiple-window text editor for writing the procedure code. To start the editor, select the **Windows/Express Basic Editor** menu item. The left pane of the editor window (Fig. 7.11) contains the object browser allowing you to navigate from module to module. To start editing the module related to a specific object, double-click that object in the object browser.

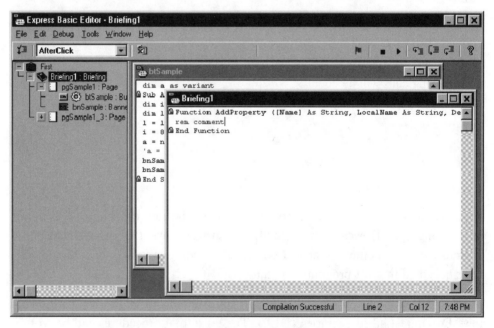

Fig. 7.11. The **Express Basic Editor** multiple-window

The drop-down list in the toolbar lists all the methods and event handlers predefined for the selected object. To override any method, select that method from the list. All required procedural parentheses with appropriate argument declarations will be inserted automatically.

Express Basic provides two types of comments continuing to the end of line. The first is designated by a single quote character ('), while the second—by the Rem directive:

```
'This is a comment
Rem This is also comment
call mysub(x,y) 'just another comment
```

Each operator consumes a separate line and therefore doesn't require the terminating character. If you need to continue the operator on the next line, you can do so using two characters: blank and underscore.

```
call musub (x, _ 'example of continuing the operator on the next line
y)
```

However, this technique is not applicable when specifying string constants. To specify that the string constant continues on the next line, use the concatenation operator:

```
mystr = "This string is too long"
mystr = mystr & " to fit within a single line."
```

To compile the active module, select the **File/Compile** menu item. If the compiler detects some errors, it will notify you of the errors by displaying warning messages in the new window. Besides the error code, the error messages specify the module name and the line number.

The specific event handler executes only when the specified event takes place. To pass control to the object method, that method must be explicitly called from the event handler or from another method.

7.4.2. Variables

Declaring Variables

Express Basic requires all the variables used in procedures to be previously declared. By visibility, all variables are classified by three categories: global variables, module-level variables, and local variables. Global variables are available from within any module of the project. They must be declared in the special Globals module. Module-level variables are declared within the module, but outside the procedure code. Such variables are global for procedures within a module, i.e., they are available from within any procedure whose source code follows the variable declaration. Local variables are declared within a procedure and can be used within that procedure only.

Variables are declared using the following directive:

```
dim variableName [as [new] type] [,variableName [as [new] type]] ...
```

where `variableName` is the name of the declared variable. If the variable name is not followed by the `as` keyword, the variable is assigned the `variant` data type by default. The variable name can be followed (without the blank separator) by one of the following type qualifiers:

Qualifier	Type
$	String
%	Integer
&	Long
!	Single
#	Double

For example,

```
dim strVar$    'this is a string of variable lenght
dim int%    'this is an integer value
```

The `as` keyword allows you to explicitly specify the variable type:

```
dim strVar as string 'this is a string of variable length
dim strFix as string*8 'this is a string of fixed length
dim d as double
```

Besides simple type, you can specify the variable type by the name of the record structure, which has to be previously declared by the `type` statement outside the procedure body, for example:

```
type record1
   staffNo as integer
   staffName as string
end type
...
dim staffInfo as record1
```

The names of Express Basic objects also can be specified as data types. If the `new` keyword is present in this case, the descendant of that object will be derived and initialized, and the declared variable will contain a reference to it. If the `new` key-word is missing, the new object will not be derived, and the variable will be initialized with an empty reference.

The `dim` directive is also used for declaring arrays. An array represents an ordered set of data of the same type. Data comprising an array can have any of the basic data types, including structures and objects. The syntax of array declaration is as follows:

```
dim variableName( [ subscriptRange, ... ] ) [as [new] type]], …
```

Here `variableName` stands for the name of the variable identifying the declared array, followed by definitions of the array dimensions enclosed in parentheses. `SubscriptRange` defines the upper and lower bounds of an array's subscripts and has the following syntax:

```
[ startSubscript to ] endSubscript
```

If the lower bound of an array's subscript (`startSubscript`) is not specified, it is assumed to be 0. Array bounds can be negative. An array can have anywhere from 1 to 60 dimensions.

If a dimension is not specified in the array declaration, this means that this array is dynamic, i.e., that the array dimension can be determined at run-time using the following statement:

```
redim[preserve] variableName(subscriptRange,...) [as [new] type] , ...
```

The `redim` statement must precede the first use of the array elements in the program code. The `redim` statement can be used multiple times to allocate and reallocate memory for storing an array. Bear in mind that the number of dimensions specified by the first `redim` statement cannot be changed in the course of subsequent reallocation operations. Repeated usage of the `redim` statement only allows you to change the subscript bounds of the dynamic array. The `preserve` keyword enables you to preserve the contents of the array. By default, the memory allocated for the array with redefined bounds will be filled with zeros for numeric arrays or empty strings ("") for string arrays.

Pay special attention to the variable lifetime. Variables declared within a procedure are dynamic. This means that when the procedure is called repeatedly, such variables will not preserve the values they were assigned during the previous call. The variables declared within a module preserve their values as long as the current module remains active. For example, you can define the click counter within the button module:

```
dim Count as integer
sub AfterClick ()
   Count = Count + 1
   ...
end sub
```

This example implies that in the course of variable declaration it is initialized by a zero value. The counter will correctly count the number of clicks as long as the page containing the button remains active. If the user navigates to another page within a briefing, and then returns to the initial page, the Count variable will be re-initialized with a 0.

The same result can be obtained for the local variable if you declare it using the static keyword. The following code:

```
sub AfterClick ()
     static Count as integer
Count = Count + 1
...
end sub
```

will be equivalent to the example presented earlier.

Global variables declared in the Globals module preserve their values both at run-time and even after the application is terminated, provided that the project remains active in the Express Objects environment. This feature distinguishes Express Objects from other development environments, and may cause some difficulties when debugging applications.

The Express Basic language has another useful feature that deserves special mention. This feature is known as name overlapping. If the object module contains a declaration of the variable with the name duplicating the name of a global variable, the global variable becomes invisible for the procedures of that module. A similar rule is applicable to declarations of local variables within procedures. If the local variable name duplicates the name of a global variable or that of a variable declared within that module, they become invisible for subsequent code. This feature allows you to abstract names from the global variable where they are not used, and also provides a certain amount of freedom when selecting names.[1]

---

[1] However, this feature is also potentially dangerous. For example, once I declared local variables differing from global variables only by case (because I got used to the C++ compiler, which is case-sensitive), and then tried to use both local and global variables within the procedure code. Obviously, the result was disappointing.

Literals and Assigning Values

Literals are words or characters within a program that define their own values rather than the name of some other element. Literals are used for specifying initial values for string and numeric variables. In comparison to other higher level languages, Express Basic has no specific rules applicable to literals. Listed below are examples of valid Express Basic literals:

```
123      'integer
12.3     'decimal
.123e+2 'decimal
.123d+2 'decimal with double precision
&o177    'octal integer
&h80FF  'hexadecimal integer
"This is a string constant"
```

For simple variables, the assignment operator works the same way as in other languages. To assign a value to an array cell, specify the array name followed by a comma-delimited list of array subscripts enclosed in parentheses, for example: myArray (0, 2) = 12. If the array consists of objects of records, record fields or object properties are referenced as follows:

```
MyBanner(3).Text = "An example of referencing the property of object array"
```

If you have two variables with the record type or that are objects, you can copy the content of the first variable into the second variable using an assignment operator.

For data representing objects, Express Basic provides the set ... =... statement, which, instead of copying data, assigns a reference to the object in the right part of the equation to the variable in the left part. For example, consider the following code:

```
dim pg1 as new Page 'derives new object from the Page ancestor,
                    'pg1 references the new object
dim pg2 as new Page 'derives another page
dim pg3 as Page     'empty reference to the object of the Page type
pg2 = pg1           'pg2 references the pg1 copy
set pg3 = pg1       'pg1 and pg3 reference the same instance of
                    'the Page object
...
```

As a result of executing this code, pg2 will become a standalone pg2 object, while the names pg1 and pg3 will become synonymous.

7.4.3. Procedures

Procedure code in Express Basic is enclosed within the procedural parentheses, namely, sub ... end sub:

```
[static] [private] sub name [([optional] parameter [as type], ...)]
...
end sub
```

The optional static keyword allows you to declare all local variables within this procedure as static (more detailed information on this topic was presented in the previous section). The private keyword disables procedure calls from other modules.

parameter — this is a comma-delimited list of procedure arguments. Parameter type can be defined using qualifiers or the As type statement. The procedure argument may be of a simple type as well as represent an array, object, or structure. The argument represents an array if its name is followed by empty parentheses. Notice, however, that arrays or user-defined data types are not allowed in object-related modules. For library modules this limitation is not applicable.

The variant object name may be preceded by the optional keyword. That means that this argument can be omitted when calling the procedure. Arguments declared using the optional keyword must follow the required arguments. This enables you to use default values for some arguments, for example:

```
sub myfunc(optional arg1)
  if ismissing(arg1) then arg1=12
end sub
```

This code determines a procedure that can be called without parameters. In this case, the optional argument will take a default value of 12.

The control is returned to the calling procedure when the end sub string is reached. The exit sub statement allows you to return control from any point within the procedure.

The function procedure is different from an ordinary procedure, in that it returns a value of the specified type. The syntax for declaring function procedures is as follows:

```
[static] [private] function name [([optional]parameter [as type] ...)]
[as functype]
      name = expression
end function
```

Here, `functype` defines the type of the return value. The return value is assigned to the function name. The `exit function` statement allows you to return control from any point within the function procedure. In all the other features, the function procedure declaration is no different from ordinary procedure declaration.

7.4.4. Passing Control

The *do* Loop

The `do` loop syntax has the following two alternative forms:

1.

```
do [{while | until} condition]
        [statementblock]
        [exit do]
        [statementblock]
loop
```

2.

```
do
        [statementblock]
        [exit do]
        [statementblock]
loop [{while | until} condition]
```

These two forms of the `do` operator have the following difference. When using the first form, the *statementblock* code enclosed by a `do ... loop` will be executed only if the logical condition specified by *condition* has a value of TRUE when entering the loop. When using the second form, the code will be executed at least once, independently from the value specified by the logical condition. In both cases, the code will be executed repeatedly until the logical condition gets a FALSE value, or until the `exit do` statement is reached.

The *for* Loop

The `for` loop allows us to repeat the series of commands enclosed by the `for ... next` parentheses for a fixed number of times:

```
for counter = start to end [step increment]
```

```
    [statementblock]

    [exit for]

    [statementblock]

next [counter]
```

Here:

counter—numeric variable representing the loop parameter

start—starting value of the loop variable

end—ending value of the loop variable

increment—increment of the loop variable

Both the loop variable and its increment may take negative values. If the increment is not specified, it is assumed to take the default value of 1.

The next statement need not necessarily be followed by the loop variable name. Express Basic allows for closing nested for loops with a single next statement, which in this case must be followed by the loop variable names (the nested loop variable name must precede the nesting loop variable name):

```
For i = 1 To 10

    [ statementblock ]

    For j = 1 To 5

        [ statementblock ]

Next j, i
```

The execution of the for loop can be interrupted by the exit for statement. Control will be passed to the operator directly following the next statement.

Conditional Jump Operator

The simplest form of the if operator has the following syntax:

```
if condition then then_statement [else else_statement]
```

The usage of this operator is no different from its usage in other programming languages. If you need to perform a conditional jump for several operators simultaneously, use another form of the conditional jump syntax:

```
if condition then
```

```
        statement_block1

    [else

        statement_block2]

   end if
```

The closing `end` `if` statement is required in any case, even if the *statement_block1* consists of a single operator.

The *goto* Operator

Unfortunately, Express Basic doesn't allow you to do without the `goto` operator, despite the fact that most users who support traditional structural programming have strong objections against its use in programs. For example, quite often it is necessary to omit some loop operators and go to a new iteration. For such situations, C++ provides a structural `continue` operator, which in our case is unavailable. Therefore, we need the `goto` operator, the syntax of which is as follows:

```
goto label

 ...

label:

 ...
```

Here, `label` is the name of the label to which control will be passed. The label must start at the first position in a row. It is separated from the remaining code by a colon.

There is also another form of the `goto` operator, allowing us to perform multiple branching of the program. It uses the following syntax:

```
on numeric_expression goto label1 [,label2 , ...]
```

In this case, before passing the control, it is necessary to calculate the integer numeric expression (*numeric_expression*) that follows the `on` statement. If this value is equal to 0 or greater than the number of labels in a list following the `goto` statement, the control is passed to the next operator; otherwise, the control will be passed to the label whose ordinal number in the list corresponds to the calculated value of the *numeric_expression*.

The *select* Switch

Similar to the `on ... goto` operator, the select switch allows you to implement multiple branching of the program:

```
select case testexpression
[case expressionlist
   [statement_block]]
[case expressionlist
   [statement_block]]
[case else
   [statement_block]]
end select
```

Here, the `testexpression` stands for an expression whose value is calculated before passing control. The calculated value is sequentially compared to the values of the expressions that follow the `case` keywords. If the test value matches one of the values in the list, the group of operators following that item is executed and control is passed to the operator following the `end select` statement. Since the text expression values are compared to the values of expressions listed in the list of allowed values, these expressions must have comparable data types.

This operator enables you to implement quite a complex branching of algorithms.

7.4.5. Procedures and Functions

A detailed description of the syntax of all Express Basic procedures and functions is provided in the on-line Help system of the Express Objects product. In this section we will provide only a brief overview of the most frequently used procedures and functions. Notice that this material is provided for reference purposes only.

Table 7.1. Date and Time Procedures

Syntax	Type	Description
Date	Variant (8)	Returns a 10-character string containing the current system date representation

continues

Table 7.1 Continued

Syntax	Type	Description
DateSerial(year%, month%, day%)	Variant (7)	Returns the date value corresponding to the specified arguments
DateValue(date$)	Variant (7)	Returns the date value corresponding to the string date representation specified as an argument
Day(date)	Variant (2)	Returns an integer from 0 to 31 corresponding to the ordinal number of the day for the date specified as an argument
Hour(time)	Variant (2)	Returns an integer from 0 to 23 corresponding to the hour for the time specified as an argument
IsDate(expression)	Boolean	Returns TRUE if the specified argument allows conversion to the date type
Minute(time)	Variant (2)	Returns an integer from 0 to 59 corresponding to the minute component of the time specified as an argument
Month(date)	Variant (2)	Returns an integer from 0 to 12 corresponding to the month for the date specified as an argument
Now()	Variant (7)	Returns the system date and time values
Second(time)	Variant (2)	Returns an integer from 0 to 59 corresponding the seconds component for the time specified as an argument
Time	Variant (8)	Returns a string representation of the current time
TimeSerial(hour%, minute%, second%)	Variant (7)	Returns the time corresponding to the specified arguments
Timer	Single	Returns the number of system time seconds elapsed since midnight
TimeValue(time$)	Variant (7)	Returns the time value for the string specified as an argument
Weekday(date)	Variant (2)	Returns the ordinal number of the day of the week (from 1 to 7) for the date specified by the argument
Year(date)	Variant (2)	Returns the ordinal number of the year (from 100 to 9999) for the date specified as an argument

The `Date` and `Time` statements allow you to set the system date and time. These statements have the following syntax:

```
Date = date_expression$
Time = time_expression$
```

The right parts of the assignments must contain string expressions representing the date (`mm/dd/yy`, `mm/dd/yyyy`, `mm-dd-yy`, `mm-dd-yyyy`) or time (`hh`, `hh:mm`, `hh:mm:ss`).

File Input/Output Procedures

Table 7.2. Disks and Directories Management

Syntax	Type	Description
`ChDir path$`	None	Changes the current directory. The string argument uses the following syntax: `[drive:] [\] directory [\directory]`...
`ChDrive drive$`	None	Changes the current drive
`CurDir [(drive$)]`	Variant (8)	Returns the current drive and directory path for the drive specified
`Dir [(pathname$ [,attributes%)]`	Variant (8)	Returns the filename corresponding to the specified template
`MkDir path$`	None	Creates a new directory

Table 7.3. File Management

Syntax	Type	Description
`FileAttr(filenumber%, returntype%)`	Integer	Returns the mode for the opened file
`FileCopy source$, destination$`	None	Copies the file
`FileDateTime(pathname$)`	Variant (7)	Returns the date and time of the most recent file modification
`FileLen(pathname$)`	Long	Returns the file size (in bytes)
`GetAttr(pathname$)`	Integer	Returns the attributes of the specified file

continues

Table 7.3 Continued

Syntax	Type	Description
`Kill pathname$`	None	Deletes the file
`Name oldfilename$ As newfilename$`	None	Renames the file
`SetAttr pathname$, attributes%`	None	Resets the file attributes

Table 7.4. File Input/Output

Syntax	Type	Description
`Close [[#] filenumber% [, [#] filenumber% ...]]`	None	Closes the file(s)
`Eof(filenumber%)`	Boolean	Returns TRUE if the EOF label is reached in the specified file
`FreeFile`	Integer	Returns the lowest free file number available for use
`Get[#] filenumber%, [recnumber&], varname`	None	Reads the record number or byte number from the file opened using random mode or binary mode
`Input[$](number%, [#]filenumber%)`	Variant (8)	Returns the string containing the specified number of characters from the file
`Input [#] filenumber%, variable [, variable]...`	None	Reads the specified portion of data from an open sequential file
`Line Input[#] filenumber%, varname$`	None	Reads the next line from the open sequential file
`Loc(filenumber%)`	Long	Returns the current offset value for the file (depends on the file mode)
`Lock[#]filenumber% [, [start&] [To end&]]`	None	Locks access by other processes to the specified part of the opened file
`Lof(filenumber%)`	Long	Returns the length of the opened file (in bytes)
`Open filename$ [For mode] [Access access] [lock] As [#] filenumber% [Len = reclen]`	None	Opens the file

continues

Table 7.4 Continued

Syntax	Type	Description
Put[#] filenumber%, [recnumber&], varname	None	Writes data to file
Reset	None	Closes all opened files
Seek(filenumber%)	Long	Returns the current position in the opened file
Seek[#] filenumber%, position&	None	Changes the current position within a file
Write[#] filenumber% [,expressionlist]	None	Writes data into the sequential file

Console Input/Output

Since Express Objects client applications run under MS Windows, screen output and keyboard input are implemented using special dialogs.

Syntax	Type	Description
Beep	None	System beep
InputBox[$](prompt$, [title$], [default$], [xpos%, ypos%])	String	Displays a dialog with the prompt and returns the string entered by the user
MsgBox(prompt$, [buttons%][, title$])	Integer	Displays a message box with the message and returns an integer corresponding to the button that the user has clicked
PasswordBox[$](prompt$, [title$], [default$] [,xpos% , ypos%])	String	Returns the string entered by the user without displaying it (i.e., using the echo off mode)

Mathematical Functions

Table 7.5. Numeric Functions

Syntax	Type	Description
Abs (number)	Depends on the argument type	Absolute value of a number

continues

Table 7.5 Continued

Syntax	Type	Description
Exp(number)	Depends on the argument type	The power of e = 2.718282...
Fix(number)	Depends on the argument type	Integer component of a number. Example: Fix(6.2) returns 6, Fix(-6.2) returns -6
Int(number)	Depends on the argument type	Integer component of a number. Example: Int(6.2) returns 6, Int(-6.2) returns -7
IsNumeric(expression)	Boolean	Returns TRUE, if the expression specified as an argument is a numeric expression
Log(number)	Depends on the argument type	Natural logarithm of a number
Rnd[(number!)]	Single	Returns a pseudo-random number evenly distributed within the (0,1) interval. The argument defines the method of randomization: <0 – use the specified value =0 – use the latest generated value >0 – use the next number from the sequence (default) Modification of the sequence can be performed using the Randomize statement
Sgn(number)	Integer	Returns an integer value determining the argument sign
Sqr(number)	Depends on the argument type	Square root of the number

Table 7.6. Trigonometric Functions

Syntax	Type	Description
Atn(number)	Depends on the argument type	The value of the circular tangent of the argument (in radians)

continues

Table 7.6 Continued

Syntax	Type	Description
Cos(number)	Depends on the argument type	Cosine of the argument
Sin(number)	Depends on the argument type	Sine of the argument
Tan(number)	Depends on the argument type	Tangent of the argument

Table 7.7. String Handling

Syntax	Type	Description
GetField[$](string$, field_number%, separator_char$)	String	Returns the substring of the specified string
Hex[$](number)	String	Text representation of a hexadecimal value
InStr([start%,] string1$, string2$)	String	Returns the starting position of the specified substring within a string
LCase[$](string$)	String	Converts the string characters to lower case
Left[$](string$, length%)	String	Returns the specified number of the starting characters from the string
Len(string$)	Integer	String length (in bytes)
string$ LIKE pattern$	Boolean	Compares the string to the pattern specified
LTrim[$](string$)	String	Deletes the leading blanks from the string and returns the trimmed string
Mid[$](string$, start%[, length%])	String	Returns the substring of the specified length and starting position within a source string
Mid(stringvar$, start%[, length%]) = string$	None	Replaces the substring with the specified string

continues

Table 7.7 Continued

Syntax	Type	Description
Oct[$](number)	String	Text representation of the octal number
Right[$](string$, length%)	String	Returns the specified number of ending characters of the string
RTrim[$](string$)	String	Deletes the trailing blanks from the string and returns the trimmed string
SetField[$](string$, field_number%, field$, separator_char$)	String	Replaces the substring with the specified one
Space[$](number)	String	Returns the substring consisting of the specified number of blanks
Str[$](number)	String	Converts the number to text
StrComp(string1$, string2$ [, compare%])	Integer	Compares two strings and returns an integer value: -1—*string1* > *string2*; 1—*string1* < *string2*; 0—*string1* = *string2*; Null—*string1* = Null or *string2* = Null
String[$](number, Character%)	String	Returns a string consisting of the specified number of specified characters
Trim[$](string$)	String	Returns the string resulting from deletion of the leading and trailing blanks
UCase[$](string)	String	Converts the string characters to upper case
Asc(string$)	Integer	Returns the ANSI code of the first character of the string
CCur(expression)	Currency	Converts the number to currency format
CDbl(expression)	double	Converts the expression to the double type
Chr[$](charcode)	String	Returns the character corresponding to the specified ANSI code

continues

Table 7.7 Continued

Syntax	Type	Description
CInt(expression)	Integer	Converts the specified expression to Integer
CLng(expression)	Long	Converts the specified expression to Long
CSng(expression)	Single	Converts the specified expression to Single
CStr(expression)	String	Converts the specified expression to String
CVar(expression)	Variant	Converts the specified expression to Variant
CVDate(expression)	Variant(7)	Converts the specified expression to Date
Format[$](expression [, format])	String	Returns the string that represents a formatted expression
Val(string$)	double	Returns the numeric representation of the first number within the specified string

Dynamic Data Exchange Procedures

Express Objects enables the developer to create applications that can interact with other Windows applications using the standard Dynamic Data Exchange (DDE) mechanism. More detailed information on this topic can be found in reference literature on the MS Windows operating system.

Table 7.8. Description of Dynamic Data Exchange Procedures

Syntax	Type	Description
DDEAppReturnCode()	Integer	Returns the code received from the application to which the DDE channel is opened
DDEExecute channel%, cmd$	None	Sends the command or commands to the applications to which the DDE channel is opened
DDEInitiate(appname$, topic$)	Integer	Opens the DDE channel to the application and returns its number
DDEPoke channel%, item$, data$	None	Sends data to the application via the DDE channel

continues

Table 7.8 Continued

Syntax	Type	Description
DDERequest[$](channel%, item$)	String	Returns the data received from the application via the open DDE channel
DDETerminate channel%	None	Closes the open DDE channel

ODBC Procedures

ODBC (Open Database Connectivity) mechanisms allow an Express Objects application to interact with relational data sources for which ODBC drivers have been installed on your computer.

Table 7.9. Description of ODBC Procedures

Syntax	Type	Description
SQLClose(connection&)	Variant	Closes connection to the ODBC data source. Returns 0 in case of success. If the data source is inaccessible, the function returns−1
SQLError(destination())	None	Allows you to get detailed information on errors caused by ODBC function calls. Destination is a two-dimensional dynamic array of variant data, each row of which contains a single error message
SQLExecQuery (connection&, query$)	Integer	Executes an SQL statement and returns the number of columns (in case of SELECT) or number of rows (in case of UPDATE, INSERT, or DELETE statements)
SQLGetSchema (connection&, action%, qualifier$, ref())	Variant	Returns various information on the ODBC data source
SQLOpen (connectStr$, [outputStr$], [prompt%])	Variant	Opens a connection to the ODBC data source and returns the connection identifier
SQLRequest (connectionStr$, query$, [outputStr$], [prompt%], [columnNames%], ref())	Variant	Simultaneously establishes a connection to the ODBC data source, executes the query, and closes the connection

continues

Table 7.9 Continued

Syntax	Type	Description
SQLRetrieve (connection&, destination(), [maxColumns%], [maxRows%], [ColumnNames%], [rowNumbers%], [fetchFirst%])	Variant	Reads the values retrieved by the current query
SQLRetrieveToFile (connection&, destination$, [columnNames%], [columnDelimiter$])	Variant	Reads and stores in the file the values retrieved by the current query

7.5. Designing the User Interface

Everything that we have said in the previous chapter when discussing briefing design principles is also applicable to applications designed using Express Objects. Because of this, we needn't discuss the design concepts and principles repetitively. We will simply proceed with discussing application development.

The Express Objects application is structured as a hierarchical tree. The root element of the tree is always a project. The project serves as a container for all objects created and placed at the briefing pages when developing an application. Each application contains at least one briefing object that has at least one page. The project file contains all information related to that project, including objects, property values, and modules written in Express Basic.

In contrast to Express Analyzer, where briefing functionality is limited to a set of predefined actions, Express Objects enables the developer to extend the functionality of standard objects by overriding their methods and event handlers using the Express Basic language.

All visual components available in the component toolbar can be considered as the building blocks of the user interface. When we discussed Express Analyzer, we described the use of some components (for example, those such as Briefing, Page, Button, Banner, OLE, Table, Graph) that can be used when designing the user interface. In this section we are going to concentrate on the additional capabilities provided by Express Objects.

Notice that all interface objects have a set of common properties:

Property	Description
Enabled	Logical variable that determines the availability of the component and its related events for the user
Text	Text variable containing the text describing the object
Visible	Logical variable specifying whether or not the component is visible to the end user
TabIndex	Integer variable that locates the position of a specific component in the general list describing the order in which the focus moves from one interface object to the next as the user presses the <TAB> key
TabStop	Logical variable allowing you to exclude the component from the **TabIndex** list. The value of this variable value indicates whether a user can use the <TAB> key to give the focus to an object

7.5.1. Creating Menus

In MS Windows, the menu is the component most often used for organizing end-user interfaces. There are two types of menus: menu bars and pop-up menus.

Normally, you insert the menu bar into your briefing or briefing page. To insert a menu bar, simply drag the menu component from the component toolbar to the briefing or page displayed in the object browser window. After you accomplish this, the component window will contain a bar representing the newly created menu. To add a new menu item, drag the CommandItem component from the component toolbar to the menu bar. A new menu item will appear in the menu, labeled as <item>. Go to the object inspector and change the text property value (for example, replace <item> with File). Now repeat this procedure three times, each time inserting the CommandItem object to the **File** object field. Thus, you'll have created three menu commands. Now change the text property for the first and the third commands to Open... and Exit..., respectively. Go to the second menu command and change the value of the ItemStale property by replacing the 0-Normal value with 2-Horizontal Separator. When you start the application, you'll notice that the newly created menu looks like a standard Windows menu (Fig. 7.12).

To test the menu, let's define the following code for the AfterItemClick () event handlers of the first and the third **File** menu commands:

```
Sub AfterItemClick ()
msgBox("The <<Open...>> command is selected")
```

```
End Sub
```

and

```
Sub AfterItemClick ()
if msgBox("Close the application?",1) = pgPROK then
   call Application.Stop
end if
End Sub
```

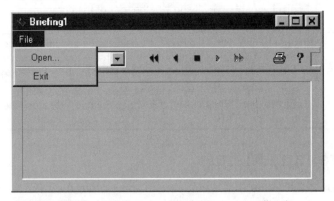

Fig. 7.12. Inserting a menu into your application

The `Stop()` method of the object named `Application` closes our application. Later in this chapter we will cover this method in more detail.

Pop-up menus are also widely used in Windows applications, perhaps even more frequently than menu bars. To convert the menu bar created in the previous example into a pop-up menu, change the `MenuStale` property of the `Menu` object by replacing the `0-Bar` value with `1-Popup` value. Now, if you start the application and right-click somewhere within the page area, you will see a pop-up menu similar to the one shown in Fig. 7.13.

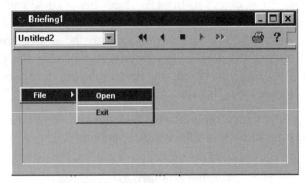

Fig. 7.13. Creating a pop-up menu

7.5.2. The Toolbar

Most contemporary applications include toolbars that contain command buttons providing quick access to the menu items and commands. To create such a toolbar in Express Objects, use the standard `ToolBar` component. You can insert toolbars into any page. Let us return to the example we started to consider in the previous section. Drag the `ToolBar` object to the briefing page. Go to the object browser and drag the first (**Open**) and the third (**Exit**) commands of the **File** menu to the newly created `Toolbar` object. Select the **Link** option from the pop-up menu that appears after you drag the command to the toolbar. Now if you go to the briefing editor window, you'll notice that our toolbar now contains two command buttons. To customize the look and functionality of your toolbar, specify an appropriate bitmap image for each button (Fig. 7.14).

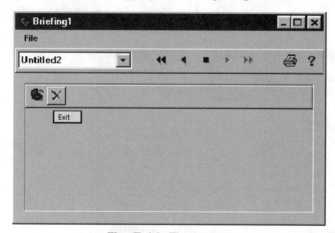

Fig. 7.14. The toolbar

To provide the user with tips that will appear any time the user positions the mouse cursor over the toolbar button, specify the tip text as the value for the `PopupTip...` property of the `CommandItem` object. The toolbar may be positioned anywhere within the window. You can also use large buttons and button labels. More detailed information on this topic is provided in the on-line Help system. For additional information, study carefully the example of the demo application (MENUBARS.XPJ).

7.5.3. Customizing the Standard Pop-Up Menu

According to the Microsoft Windows UI standard, you can associate a pop-up menu with any object. This menu appears any time the user right-clicks that object. In the previous section we demonstrated the procedure of creating a pop-up menu for the page object. Some Express components have predefined standard pop-up menus. These components include lists of dimensions, briefings, tables, and graphs.

When customizing your application, you can:

❑ Disable the popup menu for the object. To do so, set the ShowDefaultPopup property value to No. This enables you to create your own user-defined popup menu for that object.

❑ Disable the standard popup menu for all components of the selected object. To achieve this, set the ShowComponentPopups property to No.

❑ Disable some specific items of the popup menu or customize the labels of specific popup menu commands. To perform this customization, double-click the PopupMenuAttributes property. The **Popup Menu Attributes** dialog will open (Fig. 7.15), where you will be able to perform the required customization.

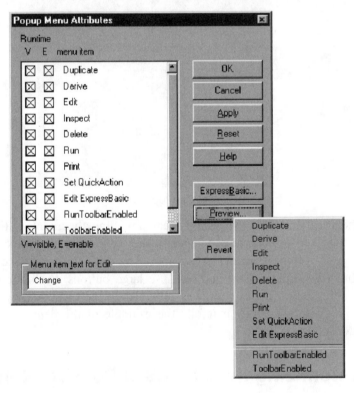

Fig. 7.15. The **Popup Menu Attributes** dialog allows you to customize the properties of the standard popup menu

The **V** (**V** stands for Visible) column in this dialog specifies whether or not the specific command will appear in the popup menu. The **E** (**E** stands for Enabled) allows you to disable the item and make it unavailable to end users. To customize the label of the selected menu item, go to the **Menu item text for**... field at the bottom of this dialog and enter the desired text there. To preview the results of your customizations, click the **Preview** button. By clicking the **Express Basic,** button you can start the Express Basic editor, which allows you to edit the code for the PopupMenuAttributes object. Notice that the code is defined for the whole PopupMenuAttributes object rather than for specific components. To define custom event handlers for this object, double click the PopupMenuAttributes value field in the object inspector, then go to the **Events** or **Methods** tab for the selected object.

7.5.4. Using Standard Dialogs

The developers of a user interface are provided with the ability to use several standard Windows dialogs. These standard dialogs are encapsulated by the appropriate visual components:

❑ ColorDialog—provides the user with the capability of using a standard color selection dialog

❑ FileDialog—provides the standard **File Open** and **Save File As** dialogs

❑ FontDialog—provides the standard font selection dialog

To preview the dialog in the course of developing your application, right-click the icon representing the desired object at the page of your application and select the **Show Dialog** command from the popup menu. At run time, dialogs are normally called from the event handler for the menu item selection or button clicking events. For example, in order to open the **File Open** dialog, insert the following line into the event handler code:

```
Call FileDialog1.ShowModal()
```

Since the ShowModal function returns a value determining the method used to close the dialog, the dialog call is normally encapsulated into the select case operator:

```
select case FileDialog1.ShowModal()
   case pgPROK
      ...
   case pgPRCancel
      ...
end select
```

Here, pgPROK and pgPRCancel are Express Objects' predefined constants, corresponding to clicking the **OK** and **Cancel** buttons, respectively.

The dialog components listed above have quite a large number of properties and methods that provide flexible capabilities for customizing the look and behavior of the standard dialogs.

7.5.5. Using Images

When implementing the UI, developers can use image files in the following formats:

- ❏ Bitmap (*.bmp)—bitmap images
- ❏ Metafile (*.wmf)—windows metafiles storing the image in vector format
- ❏ Icon (*.ico)—icon files
- ❏ Cursor—cursor files

Fig. 7.16. The dialog allowing you to specify picture properties

Images are encapsulated using the special Picture object included into the standard property sets for most visual components such as Banner, BaseControl, Briefing, Button, ComboBox, ListBox, Page, and PictureBox. To assign the value to the `Picture` property, double-click the value field for this property in object inspector. The standard dialog will open (Fig. 7.16), allowing you to define the required value. Notice that this dialog contains the **Save In project** option that allows you to specify whether the selected image will be stored in the project or if the project will only store the path to the image file. This option influences the application portability.

The **Clip**, **Scale**, and **Tile** radio buttons allow you to specify whether the selected image will be clipped, scaled, or tiled if the image size doesn't fit the size of the object encapsulating it.

Careful use of the images in your applications allows you to make your user interface more attractive, intuitive, and user-friendly. Based on user experience, one may state that these features play the key role for users evaluating your application.

7.5.6. Standard Controls

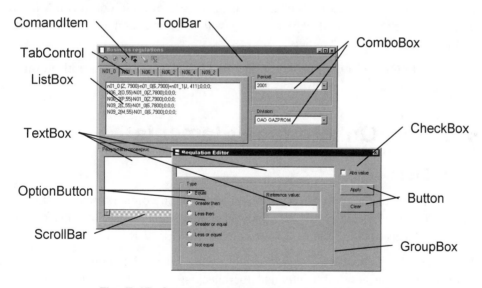

Fig. 7.17. Standard controls of the user interface

Express Objects allows developers to use standard Windows UI controls. Common Windows UI controls (Fig. 7.17) include:

❑ `Label`—multi-string text object

- ❏ Button—command button
- ❏ CheckBox—checkbox
- ❏ OptionButton—radio button
- ❏ ListBox—list field
- ❏ ComboBox—drop-down list
- ❏ TextBox—single-line text field
- ❏ ScrollBar—scroll bar
- ❏ GroupBox—visual container used for grouping other controls
- ❏ TabControl—tabbed control imitating a card box

A detailed description of the properties, event handlers, and methods provided for these controls can be found in the on-line Help system. Using these controls and customizing their properties is not a difficult task, even for beginning developers. You should just recollect that "practice is the basis of cognition". Therefore, the most efficient way of getting acquainted with the use of these controls lies in creating text applications and experimenting with customization of their properties and programming event handlers.

The CONTROLS.XPJ demo application can be used as a good illustrative example of the usage of standard controls.

7.6. Add-On Interface Elements

View Lists

The list is one of the most frequently used abstracts in computer science. In practice, it is often necessary to view two or more parallel lists. For this purpose, Express Objects provides the ListView component (Fig. 7.18).

Let's illustrate the goals of this component with a practical example. Suppose you have a set of business rules intended for checking data integrity in the database (the first list). In the course of analysis, you would like to view the result of applying each rule to the table (the second list) parallel to the rule itself. Besides which, it would be desirable to view a parallel display of actual errors or inconsistencies resulting from applying the rule (the third list). The ListView component allows you to get the desired result by proceeding as follows.

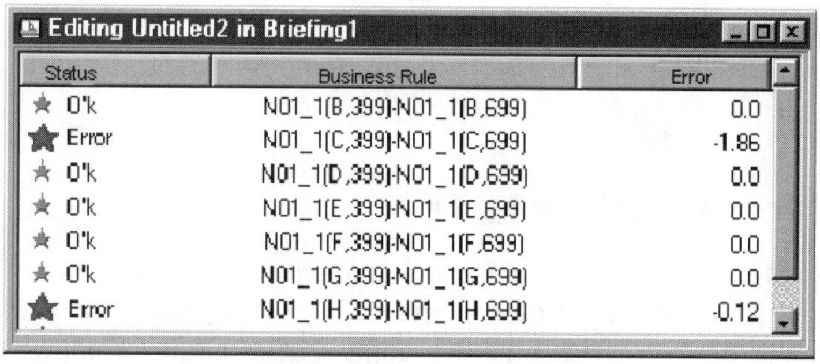

Fig. 7.18. The ListView component

First, let us specify the number and names of the columns (for example, **Status**, **Business Rule**, **Error**) in our list using a dialog that you can open by double-clicking the DefaultColumnHeaders property.

Secondly, add the following code made up of four parts to the code that will check business rules in the loop:

```
If (val(n) <> 0) then
    Stat   = "Error"
    ImgIndex    = "0"
else
    Stat  = "O'k"
    ImgIndex    = "1"
End if
CurItem = Stat & "|" & ImgIndex & "|" & rule(n) "|" & val (n)
    Call ListView1.addItem(CurItem)
```

Here, val(n) is an item of the business rules string representation list, Stat and ImgIndex are string variables, and val(n) is the decimal value of the error. The column delimiter ("|" in our case) is specified by the ColumnSepChar property of the ListView component. The ImgIndex variable defines the index of the bitmap within the list of bitmap images specified by the **SmallImages** property. An index value of 0 corresponds to the large red star, while a value of 1 corresponds to the small green star. The position within the composite CurItem string where the index will be displayed is defined by the ImageColumnIndex property, which in our case is equal to 1 (column numbering starts with 0). In principle, the bitmap image index can be located within any other column, except for the starting one (number 0). The sample result you may obtain is shown in Fig. 7.18.

Naturally, this example describes only a single employment of the `ListView` component. More detailed information on this topic is provided in the *Reference Manual.*

Hierarchical TreeView Lists

The lists used for representing hierarchical tree data structures can also be considered important elements of the user interface. The list representing the hierarchical structure of the disk file system in the standard **Open File** Windows dialog is a typical example of the hierarchical list.

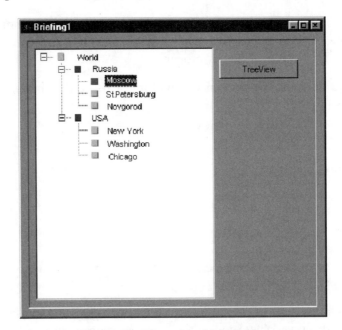

Fig. 7.19. Hierarchical list display

Express Object provides the special `TreeView` component for displaying hierarchical lists.

Let us illustrate the use of this object with an example. Insert the `TreeView` component named `Treeview1` into the briefing page. Next, add a button to that page and define the `AfterClick` event handler for this button as follows:

```
TreeView1.Clear
call TreeView1.AddTreeNode("Worldwide", "W", tvwRSNext, 0,1,2)
```

```
call TreeView1.AddTreeNode("Russia", "R","W",tvwRSChild, 0,1,2)
call TreeView1.AddTreeNode("USA", "U","W", tvwRSChild, 0,1,2)

call TreeView1.AddTreeNode("Moscow", "M", "R", tvwRSChild, 0,1,2)
call TreeView1.AddTreeNode("St.Petersburg", "P", "R", tvwRSChild, 0,1,2)
call TreeView1.AddTreeNode("Novgorod", "N", "R", tvwRSChild, 0,1,2)

call TreeView1.AddTreeNode("New York", "NN", "U", tvwRSChild, 0,1,2)
call TreeView1.AddTreeNode("Washington", "V", "U", tvwRSChild, 0,1,2)
call TreeView1.AddTreeNode("Chicago", "C", "U", tvwRSChild, 0,1,2)
```

The result is presented in Fig. 7.19. Notice that for each item it is possible to specify three possible values from the image list (the Images... property), defining individual image for each of the three possible states of the list item: 1—the item is collapsed; 2—the item is expanded; 3—the item is selected (in our case, these states are indicated by green, blue, and red squares, respectively).

The list has the TreeViewStyle property, which allows you to select one of the 8 display types for the hierarchical list:

❏ Text Only—text only

❏ Image and Text—image and text

❏ Plus/Minus and Text—plus/minus sign and text

❏ Plus/Minus, Image and Text—plus/minus sign, image, and text

❏ Lines and Text—lines and text

❏ Lines, Image, and Text—lines, image, and text

❏ Lines, Plus/Minus, and Text—lines, plus/minus sign and text

❏ Lines, Plus/Minus, Image, and Text—lines, plus/minus sign, image, and text

The *Splitter* Component

The Splitter component is very convenient if you need, for example, to place two or more data views on the same application page and provide the ability to view them either all at once or one at a time.

Using the slider between the two data views (Fig. 7.20), a business professional can view the data in parallel (a) or concentrate all attention on the table by increasing the pane that contains it (b). The elements included within the Splitter component can be placed both horizontally and vertically. The placement of the items is defined by the PaneOrientation property.

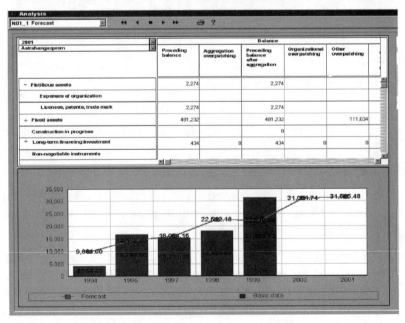

Fig. 7.20. The Splitter component usage

The *Grid* Component

The `Grid` component is used for displaying test data using table representation. Similar to the `Table` component, this object can be used for displaying data as two-dimensional tables. Notice that the content of this component is not stored in the project, but rather generated dynamically at run time.

To add a row into a `Grid` table, use the `AddItem(Item)` method, where `Item` is the string variable containing a text representation of the column data delimited by the tab characters `(Chr$(9))`. To change the contents of the specific table cell, use the `SetCellText (Col, Row, Text)` method, where `Col, Row` are long indexes of the column and row, respectively.

You can control user manipulations over the table using the `AfterClick` event handler. The `GetCellText (Col, Row)` method enables the user to view the content of the specified table cell. Besides which, Express Objects provides the `Hide-Cols`, `HideRows` methods that allow you to hide specific rows/columns or their groups. You can make the hidden rows/columns visible again using the `ShowCols`, `ShowRows` methods.

Components for Displaying Disks, Directories, and Files

If you need to provide the user with the ability to navigate the file system on the PC client, you can use the following three components—`DriveComboBox`, `DirectoryListBox`, and `FileListBox`. These components encapsulate the functions for selecting the current drive, directory, and file, respectively. Drive selection is done from the logical drives present on the local PC, including persistently mapped network drives.

7.7. Programming Express Session

At run-time, there is one automatically created root object named `Application` that corresponds to the project. This object always has the name `Application`, by which it is accessible from the application program code. Besides all of the objects that you have created within your application, the `Application` object serves as a container for:

❏ Express object instance, encapsulating the client connection to Express Server or Express Personal)

❏ The `DataDictionary` object instance, which serves to access databases and their objects

7.7.1. Express Object

The `Express` object can be used for programmatically establishing connection to the Express service. The connection is established by calling the following method:

```
Connect ([Prompt][, XCFName])
```

The `Prompt` parameter can take a logical value determining if the connection type selection dialog should be displayed to the user when creating a connection. If the application doesn't prompt the user to select a connection type, the type is determined by the `ServerType` property of the `Express` object. This property can take one of the following two values:

1—connect to the remote server

2—connect to Personal Express (version 6.1 or higher)

The `XCFName` string parameter contains the name of the connection description file.

The `Connect` method returns one of the following values:

0—connection failed

1—connection was successfully opened

2—connection was cancelled by the user (by pressing the **Cancel** button in the dialog)

To disconnect from Express, use the `Disconnect` method:

```
Disconnect ([UpdateAllDBs] [,QueryOnDBDetach])
```

Here, the `UpdateAllDBs` logical parameter defines whether the UPDATE command must be executed on the server for saving the database modifications introduced during the session. By default, this parameter is TRUE. The second optional parameter, `QueryOnDBDetach`, also takes a logical value, which is applicable if the first parameter is set to FALSE. This parameter determines if the user will be prompted to execute the UPDATE command when disconnecting each database. This method returns a logical value specifying whether the operation was completed successfully. Notice that the connection cannot be closed if the active project contains data views (tables or graphs) from attached databases.

Let's explain the discussion presented above on the example. Create a new project, open a blank page, and insert the **Connect** and **Disconnect** buttons along with the text banner named **Banner1**. Write the following program code for the AfterClick event handler for the first button:

```
Sub AfterClick ()
dim rcode as integer
if Express.Connected = True then
   Banner1.text = "Connection is already established"
else
   rcode = Express.Connect(True)
   select case (rcode)
      case 0
         Banner1.text = "Connection failed"
      case 1
         Banner1.text = "Successfully connected"
      case 2
         Banner1.text = "Cancel button clicked"
   end select
end if
End Sub
```

For the second button, create the following code:

```
Sub AfterClick ()
dim rcode as integer
if Express.Connected = True then
   rcode = Express.Disconnect()
   if rcode then
      Banner1.text = "Successfully disconnected"
   else
      Banner1.text = "Disconnection failed"
   end if
else
      Banner1.text = "Connection was not established"
end if
End Sub
```

You'll get an application that programmatically opens/closes the connection to the Express server and displays a text message informing you of the result of this operation. The code uses the logical `Connected` property of the `Express` object that determines if the connection to the server is established.

The `Execute` method of the `Express` object enables you to run any Express 4GL command or set of commands on the server.

7.7.2. The *DataDictionary* Object

Using the `DataDictionary` object, you can programmatically attach or detach the database and access objects stored in the multidimensional database.

To attach the database, use the following method:

```
AttachDatabase ([FileName][, Flags])
```

The optional `FileName` parameter contains the database file name. If this parameter is missing, the user will be prompted to select the database file using the standard **Open File** dialog. The integer `Flags` parameter determines the database access mode and can take one of the following constant values:

❐   `dbfATTReadOnly` `&H1&`—attach the database in Read-Only mode (default)

❐   `dbfATTReadWrite` `&H2&`—attach the database in Read-Write mode

❐   `dbfATTNoBrowse` `&H8&`—don't display the database in the database browser

This method returns the `DatabaseFile` object encapsulating the opened database (more detailed information will be provided in the next section). To get the `DatabaseFile` object associated to the previously opened database, use the `GetDatabase (Name)` method:

To open a floating database browser window in your application, use the following method of the `DataDictionary` object:

```
BrowseDatabases ([Flags])
```

If you want to hide the toolbar in the database browser, specify the `ddBRWNoToolbar` constant as the `Flags` parameter.

The `GetDatabaseObject(Name)` and `GetObjectDesc(Name)` methods enable you to access database objects and their descriptions.

To close the database, use the following method:

```
DetachDatabase ([Name] [, Flags])
```

If the database name is not specified, this will close an active database. The Flags parameter determines the dialog displayed to the user before closing the database. This parameter can take one of the following predefined values:

❏ dbfDETUpdate &H1&—save the changes (default)

❏ dbfDETNoUpdate &H2&—don't save the changes

❏ dbfDETQueryUpdate &H4&—prompt the user to save the changes providing the following alternatives: Yes/No/Cancel.

❏ DbfDETNoCancel &H8&—prompt the user to save the changes with the following alternatives: Yes/No

7.7.3. The *DatabaseFile* Object

The DatabaseFile object encapsulates the multidimensional database opened using the AttachDatabase method. Using the DatabaseFile object, you can sequentially access all objects (dimensions, relationships, formulae, and variables) stored in the multidimensional database. You can also access any Express Basic object encapsulating a specific database object. For example, suppose that our database named FIRST.DB contains the PRODUCT dimension and we need to sequentially view all the values of this dimension. This task can be solved using the following code:

```
dim dbFirst as DatabaseFile
dim dmProduct as Dimension
dim n as integer
dim sVal as string
dim sList as string
set dbFirst   = DataDictionary.AttachDatabase("FIRST.DB")
set dmProduct = dbFirst.GetDatabaseObject("PRODUCT")
n=1
do
   sVal = dmProduct.GetValueLabel(n,dimLBLDimValues)
   if sVal = "" then exit do
   if n<>1 then sList = sList & "," & sVal else sList = sVal
   n = n + 1
loop
```

Notice that our application did not establish a connection to the Express server. The connection will be established automatically when opening the database, if necessary. Also notice that the dim dbFirst as DatabaseFile statement only creates a blank reference to the object. To assign it a value associated to the `Da-tabaseFile` object instance, use the (`set...=...`) statement rather than just (`=`).

In a similar way, you can access Express Basic objects of the following types:

❑ Variable

❑ Relation

❑ Formula

the instances of which encapsulate objects stored in the database.

7.7.4. The *ExpressOutput* Component

This component (Fig. 7.21) is used as a functional analog of the Express Command tool available in Express Administrator. Using this object, you can run commands on the Express server and view the results of their execution.

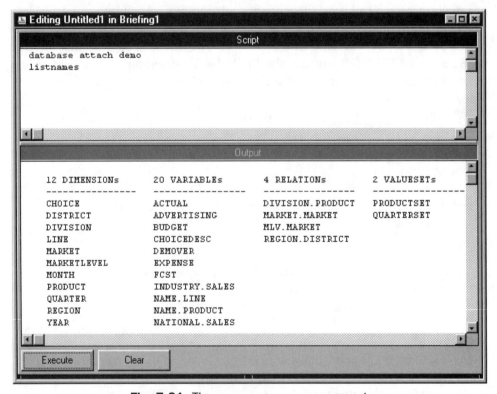

Fig. 7.21. The `ExpressOutput` component

This object can be very useful when debugging and testing client applications in Express Objects, since you are able to run commands both when developing applications and at run time. Furthermore, you can also build this component into the client application.

The component comprises two parts. The first window is used for entering Express commands, while the second represents the results of command execution. The **Execute** and **Clear** buttons enable you to start command execution and clear the output window, respectively.

To run several Express commands simultaneously, disable the **ExecuteOnEnter** option available in the popup menu of the component.

Usually this component is invisible in client applications. Execution of the required commands can be enabled using the `Execute()` method from event handlers of other interface objects, such as buttons, tables, graphs, etc. When the `Execute()` method is called, the commands specified in the `Commands` property of the current component will be executed on the server. You can set the value of the `Commands` property using the following three techniques:

❏ In the command entry field

❏ In object inspector (the `CommandScript` group property)

❏ Programmatically using Express Basic functionality

To specify the `Commands` property programmatically from the program code, separate the commands using the `Chr$(10)` character. For example, you can specify the following code in the event handler:

```
ExpressOutput1.Commands = "database attach demo" & Chr$(10)&
"listnames"
call ExpressOutput1.Execute()
```

Clicking the button at run time will result in the display of the following result in the output window:

12 DIMENSIONs	20 VARIABLEs	4 RELATIONs	2 VALUESETs
------------	------------	-----------	-----------
CHOICE	ACTUAL	DIVISION.PRODUCT	PRODUCTSET
DISTRICT	ADVERTISING	MARKET.MARKET	QUARTERSET
DIVISION	BUDGET	MLV.MARKET	
LINE	CHOICEDESC	REGION.DISTRICT	
MARKET	DEMOVER		

```
MARKETLEVEL    EXPENSE
MONTH          FCST
PRODUCT        INDUSTRY.SALES
QUARTER        NAME.LINE
REGION         NAME.PRODUCT
YEAR           NATIONAL.SALES
_DE_LANGDIM    PRICE
               PRODUCT.MEMO
               SALES
               SALES.FORECAST
               SALES.PLAN
               SHARE
               UNITS
               UNITS.M
               _DE_
```

Naturally, in order to achieve this, you need to insert the ExpressOutput component with the ExpressOutput1 name.

The ReRunInterval, ReRunIntervalUnits, and AutoExecuteOnRun properties allow you to customize your application in such a way as to run the commands specified in the Commands property on a regular basis, for example, each minute.

7.7.5. Accessing Multidimensional Data

Some applications may require that you programmatically access data stored in the multidimensional Express database. For example, if you are not satisfied with the standard data representation in a table, you can create your own custom data view using the Grid component. To solve this task, use the FETCH command of the Express Language. This command is used as a central element of the structured multidimensional API (SNAPI). The command uses the following syntax:

```
FETCH expression1 [expression2...] [TAG tag-expression] [LABELED]-

[ USING <dimensions> ]
```

or

```
[ACROSS dimensions] [ DOWN dimensions]
```

Here:

❐   *expression1* [*expression2*...]—one or more expressions of the Express language, the values of which we are accessing

❏ TAG *tag-expression*—the construct allowing you to associate an arbitrary text expression to the data block (data block label)

❏ LABELED—means that the values of indexing dimensions will be passed to the client application along with metadata

❏ USING *<dimensions>*—allows you to specify the order of variables within a block

❏ ACROSS *dimensions* and DOWN *dimensions*—allow you to organize the passed data block as a flat table

After execution of the FETCH command on the server, the data becomes available in the client application using the methods of the ExpressCommand object:

Function	Parameters	Return value
GetData (FieldIndex [, NA])	FieldIndex—cell index (starting with 0) NA—logical variable that will take a YES value if the cell is empty	The value of the current cell in the current data block
GetDataType (FieldIndex)	FieldIndex -cell index (starting with 0)	Data type for the current cell in the current data block
GetDimIndex (DimensionName)	DimensionName—name of the dimension	Index of the specified dimension by its name
GetDimName (Dimension)	Dimension—dimension index	Name of the specified dimension by its index
GetDimNumValues (Dimension)	Dimension—dimension index	Number of values of the current dimension
GetDimValueName (Dimension)	Dimension—dimension index	Value of the specified dimension
NextCell ([Dimension])	Dimension—dimension index	Navigates to the next cell within the current data block in the direction of the specified dimension
NextDataBlock ()		Navigates to the next data block

Let's illustrate the working principles of these functions in an example. Suppose that a page of our briefing contains the Grid component named Grid1 and the drop-down list named ComboBox1.

Let us define global variables:

```
dim xpCmd          as ExpressCommand    'FETCH command
dim monthIndex     as integer           'MONTH dimension index
dim prodIndex      as integer           'PRODUCT dimension index
dim regIndex       as integer           'Region dimension index
dim pageN          as integer           'number of pages
dim rowN           as integer           'number of rows
dim colN           as integer           'number of columns
```

Let us define the `AfterRun` even handler for our page as follows:

```
dim i as long
dim dimVal as string
set xpCmd = Express.Execute("limit REGION to all")
call xpCmd.Execute("limit MONTH to all")
call xpCmd.Execute("limit PRODUCT to all")
call xpCmd.Execute("FETCH SALES LABELED USING <REGION MONTH PRODUCT>")
monthIndex  = xpCmd.GetDimIndex("MONTH")
prodIndex   = xpCmd.GetDimIndex("PRODUCT")
regIndex    = xpCmd.GetDimIndex("REGION")
pageN       = xpCmd.GetDimNumValues(regIndex)-1
rowN                = xpCmd.GetDimNumValues(monthIndex)-1
colN                = xpCmd.GetDimNumValues(prodIndex)-1

'list column names
dimVal = xpCmd.GetDimValueName(prodIndex)
Grid1.TotalCols = colN+2
call Grid1.setCellText(1,0,dimVal)
for i=1 to colN
   call xpCmd.NextCell(prodIndex)
   dimVal = xpCmd.GetDimValueName(prodIndex)
   call Grid1.setCellText(i+1,0,dimVal)
next
'list row names
dimVal = xpCmd.GetDimValueName(monthIndex)
Grid1.TotalRows = rowN+2
call Grid1.setCellText(0,1,dimVal)
for i=1 to rowN
   call xpCmd.NextCell(monthIndex)
   dimVal = xpCmd.GetDimValueName(monthIndex)
```

```
      call Grid1.setCellText(0,i+1,dimVal)
next

'list page names
ComboBox1.Clear
xpCmd.ResetCell
dimVal = xpCmd.GetDimValueName(regIndex)
call ComboBox1.addItem(dimVal)
for i=1 to pageN
   call xpCmd.NextCell(regIndex)
   dimVal = xpCmd.GetDimValueName(regIndex)
   call ComboBox1.addItem(dimVal)
next

'update table data
ComboBox1.SelText = dimVal
ComboBox1.AfterClick
```

The `AfterClick` event handler for the `ComboBox1` component is as follows:

```
dim page as integer
dim row as integer
dim col as integer
dim value as string
dim region as string
region = text
xpCmd.ResetDataBlock
call xpCmd.ResetCell
for page=0 to pageN
   if (region=xpCmd.GetDimValueName(regIndex)) then goto mmm
   call xpCmd.NextCell(regIndex)
next
mmm:
for row = 0 to rowN
   call xpCmd.ResetCell(prodIndex)
   for col=0 to colN
     value = xpCmd.getData(0)
     call Grid1.setCellText(col+1,row+1,value)
     call xpCmd.NextCell(prodIndex)
   next col
   call xpCmd.NextCell(monthIndex)
next row
```

As a result, we will get a table view of the data cube corresponding to the SALES variable from the multidimensional database. This view will change according to the REGION variable value selected from the drop-down list. More detailed information on this topic is provided in the FETCH.XPJ demo application.

7.8. Programming Multidimensional Data Views

The current version of Express Objects provides two types of data views in client applications: tables and graphs. In the previous chapter of this book we have discussed in detail all the aspects related to customization of the properties of these components. In this chapter we will concentrate on programming the behavior of these objects in client applications.

7.8.1. The *DataCube* Object

The DataCube object encapsulates a multidimensional structured query to the multidimensional database. A data cube defines the content of the query and the data view structure (for example, it specifies how the GOODS dimension values are represented). Each data display contains a data cube. An important feature lies in the fact that different views can be associated to the same DataCube object. This allows you to create synchronous data views from different points of view.

As was already mentioned, a data cube always has two or three dimensions: ROWS, COLUMNS, and PAGES (the PAGES dimension may be empty). Each of these dimensions can contain one or more edge nodes (EdgeNode). The three-dimensional data cube represents the Cartesian product of all edge nodes. Each edge node has its own Selector object determining the set of values selected into the group (*edge node*). For example, the edge node can contain a subset of the REGION dimension related to USA. Fig. 7.22 illustrates the relationship between data view and data cube and the data cube structure.

Let's look at an example of data cube programming.

Suppose that we want our application to provide the user with the ability to select specific goods in the sales revenue table and select for it the 5 most profitable months for the period under analysis for the specified REGION.

To achieve this, insert the Table1 object into the page of our briefing. The Table1 object represents the sales data from our FIRST.DB database. Using the dimension bar, relate the PAGES data cube dimension to the REGION dimension. The COLUMNS and ROWS dimensions must be related to the GOODS and MONTH dimensions, respectively.

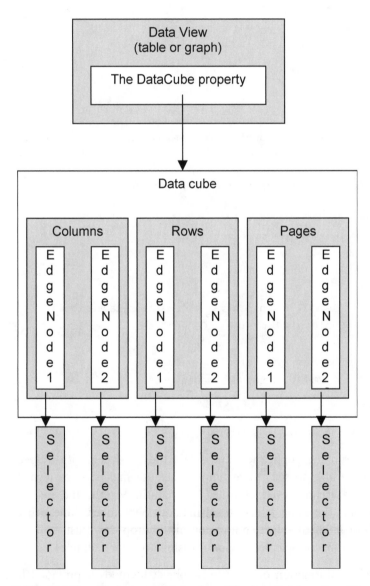

Fig. 7.22. Relationship between data view object and data cube elements

Insert the button labeled `Top 5` into the page, and define the `AfterClick` event handler for this button as follows:

```
dim objComponent as object
dim iObjectClass as integer
dim lRow as long
dim lColumn as long
dim product as string
dim cmd as string
dim er as integer


'defining the object selected in the table
er = Table1.GetSelectedObject(objComponent, iObjectClass, lRow, _
lColumn)

'make sure that the selected object corresponds to the table data
'field
if ( er = 0) or (iObjectClass <> vwOCDataBody) then
   call msgBox("Table cell not selected")
   exit sub
end if

'define the GOODS dimension value for the selected cell
product = Table1.GetDimValues(iObjectClass, lRow, lColumn, "PRODUCT")

'generating script for selecting values
cmd = "limit MONTH to top 5 basedon profit(PRODUCT '" & product & "')"

'executing selection
call Table1.SetSelection("MONTH",cmd)
```

Now, if you run the application and select the table cell with a specific type of good, you'll be able to see, for example, that the highest sales level for Ford all over the world was achieved in June, May, April, March, and February of 1999. As for Cadillac, the same selection set includes September, June, April, February, and March of 1998. By selecting a region in the drop-down list, you can perform a similar analysis for the selected region (Washington, for example).

More detailed information on the `Table` object methods is provided in the *Reference Manual.*

7.8.2. The *DimensionListBox* Component

In applications, it is often necessary to display the values of specific dimensions of the multidimensional data representation in the database. This can be achieved using the standard Express Objects component—DimensionListBox.

Let us again illustrate the usage of this component with an example.

Suppose that we have two table views: sales and sales revenue, each of which contains the PRODUCT dimension as a page. Using the DimensionListBox component, you can synchronously switch tables from one type of goods to another. To achieve this, proceed as follows:

❏   Assign the Dimension property the value of PRODUCT (the name of our dimension in multidimensional database)

❏   Determine the AfterHighlight event handler:

```
dim cmd as string
cmd = "limit PRODUCT to '" & FocusValueText & "'"
call Table1.SetSelection("PRODUCT",cmd)
call Table2.SetSelection("PRODUCT",cmd)
```

The FocusValueText property contains a value selected from the list. Notice that this property is not preceded by the name of the object to which it belongs, since we are referencing that property from the event handler of the same object.

This component has a large number of properties and methods allowing you to manage its look and behavior flexibly and efficiently. More detailed information on this topic is provided in the on-line Help system. It is also recommended that you carefully study the DIML.XBR demo application illustrating the various capabilities provided by this component.

7.8.3. Tables and Graphs

In the previous chapter we concentrated mainly on the visual tools allowing you to create and customize the properties of multidimensional data views: tables and graphs. However, we can also create data views programmatically, using Express Basic program code.

Let's consider a test application, where the following program code is used for the AfterRun event handler of the page component:

```
'create new table and data cube
```

```
dim tbSales as new table
dim dCube as new DataCube

'set table size and coordinates
tbSales.Top = 0
tbSales.Left = 0
tbSales.Height = 6000
tbSales.Width = 10000

'define the cube
dCube.addMeasures("SALES")

'build the cube into the table
set tbSales.DataCube = dCube

'insert the table into the briefing page
call Add(tbSales)
```

When you start this application, the table will appear in the page of our briefing, displaying the data on sales. Naturally, it is supposed that the database containing the SALES variable (for example, FIRST.DB) is attached to our project.

7.8.4. Data Aggregation

The aggregation mechanism is a powerful data analysis tool. Using aggregation, we are able to calculate an aggregate value for a specific set of dimension values. In other words, aggregation enables us to drill up information by excluding minor details. Summation is only a single particular case of the aggregation. Besides the sum, you can calculate, for example, average, minimum, or maximum values. Using relationships between dimension values, you can aggregate data by dimension related to the source by specific relationship. For example, you can aggregate monthly value to quarterly values or regional to country.

When performing aggregation, the data cube structure changes. EdgeNode for the source dimension is replaced by the dimension values of the dimension related to it by the specified relationship. To perform data aggregation programmatically, use the Aggregate method provided for objects such as table, graph, or data cube. This method uses the following syntax:

```
Aggregate (DimNameOrEdgeNode, AggFunction [, Dimension] [, Relation]
[, Synchronize] [, AllValues])
```

Here :

DimNameOrEdgeNode—dimension name of the reference to the EdgeNode object

AggFunction—aggregation type:

Constant	Description
DcAGGTotal	Sum
DcAGGAverage	Average
DcAGGSmallest	Minimum
DcAGGLargest	Maximum
DcAGGMedian	Median
DcAGGStdDev	Standard deviation

Dimension—name of the dimension related to the source dimension by the relationship

Relation—specifies the relation name used for aggregation

Synchronize—when aggregating by relation, the current argument defines if the source DimNameOrEdgeNode dimension will be synchronized with the relative dimension (the default value is YES)

AllValues—allows us to use all variable values during aggregation and ignore the current state

For example:

```
Call tblTable.Aggregate("CITY", dcAGGTotal, "AREA", "AREA.CITY",
False, False)
```

This call allows us to find sum values for the variable presented in the tblTable table for each value of the AREA dimension by summating the values of the current variable for all cities of the particular region.

The reverse operation is performed using the Disaggregate (DimNameOrEdgeNode) method. You can get more detailed information on using these methods by carefully studying the AGGREG.XPJ demo application.

7.9. Brief Description of the Demo Applications

If you have selected the option for installing demo applications in the course of Oracle Express Objects installation, the Windows **Start** menu will contain a shortcut for starting the standard demo examples in the **Programs/Oracle OLAP Client 2.2** program group. It is strongly recommended that you spend some time to at least get acquainted with these examples, even if you don't carefully study them. These examples present quite a large database of standard development techniques widely used for implementing the various functional capabilities of client applications. Based on practical experience, your efforts will be rewarded by a significant reduction in the time required to "reinvent the wheel" when developing your own custom applications. Besides this, these examples illustrate the capabilities of Express Objects, and in many cases can be used as a good starting point for designing applications.

The limited volume of this book does not allow us to discuss the code of these examples in detail. Hopefully, the materials presented here, along with the detailed and well-written Express Objects on-line Help system, will allow you to get a clear understanding of the working principles upon which these applications are based. For reference purposes, only brief descriptions of these examples will be provided.

Table 7.10. Demo Applications

File	Description
AGGREG.XPJ	Demonstrates the use of the `Aggregate/Disaggregate` methods for table and data cube objects
CONTROLS.XPJ	Allows you to quickly view the main controls of the user interface (UI) and investigate the influence of the component properties on their functionality
CUBEFUN.XPJ	This application illustrates the usage of a data cube by table and graph data views. The application page contains four buttons that relate, copy, derive, and create a new Selection object for the data cube related to the view
CUSTREPT.XPJ	Demonstrates the usage of the `CheckBox` control, which enables you to select the variable that will appear in the report. Illustrates the usage of the `StatusScript` property of the Selection object

continues

Table 7.10 Continued

File	Description
DIMLB.XBR	Illustrates the large number of functional capabilities of the `DimensionList` component, including its relation to other data views. Demonstrates the usage of the `SetDefaultSelection`, `GetNth`, `SetExpressStatus`, `RefreshListbox`, `RefreshSelection`, and other methods for this component
DRAWING.XPJ	Illustrates two techniques of drawing the simplest objects in the briefing page. The first one uses the `DrawCircle`, `DrawRectangle`, `DrawText`, and `DrawShapes` methods of the standard page component, while the second one directly calls the standard API functions from the following Windows DLLs: USER32 and GDI32. Can be used as a common example of using external functions implemented using other programming languages in Express Basic projects
ENABLE.XBR	Demonstrates the flexible capabilities of customizing the data display functionality (the `Table`, `Graph`, and `DimensionListBox` component), provided to the end users by means of component properties, such as `EnableSelectData`, `EnableDrilling`, `EnableHighlightData`, and `EnableAggregation`
EVENTS.XPJ	Illustrates overriding of the standard methods and event handlers in derived objects
FETCH.XPJ	Illustrates the usage of the `FETCH` command of the Express server for accessing data stored in the multidimensional database. Demonstrates the usage of various methods, such as `AttachDatabase`, `GetDatabase`, `DetachDatabase`, `Execute`, `GetDimNumValues`, `GetDimName`, `GetDimValueName`, etc.
GETSELS.XPJ	Explains the usage of the stored selections of the dimension values
GRAPHDV.XPJ	This application demonstrates the software code for changing the data values for various types of graphs
HOTSPOTS.XPJ	Usage of the `HotSpots` visual component for programming graphics to manage other objects
MDISAMP.XPJ	Demonstrates Express Basic's capabilities of imitating the Multiple-Document user interface (MDI), which is not actually supported by the objects of this language
MENUBARS.XPJ	Illustrates the usage of menu and toolbars in applications

continues

Table 7.10 Continued

File	Description
MENUDYN1.XPJ	Explains the technology of creating a dynamic menu on the basis of program code
MENUEX1.XPJ	Menu programming in Express Basic
MENUMSGS.XPJ	Demonstrates the sequence of generation of the events related to the menu and its commands. Demonstrates the capabilities of handling menu-related events within a single menu object using the `Int` variable
OUTPUT.XPJ	Illustrates the usage of the `ExpressComand` object (the supplementary documentation states that this example demonstrates the `ExpressOutput` component)
PASSWORD.XPJ	A very simple example that can be used in your application for requesting user ID and password when connecting to the Express database
REGBRWSE.XPJ	Illustrates the usage of the `TreeView`, `ListView`, and `StatusBar` components
SELECTOR.XBR	Demonstrates various capabilities of the standard `Selector` component usage, including the techniques of calling this object and its specific tools programmatically
TBLRANGE.XPJ	Demonstrates the capabilities of the `GetSelectedObjectCount`, `GetSelectedObjectInfo`, and `ConvertToDataSpace` methods for obtaining information on the object selected in a table

Chapter 8

Decision Support Systems
in the intranet/Internet

8.1. Internet and World Wide Web Overview

8.1.1. What is the Internet

The World Wide Web comprises millions of interrelated data sources distributed over computers all over the world. The Internet is a communication environment enabling computers around the globe to interact with one another. The Web is a global communication system supporting electronic data exchange via the Internet.

Networks are fundamental components of the Internet. There are two main categories of networks—local (Local Area Network, LAN) and global (Wide Area Network, WAN). Usually, Local Area Networks connect computers located not far from one another (as a rule, within a single room or building). However, LAN may also connect computers that are several miles away from one another. Wide Area Networks connect computers located in different cities, regions, and countries.

There are thousands of LANs and WANs distributed all over the world. When we connect networks with one another, we are creating an internetwork—the so-called internet (notice that here it starts with a lower-case letter) or a "network of networks". As for the Internet (notice that this time the name starts with an upper-case letter), it is the largest of internetworks known in the world. Starting from the early 1990s, the Internet is growing exponentially, and this growth has provided millions of users with the ability to access a wealth of information distributed among computers belonging to hundreds of thousands of LANs.

The concept of intranet is somewhat younger, since it first appeared in the latter half of the 1990's. The main idea of the intranet lies in using progressive and rapidly developing Internet technologies and utilities in corporate networks. The one difference between an intranet and the Internet is that an intranet is a separate network that can be accessed by internal users only.

To put this in other words, the intranet/Internet is used as a "mailing" system whose hardware and software enable data addressing and delivery. The WWW, consisting of programs and data, represents an intellectual add-on, providing us with searching and data representation capabilities.

To enable programs running on different hosts under different operating systems to exchange data, it is necessary to have a set of rules—a network protocol. TCP/IP is the basic and the most widely known family of Internet protocols. IP (Internet

Protocol) is responsible for network host addressing, while TCP (Transmission Control Protocol) ensures data delivery to the required address. Internet addresses are known as URLs (Uniform Resource Locator). The basic syntax of the URL is quite simple:

```
http://<host>:<port>/<path>?<patameters>
```

The `http://` prefix identifies the access method (more detailed information on this topic will be provided later in this chapter).

$<Host>$ specifies the IP address of the computer to which it is necessary to establish connection. The IP address consists of a dot-delimited sequence of four integers from 0 to 255, for example: 128.252.173.4. The leftmost number is the network address of the largest network; subsequent numbers (from left to right) refine this address until we get the unique address of a specific computer. To simplify the perception and memorizing of IP addresses, symbolic, human-friendly host names were introduced, known as DNS names (DNS stands for Domain Name System). Thus, the user enters a name, such as www.oracle.com, and servers processing network data traffic replace it with the appropriate address. The DNS system describes addresses in reverse order as compared to the IP address.

$<Port>$ specifies the port number by which access to the specified computer will be provided. This parameter can be omitted. By default, the HTTP protocol is assumed to access via the well-known port 80.

$<Path>$ describes the path to the requested resource (which usually represents a file). It can be followed by the '?' character and additional text, which normally is interpreted by Web applications as a parameter list.

For example, to start an application representing an imitation model of competition that is stored in the Express database (see *Chapter 9*), use the following URL:

```
http://<host>:8081/ows-
bin/oowa/ExpSrv620/dbxwdevkit/xwd_init?sharkcod/sh_start
```

However, addressing and delivering information between computers represents only a part of the solution to the data exchange problem. It is also necessary to request required information. Because of this, another protocol was created specially for Web—HTTP (Hyper Text Transfer Protocol). HTTP is often called a transaction protocol. According to this protocol, the client sends a query addressed to specific server via the Internet/intranet. The specified host will be searched for within a network by its IP address. If it is found, a connection between the client (the computer that has sent the request) and the server will be established. When the server receives and processes the query, it sends the HTTP response message and closes the client connection. Thus, the transaction is completed.

However, our overview of Web protocols is far from complete. We need another protocol to actually represent the language—HyperText Markup Language (HTML). This language not only allows you to transfer informational content from server to client, but also to specify the layout of this information. If you plan to create your own Web pages, you need to get acquainted with HTML. Fortunately for beginners, this language is not very difficult.

According to the contemporary state of the HTTP protocol, the server can send to the client text information, multimedia data (including images, audio- and video data), and programs written in Java—a special programming language intended for Internet development. Programs developed using Java are known as Java applets. After delivery to the client, Java applets are loaded and executed at the client computer using the built-in virtual Java machine. The complexity level of the transferred applets is only limited by the network throughput.

Communication between computers in the Internet is implemented using special programs: Web servers (for example, Oracle Application Server) and Web browsers (clients). A Web server receives the query from the browser and sends the requested data to it. When a Web browser receives the data, it interprets this data at the client computer. It is the browser that determines how the test information, graphics, multimedia data, and Java applets will be represented. For the moment, the most popular and widely known browsers are Netscape Communicator and MS Internet Explorer.

8.1.2. Architecture of a Web Application for an OLAP System

At the moment, OLAP and WWW are the most popular technological areas among programmers. Integration of these technologies promises to from a basis for deployment of the corporate informational systems of the 21st century, ensuring decision support 24 hours a day in any location. Currently, practically all leading manufacturers of OLAP systems are developing software tools intended to provide corporate internet/Intranet data analysis using only a common Web browser on the client side. Starting with version 6.0 of Express Server, the Oracle Corporation has also included the Express Web Agent component into the standard supply of software. The Express Web Agent component extends OLAP technology to the Web, enabling its usage on the Internet/intranet.

Our application running at a Web server not only has to create and send an HTML document, but also to populate it with data from the Express multidimensional database. This makes the above described architecture even more complicated.

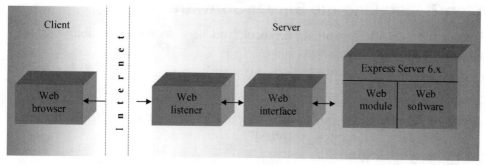

Fig. 8.1. Architecture of a Web application for an OLAP system

The query from the Web browser running on the client side is received and processed by the *Web listener* (Fig. 8.1) running on the server side and managed by the Web server. Intercommunication between the Web server and the Express server is implemented by the *Web interface* (the OOWA.EXE application or XWCRT32.DLL cartridge), which is built into the Web server using the *Web module* (a special DLL) running under the Express database server. When Express Server receives an instruction from the Web module, it opens and caches the new session, attaches the required user database, and starts the initialization program from this database. HTML code is generated by special software stored as standard objects (programs) in one or more Express databases.

8.1.3. Installing and Configuring the Software

The standard supply of the Oracle Express software includes the Oracle Express Web Agent component. This component enables us to create Express applications that run on any hardware platform using a normal Web browser, and don't require the user to install and support any additional software for the client PC.

The Oracle Express Web Publisher component is an easy-to-use development tool intended for creating simple WWW presentations.

Before you can proceed with developing a Web application, you need to install and correctly configure all the required software components.

Step 1. Installing the Client Software

On the client side, you just need to install the TCP/IP network protocol and a standard Web browser (Netscape Communicator, for example). Having accomplished this, test the Internet connection and make sure that you can browse the Internet.

Step 2. Installing the Server Software

Besides the TCP/IP networking protocol, you need to install the following software components on the server computer:

☐ A Web server, for example, Oracle Web Server 2.1

☐ Oracle Express Server 6.x

☐ The files providing Express client support (the same files are required for Express Objects and Express Analyzer)

☐ Oracle Express Web Agent

Step 3. Configuring the Express Server

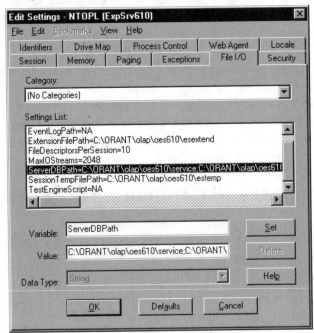

Fig. 8.2. The dialog allowing you to configure the Express server parameters (the Express Configuration Manager utility)

To enable Express Server to find the directory where we plan to store our multi-dimensional databases, it is necessary to specify the appropriate path in the default search path parameter of the Express server. To configure the default search path, proceed as follows:

1. Start the Express Configuration Manager utility.

2. In the **Edit Settings** dialog, go to the **File I/O** tab.

3. Add the required path to the **ServerDBPath** string (Fig. 8.2). Use a semicolon as the separator.

Step 4. Configuring the Web Listener

If you don't plan to use the XWCRT32.DLL cartridge for communicating with the Express server, you only need to configure virtual directories. Virtual directory names will be used when specifying local links to the files of your project. To complete this task, proceed as follows:

1. Start the Web browser and open the following URL: `http://<host>:9999/ows-abin/wladmin` (notice that in order to access the Web listener settings, it is necessary to specify the user name and password for the Web server administration tool).

2. Find the `websrv` listener (this is the standard listener name for Express Web Agent) and stop it by clicking the **Stop** link.

3. Go to the `websrv` listener settings page by clicking the **Configure** link.

4. Navigate to the **Oracle Web Listener Configuration Parameters** section, then click the **Directory Mappings** link to open the virtual directory configuration page.

5. In the virtual directory table, go to the first column of the first empty row, and enter the full pathname to the required directory, for example: `c:\orant\olap\oes620\owa200\sample\`.

6. Go to the second column and set the **NR** flag.

7. Then go to the third column and specify the name of the virtual directory, for example, `/oew-sample/`.

8. Add a new string for each additional virtual directory.

9. Click the **Modify Listener** button.

10. Make sure that the listener was successfully modified (the `Success! OWS-05700: Configuration for Web Listener on ... successfully written` message must be displayed).

11. Start the websrv listener by clicking the **Start** link.

To make sure that the listener was configured correctly, start your Web browser and open the following URL: `http://<host>/oew-sample/index.html`. If you have successfully configured the listener, the browser window will open the page containing Oracle Express Web Agent examples. Naturally, to test these examples, you need to start Express Server.

8.2. Publishing Multidimensional Data on the Web

8.2.1. The Express Web Publisher Application

Express Web Publisher enables you to create simple briefings and publish them on the intranet/Internet. Using this tool, you can easily create a Web site intended for publishing tables and graphs representing multidimensional data. You don't even need to know HTML for this! All the required HTML files will be generated automatically.

Configuring the Application

To make the sites created using Express Web Publisher accessible via a browser, you'll need to accomplish the following two steps:

First, configure the OLAP listener of the Web server by mapping the OWP virtual directory to the `<Oracle_Home>`\olap\oes620\owp200\ directory. The sequence of actions is similar to those described in the previous section.

For the second stage, go to the `<Oracle_Home>`\olap\oes620\owp200\ directory and use any text editor to modify the index.html file located there. The file itself contains editing instructions. If you don't use the XWCRT32.DLL cartridge for communications with the Express server, you need to remove the comment characters from the second of the proposed alternatives:

```
...
// 1. Oracle Web Server CARTRIDGE-mode
```

```
//location.href="/oowa/ExpSrv620/dbxwascode/runwebsite";
// 2. Oracle Web Server CGI mode
 location.href=":8081/ows-bin/oowa/ExpSrv620/dbxwascode/runwebsite";
// 3. Microsoft IIS (Microsoft Windows NT only)
 ...
```

Note that if our listener is set to listen at a port other than 80, we must specify the port number at the beginning of our link (8081 in our example); otherwise, problems may arise when accessing the Web browser from Express Web Publisher.

Starting the Application

To start the Express Web Publisher application, select the **Programs/Oracle OLAP Client 2.2/ Express Web Publisher** commands from the Windows **Start** menu. The application interface is shown in Fig. 8.3.

Fig. 8.3. The Express Web Publisher interface

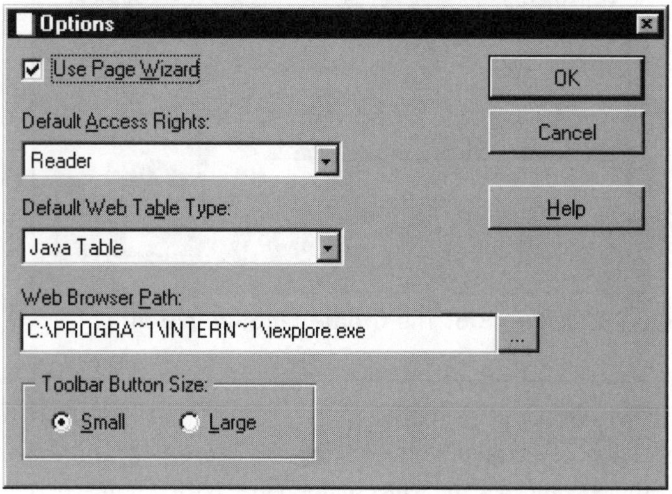

Fig. 8.4. The **Options** dialog

It is advisable to start working with the application by setting the required options. To open the dialog allowing you to configure the application options, select the **Edit/Options** commands from the main menu (Fig. 8.4).

Using this dialog, you need to specify the Web browser that will be started when debugging our Web presentations. To accomplish this, specify the path to the browser executable in the **Web Browser Path:** field.

Attaching the Database

To attach the database, select the **Database/Attach** commands from the main menu. The standard dialog for connecting Express server will appear, and then the standard **File Open** dialog. Open the FIRST.DB database. The database will be displayed in the database browser window, in a way similar to the one used in Express Analyzer and Express Objects.

Creating a Site

Next, you'll need to create a new website. Select the **File/New WebSite** commands from the main menu. The standard dialog for connecting Express server will appear. After connecting the server, the **Create WebSite** dialog will appear, allowing you to specify the parameters for the new site (Fig. 8.5).

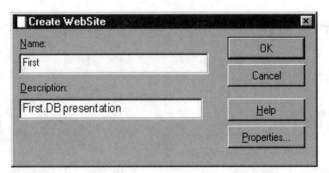

Fig. 8.5. The **Create WebSite** dialog

In this dialog, you can specify the name for the new site and provide a description string that will be displayed to the user. By clicking the **Properties** button, you'll open another dialog. By sequentially clicking the **More>>>** and **Advanced** buttons you can open the **Advanced Properties** dialog (Fig. 8.6). There you can specify the image that will be displayed in the top frame of our Web presentation.

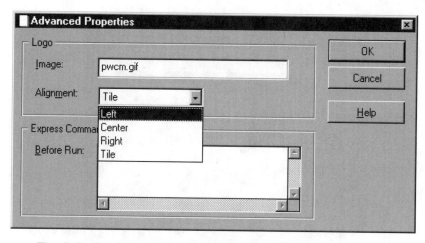

Fig. 8.6. The **Advanced Properties** dialog allows for specifying
the advanced properties of the website

Keep in mind that the image file needs to be located in the
<Oracle_Home>\olap\oes620\owp200\images directory. The **Alignment** drop-down
list enables you to position the image on the screen. For example, the image can
be centered, left- or right-aligned, or tiled. The **Before Run** editable field allows
you to specify one or more Express language commands that will be executed before displaying any website in the browser.

Creating a Briefing

To create a new briefing, select the **Insert/Web Briefing** commands from the main
menu or click the appropriate toolbar button. The newly created briefing will appear in the **Briefing Editor** window. To specify the briefing name and description,
select the **Edit/Properties** commands from the main menu.

Displaying the Data

Select the **Insert/WebTable** commands from the main menu. The following two
objects will be inserted into our briefing: WebPage and WebTable. You can view the
hierarchy of Web objects in the **Web Object Browser** window (Fig. 8.7). To open
this window, select the **Web Object Browser** menu command or click the appropriate toolbar button.

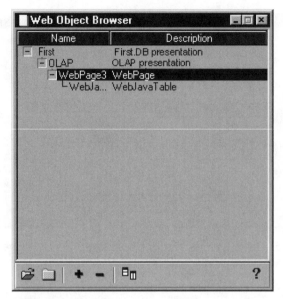

Fig. 8.7. The **Web Object Browser** window

The briefing editor window will display the newly created page with a blank table. To populate the table with the data from our database, drag the desired variable from the database browser window and drop it into the table in the briefing editor.

Publishing (Saving) a Website

After you finish all the above operations, your newly created website will be ready for publishing. To publish, select the **File/Publish All** menu commands. To view the newly created site via the Web browser, select the **Window/Web Browser** menu command. If all the settings are correct, you'll be able to view your data on the Web.

8.2.2. The WebPage component

Select the **WebPage** component in the **Web Object Browser** window and select the **Edit/Properties** menu commands. The **WebPage Properties** window will open (Fig. 8.8).

In this window, you can specify the page description that will be displayed to the user as a URL in the left frame of our site. You can also specify the text labels that will surround our table containing the data (Fig. 8.9).

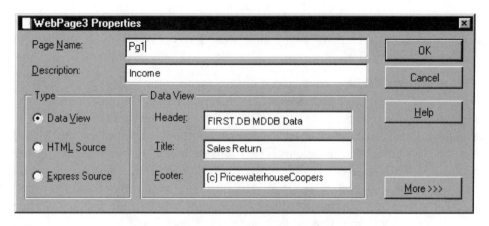

Fig. 8.8. The **WebPage3 Properties** window

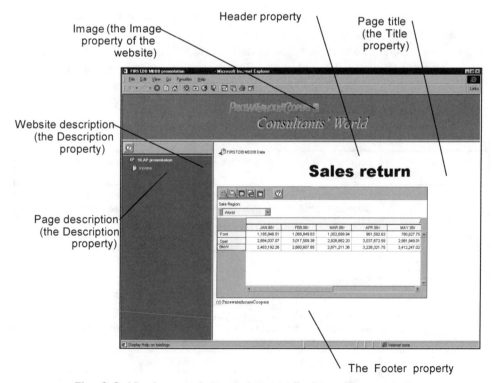

Fig. 8.9. Viewing a website via Internet Explorer. The properties
of the WebPage component

Earlier in this chapter, we looked at the procedure of creating a Web page displaying the data as a table. Besides a table view, Express Web Publisher allows you to create other data views.

Select the **Insert/WebPage** commands from the menu. A dialog will open, providing us with three possible alternatives when creating Web pages. The first alternative that we have considered above is creating a Web page containing a data view from the multidimensional database. The second alternative allows us to publish any HTML page that can be created using any HTML or text editor on our website. Furthermore, this HTML page can be a template that calls subroutines and functions from the Express database (see *Section 8.5*). The third alternative enables us to create a page that is automatically generated by the programs stored in the Express database, using the procedures from Express Web Agent Developer Tool's Kit.

8.2.3. Configuring Web Tables

Similar to Express Analyzer or Express Objects components, Express Web Publisher components have properties that enable the user to customize their view and behavior in the Web browser window. To start the object inspector, select the **WebTable** object in the object browser window, and then select the **Edit/Properties** commands from the menu. Descriptions of the main WebTable object properties are provided below:

Table 8.1. Main WebTable Properties

Property	Description
EnableSizing	Logical property that specifies whether the end user can resize the table cells
EnableDrilling	Logical property that specifies whether the end user can perform the **Drill-Down** and **DrillUp** operations over the information presented in the table
FillColor	Specifies the background color
Font	Specifies the typeface and font color that will be used to display table data
AutoIndent	Specifies the number of blank characters (from 0 to 16, 2 by default), that will be used to display rows belonging to different hierarchical levels
EnableIndent	Logical property that allows you to enable or disable the AutoIndent property when highlighting the names of the rows belonging to different hierarchical levels
ShowHGrid	Enables or disables the horizontal grid display
ShowVGrid	Enables or disables the vertical grid display

continues

Table 8.1 Continued

Property	Description
SuppressRows	Specifies whether the table will display rows consisting of the zero or blank (NA) values. It provides the following options: 0—display all rows 1—suppress rows consisting of zero values only 2—suppress rows containing blank (NA) values only 3—suppress both blank and zero rows
EnableChange Measures	Specifies whether the end user can use the selector tool to select other measures for the table
EnableChangeView Type	Specifies whether a button allowing you to change the view type will be available to the end user
EnableExport	Specifies whether a button allowing you to export table data into a flat data file will be available to the end user
EnableRotation	Specifies whether cube rotation capabilities will be available to the end user
EnableSaved Selections	Specifies whether the end user will be able to save the selection
EnableSelector	Specifies whether the Selector tool will be available to the end user
EnableToolbar	Allows you to enable or disable the toolbar display
WebHeight	Specifies the table height in the Web browser
WebWidth	Specifies the table width in the Web browser

The tables are Java applets `OwaTableApplet.class` from the `oracle.olap.webAgent.javaTable` package loaded from the server and executed on the client PC. It is therefore necessary that your Web browser support the required Java language version. For example, the current version of Express Web Agent requires Java v1.1.5. This Java version is supported by Netscape Communicator (version 4.05 or higher) and Internet Explorer (starting with version 4.0 with Service Pack 1).

As a reaction to the user input, an applet can automatically (i.e., by bypassing the Web browser) establish a connection to the Web server and request the required data from Express server. Therefore, if you select new measures or perform drill up/drill down operations, only the table area is updated, without the whole page being redrawn.

Most Web browsers cache the results of previous queries. Because of this, it is possible that the changes in properties performed and published using Web Publisher may not be displayed by the Web browser (since the browser will display the cached results). Therefore, when debugging applications, it is desirable that you disable the caching option, if possible. Also note that in most cases the problem may be corrected by simply closing and re-launching the browser.

The Table component acts as a container object for the following auxiliary objects:

ColumnEdge—field of the column names

Databody—data field

Footnote—footnote

PageEdge—field of the page names

RowEdge—field of the row names

Subtitle—the subtitle

Title—the title

Use object inspector to access properties of specific objects. To do this, select the WebJavaTable object in the briefing browser window, and then select the required object on the **Contents** page of the object inspector. For objects contained within a table, you can define the background color, font, alignment type, and contents (long or short label for dimension values, title property, etc.). These properties provide you with flexible capabilities for customizing the table view that will be presented to the end user.

8.2.4. Customizing Web Graphs

To create a graph, select the **Insert/WebPage** commands from the main menu and create a new page with the graph data view. Similar to a table, a graph also has a range of properties that enable you to manage the layout and behavior of the graph shown in the browser window. Most of the graph properties are similar to the table properties. Listed below are graph-specific properties:

Table 8.2. Graph-Specific Properties

Property	Description
BorderColor	Specifies the color of the border
BorderTransparent	Allows you to disable the border
BorderWidth	Specifies the border width
Effect3D	Specifies whether 3D effects will be available in the graph view

continues

Table 8.2 Continued

Property	Description
GraphType	Specifies the graph type. For the moment, there are 39 graph types available for graph views
Orientation	Specifies graph orientation

Besides the graph's properties, there are lots of objects contained within the graph that can be used to manage the graph's layout and behavior. The main customizable elements of a graph view are listed below:

Table 8.3. Graph Customizable Elements

Object	Description
2-D marker	Represents data as labels
3-D floor	Defines the lower edge ("floor") of 3D graphs
3-D Left Wall	Defines the left edge ("left wall") of 3D graphs
3-D Marker	Represents data as a labels in 3D graph
3-D right wall	Defines the "right wall" of 3D graphs
Area Marker, Data Line	Specifies representation for the rows of a multidimensional data cube
Data Marker	Defines the representation of the data values
Footnote	Allows you to customize the view and contents of footnotes
Legend Area	Specifies the representation of the graph legend
Legend Line	Specifies line representation for the graph legend
Legend Marker	Specifies the label representation in the graph legend
Pie Label	Specifies the representation of the labels in pie charts
Plot Area	Manages the representation of the plot area
Slice	Defines the pie chart slice representation
Slice Label	Specifies the pie chart slice label
Subtitle	Specifies the graph subtitle
Title	Specifies the graph title
X-Axis	Describes the X-axis representation
X Tick Label	Specifies the X-axis labels

continues

Table 8.3 Continued

Object	Description
X Title	Specifies the X-axis title
Y1-Axis	Describes the Y-axis representation
Y1 Title	Specifies the Y-axis title
Y2-Axis	Specifies the representation of the second Y-axis
Y2 Title	Specifies the title of the second Y-axis
Z Title	Specifies the title of the Z-axis

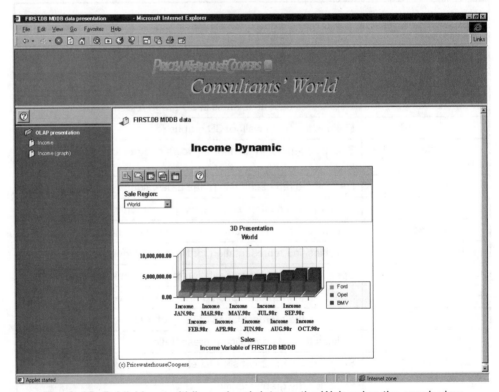

Fig. 8.10. Publishing multidimensional data on the Web using the graph view

Using the elements of the WebJavaGraph component, you can flexibly customize the graph representation of multidimensional data (Fig. 8.10). More detailed information on the properties of these elements can be found in the on-line Help system.

8.2.5. Special Features of National Languages

If you carefully study the data views presented in Figs 8.9 and 8.10, you'll notice that the time dimension values are shown in English. Note that if you want to make time dimension values appear in other language, you must use a special program, SET_NAME, written in the Express language. It starts any time you attach the FIRST.DB database to the client application (according to the `Post-Attach Program` database property). Since Oracle Express Web Publisher is a client application, the SET_NAME program runs whenever you're connecting to the FIRST.DB database. As a result, we see the month names in the language that you require. However, when the same database is attached using Express Web Agent, month names are not replaced, because this application is not identified as a client.

If you need to correct the situation and display month names in a national language, open the **Advanced Properties** dialog (Fig. 8.6) to specify the advanced website properties and enter the following code in the **Before Run** field:

```
MONTHNAMES =
'month1\nmonth2\nmonth3\nmonth4\nmonth6\nmonth7\nmonth8\nmonth9\
nmonth10\nmonth11\nmonth12'
```

where month1 ... nmonth12 are month names in the required national language.

Now, if you publish these corrections using the **File/Publish All** menu commands and then open our site in the Web browser, you'll notice that the MONTH dimension values are displayed in appropriate language.

8.3. Creating Web Applications

8.3.1. Express Web Agent Working Principles

As we have already noticed, Express Web Agent is a special program library that redirects queries from a Web browser to programs stored in Express databases. In the previous section, we discussed Web development using Express Web Publisher. To create simple websites using this application, it was sufficient to have only a superficial acquaintance with Express Web Agent. Now it is time to discuss Express Web Agent's working principles in more detail. First, let us consider the URL contained in the index.html file located in the directory corresponding to the /owp/ virtual name:

```
location.href="/ows-bin/oowa/ExpSrv620/dbxwascode/runwebsite";
```

▼

Here:

❏ ows-bin—virtual Web directory on the server where the CGI application is searched for

❏ oowa—name of the application located in this directory

❏ ExpSrv620—name of the Express server instance (note: this name is case-sensitive)

❏ dbxwascode—combined name of the database (where db is the prefix and xwascode is the database name) contained in the Express Web Publisher software

❏ runwebsite—name of the program from this database that generates HTML page and starts the published Web sites

The HTML code generated by the Express Web Agent runwebsite program is returned to the website, which, in turn, redirects it to the Web browser that sent the current query. Any other Express Web application works in a similar way.

The core of the Express Web application is formed by one or more databases containing programs responsible for Web page generation, as well as the data that needs to be published. Usually, the programs accomplish the following tasks:

❏ Start Express service programs to generate all the tags (special text markup characters) of the HTML language version 2.0.

❏ Start Express service programs to generate Web views of multidimensional data.

❏ Start Express service programs to generate HTML pages using templates. Templates are static HTML pages that include special comments containing Express commands. These HTML pages are created using a simple text editor.

Programs generating HTML code may also contain calls to any other commands and procedures of the Express language, including the commands for selecting and manipulating multidimensional data. The main goal of all these programs is to create HTML pages that display the required multidimensional data.

8.3.2. Web Developer's Toolkit

Service programs necessary for creating Express Web applications are stored in special databases:

❏ xwdevkit—contains programs for creating and manipulating pages that contain data views

- ❒ xwhtml—contains programs that generate standard HTML tags

- ❒ owagraph—contains programs that provide support for data views using the Java language

These databases together contain the tools necessary to create Web applications (Web Developer's Toolkit). The xwhtml database contains programs of two types that differ in their method of generating HTML tags, and have names starting with different prefixes:

- ❒ HTP.*—these programs output the generated tag, its attributes, and the accompanying text into the current output stream

- ❒ HTF.* – these programs return the text value containing the generated tag, its attributes, and the accompanying text to the calling program

For example, the HTF.PARA program returns the "<P>" value (opening the "New paragraph" HTML tag) to the calling program, while the HTP.PARA program directs the value returned by the HTF.PARA function to the current output stream.

Each application using the Web Developer's Toolkit must follow the requirements listed below:

- ❒ Each application must start with a call to the XWD_META.INIT service program that opens and caches the Express Server session. This program is contained in the xwdevkit database.

- ❒ Each application must end with a call to the XWD_URLCLOSE service program that signals Express Server about the session's termination and allows the server to release unused resources. If this program is not called, Express sessions will be closed anyway, when the query time-out exceeds the specified limit. The time-out value is specified by the appropriate parameter when configuring Express server.

The supplementary documentation provided with Oracle Express recommends that you separate the data to be presented on the Web pages from the software code providing the support for Web applications by storing this information in different databases. Attaching a database containing programs is accomplished using a special URL, similar to the one described in the previous section.

8.3.3. The "Hello Internet World !" Program

Any programmer knows, based on his or her own experience, that it is developing the first working application that causes the most problems when mastering new technologies. Traditionally, this is the "Hello World!" program. Let's follow this tradition and illustrate the basics of working with Web Developer's Toolkit in this simple example.

Step 1. Creating a Static HTML Page

The Web browser initializes the Express server session by sending a special URL:

```
http:/<host>:<port>/ows-
bin/oowa.exe/ExpSrv620/dbxwdevkit/xwd_init?webcode/ table
```

Here:

❏ `dbxwdevkit`—specifies the special Express database containing software tools for creating Web applications

❏ `xwd_init`—the program from the service database that initializes an Express session

❏ `?webcode/ table`—the name of the user database and the name of the program stored there and responsible for initializing the user-defined Web application ('?' is the special separator)

To hide this complex and quite long URL from the user, let's create a static HTML page (test.html) using any text editor (notepad.exe, for example). The table containing sales data will be called from this page using the **Sales Data** link:

```
<html>
<head>
<title>Express test 1.0</title>
</head>
<body>
<h1> Hello Internet World !</h1>
<a href=
"http://<host>:<port>/ows-
bin/oowa.exe/ExpSrv620/dbxwdevkit/xwd_init?webcode/table">
Sales data</a>
</body>
</html>
```

Save this file on the computer where the Web server is installed. Next, use the Web server administration utility to describe the path to the directory where this file resides by specifying a virtual directory named /workshop/.

Step 2. Creating a Table View

To create a program that will dynamically generate HTML documents, let's use the Express Administrator application. To accomplish this task, proceed as follows:

❏ Start the Express Administrator application and connect to the Express Server.

❏ Select the **File/New Database** commands from the menu to create a new database named, for example, WEBCODE. This database will contain programs for creating an HTML document (note that the database must be located in the directory whose path was specified when configuring Express server).

❏ Create a new object in this database—a program called table—by selecting the **Dictionary/Define/Program** menu items.

❏ Make the table object active and enter the program code by selecting the **Dictionary/Edit** menu items:

```
"TABLE
call xwd_meta.init        "initialize the development environment
database attach first row "attach the demo database
set_mname                 "correct the month names
call xwd_vwpg.create('TABLE', 'profit', -
'month', 'product', 'region', NA, -
'tableheader', 'tablefooter')
```

The xwd_vwpg.create service program that creates a view for multidimensional data will be covered later in this chapter. For the moment, I would like to point out that the *'tableheader'* and *'tablefooter'* parameters passed to this program define the names of the user-defined programs that create the HTML page header and footer. In our case, they look as follows:

```
"TABLEHEADER
"header output
call htp.header('1','Sales Data')
call htp.hr        "<HR>


"TABLEFOOTER
call htp.hr        "<HR>
```

```
"generating the reference to close the Express session
call htp.anchor(xwd_urlclose,'Close the session')
```

Pay special attention to the `htp.anchor` function call that generates a static reference to the required program that closes the Express session.

To start our static HTML page, we need just enter the following URL in the browser address field:

```
http://<host>:<port>/workshop/test.html
```

Now, if you follow the **Sales Data** link on this page, you'll see the data from our multidimensional database represented in a table view. Fig. 8.11 shows our dynamic HTML page displaying the multidimensional data array on sales revenue from the FIRST.DB demo database.

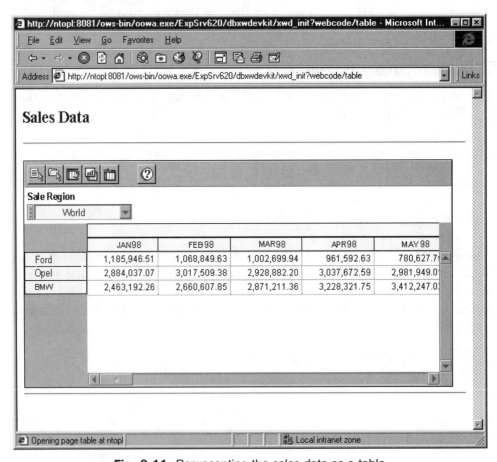

Fig. 8.11. Representing the sales data as a table

Step 3. Representing Data in a Graph View using the HTML Template

Now let us enhance our previous example by adding the **TABLEFOOTER** link to our program:

```
call htp.anchor(xwd_url('GRAPH'),'Show graph')
```

If you follow this link, the GRAPH program from our database will be executed:

```
"GRAPH
call xwd_settmppath('c:/orant/olap/oes620/owa200/sample')
"path to the file
call xwd_tmppg.create('graph.html')
     "template filename
```

The `xwd_tmppg.create` program informs Express server that to create a dynamic HTML document, it is necessary to use the template stored in the file named `graph.html`. Notice that the `xwd_settmppath` program requires you to specify the full pathname to the directory where the template file resides (the graph.html file in our example).

Express commands are included into the template using specially formatted comments:

```
<!--EXPRESS ...
...
-->
```

Now all we have to do is create the HTML document template containing the call to the program responsible for generating the Java graph:

```
<html>
<head>
<title>Express test 1.0</title>
</head>
<body>
<center>
<h1>Sales Chart</h1>
<!--EXPRESS VIEW
call xwd_view.create('JAVAGRAPH', -
'F.SALES', 'GEOGRAPHY', 'PRODUCT', -
'TIME\nCHANNEL')
-->
</center>
```

```
</body>
</html>
```

Thus, when the user clicks the **Show graph** link, the browser window will look as shown in Fig. 8.12.

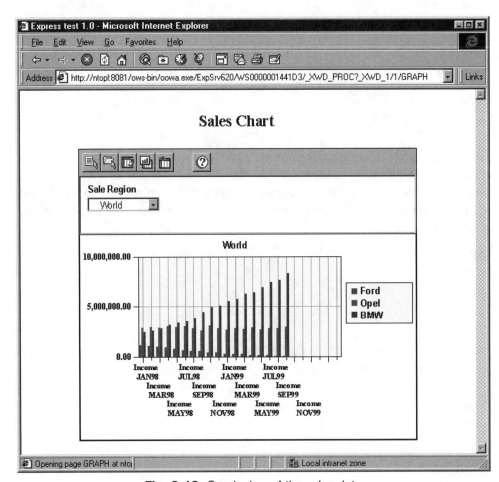

Fig. 8.12. Graph view of the sales data

Step 4. Creating the Closing Page

You might not be satisfied with the standard page displayed in the browser window after clicking the **Close session** link. This page is generated by the tablefooter program from our WEBCODE.DB database. Note that the call to this page is required to inform Express server that the current session is terminated and that it is necessary to release the resources associated with it. If you are not satisfied with this page, you can create your own custom footer page. The simplest way of accomplishing this task is to replace the standard page located in the CLOSE.HTT file residing in the *<Oracle_Home>*/olap/oes620/owp200/sample directory. This file is opened any time the `xwd_urlclose` program is executed. However, this method is not a universal one, since all Web applications that call the xwd_urlclose program will terminate by displaying the replaced HTML page. Therefore, a more convenient way of solving this problem is to create a custom program generating a user-defined closing HTML page. In order to call this program when executing the xwd_urlclose service program, you'll need to register the program in the `OOWA_CLOSE_PROC` environment variable.

Create the close_proc program in our WEBCODE.DB database:

```
call htp.print('Content-type: text/html \x0a')
call htp.htmlopen
call htp.bodyopen
call htp.print('<center>')
call htp.print('<h1>The Hello Internet World application has —
terminated</h1>')
call htp.centerclose
call htp.bodyclose
call htp.htmlclose
```

Pay special attention to the specific requirements that must be observed when creating the custom footer program:

❏ The program must start with a call to the `htp.print('Content-type: text/html \x0a')` function

❏ The program generates standard HTML tags using `HTP.*.` programs

❏ The program can't use procedures like `XWD_VWPG.CREATE` for creating pages

Add the following line of code to the table program that opens the Express session:

```
OOWA_CLOSE_PROC = 'close_proc'
```

Don't forget to save the changes introduced into the source code of the programs, along with the WEBCODE.DB database. Now re-launch the newly created Web application and make sure that all the modifications that you have introduced are correct.

8.4. Displaying Multidimensional Data

Like most other client application development tools from the Express family, Web Developer's Toolkit implements an object-oriented approach to development. HTML pages, tables, graphs, and their components are objects. Each object encapsulates either the whole HTML page or some part of it. Object properties define their contents and representation in the Web browser. However, you can't work with the Web Developer's Toolkit object like you do with objects stored in the database. The objects are referenced from the software code using special handles, with which it is possible to retrieve or modify the current property values of the specific object.

Creating a Web page using Toolkit is a two-step process:

❐ For the first stage, our application calls the Developer's Toolkit procedures that create Web objects, manipulates them using methods, and customizes their properties

❐ Next, Developer's Toolkit uses the newly created object for generating HTML pages

All objects are derived from the basic **OBJECT** object and inherit its properties:

Property	Description
DESCRIPTION	Text description of an object that can be used, for example, when displaying variables (the MEASURE object) of the multidimensional database as tables or graphs
NAME	This text property is used to identify objects. When the object is created, we assign it a name. Later, we can use this name to get a handle for a specific object

For example, when in the previous section we used the xwd_vwpg.create and xwd_view.create procedures, we created the PAGE and JAVAGRAPH objects.

8.4.1. The Data Cube

Like other products from the Express family, Express Web Agent uses the data cube as an abstract model. The data cube has three dimensions: columns, rows, and pages. Each dimension or variable of a multidimensional database is related to one of the three cube dimensions. By default, the first dimension listed is the

COLUMNS dimension, then the ROWS dimension, and lastly the PAGES dimension. When we create a data view (a table or graph), Express Web Agent automatically creates the DATACUBE object that determines the structure and contents of the data to be represented. The DATACUBE object can also be created program-matically using the XWD_CUBE.CREATE procedure. This procedure uses the following syntax:

```
XWD_CUBE.CREATE(measures, [column-edge], [row-edge], [page-edge], [cubeprops])
```

All the parameters here have the text data type.

Measures—this parameter defines the multidimensional database variables that need to be represented by the cube. This parameter is used when creating the MEASURE object, and allows us to determine its properties. The syntax for specifying this parameter is as follows:

```
'measure[;attribute=value][;attribute=value]... -

    measure[;attribute=value][;attribute=value]...'
```

where attribute specifies the name of the MEASURE object property (more details on the topic will be provided later in this chapter). If we need to create a cube con-taining more than one dimension, it is necessary to separate the dimensions with the new line character ('\n') or use the command line continuation character. For example, if we need the data cube to contain the PROFIT and SALES variables from our FIRST.DB database, we need to specify this parameter as follows:

```
'profit\nsales'
```

or

```
'profit -

sales'
```

Parameters such as column-edge, row-edge, and page-edge define the dimensions of the multidimensional variable that we need to relate to a specific dimension of the data cube. The syntax used for specifying these parameters is similar to the syntax used to specify the measures parameter. These parameters manage the proc-ess of creating EDGENODE objects, as well as define their properties. The MEASURES keyword may replace the multidimensional database dimension name, which means that the current data cube dimension is related to a set of variables defined by the measures parameter.

The `cubeprops` parameter allows for specifying the data cube's properties:

Property	Description
COMMAS	Logical property that specifies whether a comma will be used as the thousands delimiter when representing numeric data
DECIMALCHAR	Specifies the character that will be used to separate the fractional part of a number
DECIMALS	Specifies the number of characters that will be used to represent the fractional part of a number when representing numeric data
THOUSANDSCHAR	Specifies the character that will be used to delimit thousands when representing numeric data

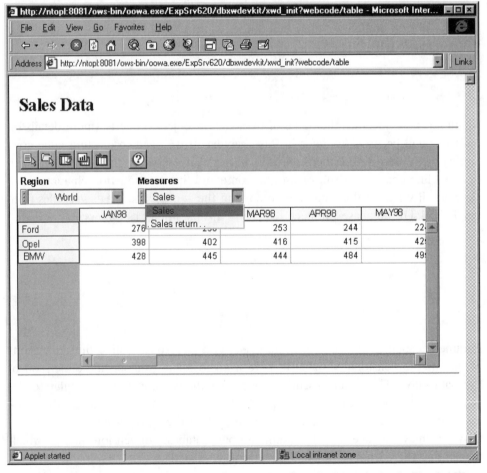

Fig. 8.13. The modified table data view (compare to the one shown in Fig. 8.12)

Now let us return to the example we started to consider in the previous section. When we called the procedure for creating a page with the table data view (call `xwd_vwpg.create`), we specified the values defining the automatically created data cube as the second, third, fourth, and fifth parameters passed to the procedure.

If we modify the code as follows:

```
call xwd_vwpg.create('TABLE', 'sales;COMMAS=NO;DECIMALS=0 -
profit;COMMAS=NO;DECIMALS=1', -
'month', 'product', 'MEASURES\nregion', NA, -
'tableheader', 'tablefooter')
```

We will get a modified table view, compared to the previous illustration (Fig. 8.13). It differs from the previous view by the presence of the additional drop-down list allowing you to navigate from variable to variable and provide different representations for the numeric values in the table cells. In the example under consideration, COMMAS and DECIMALS are the properties of the MEASURE object associated to the data cube to be created. The semantics of these properties is similar to the semantics of the data cube properties with the same names. More detailed information on the properties of the MEASURE and EDGENODE object is provided in the on-line Help system.

Developer's Toolkit contains a large number of methods that provide flexible capabilities for managing the contents and representation of the data cube. These methods have the XWD_CUBE.* prefix. More detailed information on the semantics and syntax of these methods is provided in the on-line Help system.

8.4.2. The *VIEW* Object

The current version of the Web Developer's Toolkit product provides the capability of creating three types of data views in a Web browser. These types are represented by the following objects: JAVAGRAPH, HTMLTABLE, and JAVATABLE. All these objects have a common ancestor—the VIEW object—which encapsulates their common properties:

Table 8.4. Common Properties of the View Object

Property	Description
AUTOREFRESH	Logical property that determines whether the data view will be automatically regenerated when the user selects a new value for the page dimension in the data cube. If this property is set to NO, the data view will provide the Refresh button intended for manually refreshing the data view display. This mode is advisable if we think that the user will need to introduce several modifications at once and then manually refresh the data display

continues

Table 8.4 Continued

Property	Description
DATACUBE	Defines the handle for the data cube object that is related to the specific view
ENABLECHGMEASURES	Logical property that determines if the selector tool is available to the user
ENABLECHGVIEWTYPE	Logical property that determines if the user can work with the tool for changing data view
ENABLEDRILLING	Enables or disables the **Drill Down/Drill Up** operations for the end-user
ENABLEEXPORT	Defines whether the data export tool will be available in the toolbar
ENABLEHELP	Determines whether the **Help** button will be available in the toolbar
ENABLEROTATION	Determines whether the rotation button allowing you to rotate the data view will be available in the toolbar
ENABLESAVEDSEL	Determines whether the **Save** toolbar button allowing you to save the selection results will be available
ENABLESELECTDATA	Determines whether the **Select** toolbar button allowing you to select list items will be available in the toolbar
ENABLETOOLBAR	Allows you to completely suppress the toolbar display.
HELPTOPIC	Defines the Help topic describing the current data view.
PAGECONTROLS	Specifies whether the page drop-down list allowing you to manage the page dimension will be available in the data view
RECTHEIGHT	Determines the display height (in pixels)
RECTWIDTH	Determines the display width (in pixels)
VIEWTYPE	Defines the current type of the data view
VIEWTYPELIST	Defines the subtype list corresponding to the current graph view

Fig 8.14 illustrates the hierarchy of objects related to the data views used to represent data in Web browser.

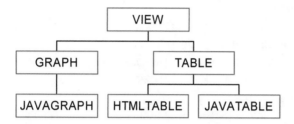

Fig. 8.14. Hierarchy of objects responsible for displaying data in Web browser

8.4.3. Creating Tables

The TABLE object is the common ancestor of the HTMLTABLE and JAVATABLE objects. It has a single SUPPRESSROWS property that allows you to manage row suppression. This property can take the following values:

0	XWC_TBL.NOSUPPRESS	Display all rows
1	XWC_TBL.ZEROSUPPRESS	Don't display rows filled with zero values
2	XWC_TBL.NASUPPRESS	Don't display blank (NA) rows
3	XWC_TBL.BOTHSUPPRESS	Don't display rows filled with zeros and NA values

The HTMLTABLE object, in turn, has the following properties:

Property	Description
ALIGN	Specifies the data alignment type. Can take the following values: LEFT, CENTER, and RIGHT
ACROSSCOLOR	Specifies the background color for the row containing column names
DATACOLOR	Specifies the background color for the table data cells
DOWNCOLOR	Specifies the background color for the column containing row names

Let us illustrate the basic principles of working with Web objects in an example of creating a HTMLTABLE object and customizing its properties. Let's then return to the example considered in the previous section. Replace the page creation procedure call (xwd_vwpg.create) with the following code:

```
call xwd_vwpg.create('HTMLTABLE', 'sales;COMMAS=NO;DECIMALS=0 -
```

```
profit;COMMAS=NO;DECIMALS=1', -
'month', 'product', 'MEASURES\nregion', NA, -
'tableheader', 'tablefooter', 'table1')
"get the table handle
h_table = XWD_GETOBJECT('table1')
"change the background color for row and column names
call XWD_SETPROPVALT(h_table, 'ACROSSCOLOR', 'FFFF00' )
call XWD_SETPROPVALT(h_table, 'DOWNCOLOR', 'FFFF00' )
"suppress the toolbar
call XWD_SETPROPVALB(h_table, 'ENABLETOOLBAR', NO )
"get the data cube handle
h_cube = XWD_VIEW.CUBE(h_table)
"rotate the table
call XWD_CUBE.ROTATE(h_cube, 'SWAP', 'PRODUCT', 'MONTH')
```

Naturally, we have added text variables at the beginning of our table program:

```
vrb h_table text
vrb h_cube text
```

Later, these variables are assigned the handles for the HTMLTABLE object and its related DATACUBE object. When calling the xwd_vwpg.create procedure, the table type is specified as 'HTMLTABLE'. The last parameter passed to the function is 'table1'. Subsequently, it will be used for getting the handle for the newly created object. Changing the object properties can be done by calling the standard XWD_SETPROPVAL*x*, method, which has the following syntax:

```
XWD_SETPROPVALx(object-handle, property-name, property-value)
```

The x suffix can take one of the following values:

B—Boolean

D—Decimal

I—Integer

O—Object

T—Text

The suffix is determined by the type of the property to be changed. The text object-handle parameter is the object handle. The property-name parameter is the name of the current object property. The type of the property-value parameter depends on the suffix of the function name. This parameter contains the value to be assigned. As a result, our multidimensional data will be represented in the Web browser (Fig. 8.15) as an ordinary HTML table and two standard SELECT HTML tags that manage page navigation. The table will be rotated as compared to the ones shown in Figs. 8.11 and 8.13.

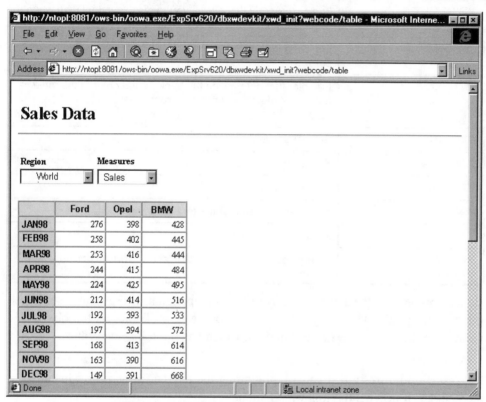

Fig. 8.15. Data represented as an HTML table

HTMLTABLE objects provide the single capability of representing multidimensional data in browsers that don't support the required Java language version. If your browser has the required virtual Java machine, then certainly representing table data using the JAVATABLE object would be more convenient and illustrative. When using this object, you can manage the following properties:

Property	Description
AUTOINDENT	Specifies the number of blank characters (from 0 to 16, the default is 2) that will be used to emphasize rows belonging to different hierarchical levels

continues

Continued

Property	Description
ENABLEINDENT	Logical property that allows you to disable indentation when emphasizing hierarchical row names
ENABLESIZING	Logical property that specifies if the end user can resize table cells
FILLCOLOR	Fill color that determines the background color of the table and some of its elements, for example: TABLE.ROWEDGE, TABLE.SUBTITLE, TABLE.TITLE, etc.
FONTBOLD	Specifies bold font
FONTCOLOR	Specifies font color
FONTITALIC	Specifies italic font
FONTNAME	Specifies the name of the font to be used
FONTSIZE	Manages the font size
SHOWHGRID and SHOWVGRID	Allows you to suppress horizontal and vertical grid lines

Besides properties, the table contains several components whose names start with the TABLE.* prefix. These objects were described earlier. To access the object elements, use the xwd_getcontent function, which has the following syntax:

```
XWD_GETCONTENT(container, [index], [object-type], [superclass])
```

This function returns a text value representing the handle to the object included in a container. It accepts the following parameters:

☐ container—handle for the container object

☐ index—integer index (starting with 0) of the object to be defined

☐ object-type—text value that specifies the type of the object to be defined

☐ superclass—logical variable that determines if the specified object type is a base class type. For example, it we don't know for sure which data view is included into the page (HTMLTABLE, JAVATABLE, or JAVAGRAPH), we can get its handle by specifying object-type = 'VIEW' and superclass = YES

To illustrate this, let's return to our example—the table program. Let's represent data using the JAVATABLE object and add a title to the table:

```
call xwd_vwpg.create('JAVATABLE', 'sales;COMMAS=NO;DECIMALS=0 -
```

```
profit;COMMAS=NO;DECIMALS=1', -
'month', 'product', 'MEASURES\nregion', NA, -
'tableheader', 'tablefooter', 'table1')
h_table = XWD_GETOBJECT('table1')
h_title = XWD_GETCONTENT(h_table,0,'TABLE.TITLE')
call XWD_SETPROPVALT(h_title, 'TEXT', 'Managing the table title' )
call XWD_SETPROPVALT(h_title, 'FILLCOLOR', 'C0C0C0' )
call XWD_SETPROPVALB(h_title, 'VISIBLE', YES )
```

Now let's execute this application using the Web browser. You'll see the JAVATABLE object with the built-in title. Additional information on the table components is provided in the on-line Help system [6].

8.4.4. Working with Graphs

The JAVAGRAPH object can be created using two functions: XWD_VIEW.CREATE and XWD_VWPG.CREATE. By default, the graph type will be set to 1 (XWC_GT.BAR_CLUSTERED) which corresponds to the clustered bar chart. To modify the graph view, it is necessary to specify an appropriate value for the VIEWTYPE property, which is inherited by JAVAGRAPH from its parent object—VIEW. You can do this using the following code, which modifies the graph program from our example:

```
"GRAPH
vrb h_graph text
limit month to first 12
call xwd_vwpg.create('JAVAGRAPH', 'profit', -
'month', 'product', 'region', NA, NA, NA,'graph1')
h_graph = XWD_GETOBJECT('graph1')
call XWD_SETPROPVALI(h_graph, 'VIEWTYPE', -
xwc_value(xwt_msgid 'XWC_GT.LINE_ABSOLUTE '))
```

Take note of the following two specific features of the code provided above. The first one relates to the usage of the limit command, which limits the time interval represented on the graph. The second peculiarity is the call to the xwc_value function instead of using the integer graph type value (8). The xwc_value function returns an appropriate integer value with the descriptive text `XWC_GT.LINE_ABSOLUTE`.

Fig. 8.16 represents the result of executing the code provided above in our application. Notice that we can now use the `xwd_vwpg.create` function when creating an HTML page, and thus we don't need the template file.

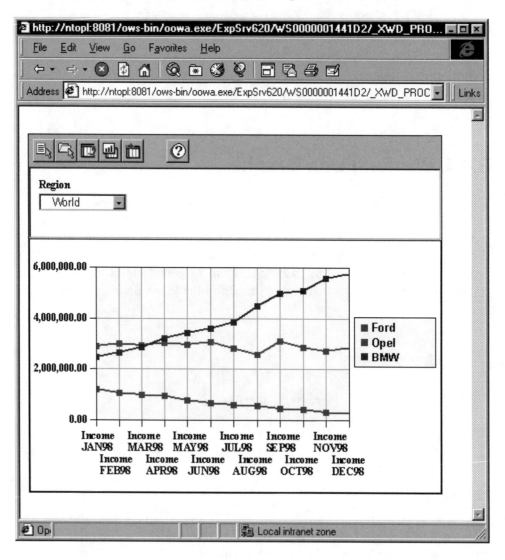

Fig. 8.16. The example of a modified graph view for representing data

As follows from the hierarchy shown in Fig. 8.14, the GRAPH object is the direct ancestor of the JAVAGRAPH object. It seems to us that the developers of the product intend for the GRAPH object to be used in the future for further improvement. The JAVAGRAPH object inherits the following properties of its parent object:

Property	Description
BORDERCOLOR	Determines the color of the border for the graph and its elements
BORDERWIDTH	Specifies the border width
EFFECT3D	Logical property that determines if the graph view will use 3D effects
FILLCOLOR	Specifies the fill color for the graph and its elements
ORIENTATION	Specifies a horizontal (0) or vertical (1) orientation for the graph
ROWOBJECTCOUNT	An integer value that specifies the number of GRAPH.ROW components

The objects contained within the GRAPH container were described in detail in *Section 8.2.* Detailed information on their types and properties is provided in the on-line Help system. The GRAPH.ROW built-in objects have some specific features. To get handles for these objects, you need to use a special function—XWD_GRP.GETROW, while other component objects can be accessed using the XWD_GETCONTENT function, as was shown in the example illustrating table title management presented in the previous section. Let's illustrate the particular features of working with the GRAPH.ROW objects in an example. Suppose that you want to make the graph presented in Fig. 8.15 more illustrative. For example, suppose that you need to emphasize the trends of the decrease in sales revenue for Opel and Ford and the steady sales growth of another product line—BMW. For this purpose, let us represent the BMW sales revenue as a filled area. This can be done using the following code:

```
"GRAPH
vrb h_graph text
vrb h_row text
limit month to first 12
call xwd_vwpg.create('JAVAGRAPH', 'profit', -
'month', 'product', 'region', NA, NA, NA,'graph1')
h_graph = XWD_GETOBJECT('graph1')
```

```
h_row = xwd_grp.getrow(h_graph, 3)
call XWD_SETPROPVALI(h_row, 'MARKERTYPE', -
xwc_value(xwt_msgid 'XWC_MT.AREA')
h_row = xwd_grp.getrow(h_graph, 2)
call XWD_SETPROPVALI(h_row, 'MARKERTYPE', -
xwc_value(xwt_msgid 'XWC_MT.LINE')
h_row = xwd_grp.getrow(h_graph, 1)
call XWD_SETPROPVALI(h_row, 'MARKERTYPE', -
xwc_value(xwt_msgid 'XWC_MT.LINE')
```

Now if you run the application, you will see the graph presented in Fig. 8.17.

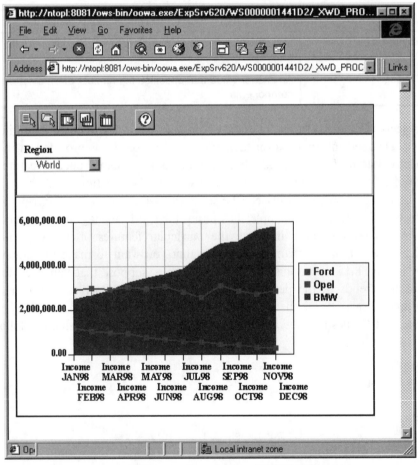

Fig. 8.17. An example of managing GRAPH.ROW objects

8.5. Creating HTML Documents

As we mentioned before, when using Developer's Toolkit there are two ways of creating HTML documents that play the role of client applications in the intranet/Internet networks.

The first option is to generate the page using the Express language only. Using this approach, we can:

❏ Use only the Express Administrator tool when developing Web applications

❏ Create custom standard fragments of HTML code (for example, headers or footnotes) that can be used within different pages without having to duplicate them in each page

❏ Work with database objects rather than with the file system of the Web server

The second option is to use HTML templates. These templates are normal HTML pages containing Express commands inserted using specially formatted comments. This method of creating HTML documents has a number of advantages:

❏ Instead of generating new HTML pages, we can reuse HTML pages created earlier by updating them with multidimensional data views

❏ We can use visual tools for rapid design of HTML documents. There are currently a large variety of such tools available on the software market

❏ We can use all the capabilities of the current HTML version and are not limited to the ones supported by Developer's Toolkit

The method used is up to the application developer. Based on experience, we would say that your Web developing will achieve maximum efficiency when you rationally combine the two above-mentioned approaches.

8.5.1. Generating HTML Documents Programmatically

Creating Pages

The PAGE object is used for logically representing HTML documents. Now let us consider the functions that allow us to create such objects.

The XWD_APPG.CREATE function creates a page that does not contain built-in views for displaying multidimensional data. The syntax of this function is as follows:

```
XWD_APPPG.CREATE([program-name [,arg1] [,arg2 ... ]])
```

This function returns the handle for the page it has created. The function's arguments are:

❏ *program-name*—name of the program contained in one of the attached databases

❏ arg1, arg2, ...—arguments of the *program-name* program

Let us provide an example that illustrates the usage of this function. For example, let us create the print_today program in our database, consisting of a single command:

```
call xwd_apppg.create('htp.print' -
    joinchars('Today: ', convert(today text '<dd>.<mm>.<yy>'), -
    ' Current time: ', tod))
```

Don't forget to store the program in the database and save the database on the hard disk. Now, if we specify the following URL in the address field of the browser:

```
http://<host>/ows-
bin/oowa.exe/ExpSrv620/dbxwdevkit/xwd_init?webcode/print_today
```

the browser window will display the following text:

```
'Today: 03.05.01 Current time: 15:03:25
```

Naturally, the date and time will correspond to the settings specified at the Express server. If you click the **Refresh** button in the browser, the page will be refreshed, and you'll see an updated time value.

Inserting Objects

Having created a page and retrieved the handle for it, you can use this handle for inserting other Web objects into this page. Let's illustrate this mechanism with an example. Modify the print_today program code as follows:

```
vrb h_page text
vrb h_cb   text
vrb h_hb   text
"initialization of the development environment
call XWD_META.INIT
```

```
"attach the FIRST.DB database
call XWD_ATTACHDB('first')

"get the handle for the newly created page
h_page = xwd_apppg.create('htp.print' -
     joinchars('Today: ', convert(today text '<dd>.<mm>.<yy>'), -
 '  Current Time: ', tod))

"create and customize the VIEW object
call XWD_VIEW.CREATE('JAVATABLE', 'sales;COMMAS=NO;DECIMALS=0 -
profit;COMMAS=NO;DECIMALS=1', 'month', 'product', -
'MEASURES\nregion', NA, NA, h_page)

"create and insert the CODEBLOCK object
h_cb = XWD_CREATE('CODEBLOCK', h_page)
call XWD_SETPROPVALT(h_cb, 'PRGTEXT', pgm_logo )

"create and insert the HTMLBLOCK object
h_hb = XWD_CREATE('HTMLBLOCK', h_page)
call XWD_SETPROPVALT(h_hb, 'HTMLSOURCE', html_logo )
```

After initializing the development environment and opening our database, this application creates a new Web page. It then inserts the JAVATABLE object into the newly created page. The next object that is inserted into the page is the block of code. After this, we assign the Express language code contained in the text variable named pgm_logo to the PRGTEXT property of this object:

```
call htp.header('3','Based on the Oracle Express OLAP')
```

Similarly, we create and insert into the page the HTMLBLOCK object, which by its HTMLBLOCK property is related to the html_logo text variable that contains HTML code:

```
<A HREF="http://www.oracle.ru/pub/prod_serv/products/olap/express/ -
index.html">
<IMG SRC="/workshop/oracle_logo.gif" HEIGHT="21" WIDTH="150"
BORDER="0" ALIGN="left" ALT="Oracle">
</A>
```

Notice that the path to the file containing the Oracle logo is specified in relation to the virtual workshop directory created earlier. It is not recommended that you specify the actual path to resources due to potential problems with porting.

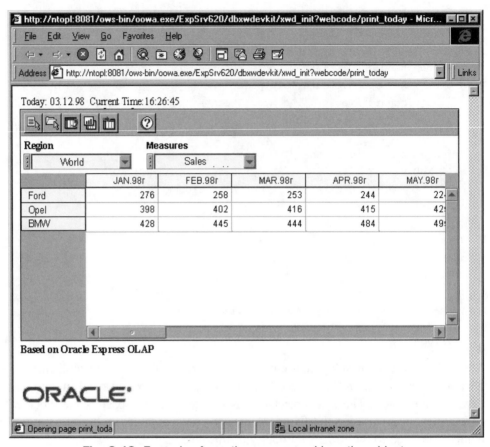

Fig. 8.18. Example of creating a page and inserting objects

Now, if you start the application using a Web browser, you'll see a result similar to the one shown in Fig. 8.18.

8.5.2. Using Templates

In *Section 8.3* we partially covered using templates when creating HTML documents. In this section we are going to discuss templates in more detail. Once again, let's use a practical example to illustrate the sequence of steps when creating a Web application using HTML templates. Suppose that we want to create an HTML document that contains two views of multidimensional data from our FIRST.DB database. Taking into consideration the quality of the design, let's place these views into an HTML table. The final view of our page is presented in Fig. 8.18.

Step 1. Application Initialization Program

We should start creating a program that would initialize the development environment, customize the specific settings of our Express session, and create an HTML page based on the template. Let's call this program "start". Its code will be as follows:

```
OOWA_CLOSE_PROC = 'close_proc'
call xwd_meta.init
database attach first ro
set_mname
call xwd_settmppath('c:/orant/olap/oes620/owa200/sample')
call xwd_tmppg.create('pg_tmp.html')
```

Step 2. Creating the Template

Using any text editor (Notepad, for example), create the following HTML document template:

```
<html>
<head>
<title>Express test 2.0</title>
</head>
<body>
<center>
<h2>Tempalte usage in Web application development</h2>
<table width=100% >
<tr>
<td align=center>
<h3>View for sales manager </h3>
<!--EXPRESS VIEW
call view_sales
-->
</td>
<td align=center>
<h3>View for regional manager</h3>
<!--EXPRESS VIEW
call view_profit
-->
</td>
</tr>
```

```
</table>
</center>
<hr>
<!--EXPRESS
call HTP.ANCHOR(xwd_urlclose,'Close the session')
-->
</body>
</html>
```

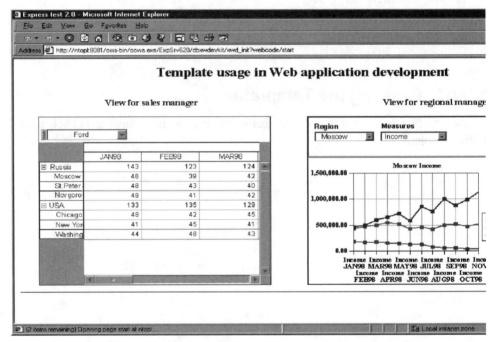

Fig. 8.19. Using two views within a single document

Notice that the text uses two types of specially formatted comments:

```
<!--EXPRESS VIEW
...
-->
```

and

```
<!--EXPRESS
...
-->
```

The Express commands that create data views (in our case these are the calls to the `view_sales` and `view_profit` programs) must be enclosed by comments of the first type. All other Express commands are enclosed by comments of the second type. As before, the URL for closing the Express session is generated by calling the `HTP.ANCHOR(xwd_urlclose, 'Close the session')` function.

Step 3. Creating Data Views

In our example, data views are created using programs that provide for flexibly adjusting the sales table and profit graph in the browser window.

The `view_sales` program used to create the table contains the following code:

```
vrb h_view text
limit month to first 12
call xp_sllimit('region', 'level', 'SELECT', 'STANDARD', 'L2')
h_view = xwd_VIEW.create('JAVATABLE', 'sales;COMMAS=NO;DECIMALS=0', -
'month', 'region', 'product', NA, 'table1')
call xwd_setpropvali(h_view, 'RECTHEIGHT', 5000)
call xwd_setpropvali(h_view, 'RECTWIDTH', 6000)
call xwd_setpropvalb(h_view, 'ENABLETOOLBAR', NO)
```

Notice that, along with the limit command, this code uses the `xp_sllimit` function, which provides more convenient capabilities of using the metadata of the dimension we are going to define (in our case these are hierarchical levels of the region dimension).

The second program, `view_profit`, creates the graph data view and contains the following code:

```
vrb h_view text
call xp_sllimit('region', 'all', 'SELECT','NONE')
h_view = xwd_VIEW.create('JAVAGRAPH', 'profit', -
           'month', 'product', 'MEASURES\nregion', NA, 'graph1')
call xwd_setpropvali(h_view, 'RECTHEIGHT', 5000)
call xwd_setpropvali(h_view, 'RECTWIDTH', 6000)
call XWD_SETPROPVALI(h_view, 'VIEWTYPE', -
xwc_value(xwt_msgid 'XWC_GT.LINE_ABSOLUTE'))
call xwd_setpropvalb(h_view, 'ENABLETOOLBAR', NO)
```

Step 4. Starting a Web Application

Now, if you have saved all the programs in the database, and then saved the database itself on the hard disk, you are ready to view the newly created application in the Web browser window. To do so, specify the following URL in the address field of the browser:

```
http://<host>/ows-
bin/oowa.exe/ExpSrv620/dbxwdevkit/xwd_init?webcode/start
```

As a result, the Web browser windows will display the HTML page shown in Fig. 8.19.

8.6. Using Java for Creating Multidimensional Data Views

The Oracle Express OLAP product line serves as an instrument for creating analytical Decision Support Systems. Even if the development toolkit is sufficient for today's tasks, each programmer pays special attention to the level of freedom they provide for implementing future ideas. For example, Oracle Express Web Agent currently allows you to use the table and Java graph types of multidimensional data views in Web applications. However, for applications intended for monitoring and managing physical processes, graphs representing smooth 3D surfaces over a specific field or isolines of the function determined by the data from multidimensional database may seem more appropriate. On the other hand, analysts investigating geographically distributed systems often need to represent a certain variable having the regional dimension as a geographical map, where specific regions are colored depending on the value of the measure under analysis. Or maybe a medical or biological investigator may need the selection instrument for selecting dimension values from a multidimensional database using a 3D picture of the human body with active points displayed on its surface. Needless to say, there is but little hope that all end-user requirements will ever be covered within one software product.

The aim of this chapter is to provide the reader with the information required for using the Java programming language to develop end-user Web applications based on Oracle Express. Having inherited most of C++'s advantages, Java also provides additional ones. This makes the Java language a most promising development tool, allowing you to design and develop applications of any complexity level. Using Java, the programmer can create applets that the Web browser will load from the server and execute on the client computer. The applet can bypass the browser and establish a direct connection to the Oracle Express server, retrieve the data from a multidimensional database, and start any procedure stored on the server.

8.6.1. Installing and Configuring the Software

Though all the required software and databases will reside on the server, experience shows that the client computer is the most appropriate place for development and debugging of client/server applications. For this purpose, the following software must be installed on the client computer

❏   Windows 95 or Windows NT operating system

❏   Oracle Express Administrator

❏   Tools for developing Java applets, such as JDK1.1.5 (or higher)

❏   Web browser, for example, Internet Explorer 4.0 with ServicePack1 (or higher)

Certainly, it is possible to develop and debug a Web application on a computer that will act as both a server and a client. In this case, however, you can't provide the required level of testing, since the mechanism responsible for providing security when running applets downloaded from remote computer will be disabled in the Web browser. Therefore, you may encounter security-related errors when attempting to remotely run the applet that you have debugged on the server.

Let's look at Java development tools in more detail. Like with any other programming language, you need to use specialized software for creating Java applets. For example, this may be integrated development environments like Java Workshop from Sun Microsystems, Microsoft Visual J++, Jbuilder from Inprise corporation, or any development tool of your choice. However, we would like to avoid using any of these software products in our examples for the following two reasons. First, if you don't have that particular product, you would be unable to reproduce the examples under discussion. Also, the software code automatically generated when using these advanced software tools is too abundant, and this mass of code may prevent you from understanding the main concepts.

Because of these reasons, and not because it is easier to use, we have chosen to use the "pure" software tool for developing Java applets—Java Developer Kit (JDK), which often is the choice of experienced programmers. The latest versions of JDK can be downloaded directly from the Sun Web server (www.javasoft.com).

JDK for Windows 95/NT is provided as a self-extracting archive (for example, the jdk115-win32.exe file contains the JDK version 1.1.5 described here). After you extract this archive, the root directory will contain a folder named jdk1.1.5 and that includes the bin, demo, include, lib, and src subdirectories. For the JDK software to function normally, you must add the path, such as C:\jdk1.1.5\bin, of the PATH environment variable. To make sure that the installation was successful, use the applet viewer utility residing in the BIN subdirectory to open the example1.html file stored under C:\JDK1.1.5\DEMO\FRACTAL\1.1. To do so, start an MS-DOS session and enter the following commands at the command prompt:

```
>cd C:\JDK1.1.5\DEMO\FRACTAL\1.1
>appletviewer example1.html
```

It is advisable to make sure that your browser (Internet Explorer, for example) supports the installed JDK version. To check, open the same file using your browser. If you get an error message after starting the applet, then you'll most likely need to update the browser version. The required software can be downloaded from the Microsoft Web site (www.microsoft.com).

For creating the source code of Java files, you can use any standard text editor, such as Notepad.exe.

As we already mentioned, the applet being developed must reside on the server. When debugging the applet, you should create a special subdirectory, for example, ORACLE_HOME\OLAP\WORKSHOP, where ORACLE_HOME is the name of the directory where you have installed the Oracle software. When configuring the Oracle Web Server listener, you must describe this directory as a virtual directory named, for example, /WORKSHOP/. If you prefer to develop applets on the client workstation, then, for the sake of convenience, it is advisable to map this directory as a network drive and make sure that you have write access to that directory.

8.6.2. Application Architecture

Like any other client/server software, our application will consist of two components (Fig. 8.20):

❏ The client-side component is the applet that the browser will download from the server and execute on the client computer

❏ The server-side software is the set of programs that will be stored in the multidimensional database named PWADDINS.DB on the Oracle Express server

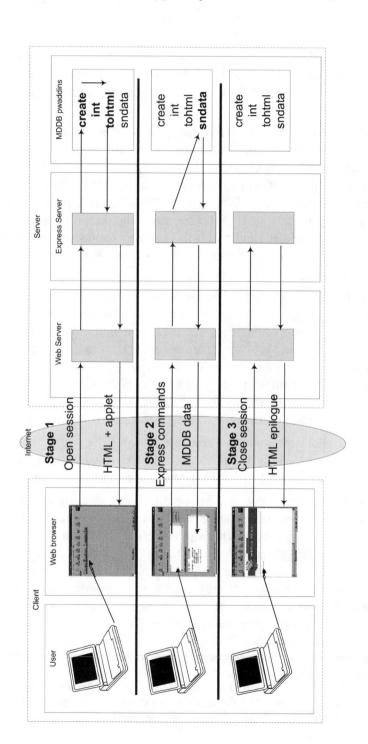

Fig. 8.20. The three stages of interaction between client-side browser and server when working with Java applet

According to the Add-In Views technology suggested by the Oracle corporation for developing an application similar to the one we are considering here, the process of interaction between the client browser and the server comprises the following three stages:

Stage 1. The Web browser sends an HTTP query to the Web server in order to initialize the Express Server session. The Express server initiates the session, opens the required database (the PWADDINS.DB database in our example), and starts the pw.xcmd.create[1] initialization program stored there, which initializes and creates the pw.xcmd software object. When the pw.xcmd.create program terminates, Express Web Agent generates an HTML page and calls the pw.xcmd.tohtml program, which inserts the applet handle with the required parameters into that page. The HTML page is then sent to the client browser via the Web server.

Stage 2. The browser receives the HTML page, then loads, initializes, and starts the built-in applet. The user enters Express Server commands in the input field and clicks the **Execute** button. The applet creates a connection to the Web server and sends it the HTTP query containing the user commands. Web server calls the pw.xcmd.sndata via Express Web Agent, and passes the string containing the user commands to it as a parameter. The result of executing commands is sent to the applet that runs at the client computer via Express Web Agent and Web server. The applet receives the result and displays it in the result window. The user then can enter new commands, and the process described above is repeated.

Stage 3. The user clicks the applet's **Terminate** button. The applet then sends a special HTTP query, according to which Express Web Agent closes the current Express Server session and sends the HTML termination page to the browser.

Finally, it should be pointed out that despite the fact that currently there is no specialized Java development environment for Express (a Web analogue of the Express Objects product), the Oracle Express product line is open to using Java technologies, and enables the programmer to create a Web application of any complexity level. The Java programming technology in Express applications will be illustrated by a practical example of creating the xCommander Java applet. This applet represents an Internet analog of the Express Commands tool intended for database administration and application debugging.

---

[1] Here we follow the naming convention according to which the names of the programs stored in the Express database are prefixed by the abbreviated name of the developer (in our case, the pw prefix is the abbreviated name of the Price Waterhouse company), the name itself is the abbreviated name of the application (xcmd is an abbreviated form of the xCommander name), and the suffix is the mnemonic name of the program.

Chapter 9

Real-World Examples

9.1. Simulation of Competition in a Limited Market

Starting in the early 60s, computerized simulation has become a widely used tool of analyzing complex economic systems—machine experiments based on mathematical models that describe the behavior of a complex system during a specified or calculated time period. Most leading US corporations, such as Xerox, Sun Microsystems, Standard Oil, Philadelphia Electronics, IBM, and others use simulation models for their purposes. At the same time, because of the competition, the results of these calculations, including the data on mathematical models, parameter classification, and working hypotheses, are practically unknown outside these corporations.

An adequate economic model of market activity under the modern conditions of uncertainty enables top management and executives of the firm to:

❐ Investigate and compare the efficiency of different long-term competition strategies

❐ Analyze the possible consequences of alternate management decisions

❐ Diagnose unfavorable trends and predict possible complications and problems

❐ Study the consequences of the likely changes in external conditions

❐ Develop intuitive skills for making management decisions under conditions of uncertainty

❐ Analyze the business skills and qualification level of personnel

In the current chapter, we will discuss the functional capabilities of the Oracle Express product line that enable us to use it as a tool for economic modeling.

9.1.1. Main Requirements for the Model

Multiple Functionality

The model must allow the investigator to perform simulation experiments using the following modes:

❐ *Prognostic mode*, when the investigator tests specific management decisions for the set of all possible external factors and variations of competitive management. Probabilistic evaluations, consisting of searching for and evaluating the most likely and the most unfavorable result.

❏ *Strategic investigations.* One or more teams determine the most important strategic decisions, while the operational management of other competing firms is determined by machine imitators, according to the selected strategic purposes.

❏ *Gaming approach,* when operational and strategic management implementation is determined by several teams of professionals. Each team is "playing" for one of the competing firms. This approach must provide the mediators with the ability to interfere in the management of external factors. Some (or all) of the players may be replaced by "dummies" (simulation models of the firms' management activity).

❏ *Diagnostic.* Analysis and detection of the reasons for the unfavorable phenomena that actually take place.

Representativity

To be useful, the model must be representative and include the key components of the economic system being modeled: *main components, determining factors, required controlling actions, condition variables,* and *their interrelationships.*

In the most common situation, the main components of the economic system include:

❏ The firm's activity in the selected field of economics

❏ The consumer market of a specific branch

❏ Raw product markets

❏ Transportation markets

❏ Financial markets

❏ Labor market

The main factors of the model are as follows:

❏ National production trends

❏ Social trends

❏ Demographic trends

❏ Inflation trends

❏ Legal trends (tax rates, custom rates, etc.)

❏ Unexpected situations (emergencies, penalties, strikes, defaults, etc.)

❏ Other factors

The economic unit being modeled (the firm or company) must be capable of defining the values of the following managing factors:

☐ Price of, amount of, and markets for the raw product (materials)

☐ Price of, amount of, and markets for the final product

☐ Increase/decrease in the production rate

☐ Hiring/firing employees

☐ Salary expenses

☐ Expenses for scientific investigation

☐ Expenses for promotion

☐ Expenses for market research

☐ Trade expenses

☐ Expenses for personnel training

☐ Corporate expenses, compensation payments

☐ Other expenses

The main *status variables* of the model must include:

☐ The demand for the product

☐ Sales amount

☐ Market segment

☐ Total revenue

☐ Raw product in stock

☐ Ready product in stock

☐ Production output

☐ Depreciation

☐ Taxes

☐ Production expenses

☐ Financial assets

☐ Credit payments

☐ Efficient trading expenses

❑   Efficient expenses for scientific investigation

❑   Other

The modeling algorithms must describe the following relationships:

❑   The influence of the following factors on the total consumer demand and on the demand for the particular firm's product:

  ❑   "External" factors

  ❑   Prices for retail products

  ❑   Promotional expenses

  ❑   Trading expenses

  ❑   Expenses for scientific investigations

  ❑   Other

❑   The influence of the following factors on labor efficiency:

  ❑   "External" factors

  ❑   Salary

  ❑   Educational expenses

  ❑   Other

Availability

The model must allow you to become acquainted with the modeling technology and prepare and perform simulation experiments within an acceptable time period. The model must have an intuitive user-friendly interface and allow the usage of lexical variables such as "increase", "significantly increase", "increase to maximum", "increase rather than decrease", etc. when specifying the initial data values.

Capabilities of Performing Parametric Analysis

When performing simulation experiments, the model must provide a sufficient set of parameters and initial states of the modeling algorithms required for shaping the model according to actual, real-world data.

Open Capabilities

Capabilities should be included for improving the model in accordance with the changing conditions of the firm's activity or for detecting new influential factors.

9.1.2. Model Description

You can fully evaluate the capabilities of Oracle Express as a tool of economic modeling only by implementing a full-scale model of a firm's economic activities, including a multidimensional database containing several gigabytes of information. In our case, the evaluation was performed on the basis of the simplified test model representing the Management economical model modification (Avalon Hill Company, Baltimore).

The Modeled Components

Economic activity of the firm. The firm's activity comprises monthly purchases of raw products on the market, and producing a certain amount of the product in existing factories. The firm can process raw products in two types of factories: normal and automated.

Raw product market. Once per month, the suggested number of raw product units and minimum purchase price are declared. Each firm provides a request for the desired quantity of raw product units and the purchase price it is ready to pay for each unit (no less than the minimum allowed on the market). The firms' requests are satisfied according to price, in descending order.

Buyer's market. Once per month, the quantity of product units and the maximum possible purchase price are declared. Each firm provides a request for purchasing a specific quantity of the product units and the price (no higher than the maximum) for which it is ready to sell each unit. The firms' requests are satisfied in ascending order according to price, starting with the minimum.

Service travel market. This market is modeled as an arbitrary stream of events—transportation crises. The firm afflicted by a transportation crisis (it is supposed that the manufacturers are located in different geographical areas) is unable to purchase raw products and sell its the products for the current month.

Financial market. Each firm can obtain a credit at the bank for up to 50% of the cost of its real estate (the existing factories) at a certain monthly interest. New credit can be obtained only when the previous one is completely paid off. Short-term credit is credit for 4 months at an interest of 1—2% per month.

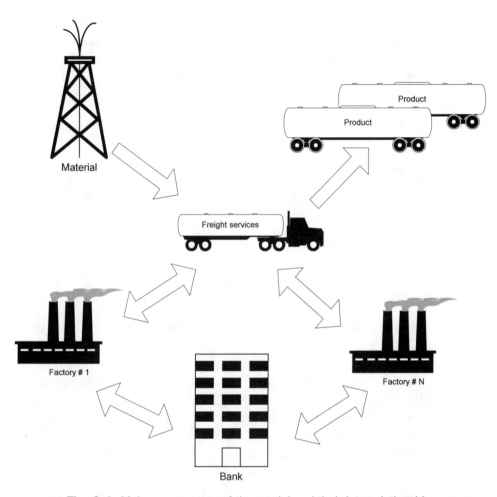

Fig. 9.1. Main components of the model and their interrelationships

Key Factors

National production trends. The supply and demand in the markets are determined depending on the general situation of the national economy (optional), which can be growing, stable, or weak.

Social. Social factors are modeled as an arbitrary stream of events—strikes. The firm afflicted with a strike can stop production for an indefinite time period (3 months average), or increase production costs by 10% (optional) until the end of the game.

Law. Each firm pays $300 for each unit not processed in the current month, $500 for each available product unit not sold during the current month, $1,000 tax for each normal factory and $1,500 for each automated factory. These payments are constant and don't depend on the amount of production (constant costs).

Emergency tax. Firms afflicted by this tax pay P% tax (optional) of the existing assets.

Unexpected events:

❏ Emergency in the factory—the factory doesn't produce any finished products this month

❏ Production improvement—the firm affected by this event decreases production cost by P%

Controls

Price and quantity of the raw product units purchased during the current month.

Price and quantity of the finished product units sold during the current month.

Production. Each firm decides how many units of finished products each of the factories will produce for the current month. The number of units of the finished product produced can't exceed the number of raw product units available. A normal factory can process one raw product unit per month at a cost of $2,000. An automated factory can do the same thing, or process two raw product units at a cost of $3,000.

Growth/decrease in production. Each firm can build factories. The process of building a normal factory lasts 5 months and costs $5,000. Building an automated factory costs $10,000 and lasts for 7 months. A normal factory can be upgraded to an automated one. Reconstruction costs $7,000 and lasts for 9 months, but during the entire reconstruction period the factory can still function as a normal one. Half of the factory cost must be paid before starting the construction, while the second half must be paid within a month before the factory starts to function.

The firm can temporarily close any of its factories. Starting from the next month, the constant production costs for the closed factory will be halved. The firm can re-open the closed factory, and it will start functioning in 2 months.

Modeling Algorithms

The demand for the finished product and the supply of the raw product is modeled as a Markovian process with five (optional) states. Market transition from state to state is defined by the $P_{n, m}$ probability matrix, which defines the probability of transition from state n to state m. Besides this, for the specific market state, the amounts of purchases and sales, along with the minimum price of the raw product unit and the maximum price of the finished product unit, are determined according to the state of the national economy (see above).

Arbitrary events (strikes, transportation crises, emergency taxes, etc.) are modeled as Poisson processes uniquely defined by the average time interval (optional) between events.

Although this model is too simplistic and doesn't reflect the situation in any real area of production, it is sufficiently representative. As can be seen from the description, by selecting a large number of parameters (options) this model can be adequately suited to fit real economic data.

9.1.3. Plan for Implementing the Model Using Oracle Express

First, let's create a multidimensional database:

```
-> database create business
```

The key elements of the multidimensional database are dimensions that determine the space within which the model variable will change. Let's define the main dimensions:

```
-> define month dimension month
-> ld Simulation time with 1 month step
"Modeling interval" with increments of 1 month

-> define owner dimension id
-> ld Owners of business list
"List of participants
```

Now let's define the main variables of the model that will change with time and describe the status of each participant during the simulation:

```
-> define factory integer <time owner >
-> ld Current quantity of factory for each owner
```

```
"Current quantity of normal factories for each participant

-> define factory_a integer <time owner >
-> ld Current quantity of automatic factory for each owner
"Current quantity of automated factories owned by each participant

-> define product integer <time owner >
-> ld Current quantity of products for each owner
"Current number of available finished product units for each participant

-> define material integer <time owner >
-> ld Current quantity of materials for each owner
"Current number of raw product units for each participant
```

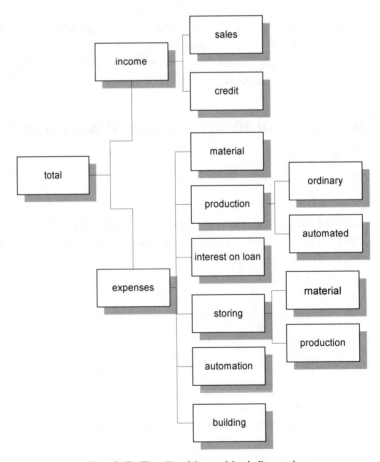

Fig. 9.2. The *line* hierarchical dimension

Introducing another hierarchical dimension—line—will enable us to reflect the structure of current income and expenses more illustratively (Fig. 9.2). It will provide the capability of analyzing with the required drilling level both our own financial status and that of the competitors using the relations and data aggregation mechanisms available in Oracle Express.

The current financial state of the participants will be evaluated by the cash variable:

```
-> define cash decimal <time owner line>
-> ld Current cash for each owner
"Current cash for each participant
```

According to the model description, it would be useful to introduce another dimension—state—by which we will distinguish the planned requests for purchase of raw products and the sales of the finished products from actual contracts:

```
-> define state dimension id
-> ld Plan/fact state
"Planned and actual contracts
```

The current state of the market will be described by requests for raw product sales and purchase of the finished products:

```
-> define m.sales integer <time state>
-> ld Plan/fact quantity of materials for sales
"Planned and actual sales of raw products


-> define m.purch integer <time state>
-> ld Plan/fact quantity of products for purchases
"Planned and actual amount of purchase of finished products


-> define m.sales_price decimal <time state>
-> ld Minimal/fact(average) price of materials for sales
"Minimum and actual (average) sales price for raw products


-> define m.purch_price decimal <time state>
-> ld Maximal/fact(average) price of products for purchases
"Minimum and actual (average) price of finished products
```

Interaction of the participants with the of raw product and finished product markets will be described by the following variables:

```
-> define o.sales integer <time owner state>
```

```
-> ld Plan/fact quantity of product sales
"Planned and actual quantity of finished product sales

-> define o.purch integer <time owner state >
-> ld Plan/fact quantity of materials purchases
"Planned and actual amount of raw product purchases

-> define o.sales_price decimal <time owner>
-> ld Price of products sales
"Planned sales price for the finished products

-> define o.purch_price decimal <time owner>
-> ld Price of products for purchases
"Planned price of raw product purchase
```

The variables describing participant requests for production, credit, and building and reconstruction of factories are described in a similar way. The constants and parameters (options) of the model are specified as normal dimensionless variables. Certainly, it is useful to define auxiliary dimensions such as `quarter` and `year` that are related to the `month` dimension by the required relationships. This hierarchy will enable you to analyze historical data more efficiently.

The main components of the model are stored in the database as the following programs:

- `setup`—model setup and initialization of the modeling variables
- `step`—the main modeling program, which sequentially starts subroutines
- `get_request`—the module responsible for processing requests
- `sales`—sales of the finished product according to the supply
- `credit`—credit servicing
- `building`—processing requests for building and reconstructing factories
- `product_tax`—payment for storage of unsold products
- `purchase`—purchase of raw products according to the supply
- `manufacturing`—product manufacturing
- `realty_tax`—real estate tax
- `material_tax`—payment for storage of the raw products

❑ event—modeling of arbitrary events (crises, strikes, etc.)

❑ balance—calculation of the current financial state of participants

❑ send_request—calculation of the states of the markets, sending requests for purchasing finished products and raw material sales

❑ destroy—model epilogue

Implementation of the above listed programs using the Express language is not a difficult task. As an illustration of the efficiency and elegance of multidimensional operations, let's look at the product_tax program:

```
"Payment for storage of unsold products

cash(line product_tax) = cash(line product_tax) - tax.product * product
```

It is suggested that the settings for the current step are set in the step main module:

```
limit time to cur_step "consider the current step only

limit owner to cash(line total) gt 0 "only creditable participants
```

Here the cur_step is a dimensionless variable specifying the current modeling step, and tax.product is the multidimensional variable determining the current value of the monthly payment for storing unsold products for each participant.

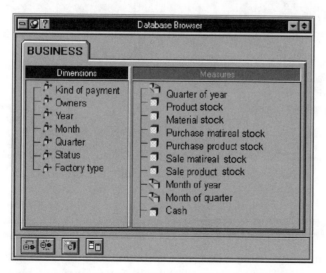

Fig. 9.3. Dimensions, relations, and variables of the multidimensional BUSINESS database

Developing the player program is a less trivial task. To implement such a program, it is preferable to use the Express Object development environment. This software product is a visual object-oriented development environment supporting the required object mechanisms and the Express Basic programming language. The standard objects enable the developer to use any MS Windows interface components, as well as all the power of *tables* and *graphs*. Tables and graphs not only display multidimensional information in a format easily readable by the end user, but also enable end users to flexibly manipulate both the screen representation of data and the informational content of the displayed data (including the time series prediction). This is the key requirement for on-line data analysis when making a business decision. Due to this fact, the main difficulty is development of the "dummy"—the machine imitator of a player. This task is purely algorithmic and is not dependent on a specific programming environment.

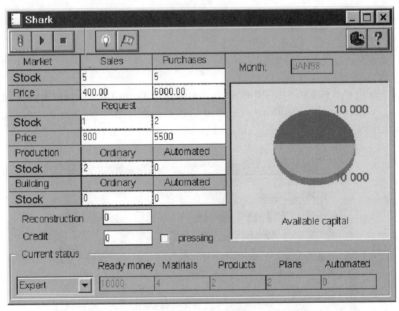

Fig. 9.4. The end-user interface implemented using Express Objects

9.1.4. Analyzing Experience

Implementation of the above-described variation of the economic model using Oracle Express took about one month. A multidimensional data view allowed us to simply and naturally describe the modeled space. The Express programming language has proven to be a powerful tool for manipulating data arrays containing all the necessary constructs required for efficiently implementing modeling algorithms. Express Objects enabled us to implement the end user interface (Fig. 9.4) that meets all the modern requirements of the MS Windows operating system. Support of the client/server technology allowed for easy implementation of the interaction between participants working at different workstations. Furthermore, the client/server technology allowed us to increase the number of players (clients) that function using different algorithms, and to manage their competition without influencing the database residing on the server. The ability to flexibly manipulate the on-screen data view and content of the displayed information can be appreciated by the professional business analyst (Fig. 9.4).

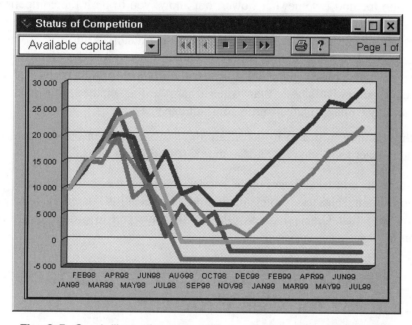

Fig. 9.5. Graph illustrating competition under conditions of oligopoly

Even this very simple economic model helped us draw important conclusions (from the point of view of the persons who are not business management professionals). First, the simulator was implemented based on the *"fair competition"* strategy, which is based on the assumption that each participant wants to make the maximum amount of profit. Management was performed according to the average market prices of the materials and finished products. This algorithm does the job adequately if the number of participants is 5 or more (oligopoly). However, after two or three games under conditions of a dual monopoly (two competitors), at least two methods of drawing the competitor to bankruptcy could be easily found (certainly this is obvious for business professionals).

The first method is much faster than the second, but it only works under conditions of aggressive competition on the finished products market, when the number of purchased units of the finished products is less than the number of the finished products owned by the market participants. This method is selling the products at dumping prices (perhaps, even at a loss). This allows us to lock the sales of the competitors and make them suffer a monthly loss related to constant expenses and payments for storing the finished products.

The second method is somewhat slower, but allows you to push the competitor out of the market regardless of the current state of the market. This method involves "cutting off the air supply", which means purchasing materials and raw products for exorbitant prices (perhaps, even suffering a loss). This makes the competitor stop production, and, consequently, sales. Thus, the competitor will be pushed out of the market, somewhat slower than when using the first method, due to the constant monthly damage related to the constant expenses.

After the "dummy" was able to detect an aggressive strategy of the competitor and adequately react to it, the program became a stronger opponent.

Developing a non-trivial economic model must be the result of serious cooperation among business professionals and IT specialists. Based on experience, one can hope that Oracle Express OLAP will allow you to produce an efficient solution for this task.

9.2. The *xCommander* Applet—Interface to Express for Web Browser

According to the Web application development schema considered in the previous chapter, we need to develop the following software:

Working location	Name	Description
Client (Java applet)	Constructor of the `xCommander()` applet	Creates and initializes the interface objects, such as input/ output window, buttons, labels, etc.

continues

Continued

Working location	Name	Description
	Overridden method of the standard `ActionListener` interface `actionPerformed(Action Event e)`	Handles button clicking events
	The `execute()` method	Reads and processes commands from the input window, creates and sends the required HTTP query, receives the answer from the server, and places it in the result field
	The `close()` method	Creates and sends an HTTP query for closing the Express server session
Server (programs stored in the Express multidimensional database)	`pw.xcmd.create`	Initializes a session and creates the Add-In object
	`pw.xcmd.init`	Initializes the Add-In object
	`pw.xcmd.tohtml`	Generates an HTML page with the `xCommander` applet handle
	`pw.xcmd.sndata`	Receives and executes user commands, formulates an answer

9.2.1. Creating a Java Applet

A detailed description of the required Java programming basics is outside the range of a single chapter. The interested reader can easily find all the required information in any book on Java. To create our applet, we will use the following Java classes: `Applet`, `FlowLayout`, `GridLayout`, `Font`, `Label`, `TextArea`, `Panel`, `Button`, `StringTokenizer`, `URL` and `URLConnection`, along with the `ActionListener` interface. Although there are a lot of classes, for our purposes it is only required that you have a general idea of the data and methods of these objects.

Open the Notepad.exe text editor and create a new file named `xCommander` with the Java filename extension. Note that the filename must exactly coincide with the class name. To give the compiler access to the listed standard language objects, specify the import statements in the starting lines of the files. These import statements must specify the required packages of Java classes (see the Listing). The title of our class specifies that it is an extension of the standard `Applet` class, and implements the `ActionListener` interface for handling button-clicking events.

The variable of the `prefixURL` class must contain the prefix of the URL address corresponding to the address of your server and the port number assigned to Web listener servicing the Express Web Agent (the value of `http://www.pw.com:8081` is provided in the list only as an example to illustrate the syntax).

When creating the user interface of the `xCommander` applet, let us take the interface implemented in the Express Command standard tool as a prototype. It consists of two text fields, appropriate labels, and the **Execute**, **Clear**, and **Close** buttons (implementation of the **Help** button will be left for future enhancements of the applet). In the `xCommander` class constructor, the new operator is used to create all the required interface elements one by one. The newly created interface elements are added to the applet panel using the add method. Additional objects, such as `Panel`, `FlowLayout`, `GridLayout`, and `Font` are used to enhance the applet interface. Calling the `addActionListener(this)` method of the `Button` class informs the current instance that the click event will be performed by the `actionPerformed` method of the `xCommander` class.

You can start debugging immediately after writing the constructor. Compile the applet by running the following command from the MS-DOS command prompt:

```
>javac xCommander.java
```

If the compiler does its job successfully and the compilation process completes without errors, the working directory will contain a file named `xCommander.class` that contains the byte-code of the applet. In the same directory, create a file named XCMDTEST.HTML that should contain the test HTML page:

```
<html>
    <head>
    <title>Express Commander</title>
    </head>
    <body >
<h3>Express Commander</h3>
<applet
    code=xCommander.class
            name=xCommander
```

```
            width=470
            height=360>
</applet>
</body>
</html>
```

Open this file using the Web browser. The browser window must display an applet similar to the one shown in Fig. 9.6.

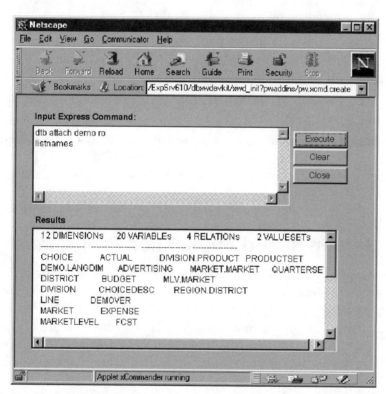

Fig. 9.6. The interface of the xCommander applet. The user has opened the connection to the demo database and retrieved the list of its stored objects

The code of other methods is quite simple and can be easily understood by readers who have at least a general understanding of Java. Some difficulties can be caused by certain lines in the execute method's code (these lines are in bold) concerning certain features of our application.

In the first code fragment, all the blanks in the user command line are replaced with the $ character, and all new line characters are replaced with two backslashes

(\ ) followed by n. The necessity to do so manifests itself when debugging the application, since the blank character in the line terminates it when transferring it as a parameter to the pw.xcmd.sndata program stored in the Express multidimensional database. The replacement of the new line characters is necessitated by the syntax of the PROGRAM command of the Express language.

The second highlighted fragment of code (from the "pw.xcmd.signature" substring included into the start of message by the pw.xcmd.sndata program) trims the service information added by Express Web Agent.

Notice that the xCommander applet must receive sndataURL and closeURL as its parameters, which are required for closing URL queries to the pw.xcmd.sndata program and to the program that closes the Express session.

When debugging the applet, it is recommended that you use the built-in Java console of the Netscape Communicator browser. This console is available from the **Communicator/Java Console** menu. Also note that if you click the **Reload** button in Netscape Communicator, you'll only reload the HTML page. To reload the applet after updating its byte-code, click the **Reload** button while pressing the <Shift> key.

9.2.2. Server-Based Application Programs

The second part of our application comprises the programs that must reside in the special Express database stored on the server in the predefined Express Web Agent directory: *ORACLE_HOME*\OLAP\OES610\OWA121\ADDINS (directory names depend on the version of the installed software). The database name is arbitrary; we have used the PWADDINS.DB database in our example. When creating the database and writing the program code, you can use the Express Administrator utility.

The first program, pw.xcmd.init, consists of only two lines of code:

```
call xwd_addtype('pw.xcmd', 'OBJECT')
call xwd_addhandler('pw.xcmd', 'TOHTML', 'pw.xcmd.tohtml')
```

This program is intended for registering our object and its method named pw.xcmd.tohtm. The code of the pw.xcmd.tohtm program is provided below:

```
call htp.appletopen('xCommander.class','/workshop/java/pwaddins/', 360, 470, 10, 0, 'left')
call htp.appletparam('sndataURL', joinchars(oowa_prefix, 'pw.xcmd.sndata'))
```

```
call htp.appletparam('closeURL', xwd_urlclose)
call htp.appletclose
return true
```

This program creates the applet handle. Descriptions of the parameters of the called functions are provided in the Express Web Agent on-line help system. Pay special attention to certain specific features. The `/workshop/java/pwaddins/'` string defines the value of the handle parameter of the CODBASE applet. Here, /workshop/ is the name of the virtual directory that we defined earlier when configuring Web listener, while the java/pwaddins/ path specifies the subdirectory of our virtual directory, where the byte-code of the newly created applet should be placed (the xCommander.class file). OWA_PREFIX is the standard text variable of the Express language. This variable contains the information necessary to create a correct HTTP query within the applet, provided that the UseCookie parameter of the Express Server is set to NO. This program will be called by Express Web Agent any time the instance of our Add-In object is created. As a result, an applet descriptor similar to the one shown below will be included into HTML page:

```
<APPLET CODE="xCommander.class" CODEBASE="/workshop/java/pwaddins/"
HEIGHT=360 WIDTH=470 HSPACE=10 VSPACE=0 ALIGN="left" >
<PARAM NAME="sndataURL" VALUE="/
ows-bin/oowa/ExpSrv610/WS0000001441D9/pw.xcmd.sndata">
<PARAM NAME="closeURL" VALUE="/
ows-bin/oowa/ExpSrv610/WS0000001441D9/close">
</APPLET>
```

The code of the pw.xcmd.sndata program is provided below:

```
arg comm text
trap on error
call htp.print('Content-type: text/html\n')
comm = CHANGECHARS(comm '$' ' ')
define pw.tmppgm program database pwaddins
call htp.prn('pw.xcmd.signature')
call pw.tmppgm
delete pw.tmppgm database pwaddins
return true
error:
delete pw.tmppgm database pwaddins
return false
```

This code changes the $ characters into blanks in the command line received from the applet and creates the pw.tmppgm temporary program based on user commands and deletes it after execution. All system output generated by the program will be returned to the applet as a reply to the HTTP query of the execute method. The HTTP protocol requires that the first line in the output stream be the `'Content-type: text/html`, followed by an empty row. The `'pw.xcmd.signature'` string is a keyword by which the applet will filter the service information.

The fact that the commands comprise a temporary program enables the user not only to execute any Express commands, but also include into his or her query any local variables and arbitrary Express Language constructs, such as DO, FOR, IF ... THEN ... ELSE, and others. This significantly enhances the functionality of your application.

The final program is as follows:

```
vrb _success boolean
vrb hpg text
trap on error
"Check to see if the metadata databases initialize
_success = xwd_meta.init
if not _success
  then goto error
call xwd_addin.init('pw.xcmd','pwaddins','pw.xcmd.init')
hpg = xwd_page.create
call xwd_create('pw.xcmd' hpg)
error:
return
```

This program initiates the Express session and the pw.xcmd program object contained in the pwaddins.db multidimensional database, creates an HTML page, and links the Add-In object instance to that page.

9.2.3. Usage of the *xCommander* Applet when Debugging Web Applications

Now that we have created both the client and server-side parts of our software, everything is ready for its usage when debugging Web applications for an Express multidimensional database. Create the xCommander.html file in the WORKSHOP directory:

```
<html>
<head>
```

```
<title>Start Express Commader</title>
</head>
<body>
<p><a href="http://www.pw.com:8081/
ows-bin/oowa/ExpSrv610/dbxwdevkit/xwd_init?pwaddins/pw.xcmd.create">
<h2>Start Express Commader</h2>
</a>
</body>
</html>
```

Note that the `www.pw.com:8081` string must be replaced according to the configuration of your network. Now start the browser and send the following URL query: `http://www.pw.com:8081/workshop/xCommander.html`. Having received the HTML page, follow the specified link: **Start Express Commader.** If all operations were successful, the applet will be loaded from the server and executed.

As we already mentioned, one of the most useful features of the `xCommander` applet lies in the fact that it allows you to control the current state of the specific Express session. As for our application, it must be created directly from the session where we plan to perform the debugging rather than from the `pw.xcmd.create` program that initiates its own session. This goal is achieved by simply adding the following code to one of the HTML templates generated by the application being debugged:

```
<!-- EXPRESS VIEW
call xwd_addin.init('pw.xcmd','pwaddins','pw.xcmd.init')
call xwd_view.create('pw.xcmd' 'fortune')
-->
```

The second parameter of the `call xwd_view.create` function defines an arbitrary variable available in the current session, since this parameter is a required one according to the syntax of this function.

You can improve the method of calling the applet. A more sophisticated method assumes that you place a link opening the applet rather than the applet itself in the new browser window on the HTML page of the debugged application (Fig. 9.7). However, this is not the only improvement that can be implemented in the application we are considering. For example, the `xCommander` class can be implemented as a Java Bean component that can be used by other applets for accessing the multidimensional database.

In the real applet that we used for debugging Web applications, we have enhanced the interface by adding the viewing function that provides the ability to view the data in table or graph form. Using this function, you can view any object stored in the database. Besides which, there is an analogue of the **Selector** tool available in Express Objects, along with some other enhancements. The limited volume of one chapter doesn't allow us to provide a detailed description of these enhancements. Hopefully, the example provided here illustrates the technology of using Java in Oracle Express, and allows the reader to reduce the time required for mastering this technology.

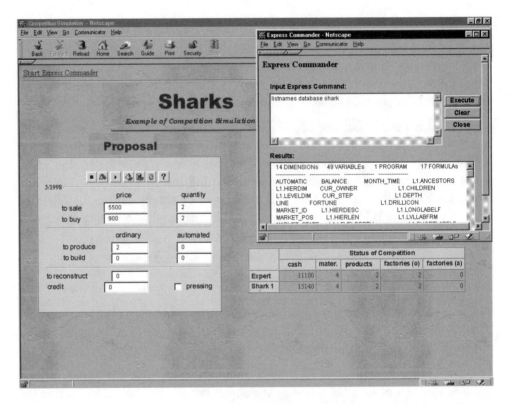

Fig. 9.7. An example of using the `xCommander` applet to debug the Web version of the competition simulation model implemented with Oracle Express

Finally, note that even despite the lack of a specialized Java development environment for Express applications (a Web analogue of Express Objects), the Oracle Express product line is still an open platform for using Java technology. It enables you to develop Web applications of any complexity level.

9.2.4. Listing of the *xCommander.java* File Containing the Applet Code

```java
import java.applet.*;
import java.awt.*;
import java.awt.event.*;
import java.net.*;
import java.util.StringTokenizer;
import java.io.*;


public class xCommander extends Applet implements ActionListener {
//variables
    private TextArea taCommand;
    private TextArea taResult:
private static String prefixURL = "http://www.pw.com:8081" ;
//====================================================
// methods
    public xCommander () {
            setBackground(Color.lightGray);
            setLayout(new FlowLayout(FlowLayout.LEFT));
            setFont(new Font("Helvetica",0,12));
            Label lb = new Label("Enter the Express command:");
            lb.setFont(new Font("Helvetica",Font.BOLD,12));
            add(lb);
            taCommand = new TextArea(6,50);
            taCommand.setBackground(Color.white);
            add(taCommand);
            Panel p1 = new Panel(new GridLayout(4,1,0,2));
            Button b1 = new Button("Execute");
            Button b2 = new Button("Clear");
            Button b3 = new Button("Close");
            b1.addActionListener(this);
            b2.addActionListener(this);
            b3.addActionListener(this);
            p1.add(b1);
            p1.add(b2);
            p1.add(b3);
            add(p1);
            lb = new Label("Command result:");
```

```
                lb.setFont(new Font("Helvetica",Font.BOLD,12));
                add(lb);
                taResult = new TextArea(10,60);
                taResult.setBackground(Color.white);
                taResult.setEditable(false);
                add(taResult);
        }
        //-----------------------------------------------------------------
        public void actionPerformed(ActionEvent e) {
                if (e.getActionCommand().equals("Execute")) {
                        execute();
                        return;
                }
                if (e.getActionCommand().equals("Clear")) {
                        taCommand.setText("");
                        taResult.setText("");
                        return;
                }
                if (e.getActionCommand().equals("Close")) {
                        close();
                        return;
                }
        }
        //-----------------------------------------------------------------
        void execute(){
                String command = taCommand.getText().replace(' ','$');
//replacing blanks with the $ character
                //replacing the new line character with two '|' followed
//by an 'n'
                StringTokenizer st = new StringTokenizer(command,"\n");
                String prm = "";
        while (st.hasMoreTokens())  prm = prm + st.nextToken() + "\\n";
                try {
        String sURL = prefixURL + getParameter("sndataURL") + "/" + prm;
                        URL url = new URL(sURL);
                        URLConnection con = null;
                        con = url.openConnection();
                        int len = con.getContentLength();
```

```
                    if (len>0){
                        StringBuffer buf = new StringBuffer (len);
                        InputStream in = con.getInputStream();
                        int i=0;
                        int ch;
        while (((ch = in.read()) != -1)&& (++i<=len)) buf.append((char)ch);
                        String text = new String(buf);
                        int ind = text.indexOf("pw.xcmd.signature");
    //search the key string
                        text = (ind>=0)? text.substring(ind+17) : text;
            //filtering the service information
                            taResult.setText(text);
                    } else {
                    taResult.setText("URL: \"" + sURL + "\" not answer");
                    }


            } catch ( Exception e) {
                    taResult.setText(e.getMessage());
            }
    }
    //-------------------------------------------------------------
    void close(){

            try {
getAppletContext().showDocument(new URL(prefixURL + getParameter("closeURL"))," top");
            } catch ( Exception e) {
                    taResult.setText(e.getMessage());
            }
    }
}//class xCommander
```

9.3. Express+Java+VRML = Regional Data Analysis System

We can observe the recent significant progress made in the field of developing decision support systems related to data warehousing technology and OLAP. The main feature of the OLAP technology is its orientation towards an intuitively abstract ("right-brained") mind that is responsible for decision making, rather than towards a logical one. Illustrative geometrical images related to the problem that has to be solved stimulate the creative mind, which results in discoveries even in such formal areas such as number theory.

Currently, the VRML language is the most powerful tool for computer graphics. The Virtual Reality Modeling Language (VRML) is the file format intended for describing 3D objects and worlds in the Internet/intranet (International Standard ISO/IEC 14772-1:1997, http://www.vrml.org/Specifications/VRML97/). From our point of view, the main achievement in this area lies in the fact that the new standard for this language (VRML97) enables the developer to create dynamically changing interactive 3D worlds. According to this standard, the developer can design virtual worlds displaying data that change with time and reside anywhere within Internet/intranet networks. Using the built-in mechanism of event generation and processing, the developer can create user interfaces of any sophistication level. This integration of the new and rapidly developing technologies of OLAP and VRML is not simply a fancy, but rather a necessity, opening new horizons (perhaps these horizons are not fully appreciated at the moment) in creating prospective Decision Support Systems. Neither small nor large business can be efficiently managed without such systems.

The main aim of this section is to illustrate the implementation of the OLAP system for geographically distributed data in a practical, real-world example, and to illustrate the role of the Java language in OLAP integration with VRML.

9.3.1. Analytical Processing System for Geographically Distributed Data

Currently, there are many examples illustrating the fact than one of the most important aspects of business is its distribution according to geographical location. This approach can be used, for example, for analyzing the activities of a bank and its affiliates, mining and processing minerals, regional economics, ecology, demography, government management, etc. According to OLAP terminology, you could say that the information being analyzed has a geographical dimension. Naturally, then, the analyst working with such information must be capable of using a geographical map in an analysis.

The most important requirement for such a system is the possibility of flexibly manipulating a map, such things as:

- Re-scaling the map

- Drilling capabilities by region, for example, according to the administrative or economic divisions

- Selecting capabilities using the mouse

- Selecting capabilities for regions according to logical conditions (for example, the capability to display the regions where bank assets have decreased by more than 10% in comparison with the previous month)

The capability of displaying the results of the analysis using the geographical map is the second important requirement for such systems. As a general rule, such a system must provide the ability to:

- Display the value of the specified variable by the fill color of the geographical region according to the specified range of values. For example, the application must be able to display a map where those regions for which income has gone down compared to the previous year are colored red, regions where income has increased by less than 10 % are yellow, and regions with an income growth of more than 10 % are green

- Display the value of a specified variable as a numeric value for each territory

- Display the value of the specified variable as a geometrical figure (for example, a cylinder, bar, or cone) for each territory

- Display the value of the specified variable as a level over a horizon

- Retrieve additional information for selected regions, to be presented in table or graph views

- Combine any of the above listed data display formats

Using these methods of displaying and representing information, the analyst can, for example, display bank assets for each region using 256 shades of grayscale, represent investment risks as red bars, and expected interest as green cylinders.

Since most measures of business activities have a time dimension, the capability of presenting time dynamics as a "cartoon" is very attractive. For example, one may produce a "cartoon" that shows the region's color and height changing with time. Analysts with experience in analyzing complicated information will appreciate the influence of such dynamic images on the intuitive mind.

As with any OLAP system, it is natural to have the ability to display not only data already stored in the database, but also to create the required variables on the spot. For example, it is very useful to calculate and display a specified functional (average, minimum, or maximum value of a specified time series), or formula, or the result of a "What if" analysis obtained using the business model stored in the database.

9.3.2. Application Architecture

According to modern trends of creating the informational systems, the system under consideration is based on "thin" client technology in Internet/intranet networks (Fig. 9.8).

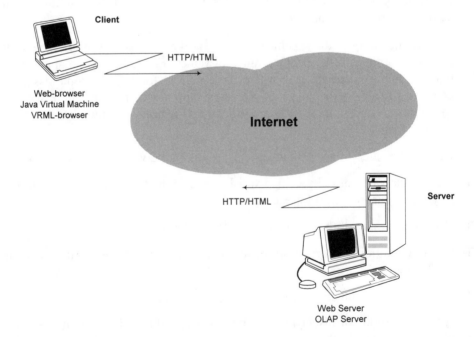

Fig. 9.8. The architecture of the system for performing analyses and processing geographically distributed data

The data warehouse located on the server side of the application accumulates retrospective geographically distributed data on business activity. The OLAP server provides for data selection and processing. The Web server accepts queries from the Web browser located on the client side and returns the requested data to it. The VRML browser is used for displaying and managing 3D informational views. The Java machine interprets the Java applet. The applet is loaded from the server and acts as a bridge connecting the OLAP server and the VRML world, and provides support for the interactive interface of the user, both with the data warehouse and with a 3D information display that has a geographical map in the background.

9.3.3. Development Tools

The system of processing and analysis of geographically distributed data is based on the OLAP server of multidimensional object-oriented data—Oracle Express Server (version 6.2). The server provides a built-in data manipulation language for processing multidimensional data—Express Language (4GL)—that provides capabilities of creating server logic of any complexity level—from simple statistic calculations to complex simulation models.

Oracle Application Server version 3.0, supplied with Oracle Express Web Agent (the component of the Oracle Express OLAP family), was used as the Web Server.

The Java applet was developed using the standard tools provided with the Java Developer's Kit (JDK) version 1.1.5. The latest version of this software can be downloaded from Sun Microsystems's website.

The client side of the application requires a Web browser that supports the required Java standard and VRML97. In the application under consideration, we are using Netscape Communicator 4.07, supplemented with JDK 1.1.5, as well as a built-in VRML browser, Cosmo Player 2.0 from Cosmo Software (Silicon Graphics Inc.).

The VRML browser from Cosmo Player has a built-in interface that provides the user with the ability to "travel" in the virtual world (Fig. 9.9). The user can fly in the 3D world, approach or move away from the objects under consideration, and fly in orbit over them. He can easily "Undo" several movements, "Redo" those movements, or go to any predefined observation point.

Fig. 9.9 shows the Netscape Communicator window. The upper part of the page contains the Cosmo Player window that recalls a view from an airplane. The "control panel" contains the controls providing the user with the tools that enable him or her to navigate in the 3D world (detailed information is provided in the Cosmo Player on-line Help system). If the user positions the mouse cursor over one of the regions, that region starts to glow from the inside.

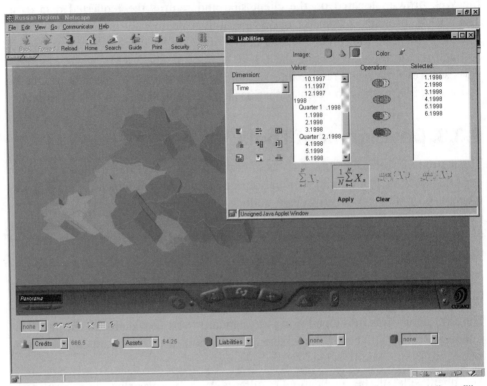

Fig. 9.9. Displaying business variables as a colored geographical map (gradient fill from green to red) and the height over the plane of the geometric view of the region

Below the Cosmo Player window there is the Java applet window, where the name of the selected (highlighted) region is displayed, along with the business variable values for that region. In this specific case, the illustration represents the region of Russia, for which we have the lowest prices for service (the region is colored green) and the highest profit (the height of the region over the horizon). Selection of the variables to be displayed is performed using lists containing all the variables from the multidimensional database that have the region dimension. The button opening the customization dialog for each region is located near each list. For example, if the variable has, besides the "region" and "time" dimensions, the "service type" dimension, the user can specify the service type he or she is interested in, or display the average (minimum, maximum, total) value for all types. Similarly, the user can display a predicted value for a specific variable for a specified date using one of the built-in prediction models available in the database.

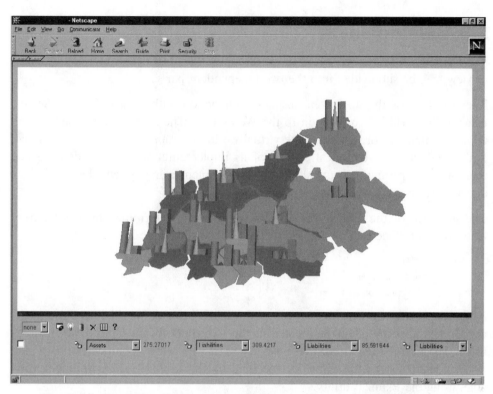

Fig. 9.10. Displaying the business variables as colored regions and heights of the geometric figures

The selected variables can be displayed for a time common to all regions (selected from the list at the upper left corner of the applet window). Time can be repre-sented dynamically as a set of sequential "frames" that display the selected business variables for the specific time interval with the specified time increment. The time for which the values of the selected variable is calculated can be specified individu-ally for each variable. For example, in Fig. 9.10, the color for each region repre-sents the value of the service cost averaged by time, the height of the yellow cylin-der specifies the profit gained from providing the service for the first half of last year, the height of the green cone specifies the profit for the same period of the current year, and the height of the blue bar shows the predicted value for the first 6 months of next year.

Naturally, the map legend, such as color palette, type, and color of the geometrical figures and other settings, can be customized and saved for use in future sessions.

9.3.4. Using Java

The "heart" of the application is the Java applet that, from the functionality point of view, can be subdivided into the two independent parts.

The first part of the applet encapsulates interaction with Oracle Express Server, using a direct HTTP connection to the Web server. The second component of the applet is intended for managing the virtual world and support of the user interface. Let's consider some technical aspects of its implementation in more detail, since there aren't very many practical examples of implementing systems based on Java and VRML interaction around.

The interface of the applet with the virtual world is determined by the External Authoring Interface (EAI) standard using the following three Java-packages:

```
vrml.external
vrml.external.field
vrml.external.exception
```

After you install the Cosmo Player v. 2.0 VRML browser, you'll find these packages in the npcosmop.zip file located in the \CosmoSoftware\CosmoPlayer directory. To make these packages available to the Java compiler, unzip the npcosmop.zip file to the directory specified by the CLASSPATH environment variable, using the Pkunzip utility.

The first thing that you need to do to install the Java applet/VRML interface is obtain the handle for that Java Browser class. This class encapsulates the virtual world. The Browser class interface contains the getNode method, which returns the handle to the object of the 3D world by its name. Besides this, the Browser class interface also contains the createVRMLFromString method that enables you to dynamically create new 3D world objects according to the user's instructions.

After obtaining the handle to the Node class (the object of the virtual world), it is controlled via the events mechanism. You access event handlers using Node class methods such as getEventOut and getEventIn. Using the event handler, it is possible to change a specific object property, such as object color or height.

The special VRML object named TouchSensor provides for the interaction between the user and 3D images. For example, when the user positions the mouse cursor over a particular region, its attached `TouchSensor` object sends the appropriate event to the Java applet. The Java applet handles this event by changing the glow of the 3D region image and displaying its name and business parameter values in the special informational string of the applet window.

Informational technologies are growing and evolving dynamically. Using these new technologies in the corporate informational systems can provide significant advantages in market competition thanks to new knowledge based on business data. This new knowledge enables business professionals to predict the future more accurately, and to make more appropriate tactical and strategic decisions. OLAP's principles were formulated in 1993, the Java language was created in June 1995, and the VRML language standard was adopted in October 1997. The integration of the illustrative capabilities provided by virtual worlds with the technology of data warehousing and OLAP using Java shows us new horizons when creating corporate decision support systems. In this chapter we have described some of the first, rather promising, examples of real-world solutions based on practical integration of the newest informational technologies.

Chapter 10

Financial Analyzer—a Special Oracle Application

10.1. Product Description

Oracle Financial Analyzer (hereafter called OFA) is a distributed multi-user application for creating financial reporting, performing financial analysis, calculating financial budgets, and forecasting. The system supports execution of basic financial functions, such as control of expenses, the analysis of efficiency, evaluating possibilities, formulating prospective strategy, the deviation analysis of planned and actual financial variables, and forming and storing several balance scenarios.

Improving the management of any organization is closely tied to the automation of business processes and reporting, and the introduction of budgeting. An analytical system based on OFA enables you to radically optimize and speed up the planning and reporting processes. This is accomplished thanks to corporate and individual processing of plans and reports at various levels of drilling, while at the same time supporting data synchronization.

OFA can be compared to a constructor that can be used in any business processes accepted by various companies participating in different business areas, such as banking, production, service provision, mining, or trading. To adopt Oracle Financial Analyzer, the company need not necessarily change its business rules, since OFA can reflect the existing business and its standard reporting rules and, obviously, bring in some new information analyzing capabilities. The structure of a data warehouse serving as a basis for OFA is flexible, and can be adapted to continuously changing business processes when and if necessary.

OFA supports budgeting and forecasting, as well as accumulation and the analysis of the actual information within the framework of the uniform system. The product coordinates and improves the budgeting process regardless of the budgeting methodology implemented—"top—bottomward", "bottom—topward" or a mixed methodology. OFA can execute budgetary functions at various aggregation levels: from the highest, such as year or regional office, to lower levels, such as month and department. Users can copy actual data for last year to the budget of the current year, and arbitrarily change individual articles (by absolute value or percentage). Users can also store specific parts of the company's financial database on their workstations (personal computers) for mobile compilation and usage of the budgets and forecasts. After completing the budgeting cycle, a final budget is compiled to provide access at the company level. The finalized budget can be locked to prevent modifications.

Information required for analyses can be presented using different slices: by time period, by product line, by regional department, by client, etc. Software tools intended for navigating multidimensional data allow users to quickly locate and identify the source of problem. Such software tools simplify analysis of the financial efficiency of a department, as well as affiliation by product, sales channel, or time period. With multidimensional analysis, users are able to control and analyze financial data, and create and store individual reports and graphs without involving technical experts. OFA allows you to solve a wide range of financial tasks thanks to its built-in financial modeling tools. The results of a "What if?" analysis performed according to the created models are displayed immediately. The large library of built-in functions enables users to make predictions, calculate efficiency correlations, and work with other complex analytical measures. In the course of analysis, users can join information from the General Ledger with other data to create new financial data for future use.

The access control capabilities enable the administrator to identify the groups of financial data that each individual user will need for viewing and editing purposes. Consequently, each user views and manages only that information which corresponds to his or her responsibilities. Upper management can receive brief informational reports created according to specified requirements, while lower-level managers can get access to more detailed information.

OFA uses a simple graphic interface oriented towards accounting and financial specialists who require a simple way of accessing complex analytical tools. After 2 or 3 days of training, even a beginning user can easily create queries of various types and perform complex analyses based on drilling and exceptions. The reports contain well-known formats and functions with which spreadsheet users are acquainted.

Besides manual data entry, OFA provides the capability of reading the required information from files, and allows you to easily download data from various sources: general ledgers, spreadsheets, relational databases and other systems.

OFA has a standard interface to the Oracle General Ledger application (hereafter referred to as OGL). This integration allows you to avoid repeated data entry, and provides for more efficient financial management. Information from OGL can be easily moved to respective OFA structures. OGL calcualted balances are fully displayed in OFA. The availability of an interface between the two applications provides the ability of automatic migration of the OGL structure modifications to OFA.

10.2. Product Architecture

OFA runs on several networked workstations and servers. Software modules known as *workstations* are installed to the end-user workstations and provide access to the OFA server and to the central shared database. The shared database is the engine of the OFA system. It contains financial data and objects shared by all users of the system. The shared database file, ofas.db, resides in the shared directory on the UNIX or Windows NT server. Besides this, each OFA workstation has its own personal (user) database, which stores objects and financial data intended for personal use. Part of the objects and data is distributed to the personal database from the shared database, while another part could be created by the user and be unavailable to other users of the system.

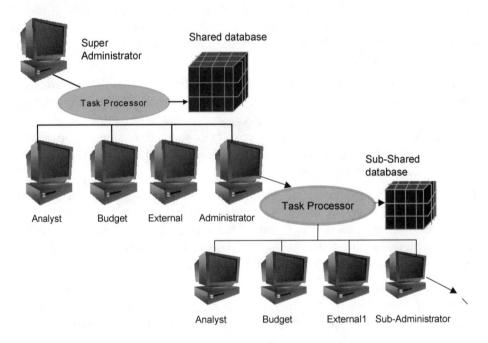

Fig. 10.1. Configuration of OFA workstations

There are two basic groups of workstations: administrator workstations and user workstations.

Administrator workstations include:

❏ *Super administration workstation.* This workstation resides at the top level of the OFA system. It has its own personal database and is connected to the super shared database. The super administration workstation allows you to perform the following tasks:

    ❏ Create other workstation users—lower level administrator, budget specialist and analyst

❏ Create database structures and distribute them to the shared database and subordinate workstations

❏ Specify user access to shared data

❏ Distribute slices of financial data to personal and shared databases

❏ Set the fiscal time for the entire system

❏ Integrate Oracle General Ledger to Oracle Financial Analyzer

❏ *Administration workstation.* Administration workstation enables you to perform the same tasks as super administration workstation, except for the last two in the list provided above. This workstation also has its own personal database and is connected to the shared database of its own level. Actually, the administrator level is a nearly autonomous system, providing all the capabilities of a super administrator, with the exception that part of the structures and data in the administrator's shared database is distributed by the super administrator (Fig. 10.1).

❏ *Task processor workstation.* Data and structures stored in the shared database are directed to the *task processor workstation,* where they are queued until the task processor processes them. This workstation:

❏ Is always connected to the *administrator workstation*

❏ Provides the administrator with the capability of controlling data migration between personal databases of individual users and the shared database

❏ Enables the administrator to manage distribution of the structures and data to subordinate workstations

The following workstation types are classified as user workstations:

❏ *Budget workstation.* The personal database contains structures (in read-only mode) and a copy of financial data from the shared database. From this workstation you can complete the following tasks:

❏ Work with objects distributed to your personal database from the shared database

❏ Create data structures for use in your personal database

❏ Create reports, forms, graphs, and folders

❏ Submit data from your personal database to the shared database

❏ Update your personal database with data from the shared database

❏ View the status of your submitted tasks in the *task processor*

❑ *Analyst workstation.* The personal database stores structures from the shared database (in read-only mode). However, there is no copy of the local financial data present in the budget workstation. From this workstation you can do the following:

  ❑ Connect to the shared database in read-only mode (or in read-write mode, if the system administrator grants you read-write access)

  ❑ Create reports, forms, graphs, and folders

  ❑ Use input forms for submitting data to the shared database

  ❑ Update data structures distributed by the administrator

❑ *External user.* This user can connect (in read-write mode) to the shared database via a Web browser or via Microsoft Excel. In contrast to workstations, the user no personal database and works with the database of other users existing in the system, or directly with the shared database.

All user workstations and external users are connected to the administrator workstation in which they were created (Fig. 10.1).

There are two possible types of client/server configurations for OFA—*thin client* (for all types of workstations), and *thick client* (only for administrator and budget workstations). The most important factors determining the client configuration are the location of the personal database and whether the Express Server to which the OFA connects runs on the server (UNIX or Windows NT) or on the user workstation.

When the workstation is installed as a thick client, the following components are installed at the user's workstation:

❑ Personal OFA database

❑ Client component of the OFA

❑ OFA code component

❑ Personal Express Server

The shared database and shared code components reside on the server.

The main distinguishing feature of the thick client configuration is the ability to work standalone. If you want, you can connect to the system and submit your data or update your personal database with the data or structures from the shared database.

If the workstation is installed as a thin client, only the client OFA component resides on the PC, and the following two options are available:

☐ The personal database resides on the same server as the shared components working in the same instance of Express Server.

☐ The personal database is attached to one Express Server instance, while the shared components run under another instance of the Express Server. This type of thin client configuration is known as a *cluster*.

10.3. Installation

The first workstation that you need to install in OFA is the super administrator workstation. The installation procedure comprises two steps:

☐ Installation of the server-side components

☐ Installation of the client-side components

10.3.1. Installing the Server-Side Components

Before you proceed with installing OFA, make sure that the software and hardware configurations meet certain requirements.

Hardware Requirements

☐ For UNIX server—dual processor and 512 RAM. For Windows NT server—dual processor and 256 MB RAM

☐ At least 40 MB of free disk space (This requirement applies only to the installation procedure; later on, as you populate the database with data, it will grow to several GB, or even larger)

Software Requirements

☐ Operating system: Windows NT 4.0 (service pack 6.0 and higher) or Unix

Access to Oracle Express Server. Installing the Server Component

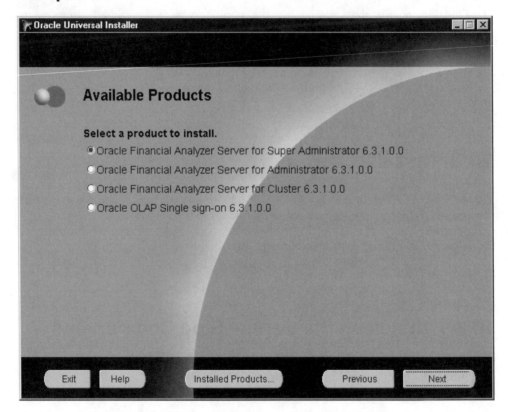

Fig. 10.2. The dialog for installing the server-side components

To install the server-side software, it is necessary to do the following:

1. Start the setup.exe program from the distribution directory or from the distribution CD containing the **OLAP Express OFA Server** product.

2. When the **File Locations** window appears, go to the **Destination** field and select the Oracle home directory (i.e., the directory where you install all Oracle products), or enter the required path manually. Then click **Next**.

3. In the **Available Products** dialog, select the **Oracle Financial Analyzer Server for Super Administrator** option and click **Next.**

4. If you plan to create Web users in your system, you'll need to enter the following information:

    ❐   In the **Web Server Location** dialog, select an option to specify, and choose whether Web Listener will run on the same server as Express Server or on a different server. If Web Listener will be running on a different server, a window will appear where you'll need to specify the installation path for OFA web files.

    ❐   In the **Web Server Information** dialog, enter the Web Server name (for example, such as www.ibs.com), and provide a description of the shared database in the **Description of Shared Data Base** field. All Web users will see the shared database under this name.

    ❐   Select the required option in the **Web Files Access Method** dialog.

5. In the dialog prompting you to specify the location of the server component of the super administrator workstation, specify the required directory (for example, C:\ofa, as shown in Fig. 10.3). Click **Next.**

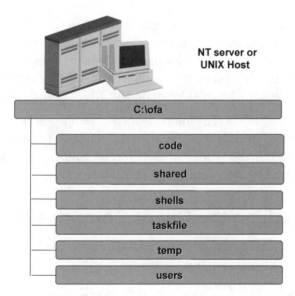

Fig. 10.3. Directory structure of the server component

6. In the next dialog, enter the name of the super administrator personal database. It is advisable to assign a name that reflects the name of the organization or department served by the system (for example, *Gccdba* for Global Computer Company). The server name and port number will be assigned by default. Click the **Next** button.

7. The next dialog relates to possible integration with Oracle General Ledger.

8. When you get to the **Summary** dialog containing all the selected components, click **Install**.

9. When the installation completes, click **Exit** to close the Setup program.

After successful installation, the new directory containing the server component of the super administrator workstation will appear on the server, named according to the directory name that you specified in the relevant dialog of the Setup program (for example, C:\ofa, see Fig. 10.3).

Besides the shared database and user databases, this directory contains a range of other system databases and files common for all system users. The shared directory contains the above-mentioned shared database (the ofas.db file) and system databases and files that control distribution of data and structures, both to the shared database and from the shared database to a personal database (the files named ofasctl.db, ofasyscf.db, ofaslck.db, etc.).

The taskfile directory serves for storing files created whenever you distribute database structures, submit data, or start calcualtions. The files created in the taskfile directory are nothing more than export files with the EIF filename extension, which are used for exchanging information between multidimensional databases. More detailed information on this topic will be provided in *Section 10.7, "Task Processor"*.

During installation of the server component, the Setup program creates the personal databases of the super administrator (the Gccdba.db file in our example) and task processor (tpm.db), along with all their related configuration files (Gccdba.cfg and tpm.cfg). These files are stored in the user directory.

10.3.2. Installing the Client Component

For successful installation, the software and hardware configuration of the computer must meet the requirements set below.

Hardware Requirements for the OFA Client Component

- ☐ 32 MB RAM or more.
- ☐ 17 MB disk space for a thin client configuration and 32 for a thick client configuration. Note that this requirement is just for successful installation. As you start working with the application and populate the database with the data, the database files will grow.

Software Requirements

☐ Operating system: Windows 95/98 or Windows NT 4.0/Windows 2000

☐ For installing a thick client configuration, you must install Personal Express Server 6.3.2

☐ TCP/IP network protocol for connecting Personal Express

Installation

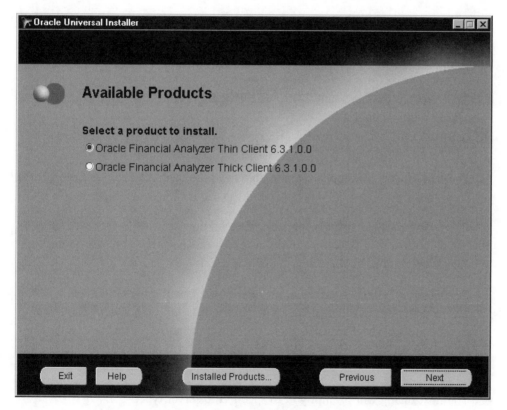

Fig. 10.4. The dialog for installing client components

To install the client component, proceed as follows:

1. From the distribution directory of the OLAP Express OFA client distribution CD, start the setup.exe application.

2. The **File Locations** window will appear. Go to the **Destination** field and specify the path to the Oracle home directory. Click **Next**.

3. In the **Available Products** window, select the required configuration—thin client or thick client—and then click **Next**.

For a thin client configuration:

1. When the **Thin Client Installation Locations** window appears, go to the **Path** field, enter the path to the installation directory, and click **Next**

2. In the next window, specify the server type

3. When the **Summary** dialog opens, displaying all the selected components, click **Install**

4. After completing the installation, click **Exit** to close the Setup application and reboot your computer

For a thick client configuration:

1. The next dialog will appear, reminding you that Personal Express Server must be installed on your computer to install the thick client configuration.

2. In the **Thick Client Installation Locations** window, go to the path field, specify the path to the installation directory, enter the personal database name, and click **Next**.

3. The **Shared Database Information** dialog will open. Specify the path to the shared database (C:\ofa\shared, in our example), and then specify the name of the server and where it resides (i.e., the name of the server where you have installed the OFA server-side software). Specify the port number or accept the default value.

4. The next dialog will prompt you to specify the server type.

5. The **Summary** dialog will appear, listing all the selected components. To continue the installation, click **Install**.

6. When the installation completes, click **Exit** to close the Setup program and reboot your computer.

10.3.3. Getting Started

Connecting to Express Server

The first login to the OFA system is done via the super administrator workstation. Actually, the super administrator personal database is the first stage in the process of creating your entire budgeting system. This workplace is used for creating database structures for the entire OFA system and performing administration tasks such as creating new users, distributing database structures and financial data to those users, and controlling changes to the shared database.

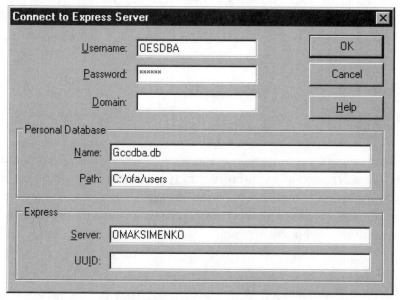

Fig. 10.5. Establishing connection to Express Server

After successful installation, you can start an OFA session (using the desktop icon or by selecting the appropriate item from the **Start** menu). The dialog shown in Fig. 10.5 will appear, where you need to specify the login information. Fill the **Username** and **Password** fields with the username and password of the operating system user of the server where the Express Server instance is running, the domain (only if you are domain user), the name of your personal database, the path to this database, and the name of the server where that particular Express Server instance is running, along with its unique ID. If there is only one Express Server instance on your server, you don't need to fill the **UUID** field at the bottom of this dialog. The system administrator must provide this information to all users. When starting subsequent sessions you'll only need to provide the password. When you login to the system for the first time, it is necessary to fill the Username and Password fields with the name of the server operating system user (the default user name is OESDBA, the default password is OESDBA). The OESDBA user is created automatically when you install Express Server, along with two other built-in users— OESguest and OESinit. Later, you can change the operating system user who is granted access to the personal database. More detailed information on this topic will be provided in *Section 10.3.2*, "*Installing the Client Component*" of this chapter. Having filled in this form, click **OK**. A dialog will appear that contains a drop-down list of national languages supported by the OFA graphical user interface. Select the desired UI language and click. The main OFA window will then open (Fig. 10.6).

Possible Errors

After filling in the login form and clicking **OK**, you might receive one of the following messages:

❑   "Cannot connect to Express. Do you want to continue?" Click **Yes** and re-enter the username and password if you typed in the information incorrectly. If you persistently receive this error message, there may be two possible sources of error: either your Express Server is not running or there are problems with the network connection.

❑   "Cannot attach personal database because it cannot be found or already attached by another user. Do you want to continue?" Click **Yes**, and make sure you have correctly specified the name of your personal database and the path to the database file. If the information is correct, it is possible that another user has already connected to your database. Only one user at a time can attach a personal database in an OFA session.

Configuring the Workstation

To configure the workstation, open the **Options** dialog (**Tools —> Options**) shown in Fig. 10.6. For each workstation, there are so-called general options. To set them, click the **General** icon, and then the **Configuration** icon.

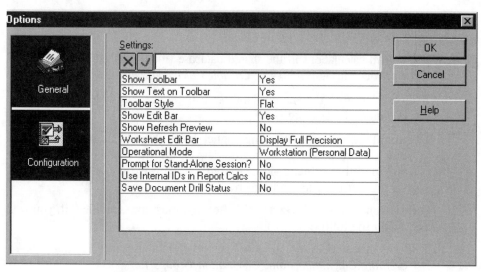

Fig. 10.6 Setting General workstation options

The general options enable you to configure the general appearance of your workstation. They include the following sections:

❐ **Show Text on Toolbar**—specifies whether text labels will be shown on the toolbar.

❐ **Show Toolbar**—specifies whether the toolbar will be shown.

❐ **Toolbar Style**—allows you to set the toolbar style.

❐ **Show Edit Bar**—specifies whether the **Edit** bar for text entry and editing will be shown.

❐ **Show Refresh Preview**—allows you to enable or disable the **Refresh Preview** dialog at the beginning of each session. (More detailed information on this option will be provided later in this chapter in *Section 10.6.5, "Receiving Information Distributed to Users".*)

❐ **Worksheet Edit Bar**—allows you to specify the precision when editing numeric data in forms.

❐ **Operational Mode**—this option appears only on the administrator workstation. It allows you to specify the working mode for the data in your personal database, in the shared database, and in the higher level shared database (if it is present). More detailed information was provided in *Section 10.2, "Product Architecture".* There are two possible settings for this option:

❑ **Administrator (Shared Data)**—this setting must be specified if you are going to perform the following tasks:

   ❑ Perform calculations in the shared database (more detailed information will be provided in *Section 10.4.8*, "*Creating Calculations and Calculation Groups*")

   ❑ Load data into the shared database using a special loader program (see *Section 10.8*, "*Loading Data*")

   ❑ Submit information into the higher-level shared database, or update your shared database with the data from the higher-level database (provided that a higher-level shared database exists, i.e., provided that you are not the super administrator)

❑ **Workstation (Personal Data)**—this setting must be specified if you will need to do the following:

   ❑ Perform calculations in your personal database (see *Section 10.4.8*, "*Creating Calculations and Calculation Groups*").

   ❑ Load data into your personal database using a special loader program (see *Section 10.8*, "*Loading Data*").

   ❑ Submit data from your personal database to the shared database, or update your personal database with data from the shared database. If you are working at the super administrator workstation, data exchange between the personal and shared databases takes place regardless of this setting.

❑ **Prompt for Stand-Alone Session**—this option displays a prompt at the beginning of each session asking you if you are going to work standalone (without attaching the shared database). This option appears only on administrator or budget workstations.

❑ **Use Internal IDs in Report Calcs**—if this option is set to **Yes**, the dimension values will appear under their internal system names in the formulae used in calculations. If this value is set to **No**, the dimension values will appear under their descriptions.

❑ **Save Document Drill Status**—this option allows you to save the drill status in your reports.

The **Configuration** settings option allows us to specify the mode in which the workstation will process specific operations.

❑ **Automatic Refresh**—if the administrator sets this option to **Yes**, and the **Show Refresh Preview** option is set to **No**, all subordinate workstations will be automatically updated by the distributed structures and data. If this option is set to **No**, users will need to manually update their personal databases.

❑ **Model Updates**—if this option is set to **Yes**, all modifications introduced to models come into force immediately. If this option is set to **No**, models are updated at the end of the session.

❑ **Allow Analysts to Use Worksheets**—if this option is set to **Yes**, all users of analyst workstations will be able to enter and edit data via worksheets.

Pay special attention to the useful capability of calling the Express Monitor dialog from the OFA interface. This dialog allows you to execute Express Language commands directly in the OFA session. To enable this option, open the configuration file *%OracleHome%* :\orant\olap\ofa6300\thinclient\client1\OFA, which appears after installing the client component of the OFA product, and enter the **ExpMonitor=yes** string to the [tools] section (Fig. 10.7).

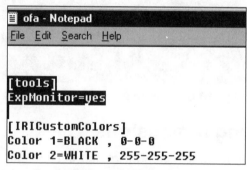

Fig. 10.7. The OFA file

Now the OFA GUI will provide the **Express Monitor** command in the **Help** menu, enabling you to open the Express Monitor dialog for entering commands.

10.4. Creating a Database Structure

Before proceeding with creation of the database structure, a financial analyst and software developer must perform many preliminary tasks to produce a document (in Word or Excel format) containing descriptions of all dimensions, their values, financial variables, hierarchies, models, and order of calculations (see *Section 2.4, "Design"*).

Database structures include dimensions, dimension values, cubes (here called financial elements), hierarchies, attributes, and data loader programs created via **Maintain** menu (Fig. 10.8). Database structures can be created by users of budget and administrator workstations in their personal databases. However, only an administrator can distribute them to the shared database.

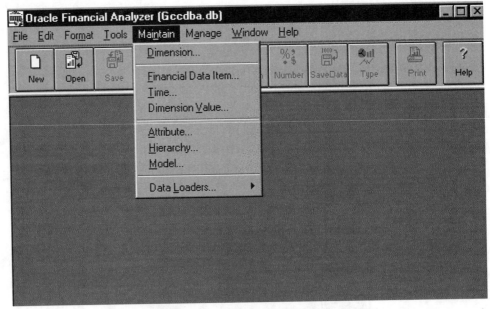

Fig. 10.8. Creating a database structure

10.4.1. Creating Dimensions

OFA has a built-in time dimension with month-quarter-year drilling. To use it, you just need to set the system fiscal time once, via the **Set a Fiscal Month** dialog (**Maintain —> Time**), and later add new financial years as necessary. This can be done via the **Maintain Time** dialog (**Maintain —> Time**). If you need drilling capabilities by days or weeks, you'll need to create a custom time dimension. Normally, budgeting and financial measures belong to a separate dimension, which in this chapter is called Line.

For maintaining dimensions, OFA provides the **Maintain Dimension** dialog (Fig. 10.9) that you can call by selecting the **Maintain —> Dimension** commands.

The options provided in this dialog are briefly described below.

1—a drop-down list with the names of existing dimensions (after the installation you'll find two system dimensions—**Users** and **Year**).

2—the name of the library to which the selected dimension belongs (**Personal** or **Shared**).

3—**Dimension Definition**: unique name of the object—system identifier (may differ from the name in field (1)), **Prefix**—system identifier used for hierarchies, models and attributes, column width—maximum number of characters allowed for dimension values, and dimension type—**Text** or **Time**.

4—**Dimension Options:** by setting or clearing the **Enable Time Aggregation** checkbox you can enable or disable time aggregation. If the **Enable B/W Variance Indicators** option is enabled, the dialog for dimension values will contain an option enabling you to specify the sign for deviations (+ or -), such as planned/actual. **Maintain DBA Sort Order**—refreshes the dimension values in your database according to their order in the administrator database. If you enable the **Control Dimension Value Scaling** option, numeric scaling can be disabled for individual values of this dimension.

5—determines the groups of users able to create their own personal objects (hierarchies, models, and attributes) for the current dimension.

6—the **Save** button—saves changes for the dimension.

7—the **Close** button—closes the dialog.

8—the **New** button—opens a dialog allowing you to create a new dimension.

9—the **Delete** button—deletes the dimension.

10—the **Rename** button—renames the dimension.

11—the **Help** button—opens the on-line Help system.

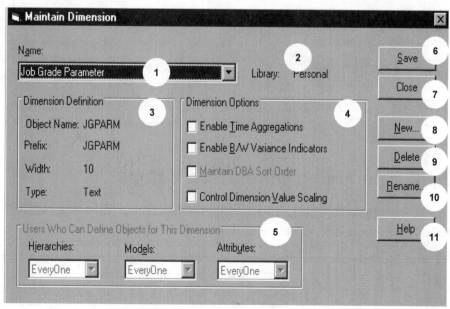

Fig. 10.9. The dialog for creating dimensions

To create a new dimension, click the **New** button. In the dialog that will open (Fig. 10.10), fill in the following fields: **Name**—specify the dimension name, **Object Name**—the unique name of the object, **Type**—dimension type, and **Column Width**—column width (maximum allowed—50 characters). In our example, we are dealing with the Job Grade dimension of the text type, with a column width of 10 characters.

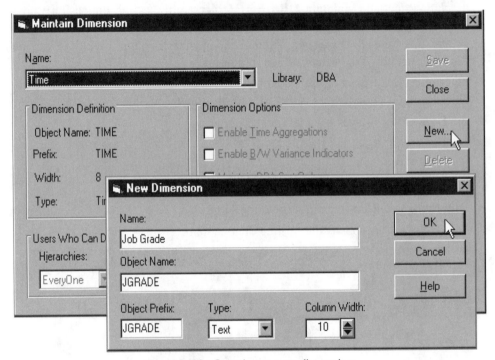

Fig. 10.10. Creating a new dimension

10.4.2. Specifying Dimension Values

Using the **Maintain Dimension Values** dialog that opens when you select the **Maintain —> Dimension Value** commands from the menu (Fig. 10.11), you can edit existing dimension values or create new ones.

The contents of this dialog are briefly described below:

1—a drop-down list with the names, of the dimensions existing in the database. You can select the needed dimension from this list, for example, Job Grade.

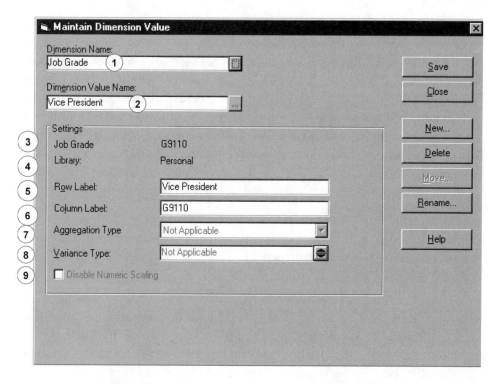

Fig. 10.11. The **Maintain Dimension Values** dialog

2—a drop-down list containing the names of existing values of the selected dimension.

3—the **Settings** area for the dimension value. Displays the name of the selected dimension and its unique name—the system identifier of the dimension value; for example, G9110, along with the following characteristics.

4—the name of the library to which the selected dimension value belongs (personal or shared).

5—the field for the row label that will appear when the current dimension is placed at the left border of the report, or in pages. By default, the dimension value name is used as a label.

6—the field for the column label that will be displayed when the current dimension will reside at the top of the report. By default, the unique name of the dimension is used as the column label.

7—time aggregation type—this drop-down list allows you to select the time aggregation type for financial elements. This list is available only when the **Enable Time Aggregation** option is set for the selected dimension (Fig. 10.11). There are 7 possible aggregation methods for financial values related to this dimension value. For example, if the dimension value is "Quantity of finished products", it would be natural to select the "Add month into quarter" type of time aggregation. If the dimension value is "Spare cash for the beginning of the period", it would be natural to select the "First month into quarter" aggregation type. If the dimension value is "Product unit price", then the recommended aggregation type will be "Average month into quarter", and so on.

8—variance type, that allows you to select the variance sign (best/worst; for example, **Actual/Budget** or **Budget/Actual**).

9—this option allows you to disable numeric scaling.

The buttons in the window shown in Fig. 10.11 have functions similar to the buttons in the **Maintain Dimension** window, with the exception of the **Move** button. This button allows you to open a new dialog and move the selected dimension value to another position within a list of values for the selected dimension.

To create a new dimension value, select the dimension to which the new value must be added from the list of available dimensions (see Fig. 10.11) and click the **New** button. The next dialog will appear (Fig. 10.12). In this dialog, fill in the following fields: **Name**—specify the name of the dimension value, **Dimension Value**—specify the internal unique identifier (it will be automatically capitalized). If you want to create a new dimension value based on an existing one, set the **Copy from** option. Notice that if you select this option, only the settings will be copied to the new dimension value, while its name and internal unique identifier must be unique within the current dimension. To continue, click the **Save** button. You'll return to the **Maintain Dimension Values** window. Here, if necessary, you can change the settings of the newly created value.

Click the **Save** button to return to the main menu.

As practice has shown, the method described above is rarely used in real-world projects. As a general rule, dimension values are created using the loader program that will be covered in detail later in this chapter.

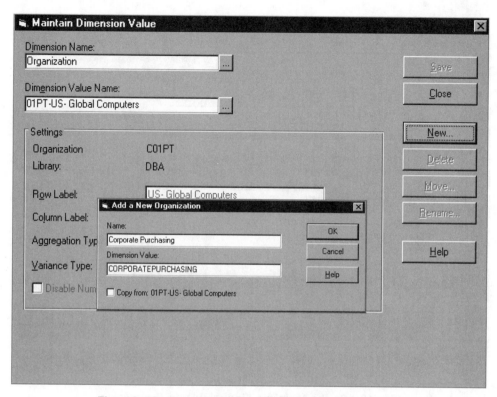

Fig. 10.12. Creating and maintaining dimension values

10.4.3. Creating Financial Data Items

In OFA documentation, measures or cubes are called Financial Data Items. To create a new financial data item, select the **Maintain Financial Data** command from the **Maintain** menu. The **Maintain Financial Data** window will open (Fig. 10.13)

The options available in this window are briefly described below:

1—a pop-up list containing the names of financial data items available in the database.

2—the library to which the selected financial data items belong.

3—a row label. By analogy to the dimension value, this label will appear when the data item shows up at the leftmost border of the report or page. By default, the financial data item name will be used as a row label.

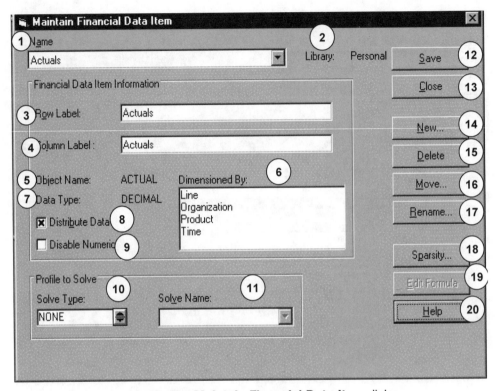

Fig. 10.13. The **Maintain Financial Data Item** dialog

4—a column label. This designates the data item when it appears at the topmost border of the report. By default, the unique identifier of the financial data item will be used as a column label.

5—an object name—the unique identifier of the financial data item.

6—the list of dimensions used in the financial data item definition.

7—the data type of the currently selected financial data item.

8—an option that enables an Administrator to specify that the data stored within the selected financial data item is available for distribution. Don't forget to enable this option, since by default all financial data items are not available for distribution. Consequently, if this option is disabled, your attempt to distribute the financial data item to the shared database will fail.

9—this option enables you to turn off numeric scaling for data associated with this financial data item.

10—solve type. The list allowing you to select the type of solve definition (**None, Solve definition,** or **Group Solve Definition**) of the financial data item.

11—solve name. A list allowing you to select the name of the solve definition or group solve definition. Solve definitions and group solve definitions are special objects that can be associated with the financial data item. These special objects are sets of models and hierarchies according to which slices of stored data are calculated on the basis of already existing ones. Later in this chapter we will cover these special objects in more detail.

The buttons at the rightmost part of the window shown in Fig. 10.13 (buttons 12—17, 20) have functions similar to the buttons in the **Maintain Dimension** and **Maintain Dimension Value** dialogs.

18—the **Sparsity** button. Opens a dialog allowing you to specify the rules of handling the sparsity of financial data items.

19—the **Edit Formula** button. Opens a dialog allowing you to edit a formula. It is available only for calcualted financial data items.

Creating a New Financial Data Item

To create a new financial data item, click the **New** button (14). The new dialog shown in Fig. 10.14 will open. Here you'll need to fill in the following fields:

❏ **Name**—the name of the new financial data item.

❏ If you want to create a new financial data item based on an existing one, set the **Copy from** option.

❏ **Object Name**—the internal unique identifier of the financial data item (it is automatically capitalized).

❏ If you create a new financial data item from scratch rather than from a copy of an existing one, you'll need to do the following:

  ❏ Select the financial data item type from the following three types of financial data items:

Type	Description
Stored	The values are copied from existing financial data, entered manually via a worksheet, or loaded using loader programs

continues

Continued

Type	Description
Manual formula	The values are calculated dynamically based on user-specified formulae in which the user specifies the data's dimensionality
Automatic formula	The values are calculated dynamically using formulae where the data dimensions are defined automatically based on the stored financial data items

☐ Select the required data type using the **Data Type** drop-down list.

☐ Use the **Add/Remove** buttons to specify the dimensions upon which the new financial data item will depend. Select the required dimensions from the **Dimensions Available** list.

☐ If the type of your financial data item is formula, specify its definition in the **Formula** field. For example, an automatic formula such as Budget-Actuals specifies dynamic calculation of the Budget-Actuals variance.

☐ Click the **Save** button to return to the **Maintain Financial Data Item** dialog.

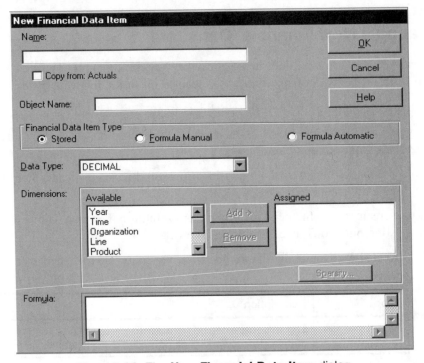

Fig. 10.14. The **New Financial Data Item** dialog

Copying Data

To copy data from one financial data item to another, select the **Tools —> Copy Data** commands. The **Copy Data** window will open (Fig. 10.15).

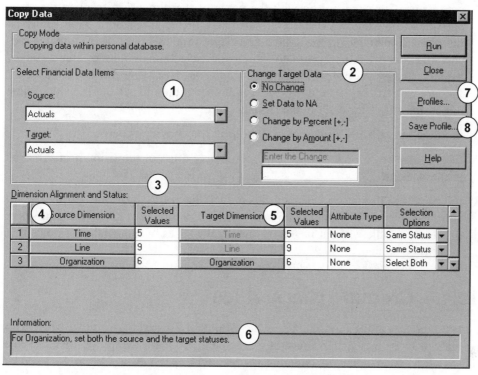

Fig. 10.15. The **Copy Data** dialog

The options available in this window are briefly described below:

1—these lists allows you to select the source financial data item from which the data is to be copied and the target financial data item to which the data is to be copied.

2—the **Change Target Data** group provides options allowing you to specify how the data must be changed during the copy operation. One of the options provided in this group—the **Set Data to NA** option—deserves special mention. As its name implies, this option sets all the data of the selected slice to NA. It provides a convenient way of clearing data that is no longer needed from financial data items.

3—the **Dimensions Alignment and Status** group enables you to set the alignment and status of the dimensions in the source and target financial data items.

4 and 5—allow you to select the dimension values for source and target financial data items. Click the button with the name of the dimension to open the standard **Selector** window, where you can select the required dimension values. If the dimension values in the source and target financial data items coincide, accept the **Same Status** option to which the **Selection options** option is set by default. If they do not, for example, if you need to copy the budget data for January to February, specify the **Select Both** option and set the individual time dimension status for each financial data item.

6—the field intended to display information on the copying process.

7—the **Profiles** button opens the dialog containing a list of the Copy profies stored in the database.

8—the **Save Profile** button opens a dialog enabling you to save the settings of the current copy profile under a unique name for future use. Later you can select the stored profile without having to specify the slices of financial data items that need to be copied.

10.4.4. Creating Hierarchies

New hierarchies must be created via the **Maintain Hierarchy** window, which can be opened by selecting the **Hierarchy** command from the **Maintain** menu. Since the newly created database contains no hierarchies, the **New Hierarchy** window will open automatically (Fig. 10.16).

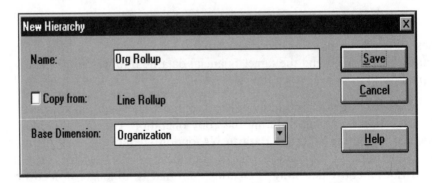

Fig. 10.16. The **New Hierarchy** window

Enter the new hierarchy name into the **Name** field. Next, go to the **Base Dimension** drop-down list, select the dimension upon which the new hierarchy will be created, and click the **Save** button. For creating subsequent hierarchies and editing existing ones, use the **Maintain Hierarchy** dialog.

The contents of the **Maintain Hierarchy** window are very much like the contents of the other **Maintain** dialogs. It contains a drop-down list with the names of hierarchies already existing in the database and the name of the library to which the selected hierarchy belongs. In the rightmost part of the window there are several buttons allowing you to close the dialog, create or delete the hierarchy, move the hierarchy to another position within a list, and rename the hierarchy, as well as a **Help** button.

To edit hierarchies, click the **Edit** button in the **Maintain Hierarchy** window. The **Edit Hierarchy** dialog will open (Fig. 10.17).

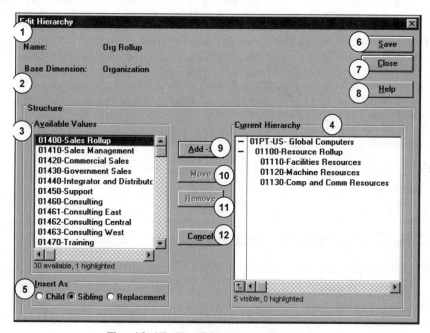

Fig. 10.17. The **Edit Hierarchy** window

The options available in this window are briefly described below:

1—name of the hierarchy.

2—name of the base dimension.

3—the **Available Values** field contains a list of available dimension values not included into the selected hierarchy. When you start editing the newly created hierarchy for the first time, this list contains all the values available in the base dimension.

4—the **Current Hierarchy** field. Contains a list of values associated with the selected hierarchy. If necessary, it provides Drill Up and Drill Down capabilities.

5—the **Insert As** group of radio buttons allows you to select the relation between the dimension values in the left list (**Available Values**) and the right list (**Current Hierarchy**). This relationship must be specified each time you add a new dimension value to the hierarchy.

6, 7, 8—the standard **Save**, **Close**, and **Help** buttons.

9—the **Add** button adds the selected values to the current hierarchy and deletes them from the **Available Values** list.

10—the **Move** button moves the selected value to another position within a hierarchy.

11—the **Remove** button deletes the selected value from the hierarchy. The value deleted from the current hierarchy will automatically reappear in the list of available dimension values.

12—the **Cancel** button cancels the current operation.

Keep in mind that operations such as **Add**, **Move**, and **Remove** can be performed by dragging with the mouse.

10.4.5. Creating Attributes

Attributes are used for establishing relationships between the values of two dimensions—the base dimension and the grouping dimension. Grouping dimensions are used for grouping the values of the base dimension. In OFA, you can specify two types of relationships: "one-to-many" and "many-to-many".

Let's look at an example of a "one-to-many" relationship. Suppose that the database has the Employees dimension containing the list of all company employees, and the Job Grade dimension. The Employees dimension is base one and can be grouped using the Job Grade dimension. For this purpose, you need to create a "one-to-many" attribute between the two dimensions, which means that for each employee there will be only one job. However, for each job in the job grade there may be more than one employee.

Now let us consider an example of a "many-to-many" relationship. As in the previous example, we will take the Employees dimension as the base, and the Projects dimension containing all the projects being implemented by the company as the grouping dimension. Since each employee can participate in several projects, and each project is implemented by a group of employees, we will create here a "many-to-many" relationship.

Attributes can be created and edited via the **Maintain Attribute** dialog. To open this dialog, select the **Attribute** command from the **Maintain** menu. If the database contains no attributes, the **New Attribute** dialog will appear automatically (Fig. 10.18). Here you need to provide a name for the new attribute, select the base and grouping dimensions from the list of available dimensions, specify the attribute type, and click **OK**. The **Maintain Attribute** dialog will then open.

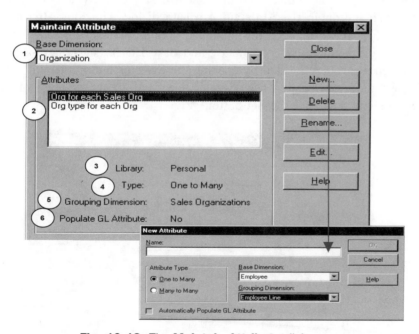

Fig. 10.18. The **Maintain Attribute** dialog

The options of the **Maintain Attribute** dialog are briefly described below:

1—the drop-down list containing the name of available base dimensions.

2—the **Attribute** field containing a list attribute created for the current dimension.

3—the name of the library to which the selected attribute belongs.

4—the attribute type—"one-to-many" or "many-to-many".

5—the name of the grouping dimension.

6—the **Populate GL Attribute** area indicator specifies whether the option instructing OFA to automatically populate the attribute from the General Ledger was selected when creating this attribute. If it is set to **Yes**, OFA automatically populates the attribute as a part of the process of loading the balance from the General Ledger.

In the right part of the is window you'll find the standard buttons, such as **Close**, **New**, **Delete**, **Rename**, **Edit**, and **Help**.

To start editing the attribute, open the **Edit Attribute** dialog (Fig. 10.19) by clicking the **Edit** button in the **Maintain Attribute** dialog. The **Edit Attribute** dialog shown in Fig. 10.19 contains the following options: **Grouping Values**—the drop-down list of grouping dimension values, and **Base Dimension Values**—a list of the base dimension values selected by clicking the **Selector** button. To edit an attribute, select the grouping dimension value, select one or more values of the base dimension, and then click the **Set** button.

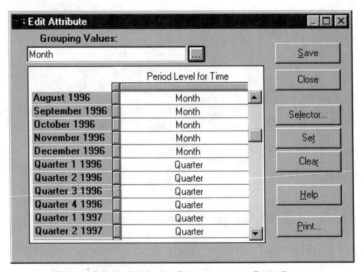

Fig. 10.19. Editing a "one-to-many" attribute

When editing a "many-to-many" attribute, select the table cell and click the **Set** button. The **Yes** indicator will appear in the cell, which indicates that the relationship exists between the values of the two dimensions.

10.4.6. Creating Models

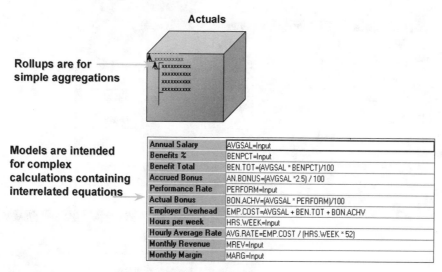

Actuals

Rollups are for simple aggregations

Models are intended for complex calculations containing interrelated equations

Annual Salary	AVGSAL=Input
Benefits %	BENPCT=Input
Benefit Total	BEN.TOT=(AVGSAL * BENPCT)/100
Accrued Bonus	AN.BONUS=(AVGSAL *2.5) / 100
Performance Rate	PERFORM=Input
Actual Bonus	BON.ACHV=(AVGSAL * PERFORM)/100
Employer Overhead	EMP.COST=AVGSAL + BEN.TOT + BON.ACHV
Hours per week	HRS.WEEK=Input
Hourly Average Rate	AVG.RATE=EMP.COST / (HRS.WEEK * 52)
Monthly Revenue	MREV=Input
Monthly Margin	MARG=Input

Fig. 10.20. Creating models

Models are objects containing groups of interrelated equations that enable you to calculate the data for dimension values. You can use them any time you need to perform calculations more complicated than simple summing (Fig. 10.20).

Models are created via the **Maintain Model** window, which you can open by selecting the **Model** command from the **Maintain** menu. If there are no models in the database, the **New Model** dialog will open first (Fig. 10.21). To create a new model, do the following:

1. Provide a name for the new model.

2. Select the base dimension from the drop-down list. Your new model will be based upon this dimension.

3. Select the time dimension from the list of time dimensions available in the database, or accept **None** (default). The time dimension must be selected when calculations using this model will be related to the time lag. For example, the value of the "Remainder for the starting time of the period" must always be

equal to another value of this dimension, "Remainder for the end of period", but for the previous month. Therefore, for the model that calculates values such as "Remainder for the start of period", you need to select the time dimension from the list.

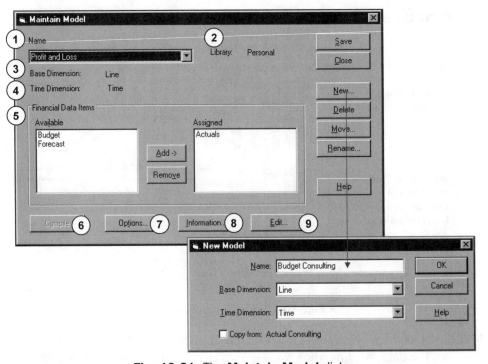

Fig. 10.21. The **Maintain Model** dialog

Model maintenance is performed via the **Maintain Model** dialog (Fig. 10.21). The contents of this dialog are briefly described below:

1—drop-down list containing the names of the models existing in the database.

2—name of the library to which the selected model belongs.

3—base dimension.

4—name of the time dimensions selected from the **Time Dimension** list when the model was created, or **None**.

5—lists of financial data items. The left field contains the list of the database financial data items shared by the base dimension of the current model. In our example, this is the `Line` dimension. The right field contains only the items that will be calculated using this model. Use the **Add/Remove** buttons to move items from field to field.

6—to compile the model, click the **Compile** button. If an error occurs, the appropriate error message will appear.

7—click the **Options** button to open a dialog where you can change the calculation settings for simultaneous equations.

8—click the **Information** button to open the window containing detailed information on compilation errors.

9—click the **Edit** button to open the **Model Definition** dialog (Fig. 10.22), where you can enter or edit the model equations.

In the right part of the **Maintain Model** window there are standard buttons, such as **Save**, **Close**, **New**, **Delete**, **Move**, **Rename**, **Edit**, and **Help**.

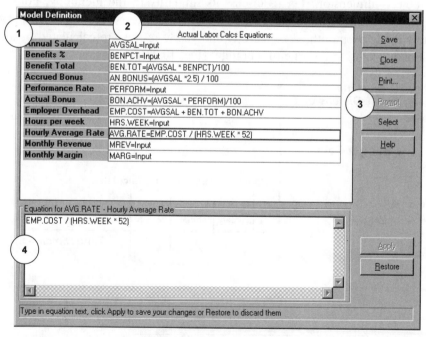

Fig. 10.22. The **Model Definition** dialog enables you to edit models

Model equations are entered via the **Model Definition** dialog (Fig. 10.22). To open this dialog, click the **Edit** button in the **Maintain Model** window. The left column of the **Maintain Definition** dialog (1) contains the names of dimension values, while the right column (2) lists their respective unique identifiers (**Dimension Value**) and equations (4). Initially, the fields for all equations contain the **Input** value. Only internal unique identifiers are used in the equations. To avoid having to enter the internal unique identifiers manually, you can click the **Prompt** button (3). Clicking the **Prompt** button will open the **Model Definition** dialog with additional components intended for simplifying the process of defining models.

10.4.7. Sample Models. Creating Programs in OFA

Creating models is one of the key and at the same time one of the most labor consuming stages of the project. Therefore, this topic deserves special attention and detailed discussion. First, let us discuss what a model is, why it is necessary, and how it can be specified. Like a hierarchy, a model is an object related to another object—dimension. Let us discuss its similarity to the hierarchy. For example, if there is a time dimension with the month-quarter-year hierarchy, and data is entered only by month, the quarterly and yearly results are calculated by simple addition according to the rule of hierarchy (Fig. 10.23).

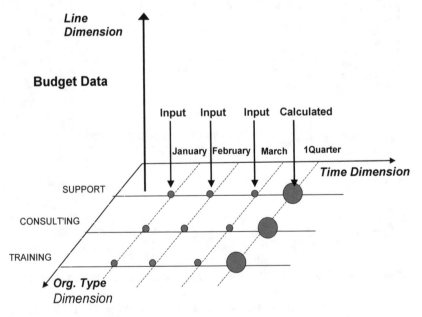

Fig. 10.23. Schema for calculating data by hierarchy

The idea behind data calculation in models is similar—data for certain dimension values is entered, while other values are calculated on the basis of the data that was entered. However, in contrast to hierarchies, models may involve much more complex calculations. One may say that hierarchies form a subset of models, since one may enter the model for the time dimension for calculating quarterly data:

```
January  |JAN=Input
February |FEB=Input
March |MAR=Input
1Quarter |Q1=JAN+FEB+MAR
```

Adding is generally performed using hierarchies, while models are used for more complex calculations. Let's consider some typical examples of the equations used in models. Notice that equations are written using the Oracle Express Language.

❑ A simple model—calculating the revenue based on income and expenses data.

```
Profit  |PROFIT=Input
Expenses |COST=Input
Revenue |REVENUE=PROFIT-COST
```

❑ The equation using a reference to the previous month—"Remainder for the beginning of the period" is always equal to another value of the same dimension—"Remainder for the end of the period" for the previous month.

```
"Remainder for the end of the period" | REST_END=Input

"Remainder for the beginning of the period" | REST_BEGIN=LAG(REST_END -
1 TIME)
```

Here, Time is the name of the time dimension specified in the **Time Dimension** field when creating the model; 1 is the number of periods. In the example provided here we are referring to the previous month. You can also use any other Express Language time functions, such as Lead, Lagdif, Lagpct.

❑ The model allows you to use conditions, for example:

```
Cost_of_Services_Support = if orgtype eq 'SUPPORT' then
Company_revenues else NA
Cost_of_Services_Consulting =if orgtype eq 'CONSULT' then
Company_revenues else NA
Cost_of_Services_Training=if orgtype eq 'TRAIN' then
Company_revenues else NA
```

Here orgtype (organization structure) is another dimension of the financial data item being calculated.

❐ The model can refer to another financial data item. For example, suppose that in order to calculate Custom expenses you need data on custom tax contained in another financial data item—Taxes. In this case, the equation may look as follows:

```
Custom expenses | COST= ALL_COUNT * TARIFF(kind_tariff
'CUSTOMS_TARIFF')
```

Here, ALL_COUNT is another value of the base dimension, TARIFF is a financial data item containing data on taxes, and 'CUSTOMS_TARIFF' is the value on the dimension kind_tariff, belonging to TARIFF.

In your model you can refer to any cell or slice of data existing in your database, either one belonging to the financial data item being calculated or to any other financial data item.

If there is a dimension that belongs to both the financial data item being calculated and to the referred financial data item, it is not necessary to refer such dimension values like this: (kind_tariff 'CUSTOMS_TARIFF'). For example, if the shared dimension is the time dimension, the loop will be executed by this dimension. In our example, the custom expenses for May will be calculated using the May tax rate value.

❐ The reference to the higher level of the hierarchy is a more complex example. For example, the tax rate is introduced quarterly, while custom expenses must be calculated monthly. In this case, the equation for our model will look as follows:

```
Custom expenses | COST= ALL_COUNT *
 TARIFF(kind_tariff 'CUSTOMS_TARIFF'
 time fmshrel.time(fmshdim.time 'FMS.TIME'))
```

Here, fmshrel.time is a relationship and fmshdim.time is a dimension. Both are internal objects related to the Time dimension. The fmshrel.time attribute describes the successor/parent relationship existing between the time dimension values. The values of the fmshdim.time attribute are all time dimension hierarchies (under their internal names). This (and many other) metadata exist for each dimension stored in the database. Their names are formulated by adding suffixes—the first letters of the dimension name—to the keyword (fmshrel, fmshdim etc.). If there is only one hierarchy on a dimension, rather than referring it you may simply write:

```
Custom expenses | COST= ALL_COUNT *
 TARIFF(kind_tariff 'CUSTOMS_TARIFF' time fmshrel.time)
```

❑ One of the most complicated cases are those where it is necessary to write an equation that refers to the data contained within the financial data item that is calculated using this model, and it is impossible to solve the problem using only the built-in time shift capability. For example, suppose that we have information on the bonus fund for the department and need to distribute it among employees for the next month. The calculated financial data item named Budget uses three dimensions—financial (Line), which is the base dimension of our model, the Time dimension, and the Orgtype dimension that describes organizational structure. The equation for calculating the bonus for each employee will refer to the data contained in the same Bonus value at the Line dimension. However, by the Orgtype dimension we take the department where the individual employee works. An attempt to include a reference within an equation to its own calcualted financial data item will result in a compilation error:

```
Budget( Line 'Bonus' Orgtype fmshrel.org)
```

Therefore, one possible workaround is to create a copy of the calculated financial data item (Budget) named, for example Budget_copy. The simplest way of doing so is to use an automatic formula. Then the correct reference in the equation will be as follows:

```
Budget_copy( Line 'Bonus' Orgtype fmshrel.org)
```

❑ Finally, models provide the capability of calling a program. For example, in the 'Budget_Bonus' model, the SET_BONUS program is called. To specify a program call for the model, open the **Express Monitor** window by calling the **Express Monitor** command from the **Help** menu (see *Section 10.3.3*, "*Configuring workstation settings*") and enter the following commands:

```
DEFINE SET_BONUS PROGRAM
INFILE 'C:/WORK/PROJECTS/SETBONUS.TXT'
LIMIT MD.ENTRY TO MD.DESC EQ 'Budget_Bonus'
MD.CATALOG(MD.PROP 'PROGRAM') = 'SETBONUS'
MD.CATALOG(MD.PROP 'COMPILE.NEEDED') = NA
MD.CATALOG(MD.PROP 'USER.PROG') = 'YES'
COMPILE SETBONUS
UPDATE
```

The first line of this code creates a new object—the SET_BONUS program. The source code of this program is stored in the SETBONUS.TXT file, the path to which is specified by the second code line. This, however, is not the only capability of writing program source code in OFA. For example, you can enter the following command in Express Monitor:

```
Edit SET_BONUS
```

The program editor window will open. However, this editor provides quite a limited set of functional capabilities. Therefore, we would advise you to use this editor only for editing small programs. As for writing and debugging programs for OFA, the most convenient way of performing these tasks is opening the OFA database via Oracle Express Administrator. Notice, however, that you can't use the Oracle Express Administrator interface for creating OFA structures, since OFA structures have their own specific metadata.

The subsequent lines of the program code provided above change the properties of the MD.CATALOG directory and relates the 'Budget_Bonus' model to the SET_BONUS program. Now the program will start automatically when you start the calculation using this model.

Notice that the source code of the program called from within a model can contain anything. This program will start any time you specify a calculation using this model.

More detailed information on the reserved OFA directories, read the following document: "*Hooks in the Oracle Financial Analyzer Application Interface*".

10.4.8. Creating Solve Definitions and Group Solve Definitions

To calculate financial data by the hierarchies and models that you have created, it is necessary to create special objects—*Solve Definitions* and *Group Solve Definitions*. The Solve Definition object is related to the specific financial data item and can include simultaneous calculations by model and hierarchy.

The data must be recalculated whenever:

☐ The source data stored in the database have changed in any way

☐ Any changes were introduced to the model or hierarchy structure

☐ New dimension values were added

☐ New time periods were added

To create or edit a solve definition, open the **Solve Definition** dialog by selecting the **Solve Definition** command from the **Tools** menu (Fig. 10.24).

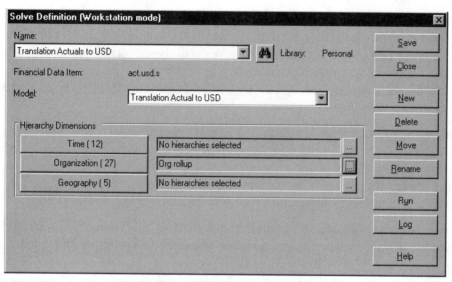

Fig. 10.24. The **Solve Definition** dialog

The main components of the **Solve Definition** dialog are briefly described below:

❏ **Name**—the name of the selected solve definition.

❏ **Financial Data Item**—the name of the calculated financial data item.

❏ **Model**—the drop-down list containing the names of models existing on the dimensions of the financial data item that needs to be calculated. Select one of the models or accept the None value.

❏ **Hierarchy Dimensions**—list of dimensions and their related hierarchies.

❏ **Other Dimensions**—list of dimensions for which there are no hierarchies (if such dimensions are present).

At the rightmost part of this dialog there are several standard command buttons. The **Run (Submit)** buttons deserve special mention. Using this button, you can start the Solve Definition for execution or submit it to the task processor. Detailed information explaining which button, **Run** or **Submit**, will appear in the **Solve Definition** dialog is provided in *Section 10.3.3, "Configuring workstation settings"*.

To specify the solve definition, select the model from the **Model** drop-down list (the model will be used within this solve definition). Next, double-click the button labeled with the dimension name to open the **Selector** window, where you can select the dimension values for which it is necessary to calculate the data.

If necessary, double-click the hierarchy button to open the **Selector** window, where you can select the hierarchy by which the data aggregation will be performed. For example, if it is necessary to perform the calculation according to the model for monthly customs expenses by quarterly taxes, only months must be present in the time dimension. The next solve definition will perform data aggregation by the time dimension.

For the moment, we have approached another object—Group Solve Definitions. This object is required in order to sequentially perform all the Solve Definitions for the financial data item or for a series of financial data items. In the example provided above, the group is formed by the two Solve Definitions—resolution by model and summing by hierarchy.

Group Solve Definitions are created and edited via the **Group Solve Definition** window that you can open by selecting the **Group Solve Definition** command from the **Tools** menu (Fig. 10.25).

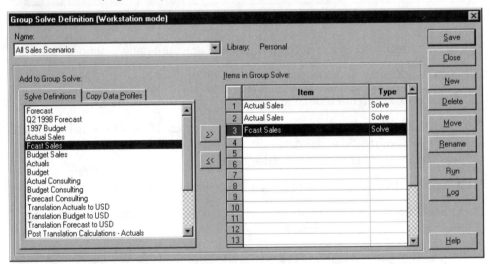

Fig. 10.25. The dialog for maintaining Group Solve definitions

The main components of the **Group Solve Definition** dialog are briefly described below:

☐ **Name**—name of the Group Solve Definition.

☐ The **Add to Group Solve** field contains the list of Solve Definitions available in the database of the Solve Definitions (the **Solve Definition** tab) and a list of Copy Profiles (at the second tab labeled **Copy Data Profiles**).

❏ The Items in the **Group Solve** field, where you select **Solve Definitions** and **Copy Profiles**.

❏ Standard buttons at the right part of the window. Besides other standard buttons, this window contains the **Run** (or **Submit**) button for starting all the **Solve Definitions** and **Copy Profiles** (see *Section 10.4.3*, *"Copying data"*) selected from the right list.

Thus, using the **Group Solve Definition** object, you can, for example, at once calculate all the data in financial data items, and then using the **Copy Profiles** copy these data slices to other financial data items. You can start the execution of solve definitions using the following methods:

❏ Use the appropriate dialog (Figs 10.24 and 10.25).

❏ Relate the financial data item to be calculated to the specific **Solve Definition** or **Group Solve Definition** via the special dialog for maintaining financial data items (see *Section 10.4.3*, *"Creating a new financial data item"*), by selecting them from the lists of the **Profile to Solve** area. Now any change of the data in the financial data item will start the specified **Solve Definition** or **Group Solve Definition**.

10.5. Creating Documents for Viewing Information Such as Reports, Worksheets, Data Entry Form, and Graphs

Documents that OFA uses to represent the data can be subdivided into the following four groups:

❏ Worksheets. These are tables used for data input

❏ Graphs

❏ Reports—the tables for viewing data

❏ Special forms for data input via the Web (Data Entry Form)—these forms are created and edited like reports

To create a new document, click the **New** button in the toolbar (Fig. 10.26), then select the document type that you are going to create and click **OK**.

To open a new document, it is necessary to click the **Open** button (1) in the toolbar (Fig. 10.27), and then go to the **Choose form** field (2) and select the required document type—**Worksheet**, **Report**, or **Graph**.

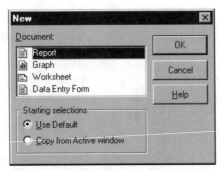

Fig. 10.26. The **New** dialog for creating new documents

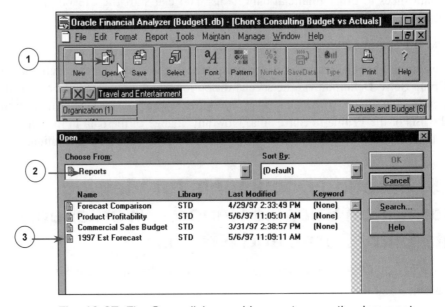

Fig. 10.27. The **Open** dialog enables you to open the document

In the lower field (3), a list of documents from the selected section will appear. Select the required one and click **OK**. You can also click the **Search** button to open the dialog containing special options intended to simplify the process of searching the required document.

10.5.1. The Selector Dialog

A new document is created by default. The first financial data item available in the database and its slice by the first dimension values is selected. Therefore, after creating the new document or changing a document that has already been created;

the **Selector** dialog appears (Fig. 10.28). Open the document and click the **Select** button at the toolbar or double-click the button labeled with the name of the required dimension. Using the **Selector** dialog, you can select one or more financial data items and a specific subset of dimension values. This can be a set of values of a group representing a hierarchical level, or a selected set based on the exclusionary criteria.

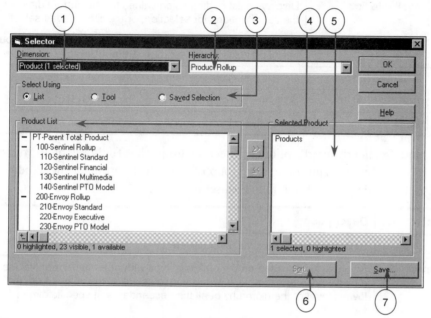

Fig. 10.28. The **Selector** dialog

This dialog contains the following components:

#	Component	Description
1	Dimension	The list of all dimensions that are required by the data in the document
2	Hierarchy	Selection of an appropriate hierarchy for the current dimension
3	Select Using	Describes the method used for selection: **List**–displays all the values for the current selected dimension or hierarchy **Tool**–displays a selection tools that help to select values from the current dimension

continues

Continued

#	Component	Description
		Saved Selection—contains the saved selections for the current dimension
4	Available list	Displays a list of dimension values for the current dimension, the set of options for selection, or the list of saved selections What will actually be displayed in this field depends on your selection in the 3 option group (**Select Using**)
5	Selected list	Contains the list of dimension values that you have selected
6	Sort	Sorts the selected values using the **Sort Select** dialog
7	Save	Saves the selection set as a Saved Selection for reuse

The most frequently used option is selection using the **Tools** set of instruments. When you select the **Tool** option, a group of icons will appear in the Product list field that provide you with the following set of options.

Tool	Description
All	Selects all available dimension values
Family	Selects values based on their relationships with other dimension values in a hierarchy. For example, it allows you to select all the values from the lowest level of the hierarchy or all the descendants of specific dimension value
Attribute	Selects according to the attribute associated to each value
Match	Character-based selection
Exception	Selection by exceptions
Top/Bottom	Top/Bottom selection based on a specified criterion

10.5.2. Folders

We advise you to actively use the capability of sorting documents by Folders. To create a new folder, open the **Maintain Folders** dialog (Fig. 10.29) by selecting the **Maintain Folders** command from the **Tools** menu. In this dialog, click the **Create** button to open the **Create Folder** dialog, and specify the new folder name. To add a document to the folder, use the **Maintain Folders** dialog. Select the folder to which you are going to add documents from the drop-down list (2), click the **Add** button to open the **Add** dialog, select the documents to be added to the folder, and click **OK**.

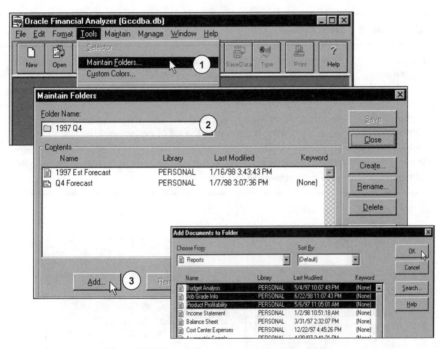

Fig. 10.29. Adding documents to a folder

10.5.3. Components of the Document Window

You can open several reports and graphs at once, but only one worksheet at a time. Within a window, you can cascade opened tables and graphs, or tile them horizontally or vertically. To set the required placement, select the appropriate option from the **Window** menu. Only one window can be active at a time. The opened document determines the content of the menu bar. To activate a document, click it with the mouse.

The **Dimension tile** buttons are the most important components of any document. In Fig. 10.30 they are marked by circles numbered 1, 2, and 3. These buttons show the names of the dimension values of the financial data item dimensions represented in the document. The number in parentheses shows the number of dimension values selected for each dimension. The button position specifies where exactly the specific dimension will appear within the table. Listed below are brief descriptions of the dimensions in positions 1, 2, and 3.

#	Component	Description
1	**Page dimensions**	The buttons in the top left corner represent page dimensions. To navigate pages, use the drop-down lists that appear when you click the top left corner of the table
2	**Column dimension**	The buttons at the top right corner specify the column dimensions, the data of which appear in the table columns
3	**Row dimension**	The buttons at the bottom left corner specify the dimension with the data that appear in the table rows

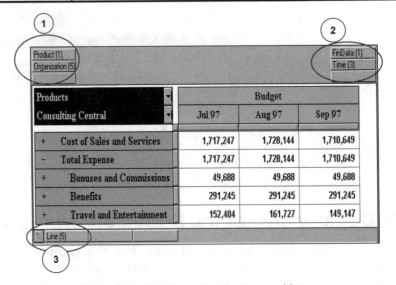

Fig. 10.30. Dimension button positions

You can easily modify your document by dragging the dimension buttons and dropping them at the desired positions.

To save the modified document under the same name, select the **File —> Save** menu commands. If you need to save the modified document under another name, select **File —> Save As**. To delete the existing document, select the document to be deleted from the list and select the **File —> Delete** commands from the menu bar. To rename the existing document, select **File —> Rename**.

10.5.4. Working with Reports

When you open a report, the Report item will appear in the menu, providing the following options.

❏ **Report Options**—options that influence the layout of the current report

❏ **Dimension Labels**—manages the dimension value labels within a report

❏ **Drill**—provides drilling capabilities

❏ **Auto Redisplay**—enables the auto-refresh option for the report

❏ **Asymmetric Format**—creates reports with an asymmetric format

❏ **Ranking/Exception**—opens the dialog that allows us to perform selection based on ranking and exception mechanisms

The **Format** menu command provides several formatting options for the report, including text formatting and alignment, font and background color selection, frame editing, etc.

To format numeric data, select the **Format —> Number** commands that work like the analogous Excel commands.

You can insert rows and columns into the report. Highlight the title of the required row or column, then select **Edit —> Insert (Delete)** commands from the menu, and specify the number of rows or columns to be inserted or deleted.

You can perform calculations within your reports. For this purpose, insert one or more rows or columns into the report, provide appropriate names for the inserted rows or columns, and specify the formula according to which the calculations will be performed on the fly (Fig. 10.31) and inserted into the new rows or columns.

The formula can calculate data both for individual cells and for entire rows or columns. The formula consists of algebraic expressions containing operators, numeric constants, dimension values, and functions. It has the following format:

```
RESULT=EXPRESSION
```

Here, RESULT is the reference to the calculated cells within the report. It appears automatically when you highlight the appropriate report cells. You can enter the formula manually or use the built-in option provided in the **Formula Tools** dialog that is opened by clicking the **f** button on the **Edit** panel.

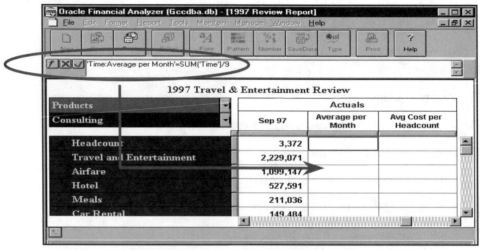

Fig. 10.31. Using calculations in reports

You can export the data from your report to an Excel file for use in other applications. To export the report data, open the report to be exported, select the **File —> Export to File** commands, and fill the form that is displayed.

To print the opened report, use the **Print Preview (File —> Print Preview)** and **Print (File —> Print)** commands from the menu. To print several documents at a time, select the **Print Multiple** command (**File —> Print Multiple**). Be careful when printing and make sure that you know how many pages are supposed to be printed.

10.5.5. Working with Worksheets

The main difference between the Worksheet and the Report lies in the fact that the worksheet allows data entry. All the other options of working with worksheets and reports — including formatting, drilling, and selection—are similar. Therefore, we won't look at these options again.

The worksheet can be used to modify data and perform calculations, such as growing, increasing, and spreading data. The worksheet is a key object for composing the budget, a forecast, or a "What if?" analysis, since it enables you to enter, modify, and calculate data.

Notice the following aspects of worksheet usage:

❐   Only one worksheet can be opened at a time.

❒ Worksheets work only with stored financial data items.

❒ Only one financial data item can be selected at a time, in contrast to reports where you can select several financial data items. To enter data into the worksheet, click the desired cell within a table. This will activate the Edit Bar, where you can enter the number. Having completed data entry, press <Enter>.

When you open the worksheet, the **Worksheet** menu item will be activated. This menu item contains a list of options similar to the options available when working with reports, with the exception of the last command—**Worksheet Tools**. This command unites the data manipulation options (Fig. 10.32).

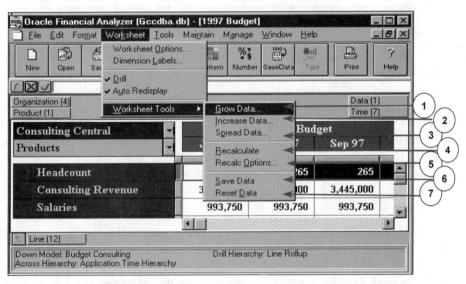

Fig. 10.32. The **Worksheet Tools** command is responsible for data manipulation

The **Worksheet Tools** commands include:

#	Command	Description
1	**Grow Data**	Grows data incrementally across the worksheet columns or down its rows by an amount or a percentage
2	**Increase Data**	Lets you increase the data within a row (column) by a constant amount or percentage
3	**Spread Data**	Spreads the data from the parents at the top hierarchical level to the lower levels (for example, the quarterly data can be spread by months)

continues

Continued

#	Command	Description
4	**Recalculate**	Allows you to recalculate the data based on the selected hierarchy or model
5	**Recalc Options**	Allows you to specify the model of hierarchy for recalculation
6	**Save Data**	Saves the data in the database
7	**Reset Data**	Resets the worksheet data to its initial state (the state that existed at the moment of the last save operation)

Now let us consider each of the above listed commands in more detail.

❑ **Grow Data**. The use of this option results in a proportional increase in the data in the specified group of cells. The value in the first cell will remain unchanged, while other values will proportionally increase (or decrease, if you have specified a negative value for the grow parameter) by the value of the specified parameter. For example, the row containing the numbers 4,5,6 after growing by 5 will contain 4,9,14. To perform the grow operation, select the required group of cells (it may be the entire row, a column, or even a combination of rows and columns). Then select the **Worksheet —> Worksheet Tools —> Grow Data** commands from the menu and specify the grow parameter when prompted. Click **OK**.

❑ **Increase Data**. As with the previous operation, select the required group of cells, then select the **Worksheet —> Worksheet Tools —> Increase Data** commands from the menu, specify the increase parameter when prompted, and then click **OK**. For example, a row containing the numbers 4,5,6, after increasing by 5, will contain 9,10,11.

❑ **Spread Data**. This command is used when it is necessary to spread the data from parents to descendants within a hierarchy (for example, the quarter is the parent for months in the time hierarchy). Select an individual column or row (naturally, a hierarchy must exist for the dimension of this row or column). Select the **Worksheet —> Worksheet Tools —> Spread Data** commands from the menu to open the **Spread Data** dialog shown in Fig. 10.33.

In the **Spread Data** dialog, the **Spread** drop-down list provides the following three options:

  ❑ **Evenly**—using this method, the "parent" value is evenly spread between all descendants

❐ **Keeping Same Profile**—if you use this method, the "parent" value will be distributed among descendants using the existing spread profile

❐ **Using Another Item's Profile**—use this option when it is necessary, for example, to spread data by months of the second quarter using the same profile that was used for the months of the first quarter

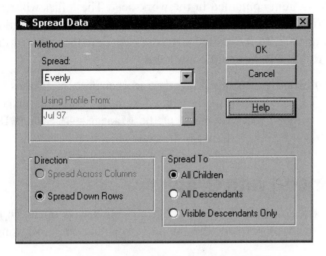

Fig. 10.33. The **Spread Data** dialog

The **Direction** options—specifies the spread direction.

It is possible to specify the values to which you need to spread the data. You can spread the data to all children, all descendants, or to all descendants of the current parent visible in the table.

❐ **Recalculate**. Starts the process of data recalculation.

❐ **Recalc Options**. Specifies the names of hierarchies and models according to which data must be recalculated in your worksheet.

❐ **Save Data**. This option is duplicated by a similarly named button in the toolbar.

❐ **Reset Data**. Resets the data to the state that existed at the moment of the last Save operation.

Like reports, you can export worksheet data to a file or print it out.

10.5.6. How Changes are Saved in the Shared Database

As we already mentioned, the Analyst user has no local data and works directly with the data stored in the shared database. When he or she fills the worksheet and clicks the **Save** button, the system will create export files containing the data slice for the financial data item contained in the worksheet. These files will reside in the taskfile directory on the server until the Task Processor processes them. After this, the files will be imported to the shared database. To view the updated data, select the **Manage —> Refresh Data** menu commands.

Budget and Administrator users save local data in their local databases by clicking the **Save** button. To submit data to the shared database and thus make this data available to other users of the system, select the **Manage —> Submit Data** menu commands, which will be covered later in this chapter.

10.5.7. Working with Graphs

Graphs are created just as reports and worksheets. When you open the graph, the **Graph** command will appear in the menu, providing the following options (Fig. 10.34):

1—**Type**—allows you to select the graph type

2—**Legend**—sets the graph legend display mode

3—**Pie Options**—options for the pie charts.

4—**Grid**—specifies the grid display mode

5—**Graph options**—manages the graph layout options

6—**Dimension Labels**—manages the dimension labels on the graph

7—**Auto Redisplay**—automatically refreshes the graph after updating the data

OFA allows you to select the following 7 graph types:

- ❑ Line
- ❑ Vertical bar
- ❑ Horizontal bar
- ❑ Bar line
- ❑ Area
- ❑ Pie chart
- ❑ Scatter

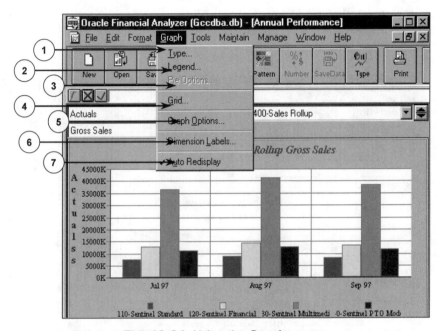

Fig. 10.34. Using the **Graph** menu

For each graph type there exist several subtypes. To modify the graph type, open the **Graph Type** dialog by selecting the **Graph —> Type** menu commands or by clicking the **Type Tool** at the toolbar.

The graph's components (Fig. 10.35) are briefly described below:

1—**Y-axis**—represents values on the Y-axis

2—**X-axis**—represents values on the X-axis

3—**Legend**—the area containing key information on the data displayed by the graph, including color choice

4—**Page Control spinner**—provides the capability of navigating the graph by dimension values placed in pages

5—**Data marker**—bar charts, lines, areas, or points used to represent the data

When working with graphs, you can apply the same formatting options as with reports and worksheets. You can use the **Selector** tool for selecting data slices for analysis, align text, and format numbers. Besides, you can change the graph color, typeface, and font color for the text labels. To perform this formatting, select the graph element and click the **Font** or **Pattern** buttons at the toolbar (depending on

the graph element that you have selected). Then specify the required options —
such as font, color, or template—based on available patterns.

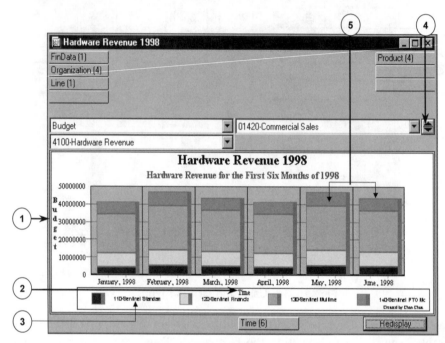

Fig. 10.35. Graph components

Graph data can also be exported to the file. To export graph data, select the
File —> Export to File menu commands, and when prompted, specify the file
name and complete path to the file.

10.6. Creating New System Users. Distributing Structures and Data. Access Control

As we said before, the first login to the OFA system must be done using the super
administrator workstation. The super administrator personal database becomes the
first step in creating the whole infrastructure of the budgeting system. We have also
already described the process of creating database structures for the whole OFA
system.

Now we will concentrate on the administrative tasks, such as creating new users, distributing database structures and financial data, and controlling changes to the shared database.

10.6.1. Creating a New User

In *Section 10.3.2*, we discussed the procedure of installing the OFA client-side software. The topic of installing a new workplace for the end user was also covered. Performing this task, however, is only the first step in the process of creating a new user. Now the new user must be added to the system.

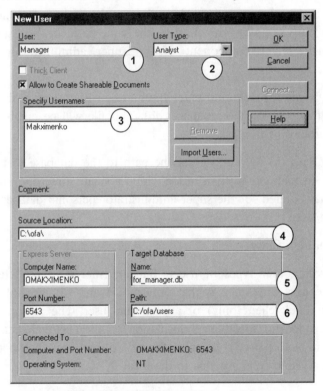

Fig. 10.36. The **New User** dialog

To create a new user, do the following:

1. Open the **Maintain Users** dialog by selecting the **Manage —> Users** menu commands.

2. Click the **New** button. The **New User** dialog will appear (Fig. 10.36).

3. Enter a name for the new user (1), for example, **Manager**. This name is used by OFA to validate the workstation at startup.

4. Select the user type from the drop-down list (2). You can select the following user types: **Analyst**, **Budget**, or **External** user. The topic was covered in detail in *Section 10.2, "Product Architecture"*.

5. Click the **Import Users** button to open the **Import Users** dialog. This dialog will contain the list of operating system users. Select one or more users. Notice that later you'll be able to change the user settings if necessary.

6. Go to the **Source Location** (4) field and enter the path to the Shells directory (C:/ofa, in our example). This must be the same path that you specified when installing the server component of the super administration workstation (Fig. 10.3).

7. Go to the **Name** (5) field and enter the name of the personal database of the new user (for example, For_manager.db). This file will be created by the system after processing the task.

8. Go to the **Path** (6) field and enter the path to the database to be created. If you want personal databases to reside within a single directory, enter the same name as was entered for the super administrator personal database (for example, C:/ofa/users).

9. Click **Save**, then **Close**.

Proceed to create other types of users—**Budget**, **Analyst**, and **External**—in the same way. The only difference is that options (5) and (6) are not available for a Budget user (thick client only) or an External user. The reason is that these options are intended for specifying information on the personal database. As you remember, there is no personal database for an External user. As for the thick client, the personal database is installed to the local PC.

To submit information on a new user to the shared database, it is necessary to start the Task Processor. This topic will be covered in *Section 10.7, "Task Processor"*.

The procedure of starting the session for the Manager user is similar to the procedure for super administrator user. This topic was covered in *Section 10.3.3, "Getting Started"*.

10.6.2. Distributing Structures

The Administrator is responsible for providing users with access to the database objects necessary to perform their jobs. The process of providing user access to the shared database objects is known as distribution. You can distribute objects from the super administrator database to the shared database and to the personal databases of the users.

The following objects are subject to distribution:

❏ Dimensions

❏ Dimension values

❏ Financial data items

❏ Hierarchies

❏ Models

❏ Attributes

❏ Solve Definitions and Group Solve Definitions

❏ Saved selections

❏ Data slices containing numeric values used to fill financial data items

You need to perform distribution in the following cases:

❏ A new object has been created in the database

❏ An existing database object has been changed

❏ An existing database object must be deleted

❏ A new database user who needs to access shared database objects has been created

❏ Data stored in the database has been changed, or new data has been saved to the database, and you need to provide users with access to this data

In a multi-level OFA system, the structures and data flow in the following way (Fig. 10.37):

❏ The Administrator creates OFA structures in his or her personal database.

❏ The Administrator creates distribution for the users, including all the objects required for the users to perform their jobs.

❑ The Task Processor to update the shared database and send the distribution to the personal user databases is started.

❑ The lower-level users submit data sliced from their personal databases to the shared database. They can submit documents such as reports, worksheets, and graphs. All the other objects they create themselves, rather than receive from the distribution procedure, remain in their personal databases for their own use. The **Library** property of the user-created objects is set to `Personal`.

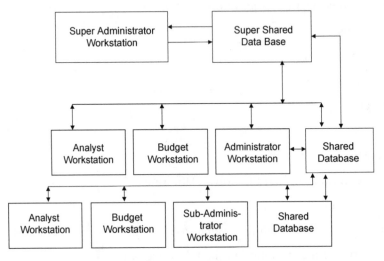

Fig. 10.37. Data flow in the OFA system

Structure distribution is performed via the **Distribute Structure** (Fig. 10.38) dialog that can be opened by selecting the **Manage —> Distribution —> Distribute Structure** commands from the menu.

From the list (1), select the items that you need to distribute, then click the **>>** button. The selected objects will move to the field on the right (2). Select the values of the items that you need to distribute. To accomplish this, double-click the required item with the mouse. The **Selector** window will open. The number of selected values appears on the right in parentheses. Next, click the **Action** button, and select the distribution type (**Add** by default). To select another action, right-click the cell containing the **Add** value to display the drop-down list of available actions, which includes the following:

❑ **Add**—adds new objects to the users.

❑ **Delete from users**—deletes objects from personal databases.

☐ **Delete from System**—deletes objects from the entire system.

☐ **Redistribute**—redistributes a changed object that was already distributed.

☐ **Add with Write Access**—this action, like the next one, appears only for reports, graphs, and worksheets. It enables users to modify these documents and then submit them back to the shared database. When working with worksheets, this option enables you to edit data directly in the shared database.

☐ **Remove with Write Access**—removes the user right granted by the previous option.

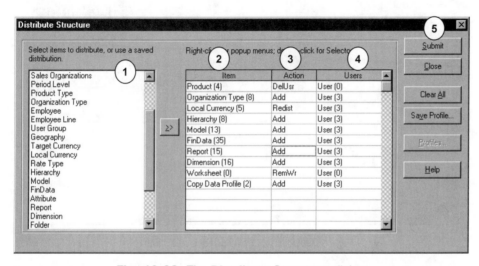

Fig. 10.38. The **Distribute Structure** dialog

For each selected item you need to specify the list of users for whom it is intended. Double-click the **Users** cell (4) to open the **Selector** dialog where you can select users. The first user in the list is Shared, which means the shared database. Notice that even if you don't select this user, all the structures will still first be exported to the shared database, and then to personal databases.

The specified distribution can be saved for future use. Click the **Save Profile** button (see Fig. 10.38) and enter the name.

To submit the distribution for processing, click the **Submit** button (5) in the dialog shown in Fig. 10.38.

10.6.3. Distributing Data

Data distribution is performed via the **Distribute Data** dialog which you can open by selecting the **Manage —> Distribution —> Distribute Data** commands from the menu (Fig. 10.39).

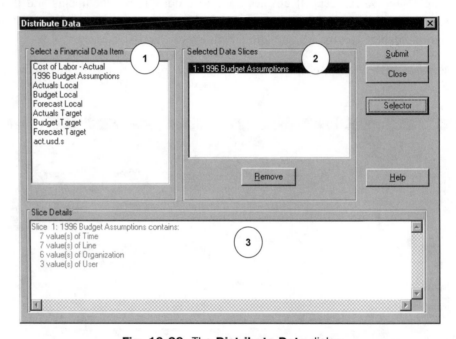

Fig. 10.39. The **Distribute Data** dialog

Notice that you can distribute only the slices of the stored financial data items determined as distributable (see option (8) in Fig. 10.13 in *Section 10.4.3, "Creating financial data items"*).

To distribute data slices, double-click the required financial data item from the list (1) and click the **Selector** button. In the **Selector** dialog select the slices by dimensions of the financial data item. The information on the selected slice will appear in the **Slice Details** field (3). Repeat this procedure if you need to distribute several financial data items.

Click **OK**. The distribution will be submitted to the Task Processor.

As practice has shown, data are rarely distributed using this method. This is partly due to the fact that this procedure is complicated and time consuming, especially if you need to load a large amount of data. As a general rule, data are loaded from external sources directly to the shared database. Users who enter data manually are generally using the Analyst workstation, from which they also enter data directly to the shared database.

Data are rarely stored in the personal database of the system administrator. This is not necessary, and, furthermore, the database grows rapidly, up to 1-2 GB even for a medium-size company. Certainly, duplicating this data in the personal database of the administrator is not particularly efficient. Therefore, this method of distributing data slices is most frequently used with budget users with a thick client installation when it is necessary to work standalone.

10.6.4. Distribution Report

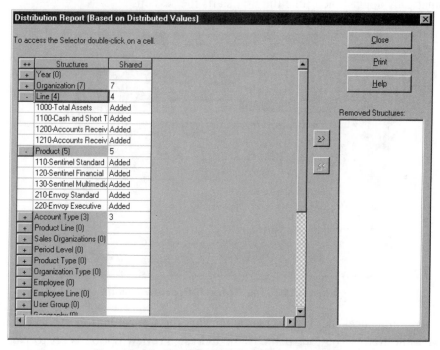

Fig. 10.40. The **Distribution Report** window

You can get a report on the distributed structures. This report will enable you to control the structures distributed to the users, and is very efficient if you have a distributed system with a large number of users. To get a distribution report, select the **Manage —> Distribution Reports —> Based on Distributed Values (or Based on All Values)** commands from the menu to open the dialog shown in Fig. 10.40.

The **Based on Distributed Values** command creates a report on the structures that were distributed to at least one user. The **Based on All Values** commands create a report on all structures available in the administrator database (however, the number of users to whom such structures are distributed will be 0).

10.6.5. Accepting Distributions

If the user has set **Show Refresh Preview** to **Yes** in his or her personal database (as you remember, this is done by selecting the **Tools —> Options** menu commands and then clicking the **General** icon), the **Refresh Preview** dialog (Fig. 10.41) will automatically appear each time the user starts the session.

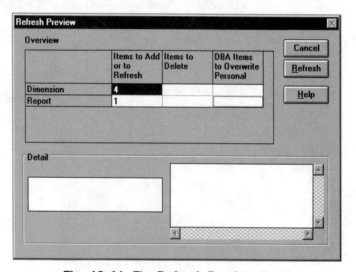

Fig. 10.41. The **Refresh Preview** dialog

The user can cancel the distribution by clicking the **Cancel** button, or accept it by clicking the **Refresh** button. If the **Show Refresh Preview** option is set to **No**, this dialog will not be displayed, and the user database will be refreshed automatically.

If some structures were distributed to the user in the course of a session, he or she will be able to receive them without closing the session by selecting the **Manage —> Refresh Structure** menu commands.

10.6.6. Updating Data in Personal Databases

To update data stored in a personal database with data from the shared database, the Analyst user needs to select the **Manage —> Refresh Data** menu commands. This will cause the shared database to be detached and the reattached to the Analyst session in read-only mode. As we already said, the Analyst has only structures, and no local data in the personal database. Therefore, he works directly with the data stored in the shared database, actual for the moment of opening the current session. If the data in the shared database was modified during the business day, the Analyst will view obsolete data until he or she performs the refresh operation.

The Budget user must import the data into his or her personal database in order to refresh them. By selecting the **Manage —> Refresh Data** menu commands, a dialog similar to the **Distribute Data** window (Fig. 10.41) will open. To accomplish the refresh operation, he or she needs to select the financial data item and its slice by dimensions, and then click **Run**.

10.6.7. Submitting Data to the Shared Database

As we said before, the Analyst submits the data to the shared database by simply clicking the **Save** button in the worksheet.

On the other hand, to submit data to the shared database, the Budget user must select the **Manage —> Submit Data** menu commands, select the financial data item and its slice by dimensions, and then click the **Submit** button.

Any data submission to the shared database is performed via Task Processor rather than directly.

10.6.8. Controlling Write Access

The Administrator can block write access to selected slices of financial data items using the **Write Access Profile** dialog (Fig. 10.42). To open this dialog, select the **Manage —> Write Access Profiles** commands from the menu.

To create a write access profile, open the **Write Access Profile** dialog, and select the required financial data item from the drop-down list. Click **New** to open the next dialog, where you can select options for the dimensions, the subset of which will be selected for the slice. Notice that the user list appears as values of another dimension—Users. For unselected dimensions, all the values will be included. Click **OK**. You'll return to the **Write Access Profile** dialog. Highlight the dimension list in the **Profile** field and click the **Edit** button. In the next dialog (Fig. 10.43), select the cells that need to be write-protected. Now any attempts by the selected users to save data in these cells will result in error messages informing the users that the cells are write-protected.

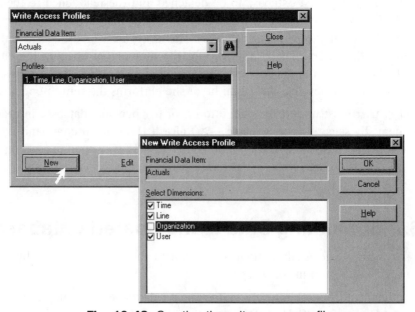

Fig. 10.42. Creating the write access profile

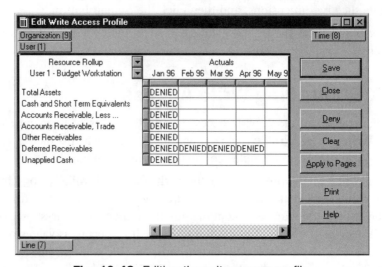

Fig. 10.43. Editing the write access profile

10.7. Task Processor

When describing the product architecture, we looked at the task processor work-station and its tasks. Remember that this workstation is always connected to the system administrator workstations and enables the administrator to control data flow from user databases to the shared database. As a matter of fact, the system administrator can refresh the shared database only via the task processor by starting it from his or her workstation or in a separate session.

To better understand the task processor, let us consider how the data submitted by the user are placed to the shared database. As you know, informational exchange (both data and structures) between multidimensional Express databases is performed via export files with the EIF filename extension. When the user submits data to the shared database, this data is exported to the files that reside in the taskfile directory. Information on each submitted task is passed to the task processor. The system administrator can use the **Manage —> Task Queue** commands to open the **Task Queue** dialog (Fig. 10.44). This dialog enables him or her to view information on financial data item slices submitted by users to the shared database. The administrator can schedule the task, change the position of tasks within a queue, suspend submitted tasks, or even delete the task from the queue. If the administrator decides that a submitted task must be processed immediately, he or she can start the task processor that executes the commands to import the files from the taskfile directory to the shared database. After importing the files, task processor deletes them. Task processor can also run in background mode. In this case, the tasks will be processed as they are submitted, i.e., as export files appear in the taskfile directory.

The components of the **Task Queue** dialog are briefly described below.

1—the **Select** options enable you to select tasks for viewing according to the following two criteria—by submission or processing time, or by submitters.

2—the **Task List** area contains information on the tasks selected using the **Select** options. It includes: the submitter (the user who submitted the current task), the type of the task (the keyword), the task status (whether or not it is already processed), date and time of submission, the start time of the task processing, the time of completion, and the task's position within a queue. If you right-click a task within the task list, a context menu with the following options will appear:

- [ ] **History**—the field (3) will display the task history

- [ ] **Details**—the field (3) will display the detailed history of the task

- ☐ **Schedule**—opens the dialog enabling you to schedule the task to be processed at the specified date and time

- ☐ **Delete**—deletes the task from the queue

3—the **Task History/Details** field provides detailed information on the selected task. If the task type is data submission, this field will display the name of the financial data item and a slice of its dimensions.

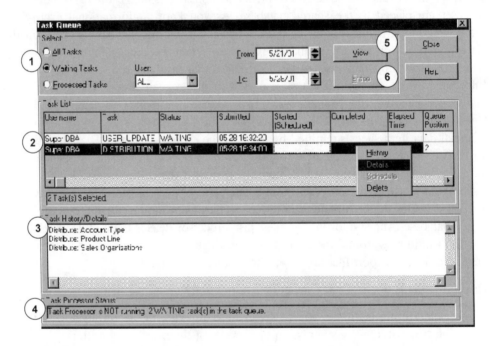

Fig. 10.44. The **Task Queue** dialog enables you to analyze the queued tasks

4—the **Task Processor Status** area contains the data on the task processor status: is it currently started, how many tasks have already been processed since starting, and how many are still waiting in the queue.

5—the **View** button displays information in the **Task List**.

6—the **Erase** button clears the history of the processed task.

All the tasks submitted for processing can have one of the following types:

Task	Keyword	Description
Data submission	SUBMIT DATA	Submits data from personal databases to the shared database
Distribution	DISTRIBUTION	Distributes structures to the users and to the shared database
Data distribution	DATA_DIST	Distributes data to the users and to the shared database
Calculation	SOLVE MODEL	Recalculates the data in the shared database based on the selected solve definition or group solve definition
Copying data	COPY DATA	Copies data slices in the shared database
Loader program loading data to the shared database	LOAD DATA	Loads data from external sources to the shared database using a program
Updating users	USER_UPDATE	Creates, edits, or deletes user accounts
Enable external users to access the shared database	ENABLE	Enables external users to access the shared database

The task processor can be started via the **Task Processor** dialog (Fig. 10.45) that you can open by selecting the **Manage —> Task Processor** commands.

The components of this dialog are briefly described below:

1—options for selecting the working mode: **Foreground**, **Background**, or the **Stop** option for stopping the task processor

2—the **Set State** button sets the state selected by the option

3—the **Task Log** area dynamically provides information on the task being processed

4—the **Task Queue Status** area contains the number of the tasks waiting in the queue and the number of completed tasks, along with completion status (success or failure)

To start the task processor in the foreground mode, select the **Start in the Foreground** option and click the **Set State** button. Notice the content of the **Task Log** and **Task Queue Status** fields. To stop the task processor, select the **Stop** option and click **Set State**.

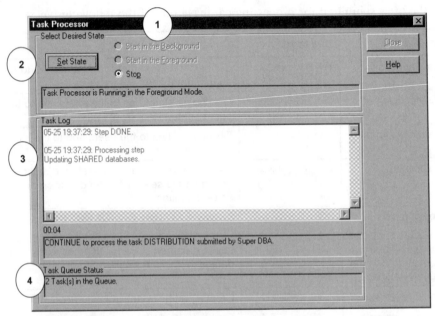

Fig. 10.45. The **Task Processor** dialog enables you to start or stop the task processor

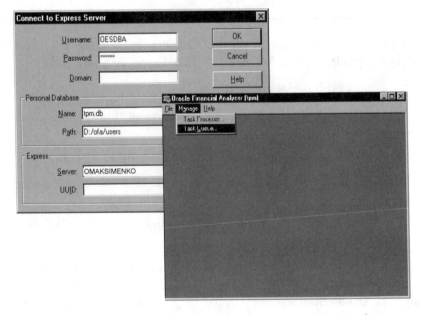

Fig. 10.46. Starting the task processor in a separate session

Since the task processor window works in interactive mode, and task processing may be time-consuming (for example, when it is necessary to load a large amount of data), it is recommended that you start the task processor in a separate session. Open a new OFA session and specify tpm.db as the database name. This is the name of the service database that is created in the course of installing the OFA server component in the user directory (Fig. 10.46).

10.8. Loading Structures and Data into the Database Using Loader Programs

Earlier in this chapter, in *Sections 10.4*, "*Creating the database structure*", and *10.5.5*, "*Working with Worksheets*", we discussed the aspects of creating dimension values, editing hierarchies using the **Maintain** menu command and data entry using Worksheets.

In practice, these methods are rarely used. In this section we will consider how dimensions values, hierarchies, and data are actually loaded into the database.

Before you start the loading procedure, you need to create dimensions, hierarchies, and financial data items in the database using the **Maintain** menu.

To create a data loader program automatically from the text file, it is necessary to install Oracle Express Administrator on your workstation.

10.8.1. Loading Dimension Values

Dimension values are loaded from the text file containing the following columns (Fig. 10.47):

❑ **ID**—unique identifier of the dimension value

❑ **Description**—dimension value name

❑ **Row Label**—row label

❑ **Column Label**—column label

We have already discussed these objects in *Section 10.4.2*, "*Specifying dimension values*".

It is advisable to use a combination of the system identifier value and row label for the description. For the column label, it is possible to take either a shortened row label or a system identifier. For example, to load one of the values of the `Line` dimension, you can specify the following parameters:

☐ System identifier (ID): **A6000**

☐ Description: **6000-Total Expense**

☐ Row label: **Total Expense**

☐ Column label: **A6000** (or **Tot_Exp**)

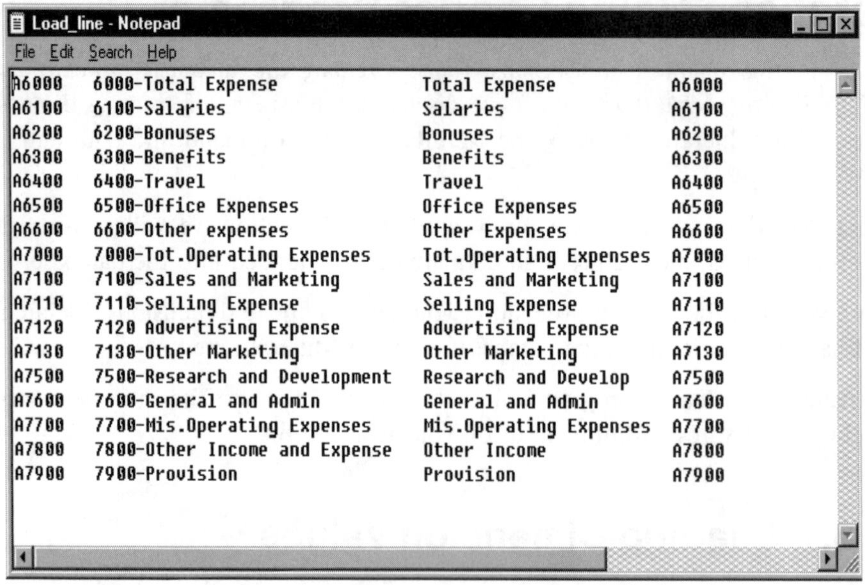

ID	Description	Row Label	Column Label

```
Load_line - Notepad                                                    _ □ X
File  Edit  Search  Help
A6000    6000-Total Expense            Total Expense            A6000
A6100    6100-Salaries                 Salaries                 A6100
A6200    6200-Bonuses                  Bonuses                  A6200
A6300    6300-Benefits                 Benefits                 A6300
A6400    6400-Travel                   Travel                   A6400
A6500    6500-Office Expenses          Office Expenses          A6500
A6600    6600-Other expenses           Other Expenses           A6600
A7000    7000-Tot.Operating Expenses   Tot.Operating Expenses   A7000
A7100    7100-Sales and Marketing      Sales and Marketing      A7100
A7110    7110-Selling Expense          Selling Expense          A7110
A7120    7120 Advertising Expense      Advertising Expense      A7120
A7130    7130-Other Marketing          Other Marketing          A7130
A7500    7500-Research and Development Research and Develop      A7500
A7600    7600-General and Admin        General and Admin        A7600
A7700    7700-Mis.Operating Expenses   Mis.Operating Expenses   A7700
A7800    7800-Other Income and Expense Other Income             A7800
A7900    7900-Provision                Provision                A7900
```

Fig. 10.47. Text file for loading dimension values

Usually, such a text file can be created by copying columns from the Excel file into the text file, using blanks or characters as delimiters.

To create a loader program, do the following:

☐ Open the **Browser** dialog by selecting the **Maintain —> Data Loader —> Create** commands. The **Browser** window is the interface of Oracle Express Administrator with, however, limited functionality.

☐ From the browser menu, select the **File —> Import —> Text** commands to open the **Import Text Data** window (Fig. 10.48).

☐ Use the **Browse** button to select the text file you have prepared.

❏   In the **File Type** option group, select the type of data file: fixed-length fields or character-delimited fields, as in our example.

❏   In the **Record** field, you'll see the first line of the text file. Now for each column select four areas, each of which will correspond to its object in the database tree displayed in the leftmost field. When you complete with the selection of the first column (ID), the bottom window labeled **File Layout** will display its row with the field number—**Field1**, the starting position of the column and its width—**Col1 Width8**, and the text pattern—A6000. The rightmost section— Express Object—remains blank for the moment.

Now expand the Line dimension in the database tree, where we are going to load the values. Drag the Line dimension to the Express Object section of the Field1 field of the ID. The dialog shown in Fig. 10.48 will appear, where you can select the settings for the loading process.

Drag other objects in the same way, and set the options for the remaining objects:

❏   Line.desc in the **Field2** field to specify the dimension value name

❏   Line.lbl.row in the **Field3** field for the row label

❏   Line.lbl.col in the **Field4** field for the column label

Click the **Save** button and specify the name of the loader program (for example, Line_load). After processing the task, the system will create a program with this name, which can be viewed in the database tree under the **Program** section.

Now select the **File —> Exit** commands from the browser menu. You'll return to the OFA window.

To start the Line_load program, open the **Run Data Loader** dialog (Fig. 10.49) that you can open by selecting the **Maintain —> Data Loader —> Run** commands from the menu. Then select our program (Line_load) from the list of available programs in the leftmost pane (**Available Program**); then click the **Run** button.

Notice that if the administrator workstation is configured in the **Workstation (Personal Data)** mode (see *Section 10.3.3, "Customizing the workstation"*), the Line_load program will load the dimension values of the Line dimension into the personal database of the system administrator. If the workstation is configured to run in the **Administrator (Shared Data)** mode, the program will load the data directly to the shared database. If this is the case, the dialog will contain the **Submit** button instead of the **Run** button. After processing the task, the system will create a task for processing by the task processor.

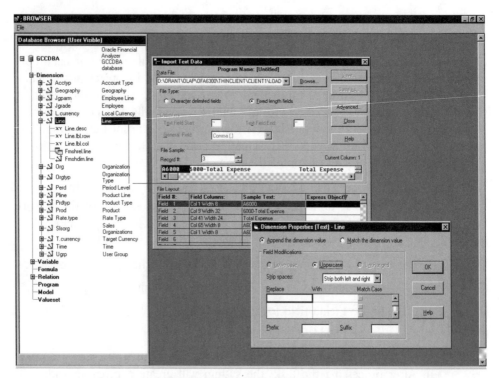

Fig. 10.48. Creating the loader program

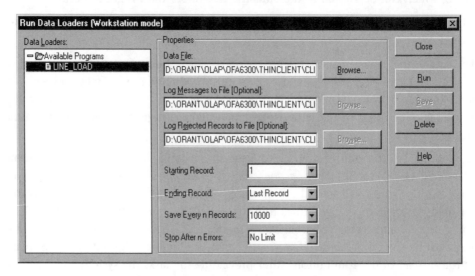

Fig. 10.49. The **Run Data Loaders** dialog

10.8.2. Loading Hierarchies

Loading hierarchies is done the same as loading dimension values, with the exception of two differences:

The text file prepared for loading hierarchies must be formatted as two columns, the first of which contains all the dimension values (under internal system names—ID) that combine the current hierarchy, while the second column, corresponding to each of these values that has the parent within the current hierarchy. If the dimension value has no parent, the second columns must be blank. An example of such a file for the hierarchy of the Line dimension is shown in Fig. 10.50.

When setting the relationship between the database objects and data columns in the text file (see Fig. 10.48), the first column maps to the dimension itself (in our example this is the Line dimension). The second column maps to the Fmshrel.line object. More detailed information on such objects was provided in this chapter in *Section 10.4.7, "Sample models. Creating programs in OFA"*. The dialog box that will appear contains an option that enables you to set the hierarchy into which the relationship must be loaded if there are several hierarchies for the current dimension.

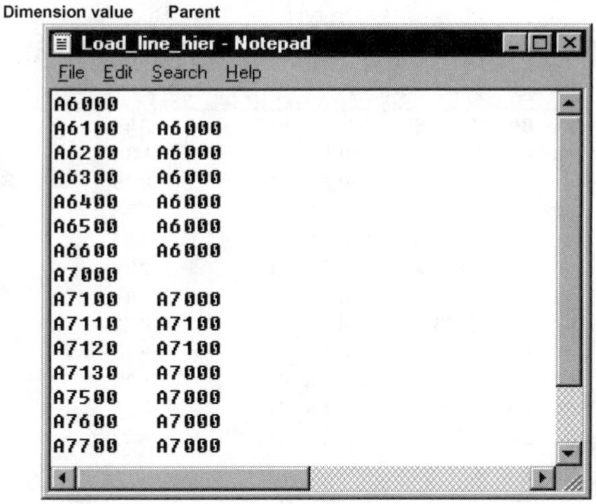

Fig. 10.50. The sample text file for loading hierarchies

10.8.3. Loading Financial Data

Loading data to financial data items can be performed using several methods:

❑ Data entry by means of Worksheets

- Data copying from one financial data item to another one
- Loading data using loader programs

In this section we will concentrate on the latter method—loading data using loader programs.

Loading Financial Data from a Text File

Creating and starting loader programs is done using the Data Loader mechanism similar to the one used for loading dimension values and hierarchies. To open the **Data Loader** window, select the **Maintain —> Data Loader —> Create** commands from the menu. Using this mechanism, you need to create the text file containing the column number equal to the number of dimensions in the financial data item, plus one extra column. For example, to load the `Budget` financial data item defined for three dimensions (`Time`, `Line`, and `Orgtype`), you need to create a file (Fig. 10. 51) where the first, second, and third columns represent the values (under system IDs) of the `Time`, `Line`, and `Orgtype` dimensions, while the fourth column represents the data of the `Budget` financial data item.

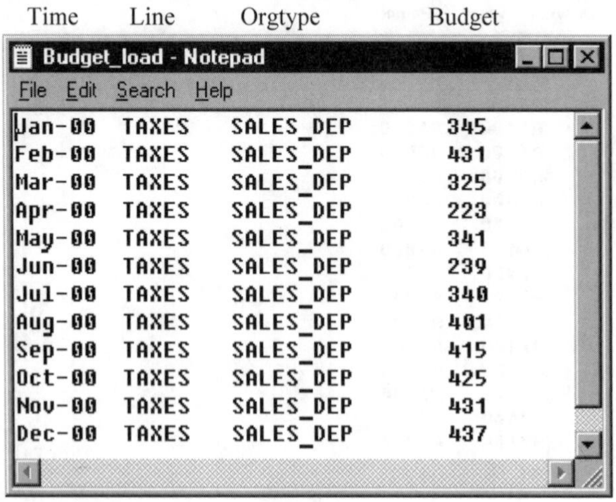

Jan-00	TAXES	SALES_DEP	345
Feb-00	TAXES	SALES_DEP	431
Mar-00	TAXES	SALES_DEP	325
Apr-00	TAXES	SALES_DEP	223
May-00	TAXES	SALES_DEP	341
Jun-00	TAXES	SALES_DEP	239
Jul-00	TAXES	SALES_DEP	340
Aug-00	TAXES	SALES_DEP	401
Sep-00	TAXES	SALES_DEP	415
Oct-00	TAXES	SALES_DEP	425
Nov-00	TAXES	SALES_DEP	431
Dec-00	TAXES	SALES_DEP	437

Fig. 10.51. An example of a text file used for loading financial data

When establishing a correlation between database objects and file columns, the first three columns are mapped to the `Time`, `Line`, and `Orgtype` dimensions, and the fourth columns is mapped to the `Budget` financial data item from the `Variables` section within the database tree displayed in the browser.

Loading Financial Data from Spreadsheets and Relational Databases

Loading data into financial data items from relational databases and spreadsheets such as MS Excel is done with the Express Administrator SQL query built-in mechanism. To create the loader program, you need to open the administrator's personal database in an Express Administrator session. Detailed instructions on the topic are provided in *Section 4.5.1, "Data Import from Oracle Relational Databases and MS Excel Spreadsheets"*.

10.9. Customizing OFA for Working via the Web

Let us return to the section where we discussed the aspects of installing an OFA server component. If you are planning to create Web users in your system, it is necessary to provide information on the location and name of the Web server and the method of loading Web files in the course of OFA installation. See *Section 10.3.1, "Installing the Server Component"*.

To customize OFA Web Publisher, it is necessary to install the following components:

☐ Oracle Express Server

☐ Oracle Financial Analyzer

☐ Express Web Agent

☐ Web Listener, for example, Oracle Web Server v. 3,4

☐ Web browser

Besides installing the required components, you'll need to do the following:

Specify the security settings for Web Agent (Enabling Web Agent Security). To achieve this, start Oracle Express Instance Manager, open the **Web Agent** window by selecting **Parameters,** and set the **WebAuthentication Type** setting to **Basic** (see Fig. 10. 52). Now when you attempt to enter the OFA site, the Web browser will open a dialog prompting the user to provide a username and password.

1. Open Web access to the OFA shared database

   ☐ Start the OFA session from the administrator workstation and select the **Tools —> Enable External Users** commands from the menu. Now external users will be able to access the OFA databases.

2. Customize Web Listener by setting the following physical (based on our example) and virtual directories:

Virtual directory	Physical directory
Ofaweb	C:/ofa/shared/web
Ofastart	C:/ofa/shared

3. Restart Web Listener.
4. Create a new external OFA user (see *Section 10.6.1, "Creating a New User"*).
5. Distribute the required database structures to the new user via the **Manage —> Distribution —> Distribution Structure** menu commands (see *Section 10.6.2, "Distributing Structures"*).

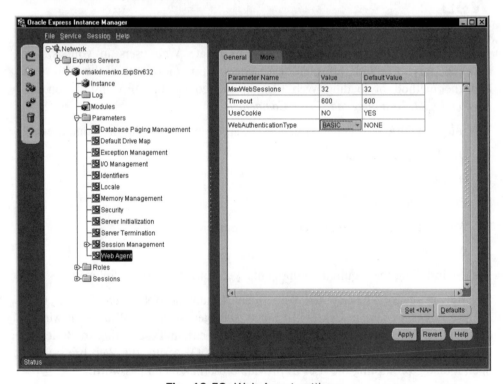

Fig. 10.52. Web Agent settings

To start the OFA Web interface, enter the URL (in our example—http://www.ibs.ru/ofastart). The OFA HTML page (Fig. 10.53) will appear. Click the **Log in** button and enter the username and password for the operating system

ton and enter the username and password for the operating system user associated to the OFA external user.

Fig. 10.53. Log in to the OFA Web interface

The new window prompts you to select the database from the list of available databases.

Finally, the third window opens. It represents the main window of the OFA Web interface (Fig. 10.54). The main components of this window are briefly described below:

1—a list of documents distributed to the external user

2—the area where opened documents are displayed

Starting with OFA version 6.3, external Web and Excel users can enter and edit data using worksheets.

The OFA Web interface provides users with functionality similar to the functionality provided to the Analyst user. However, if you organize the OFA system with Web access, it is required that you take special care to secure access to your OFA databases.

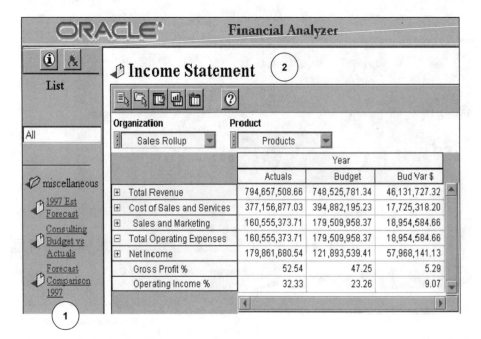

Fig. 10.54. The main window of the OFA Web interface

10.10. Advice for an OFA Administrator

To conclude this chapter, we would like to provide several recommendations and tips for the OFA system administrator:

❑ **Login to the shared database**

Users will enter data to the database on a regular basis. As a result, new tasks will appear in the queue for processing with the following keyword: SUBMIT DATA FROM <username>. The administrator can analyze the queued tasks, send them for processing, or delete them from the queue. After processing, data from export files are entered into the shared database. The administrator must bear in mind that from his or her workstation he or she views local data in his or her personal database. To view submitted information, he or she must log in under the name of the analyst user or perform the Refresh Data procedure to synchronize his local data to the data in the shared database.

If you plan to load the data from external sources on a regular basis, the administrator must start loader programs.

❏ **Aggregation and calculations using models** on the basis of solve definitions and group solve definitions.

Before performing any calculations in the shared database or loading data using external sources, it is necessary to set the following option:

Operation modes (Tools —> Options —> Operations modes) to select the option **Admin/Shared database**.

Otherwise, all these operations will be performed in the administrator's local database.

❏ **Emergency Recovery**

Just in case an emergency should occur, you'd be well advised to perform a daily backup of the whole set of information stored on the server. The tape containing the backup copy must be updated on a daily basis.

❏ Before restarting Express Server or the server operating system, the administrator must inform all the users and ask them to close their sessions. After this, he should start Express Instance Manager, open the Sessions section, and make sure that all the sessions, except for the Initial Session, are closed.

❏ If the network connection to the server is interrupted during an open session, the user gets an error message when trying to reconnect her personal database. The message informs the user that her or his personal database is connected to by another user, or is not found. This happens because the user sessions on the server are not closed, and it is necessary to delete them manually. The administrator must start Express Instance Manager, go to **Sessions,** and close these interrupted sessions by clicking the **Terminate Selected** button.

❏ If unknown error messages or system failures occur, close all sessions and restart Express Server. If errors persist, restart the operating system.

❏ There are two methods of restoring the system from the backup copy:

- Complete restoration of the ENTIRE server contents, including Windows NT settings and registry files. In this case you just need to restore the entire contents of the backup media to the server.

- Restoring only the partition storing OFA directories and the /orant directory. In this case it will be necessary to reinstall Express Server, Express Administrator, and OFA (both the client and server components). After accomplishing this, replace the directories containing OFA databases, /ofa, and /orant/olap/oes630/esextend with backup copies from the tape. Restart the server and make sure that it is up and running.

❏ **Beware of the uncorrected bug**

To avoid the consequences of an uncorrected bug that manifests itself in total destruction of the shared database after the standard operation of distributing structures to users, we need to make sure that the list of users of the personal Administrator database doesn't contain any usernames from the Analyst personal databases. Here we mean usernames at the operating system level.

For example, if the Analyst logs in to his or her personal database under a name such as ATomson, never include this username into the list of the Administrator's personal database. The problem is that it is possible to connect to the shared database in read-write mode only under the name of one of the users of the Administrator's personal database. The reason for the bug is the shared database in the Analyst session is connected incorrectly (in read-write mode rather than in read-only mode).

❏ **Read the documentation on the Express products**

❏ **Contact the technical support**

Literature

1. *Inmon W. H.* Building the Data Warehouse. John Wiley & Sons, 1996.

2. *Kimball R.* The Data Warehouse Lifecycle Toolkit. Wiley Computer Publishing, New York, 1998.

3. *Codd E. F., Codd S. B., Salley C. T.* Providing OLAP (On-Line Analytical Processing) to User-Analysts: An IT Mandate. E. F. Codd & Associates, 1993.

4. *Hill J., Laufer S.* Data Transformation: Key to Information Sharing. Strategic Analysis Report, Gartner Group, September 29, 1998.

5. *Firestone J. M.* Data Warehouses, Data Marts, and Data Warehousing: New Definitions and New Conceptions. DKMS Brief No. 6, 1999.

6. *Brooks P. L.*, Visualizing Data. DBMS, August 1997.

7. *Hofland P., Utsler J.* Data Mining at Your Desk. BYTE, July 1997.

8. *Kruchten Ph.* The Rational Unified Process: An Introduction. Addison Wesley Publishing Company, 2000.